The Harper Dictionary of Foreign Terms

The Harper Dictionary of Foreign Terms

Third Edition

Revised and edited by
Eugene Ehrlich
Based on the original edition by
C. O. Sylvester Mawson

1817

HARPER & ROW, PUBLISHERS, New York
Cambridge, Philadelphia, San Francisco, Washington
London, Mexico City, São Paulo, Singapore, Sydney

Designed by C. Linda Dingler

Library of Congress Cataloging-in-Publication Data

Mawson, C. O. Sylvester (Christopher Orlando
   Sylvester), 1870–1938.
  The Harper dictionary of foreign terms.

  Rev. ed. of: Dictionary of foreign terms.
2nd ed. 1975.
  Includes index.
  1. English language—Foreign words and phrases—
Dictionaries. I. Ehrlich, Eugene H. II. Mawson,
C. O. Sylvester (Christopher Orlando Sylvester),
1870–1938. Dictionary of foreign terms. III. Title.
PE1670.M3 1987   422'.4   86-46061
ISBN 0-06-181576-4

87 88 89 90 91 RRD 10 9 8 7 6 5 4 3 2 1

To
Hazel Ehrlich Wodehouse
and
Rebecca Ann Dally Ehrlich

Contents

Preface

English grows not only through coinage of new words and employment of existing English words in novel ways, but also through adoption of foreign words and phrases that give opportunities for colorful and precise expression. We still meet *in camera*, carry on intrigues *sub rosa*, converse *tête-à-tête*, and bid one another *adieu, adiós, arrivederci, ciao*, or *auf Wiedersehen*. And this is just the tip of the linguistic iceberg. People eager to undertake an activity are *gung ho*, the vengeful among us resort to *lex talionis*, amateur chefs (itself a foreign word taken into our language) know the implications of *cordon bleu*, and who does not speak of *charisma*? All this is just a sampling, a potpourri (the French spelling is *pot pourri*), of the tens of thousands of foreign terms borrowed by our flourishing language. Some of the terms are so well established in English that we sometimes fail to recognize them as borrowings, but others are used in full knowledge that they are of foreign origin. Thus, when someone says *annus mirabilis* or *post hoc ergo propter hoc* or *requiescat in pace*, it is clear that Latin is being used. In contrast, when people say "ad hoc" or "antebellum" or "sub rosa," they may well be unaware of the foreign origins of what now are standard English expressions.

From the time the *Dictionary of Foreign Terms* was first compiled in 1934, the intention of its editors has remained constant: to create a single-volume source that explains foreign phrases and words likely to be encountered in American and English literature. Many of these terms may no longer be current among today's speakers of the fifty-odd languages on which the dictionary draws. A good example of this group of phrases is the extensive Anglo-Indian vocabulary included in the dictionary. The British *raj* is long gone, but its rich legacy of terms is readily apparent to devotees of such writers as Rudyard Kipling, E. M. Forster, and Paul Scott.

The dictionary is not intended to serve as a guide to words now recognized as English. That responsibility is left to standard dictionaries, which usually provide etymological information along with definitions. Rather, by dealing with expressions that are foreign, the editor hopes to spare readers the trouble of searching for the meanings of word after word in a foreign-language dictionary and then attempting to put a definition together.

Aside from its utilitarian *raison d'être*, this dictionary provides other benefits. Finding out how people of other cultures express their thoughts affords insight into attitudes, prejudices, and practices—even perfunctory browsing will show that people everywhere have thoughts that are marvelously alike and astonishingly different. For this reason, the dictionary entertains and enriches the reader who discovers the variety of ways in which people express similar thoughts.

On eschewing obfuscation:
French—call a cat a cat: *appeler un chat un chat.*
German—call a thing by its right name: *das Ding beim rechten Namen nennen.*
Portuguese—bread, bread; cheese, cheese: *pão, pão; queijo, queijo.*
Spanish—call bread bread, and wine wine: *llamar al pan, pan y al vino, vino.*

On love:
French—love and smoke cannot be hidden: *l'amour et la fumée ne peuvent se cacher.*
Italian—love rules without rules: *amor regge senza legge.*
German—the illusion is brief, the repentence long: *der Wahn ist kurz, die Reu' ist lang.*
Latin—love is a kind of military service: *militiae species amor est.*
Spanish—love and prudence cannot go together: *amar y saber no puede todo ser.*

On making the most of today:
German—a sparrow in the hand is better than a pigeon on the roof: *ein Sperling in der Hand ist besser als eine Taube auf dem Dache.*
Italian—better an egg today than chicken tomorrow: *meglio un uovo oggi che una gallina domani.*
Latin—enjoy today, trusting as little as possible to what tomorrow may bring: *carpe diem, quam minimum credula postero.*

On marriage:
German—early marriage, long love: *frühe Hochzeit, lange Liebe.*
Italian—praise married life but remain single: *lauda la moglie e tienti donzello.*
Portuguese—a rich widow weeps with one eye and signals with the other: *viuva rica com um olho chora, e com outro repica.*
Spanish—marry and be tamed: *casarás y amansarás.*

On money:

French—money is a master key: *l'argent est un bon passe-partout.*

German—money rules the world: *Geld regiert die Welt.*

Italian—money is the brother of money: *il danaro è fratello del danaro.*

Latin—money, like a queen, gives rank and beauty: *et genus et formam regina pecunia donat.*

Portuguese—laws go where dollars please: *lá vão leis onde querem cruzados.*

Spanish—a golden key opens any door: *no hay cerradura donde es oro la ganzúa.*

The first edition of the dictionary was the work of the distinguished lexicographer C. O. Sylvester Mawson, who was born in England in 1870. Mawson came to the United States to join the editorial staff of the *Century Dictionary*. He later was an editor of *Roget's International Thesaurus* as well as of several Merriam-Webster dictionaries and remained active as a lexicographer until his death in 1938. The second edition of the *Dictionary of Foreign Terms* appeared in 1975. It was prepared by Charles Berlitz, a writer of foreign-language textbooks, who added terms that had come into use after Mawson's time.

The present edition has three principal goals: to correct errors in the work, particularly in the English transliteration of classical Greek entries; to add terms from languages that have come into prominence since the last revision; and to furnish an English index to the thousands of terms explained in the volume. As for how well the goal of correcting errors has been met, sharp-eyed readers will inevitably judge for themselves. The languages that contribute the bulk of the many new entries are Japanese, Russian, and modern Hebrew. Finally, it is hoped that readers will find the index helpful when they have difficulty in recalling elusive foreign words, phrases, and proverbs.

A brief summary of the classes of words and other features included in this volume indicates the scope of *The Harper Dictionary of Foreign Terms*:

Classes of Words

- Foreign words and phrases from more than fifty languages frequently used in conversation or likely to be encountered in the fields of literature, law, science, politics, music, art, diplomacy, fashion, travel, food, and dining

- Words from Asian languages, particularly Japanese and Chinese, that have been brought into use in America in recent years

- Terms from languages relatively new on the international scene, such as Swahili and modern Hebrew, and currently extending their linguistic areas of influence
- Expressions adopted into English from the American Indian languages
- Classical Greek terms given in the English or Greek alphabet, depending on the form in which they are likely to appear in most texts. Entries in the Greek alphabet include a rendering in the English alphabet, employing the modern scheme of Greek transliteration. Readers unfamiliar with the Greek alphabet will find that the English transliterations are helpful in locating entries alphabetically.
- Terms of French and Spanish origin peculiar to Canada and the southwestern United States
- Quotations from classical and modern authors frequently used in literature and public addresses, with passages from the Vulgate and the Old Testament in Greek and in English transliteration
- Folk sayings and proverbs from foreign languages that give insight into other cultures while providing pithy ways of expressing universal ideas
- Translations and definitions of foreign-language mottoes of states, institutions, and prominent families

Usage and Syntactic Data
- Translations and definitions of all foreign terms used, with the secondary meanings and popular usages indicated where necessary
- Plurals of all words that might present difficulty to the reader of English
- Feminine forms of foreign nouns and adjectives
- Foreign abbreviations and contractions

Special Terms
- Naval and military terms from foreign languages
- Menu terms in French, Italian, and other languages, with descriptions of many foreign dishes
- Archaic terms and phrases, included for the convenience of readers of old texts

New to this edition is an English index to all foreign entries.

Acknowledgments

I wish to thank all the people who helped in the preparation of this new edition of *Dictionary of Foreign Terms*, particularly Nina Davis, Christopher Dadian, David Graff, Cathy Guigui, Antje Munroe, and Ellen Sackelman, who assisted in checking entries for languages beyond my own grasp, suggesting new entries, and preparing certain definitions. They did their work enthusiastically and with the greatest care. As a result of their ministrations, the volume has been much improved.

In preparing the index for this volume, I had the cooperation of Felice Levy, indexer *par excellence*, who has collaborated with me many times. In her work on this volume, she was ably assisted by Barbara Gold, one of her associates. Since I was not cut out to be even an apprentice in the arcane art they practice, I especially value their contributions.

Sally Bunch served as editorial assistant for the project, as she has many times before for various projects developed at The Hudson Group, and I wish to thank her for her efforts. I wish also to express my admiration and gratitude for my colleagues Raymond Hand, Jr., and Hayden Carruth, who carefully worked around me during the many months in which the project cluttered my desk and occupied my attention completely.

Finally, I wish to extend thanks to Carol Cohen, my editor at Harper & Row, who suggested the project to me and saw it through to completion.

EUGENE EHRLICH

Columbia University

Abbreviations
Used in This Book

abbr.	abbreviation
adj.	adjective
adv.	adverb
aero.	aeronautics
Afrik	Afrikaans
Algon	Algonquian
Am	American
Am Sp	American Spanish
anat.	anatomy
Anglo-Ind	Anglo-Indian
Ar	Arabic
Aram	Aramaic
arch.	architecture
arith.	arithmetic
Armen	Armenian
astron.	astronomy
auto.	automobile
Beng	Bengali
biol.	biology
Bohem	Bohemian
bot.	botany
Br	British
Bulg	Bulgarian
Can	Canadian
Can Fr	Canadian French
cf.	*confer* [L, compare]
Chin	Chinese
colloq.	colloquial; colloquialism
com.	commerce
corr.	corruption

Dan	Danish
dial.	dialectal; dialect
Du	Dutch
eccl.	ecclesiastical
elec.	electricity
Eng	English
engin.	engineering
Esk	Eskimo
fem.	feminine
fig.	figuratively
Flem	Flemish
fort.	fortification
fr.	from
Fr	French
Fr Am	French American
Fr Can	French Canadian
Gael	Gaelic
geol.	geology
Ger	German
Gr	Greek
gram.	grammar
Guj	Gujarati
Hawa	Hawaiian
Heb	Hebrew
her.	heraldry
Hind	Hindi and/or Urdu (Hindustani)
hist.	historical; history
Hung	Hungarian
Icel	Icelandic
i.e.	*id est* [L, that is]
Ind	Indian
interj.	interjection
It	Italian
Jap	Japanese
Kan	Kanarese
L	Latin
LL	Late Latin
lit.	literally
Mal	Malay and Indonesian
Mar	Marathi
masc.	masculine
mech.	mechanics
med.	medicine
Mex	Mexican
Mex Sp	Mexican Spanish

mil.	military
mod.	modern
myth.	mythology
n.	noun
naut.	nautical
nav.	naval
Nav	Navajo
neut.	neuter
n.f.	noun feminine
NL	New Latin
n.m.	noun masculine
Norw	Norwegian
OF	Old French
orig.	originally
p. adj.	predicate adjective
paleog.	paleography
Pers	Persian
Pg	Portuguese
pharm.	pharmacy
philos.	philosophy
phon.	phonetics
photog.	photography
P.I.	Philippine Islands
pl.	plural
Pol	Polish
pop.	popularly
pr.	pronounced
prep.	preposition
prob.	probably
psychol.	psychology
q.v.	*quod vide* [L, which see]
R.C.Ch.	Roman Catholic Church
rhet.	rhetoric
R.R.	railroad
Rum	Rumanian
Russ	Russian
sculp.	sculpture
Serb	Serbian
sing.	singular
Sing	Singhalese
Skr	Sanskrit
Sp	Spanish
Sp Am	Spanish American
specif.	specifically
St.	Saint

Sw	Swedish
Swa	Swahili
Tag	Tagalog
Tam	Tamil
tech.	technical
Tel	Telugu
theat.	theatrical
theol.	theology
theos.	theosophy
topog.	topography
tr.	translated
Turk	Turkish
typog.	typography
univ.	university
U.S.	United States
v.	verb
v.a.	verb active
v.i.	verb intransitive
Viet	Vietnamese
v.t.	verb transitive
zool.	zoology
Zu	Zulu

The Harper Dictionary of Foreign Terms

A

ab absurdo [L], from the absurd: *geometry.*

¡abajo...! [Sp], down with...! **—¡abajo el gobierno!,** down with the government!

à bas! [Fr], down with! off with!

ab asino lanam [L], lit., wool from an ass; blood from a stone.

abatis *or* **abattis** [Fr], giblets. **—abatis de dinde,** turkey giblets: *cookery.*

abat-jour [Fr], lamp shade or reflector; *arch.,* an inclined device attached to a window, for directing daylight downward; also, a skylight or sloping aperture to admit light from above.

à bâtons rompus [Fr], lit., with sticks broken; by fits and starts; fitfully.

abat-sons [Fr], a device for throwing sound downward, as in a belfry; louver.

abattu [Fr; *fem.* abattue], dejected; cast down.

a battuta [It], lit., by the beat; in strict time: *music.*

abat-vent [Fr], any device for breaking the wind, without blocking the passage of air and sound.

abat-voix [Fr], sounding board, as over a pulpit.

abbacchio [It], lamb.

abbaye [Fr], abbey.

abbé [Fr], abbot; priest, esp. one without official ecclesiastical duties.

abbellimento [It], embellishment; ornament: *music.*

Abbildung [Ger], picture; cut: *typog.*

à beau jeu beau retour [Fr], one good turn deserves another.

à beau mentir qui vient de loin [Fr], travelers from afar can lie with impunity.

Abendessen [Ger], supper.

abends wird der Faule fleissig [Ger], in the evening the lazy man becomes industrious.

a beneplacito [It], at pleasure; *music,* at the discretion of the performer.

Aberglaube [Ger], superstition, esp. in the earlier sense of excessive reverence for that which is unknown: called by Goethe the "poetry of life."

abest [L; *pl.* absunt], he (*or* she) is absent.

abeto [Sp], spruce tree; fir tree; also, their wood; spruce.

abeunt studia in mores [L], studies change into habits; pursuits assiduously followed become habits: *Ovid.*

ab extra [L], from without.

Abhandlung [Ger; *pl.* Abhandlungen], treatise; *pl.,* transactions, as of a society: *abbr.* Abh.

ab hoc et ab hac et ab illa [L], from this man and this woman and that woman; from here, there, and everywhere; confusedly.

abiit ad plures (*or* **maiores**) [L; *pl.* abierunt], he (*or* she) has gone to the majority (i.e., is dead).

abiit, excessit, evasit, erupit [L], he has departed, gone off, escaped, broken away: *Cicero* (of Catiline).

abîmé de dettes [Fr], deep in debt.

ab imo pectore [L], from the bottom of the heart.

ab inconvenienti [L], lit., from the inconvenience (involved); designating an argument designed to show that the opposite construction is untenable because of the inconvenience or hardship it would create: *law.*

ab incunabulis [L], from the cradle; from childhood: *Livy.*

ab initio [L], from the beginning: *abbr.* ab init.

ab intra [L], from within.

ab invito [L], unwillingly.

ab Iove principium [L], from Jove is my beginning; let us commence with Jupiter; let us begin with the most important person or thing: *Virgil.*

ab irato [L], lit., from an angry man; in a fit of anger; hence, not to be taken too seriously.

à bis ou à blanc [Fr], in one way or another; by hook or by crook.

abito [Can Fr]. Same as ABOIDEAU.

abnormis sapiens [L], a natural-born philosopher: *Horace.*

abogado [Sp], advocate; lawyer.

aboideau *or* **aboiteau** [Can Fr], a sluice or tide gate in a dike: *eastern Canada.* Called also *abito* and *bito.*

à bon appétit il ne faut point de sauce [Fr], a good appetite needs no sauce.

à bon chat, bon rat [Fr], lit., to a good cat, a good rat; tit for tat; diamond cut diamond; set a thief to catch a thief.

à bon cheval point d'éperon [Fr], a good horse needs no spur; do not spur the willing horse.

à bon chien il ne vient jamais un bon os [Fr], lit., a good bone never comes to a good dog; merit rarely meets with its reward.

à bon commencement bonne fin [Fr], a good beginning makes a good end.

à bon compte [Fr], cheaply; at a low cost.

abondance de biens ne nuit pas [Fr], opulence (lit., abundance of good things) does no harm.

à bon droit [Fr], with good reason; justly.

à bon marché [Fr], at a good bargain; cheap.

abonnement [Fr], subscription.

à bonne raison [Fr], with good reason.

à bonnes enseignes [Fr], deservedly; on sure grounds.

à bon vin point d'enseigne [Fr], lit., good wine needs no signboard; good wine needs no bush.

ab origine [L], from the origin (*or* beginning).

a bove maiori discit arare minor [L], from the older ox the younger learns to plow; as the old cock crows, the young one learns.

ab ovo [L], lit., from the egg; from the beginning.

ab ovo usque ad mala [L], lit., from the egg to the apples (i.e., from the first to the last course of a Roman dinner); from beginning to end: *Horace*.

abra [Sp], orig., a bay; mountain gorge or pass; mouth of a canyon; a break in a mesa, as in Texas: *southwestern U.S.*

à bras ouverts [Fr], with open arms.

à brebis tondue Dieu mesure le vent [Fr], God tempers the wind to the shorn lamb.

abrégé [Fr], abridged; epitomized; also, a summary.

abri [Fr], shelter; cover; protection.

abricot [Fr], apricot.

abricot-pêche [Fr, *pl.* abricots-pêches], peach-apricot.

Abschied [Ger], dismissal; departure; leave; farewell.

Abschnitt [Ger; *pl.* Abschnitte], paragraph; section; division (*abbr.* Abs.): *typog.*

abscissio infiniti [L], lit., the cutting off of the infinite (*or* negative part); the systematic comparison and rejection of hypotheses till the true conclusion is reached: *logic.*

absence d'esprit [Fr], absence of mind.

absens haeres non erit [L], the absent one will not be the heir; out of sight, out of mind.

absente reo [L], the defendant being absent (*abbr.* abs. re.): *law.*

absent le chat, les souris dansent [Fr], when the cat's away, the mice will play.

absichtlich [Ger], intentional; intentionally; on purpose.

absit invidia [L], let there be no ill will; take it not amiss; envy apart.

absit omen [L], may the omen (as in a word just used) augur no evil.

absitzen! [Ger], dismount!: *mil.*

absque [L], without. —**absque hoc,** without this (a term used in a formal denial): *law.*

a buen bocado, buen grito [Sp], for a good morsel, a good groan; indulgence exacts its toll.

a buen entendedor media palabra basta [Sp], to the good listener half a word is enough.

ab uno ad omnes [L], from one to all.

ab uno disce omnes [L], from one learn all; from one sample judge the rest: *Virgil.*

a buon vino non bisogna frasca [It], good wine needs no bush.

ab urbe condita [L], from the founding of the city (i.e., Rome, founded about 753 B.C.): *abbr.* A.U.C.

abusus non tollit usum [L], abuse does not take away use; abuse is no argument against proper use.

a caballo [Sp], on horseback.

a capella [It], in the style of old church music; unaccompanied: *music.*

a capite ad calcem [L], from head to heel.

a capriccio [It], at the performer's pleasure; at will: *music.*

acariâtre [Fr], peevish; crabbed; cross-grained.

accablé [Fr; *fem.* accablée], crushed; overwhelmed; depressed; dejected.

accademia [It], academy.

accedas ad curiam [L], you may approach the court; a commonlaw writ to remove a cause to a higher court: *Eng. law.*

accelerando [It], gradually faster (*abbr.* accel.): *music.*

accentus [L], part of a ritualistic church service chanted or intoned by the priest and his assistants at the altar: distinguished from *concentus.*

accepta [L], receipts; credits.

accessit [L; *pl.* accesserunt], he (she, it) came near.

acciaccatura [It], a short grace note, one half step below a principal note: *music.*

accolade [Fr], lit., an embrace; *typog. & music,* brace; a congratulatory embrace; an award.

accompagnamento [It], accompaniment: *music.*

accompagnatore [It; *fem.* accompagnatrice], accompanist: *music.*

accordez vos flûtes [Fr], lit., tune your flutes; settle it between you.

accordo [It], agreement; harmony; *music,* chord.

accouchement [Fr], delivery in childbed; confinement.

accoucheur [Fr; *fem.* accoucheuse], obstetrician.

accroché [Fr; *fem.* accrochée], lit., hooked; deadlocked.

accueil [Fr], reception; welcome.

accusare nemo se debit, nisi coram Deo [L], no one is bound to accuse (*or* incriminate) himself, unless before God: *law.*

aceite [Sp], oil; lubricant; also, an edible oil.

aceituna [Sp], olive (fruit).

aceituno [Sp], olive tree.

a cembalo [It], for the piano: *music.*

acequia [Sp], canal; irrigation trench. —**acequia madre,** main canal or *acequia: Sp. Am. & southwestern U.S.*

acera [Sp], sidewalk.

acerbus et ingens [L], fierce and mighty.

acervatim [L], in heaps; summarily.

ac etiam [L], and also.

à chacun son fardeau pèse [Fr], everyone thinks his own burden heavy.

à chaque fou plaît sa marotte [Fr], every fool is pleased with (*or* rides) his own hobby.

à chaque oiseau son nid est beau [Fr], every bird thinks its own nest fine.

à chaque saint sa chandelle [Fr], to each saint his candle; honor to whom honor is due.

achar [Hind & Pers], pickles; any salt or tart relish: *India.*

acharné [Fr], bloodthirsty; infuriated; enthusiastic; rabid; *hunting,* fleshed.

acharnement [Fr], ferocity; blind fury; rage; fig., gusto.

achcha [Hind], good; well; opposite of *kharab.* —**bahut achcha,** all right; very well.

Acheruntis pabulum [L], food for Acheron; marked for death (said of a corrupt and depraved man): *Plautus.*

à cheval [Fr], on horseback; astride. —**à cheval!,** to horse!

a chi vuole non mancano modi [It], where there's a will, there's a way.

Achtung! [Ger], attention!

à clin [Fr], clinker-built; lapstreak: *naval.*

à coeur joie [Fr], to one's heart's content.

à coeur ouvert [Fr], with open heart; unreservedly.

à compte [Fr], on account; in part payment.

à contre coeur [Fr], reluctantly; against the grain.

à corps perdu [Fr], lit., with lost body; impetuously; headlong; with might and main.

à corsaire, corsaire et demi [Fr], set a thief to catch a thief. Cf. À FRIPON, etc.

à coups de bâton [Fr], with blows of a stick (*or* cudgel).

à coup sûr [Fr], lit., with sure stroke; surely; assuredly; unerringly; without fail.

à couvert [Fr], under cover; sheltered; secure; safe.

acqua [It], water. —**acqua cheta rovina i ponti,** stagnant water ruins bridges; still waters run deep. —**acqua lontana non spegne fuoco vicino,** distant water does not extinguish a nearby fire.

acquista buona fama e mettiti a dormire [It], acquire a good reputation and go to sleep.

acquit [Fr], receipt; discharge. —**pour acquit,** paid; settled: written on receipted bills, etc.

âcre [Fr], tart; biting; acrid.

a cruce salus [L], salvation by (*or* from) the Cross.

acta est fabula [L], the play is over; words used at the close of a dramatic performance in the ancient Roman theater; the dying words of the Emperor Augustus. Cf. LA FARCE EST JOUÉE.

acte d'accusation [Fr], bill of indictment.

actionnaire [Fr], shareholder; stockholder.

actio personalis moritur cum persona [L], a personal action dies with the person: *law.*

actualité [Fr], passing event; question of the hour.

actualmente [Sp], at the present time.

actuel [Fr; *fem.* actuelle], real; present.

actum agere [L], to do what has been already done.

actum est [L], it is all over. —**actum est de republica,** it is all over with the commonwealth.

actum ne agas [L], do not do what is done; let well enough alone: *Terence.*

actus [L], an act; actuality; in Scholastic philosophy, equivalent to ἐνέρ-γεια (henérgeia, activity, energy) as used by Aristotle. —**actus me invito factus non est meus actus,** an act done against my will is not my act: *law.* —**actus non facit reum, nisi mens est rea,** the act does not make a man guilty unless the mind (*or* intentions) be guilty: *law.*

a cuspide corona [L], from the spear a crown (i.e., honor for military exploits).

ad absurdum [L], to what is absurd: said of an argument demonstrating the absurdity of an opponent's proposition.

adagietto [It], rather slow; a short adagio: *music.*

adagio [It], slow; slowly; also, a slow movement between *largo* and *andante: music.*

adalat [Hind & Ar], a court of justice.

adam neekar bekoso, keeso, vay ka'aso [Heb], lit., a man is known by his glass, his pocket, and his anger; a man is known by what he drinks, how much money he has, and his temper.

ad amussim [L], according to a rule; accurately; exactly.

ad aperturam libri [L], at the opening of the book; wherever the book opens.

ad arbitrium [L], at will; at pleasure.

ad astra [L], to the stars; to exalted place; to high renown. —**ad astra per aspera,** to the stars through hardships (lit., rough things): motto of *Kansas.*

a dato [L], from date.

ad baculum [L], to the rod (i.e., to force rather than to reason): said of an argument or appeal.

ad captandum [L], for the sake of pleasing: said of an argument or appeal. —**ad captandum vulgus,** to catch (*or* attract) the crowd; to please the rabble.

ad clerum [L], to the clergy.

ad crumenam [L], to the purse; to one's personal interests: said of an argument or appeal.

adde parvum parvo magnus acervus erit [L], add little to little and there will be a great heap: *Ovid.*

addio [It], goodbye; adieu.

additum [L; *pl.* addita], something added.

adelig und edel sind zweierlei [Ger], noble of birth and noble of soul are two very different things.

Adel sitzt im Gemüte nicht im Geblüte [Ger], nobility lies in worth not birth.

à demi [Fr], half; by halves; in part.

a Deo et rege [L], from God and the king.

adeo in teneris consuescere multum est [L], so imperative it is to form habits in early years; as the twig is bent, the tree's inclined: *Virgil.*

a Deo lux nostra [L], our light cometh from God.

à dessein [Fr], by design; intentionally; on purpose.

ad eundem (gradum) [L], to the same (degree, *or* standing): *abbr.* ad eund.

adeus [Pg], goodbye; adieu.

à deux [Fr], for two; between two. —**à deux mains,** with both hands.

ad extra [L], in an outward direction.

ad extremum [L], to the extreme; to the last.

ad filum aquae [L], to the thread (*or* center) of the stream: *law.*

ad filum viae [L], to the center of the road.

ad finem [L], to the end; at the end; finally: *abbr.* ad fin. —**ad finem fidelis,** faithful to the end.

ad gustum [L], to the taste.

ad hanc vocem [L], at this word: *abbr.* a.h.v.

adhibenda est in iocando moderatio [L], one should employ restraint in his jests; joking should be kept within the bounds of good taste: *Cicero.*

ad hoc [L], for this (particular purpose); special: said of a body elected or appointed for a definite object.

ad hominem [L], lit., to the man (i.e., to his interests and prejudices); personal: said of an argument or appeal.

adhuc sub iudice lis est [L], the case is still before the judge (i.e., is not yet decided): *Horace.*

ad hunc locum [L], at this place: *abbr.* a.h.l.

ad idem [L], to the same (point); at one: *law.*

a die [L], from that day.

adieu [Fr], goodbye. —**faire ses (mes** *etc.*) **adieux à,** to say goodbye to.

adieu la voiture, adieu la boutique [Fr], goodbye carriage, goodbye shop; it's all over.

ad ignorantiam [L], to ignorance (i.e., of the facts): said of an argument or appeal.

ad infinitum [L], to infinity; without end or limit; endlessly: *abbr.* ad inf.

ad initium [L], at the beginning: *abbr.* ad init.

ad instar [L], after the fashion of; like. —**ad instar omnium,** in the likeness of all.

ad interim [L], in (*or* for) the meantime; meanwhile; temporary: *abbr.* ad int.

ad internecionem [L], to extermination.

ad invidiam [L], to envy (*or* prejudice): said of an argument or appeal.

adiós [Sp], goodbye; adieu.

a Dios gracias [Sp], thanks be given to God; thank God.

adiratamente [It], in an angry manner; passionately: *music*.

adiratum [L; *pl.* adirata], strayed; lost: *law*.

à discrétion [Fr], at discretion; at will; without stint (*or* limit).

ad iudicium [L], to judgment (*or* common sense): said of an argument or appeal.

adiuvante Deo labor proficit [L], with God's help, work prospers.

ad kalendas Graecas [L], at the Greek calends; never (the Greeks had no calends).

Adler brüten keine Tauben [Ger], eagles do not give birth to doves.

ad libitum [L], at pleasure; as one wishes; to any extent: *abbr.* ad lib.

ad litem [L], for the suit (*or* action): *law*.

ad maiorem Dei gloriam [L], to the greater glory of God (*abbr.* A.M.D.G.): motto of the Jesuits (the Society of Jesus).

ad manum [L], at hand; in readiness.

ad meliora vertamur [L], let us turn to better things.

ad misericordiam [L], to pity: said of an argument or appeal.

ad modum [L], in (*or* after) the manner of; like.

ad multos annos [L], for many years.

ad nauseam [L], to nausea; to the point of disgust or satiety.

Adonai [Heb], lord; God.

adorer le veau d'or [Fr], to worship the golden calf (i.e., riches).

ad patres [L], (gathered) to his fathers; dead.

ad paucos dies [L], for a few days.

ad populum [L], to the people (i.e., to their passions and prejudices): said of an argument or appeal.

ad quem [L], at (*or* to) which; opposite of *a quo*.

ad quod damnum [L], lit., to what damage; an English chancery writ to ascertain whether the grant of a certain privilege, such as holding a fair, would prove detrimental to any persons in the district: *law*.

ad referendum [L], for reference; for further consideration; specif., for (*or* subject to) the approval of a superior.

ad rem [L], to the matter in hand; to the point (*or* purpose).

à droite [Fr], to (*or* on) the right.

à droite, alignement! [Fr], right, dress!: *mil*.

adscriptus glebae [L; *pl.* adscripti glebae], (a person) bound to the soil; a serf.

ad sectam [LL], at the suit of (*abbr.* ads.): *law*.

adsum [L], I am present; here!

ad summam [L], in short; in a word.

ad summum [L], to the highest point (*or* amount).

a due voci [It], for two voices: *music*.

ad unguem [L], to a fingernail; to a nicety; to a T; highly finished (an expression borrowed from sculptors, who tested the smoothness of their work with the fingernail). Cf. εἰς ὄνυχα (eis ónykha). **—ad**

unguem factus homo, a man polished to the nail; "a man of men, accomplished and refined": *Horace* (tr. by Conington).

ad unum omnes [L], lit., all to one; all to a man; everybody without exception.

à dur âne dur aiguillon [Fr], for a stubborn ass a hard (*or* sharp) goad.

ad usum [L], according to custom: *abbr.* ad us.

ad utrumque paratus [L], prepared for either (event).

ad valorem [L], according to the value: *abbr.* ad val.

ad verbum [L], to a word; word for word; literally.

ad verecundiam [L], to modesty: said of an argument or appeal.

adversa virtute repello [L], I repel adversity by valor (*or* courage).

adversus [L], against: *abbr.* adv.

ad vitam aut culpam [L], for life or until misbehavior; during good behavior.

ad vivum [L], to the life; lifelike.

advocatus diaboli [L], Devil's advocate; a person chosen to dispute claims to canonization, before the papal court; hence, one who argues against his own convictions.

aegrescit medendo [L], he (*or* it) grows worse with the treatment; the remedy is worse than the disease: *Virgil* (adapted).

aegri somnia vana [L], a sick man's idle dreams: *Horace.*

aegrotat [L; *pl.* aegrotant], he (*or* she) is ill.

aequabiliter et diligenter [L], uniformly and diligently.

aequam servare mentem [L], to preserve an unruffled mind (adapted from the quotation *aequam memento rebus in arduis servare mentem,* remember to keep an unruffled mind in difficulties): *Horace.*

aequanimiter [L], with equanimity; composedly.

aequitas sequitur legem [L], equity follows the law (i.e., follows common-law principles, except where injustice and fraud would ensue): *law.*

aequo animo [L], with an equal (*or* calm) mind; with equanimity.

aequo pulsat pede [L], (pale Death) knocks with equal foot: *Horace.* See PALLIDA MORS.

aere perennius [L], more lasting than brass (*or* bronze): *Horace.*

aes alienum [L], money belonging to another; debt; debts.

aes triplex [L]. triple brass; strong defense.

aetatis [L], of the age: *abbr.* aet. *or* aetat. —**aetatis suae,** of his (*or* her) age.

aeternum servans sub pectore vulnus [L], nursing an everlasting wound within the breast: *Virgil.*

ἀετὸς ἐν νεφέλαισι [Gr; aetòs en nephélaisi], an eagle in the clouds; fig., an unattainable object.

afectísimo [Sp; *fem.* afectísima], most affectionate; very truly: *abbr. in a letter* af.ᵐᵒ *or* aff.ᵐᵒ, *fem.* af.ᵐᵃ *or* aff.ᵐᵃ.

afectuoso [Sp; *fem.* afectuosa], affectionate; respectful.

affabile [It], in a pleasing manner: *music.*

affaire [Fr], affair; concern; business. —**affaire d'amour,** love affair. —**affaire de coeur,** affair of the heart; love affair. —**affaire d'honneur,** affair of honor; duel. —**affaire flambée,** ruined affair (*or* business). —**les affaires sont les affaires,** business is business.

affaissement [Fr], depression; *med.,* collapse.

affanato [It], in a sorrowful manner: *music.*

affettivo [It], pathetic; affecting: *music.*

affetto [It], passion; affection; emotional warmth.

affettuoso [It], with feeling; tenderly: *music.*

affiche [Fr], poster; placard.

affichée [Fr], posted up.

affilé [Fr; *fem.* affilée], sharp; nimble; glib.

affilié [Fr], affiliated.

afflatus [L], breath; breeze; fig., inspiration; poetic impulse. —**afflatus montium,** mountain air.

afflavit Deus et dissipantur [L], God sent forth his breath and they are scattered: inscription on a medal commemorating the destruction of the Spanish Armada, 1588.

affleurement [Fr], outcrop: *geol.*

affrettando [It], quickening the tempo: *music.*

affreux [Fr; *fem.* affreuse], frightful; atrocious; shocking.

aficionado [Sp; *fem.* aficionada], a fan of a sport or other activity.

à fils de cordonnier point de chaussures [Fr], the shoemaker's son has no shoes.

à fleur d'eau [Fr], at the level of the water; between wind and water.

à fleur de terre [Fr], level with the ground.

afloramiento [Sp], outcrop; *geol.*

à fond [Fr], to the bottom; thoroughly. —**à fond de train,** at full speed.

à forfait [Fr], on speculation; *law,* by an aleatory contract.

a fortiori [L], with stronger reason; more conclusively.

à fripon, fripon et demi [Fr], against a rogue set a rogue and a half; set a thief to catch a thief.

à froid [Fr], coldly; in cold blood.

afueras [Sp], suburbs; environs.

aga *or* **agha** [Turk *aghā*], lit., great lord; commander; chief.

agaçant [Fr; *fem.* agaçante], irritating; annoying.

agacement [Fr], setting (the teeth) on edge; irritation (of the nerves).

agacerie [Fr], allurement; blandishment; flirtatious encouragement.

ἀγάπα τὸν πλήσιον [Gr; agápa tòn plésion], love thy neighbor: *Thales.*

à gauche [Fr], to (*or* on) the left.

age [Hind], in front; forward; ahead. —**age jao,** go ahead; go straight on; get on.

à genoux [Fr], on one's knees; kneeling.

agent provocateur [Fr; *pl.* agents provocateurs], lit., provoking agent; abettor; instigator; an undercover man of the secret service or the police who mixes with and abets suspected persons in their designs against society or the state.

age quod agis [L], do what you are doing; attend to the work you have in hand.

agevole [It], lightly; with ease: *music.*

aggiornamento [It], adjournment; a bringing up to date.

agitato [It], in an agitated manner: *music.*

agneau [Fr; *pl.* agneaux], lamb. —**agneau du printemps,** spring lamb.

ἀγνώστῳ θεῷ [Gr; agnóstō theô], to the Unknown God: *Acts* xvii. 23.

Agnus Dei [L], Lamb of God; *eccl.,* representation of a lamb bearing a cross or banner; also, a part of the Mass beginning with the words *Agnus Dei.*

agora [Gr ἀγορά; *pl.* agorae], public square or market place in an ancient Greek city.

agostadero [Sp], pasture; in Texas, a stretch of open country used as a pasture.

à grands frais [Fr], at great expense.

à grands pas [Fr], with great strides; at a great pace.

agréable [Fr], agreeable; pleasing.

agrément [Fr], consent; agreeableness; agreeable quality or trait; charm; also, a refined pleasure; *pl.,* embellishments, as in music. —**arts d'agrément,** accomplishments (music, painting, dancing, fencing, etc.).

agua [Sp], water; also, on the Mexican border, a stream; as, Agua Dulce in Texas. —**agua bendita,** holy water. —**agua mansa,** still water. —**agua brava,** troubled water. —**agua turbia no hace espejo,** troubled waters are no mirror. —**agua viva,** running water.

aguador [Sp], water carrier.

aguardiente [Sp], lit., burning water; an inferior brandy; *southwestern U.S.,* any distilled liquor, esp. native whisky.

aguerri [Fr], inured to war; disciplined.

à haute voix [Fr], in a loud voice; loudly; aloud.

ahava [Heb], love.

ahimè! [It], alas!

ahista [Hind], slow; slowly; opposite of *jaldi.* —**ahista jao,** go slowly.

à huis clos [Fr], with closed doors.

aide [Fr], assistant; helper.

aide de camp [Fr; *pl.* aides de camp], military aide; assistant.

aide-mémoire [Fr; *pl.* aides-mémoire], memory aid; memorandum.

aide-toi, et le ciel t'aidera [Fr], help yourself, and Heaven will help you: *La Fontaine.*

αἰδὼς ὄλωλεν [Gr; aidòs ólōlen], modesty has died out: *Theognis.*

αἰδὼς οὐκ ἀγαθή [Gr; aidòs ouk agathé], false shame: *Hesiod.*

αἰὲν ἀριστεύειν [Gr; aién aristeúein], always to excel: *Homer.*

aigre-doux [Fr; *fem.* aigre-douce], bittersweet; sourish.

aiguière [Fr], ornamental pitcher.

aiguille [Fr], needle; spire; needle-shaped peak of rock, as seen near Mont Blanc; also, a similar formation elsewhere, as in California.

aiguillette [Fr], shoulder knot or loop; aglet; also, a thin slice; strip; *naut.,* lanyard.

aileron [Fr], little wing; pinion.

aimable [Fr], lovable; pleasing; courteous.

aimer éperdument [Fr], to love passionately.

aîné [Fr; *fem.* aînée], elder; senior: often appended to surname for distinction. Cf. CADET and PUÎNÉ.

air [Fr], air; look; appearance. —**air abattu,** downcast look. —**air chagrin,** sorrowful look. —**air distingué,** distinguished appearance. —**air distrait,** absent air. —**air emprunté,** embarassed look. —**air farouche,** forbidding look. —**air noble,** air of distinction.

aire libre [Sp], open air.

αἰτεῖτε, καὶ δοθήσεται ὑμῖν· ξητεῖτε καὶ εὑρήσετε· κρούετε καὶ ἀνοιγήσεται ὑμῖν [Gr; aiteîte, kaì dothḗsetai humîn; zéteite kaì heurésete; kroúete kaì anoigésetai humîn], ask, and it shall be given you; seek, and ye shall find; knock, and it shall be opened unto you: *Matthew* vii.7.

aiuto! [It], help!

à jamais [Fr], forever.

à jour [Fr], open; in openwork.

Aktiengesellschaft [Ger], joint-stock company: *abbr.* A.G.

à la [Fr], after the manner of; after the fashion or style of: used esp. in cookery terms.

à l'abandon [Fr], in disorder; at random; left uncared for; adrift.

à la belle étoile [Fr], under the stars; in the open air (at night).

à la bonne heure [Fr], lit., at the good hour; be it so; very well.

à la bordelaise [Fr], with Bordeaux wine: *cookery.*

à l'abri [Fr], under shelter (*or* cover).

à la broche [Fr], cooked on a spit or skewer; as, eels *à la broche: cookery.*

à la campagne [Fr], in the country.

à la carte [Fr], according to the menu: distinguished from *table d'hôte.*

à la chinoise [Fr], in the Chinese style or fashion.

alacrán [Sp], scorpion: *Sp. Am.*

à la dérobée [Fr], by stealth; clandestinely; privately.

à la diable [Fr], deviled: *cookery.*

à la fin [Fr], in the end; at last.

à la française [Fr], in the French style or fashion.

à la grâce de quelqu'un [Fr], at the mercy of someone.

à la grecque [Fr], in the Greek style or fashion.

à la guerre comme à la guerre [Fr], in war as in war (i.e., one must take things as they come).

à la hollandaise [Fr], in the Dutch style or fashion.

à la jardinière [Fr]. See JARDINIÈRE.

à la lanterne! [Fr], to the lamppost with him! lynch him!

à la lettre [Fr], to the letter; literally.

à la main [Fr], to one's hand; handy; on hand; ready.

à la maison [Fr], at home; indoors.

à la maître d'hôtel [Fr], plainly prepared, with chopped parsley, butter sauce, and lemon juice: *cookery.*

alameda [Sp], shady avenue; public walk, lined with poplars or other trees: *Sp. Am. & southwestern U.S.*

à l'américaine [Fr], in the American style or fashion.

à l'amiable [Fr], amicably; by private contract.

al amigo su vicio [Sp], to a friend, his faults; make allowances for the failings of a friend.

à la militaire [Fr], in military style.

alamo [Sp *álamo*], poplar; *southwestern U.S.*, the cottonwood and other species of *Populus.*

à la mode [Fr], according to the fashion (*or* prevailing mode); fashionably; fashionable.

à l'anglaise [Fr], in the English style or fashion.

à la parisienne [Fr], in the Parisian style or fashion.

à la portée de tout le monde [Fr], within reach of everyone.

à la presse vont les fous [Fr], fools go in crowds.

à la provençale [Fr], with garlic or onions: *cookery.*

à la russe [Fr], in the Russian style or fashion.

à la sourdine [Fr], secretly; by stealth; on the sly; *music,* with the mute.

à la suédoise [Fr], in the Swedish style or fashion.

à la Tartuffe [Fr], in the style of (*or* like) Tartuffe, the hypocritical hero of Molière's comedy; hypocritically.

à la viennoise [Fr], in the Viennese style or fashion.

à la villageoise [Fr], in village style; in rustic fashion.

à la volonté de Dieu [Fr], at the will of God.

alberca [Sp], water hole; reservoir; water pocket: *southwestern U.S.*

albergo [It], inn.

al bisogno si conosce un amico [It], a friend is known in time of need; a friend in need is a friend indeed.

alcalde [Sp], mayor; in Texas and New Mexico, a justice of the peace.

alcaldía [Sp], office or jurisdiction of an *alcalde* (q.v.)

alcança quem não cansa [Pg], who tires not succeeds; success comes to him who does not give up.

alcarraza [Sp], porous earthenware vessel.

alcazaba *or* **alcazava** [Sp], fortress.

alcázar [Sp], castle; fortress; royal palace.

al d'ataift atfooch, v'sof m'tafoyich yetufun [Aram], because you drowned someone, you will be drowned, and the end of those who drowned you is they will be drowned.

aldea [Sp], village; hamlet; large farm.

aldeano [Sp], villager; rustic.

alea iacta est [L], the die is cast.

à l'échappée [Fr], by stealth.

alentours [Fr], surroundings; environs; also, associates; connections.

à l'envi [Fr], in emulation; in a spirit of rivalry.

alere flammam [L], to feed the flame.

alerte [Fr], *n.* alarm; alert. **—en alerte,** on the alert.

à l'espagnole [Fr], in the Spanish style or fashion.

à l'estragon [Fr], with tarragon: *cookery.*

à l'extérieur [Fr], without; on the outside; externally; abroad.

à l'extrémité [Fr], to extremity; without resource; at the point of death; at the last gasp.

alezan [Fr], chestnut horse; sorrel.

alfandega [Pg], custom house.

alfilaria [Mex Sp], a valuable forage plant; pin grass.

al fine [It], to the end: *music.*

alforja [Sp], saddlebag; knapsack.

al fresco [It], in the open air; open air.

algodón [Sp], cotton; cotton plant.

al hombre mayor, darle honor [Sp], to the greater man give honor; honor to whom honor is due.

alia tendanda via est [L], another way must be tried.

aliéné [Fr; *fem.* aliénée], deranged; mad.

alieni appetens [L], eager for another's property; covetous. **—alieni appetens sui profusus,** covetous of another's possessions, lavish of his (*or* one's) own: *Sallust.*

à l'immortalité [Fr], to immortality: motto of the French Academy (*Académie française*), whose forty members are consequently called "the Immortals."

à l'improviste [Fr], all of a sudden; unawares; unexpectedly.

alinéa [Fr], new paragraph; break in a paragraph: *typog.*

à l'intérieur [Fr], within; indoors; at home.

alio intuitu [L], from another point of view.

aliquando bonus dormitat Homerus [L], sometimes even the good Homer nods; even the greatest are sometimes caught napping: *Horace* (adapted).

aliquid [L], something; somewhat.

aliquis in omnibus nullus in singulis [L], a somebody in general, a nobody in particular: *Scaliger.*

à l'irlandaise [Fr], in the Irish style or fashion.

alis volat propriis [L], she flies with her own wings: motto of *Oregon.*

à l'italienne [Fr], in the Italian style or fashion.

alitur vitium vivitque tegendo [L], the taint is nourished and lives by being concealed; vice thrives when kept secret.

aliunde [L], from another source; from elsewhere.

à livre ouvert [Fr], lit., at open book; at sight; without preparation.

aljibar [Am Sp, *fr.* Sp *aljibe,* cistern], cistern; reservoir.

al-ki [Chinook], by and by: motto of the State of *Washington.*

alla breve [It], lit., by the breve (i.e., make the breves as short as semi-breves); in quick common time: *music.*

alla caccia [It], in the hunting style; in the style of the chase: *music.*

alla capella [It]. Same as A CAPELLA.

Allah [Ar], God.

Allah akbar [Ar], God is great.

all' alba [It], at daybreak.

alla salute! [It], to your health!

alla ventura [It], at one's risk; at random.

alla vostra salute! [It], to your health!

alléchant [Fr; *fem.* alléchante], alluring; attractive.

allée [Fr], narrow passage; alley; walk.

allégresse [Fr], joyousness; gladness; gaiety; sprightliness.

allegretto [It], moderately brisk (i.e., between *andante* and *allegro*); also, a movement in this time: *music.*

allegro [It], lively; brisk; also, a piece in quick time. —**allegro di molto,** very quick. —**allegro furioso,** quick and in a furious manner. —**allegro non tanto,** not too quick: *all music.*

allemand [Fr; *fem.* allemande], *adj.* German; *n.* a German; *music,* a German dance or dance movement.

allentando [It], slackening the speed: *music.*

aller Anfang ist heiter [Ger], every beginning is cheerful: *Goethe.*

aller Anfang ist schwer [Ger], every beginning is difficult.

aller à tâtons [Fr], to grope along; feel one's way.

aller au fait [Fr], to get to the point.

aller en permission [Fr], to go on leave.

aller planter ses choux [Fr], lit., to go plant one's cabbages; retire into the country (*or* into private life).

Alles zu retten, muss alles gewagt werden [Ger], to save all, we must risk all.

allez-vous-en! [Fr], be off! go away!

allmählich [Ger], gradually; little by little.

allonge [Fr], a lengthening piece; addition; leaf (of a table); *com.,* a slip of paper attached to a bill of exchange to make room for additional endorsements; a rider.

allons! [Fr], let us go! come on! come! now! now then! agreed! —**allons donc!,** well, really!

all' ottava [It], an octave higher than written (*abbr.* all' ott.): *music.*

allure [Fr], gait; manner of walking; bearing; *naut.,* trim; appearance.

almacén [Sp], warehouse; store: *mil.,* powder magazine.

almah *or* **alma** [Ar], lit., learned or knowing; Egyptian dancing girl.

alma mater [L], lit., fostering mother; university or other institution where a person has been educated.

almendra [Sp], almond.

almôço [Pg], lunch; brunch.

almud [Sp], a grain measure of capacity of varying content, equal in Texas to about a peck.

almuerzo [Sp], breakfast; luncheon, the first substantial meal of the day.

aloha [Hawa], love; hello; goodbye.

à loisir [Fr], at leisure; leisurely.

à l'ordinaire [Fr], in the ordinary manner; as usual.

alose [Fr], shad.

alouette [Fr], lark; skylark.

aloyau [Fr], sirloin or ribs of beef.

Ἄλφα καὶ Ὠμέγα [Gr; álpha kaì ōméga], Alpha and Omega (the first and last letters of the Greek alphabet); the beginning and the end.

al piacere [It], at pleasure: *music.*

al più [It], at most.

al solito [It], as usual.

al ta'am vay rayach ain leheetvakayach [Heb], one cannot argue about taste and smell.

al tedesco [It], in the German manner.

al teestakel ba kankan ella bema sheyesh do [Heb], don't look at the jug, but at what is in it; never judge a book by its cover.

alter ego [L], one's other self; bosom friend. **—alter ego est amicus,** a friend is another self.

alter idem [L], another exactly the same.

alter ipse amicus [L], a friend is a second self.

alteri sic tibi [L], do to another as to thyself.

alterum alterius auxilio eget [L], one thing needs the help of another.

alterum tantum [L], as much again; twice as much.

Altesse [Fr], Highness (*abbr.* Alt.): title of nobility.

Alteza [Sp], **Altezza** [It], Highness: title of nobility.

altiora peto [L], I seek higher things.

altiplano [Sp], the high Andean plateau.

altmodisch [Ger], old-fashioned.

alto [Sp], a height; hill; in Texas, a hill, usually treeless.

alto-rilievo [It], high relief: *sculp.*

alt wird man wohl, wer aber klug? [Ger], we all grow old, but who grows wise?

amabile [It], sweetly; gently: *music.*

amah [Pg *ama*], a children's nurse; wet nurse; also, a lady's maid or any female servant, esp. in a European household.

à main armée [Fr], lit., with armed hand; by force of arms.

a malas lenguas, tijeras [Sp], for evil tongues—scissors.

à malin, malin et demi [Fr], to the evil, (be) evil and a half.

amande [Fr], almond.

amant [Fr; *fem.* amante], lover; sweetheart; suitor. —**amant de coeur,** lit., heart's lover; preferred lover; favorite.

amantes amentes [L], lovers are lunatics: *Terence.*

amantium irae [L], lovers' quarrels. —**amantium irae amoris integratio,** the falling out of lovers is the renewal of love: *Terence.*

à ma puissance [Fr], according to my power.

amargoso [Sp], lit., bitter; bark of the goatbush, used as a tonic, febrifuge, and astringent: *Mexico & southwestern U.S.*

amari aliquid [L], something bitter; a touch of bitterness.

amar y saber no puede todo ser [Sp], love and prudence cannot go together.

amau [Hawa], tree fern.

a maximis ad minima [L], from the greatest to the least.

ambigendi locus [L], room for doubt.

à méchant chien, court lien [Fr], to a vicious dog a short chain.

âme damnée [Fr], lit., a damned (*or* lost) soul; devoted adherent; mere tool; dupe.

âme de boue [Fr], lit., soul of mud; base, mean soul.

am Ende [Ger], in the end; after all; finally.

amende [Fr], fine; penalty; reparation. —**amende honorable,** satisfactory apology; compensation; amends.

a mensa et toro [L], lit., from table and bed; from bed and board: *law.*

americanista [Sp], one who is devoted to American studies; a pro-American.

americano [Sp], American.

amertume [Fr], bitterness.

à merveille [Fr], admirably; marvelously.

a mezzo voce [It], with half the power of the voice; in a subdued tone: *music.*

ami [Fr; *fem.* amie], friend. —**ami de coeur,** bosom friend. —**ami de cour,** false friend; superficial friend. —**ami de table,** table companion; boon companion. —**ami du peuple,** friend of the people. —**ami en voie,** lit., friend on the road; friend at court.

amici probantur rebus adversis [L], friends are proved by adversity: *Cicero.*

amicitia semper prodest [L], friendship is always of benefit: *Seneca.*

amicitia sine fraude [L], friendship without deceit.

amicus curiae [L], a friend of the court; disinterested adviser.

amicus est tanquam alter idem [L], a friend is, as it were, a second self.

amicus humani generis [L], a friend of the human race.

amicus Plato, sed magis amica veritas [L], Plato is my friend, but a greater friend is truth.

amicus usque ad aras [L], a friend as far as the altars (i.e., in everything but what is contrary to one's religion).

amigo [Sp; *fem.* amiga], friend.

a minori ad maius [L], from the less to the greater.

amiral [Fr; *pl.* amiraux], admiral.

amissum quod nescitur non amittitur [L], the loss that is unknown is no loss at all: *Publilius Syrus.*

amitié [Fr], friendship; amity; kindness. **—amitié, doux repos de l'âme,** friendship, sweet resting place of the soul: *Lamartine.*

amoché [Fr], wounded: *Fr. mil. slang.*

à moi! [Fr], help! here!

à moitié [Fr], half; by half; by halves; in part.

amok [Mal], crazed with murderous frenzy; to run amok.

amole [Sp], soap plant: *Mexico & California.*

à mon avis [Fr], in my opinion.

à mon secours! [Fr], help me! help!

amor de niño, agua en cestillo [Sp], a boy's love is water in a basket.

amore [It], love; affection. **—amore è cieco,** love is blind. **—con amore,** with love; heartily; *music,* with tenderness.

amoretto [It; *pl.* amoretti], casual love affair; a flirtation.

amor gignit amorem [L], love begets love.

amor habendi [L], love of possessing.

amorino [It; *pl.* amorini], infant cupid or love: *fine arts.*

amor magnus doctor est [L], love is a great teacher: *St. Augustine.*

amor no tiene elección [Sp], love has no choice.

amor nummi [L], love of money.

amoroso [It], a lover; *music,* in a soft, loving manner; tenderly.

amor patriae [L], love of one's country; patriotism.

amor proximi [L], love of one's neighbor.

amor regge senza legge [It], love rules without rules (*or* laws).

amor sceleratus habendi [L], accursed love of possessing: *Ovid.*

amor solo d'amor si pasce [It], love feeds only on love.

amoto quaeramus seria ludo [L], setting banter aside, let us now give attention to serious matters: *Horace.*

amourette [Fr], lit., small love affair; *cookery,* marrow, esp. of calf or sheep, used in garnishing certain meat dishes. **—amourettes de veau,** calf's marrow: *cookery.*

amoureux transi [Fr], lit., chilled (*or* trembling) lover; a bashful lover.

amour fait moult (*or* **beaucoup**)**, argent fait tout** [Fr], love can do much, money can do everything; love is powerful, but money is all-powerful.

amour propre [Fr], lit., love of oneself; self-esteem; vanity.

amo ut invenio [L], I love as I find (*or* light upon).

amparo [Sp], lit., protection; a certificate protecting a claimant of land until a full title can be granted: *Texas.*

Amt ohne Geld macht Diebe [Ger], office without pay makes thieves.

anac [Tag], a son or daughter: *P.I.*

ἀνάνκη [Gr; anánkē], necessity; force; constraint.

anaqua [Mex Sp], a tree of the borage family, found in Mexico and southwestern Texas. Called also *knockaway*.

anch' io sono pittore [It], I too am a painter: *Correggio* (on beholding Raphael's *Saint Cecilia*).

anchois [Fr], anchovy. —**anchois farcis,** stuffed anchovies: *cookery*.

ancienne noblesse [Fr], ancient nobility; the French nobility before the Revolution of 1789.

ancien régime [Fr], the old regime; time before the French Revolution of 1789.

ancilla theologiae [L], the handmaid of theology; philosophy.

ancón [Mex Sp], irrigated land on the banks of a river: *southwestern U.S.*

anconada [Sp], open bay.

ancora [It], again; yet; still; also. —**ancora imparo,** I still learn: motto of *Michelangelo*. —**ancora una volta,** once again; once more; over again: *music*.

andächtig [Ger], devotional; devout; devoutly.

andante [It], moderately slow: *music*.

andantino [It], rather quicker (orig., slower) than *andante: music*.

andiamo [It], let us go.

andouillette [Fr], forcemeat ball: *cookery*.

ἀνέχου καὶ ἀπέχου [Gr; anékhou kaì apékhou], bear and forbear.

ἀνεμώλια βάζειν [Gr; anemólia bázein], to speak vain words.

ἀνήριθμον γέλασμα [Gr; anérithmon gélasma], the many-twinkling smile (of Ocean); the countless smiles (of the waves): *Aeschylus*.

Anfangsbuchstabe [Ger], initial letter: *typog*.

Anführungszeichen [Ger], quotation marks: *typog*.

anguillam cauda tenes [L], you hold an eel by the tail; you have a tiger by the tail.

anguille [Fr], eel. —**anguille de mer,** conger.

anguis in herba [L], a snake in the grass; an unsuspected danger.

angulus ridet [L], that corner of earth smiles on me; "that little nook of ground smiles to my sight": *Horace*.

Anhang [Ger], coda; appendix: *music*.

aniles fabulae [L], old wives' tales.

anima [L; *pl.* animae], breath; life; soul; spirit. —**anima bruta,** the brute soul; vital principle of the lower animals; sometimes, also, the vital principle of man as distinguished from his soul, or *anima divina*. —**anima divina,** the divine soul. —**anima humana,** the vital principle of man; the human soul. —**anima in amicis una,** one mind among friends. —**anima mundi,** spirit of the universe; the creative and energizing force that permeates all nature: *philos*.

animal bipes implume [L], a two-legged animal without feathers: Latinized form of Plato's definition of man.

animato [It], with animation: *music*.

animis opibusque parati [L], prepared in minds and resources: one of the mottoes of *South Carolina.*

animo et facto [L], in intention and fact: *law.*

animo et fide [L], by courage and faith.

animo non astutia [L], by courage, not by craft.

animum pictura pascit inani [L], with the vain (*or* shadowy) picture he feeds his soul: *Virgil.*

animus capiendi [L], the intention of taking: *law.*

animus et prudentia [L], courage and discretion (*or* prudence).

animus furandi [L], the intention of stealing: *law.*

animus meminisse horret [L], my soul shudders at the recollection: *Virgil.*

animus non deficit aequus [L], a well-balanced mind is not wanting; equanimity does not fail us.

ankus [Hind], elephant goad, with a sharp iron spike and hook at the end of a short wooden handle: *India.*

Anmerkungen [Ger], notes; annotations: *abbr.* Anm.

annales [L], chronicles; annals: *abbr.* ann.

anno [L], in the year. —**anno aetatis suae,** in the — year of his (*or* her) age: *abbr.* aet. *or* aetat. —**anno Christi,** in the year of Christ. —**anno Domini,** in the year of our Lord: *abbr.* A.D. —**anno Hegirae,** in the year of the Hegira (the flight of Muhammed from Mecca to Medina and the first year of the Muslim era, A.D. 622): *abbr.* A.H. —**anno humanae salutis,** in the year of man's redemption: *abbr.* A.H.S. —**anno mundi,** in the year of the world (i.e., when the creation of the world is said to have taken place, 4004 B.C., according to Usher): *abbr.* A.M. —**anno post Christum natum,** in the year after the birth of Christ: *abbr.* A.P.C.N. —**anno post Romam conditam,** in the year after the building of Rome (753 B.C.): *abbr.* A.P.R.C. —**anno regni,** in the year of the reign: *abbr.* A.R. —**anno salutis,** in the year of redemption: *abbr.* A.S. —**anno urbis conditae,** in the year (*or* from the time) of the founded city (Rome, founded about 753 B.C.): *abbr.* A.U.C.

annonce [Fr], announcement; advertisement.

annos vixit [L], he (*or* she) lived (so many) years: *abbr.* a.v.

annuit coeptis [L], He (God) has smiled on our undertakings: motto, adapted from Virgil, on the uncut reverse of the Great Seal of the United States.

annus [L; *pl.* anni], year. —**annus luctus,** year of mourning: *law.* —**annus magnus,** great year; *astron.,* the cycle (about 26,000 years) in which a complete revolution of the celestial bodies takes place; Platonic year. —**annus mirabilis,** wonderful year; year of wonders (esp. 1666).

à nouvelles affaires, nouveaux conseils [Fr], for new affairs (*or* occasions), new counsels.

Anschauungsunterricht [Ger], intuitive method of instruction; object lessons.

Anschluss [Ger], junction; union; as, the *Anschluss* between Germany and Austria in 1938.

ante barbam doces senes [L], you teach old men before your beard has come.

ante bellum [L], before the war.

ante Christum [L], before Christ: *abbr.* A.C.

ante cibum [L], before meals: *abbr. (in prescriptions)* a.c.

ante diem [L], before the day: *abbr.* a.d.

ante litem notam [L], before litigation has commenced: *law.*

ante lucem [L], before daybreak.

ante meridiem [L], before noon: *abbr.* A.M. *or* a.m.

ante mortem [L], before death.

ante omnia [L], before all things; in the first place.

ante partum [L], before childbirth.

antes bom Rei, que boa lei [Pg], better a good king than a good law; laws avail nothing unless ably administered.

antes de que digan [Sp], tell before they tell.

antes só, que mal acompanhado [Pg], better alone than in bad company.

ante tubam trepidat [L], he trembles before the trumpet (sounds); he cries before he is hurt: *Virgil.*

ante victoriam ne canas triumphum [L], do not sing your triumph before the victory; don't shout "hurrah" till you are out of the woods.

ἄνθρωπός ἐστι πνεῦμα καὶ σκιὰ μόνον [Gr; anthrōpós esti pneûma kaì skià mónon], man is but a breath and a shadow: *Euripides.*

antipasto [It], hors d'oeuvre; appetizer.

antonyme [Fr], a word of opposite meaning; antonym.

Anzeige [Ger; *pl.* Anzeigen], notice; announcement; advertisement.

août [Fr], August.

à outrance [Fr], to the utmost; to the death; to the bitter end

apache [Fr], Parisian gangster.

a padre guardador, hijo gastador [Sp], to a miserly father, a spendthrift son.

apage Satanas! [L], get thee hence, Satan!

aparejo [Sp], a kind of pack saddle, as used in Spanish America and in the United States army; *naut.,* tackle; rigging; *pl.,* tools, implements.

à part [Fr], apart; aside.

apartheid [Afrik], apartness; separation of races: whites, blacks, mixed and Asians.

à pas de géant [Fr], with a giant's stride.

ἅπαξ λεγόμενον [Gr; hápax legómenon], said only once. See HAPAX LEGOMENON.

à peindre [Fr], fit to paint; fit for a model.

apellido [Sp], family name; surname.

aperçu [Fr], rapid view; glance; general sketch; outline; summary.

apéritif [Fr], appetizer.

à perte [Fr], at a loss. **—à perte de vue,** beyond the range of vision; hence, at random; farfetched.

aperto vivere voto [L], to live with unconcealed desire; have one's life and progress an open book: *Persius.*

à peu de frais [Fr], at little cost; cheaply.

à peu près [Fr], nearly; almost.

a piacere [It], at pleasure; *ad lib.: music.*

à pied [Fr], on foot.

à pierre fendre [Fr], to split a stone; fig., with great intensity or rigor; as, *il gèle à pierre fendre,* it is freezing extremely hard.

à plaisir [Fr], at one's ease; freely; designedly.

à plomb [Fr], plumb; perpendicularly; hence, with assurance.

aplomb [Fr], perpendicularity; equilibrium; hence, self-possession, assurance.

a pobreza no hay vergüenza [Sp], poverty has no shame.

a poco a poco [It], little by little; by degrees.

a poco pan, tomar primero [Sp], when there is little bread, take the first slice; every man for himself.

ἀπόδοτε οὖν τὰ Καίσαρος Καίσαρι καὶ τὰ τοῦ θεοῦ τῷ θεῷ [Gr; apódote oûn tà Kaísaros Kaísari kaì tà toû theoû tô theô], render therefore unto Caesar the things that are Caesar's; and unto God the things that are God's: *Matthew* xxii. 21.

ἀπόδοτε πᾶσι τὰς ὀφειλάς [Gr; apódote pási tàs opheilás], render to all their dues: *Romans* xiii. 7.

à point [Fr], in time; just in time; opportunely; apropos; to a nicety; to a turn. **—à point nommé,** at the appointed time. **—cuit à point,** cooked to a turn.

apologia pro vita sua [L], a defense of the conduct (*or* a justification) of his life: *Cardinal Newman* (title of his autobiography).

apopo [Maori], tomorrow: *New Zealand.*

a posse ad esse [L], from possibility to realization (*or* reality).

a posteriori [L], (reasoning) from effect to cause; inductive; empirical.

apparent rari nantes in gurgite vasto [L], scattered here and there, they are seen swimming in the seething waters: often applied in criticism of a work where the few thoughts of value are engulfed in a watery waste of verbiage: *Virgil.*

apparatus belli [L], material (*or* munitions) of war.

apparatus criticus [L], information added to a text to help scholars.

appartement [Fr], an apartment or suite of rooms; a flat.

appassionato [It], with passion, in an impassioned style: *music.*

appel [Fr], a call; challenge; *fencing,* a stamp of the foot, as in commencing an attack.

appeler les choses par leur nom [Fr], to call things by their names.

appeler un chat un chat [Fr], to call a cat a cat; call a spade a spade.

appendix vermiformis [NL], the vermiform appendix: *anat.*

appetitus rationi pareat [L], let your desires be governed by reason: *Cicero.*

appoggiato [It], lit., propped; supported: applied to notes that are connected with others, as in syncopations and suspensions; also, indicating notes to be rendered without a break (i.e., with *portamento*): *music.*

appoggiatura [It], an added note of embellishment; grace note: *music.*

appui [Fr], support; prop; stay; *mil.*, defensive support.

après coup [Fr], after the event; too late.

après la mort le médecin [Fr], after death the doctor.

après la pluie le beau temps [Fr], after the rain, fair weather.

après livraison [Fr], after delivery (of goods): *abbr.* a.l.

après-midi [Fr], afternoon.

après nous le déluge [Fr], after us, the deluge: a remark attributed to Madame de Pompadour, mistress of Louis XV, who saw the signs of the approaching Revolution. The saying, in the form *après moi* (me) *le déluge,* is often attributed to Louis XV himself.

a prima vista [It], at first sight.

a primo [L], from the first.

a principio [L], from the beginning.

a priori [L], (reasoning) from cause to effect; deductive or deductively; presumptive.

à prix d'or [Fr], at the price of gold; very costly.

à propos [Fr], *adj.* reasonable; to the purpose; apropos; *adv.* opportunely; seasonably; by the way; regarding. —**à propos de bottes,** lit., speaking of boots; foreign to the subject; by the way; for no earthly reason. —**à propos de rien,** apropos of nothing; irrelevant.

apud [L], according to; in writings of.

aqua [L], water: *abbr.* aq. —**aqua bulliens,** boiling water: *abbr.* aq. bull. —**aqua caelestis,** lit., celestial water; pure rainwater; specif., rectified spirits; a cordial. —**aqua destillata,** distilled water: *abbr.* aq. dest. —**aqua et igni interdictus,** forbidden (to be provided with) water and fire; banished. —**aqua fontana,** spring water. —**aqua fortis,** lit., strong water; nitric acid. —**aqua mirabilis,** lit., wonderful water; in old pharmacy, an aromatic cordial. —**aqua profunda est quieta,** still waters run deep. —**aqua pura,** pure (distilled) water. —**aqua regia,** lit., royal water; a mixture of nitric and hydrochloric acids. —**aqua tofana,** a secret poison made by a Sicilian woman, called Tofana, in the 17th century and used by her in wholesale poisonings. —**aqua vitae,** lit., water of life; brandy; formerly, alcohol.

à quatre mains [Fr], for four hands; for two performers: *music.*

à quatre pattes [Fr], lit., on four paws; on all fours.

aquí [Sp], here.

aquila non capit muscas [L], an eagle does not catch flies.

a quo [L], from which: opposite of *ad quem.*

à quoi bon faire cela? [Fr], what's the good? what's the use?

araba [Hind & Ar], a heavy springless cart or wagon, often covered: *Oriental.*

arado [Sp *arada*], lit., plow; plowed or cultivated land: *southwestern U.S.*

à ravir [Fr], ravishingly; charmingly; admirably.

arbiter bibendi [L], lit., the judge of the drinking; master of the feast; toastmaster: *Horace.*

arbiter elegantiae *or* **elegantiarum** [L], a judge of elegance; a supreme authority in matters of taste.

Arcades ambo [L], Arcadians both; hence, two persons of similar tastes; *jocosely,* two simpletons: *Virgil.*

arcana caelestia [L], heavenly secrets; celestial mysteries.

arcana imperii [L], state secrets.

arc-boutant [Fr; *pl.* arcs-boutants], flying buttress: *arch.*

arc de triomphe [Fr; *pl.* arcs de triomphe], triumphal arch; memorial arch.

arc-en-ciel [Fr; *pl.* arcs-en-ciel], rainbow.

archon [Gr ἄρχων], ruler; chief magistrate.

arco [It; *pl.* arci], bow, as of a violin.

ardente [It], ardent; fiery; vigorous: *music.*

ardentemente [It], ardently; passionately: *music.*

ardentia verba [L], words that burn; glowing words.

ardilla [Sp], squirrel.

à (*or* **au**) **rebours** [Fr], the wrong way; against the grain; backwards.

à reculons [Fr], backwards; to the right about.

a reexpedir [Sp], please forward: direction on a letter.

arena sine ealce [L], sand without lime; incoherent speech: *Suetonius.*

arete [Gr ἀρετή], excellence; prowess; valor; virtue.

arête [Fr], lit., fishbone; ridge; *geog.,* sharp ridge or crest of a mountain or between two mountain gorges.

argent [Fr], silver; money. —**argent comptant,** cash money. —**argent comptant porte médecine,** cash money works wonderful cures. —**argent d'emprunt,** borrowed money. —**argent mignon,** pin money.

argilla quidvis imitaberis uda [L], you may easily model anything with moist clay; "soft clay, you know, takes any form you please": *Horace* (tr. by Conington).

argumentum [L], argument; proof. —**argumentum ad absurdum,** an argument to prove the absurdity of an opponent's argument. —**argumentum ad crumenam,** an argument to the purse; an appeal to one's interests. —**argumentum ad hominem,** lit., an argument to the man; an evasive argument, relying on abuse and inconsistencies or on an appeal to personal interests and prejudices. —**argumentum ad ignorantiam,** an argument based on an opponent's ignorance of the facts or on his inability to prove the opposite. —**argumentum ad invidiam,** an appeal to prejudices or low passions. —**argumentum ad iudicium,** an appeal to judgment or common sense. —**argumentum ad misericordiam,** an appeal to pity. —**argumentum ad populum,** an appeal to the people (i.e., to their lower nature rather than to their intellect). —**argumentum ad rem,** an argument bearing upon the real point at issue. —**argumentum ad verecundiam,** an appeal to modesty or one's sense of reverence; a reliance on the prestige of some great name rather than the independent consideration of the question at issue. —**argumentum baculinum** (*or* **ad baculum**), an appeal to the rod (*or* the "big stick"); conviction by force: *all logic.*

aria [It], air; a particular song within an opera.

aria parlante [It], a declamatory aria: *music.*

arietta [It], a short aria or air: *music.*

arigato [Jap], thank you: *Japan.*

arioso [It], in a gay, melodious manner: *music.*

ἄριστον μὲν ὕδωρ [Gr; áriston mèn húdōr], water is best (inscribed over the Pump Room, Bath, England): *Pindar.*

ἄριστον μέτρον [Gr; áriston métron], moderation is best: *Cleobulus.*

ἀρκετὸν τῇ ἡμέρᾳ ἡ κακία αὐτῆς [Gr; arketón tê hēméra hē kakiá autês], sufficient unto the day is the evil thereof: *Matthew* vi. 34.

ἀρχὴ ἄνδρα δείξει [Gr; arkhè ándra deíxei], power (*or* authority) will prove a man: *Bias.*

ἀρχὴ ἥμισυ παντός [Gr; arkhè hémisu pantós], the beginning is the half of the whole; well begun is half done: *Hesiod.*

arma accipere [L], to receive arms; be made a knight.

arma pacis fulcra [L], arms are the props of peace.

arma tuentur pacem [L], arms maintain peace.

arma virumque cano [L], arms and the man I sing: *Virgil* (opening words of the Aeneid).

armes à feu [Fr], firearms.

armes blanches [Fr], lit., white arms; side arms; cold steel: *mil.*

armoire [Fr], large cupboard or wardrobe.

arpeggio [It], the production of the tones in a chord in rapid succession instead of simultaneously: *music.*

arpent [Fr], an old French land measure, more or less approximating an acre; in the Province of Quebec, a linear measure, equal to about 12 rods (the length of the side of a square arpent): used also in Louisiana.

arrastre *or* **arrastra** [Sp], a drag-stone mill for pulverizing or amalgamating ore: *Mexico & southwestern U.S. also,* the pulling of a dead bull from the ring.

arrectis auribus [L], with ears pricked up: *Virgil.*

arrêt [Fr], a judgment; decree; sentence; also, arrest. —**aux arrêts,** under arrest; in confinement.

arrêtez! [Fr], stop!

arrière [Fr], rear (as of an army); stern (of a ship). **—en arrière,** in the rear; in arrears; naut., abaft.

arrière-ban [Fr], a proclamation summoning vassals to military service; also, the body so called or liable to be called; levy in mass.

arrière-garde [Fr], rearguard.

arrière-pensée [Fr], mental reservation; ulterior design; secret intention.

arrivederci *(to equals)* or **arrivederla** *(to superiors)* [It], lit., till we meet again; so long!; *au revoir.*

arriviste [Fr], person of new or uncertain social or artistic success.

arroba [Sp], a weight equal to about 25 pounds; also, a liquid measure equal to about four gallons: *Sp. Am. & Texas.*

arrondissement [Fr], district; ward; administrative subdivision of a French department.

arroyo [Sp], creek; water-course; dry gully, as in New Mexico and California.

arroz [Sp], rice.

arroz con pollo [Sp], rice with chicken.

ars artium [L], lit., art of arts; logic. **—ars artium omnium conservatrix,** the art preservative of all arts; printing.

ars est celare artem [L], (true) art is to conceal art.

ars est longa, vita brevis [L], art is long, life is short.

ars poetica [L], art of poetry.

arte magistra [L], with art the mistress (teacher): *Virgil.*

arte perire sua [L], to perish by one's own cunning; be caught in one's own trap.

artes honorabit [L], he will adorn the arts.

artichaut [Fr], artichoke.

article de fond [Fr], leading article; editorial.

artiste [Fr], artist; a highly skilled performer, esp. on the stage.

Artium Baccalaureus [LL], Bachelor of Arts: *abbr.* A.B. *or* B.A.

Artium Magister [L], Master of Arts: *abbr.* A.M. *or* M.A.

Art Nouveau [Fr], New Art: a form of decorative design introduced about 1895.

arts d'agrément [Fr], accomplishments.

aruchat [Heb], a meal. **—aruchat boker,** breakfast. **—aruchat erev,** dinner. **—aruchat tsohorayeem,** lunch.

ἄσβεστος γέλως [Gr; ásbestos gélōs], lit., unquenchable laughter; Homeric (*or* irrepressible) laughter.

à ses moments perdus [Fr], in one's spare moments.

asinus ad lyram [L], an ass at the lyre: a proverb denoting gross awkwardness or unfitness.

asinus asino, et sus sui pulcher [L], an ass is beautiful to an ass and a pig to a pig.

askari [Swa], gun bearer on safari; soldier.

asperge [Fr], asparagus.

asperges [L], thou shalt sprinkle; the sprinkling with holy water at the beginning of High Mass. —**Asperges,** the anthem (*Vulgate, Psalms* li. 7) introducing the sprinkling ceremony: *R.C.Ch.*

assai [It], enough; very.

assai basta, e troppo guasta [It], enough is enough, and too much spoils.

assegai [Zu], short stabbing spear.

assez à qui se contente [Fr], he has enough who is content.

assez bien [Fr], pretty well.

assez tôt, si assez bien [Fr], soon enough, if well enough.

assiette [Fr], a plate. —**assiettes volantes,** lit., flying plates; extra dishes; extras; small entrées.

assignatus utitur iure auctoris [L], the assignee is possessed of the rights of his principal: *law.*

assistant [Fr], bystander; onlooker.

assister [Fr], *v.t.* to assist; aid; *v.i.* to be present at; look on; attend; witness.

assumpsit [L], lit., he undertook; a suit to recover damages for breach of a contract or actionable promise, express or implied, and (formerly) not under seal: *law.*

astagh-fer Allah! [Turk & Ar], God forbid!

astra castra, numen lumen [L], the stars my camp, the Deity my light.

a su salud [Sp], to your health.

atajo [Sp], shortcut; convenience.

atalaya [Sp], watchtower.

à tâtons [Fr], gropingly; irresolutely; feeling one's way.

até a vista [Pg], until our next meeting; goodbye; *au revoir.*

atelier [Fr], workshop; studio.

a tempo [It], in time (i.e., in the original time, before a change of tempo was indicated). —**a tempo giusto,** in strict time: *music.*

a teneris (annis) [L], from tender (years).

atento [Sp], attentive; obliging: *abbr.* at.° *or* at.to. —**atento y seguro servidor,** (your) attentive and faithful servant; (yours) very truly: *abbr. in a letter* at.to y S.S.

Athanasius contra mundum [L], Athanasius against the world: referring to the stand made by Athanasius the Great against the foes of orthodox Christianity.

a tiro [Sp], within reach.

atman *or* **atma** [Skr], life principle; spirit; soul. —**Atman,** the universal Self.

atocha [Sp], esparto grass.

a toda fuerza [Sp], lit., with all power; at full speed.

atole [Mex Sp], a porridge made of cornmeal: *Sp. Am.*

à tort et à travers [Fr], at random; indiscriminately; anyhow.

à tort ou à raison [Fr], wrongly or rightly.

à toute force [Fr], lit., with all force; by every means.

à toute outrance [Fr], beyond measure; with a vengeance.

à toutes jambes [Fr], as fast as one's legs can carry one.

à tout hasard [Fr], at all hazards; at all events.

à tout prendre [Fr], on the whole; in the main.

à tout prix [Fr], at any price; cost what may.

à tout propos [Fr], at every turn; ever and anon.

atra cura [L], black care.

à travers [Fr], athwart; across; through.

at spes non fracta [L], but hope is not broken.

attacca [It], attack; begin the next part at once. —**attacca subito,** attack immediately: *both music.*

attaché [Fr; *now naturalized*], one attached to an embassy.

attorno attorno [It], all around; here, there, and everywhere.

attroupement [Fr], riotous gathering; mob.

aubade [Fr], morning serenade or concert: *music.*

aubaine [Fr], windfall; godsend.

au beau milieu [Fr], in the very middle.

auberge [Fr], inn; tavern.

aubergine [Fr], eggplant.

aubergiste [Fr], innkeeper; landlord.

au besoin [Fr], in case of need; in a pinch.

au beurre [Fr], with butter: *cookery.*

au beurre fondu [Fr], in melted butter; with butter sauce: *cookery.*

au beurre roux [Fr], with browned butter: *cookery.*

aubin [Fr], a canter; hand gallop.

au bon droit [Fr], with good (*or* just) right.

au bout de son latin [Fr], lit., at the end of his Latin; at wits' end.

au bout du compte [Fr], lit., at the end of the account; when all is said and done; after all; on the whole.

auch das Schöne muss sterben [Ger], even the beautiful must die: *Schiller.*

auch ich war in Arkadien geboren [Ger], I too was born in Arcadia (i.e., I too have aspirations towards the ideal): *Schiller.*

au contraire [Fr], on the contrary.

au courant [Fr], lit., with the current; fully acquainted with; well informed.

auctor pretiosa facit [L], the giver makes (the gifts) precious: *Ovid* (adapted).

aucun chemin de fleurs ne conduit à la gloire [Fr], it is no path of flowers that leads to glory: *La Fontaine.*

audaciter at sincere [L], boldly and frankly.

audax et celer [L], bold and swift.

audendo magnus tegitur timor [L], great fear is (often) concealed by a show of daring: *Lucan.*

audentes (*or* **audaces**) **fortuna iuvat** [L], fortune favors the bold.

au dépourvu [Fr], unawares.

au dernier les os [Fr], for the last, the bones.

aude sapere [L], dare to be wise.

au désespoir [Fr], in utter despair.

audi alteram partem [L], hear the other side.

audiatur et altera pars [L], let the other side also be heard.

audita querela [L], the complaint having been heard; a commonlaw writ giving the defendant permission to appeal: *law.*

auf! *or* **aufstehen!** [Ger], stand up!

au fait [Fr], conversant; proficient; well-instructed.

auf den Bergen ist Freiheit [Ger], on the mountains is freedom: *Schiller.*

Auffassung [Ger], comprehension; grasp.

aufgeschoben ist nicht aufgehoben [Ger], deferred is not abandoned; forbearance is not acquittance; deferred is not denied.

Aufklärung [Ger], enlightenment; an empirical movement of the 18th century: *philos.*

Auflage [Ger; *pl.* Auflagen], edition (of a book): *abbr.* Aufl.

au fond [Fr], at bottom; in the main; fundamentally.

au frais [Fr], in the cool of the evening.

aufs beste [Ger], in the best possible way.

aufs eheste [Ger], as soon as possible.

aufs Geratewohl [Ger], at random.

auf Wiedersehen [Ger], till we meet again; goodbye.

Augen rechts (*or* **links**), **richt(et) euch!** [Ger], eyes right (*or* left), dress!: *mil.*

Auge um Auge, Zahn um Zahn [Ger], eye for an eye, tooth for a tooth.

au grand sérieux [Fr], in all seriousness.

au gratin [Fr], with the burned scrapings from the pan; with a brown crust or crisp surface of buttered crumbs and, sometimes, grated cheese; as, cauliflower *au gratin: cookery.*

au jour [Fr], by daylight.

aujourd'hui roi, demain rien [Fr], today king, tomorrow nothing.

au jour le jour [Fr], from day to day; from hand to mouth.

au jus [Fr], with the natural juice or gravy, given off by the meat in cooking: *cookery.*

au lait [Fr], with milk.

au levant [Fr], to the East; eastward.

au mieux [Fr], at best; for the best; on the best of terms.

aumonier [Fr; *fem.* aumonière], almoner.

au naturel [Fr], naturally; to the life; *cookery,* (cooked) simply or plainly.

au pied de la lettre [Fr], lit., to the foot of the letter; literally; exactly.

au pis aller [Fr], at worst; if worse comes to worst; as a last resort.

au plaisir de vous revoir [Fr], to the pleasure of seeing you again.

au premier [Fr], on the first floor (i.e., the one above the ground floor).

au prix coûtant [Fr], at cost.

aura [L; *pl.* aurae], wind; breeze; air. —**aura popularis,** the popular breeze; popular favor: *Cicero.*

aurea mediocritas [L], the golden mean: *Horace* (adapted).

aurea rumpunt tecta quietem [L], golden palaces break (*or* disturb) one's rest: *Seneca.*

au reste [Fr], for the rest; besides.

au revoir [Fr], (goodbye) till we meet again!

auribus teneo lupum [L], lit., I have a wolf by the ears; I have a tiger by the tail; I have caught a Tartar: *Terence.*

auri sacra fames [L], accursed craving for gold: *Virgil.*

aurora australis [L], lit., southern dawn; in the Southern Hemisphere, a luminous polar phenomenon similar to the northern lights.

aurora borealis [L], lit., northern dawn; the northern lights.

aurora musis amica est [L], the Dawn is the friend of the Muses. Cf. Morgenstunde hat Gold im Munde.

au royaume des aveugles les borgnes sont rois [Fr], in the kingdom of the blind the one-eyed are kings.

aurum [L], gold.

aus den Augen, aus dem Sinn [Ger], out of sight, out of mind.

Ausdruck [Ger], expression: *music.*

au second [Fr], on the second floor. Cf. au troisième.

au secours! [Fr], to the rescue! help!

au sérieux [Fr], in earnest; seriously.

aus freien Stücken [Ger], of one's own accord; voluntarily.

Ausgabe [Ger; *pl.* Ausgaben], edition; revised edition: *abbr.* Ausg.

Ausgleich [Ger], agreement; compromise; esp. the political agreement between Austria and Hungary, made in 1867.

Aushaltung [Ger], the sustaining of a note: *music.*

aus nichts wird nichts [Ger], nothing comes from nothing.

Ausrufungszeichen [Ger], exclamation point: *typog.*

au soleil [Fr], in the sun (*or* sunshine).

auspicium melioris aevi [L], an omen of a better age; a pledge of better times: motto of the *Order of St. Michael and St. George.*

aus Scherz [Ger], for fun; by way of a jest.

aussitôt dit, aussitôt fait [Fr], no sooner said than done.

autant! [Fr], as you were!: *mil.*

autant de têtes, autant d'avis [Fr], so many heads, so many opinions.

autant d'hommes, autant d'avis [Fr], so many men, so many minds (*or* opinions).

aut bibat aut abeat [L], either drink or depart.

aut Caesar aut nihil [L], either Caesar or nothing; either first or nowhere.

aut disce, aut discede; manet sors tertia, caedi [L], either learn or depart; a third choice remains—to be flogged: motto in the schoolroom of *Winchester College*, one of the great English public schools.

aut insanit homo aut versus facit [L], the fellow is either mad or is composing verses: *Horace*.

aut inveniam viam aut faciam [L], I will either find a way or make one.

aut mors aut victoria [L], death or victory.

aut non tentaris, aut perfice [L], either don't attempt it, or go through with it: *Ovid*.

autocamión [Sp], truck.

auto-da-fé [Pg; *pl.* autos-da-fé], lit., edict of faith; sentence of the Inquisition; burning of a heretic.

auto-de-fe [Sp; *pl.* autos-de-fe]. Same as AUTO-DA-FÉ.

autore [It; *pl.* autori], author: *abbr.* aut.

autres temps, autres moeurs [Fr], other times, other manners (*or* customs).

au troisième [Fr], on the fourth floor. (Floors in France are calculated above the ground floor, and the next one up from the ground floor is the first floor.)

aut vincere aut mori [L], either to conquer or to die.

au voleur! [Fr], stop, thief!

aux abois [Fr], at bay; at one's wits' end; hard up.

aux aguets [Fr], on watch.

aux armes! [Fr], to arms! stand to!: *mil*.

aux arrêts [Fr], under arrest; in confinement; kept in (as at school).

aux choux [Fr], with cabbage.

aux confitures [Fr], with preserved fruit; with preserves.

aux cressons [Fr], with watercress.

aux grands maux les grands remèdes [Fr], for great ills, great remedies; desperate diseases need desperate remedies.

auxilium ab alto [L], help from on high.

auxilium non leve vultus habet [L], the face affords no inconsiderable aid; a good face is a good recommendation: *Ovid*.

aux morilles [Fr], with morels: *cookery*.

aux oignons [Fr], with onions: *cookery*.

aux petits pois [Fr], with green peas: *cookery*.

aux voix! [Fr], put it to the vote! vote!

avaler des couleuvres [Fr], lit., to swallow adders; receive indignities without protest; swallow insults.

avant-coureur *or* **avant-courrier** [Fr], forerunner; precursor; harbinger.

avant-garde [Fr], vanguard.

avanti Cristo [It], before Christ: *abbr.* av. C.

avant-propos [Fr], preliminary matter; preface.

ave! [L], hail! —**ave atque vale,** hail and farewell! —**ave, Caesar** (*or* **Imperator**)**! morituri te salutamus,** hail, Caesar (*or* Emperor)! we who are about to die salute thee: salutation of the gladiators to the Roman emperor. —**Ave Maria,** hail, Mary!: a salutation and prayer to the Blessed Virgin. —**Ave maris stella, Dei Mater alma, atque semper Virgo, felix coeli porta,**

> Hail, thou star of ocean!
> > Portal of the sky!
> Ever Virgin Mother
> > Of the Lord most high!
> > > —*Hymn to the Blessed Virgin.*

avec entrain [Fr], with a will; with enthusiasm.
avec les hommages de l'auteur [Fr], with the author's compliments.
avec nantissement [Fr], with security: *law.*
avec plaisir [Fr], with pleasure.
avec votre permission [Fr], by your leave.
avenida [Sp], avenue.
a verbis ad verbera [L], from words to blows.
avertissement [Fr], notice; warning.
avete ragione [It], you are right.
avete torto [It], you are wrong.
aviado [Sp], one who mines with means furnished by another: *Sp. Am.*
avia Pieridum loca [L], the Muses' lonely haunts: *Lucretius* (adapted).
à vieux comptes nouvelles disputes [Fr], old reckonings create new disputes; short reckonings make long friends.
avi memorantur avorum [L], my ancestors call to mind their ancestors (i.e., I have a long ancestral line).
a vinculo matrimonii [L], from the bond of marriage.
avion [Fr], airplane. —**avion de chasse,** pursuit plane.
avis [Fr], notice.
avis au lecteur [Fr], notice to the reader.
avise la fin [Fr], consider the end.
aviso [Sp], notice; information; warning.
avito viret honore [L], he flourishes on ancestral honors.
avocat [Fr], advocate; lawyer; also, avocado.
avoir de la frousse [Fr], to be in a fright: *colloq.*
avoir de l'avenir [Fr], to have good future prospects.
avoir de l'entregent [Fr], to possess tact.
avoir du guignon [Fr], to be unlucky; be down on one's luck.
avoir du toupet [Fr], lit., to have a forelock; to have a nerve: *colloq.*
avoir la langue bien pendue [Fr], lit., to have the tongue well hung; have the gift of gab.
avoir l'aller pour le venir [Fr], lit., to have the going for the coming; have one's labor for one's pains.

avoir le diable au corps [Fr], to have the devil in one; be deliberately annoying.

avoir le pas [Fr], to have precedence.

avoir les armes belles [Fr], to fence gracefully.

avoir les coudées franches [Fr], to have elbowroom; have free play.

avoir un chez soi [Fr], to have a home of one's own.

à vol d'oiseau [Fr], as the crow flies.

à volonté [Fr], at will; at pleasure.

a vostra salute! [It], to your health!

a vostro beneplacito [It], at your good pleasure; as you will.

a vostro commodo [It], at your convenience (*or* leisure).

à votre santé! [Fr], to your health!

à vous le dé [Fr], it is your throw; it's your turn to play.

à vue [Fr], at sight. —**à vue d'oeil,** by the eye; visibly. —**à vue d'oiseau,** from a bird's-eye view.

a vuelta de correo [Sp], by return mail.

a vuestra salud! [Sp], to your health! your good health!

avvocato del diavolo [It], Devil's advocate.

ἄξιος γὰρ ὁ ἐργάτης τοῦ μισθοῦ αὐτοῦ [Gr; áxios gàr ho ergátēs toû misthoû autoû], for the laborer is worthy of his hire: *Luke* x. 7.

ayah [Ango-Ind, *fr.* Pg *aia,* governess], native nurse for children; lady's maid; female attendant. Cf. AMAH.

ayeen tachat ayeen, shen tachat shen [Heb], eye for an eye, tooth for a tooth.

aymez loyauté [OF], love loyalty.

ayudante [Sp], lit, assistant; *mil.,* adjutant; also, aide-de-camp; *Sp. Am.,* helper on a ranch; *P.I.,* an assistant teacher in the elementary schools.

ayuntamiento [Sp], municipal government or its seat; town hall. —**Ayuntamiento,** central government offices in Manila.

azeite, vinho e amigo, o mais antigo [Pg], oil, wine, and friend—the oldest is the best.

azogue [Sp], quicksilver; *pl. mining,* silver ores that can be treated profitably by the mercury process: *Sp. Am.*

azote [Sp], a switch; whip; in Texas, anything used as a whip; fig., calamity.

azotea [Sp], platform on the top of a house; flat roof.

azúcar [Sp], sugar. —**azúcar de caña,** cane sugar. —**azúcar de remolacha,** beet sugar.

B

baas [Afrik], master; boss: *South Africa.*

baba [Pol & Russ], old woman; grandmother.

baba au rhum [Fr, *fr.* Pol *baba* (see above)], a rich cake soaked in rum and syrup: *cookery.*

bába [Hind & Turk], father; sire; a title of respect; also, as in Lower Bengal, a child.

babiche [Can Fr], thong of rawhide.

babillage [Fr], tittle-tattle; chit-chat; twaddle.

babillard [Fr; *fem.* babillarde], babbler; tattler; blab.

babu *or* **baboo** [Hind & Beng *bābū*, father], Hindu gentleman, esp. a Bengali; as a title, equivalent to *Mr.* or *Esquire;* specif., a native clerk who writes English; hence, formerly, a half-Anglicized Bengali: *India.*

babushka [Russ], grandmother; scarf tied under chin.

baccalauréat [Fr], baccalaureate; school-leaving certificate.

baccarat *or* **baccara** [Fr], a gambling game of cards.

bachcha [Hind], child; also, the young of any animal. Written also *bacha, bachha, butcha.*

bacio di bocca spesso cuor non tocca [It], a kiss of the mouth often touches not the heart; oft heart is missed where mouth is kissed.

Backfisch [Ger; *pl.* Backfische], lit., baked fish; a girl in her awkward teens.

badaud [Fr], a credulous idler; street lounger; booby.

badauderie [Fr], foolery; silliness; lounging.

badinage [Fr], light raillery; chaff.

badli [Hind, *fr. badal,* exchange], a substitute: *India.*

badshah [Hind & Pers], king; sovereign.

bagasse [Fr], sugar cane that has been crushed and the juice extracted; often dried and used as fuel under the sugar kettle: *southern U.S.* Called also *cane trash.*

bagh [Hind; *fem.* baghan], tiger: *India.*

baguette [Fr], rod; wand; drumstick; small loaf of bread; *arch.,* small semicircular molding; bead; chaplet.

bahadur [Hind], lit, valiant; also, hero; champion: a title of honor conferred in India.

bahía [Sp], a bay: used esp. in Spanish place names.

Bahnhof [Ger], railway station.

bahut achcha [Hind], all right; very well; the usual servant's reply on receiving an order: *India.*

bai [Hind], Hindu lady; mistress; also, dancing girl: *India.*

baia [It], bay.

baignoire [Fr], lit., bathtub; a theater box on a level with the stalls.

bail [Hind], ox; bullock. Written also *byle*. —**bail-gari,** ox cart; bullock wagon: *India.*

baile [Sp], a dance; ball: *southwestern U.S.*

bain-marie [Fr; *pl.* bains-marie], a saucepan of boiling water in which a bowl or other vessel is immersed to heat its contents: *cookery.*

baïonnette au canon! [Fr], fix bayonets!: *mil.*

bairagi [Hind], Hindu religious mendicant. Called also *vairagi.*

bairam [Ar], a Muslim festival.

baisser le drapeau [Fr], to lower the colors.

baisser le pavillon [Fr], to strike one's flag; surrender.

baissez les stores [Fr], pull down the shades; lower the blinds. *Store* is a window shade, or blind, mounted on a spring roller.

baja [Hind], musical instrument: *India.*

Bajonett ab! [Ger], unfix bayonets!: *mil.*

baken [Du], beacon; landmark.

bakra [Hind; *fem.* bakri], goat: *India.*

bakshish *or* **baksheesh** [Hind & Pers *bakhshish*], gratuity; tip: *Oriental.*

bal [Fr], ball; dance. —**bal champêtre,** country ball. —**bal masqué,** masked ball. —**bal paré** (*or* **costumé**), fancy-dress ball.

balabos [Yiddish], master.

balabustah [Yiddish], a fine housekeeper.

balayeuse [Fr], lit., female sweeper; a frill or ruffle on the inside lower edge of a skirt.

baldacchino [It], canopy of state; baldachin.

baliki [Russ], salted and smoked pieces of sturgeon.

baliverne [Fr], nonsense; stuff; humbug.

ballerina [It; *pl.* ballerine], female ballet dancer; *danseuse.*

ballet d'action [Fr], pantomimic dance.

ballon d'essai [Fr], trial balloon; device to test opinion; feeler.

bal musette [Fr], small cabaret for dancing.

baloo [Anglo-Ind], a bear; "the sleek brown bear who teaches the wolf cubs the Law of the Jungle": *Kipling.* Same as BHALU.

balourdise [Fr], stupidity; gross blunder.

bambino [It; *pl.* bambini], a child: in sacred art, a representation of the infant Jesus.

banalité [Fr], a commonplace.

Bancus Communium Placitorum [L], Court of Common Pleas: *law.*

Bancus Regis [L], King's Bench: *law.*

Band [Ger; *pl.* Bände], volume: *abbr.* Bd., *pl.* Bde.

banda [Sp], belt; sash; band.

bandar [Hind], monkey; ape.

bandarlog [Hind], the monkey people; monkeys collectively.

Bändchen [Ger], small volume.

Banddeckel [Ger], book cover.

banderilla [Sp], a small dart, carrying a streamer, used in bullfights to infuriate the bull.

banderillero [Sp], a placer of *banderillas* in a bullfight.

bandido [Sp], bandit.

bandobast *or* **bundobust** [Anglo-Ind, *fr.* Pers *band-o-bast*], lit., tying and binding; an arrangement; settlement; bargain.

bandolerismo [PI Sp], highway robbery: *P.I.*

bandolero [Sp], highwayman; robber.

banduk *or* **banduq** [Hind], musket; gun: *India.*

bandurria [Sp], stringed instrument resembling a guitar; bandore.

Bänkelsänger [Ger], itinerant ballad singer.

banlieue [Fr], suburbs; outskirts.

banquette [Fr], a long, upholstered seat; raised footway; sidewalk: *southern U.S. (local).*

banya, *pop.* **bunnia** [Hind], Hindu grain merchant; shopkeeper; money changer: *India.*

banzai [Jap], lit., ten thousand years; a cheer; a war cry.

bar [Fr], bass (fish).

bara [Hind; *fem.* bari], great; large; big; principal; elder; senior: opposite of *chhota.* —**bara haziri** *or (more correctly)* **bari haziri,** *pop.* **burra hazri,** lit., big breakfast; *déjeuner:* distinguished from *chhota haziri* (q.v.). —**bara khana,** *pop.* **burra khana,** lit., big dinner; banquet. —**bara sahib,** *pop.* **burra sahib,** lit., great sahib (*or* master; chief official; head of a firm or household: distinguished from *chhota sahib: all India.*

barachois [Fr], a rock-bound cove or small natural harbor, connected with the sea by a winding channel; in the lower St. Lawrence region, a pond or small lake separated from the sea by a sand bar.

baragouin [Fr], gibberish; jargon.

barandilla [Sp], handrail.

barato [Sp], money given to the bystanders at a gaming table by the victorious gambler to bring good luck.

barba a barba [Sp], lit., beard to beard; face to face.

barba bagnata è mezzo rasa [It], a beard well lathered is half shaved; well begun, half done.

barbae tenus sapientes [L], men wise as far as a beard (makes them appear wise); men who pretend to knowledge they do not possess.

barbera [It], a red wine made in Piedmont.

barbouillage [Fr], a daub; scribble; scrawl; also, rigmarole; twaddle.

barbu [Fr; *fem.* barbue], bearded.

barco que mandan muchos pilotos pronto va a pique [Sp], a ship directed by many pilots soon sinks.

barège [Fr], a gauzy material for veils and dresses.

barf [Hind], ice; snow. —**barf pani,** ice water: *India.*

bari haziri [Hind]. See BARA (HAZIRI).

bar mitzvah [Heb], in Judaism, a ceremony marking the religious coming of age for a male.

barra [Sp], shoal; sand bar: *southwestern U.S.*

barrage [Fr; *now naturalized*], lit., a bar or dam; a protective curtain of bursting shells: *mil.*

barranco *or* **barranca** [Sp], a deep ravine, with steep wall-like banks; gorge: common in Texas and New Mexico.

barrette [Fr], a bar, as of a watch chain; crossbar of a foil; a barlike clasp for holding hairs in place.

barrio [Sp], a political ward or municipal district; also, a village or district outside a city or town but under its administration.

bas [Hind; *pr.* bŭs], enough; that'll do.

bas bleu [Fr], a bluestocking; literary woman.

bashi-bazook [Turk], Turkish irregular soldier, noted for brutality and lawlessness.

basis virtutum constantia [L], constancy is the foundation of the virtues.

bas (*or* **bat**) **mitzvah** [Heb], in Judaism, a ceremony marking the religious coming of age for a female.

bas-relief [Fr], low relief: *sculp.*

basso [It; *pl.* bassi], bass. —**basso buffo,** a bass singer of comic parts. —**basso continuo,** thorough bass. —**basso ostinato,** lit., obstinate bass; ground bass. —**basso profondo,** a deep bass: *all music.*

basso-rilievo [It], bas-relief, low relief: *sculp.*

basta! [It], enough! hold! stop! never mind!

basta d'un pazzo per casa [It], one fool in the house is enough.

baste! [Fr], nonsense! pooh! —**baste pour cela,** well and good; let that pass; so be it.

basti *or* **bustee** [Hind *bastī*], abode; village; collection of dwellings; in southern India, a Jain temple: *India.*

bát [Anglo-Ind], word; speech; talk; hence, *slang,* "to sling the *bát,*" to talk, or be able to talk, in Hindustani.

bataille rangée [Fr], pitched battle.

batardeau [Fr], cofferdam.

bateau [Fr; *pl.* bateaux], a long, tapering, flat-bottomed river boat.

bâtir des châteaux en Espagne [Fr], to build castles in the air (lit., in Spain).

bâton [Fr], stick; staff; baton. —**tour du bâton,** perquisites; pickings; illicit profits.

batterie de cuisine [Fr], a set of kitchen utensils.

battre [Fr], to beat; strike. —**battre la campagne,** to scour the country; hence, to beat about the bush; ramble; rave. —**battre la générale,** to beat to arms; sound a general assembly: *mil.* —**battre la semelle,** lit., to strike the sole; tramp; trudge about. —**battre l'eau avec un bâton,** to beat water with a stick; make vain efforts. —**battre le fer pendant qu'il est chaud,** to strike while the iron is hot. —**battre le fusil,** to strike a light. **—battre le pavé,** lit., to beat the pavement; loaf about. **—battre les cartes,** to shuffle the cards.

battue [Fr], beating for game; fig., wanton slaughter.

batture [Fr], an alluvial elevation in the bed of a river; in Louisiana, a sandy deposit on one bank of a river, esp. of the Mississippi, formed by the action of a swift current. Private appropriation of such new ground led to the *"batture* riots" in New Orleans, Sept., 1807.

battuta [It], accented part of a bar; beat: *music.*

Bauer [Ger; *pl.* Bauern], peasant; husbandman; *cards,* jack; *chess,* pawn.

Bauernsuppe [Ger], peasant soup.

Bauhaus [Ger], lit., architecture house; German school of functional architecture.

Baukunst—eine erstarrte Musik [Ger], architecture—frozen music: *Goethe* (adapted). See DIE BAUKUNST, etc.

bavard [Fr; *fem.* bavarde], babbler; gossip; chatterer.

bavardage [Fr], babbling; cackle; idle chatter.

bavarois [Fr; *fem.* bavaroise], *adj. & n.* Bavarian.

bawarchi [Hind], a cook. **—bawarchi-khana,** cookhouse; kitchen: *India.*

bayadère [Fr], Hindu dancing girl.

bayou [Louisiana Fr, *fr.* Choctaw *bayuk*], an oxbow lake or channel of dead or sluggish water, such as is formed in level country by a river's change of course: *southern U.S.*

bayushki [Russ; *pl.* bayushek], lullaby.

beatae memoriae [L], of blessed memory: *abbr.* B.M.

Beata Maria (*or* **Virgo**) [L], the Blessed Virgin: *abbr.* B.M. *or* B.V. **—Beata Virgo Maria,** the Blessed Virgin Mary.

beati possidentes [L], happy are those who possess; possession is nine points of the law.

beau-fils [Fr; *pl.* beaux-fils], son-in-law.

beau geste [Fr; *pl.* beaux gestes], lit., beautiful gesture; a graceful or magnanimous gesture; a conciliatory gesture.

beau idéal [Fr], lit., ideal beauty; the ideal of consummate beauty or of perfection: also, **beau ideal** (without the accent and pronounced as in English).

beau monde [Fr], lit., fine world; the world of fashion; fashionable society.

beau rôle [Fr], a fine rôle; showy part.

beau sabreur [Fr], dashing cavalryman, esp. an officer.

beauséant [OF], standard and battle cry of the Knights Templar.

beauté d'emprunt [Fr], borrowed beauty; artificial beauty.

beauté du diable [Fr], lit., beauty of the devil; the bloom and freshness of youth.

beau teint [Fr], fair complexion.

beaux-arts [Fr], fine arts.

beaux esprits [Fr], men of wit. See BEL ESPRIT.

beaux yeux [Fr], fine eyes; good looks.

bébé [Fr], baby.

beca [Sp], a scholarship.

bec à bec [Fr], lit., beak to beak; face to face: *colloq.*

bécarre [Fr], the natural sign ♮ : *music.*

bécasse [Fr], woodcock; fig., idiot; imbecile.

bécassine [Fr], a snipe.

beccafico [It], lit., fig pecker; an Italian table delicacy consisting of song birds that have fed on figs and grapes: *cookery.*

becfigue [Fr]. Same as BECCAFICO.

béchamel [Fr], a variety of rich cream sauce: *cookery.*

bêche-de-mer [Fr], a trepang or sea slug, a Chinese delicacy.

Befana [It], Epiphany eve.

beg *or* **bey** [Turk], a governor; also, a Turkish title equivalent to *lord,* given to men of high rank.

Begeisterung [Ger], inspiration; spiritual enthusiasm; rapture.

Begleitung [Ger], accompaniment: *music.*

beglerbeg [Turk], lit., lord of lords *or* bey of beys; formerly, Ottoman governor next in rank to the grand vizier.

béguinage [Fr], house or community of *béguines*; fig., affected devotion; bigotry.

béguine [Fr], member of lay sisterhood in the Netherlands founded in 1180 by Lambert le Bègue (the Stammerer).

begum [Hind *begam, fr.* Turk *fem.* of *bēg*], Muslim lady of high rank; princess; queen.

Beíblatt [Ger], supplement: *abbr.* Beibl.

beige [Fr], of the natural color of wool; undyed, light tan.

beigebunden [Ger], bound up with (other matter): *abbr.* beigeb.

beignet [Fr], a fritter. —**beignets de pommes,** apple fritters: *cookery.*

Beilage [Ger; *pl.* Beilagen], addition; enclosure; supplement; appendix.

bei meiner Treu [Ger], upon my honor.

bel air [Fr], fine bearing (*or* appearance); aristocratic manners.

bel canto [It], the singing of cantabile passages with purity, smoothness, and artistic finish, in the traditional Italian manner: *music.*

belduque [Mex Sp], narrow sheath knife: *southwestern U.S.*

bel esprit [Fr; *pl.* beaux esprits], a man of wit; a wit; a brilliant mind.

bel étage [Fr], main floor (*or* story) of a house: *arch.*

bel et bien [Fr], entirely; quite; right well; in fine style.

bel hombre no es todo pobre [Sp], a handsome man is not wholly destitute.

bella, horrida bella [L], wars, horrid wars.

bellaque matribus detestata [L], and wars abominated by mothers: *Horace.* Barbier's lines regarding the Vendôme column in Paris convey a similar thought: *ce bronze que jamais regardent les mères,* this bronze on which mothers never look.

belle amie [Fr], female friend; mistress.

belle assemblée [Fr], fashionable gathering.

belle-fille [Fr; *pl.* belles-filles], daughter-in-law; stepdaughter.

belle-mère [Fr; *pl.* belles-mères], mother-in-law; stepmother.

belle montre et peu de rapport [Fr], fine show and small return (*or* crop).

belle mort [Fr], natural death.

belle parole non pascon i gatti [It], fine words do not feed cats; fine words butter no parsnips.

belle passion [Fr], the tender passion.

belles-lettres [Fr], polite or elegant literature; writings of a purely literary kind.

belle-soeur [Fr; *pl.* belles-soeurs], sister-in-law; stepsister.

belle tournure [Fr], fine figure; shapeliness.

bellum internecinum [L], internecine war; war of extermination.

bellum lethale [L], deadly war.

bellum omnium in omnes [L], a war of all against all.

bema [Gr βῆμα, bêma], in ancient Athenian assemblies, the speaker's platform or tribune; in the Eastern Church, the part of the chancel reserved for the higher clergy.

bene decessit [L], he (*or* she) died naturally (lit., well).

benedetto è quel male che viene solo [It], blessed is the misfortune that comes alone.

benedicite! [L], bless ye! bless you!

bene esse [LL], well-being.

bene est tentare [L], it is as well to try.

bene exeat [L], lit., let him (*or* her) go forth well; certificate of good character.

bénéficiaire [Fr], beneficiary; *theat.*, recipient of a benefit.

beneficium [L], lit., kindness or favor; a benefice; living; preferment: *eccl.* —**beneficium accipere libertatem est vendere,** to accept a favor is to sell one's liberty.

bene merenti [L; *pl.* merentibus], to the well-deserving.

bene meritus [L; *pl.* meriti], having well deserved.

bene orasse est bene studuisse [L], to have prayed well is to have striven well.

bene qui latuit bene vixit [L], well has he lived who has lived a retired life; he who has lived in obscurity has lived in security: *Ovid.*

benêt [Fr], booby; simpleton.

bene vale [L], farewell: *abbr.* b.v. —**bene vale vobis,** good luck to you.

ben ficcato [It], well established.

benigno numine [L], with favoring providence; by the favor of heaven: *Horace.*

benissimo [It], very well; quite right.

ben lo sai tu, che la sai tutta quanta [It], well knowest thou this, who knowest the whole of it: *Dante.*

ben marcato [It], well marked; to be played with emphasis: *music.*

ben tetragono ai colpi di ventura [It], unflinching before fortune's blows: *Dante.*

bentsh [Yiddish], to bless.

ben tornato [It], welcome home.

ben trovato [It], well found; well invented; characteristic, even if not true.

ben venuto [It], welcome.

bercail [Fr], sheepfold; shelter; fig., paternal home; also, bosom of the Church.

berceau [Fr], cradle; fig., source; infancy.

berceuse [Fr], lullaby; cradle song; soothing music.

Bereich [Ger], scope; sphere.

bereit [Ger], ready.

beret [Fr], rimless cap.

Berg [Ger; *pl.* Berge], mountain.

Bergschrund [Ger], lit., mountain cleft; deep crevasse in a mountain glacier.

beriberi [Sing], nervous disease.

berline [Fr], closed carriage.

berloque [Fr]. Same as BRELOQUE: *mil.*

berrendo [Am Sp; *fem.* berrenda], the pronghorn: *southwestern Texas.*

berretta [It], cap; hat; biretta, as worn by Catholic priests. **—berretta in mano non fece mai danno,** cap in hand never did harm; politeness costs nothing.

berrettina *or* **berrettino** [It], small cap; specif., cardinal's scarlet skullcap.

berro [Sp], watercress.

bersagliere [It; *pl.* bersaglieri], Italian sharpshooter; member of famous Italian military unit.

berserk [Old Norse], violent and frenetic; deranged.

berserker [Old Norse], warrior who fought with singular fury.

bertillonage [Fr], system of identification of criminals.

bésigue [Fr], bezique, a card game.

beso las manos [Sp], I kiss your hands: a salutation.

beso los pies [Sp], I kiss your feet: a salutation.

besser ein halb Ei als eitel Schale [Ger], better half an egg than merely a shell.

besser Rat kommt über Nacht [Ger], better counsel comes overnight: *Lessing.*

besser was als gar nichts [Ger], better something than nothing at all.

besugo [Sp], buffalo fish: *southwestern U.S.*

bêta [Fr; *fem.* bêtasse], blockhead; simpleton: *colloq.*

bet choleem [Heb], lit., house of the sick; hospital.

bête [Fr], *n.* beast; brute; fool; blockhead. —**bête noire,** lit., black beast; bugaboo; pet aversion. —**une bonne bête,** a good-natured fool.

bête [Fr], *adj.* stupid; foolish. —**bête comme un chou,** as stupid as an owl (lit., as a cabbage). —**pas si bête,** not so foolish; not such a fool.

bêtise [Fr], foolishness; absurdity; piece of folly. —**quelle bêtise!,** what an absurdity!

béton [Fr], a type of concrete.

bet sefer [Heb], lit., house of the book; a school.

betterave [Fr], beet; beetroot.

beurre [Fr], butter. —**beurre fondu,** melted butter. —**au beurre,** with butter. —**beurre roux,** browned butter.

beurré [Fr], a soft luscious pear; butter pear.

bévue [Fr], gross blunder; oversight.

bewegt [Ger], stirred; agitated; with animation: *music.*

bey [Turk]. See BEG.

bhakti [Skr], religious devotion; worship.

bhalu [Anglo-Ind]. Same as BALOO.

bhang [Hind], the hemp plant; also, an intoxicant and narcotic made from dried hemp leaves: *India.*

bhikku [Pali] *or* **bhikshu** [Skr], Brahman mendicant; also, Buddhist monk: *India.*

bhisti *or* **bheesty** [Hind], lit., celestial; Muslim water carrier: *India.*

> The finest man I knew
> Was our regimental *bhisti,* Gunga Din.
>   —KIPLING.

bibelot [Fr], trinket; curio; article of virtu.

bibere venenum in auro [L], to drink poison from a golden cup.

bibi [Hind, also Swa], Mrs., lady, woman.

bibliothécaire [Fr], librarian.

Bibliothek [Ger], library.

Bibliothekar [Ger], librarian.

bibliothèque [Fr], library.

bien [Fr], well. —**très bien,** very well.

bien-aimé [Fr; *fem.* -aimée], beloved.

bien ama quien nunca olvida [Sp], he loves well who never forgets.

bien chaussé [Fr; *fem.* chaussée], well-shod; neatly booted.

bien con bien se paga [Sp], a good deed is repaid with goodness.

bien cuit [Fr], well cooked.

bien entendu [Fr], lit., well understood; all right; to be sure; of course.

bien fendu [Fr], lit., well cleft; long-legged.

bien hablar no cuesta nada [Sp], fair words cost nothing.

bien mieux [Fr], far better.

bien obligé [Fr; *fem.* obligée], much obliged.

bien perdu, bien connu [Fr], lit., well lost, well known; once lost, then prized.

bien predica quien bien vive [Sp], he preaches best who lives best.

bienséance [Fr], decorum; propriety; good manners.

bien trouvé [Fr], lit., well found; cleverly thought of. Cf. BEN TROVATO.

bien vengas, mal, si vienes solo [Sp], welcome, misfortune, if thou comest alone: *Cervantes.*

bienvenue [Fr], welcome.

Bier [Ger], beer. **—Bierbruder,** drinking companion; fellow toper. **—Bierhaus** [*pl.* Bierhäuser], beerhouse; alehouse; tavern. **—Bierstube** [*pl.* Bierstuben], barroom.

bière [Fr], beer.

biffé [Fr], canceled; crossed off; erased; deleted.

bifteck [Fr], beefsteak.

bijou [Fr; *pl.* bijoux], jewel; trinket; any person or thing that is diminutive and attractive; pretty child; darling.

bijouterie [Fr], jewelry; trinkets.

bik'é hojoni [Nav], the trail of beauty.

billa vera [LL], true bill: *law.*

billet [Fr], note; letter; handbill; ticket. **—billet de banque,** bank note.

billet-doux [Fr; *pl.* billets-doux], love letter.

billi [Hind], cat: *India.*

Bindestrich [Ger], hyphen: *typog.*

bis [L], twice; to be repeated: *music.*

bis! [Fr & It], twice! again! encore!

bisagre [Am Sp], a spiny cactus, sometimes sliced and candied for eating: *Mexico & southwestern U.S.*

bis dat qui cito dat [L], he gives twice who gives quickly.

bise [Fr], a cold north wind of southern Europe.

bismillah! [Ar], in the name of Allah!

bisnaga *or* **biznaga** [Sp], any of several large cactaceous plants, the spines of which are used as toothpicks by some Mexicans: *Mexico & southwestern U.S.*

bis peccare in bello non licet [L], it is not permitted to blunder twice in war.

bis pueri senes [L], old men are twice children.

bis vincit qui se vincit in victoria [L], he conquers twice who conquers himself in victory: *Publilius Syrus.*

bis vivit qui bene [L], he lives twice who lives well.

bitte [Ger], please; don't mention it (*in answer to thanks*); I beg your pardon (*a request for repetition or as a polite contradiction*).

bizarre [Fr], strange, exotic, unusual.

bizarrerie [Fr], caprice; whim; eccentricity.

blagodarnee [Russ], thankful.

blagodar'yoo vas! [Russ], thank you.

blague [Fr], orig., tobacco pouch; *colloq.*, humbug; bosh; raillery; chaff; also, bragging. **—la bonne blague!,** what a joke!

blagueur [Fr], hoaxer; one who draws the long bow.

blanc-bec [Fr; *pl.* blancs-becs], lit., white beak; beardless youth; greenhorn.

blanc fixe [Fr], lit., fixed white; barium sulfate, used as a pigment and in coating paper.

blanchailles [Fr], whitebait; fry.

blanchâtre [Fr], whitish.

blanchisseuse [Fr], laundress.

blandae mendacia linguae [L], the lies of a flattering tongue.

blanquette [Fr], fricassee with white sauce: *cookery.*

blasé [Fr; *fem.* blasée], surfeited with pleasure (*or* overindulgence); cloyed; used up; sophisticated.

Bläser [Ger; *sing. & pl.*], player on a wind instrument: *music.*

Blaustrumpf [Ger; *pl.* Blaustrümpfe], a literary woman.

blessé [Fr], wounded or injured man.

bleuâtre [Fr], bluish.

bleu foncé [Fr], deep blue; dark blue.

blin [Russ; *pl.* blinok], pancake.

blinder Eifer schadet nur [Ger], blind zeal only does harm; more haste, less speed.

blintze [Yiddish], a filled pancake.

Blitzkrieg [Ger], lit., lightning war; sudden and unexpected tactics in warfare.

bloc [Fr], lit., a block; mass; specif., in a legislative body, a combination of political groups, united to attain some end; as, a farm *bloc.*

blondin [Fr; *fem.* blondine], fair-complexioned person; a blond; also, a ladies' man.

bloqué [Fr], turned, as a letter: *typog.*

Blut und Eisen [Ger], blood and iron.

boa noite [Pg], good night.

boa tarde [Pg], good afternoon; good evening.

bobèche [Fr], a perforated disk of glass or metal, to catch the drip of a candle in a candlestick; also, the similarly shaped part of a chandelier.

boca [Sp], mouth; entrance; mouth of a river or harbor.

bôca de mel, coração de fel [Pg], a mouth of honey and a heart of gall.

bocage [Fr], grove; coppice; thicket.

boche [Fr; probably from *caboche,* a square-headed nail], a German: *slang.* Cf. TÊTE CARRÉE.

bodega [Sp], lit., wine cellar; wine shop; tavern; *Am. Sp.*, grocery store.

boeuf [Fr], ox; beef.

Bogen [Ger; *pl.* Bögen], a bow, as for a violin; also, a slur or tie: *music.*

Bóg płaci, lecz nie co sobota [Pol], God pays, but not weekly wages.

bois [Fr], wood. —**bois barré,** striped maple: *Fr. Can.* —**bois blanc,** lit.,
white wood; American linden: *Fr. Can.* —**bois brûlé,** lit., burned
wood; Canadian of mixed parentage, esp. of French and Indian
parentage; also, a burned forest clearing; a *brûlée* (q.v.): *Fr. Can.*
—**bois de fer,** lit., ironwood; the hop hornbeam: *Fr. Can.* —**bois
inconnu,** lit., unknown wood; the sugarberry: *Louisiana.* —**bois pourri,**
lit., rotten wood; the whippoorwill: *Fr. Can.* —**bois puant,** lit., stinking
wood; in Louisiana, the sycamore; in Fr. Canada, the hardy catalpa.
boiteux [Fr; *fem.* boiteuse], *adj.* lame; limping; *n.* lame person.
—**attendre le boiteux,** lit., to wait for the lame; wait for confirmatory
news; bide one's time.
boi velho, rêgo direito [Pg], an old ox plows straight.
boker tov [Heb], good morning.
bolero [Sp], Spanish dance and song in three-four time: *music.*
bombance [Fr], feasting; junketing; carousal. Cf. RIPAILLE. —**faire
bombance,** to feast; junket; carouse.
bombe [Fr], bombshell; bomb; *cookery,* a bomb-shaped mold, in two
halves; also, the dessert, usually iced, with which it is filled. —**bombe
panachée,** bomb of variegated ice cream; ice bomb: *cookery.*
bombilla [Sp], a small tube, with a strainer at one end, used in drinking
maté; *elec.,* light bulb.
bom dia [Pg], good morning; good day.
bon [Fr; *fem.* bonne], good.
bona [L; *pl.*], property. —**bona fiscalia,** fiscal (*or* public) property.
—**bona mobilia,** movable goods. —**bona notabilia,** noteworthy things.
—**bona peritura,** perishable goods. —**bona vacantia,** unclaimed goods;
property without an apparent owner: *all law.*
bon accueil [Fr], good reception.
bonae notae [L], meritorious.
bona fide [L], in good faith; genuine *or* genuinely: opposite of *mala
fide.* —**bona fide polliceor,** I promise in good faith: *Cicero.*
bona fides [L], good faith; honest intention: opposite of *mala fides.*
bona gratia [L], in all kindness.
bon ami [Fr; *fem.* bonne amie], good friend; also, sweetheart.
bona roba [It], lit., a fine gown; a courtesan.
bon avocat, mauvais voisin [Fr], good lawyer, bad neighbor.
bonbonnière [Fr], a fancy dish for candy; also, a neat or snug little
house.
bon bourgeois [Fr], substantial citizen; prosperous tradesman.
bon camerade [Fr], good comrade.
bon enfant [Fr], lit., good child; good fellow.
bongo [Sp], small drum played with the fingers: *Cuba.*
bon goût [Fr], good taste.
bon gré, mal gré [Fr], with good grace (or) ill grace; willing or unwilling;
willy-nilly.

bonheur [Fr], happiness; good fortune; good luck.

bonhomie [Fr], good nature; geniality.

bonhomme [Fr; *pl.* bonshommes], good-natured fellow.

Bonhomme, Jacques [Fr], French peasant: derisive name given by the 14th-century barons.

bonis avibus [L], under favorable signs (*or* auspices); an *auspex* (*pl.* *auspices*) is someone who gets omens from the flights of certain birds.

bonis nocet quisquis pepercerit malis [L], whoever spares the bad injures the good: *Publilius Syrus*.

bonis quod bene fit haud perit [L], whatever is done for good men is never done in vain: *Plautus*.

bonjour [Fr], good day; good morning.

bon jour, bonne oeuvre [Fr], lit., good day, good work; the better the day, the better the deed.

bon marché [Fr], bargain; cheapness; a low-priced shop.

bon mot [Fr; *pl.* bons mots], a witty saying or repartee; witticism.

bonne [Fr], nursemaid; maid. —**bonne à tout faire,** maid of all work.

bonne bête [Fr], good-natured fool.

bonne bouche [Fr; *pl.* bonnes bouches], dainty morsel; toothsome tidbit, esp., to finish with.

bonne chance! [Fr], good luck!

bonne compagnie [Fr], well-bred society.

bonne et belle assez [Fr], good and fine (*or* handsome) enough.

bonne foi [Fr], good faith; honesty; plain dealing; fair play.

bonne fortune [Fr], good fortune (*or* luck); windfall. —**bonnes fortunes,** ladies' favors; success with the fair; amorous intrigues.

bonnement [Fr], plainly; frankly; honestly; simply.

bonne mine [Fr], good looks; pleasant appearance.

bonne raison [Fr], good grounds.

bonne renommée vaut mieux que ceinture dorée [Fr], a good name is worth more than a girdle of gold; a good name is better than riches.

bonnet de nuit [Fr], nightcap.

bonnet rouge [Fr], the red cap worn in the French Revolution; hence, a revolutionist; a red.

bonsai [Jap], dwarf tree or plant.

bonsoir [Fr], good evening. —**bonsoir et bonne nuit,** a good night's rest to you.

bon ton [Fr], lit., good tone; good breeding; good style; fashionable society.

bonum omen [L], a good omen.

bonum publicum [L], the public good: *abbr.* b.p.

bonum vinum laetificat cor hominis [L], good wine gladdens the heart of man.

bon vivant [Fr; *pl.* bons vivants; *fem.* bonne vivante, *pl.* bonnes vivantes], a lover of good living; gourmet.

bon viveur [Fr], free or fast liver; man about town.

bon voyage! [Fr], a good voyage to you! pleasant journey!

boondocks [Tag *bundok*, mountain], uninhabited area; *U.S. slang:* backwoods.

bordello [It], house of prostitution.

bordereau [Fr; *pl.* bordereaux], memorandum; note; document.

Borgen macht Sorgen [Ger], borrowing makes sorrowing; he who goes a-borrowing goes a-sorrowing.

borné [Fr; *fem.* bornée], limited; narrow; of limited ideas.

borracho [Sp], drunk.

borrasca [Sp], barren ground: *mining.*

borshch *or* **borscht** [Russ], beet soup.

bosan [Jap], Buddhist priest: *Japan.*

boschveld [Du], bush-covered plain: *South Africa.*

bos in lingua [L], lit., an ox on the tongue; a weighty reason for silence. Cf. βοῦς ἐπὶ γλώσσῃ (boûs epì glóssē).

bosque [Sp], wood; forest; grove.

botón [Sp; *pl.* botones], lit., button; a peculiar knot at the end of a lariat: *Mexico & southwestern U.S.*

bouc émissaire [Fr], scapegoat.

bouche [Fr], mouth; also, victuals. —**bonne bouche,** toothsome morsel; tidbit. —**bouche à bouche,** face to face. —**bouche à feu,** fieldpiece; field gun. —**bouche cousue,** lit., mouth sewn; mum's the word. —**dépense de bouche,** household expenses; living expenses.

bouchée [Fr], mouthful; morsel; *cookery,* a kind of patty. —**bouchée aux huîtres,** oyster patty.

bouderie [Fr], act of pouting; sulkiness.

boudin [Fr], an entree of seasoned forcemeat, rolled into the shape of a sausage. —**boudin de lièvre,** boudin of hare. —**boudin ordinaire** (*or* **noir**), black pudding: *all cookery.*

boudiné [Fr; *fem.* boudinée], fashioned like a sausage; *of fingers, etc.,* having the appearance of sausages: *fine arts.*

boudoir [Fr], lit., a pouting place; a woman's dressing room.

bouffant [Fr; *fem.* bouffante], puffed out; full, as a dress sleeve.

bouillabaisse [Fr], Provençal soup made of fish and various vegetables and seasonings: *cookery.*

bouilli [Fr], boiled or stewed meat: *cookery.*

bouillie [Fr], infant's food; pap. —**bouillie pour les chats,** lit., pap for cats; fruitless labor.

bouillon [Fr], clear soup or broth: *cookery.*

boulangerie [Fr], bakery.

Boule-Miche [Fr], popular name for the Boulevard St. Michel, Paris.

boulette [Fr], a small ball, as of meat or dough. **—boulettes de bachis,** forcemeat balls: *cookery.*

boulevardier [Fr], a frequenter of the boulevards, esp. in Paris.

bouleversé [Fr], overthrown; turned topsy-turvy; distracted.

bouleversement [Fr], complete overthrow; convulsion; upsetting; disorder.

bouquiniste [Fr], bookseller, esp. of secondhand books.

bourgeois [Fr; *fem.* bourgeoise], *n.* French citizen; citizen of the shopkeeping class; commoner. **—bon bourgeois,** substantial citizen; prosperous tradesman. **—bourgeois gentilhomme,** the shopkeeper turned gentleman: from the title of Molière's comedy.

bourgeois [Fr; *fem.* bourgeoise], *adj.* middle-class; fig., ordinary; commonplace; humdrum; unintellectual. **—cuisine bourgeoise,** plain cooking.

bourgeoisie [Fr], the middle class; merchant or shopkeeping class. **—haute bourgeoisie,** upper middle class; gentry.

bourgeon [Fr], bud; shoot. **—bourgeous des pins,** pine shoots; pine tips.

bourreau d'argent [Fr], lit., executioner of money; spendthrift.

bourse [Fr], lit., purse; stock exchange; *Bourse,* the Paris stock exchange.

βοῦς ἐπὶ γλώσσῃ [Gr; boûs epì glṓssē], lit., an ox on the tongue; a weighty reason for silence (as if some heavy body were holding down the tongue): *Aeschylus.*

boutade [Fr], caprice; frolic; whim. **—par boutades,** by fits and starts.

boute-en-train [Fr], the life and soul of the party.

boutez en avant [Fr], push forward.

boutique [Fr], a shop.

boutonnière [Fr], a buttonhole bouquet; buttonhole (*colloq.*).

bouts-rimés [Fr], lit., rhymed ends; rhymes given to be formed into verse.

Bouvier des Flandres [Fr], lit., cowherd of Flanders; a breed of dogs originating in Belgium.

boyar [Russ, boyárin, *pl.* boyáre], landholding nobleman.

boyau [Fr; *pl.* boyaux], a winding or zigzag trench; communication trench: *mil.*

bozza [It], printer's proof: *typog.*

bracero [Sp], one who walks arm in arm with another; a laborer; a strong man.

bragas [Sp], breeches; esp., a kind of loose wide breeches.

braguero [Sp], orig., a truss or brace; additional girth used behind the cinch: *Texas & western U.S.*

brancard [Fr], stretcher; litter.

brancardier [Fr], stretcher bearer: *mil.*

brandade *or* **brandade de morue** [Fr], a ragout of codfish: *cookery.*

brasero [Sp], a pan, usually of copper or brass, for holding lighted charcoal; brazier: *southwestern U.S.*

brasserie [Fr], brewery; also, saloon; bar that serves food.

brasseur [Can Fr], the harp seal.

brat [Russ; *pl.* bratya], brother.

Bratwurst [Ger], lit., sausage meat without waste; sausage.

brava! *(to a woman)*, **bravo!** *(to a man)* [It], well done!

bravissimo! [It; superlative of *bravo*], very well done! excellent!

¡bravo! [Sp], well done!

bravura [It], lit., bravery or spirit; a florid style of music requiring high technical skill in its rendition; virtuoso music: *music.*

bref [Fr], in short; in fine.

brelan [Fr], a card game resembling poker.

breloque [Fr], trinket; charm; ornamental attachment to a watch chain; *mil.,* a beat of drum as a signal to break ranks or as a call to meals, etc.; barrack call. Called also *berloque.*

breve orazione penetra [It], short prayers pierce (Heaven); God listens to short prayers.

brevet d'invention [Fr], certificate of invention; patent.

breveté [Fr], patented; also, patentee.

brevi manu [L], lit., with a short hand; offhand; summarily.

brevis esse laboro, obscurus fio [L], in trying to be concise, I become obscure: *Horace.*

briago [corr. of Sp. *embriagado*], drunkard: *Texas.*

Briefkasten [Ger; *pl.* Briefkästen], mailbox.

Briefmarke [Ger; *pl.* Briefmarken], postage stamp.

Briefträger [Ger; *sing. & pl.*], letter carrier; postman.

brigada [Sp], *mil.,* brigade; *mining, etc.,* shift; gang of workmen.

brigue [Fr], intrigue; bribery; cabal.

brillante [It], brilliant; sparkling: *music.*

briller par son absence [Fr], to be conspicuous by his absence.

brimade [Fr], practical joking; horseplay: *Fr. mil. slang.*

brio [It], vivacity; spirit; animation.

brioche [Fr], a roll baked from light yeast dough, eggs, and butter; fig., a blunder; mistake.

briquet [Fr], steel; tinderbox; esp., a steel used by smokers for striking a light.

brisance [Fr], the peculiar shattering effect of high explosives.

brisant [Fr], producing *brisance.*

brisé [Fr], broken.

brisons-là [Fr], let us say no more about it; enough!

brocanteur [Fr], secondhand dealer.

broche [Fr], a spit: *cookery.*

broché [Fr; *fem.* brochée], stitched (as a book, esp. a paper-covered one); embossed, as linen; woven with a raised figure.

brochet [Fr], pike (fish).

brochette [Fr], a skewer. **—en brochette,** on a skewer: *cookery.*

broder [Fr], to embroider; fig., to amplify; embellish, as a story. **—broder n'est pas mentir mais farder la vérité,** to embroider is not to lie but to gloss over the truth.

broderie à jour [Fr], openwork embroidery.

βρῶμα θεῶν [Gr; brôma theôn], food for the gods.

bronco [Sp], lit., rough, wild; untamed horse.

brosse [Fr], brush. **—en brosse,** standing erect, like the bristles of a brush; brushlike; bristling: said of a man's hair.

Brotschrift [Ger], ordinary type (i.e., not display type): *typog.*

brouhaha [Fr], hubbub; uproar.

brouillerie [Fr], misunderstanding; disagreement; a falling out.

brouillon [Fr], rough draft; rough copy.

Bruch [Ger; *pl.* Brüche], fraction: *arith.*

Bruder [Ger; *pl.* Brüder], brother.

bruit [Fr], noise; report; rumor.

brûlée [Fr], an open grassy clearing in a forest, which has been previously burned over: *Canada & parts of the U.S.*

brûler la chandelle par les deux bouts [Fr], to burn the candle at both ends.

brûler le pavé [Fr], lit., to burn the pavement; dash madly along.

Brumaire [Fr], in the Revolutionary calendar of the first French Republic, the second month of the year, from Oct. 22 to Nov. 20.

brusquerie [Fr], brusqueness; bluntness; gruffness.

brut [Fr], raw; crude; unwrought; unmanipulated: said of gems, wines, etc.; *of champagne,* very dry. **—diamant brut,** rough diamond.

brutum fulmen [L; *pl.* bruta fulmina], a harmless thunderbolt; vain display of force; empty threat.

Buch [Ger; *pl.* Bücher], book.

Buchbinder [Ger], bookbinder.

Buchbinderkunst [Ger], art of bookbinding.

Buchdruck [Ger], printing of books.

Buchdrucker [Ger], printer.

Buchhändler [Ger], bookseller.

Buchhandlung [Ger], bookstore.

Buchstabe [Ger; *pl.* Buchstaben], letter of the alphabet; type.

buena fama hurto encubre [Sp], a good reputation is a cloak for theft.

buenas noches [Sp], good evening; good night.

buenas tardes [Sp], good afternoon.

¡buena suerte! [Sp], good luck!

buenos días [Sp], good morning; good day.

buen principio, la mitad es hecha [Sp], good beginning, half is done; well begun is half done.

buey viejo surco derecho [Sp], an old ox makes a straight furrow.

buffo [It; *pl.* buffi], comic actor or singer.

bukhshi *or* **bukshi** [Anglo-Ind], paymaster: *mil.*

bukshish *or* **buksheesh** [Anglo-Ind]. Same as BAKSHISH.

Bund [Ger], league; confederacy.

Bundesrat [Ger], federal council of the German Empire (1871–1918); also, the upper house of the Austrian legislature.

bunnia [Anglo-Ind]. See BANYA.

buonamano [It], a small gratuity; tip.

buon viaggio! [It], pleasant journey! *bon voyage!*

buon vino fa buon sangue [It], good wine makes good blood.

burletta [It], burlesque operetta.

burra hazri [Anglo-Ind]. See BARA HAZIRI.

burra khana [Anglo-Ind]. See BARA KHANA.

burra sahib [Anglo-Ind]. See BARA SAHIB.

Bursch [Ger; *pl.* Burschen], lad; youth; student; in German universities, a senior student or one who has taken part in at least three duels.

Burschenschaft [Ger; *pl.* Burschenschaften], association of German university students.

Bushido [Jap], lit., military knight way; the unwritten precepts of Japanese knighthood; chivalric conduct and morals.

bustee [Anglo-Ind]. See BASTI.

butcha [Anglo-Ind]. Same as BACHCHA.

bwana [Swa], master; Mr.

byadha [Beng], hunter.

byle [Anglo-Ind]. Same as BAIL: *Kipling.*

C

cabaletta [It], a short catchy melody, commonly ending an aria or duet in Italian music.

cabalgada [Sp], cavalcade.

caballada *or* **caballad** [Sp], drove of horses or mules: *southwestern U.S.*

caballería [Sp], cavalry; knighthood; chivalry; knight-errantry.

caballero [Sp], knight; cavalier; horseman; gentleman; sir.

caballo [Sp], horse; *chess,* knight. **—a caballo,** on horseback.

cabane [Fr], cottage; shack; cabin; also, a flat-bottomed boat covered over; *aero.,* a supporting framework for the wings of an airplane.

cabaretier [Fr; *fem.* cabaretière], one who keeps a cabaret; tavern keeper.

cabello luengo, y poco seso [Sp], long hair and little brain.

cabestro [Sp], lit., halter; a lasso or lariat made of hair, used for catching horses and cattle: *southwestern U.S.*

cabillaud [Fr], cod: *colloq.* **—cabillaud farci,** stuffed cod: *cookery.*

cabine [Fr], cabin.

cabinet [Fr], office; closet **—les cabinets,** toilets.

cabo [Sp], cape; headland.

cabochon [Fr], a precious stone, highly polished but not faceted. **—en cabochon,** rounded convex on top but without facets: said of certain gems.

cabotage [Fr], coasting trade.

cabré [Fr], lit., in a rearing position; *aero.,* sharply upturned.

cabriole [Fr], a form of furniture leg.

cabriolet [Fr], a type of horse carriage; a convertible automobile.

caccia [It], the chase; also, a poem celebrating it.

cacciatore [It], lit., hunter; chicken cacciatore, sautéed with onions and mushrooms.

cachepot [Fr], ornamental covering or vase for concealing an ordinary flowerpot.

cache-poussière [Fr], dust coat; dust cloak.

cachet [Fr], small seal, as used by private individuals; fig., stamp; distinguishing mark; characteristic.

cachette [Fr], hiding place. **—en cachette,** in concealment; secretly.

cachot [Fr], dungeon; black hole.

cachucha [Sp], an Andalusian dance and song in ternary time.

cacoëthes [L, *fr.* Gr κακόηθες, kakóēthes], bad habit or propensity; itch; irrepressible desire; mania. **—cacoëthes carpendi,** mania for fault-finding. **—cacoëthes loquendi,** mania for talking. **—cacoëthes scribendi,** itch for writing; scribbling mania: *Juvenal.*

cacolet [Fr], mule litter; double pannier.

cada coisa a seu tempo [Pg], everything has its time.

cada porco tem seu S. Martinho [Pg], every pig has its Martinmas; every turkey has its Thanksgiving.

cadastre [Fr], official register of landed property.

cada uno es artífice de su ventura [Sp], each one is the maker of his own fortune: *Cervantes.*

cada uno es hijo de sus obras [Sp], every man is the child of his own works; everyone is the product of his own deeds: *Cervantes.*

cada uno tiene su alguacil [Sp], every man has his constable; every man is subject to the law.

cadeau [Fr; *pl.* cadeaux], gift; present.

cadenza d'inganno [It], a deceptive cadence; a cadence on an unexpected chord: *music.*

cadet [Fr; *fem.* cadette], younger; junior; younger brother or son: often appended to a surname for distinction. Cf. AÎNÉ.

cadi [Ar *qādī*], Muslim judge of inferior grade.

cadit quaestio [L], the question falls to the ground; there is an end of the discussion.

cadre [Fr], framework; *mil.*, the framework or skeleton of a military unit, forming a nucleus for later expansion; also, the staff or list of officers.

caeca invidia est [L], envy is blind.

caelitus mihi vires [L], my strength is from heaven.

caelum non animum mutant qui trans mare currunt [L], those who cross the sea change only their climate, not their mind: *Horace.*

caetera desunt [L]. See CETERA DESUNT.

caeteris paribus [L]. See CETERIS PARIBUS.

ça et là [Fr], here and there; to and fro.

cafardise [Fr], hypocrisy; cant.

café [Fr], coffee; coffeehouse or restaurant (in this sense, *café* is a naturalized word). —**café au lait,** coffee with hot milk in it. —**café chantant,** restaurant with music-hall entertainment. —**café noir,** black coffee; coffee without milk or cream.

cafetal [Sp], coffee plantation: *Sp. Am.*

cagnotte [Fr], money box into which is placed the percentage or fee reserved out of the stakes at a gaming table; also, the total sum so contributed.

cagoule [Fr], cowl.

cahier [Fr], copybook; notebook; also, a report of proceedings; memorial; *bookbinding,* a section ready for binding. —**cahier de croquis,** sketchbook.

cahotage [Fr], a jolting; tossing about; lurch.

cahoy [Tag], wood; timber: *P.I.*

caille [Fr], quail. —**cailles au truffes,** quails stuffed with truffles: *cookery.*

caïque [Fr], a long, narrow boat used in the Levant.

ça ira [Fr], lit., it will go on; a French Revolutionary song, with the refrain:

> Ah, ça ira, ça ira, ça ira!
> Les aristocrates à la lanterne!

(q.v., LES ARISTOCRATES À LA LANTERNE!)

caisse [Fr], box; case; cashier.

caja [Sp], case; box; receptacle; money chest; *auto.*, body.

caji [Sp], schoolmaster, a variety of snapper: *Cuba.*

calabazilla [Mex Sp], a wild squash of Mexico and California; a soap plant.

calabozo [Sp], dungeon; jail; also, a pruning knife.

calamaro [It], squid.

calando [It], decreasing in loudness; gradually becoming softer and slower: *music.*

calavera [Sp], skull; hangover.

calèche [Fr], barouche; calash; in Quebec, a two-wheeled carriage with a folding hood.

caleçon [Fr], short pants.

calembour [Fr], a pun.

calesa [Sp], carriage.

calesin [Sp], one-horse chaise, with driver's seat behind: *P.I.*

caliche [Am Sp], mineral deposit; saltpeter.

câlin [Fr; *fem.* câline], wheedling; coaxing.

calle [Sp], street; lane.

callejón [Sp], long narrow lane between high walls; narrow pass.

callida iunctura [L], skillful joining; cunning workmanship: *Horace.*

calliope [Gr Καλλιόπη, kalliópē, the beautiful-voiced], musical steam organ, named after the Muse of eloquence and epic poetry; one of the nine muses.

calmato [It], quiet; tranquil: *music.*

calore [It], heat; ardor. —**con calore,** with warmth; passionately: *music.*

caloroso [It], with warmth; animated: *music.*

calotte [Fr], skullcap, as worn by priests.

calvados [Fr], apple brandy.

calzada [Sp], paved highway; causeway: *Sp. Am.*

calzado [Sp], shoes; footgear: generic term.

camaïeu [Fr], orig., cameo; *fine arts,* a painting in monochrome, in imitation of bas-relief; fig., a monotonous play or other literary composition.

câmara [Pg], chamber; house, as of parliament.

cámara [Sp], hall; chamber; king's court (*la Cámara*).

camarade [Fr], comrade; chum; companion.

camaraderie [Fr], comradeship; fellowship; party spirit.

camarero [Sp], waiter; valet.

camarilla [Sp], orig., a small audience chamber; band of intriguers; cabal; clique; coterie.

camarín [Sp], repository behind an altar; closet; also, storehouse; shed.

camarista [Sp], member of the supreme council of *la Cámara*.

camarón [Sp], shrimp; crawfish.

camarote [Sp], cabin; stateroom: *naut.*

camastrón [Sp], cunning or crafty fellow.

camay [Tag], the hand: *P.I.*

cambio non è furto [It], exchange is no robbery.

camelot [Fr], peddler; hawker; also, newsboy.

camembert [Fr], a soft, surface-ripened cheese.

Camera Stellata [L], Star Chamber.

cameriere [It; *pl.* camerieri], waiter; valet.

camino [Sp], road; highroad; path; also, travel. **—camino de sirga,** towpath. **—camino real,** the royal road.

camion [Fr], truck; wagon; military motor truck.

camisa [Sp], a shirt; *mach.*, jacket.

camisade [Fr], night attack: *mil.*

camote [Sp], a tuber-bearing plant, esp. the yam or sweet potato.

camouflage [Fr; *now naturalized*], the disguising or concealment of military works; fig., disguise or deception.

camouflet [Fr], whiff of smoke blown in the face; hence, affront; *mil.*, a mine for blowing in the side of an enemy gun emplacement.

camoufleur [Fr], one skilled in the art of camouflage.

campagnard [Fr; *fem.* campagnarde], *adj.* rustic; rural; countrified; *n.* a rustic; countryman; clodhopper. **—à la campagnarde,** in rustic fashion; in country style.

campo [It; *pl.* campi], field; open ground. **—campo santo,** lit., sacred field; cemetery.

Campus Martius [L], Field of Mars; a grassy plain used by the ancient Romans for various contests, military exercises, and general assembly.

cañada [Sp], small canyon; glen: *western U.S.*

canaigre [Mex Sp], a large dock (*Rumex hymenosepalus*), the root of which is rich in tannic acid: *Mexico & southwestern U.S.*

canaille [Fr], rabble; riffraff; scoundrel.

canapé [Fr], sofa or divan; *cookery,* a piece of bread fried in butter and covered with anchovies, cheese, etc.

canard [Fr], duck; fig., hoax; false rumor. **—canard sauvage,** wild duck.

cancan [Fr], gossip; a woman's dance, characterized by high kicking while holding up the front of a ruffled skirt.

cancelli [L], lattice; latticed screen or railing.

candelia [Sp], bad weather, with rain, sleet, and cold, destructive to sheep and cattle: *Sp. Am. & Texas.*

candida Pax [L], white-robed Peace: *Ovid.*

candide et constanter [L], frankly and firmly.

candor dat viribus alas [L], sincerity gives wings to strength.

cane grosso [It], fat dog; *colloq.*, big shot.

cane peius et angue [L], worse than a dog or a snake.

caneton [Fr], duckling.

canevás [Sp], network of triangles in a topographical survey.

caniche [Fr], French poodle.

canis in praesepi [L], dog in the manger.

Canis Maior [L], lit., larger dog; a constellation containing Sirius, the Dog Star: *astron.*

Canis Minor [L], lit., lesser dog; a constellation to the east of Orion: *astron.*

canne-de-roche [Fr], lit., rock duck; the harlequin duck: *Fr. Can.*

cannelé [Fr], fluted; grooved; channeled.

cannelon [Fr], a fluted mold (for ices, jellies, etc.); *cookery*, a hollow roll made of puff paste; also, a fried or baked roll of mincemeat.

cañoncito [Sp], small canyon; also, esp. in southwestern Texas, a narrow lane through chaparral: *southwestern U.S.*

cantabile [It], in a flowing melodic style: *music.*

cantabit vacuus coram latrone viator [L], the penniless wayfarer will sing in the presence of the highwayman; a penniless man has nothing to lose: *Juvenal.*

cantando [It], in a singing manner: *music.*

cantante [Sp], singer.

cantate Domino [L], sing unto the Lord.

cantatore [It; *pl.* cantatori], male professional singer.

cantatrice [It & Fr; *It. pl.* cantatrici], female professional singer.

cante hondo [Sp], a style of Spanish singing.

cantera [Sp], quarry; excavation.

cantilena [It], the melody or air of a composition; a songlike melody, passage, or piece: *music.*

cantilenam eandem canis [L], you are singing the same old song; ever the same old stuff: *Terence.*

cantillatio [L], intoning or chanting portions of a religious service, as in the celebration of the Mass.

cantina [Sp], barroom; saloon; canteen: *southwestern U.S.*

cantinier [Fr; *fem.* cantinière], canteen keeper; provisioner; sutler.

cantoris [L], to be sung by the cantorial, or precentor's, side in antiphonal singing: *music.* Cf. DECANI.

cantus firmus [NL], lit., fixed song; Gregorian melody.

cantus planus [NL], plainsong; Gregorian chant.

canzone [It; *pl.* canzoni], a song; ballad; lyric.

caoba [Sp], mahogany tree.

capataz [Sp], foreman; overseer.

capias [L], lit., thou mayest take; writ of arrest: *law.*

capiat qui capere possit [L], let him take who can.

capilla [Sp], chapel.

capillaire [Fr], maidenhair fern; also, a syrup made from maidenhair, flavored with orange-flower water.

capo [It], head; beginning. **—capo d'anno,** New Year's Day. **—capo d'opera,** masterpiece. **—capo grasso, cervello magro,** fat head, lean brains. **—capo ha cosa fatta,** "the deed once done, there is an end": *Dante* (tr. by Carey). **—capo di tutti capi,** chief of chiefs: *mafia.* See also DA CAPO.

caporal [Fr], corporal; also, French shag tobacco. **—caporal postiche,** acting corporal: *mil.* **—le petit caporal,** the little corporal, an affectionate nickname of Napoleon.

caporal [Sp], an overseer, esp. of laborers: *Sp. Am. & southwestern U.S.*

capotasto [It], the bar or movable knob on the neck of a guitar, to regulate the pitch.

capote [Fr], large hooded cloak or overcoat; soldier's greatcoat; also, a woman's mantle.

câpre [Fr], caper, a shrub, the flower buds (*câpres*) of which are used for pickling.

capriccio [It], caper; fancy; freak; *music,* a caprice.

capriccioso [It], in a free, fantastic style: *music.*

captantes capti sumus [L], we catchers have been caught; the biter is bitten.

captatio benevolentiae [L], a reaching after (*or* currying of) favor.

captus nidore culinae [L], caught (*or* captivated) by the aroma of the kitchen: *Juvenal* (adapted).

capuce *or* **capuchon** [Fr], hood; cowl.

caput [L; *pl.* capita], head. **—caput inter nubila (condo),** amid the clouds (I hide) my head: *Virgil* (said of fame). **—caput lupinum,** lit., wolf's head; an outlaw (i.e., a man who may be hunted down like a wild beast). **—caput mortuum,** lit., dead head; the residuum after chemical analysis; worthless residue.

caquet [Fr], cackle, as of geese; gabble; tittle-tattle. **—caquet bon bec,** dame prattler; magpie; gossip.

caquetrie [Fr], cackling; gossiping.

carabao [PI Sp, *fr.* Mal *karbau*], water buffalo: *P.I.*

caracoler [Fr], to prance; caracole.

caractères bloqués [Fr], turned letters: *typog.*

¡caramba! [Sp], an exclamation denoting admiration or annoyance.

carapo [Sp], a South American eel.

cara sposa [It], dear wife.

caravanserai [Hind & Pers], stopping place for caravans; caravansary.

carbonaro [It; *pl.* carbonari], charcoal burner. **—Carbonari,** members of a secret anti-Austrian political organization, established in Italy in the 19th century.

carcajou [Can Fr], wolverine; also, American badger.

cárcel [Sp], prison; jail.

carême [Fr], Lent.

caret initio et fine [L], it lacks beginning and end.

cargador [Sp; *pl.* cargadores], one who loads or who has charge of freight; a freighter; in Texas, man in charge of the packs in a pack train; in P.I., a carrier or porter.

caribe [Sp], cannibal; also, any of several voracious freshwater fishes, found in South America.

carillonneur [Fr], ringer of carillons; bell ringer.

carità [It], *music,* tenderness; feeling; *fine arts,* representation of maternal love.

carmagnole [Fr], orig., a kind of jacket; later, the costume worn by French Revolutionists in 1792; also, a Revolutionary song and dance.

carmen triumphale [L], a triumphal song.

carne [Sp], flesh; meat. **—carne de vaca,** beef.

carnero [Sp], sheep; mutton.

caro cuesta el arrepentir [Sp], repentance costs dear.

caro sposo [It], dear husband.

carotte [Fr], carrot; also, a roll of tobacco.

carpe diem [L], make the most of today; enjoy the present (part of the quotation *carpe diem, quam minimum credula postero,* enjoy the present day, trusting as little as possible to what the morrow may bring): *Horace.*

carpent tua poma nepotes [L], your descendants will pluck your fruit: *Virgil.*

carpere et colligere [L], to pluck and gather.

carré [Fr], a portion of lamb, pork, or veal, cut from the fleshy part of the loin between the ribs and the leg; fillet: *cookery.*

carrefour [Fr], crossroad; intersection of streets.

carrelet [Fr], a flounder: *cookery.*

carreta [Sp], a roughly built, long, narrow, two-wheeled cart: *Mexico & southwestern U.S.*

carretera [Sp], main street; highway.

carretón [Sp], child's go-cart.

carrière [Fr], career; quarry.

carroccio [It; *pl.* carrocci], medieval Italian chariot bearing the standard and forming the rallying point in battle.

carromata [Sp], a light, two-wheeled, covered vehicle: *P.I.*

carrosse [Fr], four-wheeled carriage; coach.

carrosserie [Fr], carriage making; coach building; specif., the carriage body of an automobile.

carrozza [It; *pl.* carrozze], carriage; coach; car.

carte [Fr], pasteboard; card; ticket; bill of fare. **—carte blanche,** blank paper, esp. one bearing a signature leaving the particulars to be filled in at discretion; unlimited authority; full powers. **—carte de visite**

[*pl.* cartes de visite], visiting card; also, a small photograph, 2¼ × 3¾ inches. —**carte des vins,** wine list. —**carte du jour,** menu of the day. —**carte du pays** [*pl.* cartes du pays], map of the country; lay of the land (*lit. & fig.*). —**cartes sur table,** cards on table; aboveboard.

casa [Sp, Pg, & It], house; mansion.

casaque tourner [Fr], to turn one's coat; change sides.

casarás y amansarás [Sp], marry and be tamed.

caseta [Sp], little house; *naut.,* deckhouse.

casetta [It], little house.

casita [Sp], little house; house for a man's mistress.

casque [Fr], helmet.

casquijo [Sp], gravel.

cassette [Fr], small case or box; casket; *photog.,* plate holder.

cassetur billa [LL], let the bill be quashed: *law.*

cassis tutissima virtus [L], virtue is the safest helmet; an honest man need fear nothing.

castaña [Sp], lit., chestnut.

castello che dà orecchia si vuol rendere [It], the castle that parleys will soon surrender; fig., she who listens is going to yield.

castigat ridendo mores [L], it (comedy) corrects manners by laughing at them.

casus [L], lit., a falling; fall; hence, occasion; event; occurrence; case. —**casus belli,** an occasion for war; an act regarded as justifying war. —**casus conscientiae,** a case of conscience. —**casus foederis,** lit., a case of the treaty; a case within the stipulations of a treaty. —**casus fortuitus,** an accident; chance. —**casus omissus,** a case omitted or unprovided for, as in a law.

catalogue raisonné [Fr], descriptive catalogue arranged according to subjects.

caudillo [Sp], chieftain; chief.

causa [L], cause. —**causa causans,** the cause that causes all things; the cause in action; the Great First Cause. —**causa causata,** the cause resulting from a previous cause; an effect. —**causa essendi,** cause of being. —**causa fiendi,** cause of becoming. —**causa finalis,** final cause. —**causa latet, vis est notissima,** the cause is hidden, but its force is very well known: *Ovid.* —**causa mali,** a cause of mischief. —**causa proxima,** immediate cause. —**causa remota,** remote cause. —**causa secunda,** secondary cause. —**causa sine qua non,** indispensable cause (*or* condition). —**causa vera,** a true cause.

cause célèbre [Fr; *pl.* causes célèbres], a celebrated case; a widely debated controversial issue.

causerie [Fr], chat; informal talk; also, a chatty newspaper article, esp. on literary subjects.

causeur [Fr; *fem.* causeuse], talker; conversationalist.

causeuse [Fr], settee for two.

cautionnement [Fr], bail; security.

cavaliere servente [It], a lady's man; a gallant or lover of a married woman; lit., a serving knight.

cavatina [It], a short, simple aria, usually of a tender or sentimental kind; as, Raff's *Cavatina: music.*

caveat [L], let him beware. —**caveat actor,** let the doer beware. —**caveat emptor,** let the purchaser beware (i.e., he buys at his own risk): *law.* —**caveat viator,** let the traveler beware.

cave canem [L], beware of the dog.

cavendo tutus [L], safe by taking heed.

cave ne cadas [L], take care you do not fall; beware of falling from your high position.

cave quid dicis, quando, et cui [L], beware what you say, when, and to whom.

cavetto [It], a variety of concave molding.

cavo-rilievo [It], hollow relief: *sculp.*

cayo [Sp], a low rocky islet or reef; key: *Sp. Am.*

cazo [Sp], a large copper saucepan; specif., a cauldron in which ores are treated: *Sp. Am.*

cedant arma togae [L], let arms yield to the toga (i.e., military to civil power): *Cicero.* Motto of *Wyoming.*

cede Deo [L], submit to God.

ceia [Pg], supper.

ceinture [Fr], belt; girdle; sash.

ceja [Sp], lit., eyebrow; a long strip of chaparral: *southwestern U.S.*

cela arrive comme marée en carême [Fr], that comes like fish in Lent; that comes in the nick of time.

cela est digne de lui [Fr], lit., that is worthy of him; that's just like him.

cela est selon [Fr], that is according to circumstances.

cela laisse à désirer [Fr], there is room for improvement.

cela m'importe peu [Fr], that matters little to me.

cela saute aux yeux [Fr], lit., that leaps to the eyes; that is self-evident.

cela se laisse manger [Fr], that is good to eat; that is palatable.

cela s'entend [Fr], that is understood; of course; to be sure.

cela tombe bien [Fr], lit., that falls well; that is lucky; that is most opportune.

cela tombe mal [Fr], lit., that falls badly; that is unlucky; that is most inopportune.

cela va sans dire [Fr], that goes without saying; that is a matter of course. Cf. DAS VERSTEHT SICH VON SELBST.

cela viendra [Fr], that will come some day; all in good time.

célèbre [Fr], famous; celebrated.

céleri [Fr], celery.

celeritas et veritas [L], promptness and truth.

célibataire [Fr], bachelor; *fem.,* spinster.

celui qui veut, celui-là peut [Fr], who wills can; where there's a will there's a way.

cembalo [It; *pl.* cembali], harpsichord; pianoforte.

ce monde est plein de fous [Fr], this world is full of fools.

cena [Sp], supper.

cénacle [Fr], lit., a guest room (where the Last Supper was taken); a group with common interests, in allusion to the Last Supper; a literary coterie.

Cena Domini [L], the Lord's Supper.

cencerro [Sp], bell worn by the leading mule; hence, the leading mule in a pack train: *southwestern U.S.*

ce n'est fait de lui [Fr], it is all over with him.

ce n'est pas être bien aise que de rire [Fr], laughter is not always a sign of a mind at ease: *St. Evremond.*

ce n'est que le premier pas que coûte [Fr], it is only the first step that costs.

cenote [Sp], a natural underground reservoir of water; natural well: *Sp. Am.*

cens [Fr], annual payment or service, now usually nominal, given to the proprietor of an estate in recognition of his title: *Fr. Can. law.*

censor morum [L], a censor of morals.

central [Am Sp], a sugar mill that operates for a number of plantations.

ce qui est différé n'est pas perdu [Fr], what is put off is not lost.

cerda [Sp], hair from a horse's mane or tail; also, cow hair. A female hog; *masc.,* **cerdo**.

cérémonie [Fr], ceremony; formality; pomp.

cereza [Sp], cherry.

cerilla [Sp], wax match.

cerise [Fr], cherry; cherry color; cherry-colored.

cerrero [Sp], running wild; unbroken: said of horses.

cerro [Sp], hill.

certamina divitiarum [L], lit., struggles of riches; strivings after wealth: *Horace.*

certificado [Sp], *n.* certificate; *adj.* registered, as a letter.

certiorari [L], lit., to be certified; a writ to call up the records of a lower court: *law.*

certum est quia impossibile est [L], it is true because it is impossible: *Tertullian.*

certum voto pete finem [L], set a definite limit to your desire: *Horace.*

cervelle [Fr], brain. —**cervelles de veau en brochette,** broiled calf's brains, on skewers: *cookery.*

cerveza [Sp], beer.

cessante causa, cessat effectus [L], when the cause ceases, the effect ceases.

cessez le feu! [Fr], cease fire!: *mil.*

cessio bonorum [L], a surrender of goods: *law.*

c'est-à-dire [Fr], that is to say; namely: *abbr.* c.-à-d.

c'est à vous à donner [Fr], it is your turn to deal.

c'est à vous à parler [Fr], it is your turn to speak.

c'est bien ça [Fr], that's just it.

c'est égal [Fr], lit., it is equal; it is all one; it's all the same.

c'est la guerre [Fr], that is war; it's according to the customs of war.

c'est là le diable [Fr], there is the devil; there's the rub.

c'est la mer à boire [Fr], lit., it is the sea to drink; it is an endless task; an impossibility.

c'est le commencement de la fin [Fr], it's the beginning of the end.

c'est le premier pas qui coûte [Fr], it is the first step that costs (*or* is difficult).

c'est magnifique mais ce n'est pas la guerre [Fr], it is magnificent, but it is not war: comment of a French general on the charge of the Light Brigade at Balaklava.

c'est mon affaire [Fr], that is my affair; leave that to me.

c'est plus qu'un crime, c'est une faute [Fr], it is more than a crime, it is a blunder.

c'est selon [Fr], that depends.

c'est tout autre chose [Fr], that's quite another matter.

c'est tout dire [Fr], that is stating the whole case; that's the whole thing.

cestui [OF], he; the one. **—cestui que trust,** lit., he who trusts; the beneficiary of a trust. **—cestui que use,** lit., he who uses; the person for whose benefit real estate is granted in trust to another: *both law.*

c'est une vraie aubaine [Fr], it is a real godsend.

c'est un fin matois [Fr], he is a sly one.

c'est un sot à vingt-quatre carats [Fr], he is a twenty-four-carat fool; he is a fool of the first water.

c'est un zéro en chiffres [Fr], he is a mere cipher.

c'est vraiment incroyable [Fr], that is really incredible.

cetera desunt [L], the rest are lacking (i.e., these are all).

ceteris paribus [L], other things being equal.

cha [Chin], tea.

chabuk *or* **chabouk** [Hind], a whip; horsewhip: *India.*

chachem [Yiddish], a learned, wise, or clever person.

chacun a sa marotte [Fr], everyone has his hobby.

chacun à son goût [Fr], everyone to his taste.

chacun est l'artisan de sa fortune [Fr], everyone is the architect of his own fortune.

chacun pour soi et Dieu pour tous [Fr], everyone for himself and God for all.

chacun tire de son côté [Fr], everyone pulls for his own side.

chagrin [Fr], sorrow; grief.

chahut [Fr], a high-kicking vulgar dance of the 19th century; violent row.

chaise longue [Fr], lit., long chair; reclining chair or couch.

chal [Gypsy; *fem.* chai], man; fellow; person.

chaland [Fr], barge.

chalet [Fr], Swiss cottage; also, country house in the style of a Swiss cottage. —**chalet de nécessité,** public lavatory and toilet.

challa [Yiddish], a braided bread loaf, baked for the Sabbath.

chalumeau [Fr], a rustic flute or pipe; also, the lowest register of the clarinet.

chamade [Fr], signal for a parley or surrender made by drum or trumpet: *mil.*

chambranle [Fr], a decoration framing the sides and top of a doorway, window, fireplace, or other opening: *arch.*

chambre [Fr], chamber; room. —**chambre à coucher** [*pl.* chambres à coucher], bedroom. —**chambre d'ami,** lit., friend's room; guest room.

chambré [Fr], chambered; specif., brought to the temperature of the room: said of certain wines.

chamisal [Am Sp], a dense growth of the chamiso shrub; also, the shrub itself: *California.*

chamois [Fr], a pliant leather; mountain goat.

champak [Hind], East Indian magnolia, regarded as sacred by Hindus.

champ clos [Fr], lit., closed field; the lists (an arena for jousting).

champ de Mars [Fr], lit., Field of Mars; a large open space in Paris on the left bank of the Seine.

champignon [Fr], mushroom.

champlevé [Fr], a form of enamel work in which cells are cut in the metal, in which the enamel is laid and then fused.

Champs Élysées [Fr], Elysian Fields: name of an avenue in Paris.

chandail [Fr], sweater.

chanoine [Fr], canon (religious).

chanson [Fr], a song. —**chanson de geste,** old French epic poem, celebrating the exploits of knights, the most famous being the *Chanson de Roland.* —**chansons à boire,** drinking songs.

chansonnette [Fr], little song; ditty.

chant [Fr], song. —**chant du cygne,** swan song; the last work of a poet or musician immediately before his death. —**Chant du Départ,** Song of Departure; a French Revolutionary song.

chantage [Fr], extortion of hush money; blackmail.

chanterelle [Fr], the treble string of the violin, lute, etc.; a type of edible mushroom.

chanteur [Fr; *fem.* chanteuse], singer.

chantier [Can Fr], log hut; shack; yard; shipyard.

chapa [Sp], ornamental plate or shield, usually of silver, worn on the sombrero: *Mexico & southwestern U.S.*

chaparajos *or* **chapareras** [Mex Sp], leather or sheepskin overalls, as worn by cowboys; *colloq.*, chaps.

chaparral [Sp, *fr. chaparro,* evergreen oak], orig., a thicket of dwarf evergreen oaks; hence, any dense thicket of thorny shrubs and dwarf trees: *Mexico & southwestern U.S.* Cf. CHAMISAL.

chapati [Hind], thin unleavened bread.

chapeau [Fr; *pl.* chapeaux], hat; bonnet. **—chapeau rouge,** red cap of liberty. **—chapeaux bas!,** hats off! **—recevoir le chapeau rouge,** be made a cardinal: *R.C.Ch.*

chapeau-bras [Fr], a compressible three-cornered hat, made to be carried under the arm.

chapelle ardente [Fr], lit., a burning chapel; the chamber in which a dead body lies in state surrounded with lighted candles.

chapon [Fr], capon.

chapote [Mex Sp & Am Sp], *in southwestern U.S. and northern Mex.,* the black persimmon tree and its fruit; *in southern Mex.* (**zapote**), the sapote tree and its apple-like fruit.

chaprás [Hind], a badge; esp., the engraved brass plate attached to the shoulder belt of a messenger, or *chaprási: India.*

chaprási [Hind], the wearer of a *chaprás* or badge; messenger; orderly; sepoy; peon: *India.* Written also *chaprassy, chuprassy.* Cf. PATAWALA.

chaque pays à sa guise [Fr], each country has its own customs; lit., its own ways.

chaqueta [Sp], jacket; esp., a heavy jacket worn by cowboys.

char-à-bancs [Fr; *pl.* chars-à-bancs], a long, open, horse-drawn vehicle with transverse seats, as used by sightseers.

charbon [Fr], coal; charcoal.

charbonnier [Fr], charcoal burner.

charca [Sp], small shallow pool of standing water; puddle; in Texas, a spring gushing from a rocky ledge.

charco [Sp], a small, and usually deep, body of water, confined naturally or artificially; small lake; pond; pool.

charcuterie [Fr], pork butcher's business, shop, or supplies; dressed pork.

charcutier [Fr], pork butcher.

chargé *or* **chargé d'affaires** [Fr; *pl.* chargés], deputy ambassador.

charisma [Gk χάρισμα, favor given], personal charm; magnetism (given by God).

charmante [Fr], a charming lady.

charmeuse [Fr], enchantress; bewitching woman.

charosho [Russ], good.

charpente [Fr], framework; timber work.

charpoy [Anglo-Ind; Hind *chārpāī, fr. chār,* four, *pāī,* foot], light East Indian bedstead or cot. Cf. PALANG.

charqui [Sp], jerked beef.

charrette [Fr], cart; specif., a springless two-wheeled cart with rack sides.

charro [Sp], cowboy: *Mexico.*

châsse [Fr], shrine.

chassé [Fr], a kind of gliding step in dancing.

chasse-cousins [Fr], anything calculated to "chase away cousins" and unwelcome guests generally; cold shoulder; poor reception; meager dinner; bad wine.

chasse-marée [Fr], three-masted coasting or fishing vessel; lugger: *naut.*

chassepot [Fr], breech-loading needle gun, used in the French army from 1866 to 1874.

chasser [Fr], to hunt; chase; pursue.

chasseur [Fr; *fem.* chasseuse], hunter; sportsman; huntsman; *mil.,* lightly armed French soldier; in hotels and cafés, a liveried attendant.

chat [Fr; *fem.* chatte], cat. —**chat en poche,** lit., cat in a bag; pig in a poke. —**chat qui dort,** sleeping cat. —**n'éveillez pas le chat qui dort,** equivalent to "let sleeping dogs lie."

château [Fr; *pl.* châteaux], castle; manor house; country seat; also, designating various wine-producing estates and the wines therefrom; as, *Château-Latour, Château-Margaux,* etc.

châteaubriant [Fr], broiled fillet of beef, with fried potatoes and mushrooms or truffles: *cookery.*

chatoyant [Fr; *fem.* chatoyante], glistening or emitting changeable rays, like the eyes of a cat in the dark; shot: said of certain fabrics and precious stones.

chatti [Anglo-Ind], earthenware pot.

chaudière [Fr], boiler.

chaudron [Fr], kettle or cauldron; hence, a copperish red.

chauffage [Fr], heating.

chauffe-pieds [Fr], foot warmer.

chaufferette [Fr], foot warmer; foot stove.

chauk [Hind], market; square: *India.*

chauki [Hind], chair; bench; guard's post; watch; specif., police station; lockup.

chaukidar [Hind], watchman; patrolman.

chaumière [Fr], thatched cottage.

chaussée [Fr], causeway; ground level.

chausses [Fr], medieval breeches and hose.

chaussures [Fr], footgear; boots, shoes, etc.

chauvinist [Fr; *fem.* chauviniste], a fanatical patriot; militarist; jingoist.

chaver [Heb; *fem.* chavera], friend.

chawl [Anglo-Ind], a long narrow building divided into separate rooms for families; lodging house.

che dà orecchio si vuol rendre [It], she who listens is going to yield.

chee-chee or **chi-chi** [Anglo-Ind; cf. Hind *chhī-chhī*, nasty! fie! ugly!], East Indian of mixed racial descent or Eurasian, in allusion to the mincing English characteristic of many of them; also, this mincing English: used disparagingly.

chef or **chef de cuisine** [Fr], head cook (*male*); master cook.

chef de gare [Fr], station master.

chef-d'oeuvre [Fr; *pl.* chefs-d'oeuvre], masterpiece.

chef d'orchestre [Fr], orchestra conductor.

chela [Hind], disciple, esp. of a *guru* (q.v.); pupil; follower: *India*.

chemin de fer [Fr; *pl.* chemins de fer], lit., iron road; railroad.

chemin faisant [Fr], on the way; by the way.

che non pur ne' miei occhi è Paradiso [It], "these eyes of mine are not thy only Paradise": *Dante* (Beatrice gently chiding the poet for his wandering gaze; tr. by Cary).

cher ami [Fr; *fem.* chère amie], dear friend; lover.

chercher la petite bête [Fr], lit., to search for the little beast; be excessively finicky.

cherchez la femme [Fr], look for the woman in the case.

che sarà sarà [It], what will be will be.

cheval [Fr; *pl.* chevaux], horse. —**cheval de bataille,** war horse; charger; fig., strong point; favorite subject; hobby.

chevalier [Fr], a knight. —**le chevalier de la Triste Figure,** Don Quixote. Cf. RITTER.

chevalier d'industrie [Fr], one who lives by his wits; sharper; swindler.

chevalier sans peur et sans reproche [Fr], fearless and stainless knight.

chevaux-de-frise [Fr; *pl.*], iron spikes set in timber to repel cavalry; spikes set on top of a paling.

chevelure [Fr], head of hair; arrangement of the hair.

chevet [Fr], eastern extremity of the apse of a church: *arch.*

chevreuil [Fr], roebuck; venison.

chez lui (chez nous, chez vous) [Fr], at his (our, your) house; at home; home. —**avoir un chez soi,** to have a home of one's own.

chhota, *pop.* **chota** [Hind; *fem.* chhoti], small; little; younger; junior. —**chhota haziri** or (*more exact*) **chhoti haziri,** *pop.* **chota hazri,** lit., small breakfast; a light meal of tea, toast, and fruit, in the very early morning. —**chhota sahib,** *pop.* **chota sahib,** lit., little sahib (*or* master); subordinate official; assistant; junior; specif., assistant magistrate distinguished from *bara sahib: India*.

chhuri [Hind], knife: *India*.

chi ama assai, parla poco [It], he who loves much says little.

chi ama, crede [It], he who loves, trusts.

chiarezza [It], clearness; brightness; purity: *music*.

chiaroscuro [It], lit., bright dark; *fine arts,* disposition of light and shade; also, a drawing in black and white; fig., variety and contrast in a literary work, etc.; effective employment of light and shade; relief.

chi ben cena ben dorme [It], he who sups well sleeps well.

chibouk *or* **chibuk** [Turk], a long Turkish tobacco pipe.

chic [Fr], *adj.* stylish; smart; in good taste; *n.* smartness of style.

chicalote [Sp], a prickly poppy, with white flowers, growing in Mexico and southwestern United States.

chicane [Fr], quibbling.

chicano [Am Sp], a North American of Mexican descent, usually a member of a family with one or both parents of Mexican origin.

chicha [Sp], South American tree, with edible nutlike seeds; also, chica, or chico, a red coloring matter used by South American Indians as a stain for the skin.

chicha [Am Sp], a fermented liquor made from corn, cane sugar, etc.: *South Am.*

chichi [Fr], curls of false hair. **—faire des chichis,** to have affected manners; make a fuss.

chi-chi [Anglo-Ind]. See CHEE-CHEE.

chick [Anglo-Ind], a hanging sun blind made of narrow strips of bamboo, fastened together loosely with string.

chico [Sp; *fem.* chica], *adj.* small; little; *n.* little boy.

chicote [Sp], the end of a rope or cable; specif., a long whip, with wooden handle, used in cattle driving: *Texas.*

chi dà presto, dà due volte [It], he who gives quickly gives twice. Cf. BIS DAT QUI CITO DAT.

chien méchant [Fr], lit., wicked dog; beware of the dog.

chiffonnier [Fr; *fem.* chiffonnière], ragpicker; rag gatherer; a chest of drawers: *furniture.*

chiffré [Fr; *fem.* chiffrée], figured: *music.*

chignon [Fr], nape of the neck; knot or pad of hair worn by women at the back of the head.

chile con carne [Sp], meat in spicy sauce: *Mexico & southwestern U.S.*

chi lo sa? [It], who knows? Cf. QUI LE SAIT?

chilovek [Russ; *pl.* ludi, people], man.

chimenea [Sp], chimney; smokestack; also, air pipe; ventilating pipe. **—chimenea sin fuego, reino sin puerto,** a fireless chimney is a kingdom without a port.

chi nasca bella nasce maritata [It], she who is born beautiful is born married.

chinela [Sp], slipper.

chi niente sa, di niente dubita [It], who knows nothing doubts nothing; an ignoramus has no doubts.

chi non fa, non falla [It], he who does nothing makes no mistakes.

chi non ha, non è [It], he who has not is not.

chi non s'arrischia non guadagna [It], who risks nothing gains nothing; nothing ventured, nothing gained.

chi parla troppo non può parlar sempre bene [It], he who speaks too much cannot always speak well: *Goldoni.*

chit *or* **chitty** [Anglo-Ind], a letter; short note; signed voucher; also, certificate of character given to a servant.

chi tace acconsente [It], he who is silent consents; silence gives consent.

chi tace confessa [It], he who keeps silent confesses (*or* admits his guilt).

chi va piano va sano; chi va sano va lontano [It], he who goes softly goes safely; he who goes safely goes far.

chivarras *or* **chivarros** [Mex Sp], leggings made of stout cloth or leather: *Mexico & southwestern U.S.*

chokra [Anglo-Ind; Hind *chhokra*], boy.

chokri [Anglo-Ind; Hind *chhokri*], girl.

chômage [Fr], unemployment.

chômeur [Fr], unemployed person.

chop suey [Chin], a Chinese-American dish said to be named for the Cantonese equivalent of "odds & ends," *shap sui*, miscellaneous bits.

chor [Hind], thief.

chorea scriptorum [L], writer's cramp.

chose jugée [Fr], thing already decided and profitless to discuss; closed chapter.

chose qui plaît est à demi vendue [Fr], a thing that pleases is half sold.

chota sahib [Anglo-Ind]. See CHHOTA SAHIB.

chou [Fr; *pl.* choux], cabbage; ornamental bunch or rosette on a dress; also, a kind of light pastry; *colloq.*, a term of endearment; darling. —**chou marin,** sea kale. —**chou pour chou,** lit., cabbage for cabbage; taken all in all. —**choux de Bruxelles,** Brussels sprouts. —**mon petit chou,** my little darling.

choucroute [Fr], sauerkraut. —**choucroute garnie,** sauerkraut with sausage.

chouette [Fr], pretty; elegant; stunning: *colloq.*

chou-fleur [Fr; *pl.* choux-fleurs], cauliflower.

chow [Chin], food.

chow fan [Chin], fried rice.

chow mein [Chin], vegetables, meat, and noodles.

choza [Sp], hut; cabin; shepherd's cottage.

Christe eleison [Latinized Gr], Christ have mercy: *eccl.* Cf. KYRIE ELEISON.

Christi crux est mea lux [L], the cross of Christ is my light.

Christo et Ecclesiae [L], for Christ and for the Church.

chronique scandaleuse [Fr], scandalous reports; unsavory gossip; tittle-tattle.

chukker [Anglo-Ind; Hind *chakkar*], orig., wheel; circular course, as for exercising horses; *polo,* one of the divisions of the game.

chup! [Hind], silence! quiet! —**chup raho!,** be quiet! hold your tongue!

chupa [Sp], a dry measure, two thirds of a pint: *P.I.*

chupatty [Anglo-Ind; Hind *chapātī*], thin, unleavened cake.

chuprassy [Anglo-Ind]. See CHAPRASI.

churrasco [Sp], meat broiled over charcoal: *South Am.*

chut! [Fr], silence! hush!

chutzpah [Heb & Yiddish], brazenness; gall.

chytry jak lis [Pol], as sly as a fox.

ciao! [It], Hello! Hi! So long!

cicatrix manet [L], the scar remains.

cicerone [It; *pl.* ciceroni], a guide; one who explains antiquities, etc., to visitors.

cicisbeo [It; *pl.* cicisbei], acknowledged lover of a married woman.

ci-devant [Fr], former; late; ex-.

ciénaga *or* **ciénega** [Sp], marsh; swamp: *southwestern U.S.*

cierge [Fr], taper, church candle.

cigarillo [Sp *cigarrillo*], little cigar; cigarette.

ci-gît [Fr], here lies; *hic iacet* (q.v.).

ciguatera [Sp], disease caused by eating poisonous fish: *West Indies.*

cineri gloria sera est [L], glory paid to ashes comes too late: *Martial.*

cingulum Veneris [L], the girdle of Venus.

cinquecento [It], Italian art and literature of the 16th century.

ciò ch'io vedeva, mi sembiava un riso dell' universo [It], that which I beheld seemed unto me a laughter of the universe: *Dante* (describing the boundless joy of Paradise).

cio non vale un' acca [It], it is not worth an H; it's worth nothing.

cirage [Fr], blacking; shoe polish.

circa [L], about: *abbr.* c. *or* ca.

circiter [L], about: *abbr.* c. *or* circ.

circuitus verborum [L], lit., a circuit of words; circumlocution; *rhetoric,* a period.

circulus in probando [L], lit., a circle in the proof; reasoning in a circle; a vicious circle: *logic.*

circum [L], about: *abbr.* c. *or* circ.

ciseaux [Fr], scissors.

cito maturum, cito putridum [L], soon ripe, soon rotten.

citoyen [Fr; *fem.* citoyenne], citizen.

cittadino [It; *pl.* cittadini; *fem.* cittadina, *pl.* cittadine], citizen.

ciudad [Sp; *pl.* ciudades], city; town.

civet [Fr], a ragout of hare, venison, or other game, flavored with wine, herbs, spice, and onions. **—civet de chevreuil,** jugged venison: *both cookery.*

civilitas successit barbarum [L], civilization succeeds barbarism: territorial motto of *Minnesota.*

civis Romanus sum [L], I am a Roman citizen: *Cicero.*

clair-obscur [Fr]. Same as CHIAROSCURO.

clair semé [Fr], sparsely sown; thinly scattered.

claque [Fr], a body of hired applauders: *theat.*

claquemuré [Fr; *fem.* claquemurée], shut in; cooped up; confined to one's room.

claquer [Fr], to crack; slap; clap; applaud.

claqueur [Fr], hired applauder; claquer: *theat.*

clarior e tenebris [L], (I shine) more brightly from out of the darkness.

clarum et venerabile nomen [L], illustrious and venerable name: *Lucan.*

clavis [L; *pl.* claves], key; glossary.

cliché [Fr], stereotype plate; photographic negative plate; fig., stereotyped expression; hackneyed phrase.

clin d'oeil [Fr], twinkling of an eye; instant; a wink.

cloche [Fr], a bell.

clochette [Fr], small bell; hand bell.

cloison [Fr], partition, as of boards or masonry; division; *naut.*, bulkhead.

cloisonné [Fr], inlaid between partitions: said of enamel in which thin metal strips are bent to the outline of the design.

clôture [Fr], closure; a method of ending debate by a vote that "the question now be put": *parliamentary practice.*

clou [Fr], nail; spike; fig., nucleus; center of attraction; main point of interest.

cobre [Sp], copper.

coche [Sp], coach; carriage; car.

cocher [Fr], coachman; cabman.

cochera [Sp], coach house; *R.R.*, engine shed; round house.

cochero [Sp], coachman; driver; *P.I.*, hackney driver.

cochon [Fr], pig; hog. —**cochon de lait,** suckling pig.

cocotte [Fr], casserole; child's onomatopoetic word for "hen"; also, loose woman; prostitute.

cocu [Fr], cuckold.

codetta [It], a short coda: *music.*

codex rescriptus [L], palimpsest; wooden writing surface.

coelitus mihi vires [L]. See CAELITUS.

coelum [L]. See CAELUM.

coetus dulces valete [L], happy meetings, fare ye well: *Catullus.*

cogito ergo sum [L], I think, therefore I am (*or* exist): *Descartes.*

cognati [L], relations on the mother's side; cognates: *law.*

cognoscente [It; *pl.* cognoscenti], connoisseur.

cognovit *or* **cognovit actionem** [L], lit., he has acknowledged the action; the defendant's acknowledgment of the plantiff's claim: *law.*

cohue [Fr], noisy crowd; tumult.

coiffer Sainte Catherine [Fr], to put a headdress on St. Catherine; remain an unmarried woman after age twenty-five. —**coiffer un mari,** deceive a husband.

coiffeur [Fr; *fem.* coiffeuse], hairdresser.

coiffure [Fr], headdress; style of arranging the hair.

col [Fr], neck; a mountain pass; defile.

colazione [It], breakfast; lunch.

col canto [It], with the melody or vocal part: *music*.

colina [Sp], hill; hillock.

collaborateur [Fr; *fem.* collaboratrice], fellow worker; collaborator.

colla destra [It], with the right hand: *music*.

colla parte [It], with the part (a direction to the accompanist to follow the tempo of the principal performer): *music*.

coll' arco [It], with the bow (*abbr.* c.a.): *music*.

colla sinistra [It], with the left hand: *music*.

colla voce [It], with the voice (a direction to the accompanist to follow the voice): *music*.

collectanea [L; *pl.*], a collection of passages from various authors; miscellany; commonplace book.

collegium [L; *pl.* collegia], a body of colleagues or other persons with common pursuits, functions, and privileges; college.

collegno [It], with the wood (i.e., with the stick of the bow instead of with the hair): *music*.

colluvies vitiorum [L], vile medley of vices; sink of iniquity.

colocación [Sp], employment; job; position.

coloratura [It], runs, trills, and other embellishments in vocal music; colorature: *music*.

colubrem in sinu fovere [L], to cherish a snake in one's bosom.

comandancia [Sp], post or district under military control; a command; also, headquarters of a permanent post: *mil*.

comandante [Sp], *mil.*, commandant; commanding officer; specif., major; *nav.*, captain; commanding officer.

combien? [Fr], how many? how much?

comédie [Fr], comedy; theater. **—Comédie humaine,** The Human Comedy: title of Balzac's series of novels. **—Comédie française,** official title of Le Théâtre français. **—comédie larmoyante,** tear-producing comedy; sentimental comedy.

comédienne [Fr], comedy actress.

comendador [Sp], knight commander.

come prima [It], as at first: *music*.

comerciante [Sp], merchant; tradesman.

comes iucundus in via pro vehiculo est [L], a pleasant companion on the road is as good as a carriage: *Publilius Syrus*.

come sopra [It], as above (*abbr.* co. so.): *music*.

come state? *or* **come sta?** [It], how are you? how do you do?

come t'è picciol fallo amaro morso! [It], what bitter pain a little fault doth give thee!: *Dante*.

come va? [It], how goes it?

comida [Sp], meal; dinner.

comitadji [Serb], a band of guerrillas.

comitas inter gentes [L], comity between nations.

comité [Fr], committee; meeting; club. **—petit comité,** small party.

comitiva [It; *pl.* comitive], band of outlaws or brigands, esp. in southern Italy.

commanditaire [Fr], silent partner.

commandite *or* **société en commandite** [Fr], limited liability company, consisting of acting and one or more silent partners; limited joint-stock company. This form of partnership obtains also in Louisiana.

comme ci comme ça [Fr], so-so; middling.

comme deux gouttes d'eau [Fr], lit., as two drops of water; as alike as two peas.

comme il faut [Fr], as it should be; proper; correct; in good form; well-bred.

commencement de la fin [Fr], beginning of the end.

comment allez-vous? [Fr], how are you?

comment ça va? [Fr], how goes it?

commis [Fr; *fem.* commise], clerk; shop assistant.

commissionnaire [Fr], one entrusted with a commission, usually a small one; agent; commission agent; messenger; porter.

commis-voyageur [Fr], traveling salesman.

commodo [It], quietly; with ease: *music.*

commune bonum [L], common good; the good of all.

commune periculum concordiam parit [L], a common danger begets unity.

communibus annis [L], in common (*or* average) years; on the annual average.

communi consensu [L], by common consent.

communiqué [Fr], official communication; statement.

¿cómo está? [Sp], how are you?

¿cómo le va? [Sp], how goes it?

¿cómo se llama? [Sp], what is your (his, her) name? what is this called?

como se vive, se muere [Sp], as one lives, one dies.

cómo vai? [Pg], how goes it?

compadre [Sp], orig., godfather; friend; companion: *Sp. Am.*

compagnie [Fr], company; society; *com.,* company (*abbr.* Cie).

compagnon de voyage [Fr], traveling companion.

compañero [Sp], comrade; companion.

compañía [Sp], company; society; *com.,* company (*abbr.* C.ª *or* C.ía).

compendia dispendia [L], shortcuts are roundabout ways.

compesce mentem [L], control your temper: *Horace.*

complexus [L], lit., an embracing; aggregate of parts; complex; complicated whole; *anat.,* a broad muscle at the back of the neck.

componere lites [L], to settle disputes: *Horace.*

compositeur [Fr], *music,* composer; *printing,* compositor.

compos mentis [L], sound of mind; in one's right mind.

compos sui [L], master of himself.

compos voti [L], having gotten one's wish: *Horace*.

compote [Fr], fruit cooked with sugar; also, a savory ragout, as of pigeons.

compte rendu [Fr; *pl.* comptes rendus], an account rendered; official report.

comptoir [Fr], lit., counter; counting house; commercial agency or factory.

comte [Fr], count; earl.

comtesse [Fr], countess.

con abbandono [It], with abandon; with passionate expression: *music*.

con amore [It], with love; heartily; enthusiastically; *music*, with tenderness.

con brio [It], with vivacity; with fire: *music*.

con calore [It], with warmth or passion: *music*.

concedo [L], I admit; I grant: *logic*.

concentus [L], concord; harmony; part of the church service sung by the choir: distinguished from *accentus*.

concertante [It], a concerto in which two or more solo instruments or voices take the principal parts alternately, with orchestral or choral accompaniment: *music*.

concertino [It], a small *concerto: music*.

concerto [It; *pl.* concerti], a composition written for one (or sometimes two or three) principal instruments, with orchestral accompaniment: *music*.

concesionario [Sp], holder of a concession (as below).

concessionnaire [Fr], holder of a concession, esp. of one granted by a foreign government.

concetto [It; *pl.* concetti], a conceit; flash of wit; esp., affected and fanciful wit.

concha [Sp], lit., shell; a small cigar tapered at each end.

concierge [Fr], doorkeeper; janitor; hall porter.

conciergerie [Fr], doorkeeper's apartment; janitor's office. **—Conciergerie,** celebrated prison in Paris.

conciliatrix [L], procuress.

concio ad clerum [L], discourse to the clergy.

concitoyen [Fr; *fem.* concitoyenne], fellow citizen.

concombre [Fr], cucumber.

concordat [Fr], agreement with the church.

concordia discors [L], discordant harmony: *Horace*.

concours [Fr], concurrence; cooperation; meeting; also, competition; contest; competitive examination. **—concours hippique,** horse show. **—concours universel,** open competitive examination.

con cura [It], with care; carefully.

concurrence [Fr], competition.

condamné [Fr; *fem.* condamnée], condemned person; convict.

conde [Sp], count; earl; also, chief of gypsies.

condesa [Sp], countess.

con diligenza [It], with diligence.

condiscipulus [L], schoolfellow; fellow student; classmate.

conditio sine qua non [L], indispensable condition.

con dolcezza [It], with sweetness: *music*.

con dolore [It], with grief; sadly; mournfully: *music*.

condottiere [It; *pl.* condottieri], leader of a band of mercenaries.

con espressione [It], with expression: *music*.

confer [L], compare: *abbr.* cf.

conférence [Fr], conference; lecture; recital.

confido et conquiesco [L], I trust and am at rest.

confiteor [L], lit., I confess; a prayer of public confession: *R.C.Ch.*

confiture [Fr], jam; preserves.

con forza [It], with force: *music*.

confrère [Fr], colleague; fellow member.

con fuoco [It], with fire; spiritedly: *music*.

congé [Fr], permission; unceremonious dismissal; discharge; also, a kind of molding; *mil.*, furlough; leave. **—congé d'accorder,** permission to agree. **—congé d'aller,** permission to depart. **—congé d'appel,** permission to appeal. **—congé d'élire,** permission to elect; royal permission to elect a bishop. **—en congé,** on leave; on furlough. **—jour de congé,** holiday.

con grazia [It], with grace; gracefully: *music*.

con gusto [It], with taste; tastefully: *music*.

con impeto [It], with impetuosity: *music*.

coniunctis viribus [L], with united powers.

con latín, rocín y florín andarás el mundo [Sp], with Latin, a nag (horse), and money, you can travel all over the world.

con más miedo que vergüenza [Sp], with more fear than shame.

con molto passione [It], with much passion: *music*.

con moto [It], with movement; with animation: *music*.

con mucho gusto [Sp], with great pleasure; willingly.

connaisseur [Fr; *fem.* connaisseuse], connoisseur; critical judge.

connaître [Fr], to know; be acquainted with. **—connaître à fond,** to know thoroughly. **—connaître le dessous des cartes,** to know the underside of the cards; know the secret. **—connaître son monde,** to know one's world; know one's associates or customers.

connu! [Fr], known! that's an old story.

conocido [Sp; *fem.* conocida], acquaintance. **—conocidos muchos, amigos pocos,** many acquaintances, few friends.

con pazienza, [It], with patience; patiently.

con permesso [It], by your leave.

con piacere [It], with pleasure.

con prestezza [It], with rapidity: *music.*

conquistador [Sp], conqueror; esp., one of the Spanish conquerors of America in the 16th century.

conscia mens recti [L], a mind conscious of integrity: *Ovid.*

conscientia mille testes [L], conscience is as good as a thousand witnesses.

con sdegno [It], scornfully; disdainfully; angrily.

conseil [Fr], council. —**conseil d'administration,** board of directors. —**conseil de famille,** family council (*or* consultation). —**conseil d'état,** council of state.

con semplicità [It], with simplicity: *music.*

consensus facit legem [L], consent makes law.

consensus omnium [L], universal consent.

consequitur quodcunque petit [L], he attains whatever he attempts (*or* aims at).

conservateur [Fr], conservative: *politics;* curator.

conservatoire [Fr], academy or public place of instruction in music, elocution, and other arts; conservatory.

consilio et animis [L], by wisdom and courage.

consilio et prudentia [L], by wisdom and prudence.

consilio, non impetu [L], by deliberation, not impulse.

consommé [Fr], strong clear soup made from meat or from meat and vegetables.

con sordino [It; *pl.* sordini], with the mute (i.e., with the mutes on the string instruments to lessen the sound; in piano playing, with the soft pedal down): *music.*

con spirito [It], with spirit; with animation: *music.*

constantia et virtute [L], by firmness and courage.

consuetudo pro lege servatur [L], custom is held as law (i.e., in the absence of any specific law, custom or usage decides the point at issue): *law.*

consuetudo quasi altera natura [L], habit is, as it were, second (lit., another) nature: *Cicero.*

consule Planco [L], when Plancus was consul; in my younger days: *Horace.*

consummatum est [L], it is finished: Latin translation of Christ's words on the Cross (*John* xix. 30).

contadino [It; *pl.* contadini; *fem.* contadina, *pl.* contadine], Italian peasant.

conte [Fr], tale, esp. of imaginary adventures; short narrative. —**conte à dormir debout,** story that would put one to sleep on one's feet; rigmarole; old wives' tale.

contentement passe richesse [Fr], contentment surpasses riches; enough is as good as a feast.

conter [Fr], to tell; relate. —**conter des fagots,** to tell idle stories. —**conter fleurettes,** to whisper sweet nothings; make love to.

continuato [It], continued; sustained: *music.*

conto [Pg], lit., a million: specif., in the modern Portuguese monetary system, 1000 escudos. [It], account; bill.

contrabandista [Sp], smuggler.

contrabasso *or* **contrabbasso** [It], double bass: *music.*

contra bonos mores [L], contrary to good manners: *abbr.* cont. bon. mor.

contradictio in adiecto [L], contradiction in terms: *logic.*

contrafagotto [It], double bassoon.

contra formam statuti [L], against the form of the statute: *law.*

contrainte par corps [Fr], arrest for debt: *Fr. law.*

contra ius gentium [L], against the law of nations.

contra mundum [L], against the world.

contra pacem [L], against the peace: *law.*

contraria contrariis curantur [L], opposites are cured by opposites (the principle of allopathy).

contrat [Fr], contract; agreement. **—contrat aléatoire,** conditional contract: *Fr. law.* **—contrat de vente,** contract of sale. **—contrat social,** social compact.

contrecoup [Fr], counterblow; rebound; repercussion; result; effect; *billiards,* a kiss. **—par contrecoup,** as a consequence.

contretemps [Fr], untoward accident; vexatious happening; mischance; hitch.

contrôlé [Fr], registered; hallmarked.

convenance [Fr], conformity; fitness; propriety; also, convenience; *pl.,* conventional proprieties; good manners; etiquette. **—mariage de convenance,** marriage contracted primarily from material considerations; marriage of convenience.

conversazione [It; *pl.* conversazioni], lit., conversation; an evening assembly for conversation or discussion.

copain [Fr; *fem.* copine], chum; companion; buddy; crony.

copia fandi [L], abundance (*or* great flow) of talk.

copia verborum [L], abundance of words; prolixity.

coq [Fr], cock; rooster. **—coq de bruyère,** grouse. **—coq de combat,** gamecock. **—coq d' Inde,** lit., cock of India; turkey cock.

coq-à-l'âne [Fr], lit., rooster to the ass; cock-and-bull story; nonsense.

coquillage [Fr], shellfish; shellwork.

coquille [Fr], shell; scallop; ragout; pat, as of butter; *typog.,* wrong letter. **—coquilles de moules,** scalloped mussels: *cookery.* **—coquille St.-Jacques,** prepared scallops baked and served in a *coquille: cookery.*

coquin [Fr], knave; scamp; rascal. **—tour de coquin,** knavish trick.

coraggio! [It], courage!

coram [L], before; in the presence of. **—coram domine rege,** before our lord the king. **—coram iudice,** before a judge: *law.* **—coram nobis,** before us (i.e., the sovereign); in the Court of King's Bench: *law.* **—coram non iudice,** before a judge without jurisdiction; before one not the proper judge: *law.* **—coram paribus,** before equals; before one's peers. **—coram populo,** in public; in sight of spectators: *Horace.*

cor anglais [Fr], English horn; also, a corresponding organ stop: *music.*

corbeau [Fr], crow; raven; also, a very dark shade of green.

corbeille [Fr], basket. **—corbeille de mariage** (*or* **de noces**), wedding presents.

corda [It; *pl.* corde], a string: *music.* See also TRE CORDE and UNA CORDA.

cordelle [Fr], towline; towrope: *Canada & U.S. (local).*

cordon bleu [Fr], formerly, the blue ribbon worn by knights of the Holy Ghost; hence, a person of distinction; a first-rate cook.

cordon sanitaire [Fr], sanitary cordon; a line of guards stationed between infected and uninfected districts.

corno [It; *pl.* corni], horn. **—corno di bassetto,** tuba. **—corno inglese** [*pl.* corni inglesi], English horn: *all music.*

cornuto [It], a cuckold.

corona lucis [L], lit., crown of light; circular chandelier as hung from the roof of a church; corona.

corpora lente augescunt cito extinguuntur [L], bodies grow slowly (and) die quickly; bodies are slow in growth, rapid in decay: *Tacitus.*

corps [Fr], body. **—corps-à-corps,** body to body; hand to hand. **—corps d'armée,** army corps: *mil.* **—corps de ballet,** ensemble of ballet dancers. **—corps de bâtiment** *or* **corps de logis,** main mass of a building; also, a detached building. **—corps de bâtiments,** block of buildings. **—corps de cheminée,** chimney stack. **—corps de garde,** formerly, a body of men forming a guard; now, guardhouse; guardroom; military post. **—corps d'élite,** body of picked men: *mil.* **—corps de réserve,** a body of reserves: *mil.* **—corps de santé,** medical staff. **—corps des lettres,** the body of the type: *typog.* **—corps diplomatique,** diplomatic corps. **—corps dramatique,** theatrical company.

corpus [L; *pl.* corpora], body; dead body (now chiefly humorous in this sense); body, or collection, of writings; main body or material substance. **—Corpus Christi,** lit., body of Christ; festival in honor of the Holy Eucharist, observed on the Thursday after Trinity Sunday. **—corpus delicti,** the body of the crime; the substance or fundamental facts of a crime or offense: *law.* **—corpus iuris,** a body of law: a collection of laws of a country or jurisdiction. **—Corpus Iuris Canonici,** the body of canon law. **—Corpus Iuris Civilis,** the body of civil or Roman law. **—corpus omnis Romani iuris,** compendium of all Roman law: *Livy.* **—corpus sine pectore,** a body without a soul: *Horace.* **—corpus vile,** worthless matter.

correcteur [Fr], corrector of the press; proofreader.

corregidor [Sp], magistrate; esp., the chief magistrate of a Spanish town.

corregimiento [Sp], the office or jurisdiction of a *corregidor;* Spanish magistracy.

corre lontano chi non torna mai [It], he runs far who never turns.

correo [Sp], post office. **—en lista de correos,** general delivery. **—correo aereo,** air mail.

corrida de toros [Sp], bullfight.

corriente [Sp], this month (week, year); the present month (week, year): *abbr.* cte.

corrigendum [L; *pl.* corrigenda], error to be corrected, as in a book.

corruptio optimi pessima [L], the corruption of the best is the worst; "lilies that fester smell far worse than weeds": *Shakespeare.*

corruptissima re publica plurimae leges [L], in the most corrupt state the most laws: *Terence.*

corso [It; *pl.* corsi], course; broad thoroughfare.

cortège [Fr], train of attendants; retinue; procession.

cortesias engendran cortesias [Sp], courtesy begets courtesy.

cortile [It; *pl.* cortili], enclosed courtyard.

cor unum, via una [L], one heart, one way.

corvée [Fr], unpaid labor due to a feudal lord; statute labor; duty service; *mil.,* fatigue duty or party; fig., extra duty.

coryphée [Fr], leading ballet dancer.

cosa ben fatta è fatta due volte [It], a thing well done is twice done.

cosa mala nunca muere [Sp], a bad thing never dies.

cosaque [Fr], cossack; fierce or brutal man.

cosecha [Sp], harvest; harvest time; crop.

così fan tutti [It], thus do they all; that is the way of the world. **—così fan tutte,** that's the way all women behave.

cos ingeniorum [L], a whetstone for the wits.

cospetto! [It], confound it!

costumé [Fr; *fem.* costumée], in costume.

coteau [Fr; *pl.* coteaux], hillock; rising ground; *in Canada and U.S.,* upland or ridge between two valleys.

côtelette [Fr], cutlet; chop. **—côtelette de filet,** loin chop. **—côtelette en papillote,** cutlet cooked in a paper wrapper. See PAPILLOTE.

côtes de boeuf [Fr], ribs of beef.

cotillon [Fr], orig., petticoat, as worn by peasants; cotillion (dance and music).

couci-couci [Fr], so-so; indifferently.

coulé [Fr], a slur: *music.*

coulée [Fr], bed of a deep stream, having inclined sides; arroyo: *western Canada & U.S.*

couleur de rose [Fr], rose color; rose-colored; fig., bright side of things.

couleuvre [Fr], adder; fig., mortification; bitter pill. **—avaler des couleuvres,** to swallow insults; pocket affronts.

couloir [Fr], steep gorge; Alpine gully.

coup [Fr], a blow; stroke; act; shot; report; sudden motion or action.
—**coup d'aile,** flap (of the wings); fig., a flight of the imagination.
—**coup d'archet,** stroke of the bow: *music.* —**coup de bec,** peck; fig.,
taunt; gibe. —**coup de bonheur,** stroke of luck; lucky hit. —**coup de
bourse,** successful stock speculation. —**coup de boutoir,** a blow from
the snout of a wild boar; fig., a gibe; rough answer; crushing attack
in an argument. —**coup de chapeau,** a salute with the hat; raising
the hat in salute. —**coup de coude,** nudge. —**coup d'éclat,** brilliant
exploit; bold stroke. —**coup de dés,** throw of the dice. —**coup de
fond,** home thrust: *fencing.* —**coup de foudre,** thunderclap; love at
first sight. —**coup de grâce,** lit., stroke of mercy; finishing stroke;
death blow. —**coup de langue,** backbiting; slander; invective. —**coup
de main,** sudden, vigorous onslaught; surprise attack; bold stroke.
—**coup de maître,** master stroke. —**coup de malheur,** unlucky stroke;
piece of bad luck. —**coup de pied,** a kick; stamp. —**coup de plume,**
literary attack. —**coup de poing,** blow with the fist; punch. —**coup
de soleil,** sunstroke; *colloq.,* flush; blush. —**coup d'essai,** first attempt.
—**coup d'état,** violent change in government. —**coup de tête,** butt;
fig., a capricious, spiteful, or desperate act; freak. —**coup de théâtre,**
an unexpected and sensational turn or action; theatrical effect; stage
trick. —**coup de tonnerre,** peal of thunder. —**coup de vent,** gust of
wind; gale. —**coup d'oeil,** rapid and comprehensive glance; general
view. —**coup du ciel,** providential stroke; special providence. —**coup
manqué,** abortive attempt; failure.

coupé [Fr], a step, or salutation, in dancing.

coupure [Fr], a cutting; cut; incision; also, small banknote; bond; coupon;
fig., deletion of certain passages in a play or other composition.

courage sans peur [Fr], courage without fear; fearless courage.

coureur [Fr], runner; hunter; *mil.,* scout; skirmisher. —**coureur de bois,**
French-Canadian trapper. —**coureur de nuit,** a man who keeps late
hours; also, a woman chaser.

courge [Fr], gourd; pumpkin. —**courge à la moelle,** squash; vegetable
marrow.

court-bouillon [Fr; *pl.* courts-bouillons], a wine bouillon in which fish,
etc., is boiled: *cookery.*

court plaisir, long repentir [Fr], short pleasure, long repentance.

couru [Fr; *fem.* courue], run after; in demand; popular.

couscous [Fr, *fr.* Ar *kuskus, fr. kaskasa,* to pound to a small size], a North
African dish of steamed semolina, served with meat and vegetables
or with fruit.

coûte que coûte [Fr], cost what it may; at any cost; come what may.

couturier [Fr], *n.m.* ladies' tailor; dress designer.

couturière [Fr], *n.f.* dressmaker; seamstress; needlewoman.

crabe [Fr], crab.

craignez (la) honte [Fr], fear shame (*or* disgrace).

crains Dieu tant que tu vivras [Fr], fear God as long as you live.

crambe repetita [L], warmed-over cabbage; stale repetitions; harping on the same string: *Juvenal.*

craquelé [Fr], crackled, as china.

cras credemus, hodie nihil [L], tomorrow we will believe, but not today.

cras mane summendus [L], to be taken tomorrow morning: *med.*

cras mihi [L], my turn tomorrow.

crassa negligentia [L], gross (*or* criminal) negligence: *law.*

cravate [Fr], necktie; originally named for the Croat mercenaries, who wore a scarf around the neck in battle.

crèche [Fr], manger; crib; day nursery. —**Crèche,** the manger in which the newborn Christ was laid; also, a representation of this, displayed in churches at Christmas: *eccl.*

crecida [Sp], freshet.

credat Iudaeus Apella [L], let Apella the Jew (i.e., a credulous person) believe it (I won't): *Horace.*

crede Deo [L], trust to God.

credendum [L; *pl.* credenda], a thing to be believed; article of faith: *theol.*

crede quod habes, et habes [L], believe that you have it, and you have it.

credite posteri [L], believe it, future generations (*or* posterity): *Horace.*

crédit foncier [Fr], an association that makes loans on real estate.

crédit mobilier [Fr], a banking corporation that makes loans on personal property.

credo quia absurdum [L], I believe it because it is absurd (*or* so unlikely).

credo quia impossibile [L], I believe it because it is impossible.

credula res amor est [L], a credulous thing is love: *Ovid.*

crème [Fr], cream. —**crème à la glace** *or* **crème glacée,** ice cream. —**crème de la crème,** cream of the cream; the choicest. —**crème de menthe,** lit., cream of mint; a green peppermint liqueur. —**crème fouettée,** whipped cream.

créole [Fr], person descended from French or Spanish parents but born in the New World.

crêpe [Fr], *n.m.* crape or crapelike fabric. —**crêpe de Chine,** Chinese silk crape.

crêpe [Fr], *n.f.* pancake. —**crêpes suzette,** pancakes cooked with brandy.

crêpé [Fr], frizzed, as hair.

crépon [Fr], a thick crapelike fabric.

crescendo [It], with gradually increasing loudness and power (*abbr.* cr. *or* cresc.): *music.*

crescit amor nummi quantum ipsa pecunia crescit [L], the love of money grows as our wealth increases: *Juvenal.*

crescite et multiplicamini [L], increase and multiply: motto of *Maryland.*

crescit eundo [L], it grows by going (*or* as it goes): motto of *New Mexico.*

crescit sub pondere virtus [L], virtue grows under oppression.

cresson [Fr], cress; watercress.

crestón [Sp], outcrop: *geol.*

crève-coeur [Fr], heartbreak; crushing sorrow; heartbreaking thing.

crever de rire [Fr], to burst with laughter; split one's sides.

crevette [Fr], shrimp; prawn.

criada [Sp], maid; domestic servant.

criaillement [Fr], wrangling; brawling; clamor.

criard [Fr; *fem.* criarde], crying; shrill; *painting,* discordant. —**voix criarde,** shrill voice.

cribro aquam haurire [L], to draw water in a sieve.

crier famine sur un tas de blé [Fr], to cry famine (*or* "I am famished") on a heap of corn.

crimen [L; *pl.* crimina], a crime: *law.* —**crimen falsi,** the crime (*or* charge) of perjury. —**crimen laesae maiestatis,** high treason.

crinière [Fr], mane, of a horse or lion; *colloq.,* long hair; shock of hair.

criollo [Sp], person descended from Spanish parents but born in the Americas.

critique [Fr], critical estimate of a work of art or literature; critical dissertation; a criticism; review; also, art of criticism; *philos.,* analysis of the foundations of knowledge, as Kant's *Critique of Pure Reason.*

croissant [Fr], pastry roll shaped like a crescent.

croix [Fr], cross. —**croix de guerre,** war cross; French decoration for bravery.

croquante [Fr], a crisp tart or pie; crisp almond cake: *cookery.*

croque-mitaine [Fr], bugbear; bugaboo.

croque-monsieur [Fr], grilled sandwich of ham and cheese.

croquer le marmot [Fr], to dance attendance.

croqueur [Fr], glutton; gormandizer.

croquis [Fr], sketch; outline; rough draft: *fine arts.* —**cahier de croquis,** sketchbook.

crore [Anglo-Ind], ten millions, esp. of rupees; one hundred lacs. Cf. LAC.

croustade [Fr], a kind of patty: *cookery.*

croûte [Fr], crust; toast; piece of toast; fig., a bad painting; daub.

croûton [Fr], small cube of toasted or fried bread, as used in soups: *cookery.*

cruce, dum spiro, fido [L], while I breathe, I trust in the Cross.

crux [L; *pl.* cruces], cross; fig., perplexing problem; puzzle. —**Crux,** the Southern Cross: *astron.* —**crux ansata,** a T-shaped cross with a loop on the top, representing enduring life; in Egyptian archaeology, called *ankh.* —**crux commissa,** the tau cross. —**crux criticorum,** the crux (*or* puzzle) of critics. —**crux decussata,** an X-shaped cross; cross of St. Andrew or St. Patrick. —**crux medicorum,** the puzzle of the doctors. —**crux mihi ancora,** the Cross is my anchor. —**crux stellata,** the cross with arms ending in stars.

cuadrilla [Sp], gang; crew; troop; specif., the attendants of a matador.

cual el cuervo, tal su huevo [Sp], as the crow, so the egg; like father, like son.

cuan lejos de ojo, tan lejos de corazon [Sp], as distant from the heart as from the eye; out of sight, out of mind.

cuartel [Sp], barracks: *mil.*

cuatro ojos ven mejor que dos [Sp], four eyes see better than two.

cuchillo [Sp], knife; *engin.*, girder; truss.

cucullus non facit monachum [L], the cowl does not make the monk.

cuenta corriente [Sp], account current: *abbr.* c/c *or* c/cte.

cuéntaselo a tu abuela [Sp], tell it to your grandmother; tell it to the Marines; tell it to someone who is gullible.

cuerpo [Sp], the body. —**in cuerpo,** revealing the shape of the body, through not wearing a cloak; fig., uncovered; unprotected; naked.

cuesta [Sp], a low ridge, steep on one side and gently sloping on the other; sloping upland; slope: *southwestern U.S.*

cui bono? [L], who benefits by it? for whose advantage?

cuidado! [Sp], look out! take care!

cui Fortuna ipsa cedit [L], to whom Fortune herself yields: *Cicero.*

cuilibet in arte sua perito credendum est [L], every skilled man is to be trusted in his own art.

cui malo? [L], whom will it harm?

cuique suum [L], to each his own.

cuir-bouilli [Fr], boiled leather pressed or molded into permanent shape: used originally for armor.

cuisine [Fr], the kitchen; art or manner of cooking; also, the dishes themselves. —**cuisine bourgeoise,** plain cooking.

cuisse [Fr], thigh; rump (of beef); leg, as of a goose.

cuissot [Fr], haunch, as of venison.

cuistot [Fr], army cook: *Fr. mil. slang.*

cuit à point [Fr], lit., cooked to a point; done to a turn.

cuius [L], of which.

culbute [Fr], somersault; fall; failure.

culbuter [Fr], to upset; overthrow violently; ruin.

cul-de-four [Fr; *pl.* culs-de-four], lit., bottom of an oven; a vault shaped like a quarter sphere; sometimes, a demicupola: *arch.*

cul-de-lampe [Fr; *pl.* culs-de-lampe], *arch.*, a bracket or pendant suggestive of the bottom of an ancient church lamp; *printing,* tailpiece.

cul-de-sac [Fr; *pl.* culs-de-sac], lit., bottom of a bag; passage with only one outlet; blind alley; dead-end street; *mil.,* the position of a hemmed-in army with no exit except in front; trap; fig., a route that leads nowhere.

culotte [Fr], breeches; *cookery*, rump, as of beef. —**culotte de peau,** lit., leather breeches; old military officer; old fogy: *colloq.*

culpa [L], fault; negligence. —**culpa lata,** gross negligence. —**culpa levis,** ordinary negligence; excusable neglect: *all law.*

culpam poena premit comes [L], punishment presses hard upon the heels of crime: *Horace.*

culteranismo [Sp], cultism; Gongorism; affected literary elegance.

cultos [Sp], Spanish writers of the cultist school; Gongorists.

cum [L], with: used in various phrases, as in *cum* dividend (*abbr.* cum div.), also in the names of combined English parishes, as in Stow-*cum*-Quy.

cum bona venia [L], with your good favor; with your kind indulgence.

cumbre [Sp], top; summit.

cum grano salis [L], with a grain of salt; with allowance or reservation.

cum laude [L], with praise; with distinction: used esp. in a diploma to designate work of special merit; the first (lowest) grade of honors. Cf. MAGNA CUM LAUDE and SUMMA CUM LAUDE.

cummerbund [Anglo-Ind; Hind *kamarband*], waistband or sash.

cum multis aliis [L], with many others.

cum notis variorum [L], with the notes of various commentators.

cum privilegio [L], with privilege.

cumshaw [Pidgin], *in Chinese*, lit., grateful thanks; gratuity; present; bonus: *China.*

cum tacent, clamant [L], when they are silent they cry loudest; their silence speaks louder than words.

cuneta [Sp], drain; gutter; ditch.

cuneus cuneum trudit [L], wedge drives wedge.

curae leves loquuntur, ingentes stupent [L], light griefs find utterance, great ones are dumb: *Seneca.*

cura facit canos [L], care brings gray hairs.

cur ante tubam tremor occupat artus [L], why should fear seize the limbs before the trumpet sounds: *Virgil.*

curateur [Fr], trustee.

curé [Fr], parish priest; rector; vicar.

cure-dent [Fr], toothpick.

curia advisari vult [LL], the court wishes to be advised; the court wishes to consider (*abbr.* cur. adv. vult *or* c.a.v.): *law.*

curiosa felicitas [L], nice felicity of expression: *Petronius.*

currente calamo [L], with a running pen; fluently; offhand.

currus bovem trahit [L], the cart draws the ox; put the cart before the horse.

cursus curiae est lex curiae [L], the practice of the court is the law of the court: *law.*

curta supellex [L], scanty supply of furniture; meager stock of knowledge.

cushy *or* **kushi** [Hind *khūshī*]. See KHUSHI.

custodia legis [L], in the custody of the law: *law.*

custos [L; *pl.* custodes], guardian; keeper; custodian. **—custos morum,** guardian of morals. **—custos rotulorum,** custodian of the rolls, principal justice of the peace in an English county: *abbr.* C.R.

cutis anserina [NL], gooseflesh; a roughening of the human skin, as by cold.

cuvée [Fr], contents of a vat (of wine).

cuyas manos beso [Sp], whose hands I kiss: *abbr.* c.m.b. *or* C.M.B.

cuyos pies beso [Sp], whose feet I kiss: *abbr.* c.p.b. *or* C.P.B.

cygne noir [Fr], black swan; rarity.

cyma recta [L], a cornice molding forming a double curve, concave above and convex below: *arch.*

cyma reversa [L], a molding in which the curve is convex above and concave below: *arch.*

cy près [OF], lit., so nearly (as may be); as near as practicable to the testator's wishes: *law.*

D

da [Russ], yes.

daan [Tag], a road: *P.I.*

daar niets goeds in is, gaat niets goeds uit [Du], where no good is in, no good comes out.

da ballo [It], in dance style: *music.*

dabit Deus his quoque finem [L], God will put an end to these (troubles) also: *Virgil.*

dabit qui dedit [L], he will give who gave.

da capo [It], from the beginning: *abbr.* D.C. —**da capo al fine,** from the beginning to the end (or to where the word "Fine" or a ⌒ stands). —**da capo al segno,** from the beginning to the sign ;∫: or 𝄋 : *all music.* Cf. CAPO.

da cappella *or* **da chiesa** [It], in church style: *music.*

d'accord [Fr], in accord; in agreement; agreed; granted.

dacha [Russ dácha; *pl.* dáchi], villa or small house in the country for use in summer.

dacoit [Anglo-Ind; Hind *dakait*], member of a gang of armed robbers and outlaws.

dada [Fr], hobby; horse. —**Dadaism,** an art movement begun c. 1920 whose purpose was to overthrow traditional art forms.

dádivas quebrantan peñas [Sp], gifts break rocks; a golden key will open any door.

da fidei quae fidei sunt [L], give to faith that which belongs to faith.

daftar [Hind & Pers], a record; register; journal; also, office. —**daftar khana,** office; countinghouse: *India.*

dah *or* **dao** [Anglo-Ind], a heavy knife, used as a tool and weapon in Assam and Burma. Cf. KUKRI.

dai ichi [Jap], number one; very good.

d'ailleurs [Fr], from another cause; besides; moreover.

daimio *or* **daimyo** [Jap], Japanese feudal lord, under old regime.

dak [Hind], transport by relays of runners, horses, etc.; esp., transport of mail in this manner; hence, mail. —**dakghar,** post office: *both India.*

δάκρυ’ ἀδάκρυα [Gr; dákru’ adákrua], tearless tears: *Euripides.*

dal [Hind], a kind of pea: *India.*

dalbhat [Hind], cooked *dal* and rice: *India.*

dalla rapa non si cava sangue [It], you cannot get blood from a turnip; you cannot get blood out of a stone.

da locum melioribus [L], give way to your betters: *Terence.*

dal segno [It], lit., from the sign; repeat from the sign 𝄋 : *music.*

dame de compagnie [Fr], lady's companion.

dame d'honneur [Fr], maid of honor; bridesmaid.

dame du palais [Fr], lady-in-waiting.

dames de la halle [Fr], market women.

dames seules [Fr], ladies only; ladies' compartment.

damit ist es Essig [Ger], lit., therewith is it vinegar; it's all up! the thing has proven a failure: *colloq.*

Dämmerschlaf [Ger], twilight sleep.

damna minus consulta movent [L], afflictions (*or* losses) to which we are accustomed affect us less deeply: *Juvenal.*

damnant quod non intelligunt [L], they condemn what they do not understand.

damnosa hereditas (*or* **haereditas**) [L], lit., a damaging inheritance (i.e., one that entails loss).

damnum [L; *pl.* damna], loss; damage; harm. —**damnum absque iniuria,** loss without injury (*or* actionable wrong); loss due to lawful competition.

Dampfboot [Ger; *pl.* Dampfboote & -böte], steamboat.

dangereux [Fr; *fem.* dangereuse], dangerous.

danke *or* **danke schön!** [Ger], thanks! thanks very much!

dansant [Fr], dancing.

danse [Fr], dance; dancing. —**danse de corde,** rope dancing. —**danse du ventre,** lit., belly dance. —**danse macabre,** dance of death.

danseur [Fr], a male dancer, esp. a professional.

danseuse [Fr], a female dancer; figurante; woman ballet dancer.

dante Deo [L], by the gift of God.

danzón [Sp], a Latin American dance.

dapes inemptae [L], unbought feasts (i.e., home produce).

darbar [Hind & Pers]. Same as DURBAR.

dare in guardia la lattuga ai paperi [It], to give the lettuce to the keeping of the geese.

dare pondus idonea fumo [L], fit only to give weight to smoke; absolutely worthless: *Persius.*

dari [Hind]. Same as DHURRIE.

dariole [Fr], a kind of rich cream cake; duchess cake: *cookery.*

darmoyed [Russ; *fem.* darmoyedka], freeloader.

darne [Fr], slice of fish: *cookery.*

darunter und darüber *or* **drunter und drüber** [Ger], topsy-turvy.

darwaza [Hind], door. —**darwaza band,** lit., the door (is) shut; East Indian equivalent of "not at home": *India.*

das Alter wägt, die Jugend wagt [Ger], age weighs (*or* considers), youth essays.

das Beste ist gut genug [Ger], the best is good enough: *Goethe.*

das Ding beim rechten Namen nennen [Ger], call a thing by the right name; call a spade a spade.

das Ewig-Weibliche [Ger], the eternal feminine: *Goethe.* See EWIG-WEIBLICHE.

das freut mich [Ger], I am glad of it.

das geht nicht [Ger], that will never do.

das heisst [Ger], that is to say; that is: *abbr.* d.h.

das irdische Glück [Ger], earthly happiness (*or* fortune).

das ist [Ger], that is; *id est.: abbr.* d.i.

das ist aber schade [Ger], that is too bad.

das ist eine Pracht [Ger], that's splendid.

das ist keine Kunst [Ger], that is easy enough.

das ist Pech! [Ger], lit., that is pitch; how annoying!

das kannst du deiner Grossmutter erzählen [Ger], you can tell that to your grandmother; tell it to someone gullible.

das kommt mir spanisch vor [Ger], it sounds like Spanish to me; it's Greek to me.

das Leben ist die Liebe [Ger], life is love: *Goethe.*

das schadet nichts [Ger], never mind.

das schöne Geschlecht [Ger], the fair sex.

das Seitengewehr pflanzt auf! [Ger], fix sidearms! fix bayonets!: *mil.*

das tut nichts [Ger], it doesn't matter; never mind.

das tut's [Ger], that will do; that is enough.

das versteht sich von selbst [Ger], that goes without saying; that is understood. Cf. CELA VA SANS DIRE.

data et accepta [L], things given and received; expenditures and receipts.

data fata secutus [L], following what is decreed by fate: *Virgil.*

date et dabitur vobis [L], give and it shall be given unto you: *Vulgate.*

dà tempo al tempo [It], give time to time; give things time to mature.

date obolum Belisario [L], give a penny to Belisarius (a great general of the Emperor Justinian, reduced to beggary in his old age—a story denied by Gibbon).

dato *or* **datto** [Tag], headman of a town or district; also, Moro chieftain: *P.I.*

daube [Fr], a manner of stewing and seasoning certain braised dishes; also, the dish itself: *cookery.*

d'aujourd'hui en huit [Fr], this day a week; a week from today.

d'aujourd'hui en quinze [Fr], this day a fortnight; two weeks from today.

dauphin [Fr], crown prince; dolphin.

Davus sum, non Oedipus [L], I am Davus, not Oedipus; I am a plain man and no genius: *Terence.*

de auditu [L], from hearsay.

débâcle [Fr], the breakup of ice in a river; hence, a confused rush; stampede; rout; collapse.

debaixo de boa palavra, ahi está o engano [Pg], under fair words a trick is hidden.

debellare superbos [L], to overthrow the proud: *Virgil.*

debitum [L.; *pl.* debita], a debt: *law.* **—debitum naturae,** the debt of nature; death.

de bon augure [Fr], of good omen.

de bon genre [Fr], gentlemanly; ladylike; well-bred.

de bon gré [Fr], willingly.

de bonis asportatis [L], of goods carried away: *law.*

de bonis non (administratis) [L], of the goods not (yet administered): *law.*

de bonis propriis [L], out of his own goods (*or* pocket).

de bonne foi [Fr], in good faith.

de bonne grâce [Fr], with a good grace; willingly.

de bonne guerre [Fr], according to the laws of war; by fair play; by fair means; fairly.

de bonne lutte [Fr], by fair play.

de bonne part (*or* **source**) [Fr], on good authority.

de bonne volonté [Fr], with good will; willingly.

de bon vouloir servir le roy [OF], to serve the king with right good will.

débouché [Fr], opening; outlet; *com.*, market; sale; trade outlet.

déboutonné [Fr; *fem.* déboutonnée], unbuttoned; careless.

de bric et de broc [Fr], by hook or by crook.

débris [Fr], remains, esp. of something broken or destroyed; ruins; leavings; rubbish.

début [Fr], first appearance before the public; entrance into society; *colloq.*, coming out.

débutant [Fr; *fem.* débutante], one appearing before the public or in society for the first time.

de but en blanc [Fr], bluntly; point-blank.

decani [L], to be sung by the decanal, or dean's, side in antiphonal singing: *music.* Cf. CANTORIS.

décédé [Fr; *fem.* décédée], deceased: *abbr.* déc.

décence [Fr], propriety; decorum; decency.

deceptio visus [L], optical illusion.

décharnement [Fr], emaciation; *of style,* baldness; poverty.

déchéance [Fr], forfeiture; loss; downfall.

déchirant [Fr; *fem.* déchirante], heartrending; harrowing.

decies repetita placebit [L], though ten times repeated, it will continue to please: *Horace.*

décime [Fr], French copper coin, the tenth part of a franc. —**décime de guerre,** war tax.

decipimur specie recti [L], we are deceived by the semblance of what is right: *Horace* (adapted).

decipit frons prima multos [L], the first appearance deceives many.

deciso [It], decidedly; boldly: *music.*

déclassé [Fr.; *fem.* déclassée], declassed; socially degraded; cashiered; struck off the rolls.

décolletage [Fr], *of a dress*, a low neckline; also, the state of being *décolleté*.

décolleté [Fr; *fem.* décolletée], low-necked, as a woman's evening gown; low-cut; wearing a low-necked dress.

décoré [Fr], decorated; knighted; wearing the insignia of an order of merit.

decori decus addit avito [L], he adds honor to the ancestral honor.

decoucher [Fr], to sleep out, away from home; stay out all night.

décousu [Fr.; *fem.* décousue], unsewn; unstitched; *of literary style,* unconnected; desultory; loose.

decrescendo [It], with a gradual decrease in loudness (*abbr.* dec. *or* decres.): *music.*

decretum [L; *pl.* decreta], decree; ordinance: *abbr.* d.

décrotté [Fr], brushed up; cleaned.

decus et tutamen [L], honor and defense.

dédicace [Fr], dedication; inscription.

de die in diem [L], from day to day: *abbr.* de d. in d.

dédit [Fr], lit., retracted; retraction; forfeiture; forfeit; penalty for breach of contract: *Fr. & Can. law.*

de duobus malis, minus est semper eligendum [L], of two evils, the lesser is always to be chosen: *Thomas à Kempis.*

de facto [L], in fact; actual *or* actually: distinguished from *de iure.*

defectus sanguinis [L], failure of issue: *law.*

défense d'afficher [Fr], post no bills.

défense de fumer [Fr], no smoking.

défense d'entrer [Fr], no admittance.

deficit omne quod nascitur [L], everything that is born passes away: *Quintilian.*

de fide [L], lit., of the faith; required to be held as an article of faith.

de fide et officio iudicis non recipitur quaestio [L], concerning the good faith and duty of the judge, no question can be allowed: *law.*

defiéndame Dios de mí [Sp], may God defend me from myself.

definitum [L; *pl.* definita], a thing defined.

de fond en comble [Fr], from top to bottom; wholly.

de fumo in flammam [L], out of the smoke into the flame; out of the frying pan into the fire.

dégagé [Fr.; *fem.* dégagée], easy; free; unconstrained.

de gaieté de coeur [Fr], from lightness of heart; sportively; wantonly.

d'égal à égal [Fr], on equal terms.

dégât [Fr], damage.

degeneres animos timor arguit [L], fear betrays ignoble souls: *Virgil.*

dégoût [Fr], distaste; loathing; disgust.

dégoûté [Fr; *fem.* dégoûtée], *adj.* fastidious; squeamish; *n.* fastidious person.

dégras [Fr], a dressing for leather; dubbing.

de gratia [L], by favor: *law.*

de gré à gré [Fr], by private contract.

de gustibus non est disputandum [L], there is no disputing about tastes.

de haute lutte [Fr], by main force; with a high hand.

de haut en bas [Fr], from top to bottom; from head to foot; scornfully; superciliously.

dehors [Fr], outside; out of; foreign to.

Dei gratia [L], by the grace of God.

Dei iudicium [L], lit., judgment of God; trial by ordeal.

Dei memor, gratus amicis [L], mindful of God, grateful to friends.

de integro [L], afresh; anew.

de iure [L], by right; by law; rightful or rightfully: distinguished from *de facto.*

déjà vu [Fr], seen before; an illusion of something previously experienced.

déjeuner [Fr], breakfast; lunch. **—petit dejeuner,** breakfast.

dejuma [Rum], breakfast.

δέχεται κακὸν ἐκ κακοῦ αἰεί [Gr; dékhetai kakòn ek kakoû aieí], one evil always succeeds another: *Homer.*

dekko [Hind.; imperative of *dekhna,* to see; look at], look! look here!

délabrement [Fr], ruin; decay; dilapidation.

del agua mansa Dios me libre; del agua brava, me libraré yo [Sp], from still waters God save me; from rough waters I can save myself. (Still waters run deep.)

de lana caprina [L], lit., about goat's wool (a nonexistent thing, since goats have hair); hence, about any worthless object: *Horace* (adapted).

de l'audace, encore de l'audace, et toujours de l'audace [Fr], audacity, again audacity, and always audacity: the closing words of Danton's speech in 1792, before the Legislative Assembly, hurling defiance at the foes of France.

del credere [It], designating an agent's guarantee that the buyer is solvent and dependable: *mercantile law.*

delectando pariterque monendo [L], by giving pleasure and at the same time instructing: *Horace.*

delenda [L], things to be deleted.

delenda est Carthago [L], Carthage must be destroyed; the war must be carried on to the bitter end: the repeated advice of Cato the Elder to the Roman Senate.

délicat [Fr; *fem.* délicate], agreeable to the taste; delicate; exquisite; fastidious; scrupulous; dainty; nice; fig., feeble; frail; fragile.

délicatesse [Fr], delicacy; a delicate touch.

delicato [It], in a delicate manner: *music.*

deliciae humani generis [L], the delight of mankind: appellation of the Emperor Titus.

delictum [L; *pl.* delicta], offense; misdemeanor.

délié [Fr], lit., untied; loose; *of style,* easy, flowing.

delineavit [L], he (*or* she) drew it: *abbr.* del.

délit [Fr], transgression; misdemeanor.

de los enemigos los menos [Sp], the fewer enemies, the better.

delphinum natare doces [L], you are teaching a dolphin to swim; you are teaching your grandmother to suck eggs.

delphinum silvis appingit, fluctibus aprum [L], he portrays a dolphin in the woods and a wild boar in the waves; he introduces objects unsuited to the scene: *Horace.*

de lunatico inquirendo [L], a writ to inquire into the sanity of a person: *law.*

de luxe [Fr], sumptuous; elegant.

de mal en pis [Fr], from bad to worse.

démarche [Fr], gait; walk; fig., course of action, esp. one implying a change of policy; step; attempt; overture; as, a diplomatic *démarche* to a foreign government.

de mauvais augure [Fr], of ill omen; ominous; portentous.

de mauvais genre [Fr], ungentlemanly; unladylike; ill-bred.

démêlé [Fr], altercation; quarrel; dispute.

démenti [Fr], contradiction; official denial.

dementia [L], insanity. —**dementia a potu,** insanity from drinking; delirium tremens. —**dementia praecox,** a form of early insanity.

deme supercilio nubem [L], remove the cloud from your brow.

demeure [Fr], abode; dwelling.

demi [Fr], half.

demi-jour [Fr; *pl.* demi-jours], lit., half day; twilight.

demi-mondaine *or* **demimondaine** [Fr], a woman of the *demi-monde;* woman of dubious character.

demi-monde *or* **demimonde** [Fr], lit., half-world; the world of women supported by their lovers; women of doubtful reputation, on the outskirts of society.

demi-mot [Fr], half-word; hint.

de minimis non curat lex [L], the law does not concern itself with trifles.

demi-solde [Fr], half pay.

démodé [Fr; *fem.* démodée], out of fashion; antiquated; behind the times.

de mortuis nil nisi bonum [L], of the dead (say) nothing but good.

demos [Gr δῆμος, dêmos], township; the commons; commonalty; people; populace.

de nihilo nihil [L], from nothing nothing (can come): *Persius.*

denique caelum [L], heaven at last: battle cry of the Crusaders.

denique non omnes eadem mirantur amantque [L], all men, in short, do not admire and love the same things: *Horace.*

dénouement [Fr], the unraveling of a plot or story; issue; catastrophe; final solution.

de nouveau [Fr], anew; afresh; once again.

de novo [L], anew; afresh.

dente lupus, cornu taurus petit [L], the wolf attacks with his teeth, the bull with his horns; people make use of their natural weapons: *Horace.*

dente superbo [L], with a disdainful tooth: *Horace.*

den Ton angeben [Ger], to set the fashion.

Deo adiuvante non timendum [L], with God helping, nothing need be feared.

Deo date [L], give ye to God (*or* give unto God).

deo dignus vindice nodus [L], a knot worthy of a god to untie; a crucial difficulty. Cf. DEUS EX MACHINA.

Deo duce, ferro comitante [L], with God as my leader and my sword my companion.

Deo et regi fidelis [L], loyal (*or* faithful) to God and king.

Deo favente [L], with God's favor.

Deo gratias [L], thanks to God.

de oídos [Sp], by ear; by hearsay.

Deo iuvante [L], with God's help: motto of *Monaco.*

de omnibus rebus et quibusdam aliis [L], concerning all things and certain other matters: said of books marked by rambling prolixity.

de omni re scibili et quibusdam aliis [L], concerning everything knowable and a few other things besides: designating one who thinks he knows it all.

Deo monente [L], God warning; God giving warning.

Deo, non fortuna [L], from God, not chance (*or* fortune).

Deo, Optimo, Maximo [L], to God, the Best, the Greatest (*abbr.* D.O.M.): motto of the *Benedictines.*

Deo, patriae, amicis [L], for God, fatherland, and friends.

deorum cibus est [L], it is food for the gods.

deos fortioribus adesse [L], the gods (are said) to aid the stronger: *Tacitus.*

Deo volente [L], God willing: *abbr.* D.V.

de palabra [Sp], by word of mouth.

de par le roy [OF], in the king's name.

département [Fr], territorial division; department; *abbr.* dep.

dépêche [Fr], message; dispatch.

dependiente [Sp], clerk.

dépense de bouche [Fr], living (*or* household) expenses.

de pied en cap [Fr], from head to foot.

de pilo pendet [L], it hangs by a hair (like the sword of Damocles).

de pis en pis [Fr], from worse to worse; worse and worse.

dépit [Fr], spite; vexation.

déplacé [Fr], displaced; misplaced; ill-timed.

de plano [L], with ease; easily; without difficulty; *law,* clearly; manifestly.

de plein gré [Fr], voluntarily.

de plus belle [Fr], with renewed ardor; with increased vigor; more than ever.

depósito [Sp], depository; tank; reservoir.

de praesenti [L], of (*or* for) the present.

deprendi miserum est [L], it is wretched to be detected (*or* found out).

de prix [Fr], valuable; precious.

de profundis [L], out of the depths: *Vulgate* (*Psalms* cxxx. 1).

de proprio motu [L], of one's (*or* its) own motion; spontaneously.

député [Fr], deputy; delegate; member of the lower French Chamber.

dérangé [Fr.; *fem.* dérangée], out of order.

dérangement [Fr], confusion; disorder.

der Ausgang gibt den Taten ihre Titel [Ger], it is the issue (*or* outcome) that gives deeds their title: *Goethe.*

derecha [Sp], right hand (side); on the right: *abbr.* dcha.

de règle [Fr], customary; proper.

de retour [Fr], back again; back; returned; homeward bound.

derévnya [Russ; *pl.* derevén], village.

der Führer [Ger], the leader; specif., the head of the Nazis (National Socialist Party) in Germany; the official title of Chancellor Adolf Hitler within his party, and popularly. Cf. IL DUCE.

der Fürst ist der erste Diener seines Staats [Ger], the prince is the first servant of his state: *Frederick the Great.*

der Hahn im Korbe sein [Ger], lit., to be the rooster in the basket; be the cock of the walk.

der Heiland [Ger], the Savior.

der Historiker ist ein rückwärts gekehrter Prophet [Ger], the historian is a prophet looking backwards: *Schlegel.*

de rigueur [Fr], obligatory; indispensable; required by etiquette.

der Krieg ernährt den Krieg [Ger], war fosters war: *Schiller.*

der Mensch ist was er isst [Ger], man is what he eats: *Feuerbach.*

dernier cri [Fr], lit., the last cry; the last word; latest thing.

dernier ressort [Fr], a last resort; desperate expedient.

derrière [Fr], behind; buttocks: *colloq.*

der Stärkste hat Recht [Ger], lit., the strongest is right; right is with the strongest; might makes right.

der Teufel ist los! [Ger], there's the devil to pay!: *colloq.*

der Wahn ist kurz, die Reue ist lang [Ger], the illusion (of love) is brief, the regret long: *Schiller.*

der Weg des Verderbens [Ger], the road to ruin.

désagrément [Fr], something disagreeable; unpleasantness.

désarroi [Fr], disorder; confusion.

déshabillé [Fr], being negligently attired; undressed; in dishabille.

desideratum [L; *pl.* desiderata], anything desired or needed; a felt want.

desierto [Sp], desert; wilderness.

desinit in piscem mulier formosa superne [L], a woman, beautiful above, with a fish's tail: *Horace.*

desipere in loco [L], to indulge in trifling at the proper time; unbend on occasion: *Horace.*

des Lebens Mai [Ger], lit., the May of life; the springtime of life.

désobligeant [Fr; *fem.* désobligeante], disobliging; unaccommodating; ungracious; also, a two-wheeled vehicle for one person; a sulky.

de sobra [Sp], over and above.

désoeuvré [Fr; *fem.* désoeuvrée], unoccupied; idle.

désoeuvrement [Fr], lack of occupation; idleness.

désolé [Fr; *fem.* désolée], disconsolate; broken-hearted.

de son état [Fr], by profession; by trade.

désorienté [Fr.; *fem.* désorientée], having lost one's bearings; astray; bewildered.

dessein [Fr], design; intention; plan.

dessin [Fr], a drawing; design; *music,* arrangement.

dessous des cartes [Fr], lit., underside (i.e., face) of the cards; a secret.

dessus [Fr], *adv.* on; upon; uppermost; *n.* top; upper part; *music,* soprano; treble.

desto [It], sprightly; lively: *music.*

destra [It], right-hand side: *abbr.* d. —**destra mano,** right hand (*abbr.* D.M.): *music.*

desuetudo [L], disuse.

desunt caetera (*or* **cetera**) [L], the remainder (as of a quotation) is wanting.

desunt multa [L], many things are wanting.

détaché [Fr; *fem.* détachée], detached; isolated; *music,* staccato.

de tal arvore, tal fructo [Pg], like trees, like fruit.

de te fabula narratur [L], the story is told of (*or* relates to) you: *Horace.* See MUTATO NOMINE, etc.

de temps en temps [Fr], from time to time.

détente [Fr], an unbending or relaxing; specif., relaxation of international tension.

détenu [Fr; *fem.* détenue], a detained person; prisoner.

détonner [Fr], to sing or play out of tune.

détour [Fr], deviation; circuitous route; detour; fig., subterfuge; evasion. —**sans détour,** straightforward; sincere; sincerely.

detrás de la Cruz está el diablo [Sp], the devil stands behind the Cross.

de trop [Fr], too much (*or* too many); superfluous; unwanted; in the way; unwelcome.

detur [L], lit., let it be given; a book prize given to meritorious undergraduates at Harvard. —**detur aliquando otium quiesque fessis,** let ease and rest be sometimes granted to the weary: *Seneca.* —**detur**

digniori, let it be given to the more worthy. **—detur pulchriori,** let it be given to the fairest: inscription on the apple of discord.

Deum cole, regem serva [L], worship God and serve the king.

de un golpe [Sp], at one blow.

de un tirón [Sp], at one stroke.

Deus avertat! [L], God forbid!

Deus det! [L], God grant!

Deus est regit qui omnia [L], there is a God who rules all things.

Deus est summum bonum [L], God is the chief good.

deus ex machina [L], a god out of a machine (alluding to a favorite stage trick in classical tragedies of introducing a god, usually lowered in a crane, to solve the entanglement of the plot); providential intervention, esp. in a play or novel. Cf. θεὸς ἐκ μηχανῆς (theòs ek mēkhanês).

Deus gubernat navem [L], God steers (*or* is the pilot of) the ship.

Deus misereatur [L], God be merciful.

Deus nobiscum, quis contra? [L], God with us, who (can avail) against us?

deus nobis haec otia fecit [L], a god has wrought for us this repose; a deity has conferred these comforts upon us: *Virgil.*

Deus providebit [L], God will provide.

Deus vobiscum [L], God be with you.

Deus vult [L], God wills (it): rallying cry of the First Crusade.

Deutsches Reich [Ger], German Empire; official name of the former German Empire and Republic.

Deutschland über alles [Ger], Germany above all.

deva [Skr], a god.

devalaya [Skr], temple; shrine: *India.*

devi [Skr], a goddess.

devochka [Russ; *pl.* devochik], girl.

devoir [Fr], duty; task; courteous attentions: usually in *pl.* **—devoir pascal,** Easter communion.

de vuelta [Sp], returned; back again.

dewan [Anglo-Ind]. See DIWAN.

dextras dare [L], lit., to give right hands; shake hands as a pledge of faith.

dextro tempore [L], at the right time; at the opportune moment: *Horace.*

dey [Fr, *fr.* Turk *dāi*, lit., maternal uncle; a title given to elderly men by the Janissaries, and esp. to their commanding officer in Algiers], the title of the former rulers of Algiers, Tunis, and Tripoli.

dharma [Skr], law; religious obligation; duty; religion: *Hinduism.*

dharna [Hind], enforcement of payment of a debt or of compliance with any demand by sitting fasting at the offender's door: *India.*

Dhia bith leat chun an ath chlach mhile agus na's fada [Gael], God be with you to the last milestone—and beyond.

Dhia duit [Gael], good morning.

dhoti [Hind], a cloth worn by Hindus round the waist, passing between the legs and fastened behind; loincloth: *India.*

dhu [Irish & Gael], black: used esp. in Celtic personal and place names.

diable [Fr], devil; the Devil. **—diable à quatre,** the devil to pay; uproar; rumpus.

diablerie [Fr], deviltry; witchcraft; malice; also, wanton mischief, as of a child.

διὰ δυσφημίας καὶ εὐφημίας [Gr; dià dusphēmías kaì euphēmías], by evil report and good report: *II Corinthians* vi. 8.

diamant brut [Fr], rough diamond.

diantre! [Fr], the devil! the deuce!

diapason normal [Fr], French standard pitch: *music.*

diavolo [It], devil.

di bravura [It], with brilliance; in a florid style: *music.*

dibujo [Sp], drawing; sketch.

di buona volontà sta pieno l'inferno [It], hell is full of (*or* paved with) good intentions.

dicamus bona verba [L], let us speak words of good omen: *Terence.*

dic bona fide [L], tell me in good faith: *Plautus.*

dicho y hecho [Sp], said and done.

Dichter [Ger], poet.

Dichtung und Wahrheit [Ger], poetry and truth: subtitle of Goethe's autobiography.

dicitur [L], it is said; they say.

dictis facta suppetant [L], let deeds correspond to words.

dicton [Fr], proverb; saying.

dictum ac factum *or* **dictum factum** [L], said and done; no sooner said than done: *Terence.*

dictum de dicto [L], report upon hearsay; secondhand story.

dictum sapienti sat est [L], a word to the wise is enough: *Plautus.*

die Baukunst ist eine erstarrte Musik [Ger], architecture is frozen music: *Goethe.*

die een ander jaagt zit zelfs niet stil [Du], he who chases another does not sit still himself.

die Gegenwart ist eine mächtige Göttin [Ger], the present is a mighty goddess: *Goethe.*

die geistige Welt [Ger], the intellectual world; the intelligentsia.

die höchste Not [Ger], the direst need.

die Hölle selbst hat ihre Rechte? [Ger], has even Hell its rights?: *Goethe.*

die Kunst geht nach Brot [Ger], lit., art goes after bread; the artist must live: *Luther.*

die Luft ist rein [Ger], the coast (lit., air) is clear.

die lustige Witwe [Ger], the merry widow.

die Meisterschaft gilt oft für Egoismus [Ger], mastery passes often for egoism: *Goethe.*

die Mensur [Ger], lit., measurement; students' duel.

diem perdidi [L], I have lost a day: attributed to the Emperor Titus, characterizing a day in which he had done nothing for his subjects.

die Natur weiss allein was sie will [Ger], Nature alone knows what her purpose is: *Goethe.*

die Probe eines Genusses ist seine Erinnerung [Ger], the test of pleasure is the memory it leaves behind: *Jean Paul Richter.*

die Rachegötter schaffen im Stillen [Ger], the gods of vengeance act in silence: *Schiller.*

dies [L], day. **—dies datus,** a day given; a day appointed for the hearing of a lawsuit: *law.* **—dies faustus,** a lucky day. **—dies infaustus,** an unlucky day. **—Dies Irae,** day of wrath; Day of Judgment: a Latin hymn sung at solemn requiems. **—dies iuridicus,** a day on which courts sit: *law.* **—dies non** (short for **dies non iuridicus,** nonjudicial day), a day on which the courts do not sit; hence, a day that does not count: *law.*

die Saiten zu hoch spannen [Ger], lit., to tighten (*or* tune) the strings too high; take too high a tone; make pretensions.

die schönen Tage in Aranjuez sind nun zu Ende [Ger], the beautiful days in Aranjuez (Spain) are now at an end (*or* are past and gone): *Schiller.*

die schöne Welt [Ger], the fashionable world.

die schöne Zeit der jungen Liebe [Ger], the happy days of early love: *Schiller.*

Dieu avec nous [Fr], God with us.

Dieu défend le droit [Fr], God defends the right.

Dieu et mon droit [Fr], God and my right: motto of the English monarchs since Henry VI.

Dieu le veuille [Fr], God grant it.

Dieu m'en garde [Fr], God forbid! Heaven preserve me from it!

Dieu vous garde [Fr], God keep you.

die Wacht am Rhein [Ger], the watch on the Rhine: German national song.

die Weltgeschichte ist das Weltgericht [Ger], the world's history is the world's tribunal: *Schiller.*

die Zeit bringt Rosen [Ger], time brings roses; all things come to those who wait.

difficile [Fr], difficult; trying; hard to please; hard to deal with; *of horses,* skittish.

difficiles nugae [L], laborious trifles: *Martial.*

difficilia quae pulchra [L], things that are excellent are difficult (of attainment).

di fresco [It], lately; just now.

di giovinezza il bel purpureo lume [It], the lovely purple light of youth: *Tasso.*

digito monstrari [L], to be pointed out with the fingers; be famous: *Persius.*

dignus vindice nodus [L], a knot worthy of (such) a liberator; a difficulty that needs the intervention of a god to solve: *Horace.*

di grado in grado [It], step by step; by degrees; gradually.

dii [L.; *pl.* of *deus,* god]. For phrases beginning with *dii,* see preferred form DI.

diligence [Fr], stagecoach.

diluendo [It], dying away: *music.*

di (*or* **dii**) **maiores** [L], the greater gods; fig., men of outstanding eminence.

dime con quien andas y te diré quien eres [Sp], tell me with whom you associate and I will tell you who you are.

di meliora [L], heaven send better times.

dimidium facti qui coepit habet [L], he who has begun has the work half done; what is well begun is half done: *Horace.*

di (*or* **dii**) **minores** [L], the lesser gods; fig., men of lesser merit.

diminuendo [It], with gradually diminishing power (*abbr.* dim.): *music.*

di molto [It], very; as, allegro *di molto,* very quick: *music.*

dim sum [Chin], lit., a dot (*or* refreshment) on the heart; a snack; refreshment.

dinde [Fr], turkey hen. **—dinde en daube,** stewed turkey hen: *cookery.*

dindon [Fr], turkey cock; tom turkey.

dîner [Fr], dinner. **—dîner par coeur,** to go without dinner.

dinero [Sp], coin; money.

dineros y no consejos [Sp], money and not advice.

Ding an sich [Ger], thing in itself: *Kant.*

ding hao [Chin], very good.

di novello tutto par bello [It], everything new appears beautiful.

Dios ayuda a los mal vestidos [Sp], God helps the poorly dressed.

Dios me libre de hombre de un libro [Sp], God deliver me from a man of one book.

Dios que da la llaga, da la medicina [Sp], God who gives the wound gives the medicine: *Cervantes.*

Dios unión libertad [Sp], God, union, liberty: motto of *El Salvador.*

Dios y federación [Sp], God and federation: motto of *Venezuela.*

Dio vi benedica [It], God bless you.

di (*or* **dii**) **penates** [L], household gods.

di (*or* **dii**) **pia facta vident** [L], the gods see virtuous deeds: *Ovid.*

Directoire [Fr], the French Directory (1795-1799).

direttore [It; *pl.* direttori], director.

dirige nos Domine [L], direct us, O Lord.

dirigo [L], I lead: motto of *Maine.*

diruit, aedificat, mutat quadrata rotundis [L], he pulls down, he builds up, he changes square things into round: *Horace*.

dis aliter visum [L], to the gods it has seemed otherwise: *Virgil*.

di salto [It], at a leap; by leaps and bounds.

disce pati [L], learn to endure.

discere docendo [L], to learn through teaching.

discothèque [Fr], small intimate nightclub.

dis ducibus [L], under the direction of the gods.

diseur [Fr; *fem*. diseuse], talker; teller; speaker. **—diseur de bons mots,** joker; jester. **—diseur de riens,** lit., talker about nothings; idle talker.

disiecta membra [L], scattered parts (*or* remains).

disiecti membra poetae [L], limbs of the dismembered poet: *Horace*.

disinvolto [It], free; easy; graceful; spirited.

δὶς κράμβη θάνατος [Gr; dìs krámbē thánatos], cabbage, twice over, is death. Cf. CRAMBE REPETITA.

dis-moi ce que tu manges, et je dirai ce que tu es [Fr], tell me what you eat, and I will tell you what you are: *Brillat-Savarin*.

dispendia morae [L], loss of time: *Virgil*.

distingué [Fr; *fem*. distinguée], distinguished; of aristocratic air or bearing; remarkable; eminent.

distrait [Fr; *fem*. distraite], absentminded; abstracted.

dit [Fr], said; called; surnamed; alias.

ditat Deus [L], God enriches: motto of *Arizona*.

diti [Russ; *sing*. ribyonik], children.

diva [It.; *pl*. dive], lit., goddess; prima donna.

divertissement [Fr], entertainment; diversion; amusement; *theat.*, interlude; *music*, a light, entertaining composition or medley.

dives agris, dives positis in faenore nummis [L], rich in lands, rich in money put out at interest: *Horace*.

divide et impera [L], divide and rule.

Divina Commedia [It], *Divine Comedy*: title of Dante's great epic poem.

divinae particula aurae [L], a particle of divine spirit (lit., air, breath): *Horace*.

Divis [Ger; *pl*. Divise], hyphen: *typog.*

divisi [It], divided; separate; a direction that two or more parts on the same staff are to be divided among several performers: *music*.

divitiae virum faciunt [L], riches make the man.

divorcé [Fr.; *fem*. divorcée], a divorced person.

diwan [Pers], orig., a royal court, council of state, or tribunal of justice; in Indian native states, a minister of state.

dixi [L], I have said (all that I am going to); I have spoken.

dizer mentira por tirar a verdade [Pg], to lie to discover the truth.

djinn [Ar], spirit; genie.

dobre din [Russ], good afternoon.

dobre utra [Russ], good morning.

d'occasion [Fr], accidentally; also, secondhand.

docendo discimus [L], we learn by teaching.

Docent *or* **Dozent** [Ger], licensed university teacher or lecturer; tutor; *privatdocent* (q.v.).

doce ut discas [L], teach that you may learn.

doch [Russ; *pl.* dochiree], daughter.

doctor utriusque legis [L], doctor of both laws (canon and civil).

dogana [It], customhouse; also, a customs duty.

dogaressa [It], wife of a doge.

dojo [Jap], school for teaching judo, kendo, etc.

dolce [It], sweet; soft; agreeable. —**dolce far niente,** sweet doing nothing; pleasant idleness. —**dolce maniera,** delightful manners.

dolcemente [It], sweetly; softly: *music.*

dolce-piccante [It], bittersweet.

dolce vita [It], sweet life; specifically, the indolent, luxurious life of the idle rich or jet set.

dolente [It], doleful; sad, plaintive.

dolium volvitur [L], an empty cask is easily rolled.

doloroso [It; *fem.* dolorosa], pathetic; doleful: *music.*

dolus [L], deceit; fraud. —**dolus bonus,** permissible deceit. —**dolus malus,** unlawful deceit: *all law.*

Dom [Ger; *pl.* Dome], cathedral.

dom [Russ], house; domicile.

Domchor [Ger], cathedral choir.

domina [L; *pl.* dominae], lady.

Domine, dirige nos [L], O Lord, direct us: motto of the *City of London.*

Dominus illuminatio mea [L], the Lord is my light (*Psalms* xxvii. 1): motto of *Oxford University.*

Dominus providebit [L], the Lord will provide.

Dominus vobiscum [L], the Lord be with you.

domus et placens uxor [L], home and a pleasing wife: *Horace.*

Domus Procerum [L], the House of Lords: *abbr.* D.P. *or* Dom. Proc.

Don [Sp], Spanish nobleman; gentleman: a title, equivalent to Sir or Mr., prefixed to the given name. Cf. SEÑOR.

Dona [Pg], lady; madam: a title given to Portuguese ladies. —**dona,** a Portuguese lady.

Doña [Sp], lady; madam: a title prefixed to the given name of a Spanish lady: *abbr.* D.ª. —**doña,** a Spanish lady.

donde está la verdad está Dios [Sp], where truth is, there is God: *Cervantes.*

donec eris felix multos numerabis amicos [L], as long as you are prosperous, you will number many friends: *Ovid.*

donga [Zulu], gully: *South Africa.*

Donna [It], lady; madam: a title prefixed to the given name of an Italian lady. **—donna,** an Italian lady; woman; wife; mistress. **—la donna è mobile,** woman is changeable.

donnée [Fr], known fact; idea; theme of a play, story, or poem; motif; *math.,* known quantity.

Donner [Ger], *n.* thunder; *interj.* zounds! hang it! **—Donner Blitz,** thunder and lightning: *an expletive.* **—Donnerwetter!,** thunderation!

donner dans le piège (*or* **panneau**) [Fr], to fall into a trap.

donner un oeuf pour avoir un boeuf [Fr], to give an egg to have an ox; a sprat to catch a mackerel.

dono dedit [L], gave as a gift: *abbr.* d.d.

dooli, doolie, *or* **dooly** [Anglo-Ind; Hind *dōlī*], a light litter, used for women and for the sick and wounded.

dopo [It], after: *music* **—dopo Cristo,** after Christ: *abbr.* d.C.

Doppelgänger [Ger], wraith; lit., double walker; the ghostly double of a living being, whose appearance is said to presage that person's death.

Doppelpunkt [Ger], lit., double point; colon.

doppio [It], double; twofold. **—doppio movimento,** double movement (i.e., twice as fast as the preceding movement): *music.*

dorer la pilule [Fr], to gild the pill.

Dorf [Ger], village.

dormeuse [Fr], a traveling carriage adaptable for sleeping.

dormitat Homerus [L], (even) Homer nods. See ALIQUANDO BONUS DORMITAT HOMERUS.

doróga [Russ], road; way; path.

Dorp [Du], village.

dos à dos [Fr], back to back; the original of the do-si-do of square dancing.

dos aves de rapiña no mantienen compañía [Sp], two birds of prey soon part company.

δός μοι ποῦ στῶ καὶ κινῶ τὴν γῆν [Gr; dós moi poù stô kaì kinô tèn gén], give where I may stand and (with a lever) I can move the earth: *Archimedes.*

dossier [Fr], bundle of papers; file; official record; all the documents relating to a case or individual.

do svidaniya [Russ], till we meet again; *au revoir.*

dotación [Sp], endowment; *nav.,* crew.

douane [Fr], customhouse; customs.

douanier [Fr], customs official.

doublé [Fr; *fem.* doublée], lit., doubled; lined: said of clothes.

double entente *or, esp. in English,* **double entendre** [Fr], ambiguous expression; indelicate play on words.

doublure [Fr], ornamental lining on the inner side of the cover of a sumptuously bound book: usually of tooled leather, vellum, silk, velvet, or brocade.

doucement [Fr], gently; softly: *music*.

douceur [Fr], sweetness; mildness; agreeableness of manner; kindness; specif., a gratuity; tip; *pl.*, dainties; tidbits; delights, as of society; comforts, as of home; also, gallant remarks; compliments.

do ut des [L], lit., I give that you may give; a form of contract: *law*.

do ut facias [L], lit., I give that you may do; a form of contract: *law*.

douzaine [Fr], dozen: *abbr.* dzne.

dove Dio si trova nulla manca [It], where God is, nothing is lacking.

dove l'oro parla, ogni lingua tace [It], where gold speaks, every tongue is silent.

δόξα ἐν ὑψίστοις θεῷ καὶ ἐπὶ γῆς εἰρήνη ἐν ἀνθρώποις εὐδοκίας [Gr; dóxa en hupsístois theô kaì epì gês eirḗnē en anthrṓpois eudokías], glory to God in the highest, and on earth peace, good will toward men (*or* peace among men in whom he is well pleased; lit., men of good pleasure): *Luke* ii. 14.

doyen [Fr; *fem.* doyenne], dean; senior member of a group; oldest member.

dozho [Jap], if you please.

dramatis personae [L], the characters in a play; cast.

drame [Fr], drama. **—drame lyrique,** opera.

Drang nach Osten [Ger], lit., pressure toward the East; the Eastern trend of traditional German expansionists.

drap d'or [Fr], cloth of gold.

drapeau [Fr; *pl.* drapeaux], flag; standard. **—drapeau tricolore,** flag of the French Republic; tricolor.

Dreibund [Ger], triple alliance; notably, the alliance of Germany, Austria-Hungary, and Italy, formed in 1882.

Dreikönige [Ger], the Three Kings of Cologne; the Wise Men of the East (whose bodies were said to have been brought to Cologne).

Dreikönigsabend [Ger], the eve of the Epiphany; Twelfth Night.

droit [Fr], *adj.* right; straight; erect; just. **—droit et avant,** right and forward. **—droit et loyal,** just and loyal.

droit [Fr], *n.* right; law; authority. **—à bon droit,** with good reason; justly. **—droit d'aînesse,** birthright. **—droit d'aubaine,** the right of confiscation. **—droit des gens,** the law of nations; international law. **—droit de seigneur,** right of the first night; the right of the feudal lord to deflower the bride of a vassal. Cf. IUS PRIMAE NOCTIS. **—droits civils,** private rights.

droite [Fr], right hand; right: *abbr.* d.

drôle [Fr], *adj.* droll; ludicrous; comical; odd.

drôle [Fr], *n.* knave; rascal; scoundrel. **—mauvais drôle,** thorough blackguard.

droog [Russ; *fem.* padrooga, *pl.* droozhya], friend.

Druck [Ger.; *pl.* Drucke], printing; print; proof. —**Druck und Verlag,** printed and published by (*abbr.* Dr.u.Vrl.): *both typog.*

Druckfehler [Ger], printer's error; misprint: *typog.*

drunter und drüber [Ger], topsy-turvy.

duabus sellis sedere [L], to sit in two saddles; wear two hats; take both sides in a dispute.

duas tantum res anxius optat, panem et circenses [L], two things only do the people earnestly desire, bread and the circus (i.e., food and amusement): *Juvenal.*

dubash [Anglo-Ind; Hind & Mar *dubhāshī*, lit., one who speaks two languages], interpreter.

du bist am Ende was du bist [Ger], thou art in the end what thou art: *Goethe.*

duc [Fr], duke.

duce [It], leader; commander. See IL DUCE.

duces tecum [L], lit., you shall bring with you; a subpoena.

duchesse [Fr], duchess.

ducit amor patriae [L], love of country leads me.

due [It], two. —**due punti,** lit., two points; colon. —**due volte,** twice: *music.*

due capitani mandano a fondo la nave [It], two captains send the ship to the bottom.

dueña [Sp], married lady; mistress.

dueño [Sp], master; owner.

du fort au faible [Fr], lit., from the strong to the weak; one thing with another; on an average.

du jour [Fr], of the day; today's.

dukan [Hind], a shop: *India.*

dulce bellum inexpertis [L], war is sweet to those who never have tried it.

dulce "Domum" [L], sweet "Home" (*or* "Homeward"): from the song sung by students of Winchester College and other English schools at the close of the term.

dulce est desipere in loco [L], it is sweet to unbend on occasion; a little nonsense now and then is relished by the wisest men: *Horace.*

dulce et decorum est pro patria mori [L], it is sweet and fitting to die for one's country: *Horace.*

dulce quod utile [L], what is useful is sweet.

dulces moriens reminiscitur Argos [L], as he dies, he remembers his beloved Argos (the home of his childhood): *Virgil.*

dulce sodalicium [L], sweet companionship; pleasant association of friends.

dulcis amor patriae [L], sweet is the love of one's fatherland.

dum fortuna fuit [L], while fortune lasted.

dum loquimur fugerit invida aetas [L], "even as we speak, grim Time speeds swift away": *Horace* (tr. by Marshall).

dum loquor, hora fugit [L], time is flying while I speak: *Ovid.*

Dummkopf [Ger], blockhead; stupid.

dum sola [L], while unmarried: *law.*

dum spiro, spero [L], while I breathe I hope: one of the mottoes of *South Carolina.*

dum vita est, spes est [L], while there is life, there is hope.

dum vitant stulti vitia in contraria current [L], in shunning (one kind of) vices, fools run to the opposite extremes: *Horace.*

dum vivimus, vivamus [L], while we live, let us live.

dungaree [Hind *dungrī*], blue denim fabric pants.

duo [It; *pl.* dui], duet; instrumental duet: *music.*

duolo [It], grief; sorrow; pathos.

duomo [It; *pl.* duomi], Italian cathedral.

duplici spe uti [L], to have a double hope; have two strings to one's bow.

dur [Fr; *fem.* dure], hard; tough; hard-boiled (eggs).

dura lex, sed lex [L], the law is hard, but it is the law.

duramente [It], harshly: *music.*

durante [L], during: *law.* —**durante absentia,** during absence. —**durante beneplacito,** during (our) good pleasure: said of certain Crown appointments in Great Britain. —**durante minore aetate,** during minority. —**durante vita,** during life.

durate et vosmet rebus servate secundis [L], carry on (*or* endure) and preserve yourselves for better times: *Virgil.*

durbar [Anglo-Ind; Hind & Pers *darbar*], audience hall; court; hence, assembly; reception; levee.

Durchgangszug [Ger], a through train.

durch Schaden wird man klug [Ger], lit., through injury one becomes wise; a burned child dreads the fire; experience is the mistress of fools.

duro de cozer, duro de comer [Pg], hard to boil, hard to eat.

du sublime au ridicule il n'y a qu'un pas [Fr], from the sublime to the ridiculous is but a step: *Napoleon.*

duvet [Fr], eiderdown quilt.

du vieux temps [Fr], quite old-fashioned.

dux femina facti [L], the leader (*or* originator) of the deed was a woman: *Virgil.*

dux gregis [L], leader of the flock (*or* herd).

E

eau [Fr; *pl.* eaux], water. **—eau bénite,** holy water. **—eau bénite de cour,** court holy water; flattery; empty promises; blarney. **—eau courante,** running water. **—eau de vie,** lit., water of life; brandy. **—eau dormante,** stagnant water. **—eau morte,** still water. **—eau rougie,** red wine and water. **—eau sucrée,** water sweetened with sugar. **—eau vive,** spring water; running water.

ébauche [Fr], first rough outline, showing the principal parts of a work of art or literature; a rough commencement or blocking out of an actual work: distinguished from *esquisse,* or separate and preliminary sketch.

éboulement [Fr], falling down, as of a rampart; landslide; landslip.

è buon orator chi a se persuade [It], he is a good orator who convinces himself.

écart [Fr], lit., a setting or stepping aside; deviation; digression, as in a discourse; hence, mistake; error.

è cattivo vento che non è buono per qualcheduno [It], it is an ill wind that blows nobody good.

ecce [L], behold. **—ecce agnus Dei,** behold the lamb of God. **—ecce iterum Crispinus,** here's that fellow Crispin again; here's that bore again (used of persons and things): *Juvenal.* **—ecce signum,** behold the sign; here is the proof. **—Ecce Homo,** behold the man (*John* xix. 5): a representation of Christ crowned with thorns.

écervelé [Fr], harebrained; lacking in judgment; rash.

échafaudage [Fr], scaffolding; fig., great reparations; display.

échantillon [Fr], simple; specimen; pattern.

échappée [Fr], escape; prank; sally; space to turn in, as for carriages; also, vista. **—échappée de lumière,** accidental light: *fine arts.*

echar el mango tras el destral [Sp], lit., to throw the handle after the hatchet; give up in despair; throw something away with all means of retrieving it.

écharpe [Fr], scarf.

échauffourée [Fr], affray; skirmish: *mil.*

échec [Fr], check; defeat; failure; repulse.

échelle [Fr], ladder; *music,* scale.

éclaircissement [Fr], clearing up; elucidation; explanation.

éclat [Fr], orig., splinter or fragment, as the result of violent breakage; crash, as of thunder; also, brilliant light; fig., splendor; striking effect; glory. **—éclat de rire,** burst (*or* roar) of laughter.

école [Fr], school. **—école de droit,** law school. **—École des beaux-arts,** school of fine arts, esp. the famous institution in Paris, founded in

1648. **—école militaire,** military school. **—haute école,** high military horsemanship.

e contra [L], on the other hand.

e contrario [L], on the contrary.

écorcher les oreilles [Fr], to grate on one's ears.

écran [Fr], screen.

écrasé de travail [Fr], overwhelmed with work.

écrasement [Fr], lit., a crushing; surgical operation performed with an *écraseur* (q.v.).

écraseur [Fr], lit., crusher; a surgical instrument, used esp. in the removal of tumors.

écrasez l'infâme [Fr], crush the abomination (i.e., the persecuting and entrenched orthodoxy of pre-Revolutionary France): *Voltaire.*

écrevisse [Fr], crawfish; specif., a piece of armor consisting of splints sliding over one another in the manner of a crawfish's tail.

écrivain [Fr], writer.

écroulement [Fr], collapse.

écru [Fr], lit., unbleached; of a pale brown or neutral color, like that of raw or unbleached fabrics; also, materials of this color or the color itself.

écu [Fr], orig., a small shield; any of several old French coins, esp. the silver coin in use in the 17th and 18th centuries, equivalent to an English crown or the French five-franc piece. **—père aux écus,** moneyed man, a man made of money.

edel ist der edel tut [Ger], noble is that noble does.

éditeur [Fr], publisher.

édition de luxe [Fr], a sumptuous edition.

editio princeps [L; *pl.* editiones principes], the first printed edition of a book.

eenostrahnyets [Russ; *fem.* eenostrahnka], foreigner.

effleurer [Fr], to graze; skim over; glance at; touch lightly.

efharisto [Mod Gr, *fr.* Gr εὐχαριστῶ, eukharisto], thank you.

e flamma petere cibum [L], to snatch (*or* fetch) food out of the flame; to live by desperate means: *Terence.*

égalité [Fr], equality.

égards [Fr], regards; respects.

égaré [Fr; *fem.* égarée], strayed; roving; wild; bewildered.

égarement [Fr], losing one's way; blunder; error; also, wildness of look; bewilderment. **—égarement d'esprit,** mental alienation.

ego et rex meus [L], my king and I: *Cardinal Wolsey* (the correct order in Latin, but commonly translated "I and my king" in keeping with Wolsey's character).

egomet mihi ignosco [L], I myself pardon myself: *Horace.*

ego spem pretio non emo [L], I do not purchase hope for a price; I do not buy a pig in a poke: *Terence.*

egualmente [It], equally; evenly: *music.*

eheu! fugaces labuntur anni [L], alas! the fleeting years slip by: *Horace.*

ehrlich währt am längsten [Ger], to be honest lasts longest; honesty is the best policy.

eidos [Gr εἶδος, eîdos; *pl.* εἴδη], form; species; *philos.,* idea.

eiectamenta [L; *pl.*], ejected matter.

eigner Herd ist Goldes werth [Ger], one's own hearth is of golden worth; there's no place like home.

eile mit Weile [Ger], lit., hasten with leisure; more haste, less speed. Cf. FESTINA LENTE.

eine Hand wäscht die andere [Ger], one hand washes the other.

ein Esel bleibt ein Esel [Ger], an ass remains an ass.

einfach [Ger], simple; plain; homely.

Ein' feste Burg ist unser Gott [Ger], A Mighty Fortress Is Our God: hymn by *Luther.*

ein Gelehrter hat keine lange Weile [Ger], lit., a scholar has no long leisure; time never hangs heavy on a scholar's hands: *Jean Paul Richter.*

ein gutes Mädchen [Ger], a good-natured girl.

Einleitung [Ger], introduction, as to a book; preamble.

ein lustiger Bruder [Ger], a jolly fellow.

einmal ist keinmal [Ger], lit., once is not-once (*or* never); once does not count; the exception proves the rule.

ein Mann, ein Wort [Ger], lit., one man, one word; word of honor! honor bright!

Einsamkeit [Ger], loneliness; solitude.

ein Sperling in der Hand ist besser als eine Taube auf dem Dache [Ger], a sparrow in the hand is better than a pigeon on the roof.

ein starker Geist [Ger], a powerful intellect.

ein unbedeutender Mensch [Ger], an insignificant fellow; a man of no account.

ein Unglück kommt selten allein [Ger], misfortunes seldom come singly.

ein wenig schneller [Ger], a little faster: *music.*

Eirēann go Brat! [Gael], long live Ireland!

εἰς αὔριον τὰ σπουδαῖα [Gr; eis aúrion tà spoudaîa], serious affairs tomorrow; business tomorrow (i.e., don't bother me today): saying of *Archias,* a Spartan general noted for his procrastination.

Eisenbahn [Ger], railroad; railway.

Eisen und Blut [Ger], iron and blood: *Bismarck* (words used by him in a speech, Sept. 1862; hence his common appellation, "the man of blood and iron," the order being usually reversed in English).

εἰς ὄνυχα [Gr; eis ónykha], lit., to a fingernail; to a hair; to a nicety; to a T.

eiusdem farinae [L], of the same flour; of the same kind.

eiusdem generis [L], of the same kind.

ejido [Sp], a common, or public, tract of land; also, in Spanish and Mexican settlements, esp. in Texas, land allocated for the laying out of a town: *Sp. & Mex. law.*

ἐκεῖνος ἦν ὁ λύχνος ὁ καιόμενος καὶ φαίνων [Gr; ekeînos hên ho lúkhnos ho kaiómenos kaì phaínōn], he was a burning and a shining light: *John* v. 35.

ἐκ γὰρ τοῦ περισσεύματος τῆς καρδίας τὸ στόμα λαλεῖ [Gr; ek gàr toû perisseúmatos tês kardías tò stóma laleî], for out of the abundance of the heart the mouth speaketh: *Matthew* xii. 34.

ἐκ τοῦ στόματός σου κρίνω σε [Gr; ek toû stómatós sou krínō se], out of thine own mouth will I judge thee: *Luke* xix. 22.

élan [Fr], impetuosity; ardor; dash; rush; sally. **—par élans,** by starts.

élan vital [Fr], the vital, creative force; a creative force in all organisms, said to be responsible for evolution: *Henri Bergson.*

elapso tempore [L], the time having elapsed.

el buen paño en el arca se vende [Sp], good cloth sells itself in the box; good wine needs no bush.

el deseo vence al miedo [Sp], desire conquers fear.

ἐλέησόν με [Gr; eléēsón me], have mercy on me; pity me.

élégant [Fr; *fem.* élégante], stylish or fashionable person; gentleman (*or* lady) of fashion.

elegantemente [It], elegantly: *music.*

elephantem ex musca facis [L], you are making an elephant out of a fly; you are making a mountain out of a molehill.

élève [Fr], pupil; scholar; student.

el hijo del tigre nace rayado [Sp], the son of the tiger is born with stripes; like father like son.

el honor es mi guía [Sp], honor is my guide.

Eli, Eli, lama sabachthani? [Aram], my God, my God, why hast thou forsaken me? (Christ's words on the Cross): *Matthew* xxvii. 46.

élite [Fr], choice; pick; flower; select few.

elixir vitae [L], elixir of life.

el malo siempre piensa engaño [Sp], the knave always suspects knavery.

éloge [Fr], eulogium; panegyric; funeral oration.

éloignement [Fr], distance; aversion; estrangement.

el olvido, la muerte de la muerte! [Sp], to be forgotten is the death of death: *Ramon de Campoamor.*

el río pasado, el santo olvidado [Sp], the river crossed, the saint forgotten.

el tiempo corre, y todo tras él [Sp], time runs and everything runs after it.

el tiempo es oro [Sp], time is gold.

embarcación [Sp], lit., embarkation; vessel; ship; boat: *naut.*

embarcadero [Sp], quay; wharf.

embarras [Fr], encumbrance; obstacle; embarrassment; trouble; difficulty; fig., pretensions; fine airs. **—embarras de choix,** embarrassment
of choice; too much to choose from. **—embarras de richesses,** an
embarrassment of riches; encumbrance of wealth.

embêtant [Fr], annoying; vexing; wearying: *colloq.*

embonpoint [Fr], plumpness; stoutness; corpulence.

embuscade [Fr], ambush.

embusqué [Fr], lit., one who lurks in ambush; *mil.,* a slacker.

è meglio domandar che errare [It], better ask than lose your way.

è meglio donar la lana che la pecora [It], better give the wool than
the sheep.

è meglio esser mendicante che ignorante [It], better be a beggar than
a fool.

è meglio una volta che mai [It], better once than never.

è meglio un buon amico che cento parenti [It], better one good friend
than a hundred relatives.

emeritus [L; *fem.* emerita], retired or superannuated after long and
honorable service: a title given esp. to clergymen and college pro-
fessors.

émeute [Fr], riot; seditious outbreak; popular rising.

émigré [Fr; *fem.* émigrée], emigrant; refugee; esp., a Royalist refugee
at the time of the French Revolution.

éminement [Fr], in a high degree; eminently.

emir [Ar], military commander; also, a title.

ἐμοῦ θανόντος γαῖα μιχθήτω πυρί [Gr; emoû thanóntos gaîa mikhthéto
purí], when I am dead, let the earth be mingled with fire: anonymous
Greek writer quoted by *Suetonius.*

empesé [Fr; *fem.* empesée], starched; *of style,* stiff; formal; affected.

Empfindung [Ger], feeling; sensitiveness; perception.

emplastrum [L; *pl.* emplastra], a plaster: *pharm.*

empleado [Sp], employee; clerk; official.

ἐμποδίζει τὸν λόγον ὁ φόβος [Gr; empodízei tòn lógon ho phóbos], fear
hinders speech; fear curbs the tongue: *Demades.*

emportement [Fr], transport; passion; violent rage.

empressé [Fr; *fem.* empressée], eager; keen; assiduously attentive.

empressement [Fr], eagerness; ardor; demonstrativeness; excessive cordiality; assiduous attention.

empta dolore docet experientia [L], experience bought with pain teaches
effectually; a burned child dreads the fire.

emptor [L], buyer; purchaser. **—caveat emptor,** let the purchaser beware:
law.

emunctae naris [L], lit., of wiped nose; of mature judgment; of nice
discernment: *Horace.*

en alerte [Fr], on the alert.

en ami [Fr], as (*or* like) a friend.

en arrière [Fr], in (*or* to) the rear; in arrears; *naut.,* abaft.

en attendant [Fr], in the meantime.

en avant! [Fr], forward! march on! —**en avant de,** in front of, before.

en badinant [Fr], in jest; in sport; by way of a joke; in fun.

en bloc [Fr], in a lump; as a whole; wholesale.

en boca cerrada no entra mosca [Sp], a fly does not enter a closed mouth.

en bon français [Fr], lit., in good French; in plain terms; without mincing matters; like a true Frenchman.

en brochette [Fr], on a skewer; skewered: *cookery.*

en brosse [Fr], brushlike; bristling. See BROSSE.

en cabochon [Fr], polished but without facets.

encabritada [Sp], lit., rearing; the sharp upward tilt of an airplane in flight: *aero.* Cf. CABRÉ.

en cachette [Fr], in concealment; secretly; stealthily.

en cada tierra su uso [Sp], each country has its own custom.

en caracole [Fr], winding; spiral, as a staircase.

en casa de [Sp], in care of; in (*or* at) the house of.

en cas d'événement [Fr], in (*or* in case of) an emergency.

encastré [Fr], fitted in; built in at the supports (as a beam): *engin.*

enceinte [Fr], *n.* enclosure (as within town walls); precincts; main enclosure of a fortress; *adj.* pregnant; with child.

enchanté [Fr; *fem.* enchantée], enchanted; delighted.

enchère [Fr], bidding (at an auction); auction.

en cheveux [Fr], bare-headed: said of a woman.

enchilada [Sp], dish of tortilla, chili, meat, and cheese: *Mexico.*

enclave [Fr], area enclosed within a larger area: *geog.*

en coeur [Fr], heart-shaped.

en condition [Fr], in service: said of servants.

en congé [Fr], on leave; on furlough.

en connaissance de cause [Fr], with full knowledge of the subject.

encore [Fr], yet; still; again; once more.

en courroux [Fr], in anger; wrathfully.

en cueros [Sp], stark naked.

en cuerpo [Sp], with the shape of the body exposed, through not wearing a cloak; fig., uncovered; naked.

Ende gut, alles gut [Ger], all's well that ends well.

en dernier ressort [Fr], as a last resort; *law,* without appeal.

en désespoir de cause [Fr], as a last resource.

en déshabillé [Fr], in a state of undress.

en Dieu est ma fiance [Fr], in God is my trust.

en Dieu est tout [Fr], in God is everything.

endimanché [Fr], dressed in Sunday clothes; in Sunday best.

en échelle [Fr], ladderlike.

en effet [Fr], in effect; in reality; substantially; really.

energicamente [It], with energy (*abbr.* energ.): *music.*

energico [It], energetic; forcible: *music.*

en évidence [Fr], in evidence.

en famille [Fr], in (*or* with) one's family; among ourselves; informally.

enfance [Fr], childhood.

enfant [Fr], child. —**enfant de famille** [*pl.* enfants de famille], lit., child of the family; child (*or* young person) of good family. —**enfant gâté** [*fem.* gâtée], a spoiled child. —**enfants perdus,** lit., lost children; a forlorn hope: *mil.* —**enfant terrible,** a terrible child; a child who makes disconcerting remarks. —**enfant trouvé,** a foundling.

enfaticamente [It], emphatically: *music.*

enfer [Fr], hell.

en fête [Fr], in holiday dress or mood; in the act of holiday merrymaking.

enfilade [Fr], suite (of rooms); string (of phrases); *mil.,* enfilade.

enfin [Fr], in fine; in short; at last.

en fin de compte [Fr], lit., in the end of the account; in the end; when all is told.

en flagrant délit [Fr], in the very act; red-handed.

en flûte [Fr], like a flute, or naval transport; armed with guns on the upper deck only: *nav.*

en foule [Fr], in a crowd; in crowds.

en fuego [Sp], under fire; in action: *mil.*

en garçon [Fr], as a bachelor.

en grand [Fr], on a large scale; in grand style; *portrait painting,* full-sized; at full length.

en grande tenue [Fr], in full dress; *mil.,* in full uniform; in review order.

en grande toilette [Fr], in full dress.

en grand seigneur [Fr], like a great lord; in lordly style.

en guerre [Fr], at war; at variance.

en habiles gens [Fr], like able men.

en haut [Fr], on high; aloft; above; overhead.

en joue! [Fr], lit., at the cheek! aim! take aim!

en la rose je fleuris [Fr], in the rose I flourish: motto of the *Duke of Richmond.*

en ligne [Fr], in line; *mil.,* fall in!

en lista *or* **en lista de correos** [Sp], general delivery; to be kept till called for: *postal direction.*

enluminure [Fr], the art of coloring or illuminating; illuminated design; colored print; *colloq.,* high color (of the face); fig., false brilliancy of style.

en masse [Fr], in a mass; in a body; all together.

ennui [Fr], boredom.

ennuyé [Fr; *fem.* ennuyée], mentally wearied; bored.

ennuyeux [Fr], boring, dull.

ἐν οἴνῳ ἀλήθεια [Gr; en oínō alḗtheia], in wine there is truth. Cf. IN VINO VERITAS.

en papillotes [Fr], in curl papers; in papillotes.

en parole je vis [Fr], I live in the word.

en partie [Fr], in part; partly.

en passant [Fr], in passing; by the way.

en paz descanse [Sp], may he rest in peace: *abbr.* E.P.D.

en pension [Fr], as a boarder.

en petit [Fr], in miniature; on a small scale.

en peu de mots [Fr], in a few words; briefly.

en plein [Fr], fully; completely; in the midst; right in. **—en plein air,** in the open air. **—en pleine-eau,** in deep water. **—en plein été,** in the height of summer. **—en plein hiver,** in the depth of winter. **—en plein jour,** in broad daylight; openly.

en poco tiempo [Sp], in a short time.

en prince [Fr], in princely fashion; like a prince.

en prise [Fr], in danger of capture; exposed.

en propia mano [Sp], into (his) own hands; to be delivered in person: *abbr.* E.P.M.

en pure perte [Fr], to no purpose; in vain.

enquête [Fr], inquiry; investigation.

en queue [Fr], in the rear; behind; at one's heels; in a line.

enragé [Fr; *fem.* enragée], mad; enraged; fig., irritated; violent; also, excessive, as thirst.

en rapport [Fr], in accord; in sympathy.

en règle [Fr], according to rule; in due form; in order.

enrejado [Sp], latticework; trelliswork.

en résumé [Fr], to sum up; on the whole.

en revanche [Fr], in requital; in return; in retaliation.

en route [Fr], on the way.

ens [LL; *pl.* entia], being, in the abstract; existence; entity: *philos.* **—Ens Entium,** Being of Beings; the Supreme Being. **—ens rationis,** a creature of reason; a product of mental action.

en scène [Fr], on the stage: *theat.*

ense et aratro [L], with sword and plow.

ensemble [Fr], *adj.* together; at the same time; *n.* the whole; all the parts taken together. **—tout ensemble,** the general effect.

ensenada [Sp], cove; inlet.

ense petit placidam sub libertate quietem [L], by the sword she seeks calm repose under liberty: motto of *Massachusetts*. The second line of a couplet attributed to Algernon Sidney (1622-83), the first being *manus haec inimica tyrannis* (q.v.).

en somme [Fr], in the main; in short; finally.

en suite [Fr], in company; in a series or set.

en suivant la vérité [Fr], in following the truth.

en tablier [Fr], apronlike.

entbehren sollst du! sollst du entbehren [Ger], refrain thou must! thou must refrain: *Goethe*.

entente [Fr], an understanding; agreement. **—entente cordiale,** friendly understanding, esp. between two nations, notably that between England and France established in 1904.

entêté [Fr; *fem.* entêtée], *adj.* headstrong; obstinate; self-willed; infatuated; *n.* stubborn person.

en tête-à-tête [Fr], face to face; in private.

entêtement [Fr], stubbornness; obstinacy; infatuation.

entourage [Fr], surroundings; attendant persons; associates (collectively); circle; *jewelry,* setting; mounting.

en tout cas [Fr], in any case; at all events.

en-tout-cas [Fr], umbrella-sunshade.

entracte [Fr], interval between two acts; interlude.

entrada [Sp], entrance; entry; also, receipts; revenue.

en train [Fr], in progress.

entrain [Fr], high spirits; heartiness; life; go. **—avec entrain,** with a will.

entrata [It], lit., entrance; prelude: *music.*

entrechat [Fr], a leap from the floor in which the ballet dancer's feet are repeatedly struck together: *dancing.*

entre chien et loup [Fr], lit., between dog and wolf (i.e., when it is impossible to distinguish one from the other); in the twilight; at dusk.

entrecôte [Fr], steak cut from between the ribs; tenderloin: *cookery.*

entre deux [Fr], between two. **—entre deux âges,** lit., between two ages; middle-aged. **—entre deux feux,** between two fires. **—entre deux vins,** lit., between two wines; half drunk; tipsy.

entre dos aguas [Sp], between two waters; in doubt.

entre la espada y la pared [Sp], between the sword and the wall (between the devil and the deep).

entre l'enclume et le marteau [Fr], between the anvil and the hammer (see above).

entremets [Fr], a dainty side dish or dishes, usually following the main course: *cookery.*

entremetteuse [Fr], go-between; procuress.

entre nous [Fr], between ourselves; in confidence.

entrepôt [Fr], warehouse; temporary storehouse; emporium; mart; commercial center.

entrepreneur [Fr], contractor; organizer, esp. of musical and other public entertainments.

entre quatre yeux [Fr], lit., between four eyes; between ourselves.

entresol [Fr], a low story between the ground floor and the floor above; mezzanine.

en un clin d'oeil [Fr], in the twinkling of an eye.

en vélin [Fr], in vellum.

en vérité [Fr], in truth; truly; indeed.

en vieillissant on devient plus fou et plus sage [Fr], as we grow old, we become more foolish and more wise: *La Rochefoucauld.*

en vigueur [Fr], in force; operative, as a law.

envoi [Fr], shipment; concluding stanza: *poetry.*

en voiture! [Fr], take your seats! all aboard!

envoyé [Fr; *fem.* envoyée], messenger; envoy.

eo animo [L], with that intention.

eo instante [L], at that moment.

eo ipso [L], by that itself; by that fact.

eo loci [L], at that very place: *Cicero.*

eo nomine [L], by (*or* under) that name; on this account.

épanchement [Fr], outpouring; effusion; overflowing. **—épanchement de coeur,** opening of one's heart.

épaule [Fr], shoulder.

ἔπεα πτερόεντα [Gr; épea pteróenta], winged words: *Homer.*

éperdu [Fr; *fem.* éperdue], distracted; bewildered. **—éperdu d'amour,** madly in love.

éperdument [Fr], distractedly; desperately.

éperlan [Fr], European smelt.

épice [Fr], spice. **—fine épice,** fig., sharp-witted fellow.

épicier [Fr; *fem.* épicière], grocer; fig., vulgar fellow.

Epicuri de grege porcus [L], a hog from the drove of Epicurus; glutton: *Horace.*

ἐπὶ γήραος οὐδῷ [Gr; epì géraos oudô], on the threshold of old age: *Homer.*

épigramme [Fr], epigram; *cookery,* ragout, as of lamb; also, small cutlet.

épinard [Fr], spinach.

épinette [Can Fr], any of several trees of the fir and larch families, esp. the white spruce (*Picea canadiensis*) and the red larch (*Larix americana*).

ἢ πῖθι ἢ ἄπιθι [Gr; ề pîthi ề ápithi], either drink or depart.

e pluribus unum [L], one out of many: motto of the *U.S.A.*

eppur si muove [It], nevertheless, it does move: words popularly attributed to *Galileo,* after he had been compelled by the Inquisition to swear that the earth stood still.

épreuve [Fr], proof; trial; ordeal; *printing,* proof.

épris [Fr; *fem.* éprise], enamored; taken with.

éprouvette [Fr], a testing apparatus, as for gunpowder; test tube.

épuisé [Fr; *fem.* épuisée], exhausted; spent; worn out; *typog.,* out of print.

epulis accumbere divum [L], to recline at the feasts of the gods: *Virgil.*

épure [Fr], working drawing (of a building); diagram: *arch.*

è pur troppo vero [It], it is but too true.

equabilmente [It], equably; smoothly: *music.*

équivoque [Fr], *adj.* ambiguous; doubtful; equivocal; *n.* ambiguity; equivocation; quibble; also, an ambiguous word or phrase.

e re nata [L], under the present circumstances; as matters stand.

erev tov [Heb], good evening.

ergebet euch *or* **ergeben Sie sich!** [Ger], surrender!

ergo [L], therefore; hence.

erhaben [Ger], elevated; lofty; stately.

er hat Haare auf den Zähnen [Ger], lit., he has hairs on his teeth; he knows what's what; he's aggressive.

Erin go bragh [Irish], Erin (*or* Ireland) forever: ancient battle cry of the Irish.

Erinnerung [Ger], recollection; reminiscence; reminder.

eripuit caelo fulmen sceptrumque tyrannis [L], he snatched the thunderbolt from heaven and the scepter from tyrants: inscription under the bust of Benjamin Franklin by Houdon.

erlaubt ist was gefällt [Ger], what pleases us is permissible; what a man likes to do, that he thinks right to do: *Goethe.*

ernst [Ger], earnest; grave; serious: *music.* —**ernst ist das Leben, heiter ist die Kunst,** life is earnest, art is joyous: *Schiller.*

eroico [It; *fem.* eroica], heroic: *music.*

errare humanum est [L], to err is human.

erreur ou omission exceptée [Fr], error or omission excepted: *abbr.* e.o.o.e.

Ersatz [Ger], amends; compensation; reparation; substitute.

erstens [Ger], in the first place.

erstgeboren [Ger], *adj.* first-born.

erst wägen, dann wagen [Ger], first consider, then venture.

erubuit; salva res est [L], he blushed; the affair is safe: *Terence.*

Erzherzog [Ger; *fem.* Erzherzogin], archduke.

esa es la herencia de Adán [Sp], that is the heritage of Adam: *Calderón* (said of misery).

es bildet ein Talent sich in der Stille, sich ein Charakter in dem Strom der Welt [Ger], a talent is developed in quiet (*or* solitude), a character in the stream of the world: *Goethe.*

es bleibt dabei! [Ger], agreed!

escadrille [Fr], naval or aviation squadron; as, the Lafayette *escadrille.*

escalier [Fr], staircase; stairs. —**escalier dérobé,** private staircase.

escamotage [Fr], juggling; sleight of hand; fig., pilfering.

escargot [Fr], edible snail.

escarmouche [Fr], skirmish; brush; running fight: *mil.*

esclandre [Fr], uproar; scandal; a quarrel in public.

escouade [Fr], squad; gang (of workmen).

escribiente [Sp], clerk; amanuensis.

escrime [Fr], fencing. —**salle d'escrimer,** fencing school.

escritura, buena memoria [Sp], writing, the best memory.

escroquerie [Fr], dishonest action, swindle.

escudo [Sp & Pg], lit., shield; a currency unit in Portugal and Chile.

es de vidrio la mujer [Sp], woman is made of glass: *Cervantes.*

è sempre l'ora [It], it is always the hour; it is always the right time.

esencia [Sp], fuel; generic name for gasoline, alcohol, and other inflammable liquids. Cf. *Fr.* ESSENCE.

es gibt für die Kammerdiener keine Helden [Ger], valets have no heroes: no man is a hero to his valet: *Goethe.*

es ist ewig schade [Ger], it is a thousand pities; lit., an unending pity.

es ist nicht alles Gold was glänzt [Ger], all is not gold that glitters.

es ist rein aus mit uns [Ger], it is all over with us.

eso es chino para mi [Sp], that is Chinese to me; it's Greek to me.

espada [Sp], sword; also, matador.

espadrille [Fr], rope-soled canvas shoe.

español [Sp; *fem.* española], *adj.* Spanish; *n.* Spaniard. **—el español,** Spanish (the language).

espérance en Dieu [Fr], hope in God.

espérance et Dieu [Fr], hope and God.

espiègle [Fr], roguish; waggish; frolicsome.

espièglerie [Fr], roguish trick; waggishness.

espionnage [Fr], spying; espionage.

esposa [Sp], wife; spouse.

esposo [Sp], husband; spouse.

espressione [It], expression; feeling: *music.*

espressivo [It], expressive; with expression: *music.*

esprit [Fr], spirit; soul; mind; wit; sprightliness. **—esprit borné** (*or* **étroit**), narrow mind. **—esprit de corps,** animating spirit of a collective body and devotion to its honor and interests; a spirit of comradeship and loyalty to the body or association to which one belongs. **—esprit de parti,** party spirit. **—esprit dérangé,** disordered mind. **—esprit de suite,** consistency. **—esprit d'ordre,** orderliness. **—esprit follet,** goblin; elf; esp. one attached to a house or person. **—esprit fort** [*pl.* esprits forts], lit., a strong spirit; strong-minded person; freethinker. **—esprit présent,** ready wit.

esquisse [Fr], first rapid sketch or a design, painting, or of a model of a statue; rough drawing; outline or general delineation, as of a novel; preliminary study of a projected work: distinguished from *ébauche,* or rough commencement of the actual work itself.

essayage [Fr], testing; trying on.

esse [L], to be; exist; being.

essence [Fr], fuel; specif., gasoline. Cf. *Sp.* ESENCIA.

esse quam videri [L], to be rather than to seem: motto of *North Carolina.* **—esse quam videri bonus malebat,** he preferred to be rather than to seem good: *Sallust.*

es soberbia la hermosura [Sp], beauty is pride (*or* haughtiness); beauty and pride go hand in hand: *Lope de Vega.*

estação [Pg], railroad station; season; time of year.

estado [Sp], state. —**los Estados Unidos,** the United States: *abbr.* EE.UU. *or* E.U.

estafa [Sp], swindling: *Sp. law.*

estafette [Fr], courier; mounted messenger.

estaminet [Fr], a cafe and smoking room; barroom.

estampe [Fr], print.

estancia [Sp], cattle ranch; stock farm; country estate: *Sp. Am.*

estanciero [Sp], owner of an *estancia: Sp. Am.*

estanco [Sp], lit., monopoly; hence, a store where government monopoly goods are on sale. —**estanco de tabaco,** tobacco store.

estanque [Sp], pond; reservoir.

estaño [Sp], tin.

est ars etiam male dicendi [L], there is an art even to maligning.

est brevitate opus, ut currat sententia [L], terseness is needed that the thought may run free: *Horace.*

est deus in nobis [L], there is a god within us: *Ovid.*

estimo muito [Pg], I appreciate it very much.

est modus in rebus [L], there is a medium (*or* due measure) in all things: *Horace.*

esto perpetua! [L], be thou eternal! may she (*or* it) be everlasting: motto of *Idaho.*

esto perpetuum [L], let it be everlasting.

estoque [Sp], sword used in killing the bull in a bullfight.

esto quod esse videris [L], be what you seem to be.

est quaedam flere voluptas [L], there is a certain pleasure in weeping: *Ovid.*

estrade [Fr], raised platform; stand.

estrella [Sp], star.

estro [It], ardor; enthusiasm. —**estro poetico,** poetic fire; outburst of genius; fervent enthusiasm.

esturgeon [Fr], sturgeon.

es tut mir leid [Ger], I am sorry (an expression of grief).

étage [Fr], story; floor.

étagère [Fr], a whatnot; ornamental stand, with shelves.

étalage [Fr], exposing for sale; ostentatious display; show.

et alibi [L], and elsewhere: *abbr.* et al.

et alii (*masc.*) *or* **et aliae** (*fem.*) [L], and others: *abbr.* et al.

ἢ τὰν ἢ ἐπὶ τάν [Gr; ḕ tàn ḕ epì tán], either this or upon this: the Spartan mother to her son on giving him his shield.

étape [Fr], public storehouse; *mil.,* halting place; stage.

état-major [Fr; *pl.* état-majors], staff; staff office: *mil.*

eta vazmozhna [Russ], that's impossible.

et campos ubi Troia fuit [L], and the plains where once was Troy: *Virgil.*

et cum spiritu tuo [L], and with thy spirit: liturgical response to *Dominus vobiscum,* the Lord be with you.

et decus et pretium recti [L], both the ornament and the reward of virtue.

été [Fr], summer; also, prime (of life).

et ego in Arcadia [L], I too have been in Arcadia (the ideal region of rural happiness); *funerary inscription,* I (Death) am even in Arcadia; fig., Death is everywhere.

et genus et formam regina pecunia donat [L], money, like a queen, gives both rank and beauty: *Horace.*

ἢ θηρίον, ἢ θεός [Gr; ĕ thēríon, ĕ theós], (man is) either a brute or a god: *Aristotle.*

et hoc genus omne [L], and everything of this kind.

etiam atque etiam [L], again and again.

etiam perire ruinae [L], even the ruins have perished: *Lucan.*

et id genus omne [L], and everything of the kind.

et l'avare Achéron ne lâche point sa proie [Fr], and grasping Acheron never lets go of his prey: *Racine.*

et mihi res, non me rebus subiungere conor [L], I endeavor to make circumstances yield to me, not me to circumstances: *Horace.*

et nos quoque tela sparsimus [L], we too have hurled javelins.

et nunc et semper [L], now and always.

étoile [Fr], star; central point where several paths converge, as in a public garden; specif., a kind of satin material; *typog.,* asterisk. —**étoile de mer,** starfish. —**Étoile du Nord,** Star of the North: motto of *Minnesota.*

étourderie [Fr], thoughtless act; heedlessness; thoughtlessness.

être à jour [Fr], to be up-to-date.

être cousu d'argent [Fr], to be rolling in money.

être de jour [Fr], to be on duty.

être en goguettes [Fr], to be in a merry mood. See GOGUETTE.

être gris [Fr], to be fuddled (*or* tipsy).

être sur la sellette [Fr], to be on the culprit's stool; be hauled over the coals.

être un sot fieffé [Fr], to be a downright fool.

è troppo [It], it is too much.

et sceleratis sol oritur [L], the sun shines even on the wicked (on everybody): *Seneca.*

et semel emissum volat irrevocabile verbum [L], and a word once uttered flies onward never to be recalled; "you can't get back a word you once let go": *Horace.*

et sequens [L; *pl.* et sequentes *or* et sequentia], and the following: *abbr.* et seq., *pl.* et seqq. *or* et sqq.

et sic de ceteris [L], and so of the rest.

et sic de similibus [L], and so of the like.

et similia [L], and the like.

et tu, Brute [L], and you too, Brutus! (implying betrayal by a friend): *Shakespeare* (last words of Caesar, when he beheld Brutus among his assassins). Cf. καὶ σύ, τέκνον (kaì sú, téknon).

étude [Fr], a study; esp., a musical composition intended to afford practice in mastering certain technical difficulties. **—étude de concert,** a concert piece.

étui [Fr], small case.

étuvée [Fr], stewed meat; stew: *cookery*.

etwas [Ger], somewhat; rather; some; a little.

Etwas ist faul in Staate Dänemark [Ger], something's rotten in Denmark.

euge! [L], well done! bravo! good!

eureka [Gr εὕρηκα, heúrēka], I have found it: *Archimedes* (on finding a way to test the purity of Hiero's crown). "Eureka" is the motto of *California*.

εὐτυχία πολύφιλος [Gr; eutukhía polúphilos], prosperity is many-friended; prosperity has many friends.

εὐτυχῶν μὴ ἴσθι ὑπερήφανος, ἀπορήσας μὴ ταπεινοῦ [Gr; eutukhôn mè ísthi hyperéphanos, aporésas mè tapeinoû], be not arrogant in prosperity nor abject in adversity: *Cleobulus*.

événement [Fr], event; occurrence; emergency. **—en cas d'événement,** in (*or* in case of) an emergency.

eventus stultorum magister [L], the result is the instructor of fools; fools must be taught by experience: *Livy* (adapted).

évêque [Fr], bishop.

evviva! [It], hurrah!

Ewigkeit [Ger], eternity.

Ewig-Weibliche [Ger], eternal feminine: *Goethe* (part of the line from *Faust*: *Das Ewig-Weibliche zieht uns hinan,* the eternal feminine doth draw us on).

ex abrupto [L], abruptly; without preparation.

ex abundante cautela [L], from excessive caution.

ex abundantia [L], out of the abundance.

ex abusu non arguitur in usum [L], from the abuse of a thing there is no arguing against its use: *law*.

ex acervo [L], out of a heap.

ex adverso [L], from the opposite side; in opposition.

ex aequo et bono [L], according to what is right and good.

ex Africa semper aliquid novi [L], out of Africa there is always something new.

exalté [Fr; *fem.* exaltée], *adj.* elated; overexcited; enthusiastic; *n.* enthusiast; fanatic.

ex animo [L], from the heart; heartily; sincerely. —**ex animo effluere,** to escape from the mind.

ex auctoritate mihi commissa [L], by virtue of the authority entrusted to me.

ex bona fide [L], on one's honor.

ex capite [L], out of the head; from memory.

ex cathedra [L], from the chair; authoritatively.

Excelentísimo [Sp], Most Excellent; Honorable: *abbr.* Ex.ᵐᵒ.

excellence [Fr], excellency.

excelsior [L], higher; ever higher: motto of *New York State.*

exceptio probat regulam de rebus non exceptis [L], an exception proves the rule as to things not excepted.

exceptis excipiendis [L], due exceptions being made.

excerpta [L], excerpts; selections; clippings.

excitari, non hebescere [L], to be spirited, not dull (*or* sluggish).

ex commodo [L], conveniently.

ex concesso [L], from what has been granted (*or* conceded).

excudit [L], he (*or* she) fashioned it: *abbr.* exc.

ex curia [LL], out of court: *law.*

ex delicto [L], of (*or* by reason of) an actionable wrong: *law.*

ex desuetudine amittuntur privilegia [L], rights are lost (*or* forfeited) by disuse: *law.*

ex dono [L], by the gift; as a present. —**ex dono Dei,** by the gift of God.

exegi monumentum aere perennius [L], I have raised a monument more enduring than bronze: *Horace* (prophesying the permanence of his work).

exemplaire [Fr], copy, as of a book or engraving; specimen.

exempla sunt odiosa [L], examples are odious.

exemple [Fr], example; instance. —**par exemple,** for instance (*abbr.* p.ex.); indeed! the idea!

exempli gratia [L], for the sake of example; for example: *abbr.* e.g.

exemplum [L; *pl.* exempla], sample; copy.

exercitatio optimus est magister [L], practice is the best master.

exeunt [L], they go out (*or* leave the stage). —**exeunt omnes,** all go out; all leave the stage.

ex facie [L], from the face; on its face; evidently: said of legal documents, etc.

ex facto ius oritus [L], the law arises out of the fact: *Blackstone.*

ex fide fortis [L], strong through faith.

ex granis fit acervus [L], many grains make a heap; every little bit helps.

ex gratia [L], of or by favor (i.e., in the absence of legal right): *law.*

ex hypothesi [L], by hypothesis.

exigeant [Fr; *fem.* exigeante], exacting; unreasonable; hard to please.

exit [L; *pl.* exeunt], he goes out (*or* goes off the stage).

exitus acta probat [L], the issue proves (*or* justifies) the deeds; all's well that ends well.

ex lege [L], arising from the law; as a matter of law.

ex libris [L], lit., from the books (of); an inscription used, with the owner's name, in a book; bookplate.

ex longinquo [L], from a distance.

ex malis moribus bonae leges natae sunt [L], from bad usages, good laws have sprung: *Coke.*

ex mera gratia [L], through mere favor.

ex mero motu [L], out of mere impulse; of one's own accord.

ex more [L], according to custom.

ex necessitate rei [L], from the necessity of the case; necessarily.

ex nihilo nihil fit [L], from nothing, nothing is made; nothing produces nothing.

ex officio [L], by virtue of one's office.

ex ore parvulorum veritas [L], out of the mouth of little children (comes) truth.

exoriare aliquis nostris ex ossibus ultor [L], may some avenger arise from my bones: *Virgil* (imprecation of the dying Dido).

ἔξω τοῦ πράγματος [Gr; *éxō toû prágmatos*], beside the question.

ex parte [L], from one party (*or* side); in the interests of one side only.

ex pede Herculem [L], from the foot (we can judge) Hercules; from a part we can divine the whole.

expende Hannibalem [L], weigh (the dust of) Hannibal: *Juvenal.*

experientia docet [L], experience teaches. —**experientia docet stultos,** experience teaches fools.

experimentum crucis [L], a crucial experiment (*or* test); an attempt to solve a difficult problem.

experto crede (*or* **credite**) [L], believe one who has had experience.

expertus metuit [L], having had experience, he is afraid; the burned child fears fire: *Horace.*

explicit [LL], here ends: a word formerly written at the end of a manuscript book.

explorador [Sp], explorer; *mil.* scout.

explorant adversa viros [L], misfortune tries men.

exposé [Fr], exposure (of something discreditable); showing up; revelation; statement of facts. —**exposé des motifs,** explanatory statement.

ex post facto [L], after the deed is done; retrospective.

expressio unius est exclusio alterius [L], the express mention of the one is the exclusion of the other: *law.*

expressio verbis [L], in express terms; expressly.

ex professo [L], avowedly; openly; professedly.

ex proposito [L], by design; of set purpose.

ex propriis [L], from one's own resources.

ex proprio motu [L], of one's (*or* its) own accord.

ex quocunque capite [L], for whatever reason.

ex tacito [L], tacitly.

ex tempore [L], without premeditation; offhand; impromptu.

externat [Fr], day school.

externe [Fr], nonresident; day pupil; in hospitals, a medical assistant who lives outside; an extern.

extincteur [Fr], fire extinguisher.

extinctus amabitur idem [L], the same man (though hated while he lives) will be loved after he is dead: *Horace.*

extortor bonorum legumque contortor [L], a blackmailer of good citizens and a twister of laws: *Terence.*

extrait [Fr], an extract; abstract; copy of certificate. **—extrait authentique,** certified copy of a document. **—extrait de mariage,** marriage certificate. **—extrait de naissance,** birth certificate. **—extrait mortuaire,** death certificate.

extra modum [L], beyond measure.

extra muros [L], beyond (*or* outside) the walls.

extranjero [Sp; *fem.* extranjera], stranger; foreigner.

ex ungue leonem [L], by his claw (we know) the lion.

ex uno disce omnes [L], from one learn all; from one judge of the rest.

ex usu [L], of use; serviceable; advantageous.

ex utraque parte [L], on either side.

ex vi termini [LL], by force of the term.

ex voto [L], according to (*or* in pursuance of) one's vow.

F

faber est quisque fortunae suae [L], everyone is the architect of his own fortune: *Sallust.*

fabliau [Fr; *pl.* fabliaux], one of the short metrical tales or *contes* told by the *trouvères* (minstrels) in the 12th and 13th centuries.

fábrica [Sp], factory; plant; mill; *elec.*, powerhouse.

façade [Fr], front, usually of building; also a false front; something intended to create a false impression: a *façade* of gentility.

fâcheux [Fr; *fem.* fâcheuse], grievous; vexatious; troublesome.

facies non omnibus una nec diversa tamen [L], the features are not the same in all respects, nor are they quite different: *Ovid.*

facile [Fr & It], easy; light; fluent: *music.*

facile est inventis addere [L], it is easy to add to things already invented.

facile largire de alieno [L], it is easy to be generous with what is another's.

facile princeps [L], easily chief (*or* first).

facilis descensus Averno (*or* **Averni**) [L], the descent to Avernus (*or* hell) is easy: *Virgil.*

facilité de parler, c'est impuissance de se taire [Fr], fluency of speech is (often) inability to hold the tongue: *Rousseau.*

facinus quos inquinat aequat [L], crime equalizes those whom it contaminates: *Lucan.*

facio ut des [L], lit., I do that you may give; a form of contract: *law.*

facio ut facias [L], lit., I do that you may do; a form of contract: *law.*

Facit [Ger], result; product; sum: *arith.*

facit indignatio versum [L], indignation produces verse; righteous anger flames into verse: *Juvenal.*

façon [Fr], fashion; manner; way; style. **—façon de parler,** way of speaking; manner of speech.

facta non verba [L], deeds, not words.

facteur [Fr], agent; postman; letter carrier.

factum est [L], it is done.

factura [Sp], invoice.

fac ut sciam [L], lit., make me know (*or* be aware); tell me.

fade [Fr], insipid; stale; flat; dull; pointless.

faenum habet in cornu, longe fuge [L], he has hay on his horn (the mark of a dangerous bull); stay away from him; beware of him, he is vicious: *Horace.*

faex populi [L; *pl.* faeces populi], dregs (*or* scum) of the people; the rabble: *Cicero.*

Fahlband [Ger], lit., fallow band; a zone or stratum of rock, permeated with metallic sulfides and become a rusty brown through oxidation.

faïence [Fr], glazed and painted earthenware or porcelain made esp. in France but originating in Faenza, Italy.

fainéant [Fr; *fem.* fainéante], *adj.* idle; slothful; lazy; apathetic; *n.* idler; do-nothing; sluggard.

fainéantise [Fr], idleness; sloth.

faire accueil [Fr], to welcome; *com.,* to meet, as a bill; honor, as a draft.

faire antichambre [Fr], to dance attendance.

faire bonne mine [Fr], to put a good face on it; give a good reception to.

faire claquer son fouet [Fr], lit., to crack one's own whip; sound one's own trumpet; blow one's own horn.

faire des frais [Fr], to incur expenses.

faire des siennes [Fr], to be at one's old tricks; play pranks.

faire du feu [Fr], to light a fire.

faire école [Fr], to found a school or sect.

faire faux bond [Fr], to fail to meet an appointment.

faire feu [Fr], to fire: *mil.*

faire l'amant [Fr], to act the lover.

faire l'amende honorable [Fr], to make amends; apologize.

faire la moue [Fr], to pout.

faire la noce [Fr], to go on a spree.

faire la sourde oreille [Fr], to turn a deaf ear.

faire l'école buissonnière [Fr], to play truant; play hooky.

faire le diable à quatre [Fr], to play the devil; play all kinds of tricks.

faire le malade [Fr], to feign sickness; malinger.

faire le pied de grue [Fr], to stand on one leg like a crane; dance attendance.

faire le possible [Fr], to do everything possible.

faire le savant [Fr], to act the learned man.

faire les yeux doux [Fr], to cast loving glances (at); ogle.

faire l'homme d'importance [Fr], to play the man of importance; put on airs; presume.

faire l'ingénu (*or, fem.,* **ingénue**) [Fr], to affect simplicity.

faire mon devoir [Fr], to do my duty.

faire pattes de velours [Fr], to draw in one's claws; fig., to cajole; flatter.

faire ripaille *or* **faire bombance** [Fr], to feast; junket; live sumptuously.

faire sa malle [Fr], to pack one's trunk; pack up.

faire sans dire [Fr], to act without talking; act unostentatiously.

faire ses choux gras [Fr], lit., to make one's cabbages fat; make a profit; feather one's nest.

faire ses frais [Fr], to cover one's expenses.

faire ses paquettes [Fr], to pack up one's traps; pack up.

faire son coup [Fr], to make one's success; succeed.

faire suivre [Fr], to be forwarded; please forward.

faire un esclandre [Fr], to make a scene; create an uproar.

faire une trouée [Fr], to make an opening; fig., to dislodge skepticism; break down opposition; make one's point.

faire un impair [Fr], to make a tactless blunder in conversation.

faire un trou à la lune [Fr], lit., to make a hole in the moon; flee one's creditors; decamp; skip town.

faire venir l'eau à la bouche [Fr], to make the mouth water.

faisan [Fr; *fem.* faisane], pheasant.

fais ce que dois, advienne que pourra [Fr], do your duty, come what may.

fait accompli [Fr], an accomplished fact; a thing already done.

fait à peindre [Fr], lit., made to paint; pretty as a picture.

fakir [Hind & Ar; *pr.* fa-kēr], Muslim religious mendicant: *India.* Cf. SANNYASI.

falando no diabo, ele aparece [Pg], speaking about the devil, he appears.

falda [Sp], side of a hill or mountain; skirt.

faldetta [It], hooded cape worn by women: *Malta.*

falla [Sp], fissure; open fault: *geol.*

fallacia consequentis [L], fallacy of the consequent; *non sequitur: logic.*

fallentis semita vitae [L], the narrow path of an unnoticed life: *Horace.*

falsa lectio [L; *pl.* falsae lectiones], an erroneous reading.

falsi crimen [L], the crime of falsification: *law.*

falsus in uno, falsus in omnibus [L], false in one thing, false in everything.

faltóle lo mejor, que es la ventura [Sp], he lacked the best of all—good luck.

fama clamosa [L], noisy rumor; current scandal.

fama malum quo non aliud velocius ullum [L], rumor is an evil than which there is nothing swifter: *Virgil.*

famam extendere factis [L], to spread abroad his fame by deeds: *Virgil.*

fama nihil est celerius [L], nothing is swifter than rumor.

fama semper vivat! [L], may his (*or* her) fame live forever!

fama volat [L], the report flies: *Virgil.*

fanatico [It; *pl.* fanatici], fanatic; visionary.

fanático [Sp], sports fan; enthusiast.

fanega [Sp], in Spain and Spanish America, a dry measure equal to about 1.5 bushels; also, a Spanish land measure equal to about 1.6 acres.

fango [Sp], mud; mire.

fantaisiste [Fr], *adj.* fanciful; whimsical; capricious; imaginative; *n.* a writer or artist who obeys only the caprices of his imagination.

fantoccino [It; *pl.* fantoccini], doll; puppet; marionette; also, simpleton.

farallon [Sp; *pl.* farallones], rocky islet, usually found in groups, as in the *Farallon Islands,* or *Farallones,* off the coast of California.

far almanacchi [It], lit., to make calendars; build castles in the air.

farandole [Fr], a rapid Provençal dance, in which a large number take part.

farash [Hind & Ar], a servant who attends to the carpets and mats; also, one who sweeps an office. Spelled *ferrash* by Fitzgerald.

> 'Tis but a Tent where takes his one day's rest
> A Sultan to the realm of Death addrest;
>   The Sultan rises, and the dark *Ferrash*
> Strikes, and prepares it for another Guest.
>   *—Rubaiyat of Omar Khayyám* (tr. by Fitzgerald).

farce [Fr], forcemeat: *cookery.*

farceur [Fr; *fem.* farceuse], joker; jester; wag; practical joker; also, a farce writer or player.

fardé [Fr; *fem.* fardée], painted, as the face; rouged; fig., given a false brilliance; glossed over; dissimulated; disguised.

fari quae sentiat [L], to say what one feels (*or* thinks): *Horace.*

far niente [It], doing nothing.

farouche [Fr], wild; fierce; intractable; *colloq.,* unsociable; shy. **—regard farouche,** fierce look.

farrago libelli [L], the medley of that little book of mine: *Juvenal.*

Fascio [It; *pl.* Fasci], lit., a bundle; group; specif., a local branch of *Fascisti.*

Fascismo [It; *pl.* Fascismi], a nationalistic and antiradical movement begun in Italy in 1919.

Fascista [It; *pl.* Fascisti], member of an Italian antiradical organization established in 1919; member of the *Fascismo;* Fascist.

fas est ab hoste doceri [L], it is permissible to learn even from an enemy: *Ovid.*

faste [Fr], pomp; show; ostentation.

fasti [L; *pl.*], calendar of events; annals.

fasti et nefasti dies [L], lucky and unlucky days.

fastoso [It], pompous; stately: *music.*

Fata obstant [L], the Fates oppose: *Virgil.*

Fata viam invenient [L], the Fates will find a way: *Virgil.*

Fata volentem ducunt, nolentem trahunt [L], the Fates lead the willing and drag the reluctant.

fatihah [Ar], lit., beginning or opening; the opening chapter of the Koran: (used as a prayer, esp. for the dying): *Islam.*

fatras [Fr], medley; jumble; farrago; trash.

fatti maschi, parole femmine [It], deeds (are) manly, words womanly: one of the mottoes of *Maryland.*

faubourg [Fr], suburb; outskirt.

faujdar [Hind & Pers], orig., a commander of a body of troops; under the Moguls, an officer with police and magisterial powers; under the

British, chief of police; in some parts of India, a village constable: *India.*

fausse tortue [Fr], mock turtle: *cookery.*

faute [Fr], fault; imperfection; mistake; also, lack; want. —**faute de mieux,** for want of something better. —**sans faute,** without fail.

fauteuil [Fr], armchair; theater stall.

faux [Fr; *fem.* fausse], false; erroneous; wrong; sham. —**faux brave,** swaggerer; braggart. —**faux feu,** flash in the pan. —**faux frais,** incidental expenses. —**faux jour,** false light; *arch.,* borrowed light. —**faux pas,** false step; slip in behavior; social indiscretion.

favete linguis [L], lit., favor with your tongues (i.e., utter no ill-omened word to mar the religious rite); be silent: *Horace.*

fax mentis incendium gloriae [L], the passion for glory is the torch of the mind.

faze bem, não cates a quem [Pg], do good, never mind to whom.

fecit [L; *pl.* fecerunt], lit., he (*or* she) made (it): appended to the artist's name on a picture; *abbr.* fec., *pl.* ff.

fedaya [Ar; *pl.* fedayeen *or* fedayin], member of Arab anti-Israel organization.

Feiertag [Ger; *pl.* Feiertage], holiday.

felice ritorno! [It], happy return!

felicitas multos habet amicos [L], happiness (*or* prosperity) has many friends.

feliciter [L], happily; fortunately.

felix culpa! [L], O fault most fortunate!: *St. Augustine* (alluding to the fall of our first parents, and the consequent coming of the Redeemer).

felix qui potuit rerum cognoscere causas [L], happy is he who has been able to penetrate into the causes of things: *Virgil.*

fellah [Ar; *pl.* fellahin], peasant; cultivator.

felo-de-se [LL; *pl.* felos-de-se], a committer of felony by self-murder; self-murderer; also, self-murder; suicide: *law.*

femme [Fr; *pl.* femmes], woman; wife. —**femme célibataire,** unmarried woman. —**femme couverte** *or* **femme mariée,** married woman: *law.* —**femme de chambre,** lady's maid; chambermaid. —**femme de charge,** housekeeper. —**femme de journée,** a cleaning woman. —**femme galante,** prostitute; courtesan. —**femme incomprise,** a woman unappreciated or not understood. —**femme sage,** a virtuous woman. —**femme savante,** a learned woman; a woman of literary interests.

fendre un cheveu en quatre [Fr], to split a hair into four; make overly subtle distinctions.

fendu [Fr; *fem.* fendue], lit., split; cut open; slashed: said of a style of dress decoration. —**bien fendu,** long-legged.

fenouil [Fr], fennel.

ferae naturae [L], of a wild nature; not domesticated.

feria [Sp], a fair; fiesta.

fermage [Fr], the farming of land leased for a fixed rent; tenant farming. Cf. MÉTAYAGE.

fermata [It], the pause (⌒): *music*.

fermatevi! [It], stop!

ferme [Fr], farm; farmstead. —**ferme école,** agricultural school. —**ferme modèle,** model farm. —**ferme ornée,** a fancy or model farm.

fermeté [Fr], firmness; stability.

fermier [Fr], tenant farmer.

ferrocarril [Sp], railroad; railway. —**por ferrocarril,** by rail.

ferrovia [It], railroad; railway.

ferrum ferro acuitur [L], iron is sharpened by iron.

fertig [Ger], ready; prepared; skillful; accomplished.

Fertigkeit [Ger], skill; dexterity; *music,* skill in execution; technical accomplishment.

fervens difficili bile tumet iecur [L], my hot passion (lit., liver, the seat of the passions) swells with savage wrath: *Horace*.

fervet olla, vivit amicitia [L], while the pot boils, friendship lives (*or* endures).

fervet opus [L], the work boils (*or* is carried on briskly): *Virgil*.

Fervidor [Fr]. See THERMIDOR.

fessus viator [L], a weary traveler.

festa [It; *pl.* feste], holiday; feast; festival; *fête*.

festina lente [L], make haste slowly: attributed to the emperor Augustus by *Suetonius*.

festivamente [It], in a gay manner: *music*.

fête [Fr], festival; feast day. —**fête champêtre,** outdoor *fête*. —**Fête-Dieu,** feast of Corpus Christi.

fêté [Fr; *fem.* fêtée], well entertained.

feu [Fr; *fem.* feue], *adj.* late; deceased.

feu [Fr; *pl.* feux], *n.* fire. —**feu de joie,** lit., fire of joy; a firing of guns at a time of public rejoicing; salute; also, bonfire. —**feu d'enfer,** lit., fire of hell; a scathing fire. —**feux d'artifice,** an exhibition of fireworks.

Feuer [Ger], fire; passion; ardor.

feuerig *or* **feurig** [Ger], fiery; passionate; ardent.

feuille [Fr], leaf; *typog.,* sheet, as of paper.

feuille-morte [Fr], of the color of a dead leaf; pale yellow or yellowish brown.

feuillet [Fr], leaf (i.e., two pages). —**feuillet blanc,** blank leaf: *both typog*.

feuilleton [Fr], a ruled-off section at the foot of a French newspaper, devoted to fiction, criticism, etc.; also a serial.

fève [Fr], bean. —**fève de marais,** broad bean.

fiacco [It], feeble; weak; languishing.

fiacre [Fr], hackney coach; cab.

fiancé [Fr; *fem.* fiancée], a betrothed.

fiaschetta [It], a little flask or bottle.

fiat Dei voluntas [L], God's will be done.

fiat experimentum in corpore vili [L], let the experiment be made upon a worthless body (*or* object).

fiat haustus [L], let a draft be made: *abbr.* (*in prescriptions*) ft. haust.

fiat iustitia, ruat caelum [L], let justice be done, though the heavens fall.

fiat lux [L], let there be light: *Vulgate* (*Genesis* i. 3).

fiat mistura [L], let a mixture be made: *abbr.* (*in prescriptions*) ft. mist.

fiato [It], breath; respiration. **—stromenti da fiato,** wind instruments: *music.*

fiat voluntas tua [L], Thy will be done: *Vulgate* (*Matthew* vi. 10).

ficelle [Fr], packthread; twine; hence, of the color of pack thread.

ficta voluptatis causa sint proxima veris [L], fictions if they are to please should bear the semblance of truth: *Horace.*

fictilia [L], pottery.

fictilis [L], made of pottery: *abbr.* fict.

fidalgo [Pg], Portuguese noble, corresponding to Spanish *hidalgo.*

fide et amore [L], by faith and love.

fide et fiducia [L], by fidelity and confidence.

fide et fortitudine [L], by fidelity and fortitude.

fidei coticula crux [L], the cross is the touchstone of faith.

fidei defensor [L], Defender of the Faith (a title of the monarchs of England): *abbr.* F.D. *or* fid. def.

fideli certa merces [L], to the faithful one, reward is sure.

fidelis ad urnam [L], lit., faithful to the urn; true till death.

fidélité est de Dieu [Fr], fidelity is of God.

fideliter [L], faithfully.

fide, non armis [L], by faith, not by arms.

fides ante intellectum [L], faith before understanding.

fide, sed cui vide [L], trust, but take care whom.

fides et iustitia [L], fidelity and justice.

fides facit fidem [L], faith creates faith; confidence begets confidence.

fides non timet [L], faith does not fear.

fides probata coronat [L], approved faith confers a crown.

fides Punica [L], Punic faith; treachery.

fides servanda est [L], faith must be kept.

fi donc! [Fr], fie! for shame!

fidus Achates [L], faithful Achates; hence, a trusted friend; devoted follower: *Virgil.*

fidus et audax [L], faithful and courageous.

fiel pero desdichado [Sp], faithful but unlucky.

fier [Fr; *fem.* fière], proud; haughty.

fieramente [It], ferociously; haughtily: *music.*

fieri facias [L], lit., cause it to be done; a writ commanding the sheriff to execute judgment: *abbr.* fi.fa.

fiesta [Sp], religious festival; feast; festivity; fair; holiday.

figlia [It; *pl.* figlie], daughter.

figlio [It; *pl.* figli], son.

figurant [Fr; *fem.* figurante], ballet dancer; also, a supernumerary actor; super.

filar la voce *or* **filar il suono** [It], to spin out or prolong a tone, usually with a gradual increase and decrease of force: *music.*

filer à l'anglaise [Fr], to slip away unnoticed; take French leave; skip town.

filet [Fr], fillet: *cookery.*

filho [Pg; *pl.* filhos], son. —**filhos casados, cuidados dobrados,** married children, double cares.

filius [L; *pl.* filii], son. —**filius nullius,** a son of nobody; a bastard. —**filius populi,** lit., son of the people; a bastard. —**filius terrae,** a son of the earth; man of low origin.

fille [Fr; *pl.* filles], daughter; girl; maid. —**fille de chambre,** chambermaid; formerly also, lady's maid (z*femme de chambre*). —**fille de joie,** prostitute; courtesan. —**fille d'honneur,** maid of honor.

filon [Fr], mineral vein; lode: *geol.*

fils [Fr], son: often used after a French surname to distinguish son from father. Cf. PÈRE.

filum [L; *pl.* fila], a thread; filament; filar structure.

fin [Fr], end; termination; close. —**fin de siècle,** lit., end of century; characteristic of the close of the 19th century; ultramodern; advanced.

finca [Sp], fixed property; real estate; plantation; as, a coffee *finca: Sp. Am.*

fine [It], the end; finish (*abbr.* fin): *music.*

fine épice [Fr], sharp-witted fellow.

finem respice [L], consider (*or* have regard for) the end (*or* outcome).

finis coronat opus [L], the end crowns the work.

finjan [Ar], Oriental coffee cup, without handle.

fiochetto [It], somewhat hoarse.

fiochezza [It], hoarseness.

fioco [It], hoarse; dim; faint: *music.*

fioreggiante [It], in a florid style: *music.*

fiorito [It], flowery; florid: *music.*

fioritura [It; *pl.* fioriture], lit., flowering; melodic ornaments introduced into a composition; flourishes: *music.*

firma [Sp], signature.

firme [Sp], pavement; roadway of a bridge: *engin.*

fit via vi [L], a way is made by force.

fiumara [It], torrent; also, bed of a stream.

fiume torbo guadagno de' pescatori [It], a troubled stream is the fisherman's gain.

fixe! [Fr], eyes front!: *mil.*

fjord [Norw], sea inlet between high cliffs.

flacon [Fr], flask; phial. **—flacon d'odeur,** scent bottle.

flagrante bello [L], lit., while the war is blazing; during hostilities.

flagrante delicto [L], lit., while the crime is blazing; in the very act; red-handed.

flair [Fr], keen sense of smell; scent, as of a hunting dog; fig., intuitive perception; instinctive sense of discrimination; keen critical discernment.

flak [Ger], anti-aircraft fire; from German *Fliegerabwehrkanone* (anti-aircraft gun); *colloq.,* excessive criticism.

flambé [Fr; *fem.* flambée], lit., singed; set afire; ruined; done for; undone.

flamenco [Sp], a Spanish dance.

flamma fumo est proxima [L], flame is very close to smoke; where there's smoke, there's fire: *Plautus.*

Flammenwerfer [Ger], flame thrower: *mil.*

flan [Sp], custard.

flânerie [Fr], lounging; loafing; aimlessness.

flâneur [Fr; *fem.* flâneuse], lounger; idler.

flatteur [Fr; *fem.* flatteuse], *adj.* flattering; gratifying; *n.* flatterer.

flebile [It], plaintive; mournful: *music.*

flebile ludibrium [L], a lamentable mockery; tragic farce.

flebilmente [It], dolefully; mournfully: *music.*

flèche [Fr], lit., arrow; *arch.,* slender spire, esp. at the intersection of the nave and transepts of a church; *fort.,* a kind of redan. **—en flèche,** tandem: *driving.*

fléchette [Fr], small arrow or dart; *mil.,* a small steel dart (encased in an explosive projectile) to be dropped from an airplane in warfare.

flectere si nequeo superos, Acheronta movebo [L], if heaven I cannot bend, then hell I'll stir: *Virgil.*

flecti, non frangi [L], to be bent, not broken.

flétri [Fr; *fem.* flétrie], withered; faded; tarnished.

fleur [Fr], flower. **—à fleur d'eau,** at water level; level with the water. **—à fleur de terre,** level with the ground. **—fleur-de-lis** [*pl.* fleurs-de-lis], lily flower; iris; *her.,* heraldic lily, emblem of the royal family of France.

fleuret [Fr], fencing foil.

fleurette [Fr], little flower; floweret; *colloq.,* gallant speech; amorous nonsense.

fleuron [Fr], in ornamental art, a conventional flower design; floral ornament; flower work.

fliegende Blätter [Ger], lit., flying leaves; flyleaves; pamphlets; occasional papers.

Fliegenkopf [Ger; *pl.* Fliegenköpfe], turned letter: *typog.*

flingot [Fr], gun; rifle: *Fr. mil. slang.*

floración [Sp], outcrop: *geol.*

Floréal [Fr], in the Revolutionary calendar of the first French Republic, the eighth month of the year, from April 20 to May 19.

floreat [L], may (it) flourish. —**floreat Etona,** may Eton flourish: motto of *Eton College.*

flores [L], flowers: *abbr.* fl. —**flores curat Deus,** God takes care of the flowers.

floruit [L], flourished: *abbr.* fl. *or* flor.

flosculi sententiarum [L], flowerets of thought.

fluctuat nec mergitur [L], she is tossed by the waves but she does not sink: motto of *Paris,* which has a ship as its emblem.

Flügelhorn [Ger], bugle horn; bugle.

fluidus [L], liquid; fluid.

flux [Fr], a flow; flux; *cards,* a flush. —**flux de bouche,** salivation; also, flow of words; loquacity. —**flux de mots** (*or* **paroles**), flow of words.

focosamente [It], in a fiery manner; vehemently: *music.*

focoso [It], fiery; passionate: *music.*

Föhn *or* **Foehn** [Ger], Alpine south wind.

foie [Fr], liver. —**foie de veau,** calf's liver. —**foie gras,** fattened liver, esp. goose liver.

foi en tout [Fr], faith in everything.

folâtre [Fr], frolicsome; playful; wanton.

folio verso [L], on the back of the page: *abbr.* f.v.

Folketing [Dan], lower house of the Danish legislature.

fonctionnaire [Fr], functionary; public official.

fonda [Sp], hotel; inn; restaurant.

fondre en larmes [Fr], to burst into tears; dissolve in tears.

fondue [Fr], dish of melted cheese, eggs, etc.: *cookery.*

fons et origo [L], the source and origin.

fons malorum [L], the fountain (*or* source) of evils.

fontein [Du], spring of water: *South Africa.*

foramen magnum [L], lit., great opening; the passage from the cranial cavity to the spinal canal: *anat.*

forçat [Fr], criminal condemned to hard labor; galley slave; convict.

force majeure [Fr], superior force; irresistible compulsion.

forcené [Fr; *fem.* forcenée], *adj.* furious; infuriated; beside oneself; mad; *n.* madman.

forensis strepitus [L], the clamor of the forum.

forma bonum fragile est [L], beauty is a transitory blessing: *Ovid.*

forma flos, fama flatus [L], beauty is a flower, fame a breath.

formez les faisceaux! [Fr], stack arms!: *mil.*

forsan et haec olim meminisse iuvabit [L], perchance some day it may be a pleasure to remember even these things (*or* sufferings): *Virgil.*

forte [It], loud: *abbr.* f. —**forte forte,** very loud: *abbr.* ff. —**forte-piano,** loud and then soft: *abbr.* fp. —**forte possible,** as loud as possible: *all music.*

forte è l'aceto de vin dolce [It], strong is the vinegar from sweet wine.

fortem posce animum [L], pray for a strong will (*or* soul): *Juvenal.*

fort en train [Fr], in high spirits; in fine fettle.

forte scutum, salus ducum [L], a strong shield is the safety of leaders.

fortes fortuna iuvat [L], fortune favors the brave.

forti et fideli nihil difficile [L], to the brave and faithful, nothing is difficult.

fortis cadere, cedere non potest [L], the brave man may fall, but cannot yield.

fortis et fidelis [L], brave and faithful.

fortissimo [It], very loud (*abbr.* ff.): *music.*

fortiter et recte [L], bravely and uprightly.

fortiter, fideliter, feliciter [L], fearlessly, faithfully, fruitfully.

fortiter geret crucem [L], he will bravely bear the cross.

fortiter in re, suaviter in modo [L], strongly (*or* courageously) in deed, gently in manner; resolute in action, but gentle in manner.

fortitudine et prudentia [L], by courage and sagacity (*or* prudence).

fortitudini [L], for bravery.

fort peu [Fr], very little.

fortunae cetera mando [L], I commit the rest to fortune.

fortunae filius [L], a child (*or* favorite) of fortune: *Horace.*

fortuna favet fatuis [L], fortune favors fools.

fortuna favet fortibus [L], fortune favors the brave.

fortuna mea in bello campo [L], lit., my fortune in a fair (beautiful) field; the fortune is mine in fair fight: punning motto of the *Beauchamp* family.

fortuna meliores sequitur [L], fortune follows the better man: *Sallust.*

fortuna multis dat nimium, nulli satis [L], to many fortune gives too much, to none enough: *Martial.*

fortuna nimium quem fovet, stultum facit [L], fortune makes a fool of him whom she favors too much: *Publilius Syrus.*

fortuna sequatur [L], let fortune follow.

forza [It], force; power; vigor: *music.*

forzando [It], lit., forcing; *music,* forced (*abbr.* fz.): same as SFORZANDO.

fossoribus orti [L], sprung from ditch diggers; of humble origin.

fossoyeur [Fr], ditchdigger; gravedigger; sexton.

fougade *or* **fougasse** [Fr], a small mine in the form of a covered well: *mil.*

foulard [Fr], scarf; square scarf.

fou qui se tait passe pour sage [Fr], the fool who holds his tongue passes for a wise man.

fourchette [Fr], fork; *Fr. mil. slang,* bayonet.

fourgon [Fr], baggage or ammunition wagon: *mil.*

fourragère [Fr], an ornamental braided cord looped under the left arm and attached to the shoulder of the uniform: *mil.*

foy est tout [OF], faith is all.

foy pour devoir [OF], faith for duty.

Fragezeichen [Ger], question mark: *typog.*

fraîcheur [Fr], freshness; coolness; chill; also, bloom; brilliance of color.

fraile [Sp], friar; monk.

frailejon [S Am Sp], a growth of tall composite plants found on the *páramos* of the Andes.

frais [Fr], expense; cost; expenses. **—faux frais,** incidental expenses.

fraise [Fr], strawberry. **—fraises des bois,** wild strawberries.

Fraktur [Ger], Gothic characters; German text: *typog.*

framboise [Fr], raspberry.

franco [It], franked; postage free: *abbr.* fco.

franc-tireur [Fr; *pl.* francs-tireurs], a French irregular light infantry soldier: *mil.*

frangas, non flectes [L], you may break, you will not bend (me).

frangin [Fr], brother; buddy: *Fr. mil. slang.*

frangine [Fr], sister; nurse; also, any woman: *Fr. mil. slang.*

frappant [Fr; *fem.* frappante], striking; impressive.

frappé [Fr], iced, frozen, or artificially chilled (said of certain beverages and fruit juices); also, a liquefied fruit mixture or the like served frozen.

frate [It; *pl.* frati], brother; friar.

frater [L; *pl.* fratres], brother.

Frau [Ger; *pl.* Frauen], married woman; wife; a German title of courtesy equivalent to *madam* or *Mrs.*

Fräulein [Ger; *sing. & pl.*], an unmarried woman; young lady; a German title of courtesy equivalent to *Miss.*

fraus est celare fraudem [L], it is fraud to conceal a fraud.

fraus pia [L], a pious fraud.

fredaine [Fr], youthful folly; prank. **—faire les fredaines,** to sow one's wild oats.

freddamente [It], coldly; with coldness: *music.*

fredonnement [Fr], humming.

fregiatura [It; *pl.* fregiature], embellishment: *music.*

Freihandel [Ger], free trade.

Freiheit ist nur in dem Reich der Träume [Ger], freedom exists only in the realm of dreams: *Schiller.*

Freiherr [Ger], lit., free lord; German or Austrian baron: *abbr.* Frhr.

Fremd [Ger; *pl.* Fremde], stranger; foreigner; also, guest. **—Fremde haben,** to have guests (*or* company).

Fremmed [Dan], stranger.

freno [Sp], bridle; brake, as of an automobile.

frérot [Fr], little brother: *familiar.*

frescamente [It], freshly; vigorously: *music.*

fresser [Yiddish], a glutton.

freudig [Ger], joyously; cheerfully: *music.*

friandise [Fr], taste for delicacies; epicurism; also, a dainty; *pl.,* sweet-meats; sweets.

Friedensbruch [Ger], breach of the peace.

Friedhof [Ger], lit., peace yard; churchyard; cemetery.

frijol *or* **frijole** [Sp; *pl.* frijoles], a cultivated bean of the genus *Phaseolus,* an important staple of food in Spanish America and southwestern U.S.

Frimaire [Fr], in the Revolutionary calendar of the first French Republic, the third month of the year, from Nov. 21 to Dec. 20.

fripier [Fr; *fem.* fripière], dealer in old clothes, furniture, etc.

fripon [Fr], knave; rogue; swindler. **—fripon fieffé,** arrant knave.

frisch [Ger], fresh; cheerful; lively: *music.*

frisch auf! [Ger], look alive! cheer up!

frisch, fromm, frei, froh [Ger], brisk, good, free, cheerful: motto of German gymnastic clubs.

frit [Fr; *fem.* frite], *cookery,* fried; *colloq.,* ruined; done for. **—tout est frit,** it's all over.

friture [Fr], frying; thing fried; fry; fried fish: *cookery.*

fröhliche Weihnachten! [Ger], Merry Christmas!

froides mains, chaud amour [Fr], cold hands, warm heart.

Frokost [Dan], breakfast.

Fronde [Fr], a political party comprising rebellious French malcontents during the minority of Louis XIV.

fronder [Fr], lit., to throw with a sling; blame; censure; find fault with.

frondeur [Fr; *fem.* frondeuse], lit., slinger; faultfinder; a member of the *Fronde* (q.v.); hence, a malcontent; rebel.

frons est animi ianua [L], the forehead is the door of the mind: *Cicero.*

front à front [Fr], face to face.

fronti nulla fides [L], there is no trusting to appearances: *Juvenal.*

frottée [Fr], a drubbing; beating: *colloq.*

frottola [It; *pl.* frottole], ballad.

frou-frou [Fr; *pl.* frou-frous], rustle or swish, as of a silk skirt. **—faire du frou-frou,** to show off.

frousse [Fr], fright; shock: *colloq.*

Fructidor [Fr], in the Revolutionary calendar of the first French Republic, the twelfth month of the year, from Aug. 18 to Sept. 21.

fructu non foliis arborem aestima [L], judge a tree by its fruit, not by its leaves: *Phaedrus.*

fruges consumere nati [L], born (merely) to consume the fruits of the earth: *Horace.*

frühe Hochzeit, lange Liebe [Ger], early marriage, long love.

Frühlingslied [Ger], spring song.

Frühschoppen [Ger], beer drunk before luncheon, esp. after a great feast the night before: *Ger. students' slang.*

Frühstuck [Ger], breakfast.

Frühzug [Ger], early train; morning train.

frusques [Fr], clothes; togs; toggery: *colloq.*

frustra laborat qui omnibus placere studet [L], he labors in vain who tries to please everybody.

fservyo charoshevo [Russ], all the best!

fuego [Sp], fire. —**en fuego,** under fire: *mil.*

fuente [Sp], fountain; spring; source.

fuero [Sp], statute law; usage having the force of law; privileges granted to a province; also, jurisdiction of a tribunal: *Sp. law.*

fuerza [Sp], force, power. —**a fuerza de,** by dint of; by means of. —**a toda fuerza,** at full speed. —**fuerza electromotriz,** electromotive force: *abbr.* f.e.m.

fuése por lana, y volvió trasquilada [Sp], she went for wool and returned shorn.

fuga [It; *pl.* fuge], a fugue: *music.*

fughetta [It], a short fugue: *music.*

fugit hora [L], the hour flies: *Ovid.*

fugit irreparabile tempus [L], irrecoverable time flies (*or* glides away): *Virgil.*

Führer *or* **Fuehrer** [Ger], leader; chief; specif., leader of the Nazis in Germany. See DER FÜHRER.

Führerschaft [Ger], leadership; direction; command.

fuimus [L], we have been. —**fuimus Troes,** we (once) were Trojans; our day is over: *Virgil.*

fuit Ilium [L], Troy was (i.e., exists no longer); its day is over: *Virgil.*

fulmen brutum [L], a senseless thunderbolt; empty threat.

fumum et opes strepitumque Romae [L], the smoke, the wealth, and the din of Rome: *Juvenal.*

functus officio [L], having performed his office; hence, resigned from office.

fundamentum iustitiae est fides [L], the foundation of justice is good faith: *Cicero.*

funzioni [It], functions; offices; religious services; Masses.

fuoco [It], fire; passion: *music.*

furiosamente [It], passionately; vehemently: *music.*

furioso [It], furious; passionate; vehement.

furor arma ministrat [L], rage supplies arms: *Virgil.*

furor loquendi [L], a rage for speaking.

furor poeticus [L], poetic frenzy.

furor scribendi [L], a rage for writing.

Fürst der Schatten [Ger], Prince of Shades; Death.

fusain [Fr], orig., the spindle tree or the charcoal made from it; *fine arts,* specially prepared charcoal; also, a charcoal drawing.

fuste [Sp], a strong wooden saddletree, covered with rawhide, as used for lassoing: *California.*

fuyez les dangers de loisir [Fr], shun the perils of leisure.

G

gaddi [Hind], cushion; throne. See GUDDEE.

gaffe [Fr], boat hook; fig., maladdress; tactless behavior; *faux pas;* gross blunder.

gage d'amour [Fr], a love pledge; love token.

gageure est la preuve des sots [Fr], a wager is a fool's argument; betting marks the fool.

gaiamente [It], gaily; merrily: *music.*

gaiement [Fr], gaily; blithely; merrily.

gaieté de cœur [Fr], gaiety of heart; lightheartedness; flow of spirits.

gaku [Jap], a Japanese framed picture; ornamental panel.

gál [Wolof], boat: *West Africa.*

galantemente [It], gallantly; pleasingly; gracefully: *music.*

galant homme [Fr], man of honor.

galantuomo [It], man of honor; gentleman.

galbe [Fr], outline; outward form; conformation: *fine arts.*

galimatias [Fr], confused talk; gibberish.

Gallice [L], lit., in Gaulish; in French.

gamache [Fr], a kind of leather legging, worn in the 16th century.

gambade [Fr], skip; gambol; antic; fig., blarney.

γαμεῖν ὁ μέλλων εἰς μετάνοιαν ἔρχεται [Gr; gameîn ho méllōn eis metánoian érkhetai], he who is about to marry is on the road to repentance.

γάμος γὰρ ἀνθρώποισι εὐκταῖον κακόν [Gr; gámos gàr anthrṓpoisi euktaîon kakón], marriage is an evil that most men welcome: *Menander.*

ganado [Sp], cattle; flock; herd.

gancho [Sp], lit., a hook or crook; a crooked branding iron: *southwestern U.S.*

Gänsefüsschen [Ger], lit., goose feet; quotation marks: *typog.*

garbure [Fr], a soup of Gascon origin, made of cabbage and other vegetables, with slices of bread, ham, salt pork, etc., and often grated cheese. When made with meat, it is called *garbure au gras;* when without meat, *garbure au maigre: cookery.*

garçon [Fr], boy; lad; youth; bachelor; waiter; servant. —**en garçon,** as a bachelor. —**garçon d'honneur,** best man (at a wedding).

garçonnière [Fr], bachelor's apartment.

garde [Fr], guard; guardsman. —**garde à cheval,** mounted guard. —**garde champêtre** [*pl.* gardes champêtres], rural guard. —**garde de nuit,** night watchman; watchman. —**garde du corps,** bodyguard. —**garde mobile,** French militia.

garde à vous! [Fr], attention!: *mil.*

garde-chasse [Fr; *pl.* gardes-chasse *or* gardes-chasses], gamekeeper.

garde-côte [Fr; *pl.* garde-côtes *or* gardes-côtes], coast guard.

garde-feu [Fr; *pl.* garde-feu *or* garde-feux], fire guard; fender; fire screen.

garde-fou [Fr; *pl.* garde-fous], parapet; railing; handrail.

garde-port [Fr; *pl.* gardes-port *or* gardes-ports], harbor master.

gardez bien [Fr], take good care.

gardez la foi [Fr], keep the faith.

gare [Fr], railway station; also platform. —**chef de gare,** station master. —**gare d'arrivée,** arrival platform. —**gare de départ,** departure platform.

gare! [Fr], take care! look out! —**gare de là!,** clear the way there!

gari [Hind]. See GHARRY.

gariwala [Hind]. See GHARRY WALLAH.

gark [Armen], a carriage.

garm [Hind], hot; warm: *India.*

garnement [Fr], a good-for-nothing; scamp; scapegrace. Cf. VAURIEN.

garni [Fr; *fem.* garnie], furnished. —**chambres garnies,** furnished apartments.

gasconnade [Fr], boasting; bragging; braggadocio: so called from *gascon,* a native of Gascony, proverbial home of braggarts.

gaspillé [Fr; *fem.* gaspillée], squandered; frittered away.

Gasthaus [Ger; *pl.* Gasthäuser], restaurant; inn.

Gasthof [Ger; *pl.* Gasthöfe], hotel; inn.

gâté [Fr; *fem.* gâtée], spoiled. —**enfant gâté,** spoiled child.

gâteau [Fr; *pl.* gâteaux], a cake. —**partager le gâteau,** lit., to share the cake; go halves.

gâterie [Fr], pampering, as of a child; excessive indulgence.

gâte-sauce [Fr], lit., a spoil-sauce; a bad cook.

gato [Sp; *fem.* gata], cat.

gato escaldado de água fria tem mêdo [Pg], a scalded cat is afraid of cold water.

gato que duerme no caza ratón [Sp], the sleeping cat doesn't catch a mouse.

Gau [Ger; *pl.* Gaue], district; county; stretch of country.

gauche [Fr], lit, left; clumsy; awkward, esp. in society; tactless.

gaucherie [Fr], awkwardness; uncouth manners; tactlessness; social blunder.

gaucho [Sp], cowboy: *Argentina.*

gaudeamus igitur [L], let us then be joyful.

gaudet tentamine virtus [L], virtue rejoices in trial.

gaudioso [It], joyous; merry: *music.*

gaudium certaminis [L], delight of battle.

gavage [Fr], forced feeding or fattening, as of poultry.

gavroche [Fr], street arab; gamin: from *Gavroche,* a Parisian gamin in Victor Hugo's *Les Misérables.*

Gebirg [Ger; *pl.* Gebirge], mountain; mountain chain.

geboren [Ger], born: *abbr.* geb.

gebranntes Kind scheut das Feuer [Ger], a burned child fears the fire.

Gebraucht der Zeit! sie geht so schnell von hinnen; doch Ordnung lehrt euch Zeit gewinnen [Ger],

> Use then each hour—fast, fast they glide away;
> But learn, through Order, Time's swift flight to stay.
> —GOETHE.

Gebrüder [Ger], brothers: *abbr.* Gbr. *or* Geb.

gedämpft [Ger], muffled; muted: *music.*

Gedicht [Ger; *pl.* Gedichte], poem.

geflügelte Worte [Ger], winged words. Cf. ἔπεα πτερόεντα (épea pteróenta).

Gefühl [Ger], feeling; sentiment; *music,* expression.

gehend [Ger], at a walking pace; andante: *music.*

geisha [Jap], lit., art person; a young woman trained to entertain and provide company for men: *Japan.*

Geist [Ger], spirit; animating principle.

geistig [Ger], spiritual; intellectual; witty.

geläufig [Ger], fluent; voluble; facile.

Geld oder Tod [Ger], lit., money or death; your money or your life.

Geld regiert die Welt [Ger], money rules the world.

gelée [Fr], frost; *cookery,* jelly. **—gelée de groseille,** currant jelly.

Gelehrten-verein [Ger], a literary society or club.

γέλως ἄκαιρος ἐν βροτοῖς δεινὸν κακόν [Gr; gélōs ákairos en brotoîs deinòn kakón], ill-timed laughter in mortals is a grievous evil: *Menander.*

gemach [Ger], comfortable; easy. **—gemach!,** stop! hold on! easy there! not so fast!

gemütlich [Ger], good-natured; kindly.

Gemütlichkeit [Ger], good nature; kindliness; cordiality; easygoing disposition; freedom from financial worries.

gendarme [Fr], a soldier employed as a policeman, esp. in France.

gendarmerie [Fr], force of gendarmes; constabulary.

génépi [Fr], a sweet absinthe, made from alpine wormwood.

generalia [L], general principles.

géneros [Sp], goods; commodities.

genius loci [L; *pl.* genii loci], the genius (*or* presiding deity) of a place.

genre [Fr], kind; sort; species; style; *fine arts,* portrayal of scenes from everyday life. **—de bon genre,** gentlemanly; ladylike. **—de mauvais genre,** ungentlemanly; unladylike.

gens [Fr], people; persons; domestics; nations. **—gens d'affaires,** business people. **—gens d'armes,** men at arms: *hist.* **—gens de condition,** people of rank. **—gens d'église,** clergymen; churchmen. **—gens de**

guerre, military men. **—gens de lettres,** writers; literary people. **—gens de loi,** lawyers. **—gens de maison,** domestic servants. **—gens de même famille,** people of the same family; birds of a feather. **—gens de mer,** seafaring men; mariners; sailors. **—gens de peu,** people of small account; the lower classes. **—gens de robe,** attorneys; magistrates. **—gens du monde,** people of fashion. **—les petites gens,** humble folk.

gens togata [L], the togaed nation; Roman citizens; hence, civilians generally: *Virgil.*

gentile [It], graceful; delicate: *music.*

gentilhomme [Fr; *pl.* gentilshommes], nobleman; gentleman; squire. **—gentilhomme à lièvre,** small country squire.

genus est mortis male vivere [L], to live evilly (*or* an evil life) is a kind of death: *Ovid.*

genus irritabile vatum [L], the irritable race (*or* tribe) of poets; "those wasplike creatures, our poetic bees": *Horace* (tr. by Conington).

gerade aus! [Ger], straight on!

gérance [Fr], management; managership; editorship.

gérant [Fr], business manager; managing editor.

geratewohl [Ger], haphazard.

Germinal [Fr], in the Revolutionary calendar of the first French Republic, the seventh month of the year, from March 21 to April 19.

gesagt, getan [Ger], said, done; no sooner said than done.

Gesang [Ger; *pl.* Gesänge], singing; song; melody; lay.

geschäftiger Müssiggang [Ger], busy idleness.

Geschichte [Ger], history: *abbr.* Gesch.

Geschlecht [Ger; *pl.* Geschlechter], species; sex.

Gesellschaft [Ger], company; society; association: *abbr.* Ges.

Gesetz ist mächtig, mächtiger ist die Not [Ger], law is mighty, necessity is mightier: *Goethe.*

gesso [It], lit., plaster; chalk; *fine arts,* a prepared surface of plaster of Paris or other material, as a ground for painting.

Gestalt [Ger], a unified configuration with properties that cannot be derived from its components.

Gestapo [Ger], secret police of the Nazi regime in Germany, from the first syllables of *Geheime Staats-Polizei.*

gestorben [Ger], deceased: *abbr.* gest.

Gesundheit! [Ger], to your health! (a toast); also, an exclamation to a person sneezing, short for *Gesundheit ist besser als Krankheit,* health is better than sickness.

geta [Jap], a wooden sandal, mounted on two high crosspieces, used by the Japanese when roads are wet and muddy.

geteilte Freude ist doppelt Freude [Ger], a joy shared is a joy doubled: *Goethe.*

Gewehre wegwerfen! [Ger], throw down your arms!: *mil.*

gharry *or* **gari** [Anglo-Ind; Hind *gārī*], a carriage or cart (a generic name in India for any vehicle drawn by horse or bullock).

gharry-wallah *or* **gariwala** [Anglo-Ind], driver of a gharry; hackney driver.

ghat *or* **ghaut** [Anglo-Ind], mountain pass; also, flight of steps leading down to a river; landing place; *pl.* either of two mountain ranges in India (*Eastern Ghats* and *Western Ghats*).

ghawazi [Ar], public dancer: *Egypt.*

ghazal [Ar], Oriental love lyric.

ghazi [Ar], a Muslim champion or slayer of infidels.

ghee *or* **ghi** [Anglo-Ind], a semiliquid butter clarified by boiling.

ghiribizzo [It; *pl.* ghiribizzi], whim; caprice; fancy.

ghiribizzoso [It], whimsical; capricious: *music.*

ghurry [Anglo-Ind; Hind *gharī*], among the Hindus, a measure of time equal to the sixtieth part of a day (24 minutes); among Anglo-Indians, an hour; by extension, a water clock; also, a gong on which the hours are struck; hence, a watch; clock.

ghusl [Hind], bath: *India.*

giallo antico [It], lit., ancient yellow; a rich yellow marble found among ancient Italian ruins.

gibelotte [Fr], rabbit stew: *cookery.*

gibier [Fr], game. —**gibier à plume,** feathered game. —**gibier de potence,** jailbird; gallows bird. —**menu gibier,** small game.

gigot [Fr], leg of mutton: *cookery.* —**gigots,** hind legs of a horse.

gin-zaiku [Jap], silverware: *Japan.*

giochevole [It], playful; jocose; merry: *music.*

giocondo [It], playful; gay; joyous: *music.*

giocoso [It], gay; lively; mirthful; playful: *music.*

giovane ozioso, vecchio bisognoso [It], a lazy young man, a needy old one.

giovane santo, diavolo vecchio [It], a young saint, an old devil.

giovanezza [It], youth.

gioviale [It], jovial; gay: *music.*

giro [Sp], draft; money order. —**giro postal,** postal money order.

girouette [Fr], weathercock; fig., timeserver; timeserving politician.

gitano [Sp; *fem.* gitana], a gypsy.

gîte [Fr], stopping place; refuge; shelter, as in mountaineering; home.

giuoco di mano, giuoco di villano [It], practical jokes are the jokes of boors; horseplay is roughs' play.

giustamente [It], exactly; with precision: *music.*

giusto [It], in exact or appropriate time: *music.*

glace [Fr], ice; ice cream.

glacé [Fr], smooth; polished; highly polished; *cookery,* iced; glazed; frosted (said of fruit, cakes, etc.).

glacière [Fr], ice cave; ice house; also, refrigerator.

glänzendes Elend [Ger], glittering pauperism.

glasnost' [Russ], lit., publicity; increased openness to criticism.

glaube dem Leben [Ger], have faith in life.

γλαῦκας εἰς 'Αθήνας [Gr; glaûkas eis Athénas], owls to Athens; coals to Newcastle.

glebae ascriptus [L], attached to the soil.

gli assenti hanno torto [It], the absent are (always) in the wrong.

glissando [It], in a gliding manner: *music*.

glissant [Fr; *fem.* glissante], slippery; fig., ticklish; delicate; precarious. —**pas glissant,** dangerous step; ticklish affair.

Glocke [Ger; *pl.* Glocken], bell.

Glockenspiel [Ger], lit., play of bells; chimes; carillon.

Gloria [L], Glory: the first word in certain doxologies. —**Gloria in Excelsis (Deo),** Glory be (to God) on high (*Luke* ii. 14): the "greater doxology." —**Gloria Patri,** Glory be to the Father: the "lesser doxology." —**Gloria Tibi, Domine,** Glory be to Thee, O Lord.

gloria virtutis umbra [L], glory is the shadow of virtue.

Glück auf den Weg [Ger], good luck on the way; a pleasant journey to you!

Glück auf! Glück zu! viel Glück! [Ger], good luck! God speed!

glückliche Reise! [Ger], a prosperous journey! *bon voyage!*

Glück und Glas, wie bald bricht das [Ger], lit., luck and glass, how soon it breaks; glass and luck, brittle muck.

glupi nie posiwieje [Pol], a fool's head never grows gray.

γνῶθι σεαυτόν [Gr; gnôthi seautón], know thyself: inscribed over the entrance of the temple of Apollo at Delphi.

gobe-mouches [Fr], flycatcher (bird); fig., one who swallows anything; credulous person; simpleton.

godiveau [Fr], a kind of forcemeat ball: *cookery*.

goguette [Fr], a singing society, usually meeting in a tavern; free-and-easy party; hence, mirth; merry mood. —**être en goguette,** to be in a convivial mood; be on a spree.

goma [Sp], gum; India rubber. —**goma laca,** shellac.

gommeux [Fr], fop; swell; man about town.

gonif [Yiddish], a crook; an untrustworthy person; a clever person.

goon [Hind *gunda*], hired thug.

gora [Hind], fair-complexioned, hence, Caucasian, esp. of inferior rank; specif., European soldier: *India*.

górdym protivitsya Bóg [Russ], God opposes the haughty ones.

gorge-de-pigeon [Fr], iridescent, like the throat of a pigeon; shot, as silk.

gorgheggio [It; *pl.* gorgheggi], trill; florid passage: *music*.

gorgio [Romany], gypsy name for a non-gypsy.

górod [Russ], city; town: common in place names.

gospodar [Russ], gentlemen.

gospodin [Russ; *fem.* gospozha], lord; master; gentleman; a Russian title of courtesy equivalent to *Sir* or *Mr.*

gosse [Fr], urchin; brat; youngster: *colloq.*

gostínnitsa [Russ], hotel.

Gott bewahre! [Ger], God forbid!

Gott mit uns [Ger], God with us: motto of the *Order of the Crown,* Prussia.

Gott sei dank! [Ger], thank God!

Gott will es [Ger], God wills it: Crusaders' cry.

gouache [Fr], method of painting with opaque colors, ground in water and mixed with gum, honey, etc.; also, a painting done by this method: *fine arts.*

gourmand [Fr; *fem.* gourmande], excessive eater; glutton.

gourmandise [Fr], excessive love of eating; gluttony.

gourmet [Fr], a connoisseur of food and wines; epicure.

goût [Fr], taste; relish. **—goût raffiné,** refined taste.

goûter [Fr], *n.* a snack; *v.t.* to taste.

goutte [Fr], a drop; small quantity; dram; *med.*, gout. **—goutte à goutte,** drop by drop. **—payer la goutte,** to stand a drink.

gouvernante [Fr], governor's wife; also, governess.

gouverneur [Fr], governor; ruler.

goy [Yiddish; *pl.* goyim], a Gentile.

grâce à Dieu [Fr], thanks to God.

gracias [Sp], thanks.

gracias a Dios [Sp], thanks to God.

gradatim [L], step by step; gradually. **—gradatim vincimus,** we conquer by degrees.

gradu diverso, una via [L], with different pace, (but) on the same road; the same way by different steps.

gradus ad Parnassum [L], a step to Parnassus; dictionary of prosody to aid in writing Latin verse; gradus.

Graeculus esuriens [L], hungry Greekling; parasite: *Juvenal.*

Graf [Ger; *pl.* Grafen], a German, Austrian, and Swedish title of nobility, equivalent to *earl* in Great Britain or *count* on the Continent.

graffiti [It], writings (often obscene) by passersby on walls of monuments, buildings, etc.

Gräfin [Ger], countess.

grammatici certant, et adhuc sub iudice lis est [L], the grammarians (*or* critics) wrangle, and the question is still undecided: *Horace.*

granada [Sp], pomegranate; *mil.*, shell; hand grenade.

gran casa, gran croce [It], a great house is a great cross.

grande [Sp], great. **—grande de españa,** grandee; great lord of Spain.

grande chère et beau feu [Fr], good fare (*or* cheer) and a good fire.

grande fortune, grande servitude [Fr], a great fortune is a great slavery.

grande nao, gran cuidado [Sp], great ship, great anxiety.

grande passion [Fr], great passion; love; serious love affair.

grande tenue [Fr], full dress.

grande toilette [Fr], ceremonial dress (*or* costume); full dress.

grandeur naturelle [Fr], life-size.

grandioso [It], in a grand or majestic style: *music.*

grand merci [Fr], many thanks! much obliged!

grand-mère [Fr; *pl.* grand-mères], grandmother.

grand'messe [Fr], High Mass.

grand monde [Fr], great world; high society.

grand-père [Fr; *pl.* grands-pères], grandfather.

grand seigneur [Fr], great nobleman; man of eminence. **—en grand seigneur,** like a great lord; in lordly style.

gran placer comer y no escotar [Sp], it is a great pleasure to dine without paying the bill.

gras [Fr; *fem.* grasse], fat; plump; fleshy. **—soupe grasse,** meat soup: *cookery.*

grasseyé [Fr], pronounced in the throat; rolled: said esp. of the letter *r.*

gratia Dei [L], by the grace of God.

gratia gratiam parit [L], kindness produces kindness.

gratia placendi [L], the grace of pleasing.

gratias agere [L], to give thanks.

gratificación [Sp], recompense; gratuity.

gratin [Fr], burned part; a gratinated dish and the manner of preparing it. **—au gratin,** cooked with a brown crust or crisp surface of buttered crumbs; as, cauliflower *au gratin: both cookery.*

gratior et pulchro veniens in corpore virtus [L], and worth that wins more favor in a comely form: *Virgil.*

gratis dictum [L], a mere assertion.

grave [It], very slow and solemn: the slowest musical tempo.

graviora manent [L], more grievous perils remain; the worst is yet to come: *Virgil* (adapted).

graviora quaedam sunt remedia periculis [L], some remedies are worse than the disease: *Publilius Syrus.*

gravis ira regum est semper [L], the wrath of kings is always heavy: *Seneca.*

gravissimum est imperium consuetudinis [L], the power of custom is most weighty: *Publilius Syrus.*

grazhdanyin [Russ; *fem.* grazhdanka], citizen.

grazia [It], grace, elegance; charm.

grazie! [It], thanks!

graziosamente [It], gracefully: *music.*

grazioso [It], graceful; flowing (*abbr.* graz.): *music.*

gré [Fr], will; inclination; pleasure. **—bon gré, mal gré,** willing or unwilling; willy-nilly. **—de bon gré,** willingly. **—de gré à gré,** by private contract.

greffier [Fr], registrar; recorder; clerk of the court; notary: *France and the Channel Islands.*

gregatim [L], in flocks or herds; in droves.

grenat [Fr], garnet.

grex venalium [L], a venal throng.

griffonnage [Fr], scrawl; scribble.

grillé [Fr; *fem.* grillée], broiled: *cookery.*

gringo [Sp], derisive word for a foreigner, particularly one from the United States, heard especially in Mexico.

grisette [Fr], a young working-class woman, so-called because orig. dressed in gray (*gris*).

grivois [Fr; *fem.* grivoise], too free and bold; coarsely jolly; broad; indelicate. —**conte grivois,** an indelicate story.

groente [Du; *pl.* groenten], vegetable.

gros [Fr; *fem.* grosse], big; large; stout; pregnant; dark (of color). —**gros bleu,** dark blue. —**gros mots,** high words; oaths. —**gros poisson,** fat fish; important person. —**gros rhume,** bad cold. —**grosse tête, peu de sens,** big head, little sense (*or* wit). —**gros temps,** foul weather. —**une femme grosse,** a pregnant woman. —**une grosse femme,** a stout woman.

groseille [Fr], currant. —**groseille à maquereau** (lit., mackerel currant) *or* **groseille verte** (lit., green currant), gooseberry.

grosse Seelen dulden still [Ger], great souls suffer in silence: *Schiller.*

grossièreté [Fr], coarseness; grossness; rudeness; vulgarity.

grosso [It], great; grand; full; deep: *music.*

gruppetto [It; *pl.* gruppetti], lit., small knot; a turn: *music.*

guano [Sp], fertilizer from bird droppings: *Peru.*

guarapo [Am Sp], cane juice; a fermented beverage made from the sugar cane.

guardacoste [It; Sp *guarda-costas*], coast guard.

guardatevi! [It], take care!

guarde-vos Deus de amigo reconciliado [Pg], God preserve you from a reconciled friend.

guazzo [It], lit., puddle; splash; *fine arts,* a method of watercolor painting. Cf. GOUACHE.

guberniya [Russ], a government, or territorial subdivision, of the former Russian empire; in Soviet Russia, a provincial soviet.

guddee [Anglo-Ind; Hind *gaddī*], cushion; specif., a king's cushion; throne. Cf. MUSNUD.

guerra a la cuchilla [Sp], war to the knife.

guerra cominciata, inferno scatenato [It], war commenced, hell unchained.

guerre [Fr], war. —**guerre à mort,** war to the death. —**guerre à outrance,** war to the utmost; war to the death; war without mercy. —**guerre de plume,** paper warfare.

guerrero [Sp], warrior.

guerrilla [Sp], lit., little war; a wager of hit-and-run warfare; the description of such warfare.

guet-apens [Fr; *pl.* guets-apens], a lying in wait; ambush; fig., premeditated design to injure.

guillemet [Fr], inverted comma; quotation mark: *typog.*

guillotine [Fr], machine for executing criminals by decapitation; named after *Dr. Guillotin.*

guindé [Fr; *fem.* guindée], stiff; affected; unnatural; *of style,* stilted; bombastic.

guingette [Fr], roadside inn; tea garden or cabaret.

gung ho [Chin], work together (said, for example, by the foreman of a work crew to ensure full use of each worker's strength in a heavy task of lifting or pulling).

guru [Hind & Skr], Hindu religious teacher; spiritual guide: *India.*

gustosamente [It], tastefully: *music.*

gustoso [It], tasteful; agreeable: *music.*

gute Besserung [Ger], I wish you a quick recovery.

guten Abend [Ger], good evening.

gute Nacht [Ger], good night.

guten Morgen [Ger], good morning.

guten Tag [Ger], good day.

gutta cavat lapidem, non vi, sed saepe cadendo [L], the drop hollows the stone, not by force, but by constant dropping.

Gymnasium [Ger], German classical school, preparing students for university.

H

haba [Sp], bean; esp., lima bean.

habemus confitentem reum [L], we have (before us) an accused person who pleads guilty: *Cicero.*

habent sua fata libelli [L], books have their own destiny: *Terentius Maurus* (the only fragment of his verse that lives in quotation—and is then commonly attributed to Horace or another).

habere et dispertire [L], to have and to distribute.

habere, non haberi [L], to hold, not to be held.

habet! [L], he has it! he is hit! See HOC HABET.

habet et musca splenem [L], even a fly has its spleen (*or* anger).

habitant [Fr; *now naturalized*], inhabitant; specif., a Canadian or Louisianan of French descent, esp., of the farming or laboring class.

habitué [Fr; *fem.* habituée], frequenter; regular customer.

hablando del rey de Roma pronto se asoma [Sp], speaking of the king of Rome, suddenly he appears.

hablar sin pensar es tirar sin encarar [Sp], to speak without thinking is to shoot without taking aim.

hâblerie [Fr], bragging; drawing the long bow.

hâbleur [Fr; *fem.* hâbleuse], braggart; boaster.

hacendado [Sp], proprietor of a *hacienda;* man of property.

hacendero [Sp], a farmer.

hachis [Fr], minced meat; hash: *cookery.*

hacienda [Sp], a large country estate, or plantation, with its dwelling house; landed estate; ranch; also, any large works or industrial establishment in the country: *Sp. Am.*

hac lege [L], with (*or* under) this law (*or* condition); with this proviso.

hac mercede placet [L], I accept the terms.

hac urgent lupus hac canis [L], on one side menaces a wolf, on the other a dog: *Horace.*

hadj *or* **haj** [Ar *hajj*], pilgrimage; esp., a pilgrimage to Mecca made by devout Muslims.

hadji *or* **haji** [Ar *hājī*], one who has completed the *hadj,* or pilgrimage to Mecca; also, a title conferred on such a Muslim.

haec generi incrementa fides [L], this faith will bring new increase to our race.

haec olim meminisse iuvabit [L], it will be a pleasure to remember these things hereafter: *Virgil.*

haec tibi dona fero [L], these gifts I bear to thee: motto of *Newfoundland.*

hae nugae in seria ducent mala [L], these trifles will lead to serious evils: *Horace.*

haere [Maori], go; also, come. **—haere atu,** go away. **—haere e hoki,** go back again. **—haere mai,** come here: *all New Zealand.*

haerent infixi pectore vultus [L], (his) looks are deep imprinted in (her) breast; (his) face is graven on (her) heart: *Virgil,* writing of Dido and Aeneas.

hafiz [Pers], one who knows the Koran by heart; a Muslim title.

haiduk *or* **heyduck** [Ger *Heiduck, fr.* Hung *hajdu*], orig., a brigand mountaineer; *Hung. hist.,* one of a class of mercenaries who received the rank of nobles in 1605; Hungarian foot soldier; formerly, in France and Germany, an outrider or footman in Hungarian costume.

haik [Ar], a strip of woolen or cotton cloth worn over the head and body by Arabs.

haiku [Jap], a three-line poem of seventeen syllables.

haji [Ar]. See HADJI.

hakeem *or* **hakim** [Ar *hakīm*], lit., wise one; Muslim physician.

haki-dame ni tsuru [Jap], a stork on a dust heap; a jewel in a dunghill.

hakim [Ar *hakīm*], Muslim judge or governor.

halachah [Heb], lit., the way; the body of Jewish law supplementing scriptural law.

Hälfte [Ger; *pl.* Hälften], half; moiety.

Hals über Kopf [Ger], lit., neck over head; head over heels; headlong.

halte-là! [Fr], halt!: *mil.*

hamal *or* **hammal** [Turk, Ar, & Hind], Oriental porter; palanquin bearer.

ha matseel nefesh achat mee Israel, ke eeloo heetseel et ha olam koolo [Heb], whoever saves one soul of Israel has done the equivalent of saving the entire world.

hammam [Turk & Ar], Turkish bath.

Handbuch [Ger; *pl.* Handbücher], handbook; manual.

Hände hoch! [Ger], hands up!

Handelsblatt [Ger; *pl.* Handelsblätter], trade journal.

Handelshochschule [Ger; *pl.* -schulen], commercial high school; commercial college.

Händler [Ger; *sing. & pl.*], dealer.

Handschrift [Ger; *pl.* Handschriften], manuscript: *abbr.* Hs., *pl.* Hss.

Handwörterbuch [Ger; *pl.* -bücher], handy dictionary.

Hannibal ad portas [L], Hannibal is at the gates; the enemy is close at hand: *Cicero* (adapted).

haole [Hawa], white man; foreigner to the Hawaiian Islands.

hapax legomenon [Gr ἅπαξ λεγόμενον], said only once; a word or phrase used but once in a book; a rare word or form.

hara-kiri [Jap], lit., belly cutting; Japanese method of suicide by piercing the abdomen; disembowelment; happy dispatch (*a euphemism*). Called also *seppuku.*

hardi comme un coq sur son fumier [Fr], bold as a rooster on his own dunghill.

hardiesse [Fr], hardihood; daring; *of style*, boldness.

hare! [Skr], hail! —**hare Krishna,** hail to the god Krishna.

hareng [Fr], herring. —**hareng frais,** fresh herring. —**hareng fumé,** smoked herring.

haricots verts [Fr], French beans.

hari-nuki [Jap], Japanese papier-mâché.

haro [Fr], hue and cry; outcry. —**haro!,** shame! out upon!

hartal [Hind], closing of the shop; specif., a general stoppage of work and business as a protest against some governmental act or policy: *India*.

hasard [Fr], chance; risk; hazard. —**par hasard,** by chance; accidentally. —**un coup de hasard,** a stroke of luck.

hasardé [Fr], lit., hazarded; *of food*, tainted; stale.

Hasenpfeffer [Ger], stew of hare in pepper and vinegar sauce.

hasta la muerte todo es vida [Sp], until death comes, all is life; while there is life, there is hope: *Cervantes*.

hasta luego [Sp], lit., until soon; farewell for a little while.

hasta mañana [Sp], till tomorrow: *leave taking*.

hasta otra vez [Sp], until another time.

haud ignota loquor [L], I speak of things by no means unknown; I speak of well-known events.

haud longis intervallis [L], at intervals by no means long; at frequent intervals.

haud passibus aequis [L], not with equal steps; with unequal steps: *Virgil*.

Hauptpost [Ger], general post office.

Hauptstadt [Ger], metropolis; capital.

Hausfrau [Ger; *pl.* Hausfrauen], housewife; lady of the house; mistress; landlady.

Hausglück [Ger], domestic happiness.

Hausherr [Ger; *pl.* Hausherren], master of the house; landlord.

haussier [Fr], bull: *stock exchange*.

Haus und Hof [Ger], house and home; one's all.

Haut-Canada [Fr], upper Canada.

haute bourgeoisie [Fr], upper middle class; gentry.

haute école [Fr], high horsemanship, as practiced in a military riding school.

haut et bon [Fr], great and good.

hauteur [Fr], haughtiness; arrogance; loftiness.

haut goût [Fr], high flavor; high seasoning; slight taint.

haut monde [Fr], high society.

haut-relief [Fr], high relief: *sculp*.

hauts faits [Fr], great deeds; exploits.

haut ton [Fr], high tone; high fashion; high social standing.

hay más estacas que tocino [Sp], there are more hooks than bacon; there are more mouths than food to fill them.

hay un gato encerrado [Sp], there is a cat shut up; there's something rotten in Denmark.

ἡ ἀλήθια ἐλευθερώσει ὑμᾶς [Gr; hē aléthia eleutherósei humâs], the truth shall make you free: *John* vii. 32.

Heauton Timoroumenos [Gr ἑαυτὸν τιμωρούμενος], self-tormentor: title of play by Menander and of Terence's adaptation.

ἡ ἀξίνη πρὸς τὴν ῥίζαν τῶν δένδρων [Gr; hē axínē pròs tèn rhízan tôn déndrōn], the axe is laid unto the root of the trees: *Luke* iii. 9.

heb' dich weg von mir, Satan [Ger], get thee behind me, Satan.

ἡδὺ δούλευμα [Gr; hēdu doúleuma], sweet service (*or* bondage): said of love.

Heft [Ger; *pl.* Hefte], a stitched or paper-covered book; also, part of a serial publication: *abbr.* H.

heftig [Ger], vehement; violent; impetuous.

hegira [Ar *hijrah*, flight], the beginning of the Muslim calendar, commemorating the flight of Muhammad from Mecca to Medina (A.D. 622).

Heiland, der [Ger], the Savior.

Heilanstalt [Ger], sanatorium.

heilig [Ger; *fem.* heilige] holy; sacred; *abbr.* hl. —**heilige Jungfrau,** the Blessed Virgin. —**heilige Nacht,** Holy Night; the night of Christ's birth.

Heiligenschein [Ger], lit., holy light; halo; specif., in certain atmospheric conditions, the bright light surrounding the shadow of one's head, due to diffraction.

Heimat [Ger], home; birthplace.

Heimgang [Ger], home-going; fig., death.

Heimweh [Ger], homesickness; nostalgia.

heiter [Ger], serene; clear; calm; cheerful.

hélas! [Fr], alas!

helluo librorum [L; *helluo*, a person who spends money immoderately on eating], a devourer of books; bookworm.

ἕως κόρακες λευκοὶ γένωνται [Gr; héōs kórakes leukoì génōntai], till the crows turn white (i.e., never).

ἡ πίστις σου σέσωκέν σε [Gr; hē pístis sou sésōkén se], thy faith hath saved thee: *Luke* vii. 50.

Herausgeber [Ger], lit., giver forth; editor (of a book); publisher.

heredad [Sp], lit., inherited property; farm; cultivated land.

heres [L; *pl.* heredes], heir (*abbr.* her.): *law.*

hermana [Sp], sister.

hermano [Sp], brother.

heroum filii [L], sons of heroes: motto of *Wellington College,* England.

Herr [Ger; *pl.* Herren], lord; master; gentleman; a German title of courtesy equivalent to *Sir* or *Mr.*

Herrenhaus [Ger], House of Lords; esp., the upper house of the Prussian and Austrian legislatures before 1918.

Herzog [Ger; *pl.* Herzoge; *fem.* Herzogin], duke.

εἷς ἀνήρ, οὐδεὶς ἀνήρ [Gr; hês anér, oudeìs anér], one man, no man; two heads are better than one.

hesterni quirites [L], citizens of yesterday (i.e., slaves recently set free): *Persius.*

heu pietas! heu prisca fides! [L], alas for piety! alas for the ancient faith!: *Virgil.*

heures perdues [Fr], leisure hours; spare time.

heureusement [Fr], happily; fortunately.

heute mir, morgen dir [Ger], today mine, tomorrow thine; my turn today, yours tomorrow.

heute rot, morgen tot [Ger], today red, tomorrow dead; here today, gone tomorrow.

Hexerei [Ger], witchcraft; sorcery; voodooism; esp., the practice of hexing, as in Pennsylvania.

hiatus valde deflendus [L], a gap (*or* deficiency) much to be regretted: used to mark a blank in a work, also used of persons whose achievements fall short of earlier promise.

hibachi [Jap], lit., fire bowl; charcoal brazier: *Japan.*

hibakusha [Jap], lit., bomb-affected people; survivors.

hic domus, haec patria est [L], here is our home, this our country: *Virgil.*

hic et nunc [L], here and now.

hic et ubique [L], here and everywhere. —**hic et ubique terrarum,** here and everywhere throughout the world: motto of the *University of Paris.*

hic finis fandi [L], here was an end of the speaking; here the speech ended: *Virgil.*

hic funis nihil attraxit [L], this line has taken no fish; the scheme is a failure.

hic iacet [L], here lies (*abbr.* H.I.): used in epitaphs. —**hic iacet sepultus,** here lies buried (*abbr.* H.I.S.): used in epitaphs. —**hic iacet lepus,** here lies the hare; fig., here lies the difficulty.

hic sepultus [L], here is buried: used in epitaphs.

hidalgo [Sp; *fem.* hidalga], Spanish nobleman of lower rank. Cf. *Pg.* FIDALGO.

hidalguía [Sp], nobility.

hier geht kein Weg [Ger], no thoroughfare.

hier stehe ich! ich kann nicht anders [Ger], here I stand! I cannot act otherwise: *Luther* (at the Diet of Worms).

hija [Sp], daughter. —**hija desposada hija enajenada,** a daughter married is a daughter lost.

hijo [Sp], son. —**hijo de tigre nace rayado,** the tiger's son is born with stripes; like father, like son.

Himmel! [Ger], heavens!

hinc illae lacrimae [L], hence these tears: *Terence.*

hinc lucem et pocula sacra [L], from hence (we receive) light and sacred libations: motto of *Cambridge University.*

hin ist hin [Ger], gone is gone; no use in crying over spilled milk.

hinlegen! [Ger], lie down!

hin und her [Ger], here and there; there and back.

hin und zurück [Ger], there and back.

hirtlich [Ger], pastoral; rustic: *music.*

his non obstantibus [L], notwithstanding these things.

hízonos Dios y maravillámonos [Sp], God made us and we are struck with wonder.

ὁ βίος βραχὺς, ἡ δὲ τέχνη μακρή [Gr; ho bíos brakhùs, hē dè tékhnē makrē], life is short, art is long. Cf. ARS LONGA, VITA BREVIS.

hoc age [L], do this; mind what you are about; attend.

hoc anno [L], in this year: *abbr.* h.a.

hoc erat in more maiorum [L], this was in the manner of our ancestors.

hoc erat in votis [L], this was among my wishes; this was one of my desires: *Horace.*

hoc genus omne [L], all of this class (*or* sort): *Horace.*

hoch! [Ger], hurrah!

hoc habet! [L], he has it! he is hit!: the cry of the spectators at a gladiatorial combat.

Hochamt [Ger], High Mass.

hoch lebe der König! [Ger], long live the king!

hoch soll er (sie) leben! [Ger], long may he (she) live; lit., high may he live.

hoc indictum volo [L], I wish this unsaid; I withdraw the statement.

hoc loco [L], in this place: *abbr.* h.l.

hoc mense [L], in this month: *abbr.* h.m.

hoc monumentum posuit [L], he (*or* she) erected this monument: *abbr.* H.M.P.

hoc opus, hic labor est [L], this is the task, this the toil; this is the real difficulty; there's the rub: *Virgil.*

hoc opus, hoc studium [L], this work, this pursuit: *Horace.*

hoc quaere [L], look for this: *abbr.* h.q.

hoc sensu [L], in this sense: *abbr.* h.s.

hoc sustinete, maius ne veniat malum [L], endure this evil, lest a greater come upon you: *Phaedrus.*

hoc tempore [L], at this time: *abbr.* h.t.

hoc titulo [L], under this title: *abbr.* h.t.

hoc volo, sic iubeo, sit pro ratione voluntas [L], this I write, thus I command, let my will stand for reason: *Juvenal.*

hodie mihi, cras tibi [L], today for me, tomorrow for thee; my turn today, yours tomorrow.

hodie, non cras [L], today, not tomorrow.

ὁ ἐλέφας τὴν μυῖαν οὐκ ἀλεγίζει [Gr; ho eléphas tèn muîan ouk alegízei], the elephant does not trouble itself about the fly.

Hof [Ger; *pl.* Höfe], courtyard; court; hotel.

Hofdichter [Ger], court poet; poet laureate.

Hoffnung [Ger], hope.

hogan [Nav], a conical hut of the Navajo Indians, covered with bark and earth.

οἳ ἀρούρης καρπὸν ἔδουσιν [Gr; hoì arourēs karpòn édousin], they who eat the fruit of the soil: *Homer*

hoi polloi [Gr οἱ πολλοί], the many; the multitude; the masses.

ὁ κόσμος οὗτος μία πόλις ἐστι [Gr; ho kósmos hoûtos mía pólis esti], this world of ours is one city: *Epictetus.*

Holi *or* **Hoolee** [Hind], Hindu spring festival in honor of Krishna: *India.*

hollandais [Fr; *fem.* hollandaise], *adj.* Dutch; *n.* Hollander; Dutchman: *abbr.* holl.

homard [Fr], lobster.

hombre [Sp], man; fellow. **—hombre de barba,** man of intelligence. **—hombre de un libro,** a man of one book.

homem pobre com pouco se alegra [Pg], a poor man is happy with little.

ὁ μὲν θερισμὸς πολύς, οἱ δὲ ἐργάται ὀλίγοι [Gr; ho mèn therismòs polús, hoi dè ergátai olígoi], the harvest truly is bountiful but the laborers are few: *Matthew* ix. 27.

ὁ μὴ ὢν μετ᾽ ἐμοῦ κατ᾽ ἐμοῦ ἐστίν [Gr; ho mè òn met᾽ emoû kat᾽ emoû estín], he that is not with me is against me: *Luke* xi. 23.

hominem quaero [L], I am looking for a man: *Phaedrus* (after Diogenes).

hominis est errare [L], to err is human; it is the nature of man to err.

hommage [Fr], homage; respect. **—avec les hommages de l'auteur,** with the author's compliments. **—hommage de reconnaissance,** token of gratitude.

homme [Fr], man. **—homme à tout faire,** jack of all trades. **—homme comme il faut,** gentleman. **—homme d'affaires,** man of business; agent; steward; middleman. **—homme de bien,** honest, respectable man. **—homme de cour,** courtier. **—homme d'église,** churchman; ecclesiastic. **—homme de lettres,** man of letters; literary man. **—homme de paille,** straw man. **—homme de parti,** party man. **—homme d'épée,** swordsman; military man. **—homme de plume,** writer; author. **—homme de robe,** magistrate; lawyer. **—homme d'esprit,** man of intellect; man of wit. **—homme d'état,** statesman.

—**homme de tête,** resourceful man. —**homme d'hier,** lit., man of yesterday; upstart. —**homme d'honneur,** man of honor; gentleman. —**homme du monde,** man of the world; man of society. —**homme honnête,** civil man.

homo [L; *pl.* homines], man. —**homo antiqua virtute ac fide,** a man of the old-fashioned virtue and loyalty. —**homo homini aut deus aut lupus,** man is to man either a god or a wolf: *Erasmus.* —**homo multarum literarum,** lit., a man of many letters; man of great learning. —**homo nullius coloris,** a man of no political party. —**Homo sapiens,** lit., wise (*or* reasoning) man; the single human species of the genus *Homo.* —**homo sum; humani nihil a me alienum puto,** I am a man; nothing that relates to man do I deem alien to me: *Terence.* —**homo trium literarum,** a man of three letters (*f u r,* Latin for "thief"); a thief: *Plautus.* —**homo unius libri,** a man of one book: Thomas Aquinas's definition of a man of learning. —**homo vitae commodatus non donatus,** a man is lent, not given, to life: *Publilius Syrus.*

homunculi quanti sunt [L], what insignificant creatures men are: *Plautus.*

hondonada [Sp], dale; glen; *geol.,* depression.

honesta mors turpi vita potior [L], an honorable death is better than a base life: *Tacitus.*

honesta quam splendida [L], honorable things rather than brilliant ones; reputable rather than showy.

ὃν γὰρ ἀγαπᾷ Κύριος παιδεύει [Gr; hòn gàr agapâ Kúrios paideúei], for whom the Lord loveth he chasteneth: *Hebrews* xii. 6.

ὃν οἱ θεοὶ φιλοῦσιν ἀποθνήσκει νέος [Gr; hòn hoi theoì philoûsin apothnḗskei néos], he whom the gods love dies young: *Menander.*

honi soit! [Fr], an abbreviated form of **honi soit qui mal y pense,** shame to him who thinks evil of it: motto of the *Order of the Garter.*

honnête [Fr], honest; upright; virtuous; civil; reasonable. —**homme honnête,** civil man. —**honnête garçon,** honest fellow. —**honnête femme,** virtuous woman. —**honnête homme,** worthy man; honest man. —**prix honnête,** reasonable price.

honneur et patrie [Fr], honor and fatherland: motto of the *Legion of Honor,* France.

honoraires [Fr], professional fee; honorarium.

honores mutant mores [L], honors alter manners.

honor est a Nilo [L], honor is from the Nile: anagram on "Horatio Nelson," victor in the battle of the Nile.

honoris causa (*or* **gratia**) [L], for the sake of honor; honorary.

honor virtutis praemium [L], honor is the reward of virtue (*or* valor): *Cicero.*

honos alit artes [L], honor nourishes the arts: *Cicero.*

honos habet onus [L], honor has its burden; honor carries responsibility.

ὃ οὖν ὁ θεὸς συνέζευξεν ἄνθρωπος μὴ χωριζέτω [Gr; ho oûn ho theós synézeuxen ánthrōpos mḕ khōrízeto], what therefore God hath joined together, let not man put asunder: *Matthew* xix. 6 and *Mark* x. 9.

ὁ φίλος ἕτερος ἐγώ [Gr; ho phílos héteros egó], a friend is a second self: *Aristotle*.

hôpital [Fr], free hospital; also, hospice; refuge.

ὅπου γάρ ἐστιν ὁ θησαυρός σου, ἐκεῖ ἔσται ἡ καρδία σου [Gr; hópou gár estin ho thēsaurós sou, ekeî éstai hē kardía sou], for where your treasure is, there will your heart be also: *Matthew* vi. 21.

hora decubitus [L], at bedtime: *abbr.* (*in prescriptions*) hor. decub.

horae canonicae [L], canonical hours; hours for prayer.

horae subsicivae [L], leisure hours.

hora fugit [L], the hour flies.

horas non numero nisi serenas [L], I number (*or* mark) none but shining hours: *for a sun dial*.

ὅρα τέλος μακροῦ βίου [Gr; hóra télos makroû bíou], look to (*or* consider) the end of a long life: *Solon* (to Croesus).

horresco referens [L], I shudder to relate it (generally used in a playful sense): *Virgil*.

horribile dictu [L], horrible to relate.

horribile visu [L], horrible to see.

horror ubique [L], terror everywhere: motto of the *Scots Guards* (with a thunderbolt as crest).

hors concours [Fr], not competing for prize: said of a picture in an exhibition.

hors de combat [Fr], out of the combat; disabled.

hors de ligne [Fr], out of line; out of the common; exceptional.

hors de pair [Fr], without equal; peerless.

hors de prise [Fr], out of reach (*or* danger).

hors de prix [Fr], extravagantly dear.

hors de saison [Fr], out of season; inopportune.

hors d'oeuvre [Fr; *usually in pl.* hors d'oeuvres], a side dish served as an appetizer at the beginning of a meal.

hors la loi [Fr], outlawed.

hortus siccus [L], lit., a dry garden; herbarium.

hos ego versiculos feci, tulit alter honores [L], I wrote these lines, another has carried off the honors (*or* the credit): *Virgil*.

hospes, hostis [L], stranger, enemy.

hospice [Fr], religious establishment serving as an aid to travelers; lodging.

hospodar [Russ], lord: a title formerly born by the vassal princes or governors of Wallachia and Moldavia. Cf. GOSPODAR.

hostis honori invidia [L], envy is the foe (*or* bane) of honor.

hostis humani generis [L], an enemy of the human race.

hôte [Fr; *fem.* hôtesse], host; innkeeper; landlord, also, guest; fig., inhabitant; denizen.

Hôtel des Invalides [Fr], a hospital in Paris, founded by Louis XIV, for aged and infirm soldiers.

hôtel des postes [Fr], general post office.

hôtel de ville [Fr], town hall.

hôtel-Dieu [Fr; *pl.* hôtels-Dieu], chief hospital of a town.

hôtel garni (*or* **meublé**) [Fr], lodging house; furnished apartments or lodgings.

houppelande [Fr], greatcoat; cloak.

hubris [Gr ὕβρις, húbris], wanton violence; overweening or arrogant behavior.

hübsch [Ger], pretty.

huerta [Sp], orchard; kitchen garden.

huevo [Sp], egg; spawn.

huissier [Fr], usher or doorkeeper, esp. for a king or nobleman; also, sheriff's officer; bailiff.

huître [Fr], oyster; fig., dunce; blockhead.

huius anni [L], of this year.

huius mensis [L], of this month.

hukm [Hind & Ar], order; command: *India.*

humani nihil alienum [L], nothing that relates to man is alien to me: *Terence* (adapted).

humanum est errare [L], to err is human.

ὑμεῖς ἐστε τὸ ἅλας τῆς γῆς [Gr; humeîs este tò hálas tês gês], ye are the salt of the earth: *Matthew* v. 13.

ὑμεῖς ἐστε τὸ φῶς τοῦ κόσμου [Gr; humeîs este tò phôs toû kósmou], ye are the light of the world: *Matthew* v. 14.

humo [Sp], smoke; fume.

hunc tu, Romane, caveto [L], of him, Roman, do thou beware: *Horace.*

Hund [Ger; *pl.* Hünde], dog.

ὕπαγε ὀπίσω μου Σατανᾶ [Gr; húpage opísō mou Satanâ], get thee behind me, Satan: *Matthew* xvi. 23 and *Mark* viii. 33.

hure [Fr], head of a boar, salmon, etc. —**hure de sanglier,** boar's head: *cookery.*

hurler à la lune [Fr], to howl at the moon; raise a futile voice against a person in high position.

hurler avec les loups [Fr], lit., to howl with the wolves; do as others do.

hurtar el puerco, y dar los pies por Dios [Sp], to steal the pig and give away the feet for God's sake.

hurtar para dar por Dios [Sp], to steal in order to give to God.

hurtig [Ger], quick; presto: *music.*

Hut ab! [Ger], off with your hat! hats off!

hutzpah [Yiddish]. See CHUTZPAH.

huurder [Du], a lessee: *Dutch law.*

huyendo del toro, cayó en el arroyo [Sp], fleeing from the bull, he fell into the brook.

huzur [Ar], lit., presence; a respectful form of address equivalent to *your honor: India.*

ὕδραν τέμνεις [Gr; hýdran témneis], you are wounding a Hydra (a many-headed water snake slain by Hercules, two heads immediately growing in place of each one cut off); you are making a bad matter worse.

hypotheses non fingo [L], I frame no hypotheses; I deal entirely with facts: *Isaac Newton.*

hysteron proteron [Gr ὕστερον πρότερον], lit., the latter before others; inversion of the natural or logical order: *rhet. & logic.*

I

iacta est alea [L], the die is cast (exclamation attributed to Julius Caesar on crossing the Rubicon): *Suetonius*.

iam proximus ardet Ucalegon [L], already Ucalegon's house next door is on fire: *Virgil*.

iam redit et Virgo, redeunt Saturnia regna [L], now returns the Virgin (Astraea, goddess of justice, who was said to have left the earth in the iron age), now the Saturnian (or Golden) Age returns: *Virgil*.

iam satis [L], already enough.

ianuae mentis [L], gates of the mind; inlets of knowledge.

ianuis clausis [L], with closed doors; in secret.

ἰατρέ, θεράπευσον σεαυτόν [Gr; iatré, therápeuson seautón], physician, heal thyself: *Luke* iv. 23. Cf. MEDICE.

ibidem [L], in the same place (in a book): *abbr.* ib. *or* ibid.

ich bin der Geist der stets verneint [Ger], I am the spirit that always denies: *Goethe* (reply of Mephistopheles to Faust).

ich bin ganz ab [Ger], I am quite exhausted.

ich danke Ihnen [Ger], thank you.

ich dien [Ger], I serve: motto of the *Prince of Wales*.

ich habe genossen das irdische Glück; ich habe gelebt und geliebet [Ger], I have known earthly fortune (*or* I have experienced earthly happiness); I have lived and loved: *Schiller*.

ici on parle français [Fr], French is spoken here.

idée fixe [Fr], fixed idea; monomania.

idem [L], the same; the same as above: *abbr.* id. **—idem quod,** the same as: *abbr.* i.q. **—idem sonans,** sounding alike; having the same sound (*or* meaning).

idem velle atque idem nolle [L], to like and dislike the same things: *Sallust*.

id est [L], that is; that is to say: *abbr.* i.e.

id genus omne [L], all of that kind.

idhar ao [Hind], come here.

idoneus homo [L], a fit man; a man of proven ability.

ἰδοὺ ὁ ἄνθρωπος [Gr; idoù ho ánthrōpos], behold the man: *John* xix. 5. Cf. ECCE.

ieiunus raro stomachus vulgaria temnit [L], an empty stomach seldom scorns common food: *Horace*.

Iesus Hominum Salvator [L], Jesus Savior of Mankind.

i frutti proibiti sono i più dolci [It], forbidden fruits are the sweetest.

igloo [Esk], Eskimo house, often built of ice.

ignavis semper feriae sunt [L], to the indolent it is always holiday.

ignis aurum probat, miseria fortes viros [L], fire tests gold, misery tests brave men: *Seneca*.

ignis fatuus [L; *pl.* ignes fatui], will-o'-the-wisp; delusive hope.

ignobile vulgus [L], the baseborn multitude.

ignorance crasse [Fr], gross ignorance.

ignorantia facti excusat, ignorantia iuris non excusat [L], ignorance of fact excuses, ignorance of law does not excuse: *law*.

ignorantia legis neminem excusat [L], ignorance of the law excuses no one.

ignoratio elenchi [L], ignorance of the point in dispute; the fallacy of appearing to refute an opponent by arguing an unraised point: *logic*.

ignoscito saepe alteri nunquam tibi [L], forgive others often, yourself never.

ignoti nulla cupido [L], no desire (is felt) for a thing unknown; where ignorance is bliss, 'tis folly to be wise: *Ovid*.

ignotum per ignotius [L], the unknown (explained) by the still more unknown.

ignotus [L], unknown: *abbr.* ign.

i gran dolori sono muti [It], great griefs are silent.

ikebana [Jap], lit., living flowers; the art of Japanese flower arrangement, sometimes exhibiting cut flowers with other natural objects.

il a beaucoup de moyens [Fr], he has plenty of brains; he is a clever fellow.

il aboie après tout le monde [Fr], he snarls at everybody.

il a le diable au corps [Fr], the devil is in him.

il brode très bien [Fr], lit., he embroiders very well; he can spin a good yarn.

il conduit bien sa barque [Fr], he steers his boat well; he is getting on very well.

il danaro è fratello del danaro [It], money is the brother of money.

Il Duce [It], lit., the leader; the head of the Fascisti in Italy; specif., Mussolini.

île [Fr], island.

il est bas percé [Fr], he is low in funds; he is down at the heel.

il est plus aisé d'être sage pour les autres que pour soi-même [Fr], it is easier to be wise for others than for oneself: *La Rochefoucauld*.

il est plus honteux de se défier de ses amis que d'en être trompé [Fr], it is more shameful to distrust one's friends than to be deceived by them: *La Rochefoucauld*.

il faut cultiver son jardin [Fr], one must cultivate one's garden; attend to one's own affairs: *Voltaire*.

il faut de l'argent [Fr], money is necessary; you must have money.

il faut laver son linge sale en famille [Fr], soiled linen should be washed in private.

il faut souffrir pour être belle [Fr], to be beautiful, it is necessary to suffer.

il fuoco non s'estingue con fuoco [It], fire is not extinguished by fire.

Ἰλιὰς κακῶν [Gr; Iliàs kakôn], an Iliad of woes.

Ilias malorum [L], an Iliad of woes; a series of calamities.

il jette feu et flamme [Fr], lit., he throws fire and flame; he frets and fumes.

illaeso lumine solum [L], with undazzled eye to the sun.

illotis manibus [L], with unwashed hands; unprepared.

il m'aime — un peut — beaucoup — passionnément — pas de tout [Fr], He loves me — a little — a lot — passionately — not at all. Equivalent to "He loves me; he loves me not."

il m'a poussé à bout [Fr], he has provoked me beyond endurance.

il meglio è l'inimico del bene [It], better is the enemy of good; leave well enough alone.

il mondo è di chi ha pazienza [It], the world is his who has patience.

il n'a pas inventé la poudre [Fr], lit., he has not invented powder; he will never set the world on fire.

il n'appartient qu'aux grands hommes d'avoir de grands défauts [Fr], it belongs only to great men to have great defects; only great men have great defects: *La Rochefoucauld.*

il ne faut jamais défier un fou [Fr], one should never defy a madman.

il ne faut pas éveiller le chat qui dort [Fr], don't wake a sleeping cat; let sleeping dogs lie.

il ne faut pas vendre la peau de l'ours avant de l'avoir tué [Fr], one must not sell the bear's skin before one has killed him; don't count your chickens before they're hatched.

il n'est chère que d'appétit [Fr], lit., it is dear only with appetite; hunger is the best sauce.

il n'est sauce que d'appétit [Fr], there is no sauce like appetite.

il n'y a pas à dire [Fr], there is nothing to be said; the thing is settled.

il n'y a pas de héros pour son valet de chambre [Fr], no man is a hero to his valet.

il n'y a pas de quoi [Fr], there is no occasion for it; don't mention it.

il n'y a plus de Pyrénées [Fr], there are no longer any Pyrenees: attributed to *Louis XIV.*

il n'y a que le premier pas qui coûte [Fr], it is only the first step that costs.

il n'y en a plus [Fr], there is no more.

il penseroso [Old It], the pensive (*or* melancholy) man.

il porte lanterne à midi [Fr], he carries a lantern at noon.

il rit bien qui rit le dernier [Fr], he laughs best who laughs last.

il s'en faut de beaucoup [Fr], it is very much lacking; it falls far short.

il sent le fagot [Fr], he smells of the fagot (burning at the stake); he is suspected of heresy.

il se recule pour mieux sauter [Fr], he draws back in order to leap better.

ils ne passeront pas [Fr], they shall not pass: World War rallying cry, originating in the determined stand of the French at Verdun, 1916.

ils n'ont rien appris ni rien oublié [Fr], they have learned nothing and forgotten nothing: said of the Bourbons, supposedly by Talleyrand.

il tempo buono viene una volta sola [It], the good time comes but once.

il tondrait sur un oeuf [Fr], lit., he would shave an egg; he is a skinflint.

il va sans dire [Fr], it goes without saying.

il vaut mieux tâcher d'oublier ses malheurs que d'en parler [Fr], it is better to try to forget one's misfortunes than to talk about them.

il volto sciolto ed i pensieri stretti [It], the countenance open, but the thoughts withheld.

il y a anguille sous roche [Fr], there is an eel under the rock; there is more to it than meets the eye.

imagines maiorum [L], portraits of ancestors.

imam [Per], Muslim priest; title conferred on certain Muslim leaders, both spiritual and temporal.

im Auftrage [Ger], by order of: *abbr.* i.A.

im Freien [Ger], in the open air; outdoors.

im Ganzen, Guten, Wahren, resolut zu leben [Ger], to live resolutely in the whole, the good, the true: *Goethe.*

im Gegenteil [Ger], on the contrary.

imitatores, servum pecus [L], ye imitators, servile herd: *Horace.*

im Jahre [Ger], in the year: *abbr.* i.J. **—im Jahre der Welt,** in the year of the world: *abbr.* i.J.d.W.

immedicabile vulnus [L], an incurable wound: *Ovid.*

immer schlimmer [Ger], worse and worse.

imo pectore [L], from the bottom of one's heart.

impari Marte [L], with unequal military strength.

impasse [Fr], blind alley; inextricable difficulty; dilemma.

impavidum ferient ruinae [L], the ruins (of the world) will strike him undismayed; nothing can shatter the steadfastness of the upright man: *Horace.*

impayable [Fr], invaluable; matchless; priceless; inimitable; *colloq.,* beyond anything; beyond ordinary limits.

impazientemente [It], impatiently: *music.*

imperat aut servit collecta pecunia cuique [L], money amassed either rules or serves us; money is either our master or our slave: *Horace.*

imperioso [It], imperious; haughty: *music.*

imperium et libertas [L], empire and liberty.

imperium in imperio [L], a sovereignty within a sovereignty; an absolute authority within the jurisdiction of another: motto of *Ohio.*

imperméable [Fr], raincoat.

impeto [It], impetuosity. **—con impeto,** with impetuosity: *music.*

impetuoso [It], impetuous; dashing: *music.*

impi [Zulu], a body of Zulu warriors: *South Africa.*

implicite [L], by implication.

imponere Pelion Olympo [L], to pile Pelion on Olympus.

impos animi [L], having no power over the mind; imbecile.

impotens sui [L], having no power over one's self; without self-control; unrestrained; passionate.

impresos [Sp], printed matter.

imprevisto [Sp], unforeseen.

imprimis [L], in the first place; first in order.

improvvisata [It], impromptu composition; improvisation: *music.*

improvvisatore [It; *fem.* improvvisatrice], an improviser; one who composes extemporaneously.

im Rausche [Ger], in one's cups; tipsy.

imshi! [Ar], go away! be off!

i mucha nie bez brzucha [Pol], even a fly has a belly.

in abstracto [L], in the abstract.

in actu [L], in act or reality; in the very act.

in aeternum [L], forever; everlastingly.

in alio loco [L], in another place.

in altissimo [It], in the register above F in alt (g′′′—f′′′′): *music.*

in alto *or* **in alt** [It], in the octave above the treble staff (g′′—f′′′): *music.*

in ambiguo [L], in doubt; in a doubtful manner.

in aqua scribis [L], you are writing in water; you are wasting your time on something that will not last.

in arena aedificas [L], you are building on sand.

in armis [L], in arms; under arms.

in articulo mortis [L], at the point (*or* at the moment) of death.

in banco [LL], in full court: *law.*

in banco regis [LL], in the King's Bench.

in beato omnia beata [L], with the fortunate all things are fortunate: *Horace.*

in bianco [It], in white (*or* in blank); blank.

in bonis [L], in (*or* among) the goods or property: *law.*

in caelo quies [L], in heaven is rest.

in caelo salus [L], in heaven is salvation.

in camera [L], in chamber; in private; *law,* at chambers; not in open court.

in capite [L], in chief (i.e., holding directly from the Crown): *feudal law.*

Incarnatus [L], a part of the Nicene Creed, containing the words *Et incarnatus est de Spiritu Sancto, ex Maria Virgine,* "and was incarnate by the Holy Ghost of the Virgin Mary."

incartade [Fr], a brusque and wanton affront; insult; outburst; also, prank; folly; extravagance.

in casa [It], at home.

incessu patuit dea [L], by her gait the goddess was revealed: *Virgil.*

in Christi nomine [L], in Christ's name.

incidis in Scyllam cupiens vitare Charybdim [L], you fall prey to Scylla in trying to avoid Charybdis.

incipit [L], here begins (book, poem, etc.).

in commendam [L], in trust for a time: said of the tenure of a benefice in the absence of a regular incumbent: *eccl. law.*

inconnu [Fr; *fem.* inconnue], unknown; specif., a large food fish (*Stenodus mackenziei*) of Alaska and N. W. Canada.

incordamento [It], tension of the strings of a musical instrument.

incredulus odi [L], being skeptical, I detest it: *Horace.*

incroyable [Fr], incredible; also, a dandy, esp. of the time of the French Directory.

in cruce spero [L], I hope in the Cross.

incudi reddere [L], to return to the anvil (i.e., to revise or retouch): *Horace.*

in cumulo [L], in a heap.

in curia [LL], in open court.

in custodia legis [L], in the custody of the law.

inde irae et lacrimae [L], hence this anger and these tears: *Juvenal.*

in Deo speravi [L], in God have I trusted.

in deposito [L], on deposit; as a pledge.

Index Expurgatorius [L], a list of books from which condemned passages must be expunged before the books may be read by Catholics: *R.C.Ch.*

Index Librorum Prohibitorum [L], a catalogue of prohibited books: *R.C.Ch.*

index rerum [L], an index of matters (*or* subjects); reference notebook.

index verborum [L], an index of words.

indicium [L; *pl.* indicia], indicating mark or sign; indication; symptom.

indictum sit [L], be it unsaid.

in diem vivere [L], to live for the day; live from hand to mouth.

indignante invidia florebit iustus [L], the just man will flourish in spite of envy.

indio [Sp], an Indian; American Indian.

in disparte [It], aside; apart; secretly.

indocilis pauperiem pati [L], one who cannot learn to endure poverty: *Horace.*

in dubio [L], in doubt; undetermined.

induna [Zulu], leader of an *impi: South Africa.*

industriae nil impossibile [L], to industry (hard work), nothing is impossible.

inédit [Fr; *fem.* inédite], unpublished.

inedita [L], unpublished compositions.

in equilibrio [L], in equilibrium.

in esse [L], in being; in actual existence: contrasted with *in posse*.

inest clementia forti [L], clemency belongs to the brave.

inest sua gratia parvis [L], even little things have a grace (*or* charm) of their own; trifles are not to be despised.

in excelsis [L], in the highest.

in extenso [L], at full length.

in extremis [L], in the last extremity; at the point of death.

in facie curiae [LL], in the presence of (*or* before) the court: *law.*

infandum, regina, iubes renovare dolorem [L], unspeakable, O queen, is the grief thou bidst me renew: *Virgil* (reply of Aeneas to Dido, when requested to relate the history of Troy's destruction).

infandum renovare dolorem [L], to renew an unspeakable grief: *Virgil* (adapted). See previous entry.

infecta pace [L], without effecting a peace: *Terence.*

in ferrum pro libertate ruebant [L], for freedom they rushed upon the sword.

infiel [Sp; *pl.* infieles], infidel; unfaithful.

in fieri [L], pending; in course of completion: *law.*

infima species [L; *pl.* infimae species], the lowest species (i.e., of a genus or class).

infixum est mihi [L], I have firmly resolved; I am determined.

in flagrante delicto [L], lit., while the crime is blazing; in the very act; red-handed.

inflatilia [L], wind instruments: *music.*

in-folio [Fr, *fr.* L *in folio,* in the form of a sheet folded once], a folio volume; folio.

in forma pauperis [L], in the form of a pauper; as a poor man, not liable to costs: *law.*

in foro conscientiae [L], in the court (*or* before the tribunal) of conscience.

in foro domestico [L], in a domestic (i.e., nonforeign) court.

infra [L], below; beneath; after; further on (in book or manuscript). **—infra dignitatem,** beneath one's dignity; unbecoming; *abbr.* infra dig.

in fretta [It], in haste; hurriedly: *music.*

in fumo [L], in smoke.

in futuro [L], in (*or* for) the future.

inganno [It], deceit; trick; deception. **—cadenza d'inganno,** a deceptive cadence; a cadence on an unexpected chord: *music.*

in genere [L], in kind.

ingenio sin prudencia, loco con espada [Sp], wit without discretion is a fool (*or* madman) with a sword.

ingens aequor [L], the mighty ocean.

ingens telum necessitatis [L], necessity is a powerful weapon.

ingénue [Fr], artless girl or young woman; an actress representing such a type.

in gremio legis [L], in the bosom (*or* lap) of the law; under the protection of the law.

in hoc parte [L], on this part.

in hoc salus [L], there is safety in this.

in hoc signo spes mea [L], in this sign (i.e., the Cross) is my hope.

in hoc signo vinces [L], in (*or* by) this sign thou shalt conquer: motto of *Constantine the Great.*

in infinitum [L], forever; to infinity.

in intellectu [L], in the mind.

in invidiam [L], in ill-will; to excite prejudice.

in invitum [L], against the unwilling; compulsory.

initio [L], in (*or* at) the beginning (referring to a passage in a book, etc.): *abbr.* init.

inkomo [Zulu], cow: *South Africa.*

in limine [L], on the threshold; at the beginning: *abbr.* in lim. —**in limine belli,** at the outbreak of war: *Livy.*

in loco [L], in the place; in place of; in the proper or natural place. —**in loco citato,** in the place cited: *abbr.* loc. cit. —**in loco parentis,** in the place of a parent.

in manus tuas commendo spiritum meum [L], into Thy hands I commend my spirit: Christ's last words on the Cross (*Vulgate, Luke* xxiii. 46).

in medias res [L], in the midst of things (*or* affairs): *Horace:* a story that begins in the midst of action or plot.

in mediis rebus [L], in the midst of things.

in medio [L], in the middle. —**in medio tutissimus ibis,** in a middle course, you will go most safely. See MEDIO TUTISSIMUS IBIS (the correct form).

in meditatione fugae [L], in contemplation of flight.

in memoriam [L], lit., into memory; in memory of.

in mora [L], in delay; in default: *law.*

innamorato [It; *fem.* innamorata], *adj.* loving; in love; *n.* lover; beloved.

in necessariis unitas, in dubiis libertas, in omnibus caritas [L], in things essential unity, in things doubtful liberty, in all things charity.

innig [Ger], sincere; heartfelt; fervent: *music.*

in nocte consilium [L], in the night is counsel; sleep on it.

in nomine [L], in the name of. —**in nomine Domini,** in the name of the Lord.

in notis [L], in the notes.

in nubibus [L], in the clouds; befogged.

in nuce [L], in a nutshell.

in oculis civium [L], in the eyes of citizens; in public.

in omnia paratus [L], ready (*or* prepared) for all things.

inopem me copia fecit [L], abundance made me poor: *Ovid.*

i no uchi no kawazu [Jap], like a frog in a well (i.e., knowing nothing of the world).

in ovo [L], in the egg; undeveloped.

in pace [L], in peace.

in pari materia [L], in an analogous case.

in partibus infidelium *or* **in partibus** [L], in the lands of the unbelievers (*abbr.* i.p.i.); specif., *bishop in partibus infidelium,* a titular bishop who bears the title of an extinct see: *R.C.Ch.*

in pectore [L], in the breast; in reserve.

in perpetuam rei memoriam [L], in everlasting remembrance of the event (*or* affair).

in perpetuum [L], forever.

in persona [L], in person.

in personam [L], against a particular person (said of enforceable rights); also, against the person, as distinguished from things (in both senses, opposed to *in rem*): *law.*

in petto [It], within one's own breast; in secret; in reserve.

in piccolo [It], in little.

in plano [L], on a level surface.

in pleno [L], in full.

in pontificalibus [LL], in pontificals; in episcopal robes.

in posse [LL], potentially; in possibility: contrasted with *in esse.*

in posterum [L], for the future.

in potentia [L], in possibility; potentially.

in praesenti [L], at the present time; now.

in praesentia [L], for the present.

in principio [L], in the beginning: *abbr.* in pr.

in procinctu [L], with loins girded; in readiness for the fray.

in promptu [L], in readiness.

in propria causa [L], in his (*or* her) own suit.

in propria persona [L], in one's own person (*or* character).

in prospectu [L], in prospect.

in puris naturalibus [L], stark naked.

inquirendo [L], lit., by inquiring; authority to inquire into something for the benefit of the Crown: *Eng. law.* —**de lunatico inquirendo,** a writ to inquire into the sanity of a person: *law.*

in re [L], in the matter of; concerning.

in rem [L], lit., in or against a thing: said of a right available against all persons, or of an action against a thing, as, for example, against a ship or cargo for the enforcement of a maritime lien (opposed to *in personam*): *law.*

in rerum natura [L], in the nature of things.

in saecula saeculorum [L], for ages of ages; forever and ever.

insalutato hospite [L], without saluting one's host; without saying goodbye.

insanus omnis furere credit ceteros [L], every madman thinks everybody else mad: *Publilius Syrus.*

insculpsit [L], he (*or* she) engraved it.

in se [L], in itself.

insensibilmente [It], insensibly; imperceptibly; gradually: *music.*

inshallah [Ar], lit., if Allah wills; a pious interjection among Muslims, akin to "God willing."

in silvam ligna ferre [L], to carry wood to the forest; carry coals to Newcastle.

in situ [L], in its (original) place.

in solidum *or* **in solido** [L], for (*or* in) the whole; jointly: *law.*

insolite [Fr], unusual; unprecedented; unwonted.

in solo Deo salus [L], in God alone is salvation.

insouciance [Fr], indifference; nonchalance; unconcernedness; apathy.

instar omnium [L], worth all of them.

in statu pupillari [L], as a pupil.

in statu quo [L], in the same state as formerly. **—in statu quo ante bellum,** in the same state as before the war.

intaglio rilevato [It], hollow relief.

in te, Domine, speravi [L], in thee, O Lord, have I put my trust.

integer vitae scelerisque purus [L], blameless of life and free from crime (*or* guilt): *Horace.*

integra mens augustissima possessio [L], a sound and vigorous mind is the most honored possession.

integros haurire fontes [L], to drink from pure fountains.

intelligenti pauca [L], to the understanding, few words suffice.

intelligentsia [Russ *fr.* L], the intellectual elite.

intendencia [Sp], office of an intendant, esp. of a province.

intendente [Sp], an intendant; chief administrative official.

in tenebris [L], in darkness; in a state of doubt.

inter [L], between; among. **—inter alia,** among other things. **—inter alios,** among other persons. **—inter arma leges silent,** in time of war, the laws are silent: *Cicero.* **—inter canem et lupum,** between dog and wolf; twilight. **—inter malleum et incudem,** between the hammer and the anvil. **—inter nos,** between ourselves. **—inter pocula,** between cups; over drinks. **—inter regalia,** among (*or* part of) the regalia. **—inter se,** between (*or* among) themselves. **—inter spem et metum,** between hope and fear. **—inter vivos,** among the living.

interdum vulgus rectum videt [L], sometimes the common people see aright: *Horace.*

intermezzo [It], an entr'acte; a movement separating sections of a symphonic work.

in terminis [L], in express terms; definitely.

Internat [Ger; *pl.* Internate], boarding school.

in terrorem [L], as a warning.

in testimonium [L], in witness.

intonaco [It], finishing coat of plastering in fresco painting.

in totidem verbis [L], in so many words.

in toto [L], in the whole; entirely. —**in toto caelo,** lit., in the whole sky (*or* heavens); as far as possible.

intrada [It], prelude; introductory piece: *music.*

intra muros [L], within the walls (esp. city walls).

intransigeance [Fr], ultraradicalism; irreconcilability. See INTRAN-SIGEANT.

intransigeant [Fr], *adj.* ultraradical; uncompromising; irreconcilable, esp. in political views; revolutionary; *n.* one who holds ultraradical or revolutionary opinions in politics, art, etc.; an irreconcilable; intransigent.

in transitu [L], on the way: *abbr.* in trans.

intra parietes [L], within the walls (of a house).

intra verba peccare [L], to offend in words only.

intra vires [L], within the powers (of).

intrigant [Fr; *fem.* intrigante], intriguer; schemer; plotter.

intuitu [L], in respect of.

intus et in cute novi hominem [L], lit., I know the man within and in the skin (i.e., inside and out; thoroughly): *Persius.*

in usu [L], in use.

in usum Delphini [LL], for the use of the Dauphin; hence, expurgated.

in utero [L], in the womb.

in utroque fidelis [L], faithful in both.

in utroque iure [L], under both laws (canon and civil): *law.*

in utrumque paratus [L], prepared for either event: *Virgil.*

in vacuo [L], in a vacuum.

in vadio [LL], in pledge.

invenit [L], he (*or* she) designed it: *abbr.* inv.

inventario [Sp], an inventory: *Sp. Am. & P.I.*

in ventre [L], in the womb: *law.*

inverso ordine [L], in inverse order.

invictus maneo [L], I remain unconquered.

in vino veritas [L], in wine there is truth; truth is told under the influence of intoxicants.

invita Minerva [L], Minerva being unwilling; artistic or literary inspiration being lacking: *Cicero.* Cf. TU NIHIL INVITA DICES FACIESVE MINERVA.

in vitro [L], in glass: *med.*, describing a reaction carried out in a culture dish or test tube.

invitum sequitur honor [L], honor follows him unsolicited.

in vivo [L], in the living organism: *med.*

Ioannes est nomen eius [L], his name is John: motto of *Puerto Rico.*

ioci causa [L], for the sake of the joke.

io dirò cosa incredibile e vero [It], I'll tell a thing incredible yet true: *Dante.*

io Triumphe! [L], hail, god of Triumph! (the shout of the Roman soldiers and populace on the occasion of a triumphal procession in honor of a victorious general).

i pazzi per lettera sono i maggiori pazzi [It], learned fools are the biggest fools.

ipse dixit [L], lit., he himself said it; a dogmatic statement supported by bare authority; dictum.

ipsissima verba [L], the very words. —**ipsissimis verbis,** in the very words; quoted exactly.

ipso facto [L], by that very fact.

ipso iure [L], by the law itself.

ira de irmãos, ira de diabos [Pg], the wrath of brothers, the wrath of devils.

ira furor brevis est [L], anger is a brief madness: *Horace.*

irato [It], angry; passionate: *music.*

ir por lana y volver trasquilado [Sp], to go for wool and come back shorn.

irrevocabile verbum [L], a word beyond recall.

irritabis crabrones [L], you will stir up the hornets: *Plautus.*

Irrlicht [Ger], will-o'-the-wisp.

Irrtümer vorbehalten [Ger], errors excepted.

Irrwahn [Ger], delusion; erroneous opinion.

ispravnik [Russ], chief police official in local districts.

issei [Jap], lit., first generation; a Japanese immigrant to America.

istesso [It], the same: *music.*

ita est [L], it is so.

ita lex scripta est [L], thus the law is written; such is the law.

Italia irredenta [It], unredeemed Italy (i.e., neighboring regions, largely Italian in population but subject to other powers).

italice [L], in Italian; in the Italian manner.

italien [Fr; *fem.* italienne], *adj. & n.* Italian.

ite missa est [L], go, the mass is over.

iterum [L], again; anew.

i tiranni fanno i ribelli [It], tyrants make rebels.

Iubilate Deo [L], rejoice in God; be joyful in the Lord.

iucundi acti labores [L], past labors are pleasant; the memory of mastered difficulties is sweet: *Cicero.*

iudex damnatur cum nocens absolvitur [L], the judge is condemned when the guilty is acquitted: *Publilius Syrus.*

iudicium Dei [L], judgment of God.

iudicium parium aut leges terrae [L], the judgment of one's peers or the laws of the land: from *Magna Charta.*

iuncta iuvant [L], things united aid each other; union is strength.

iuniores ad labores [L], the younger men for labors.

Iupiter (*or* **Iuppiter**) **Tonans** [L], Jupiter the Thunderer.

iurare in verba magistri [L], to swear to the words of the master: *Horace.* See NULLIUS ADDICTUS etc.

iure [L], by right. —**iure coronae,** by the right of the crown. —**iure divino,** by divine right (*or* law). —**iure humano,** by human law; by the will of the people. —**iure mariti,** by a husband's right. —**iure non dono,** by right, not by gift. —**iure propinquitatis,** by right of relationship. —**iure sanguinis,** by right of blood: *all law.*

iurisdictionis fundandae causa (*or* **gratia**) [L], for the sake of establishing jurisdiction: *law.*

iuris peritus [L], learned (*or* skilled) in the law.

Iuris Utriusque Doctor [L], Doctor of Both Laws (i.e., of canon and civil law): *abbr.* J.U.D.

ius [L; *pl.* iures], law; legal right. —**ius canonicum,** canon law. —**ius civile,** civil law. —**ius commune,** the common law. —**ius divinum,** divine law. —**ius et norma loquendi,** the law and rule of speech; ordinary usage: *Horace.* —**ius gentium,** law of nations; international law. —**ius gladii,** the right of the sword; supreme jurisdiction. —**ius in re,** a real right. —**ius mariti,** the right of a husband. —**ius naturae,** the law of nature. —**ius pignoris,** right of pledge or hypothecation. —**ius possessionis,** right of possession. —**ius postliminii,** the right of resumption of their former status by persons and things taken by an enemy in war, on their coming again under the control of the nation to which they originally belonged: *international law.* —**ius proprietatis,** right of property. —**ius regium,** right of the crown; royal right. —**ius relicti,** the right of the widow. —**ius sanguinis,** law or right of consanguinity (*or* blood); specif., the rule of law that the citizenship of the parents determines that of the child. —**ius soli,** law or right of the soil; specif., the rule of law that the citizenship of a child is determined by the place of his birth. —**ius summum saepe summa malitia est,** extreme law is often extreme wrong: *Terence.*

iusiurandum [L; *pl.* iusiuranda], an oath.

ius primae noctis [L], the right of the first night. Cf. DROIT DE SEIGNEUR.

iustitiae soror fides [L], faith is the sister of justice.

iustitiae tenax [L], tenacious of justice.

iustitia omnibus [L], justice to all: motto of the *District of Columbia*.

iusto tempore [L], at the right time.

iustum et tenax propositi vir [L], a man who is upright and firm of purpose: *Horace* (adapted).

iuvante Deo [L], God helping.

izquierda [Sp], on the left: *abbr.* izq.ª.

izvestiya (*or* **izvestia**) [Russ], news; information; reports. —**Izvestia,** name of official U.S.S.R. newspaper.

izzat [Hind], honor; reputation; public esteem.

J

Jacquerie [Fr], revolt of French peasants in 1358; hence, any peasant uprising.

jadu *or* **jadoo** [Hind & Pers], conjuring; magic.

jahannan [Hind], hell.

jai alai [Basque], lit., merry festival; a handball game played with basketlike attachments strapped on the arm.

j'ai vécu [Fr], I lived; I existed through it all (i.e., the Reign of Terror): *Abbé Sieyès.*

jaldi [Hind], quickness; haste; speed. —**jaldi karo,** make haste. —**jaldi jao,** go quickly: *all India.*

jalousie [Fr], jealousy; envy; specif., Venetian blind; latticed shutter. —**jalousie de métier,** professional jealousy.

jamais arrière [Fr], never behind.

jamais bon coureur ne fut pris [Fr], a good runner was never captured; old birds are not to be caught with chaff.

jamais de ma vie [Fr], never in my life; never, never.

jambière [Fr], legging; leg guard.

jambo [Swa], hail; greetings.

jambon [Fr], ham.

jamón [Sp], ham or bacon; also, a guitar: *southwestern U.S.*

jampan [Anglo-Ind], a sedan chair with two poles, borne on the shoulders of four people.

jantar [Pg], dinner.

janvier [Fr], January: *abbr.* janv.

jao [Hind; imperative of *jāna*, to go], go! begone!

ja, prosit! [Ger], don't you wish you may get it!: *colloq.*

jaquima [Sp *jáquima*], head portion of a halter, as used for breaking wild horses: *southwestern U.S.*

jarabe [Sp], syrup.

jarabe tapatio [Mex], popular dance.

jardin [Fr], garden. —**jardin des plantes,** lit., garden of plants; botanical garden; notably, the *Jardin des Plantes* in Paris.

jardinière [Fr], ornamental flower stand; *cookery,* a dish composed of various vegetables cut into cubes and combined with a thick sauce. —**à la jardinière,** prepared in the above manner; as, lamb cutlets *à la jardinière: cookery.*

ját [Hind], caste; clan; also, sort; kind.

jaune [Fr], yellow. —**rire jaune,** laugh on the wrong side of one's face.

jawohl [Ger], yes indeed; quite so; certainly.

j'ay bonne cause [OF], I have good cause (*or* reason).

jedenfalls [Ger], in any case; at all events.

173

jeder fege vor seine Tür [Ger], everyone should sweep before his own door.

jeder ist seines Glückes Schmied [Ger], every man is the architect of his own fortune.

jeder Krämer lobt seine Ware [Ger], every shopkeeper praises his own wares.

jeder Tag ist ein kleines Leben [Ger], every day is a little life.

jeder Vorteil gilt [Ger], every advantage is permitted; all's fair in love and war.

jefe [Sp], chief; leader.

je gage que si [Fr], I bet it's so.

jehad [Ar]. Same as JIHAD.

jemadar *or* **jamadar** [Hind], a subaltern native officer, corresponding to a lieutenant; also, the head of a staff of attendants and messengers: *India.*

je maintiendrai [Fr], I will maintain: motto of the *Netherlands.* —**je maintiendrai le droit,** I will maintain the right.

j'embrasse mon rival, mais c'est pour l'étouffer [Fr], I embrace my rival, but only to choke him: *Corneille.*

je me fie en Dieu [Fr], I trust in God.

je mehr, je besser [Ger], the more the better; the more the merrier.

je m'en fous [Fr], I don't care; I don't give a damn.

je m'en vais chercher un grand Peut-être [Fr], I am going to seek a great Perhaps: *Rabelais* (on his deathbed).

je m'en vais voir le soleil pour la dernière fois [Fr], I am going to see the sun for the last time: *Rousseau* (last words).

je ne cherche qu'un [Fr], I seek but one (i.e., God only do I seek).

je ne sais quoi [Fr], I don't know what; an indescribable something.

je ne sais trop [Fr], I don't know exactly; I am not quite sure.

je n'oublierai jamais [Fr], I shall never forget.

je prends mon bien où je le trouve [Fr], I take my property (*or* I take what is useful to me) where I find it: *Molière* (replying to those who accused him of plagiarism).

je suis prêt [Fr], I am ready.

jet d'eau [Fr; *pl.* jets d'eau], an ornamental jet of water; fountain.

jetée [Fr], jetty; pier; *lumbering,* place on a river bank where logs are piled during the winter.

jeter de la poudre aux yeux [Fr], to throw dust in the eyes; mislead.

jeter le manche après la cognée [Fr], to throw the handle after the hatchet; give up in despair. Cf. ECHAR EL etc.

jeu [Fr; *pl.* jeux], play; sport; game; jest. —**jeu de hasard,** game of chance. —**jeu de mains,** horseplay. —**jeu de mots,** a play on words; pun. —**jeu d'esprit,** a witticism; humorous trifle, usually literary. —**jeu de théâtre,** stage trick or attitude; claptrap. —**jeu du hasard,** freak of fortune.

jeune premier [Fr; *fem.* jeune première], lit., first young (person); juvenile lead; stage lover: *theat.*

jeunesse dorée [Fr], gilded youth; rich and fashionable young men.

je vais rejoindre votre père [Fr], I am going to rejoin your father: *Marie Antoinette* (parting words to her children, on her way to the guillotine).

je vis en espoir [Fr], I live in hope.

jezail [Pers], a long, heavy Afghan rifle, fired from a forked rest.

jheel *or* **jhil** [Anglo-Ind], a pool, marsh, or shallow lake.

jhuta [Hind], *adj.* false; untrue; not genuine; *n.* liar.

jiang [Chin]. Same as KIANG.

jihad *or* **jehad** [Ar], a Muslim war against heretics or enemies of Islam; hence, a holy war, or crusade, waged for a principle or belief.

jinete [Sp], cavalier; horseman; *mil.,* trooper; cavalryman; *in southwestern U.S.,* bronco buster.

jingal [Anglo-Ind], a small portable piece of ordnance, mounted on a swivel.

jipijapa [Sp, *fr. Jipijapa,* a town in Ecuador], a tropical plant, from which the so-called "Panama" hats are made; hence, a hat made from this plant; a Panama hat (the name by which the *jipijapa* is known outside Latin America).

jiu jitsu [Jap], lit., gentle struggle; Japanese wrestling.

jodhpurs [Hind], riding breeches of heavy cloth fitting closely at knees and ankles.

Johannistag [Ger], St. John the Baptist's Day; Midsummer Day.

joie de vivre [Fr], joy of living.

joli [Fr; *fem.* jolie], pretty; attractive.

jornada [Sp], a journey or the like performed in a day; also, a land measure, equivalent to as much land as can be plowed in one day; specif., a long waterless stretch of desert country; as, the *Jornada del Muerto* in New Mexico: *Mexico & southwestern U.S.*

joro [Jap], a prostitute.

joss [Pidgin, *fr.* Pg *deos*], god; a Chinese idol or cult image. —**joss house** [Eng], a Chinese shrine or temple.

jour [Fr], day. —**au jour,** by daylight. —**au jour le jour,** from day to day. —**jour de congé,** a day's leave; holiday. —**jour de fête,** fete day; festival. —**jour de l'an,** New Year's Day. —**jour maigre,** lit., lean day; meatless day; fish day; fast day. —**c'est le jour et la nuit,** they are as different as day and night.

journal intime [Fr], private diary.

joya [Sp], jewel.

Joyeux Noël [Fr], Merry Christmas.

jubbah *or* **jubba** [Hind & Ar], a long robe worn by Muslims of both sexes.

judo [Jap], lit., way of gentleness; Japanese wrestling.

juego [Sp], game.

juego de naipes [Sp], card game.

juez [Sp; *pl.* jueces], a judge. **—juez de paz,** justice of the peace.

juge [Fr], judge; justice. **—juge de paix,** justice of the peace. **—juge d'instruction,** examining magistrate.

Jugendsünde [Ger], youthful offense.

juillet [Fr], July.

juin [Fr], June.

juiz piedoso faz o povo cruel [Pg], a merciful judge makes a cruel people.

julienne [Fr], a clear soup made of chopped vegetables cooked in meat broth: *cookery.*

jumelle [Fr], *adj.* twin; paired; *n. pl.* pair of opera glasses (*jumelles de théâtre*) or field glasses (*jumelles de campagne*); *carpentry,* side beams.

Junge [Ger; *pl.* Jungen], boy; youth; apprentice.

Jünger [Ger; *fem.* Jüngerin], disciple.

Jüngling [Ger; *pl.* Jünglinge], young man.

Junker [Ger; *sing. & pl.*], young nobleman or squire; young German aristocrat.

Junkerei [Ger], behavior of the younger nobility in Germany; aristocratic arrogance.

junta [Sp], collective leadership, often in a *coup d'état.*

juramentado [Sp], lit., bound by an oath; a Moro who takes a Muslim oath to die in the slaying of Christians: *P.I.*

juramento [Sp], oath.

jus [Fr], juice; gravy. **—au jus,** with the natural juice or gravy, given off by the meat in cooking: *both cookery.*

justaucorps [Fr], lit., close to the body; a close-fitting coat or doublet, with long skirts, popular in the 17th and early 18th centuries.

juste-milieu [Fr], the just (*or* golden) mean; specif., a method of government that steers a middle course between extremists.

justicia [Sp], justice.

justicia, mas no por mi casa [Sp], a court of justice by all means, but not for my family.

j'y suis, j'y reste [Fr], here I am, here I stay: *Marshal MacMahon* (when urged to abandon the Malakoff Tower in 1855).

K

kabab [Hind & Pers], roasted meat; a roast.

Καδμεία νίκη [Gr; kadmeía níkē], a Cadmean victory (i.e., one that ruins the victor); Pyrrhic victory.

Kaffeeklatsch [Ger], afternoon coffee party, esp. for women.

kaffiyeh [Ar], Arab headdress, as worn esp. by Bedouins.

kafir [Ar], a non-Muslim; infidel.

kai [Maori & Polynesian], food.

καὶ ἐδικαιώθη ἡ σοφία ἀπὸ τῶν ἔργων αὐτῆς [Gr; kaì edikaióthē hē sophía apò tôn érgōn autês], but wisdom is justified of her children (*or* by her works): *Matthew* xi. 19.

καὶ κεραμεὺς κεραμεῖ κοτέει καὶ τέκτονι τέκτων [Gr; kaì keramèus keramei kotéei kaì téktoni téktōn], a potter has a grudge against a potter, and a smith against a smith: *Hesiod.*

καιρὸν γνῶθι [Gr; kairòn gnôthi], know your opportunity: *Pittacus.*

καὶ σύ, τέκνον [Gr; kaì sú, téknon], thou, too, my son (lit., child): *Plutarch* (reporting Caesar's dying words to Brutus). Cf. ET TU, BRUTE.

καὶ τὰ λοιπά [Gr; kaì tà loipá], and the rest; and so forth; et cetera: *abbr.* κ. τ. λ.

kajawah [Hind & Pers], a litter or pannier used in pairs on camels, horses, and mules, esp. for the transport of women and children.

kak delah? [Russ], how are you getting on?

kakemono [Jap], a Japanese unframed picture for hanging on a wall, usually mounted on rollers for convenience when not in use. Cf. MAKIMONO.

κακοῦ κόρακος κακὸν ᾠόν [Gr; kakoû kórakos kakòn ōón], from a bad crow a bad egg; like father, like son.

kala [Hind], black. —**kala admi,** black man. —**kala azar,** lit., black disease; a virulent form of malarial fever; "black sickness." —**kala jagah,** lit., black place; shady nook; retreat, esp. one with romantic appeal. —**kala pani,** lit., black water; the open sea: *all India.*

καλόν ἐστιν ἡμᾶς ὧδε εἶμι [Gr; kalón estin humâs hôde eîmi], it is good for us to be here: *Matthew* xvii. 4.

καλῶς [Gr; kalôs], well said! bravo! good! Cf. EUGE. —πάνυ καλῶς, pánu kalôs, no, thank you.

kam [Hind], work; task; occupation; business.

kamaina [Hawa], long-time resident of the Hawaiian Islands.

kama rupa [Skr], lit., desire form; the form of a body after death; astral body: *theos.*

kameel [Cape Du], lit., camel; giraffe: *South Africa.*

Kamerad [Ger; *pl.* Kameraden], comrade: used by German soldiers in appealing for mercy (W.W. I).

kami [Jap], in Shintoism, a god; a divinity; also, a Japanese title of nobility, equivalent to *lord*.

kammal [Hind], blanket: *India*.

Kampf der Anschauungen [Ger], conflict of opinions.

Kampf ums Dasein [Ger], struggle for existence.

kanat [Anglo-Ind], the walls of a tent.

kang [Chin], in Chinese houses, a brick platform for sleeping upon, with space underneath for a fire in cold weather; also, a large water jar: *China*.

kannushi [Jap], Shinto priest: *Japan*.

kantikoy [Algon], Indian tribal dance.

kan pei! [Chin], lit., dry cup; to your health! bottoms up!

kanwa [Beng], a Hindu sage: *India*.

Kapelle [Ger], lit., chapel; hence, a private choir or orchestra.

Kapellmeister [Ger], orchestra conductor or choir leader.

kapra [Hind; *pl.* kapre], cloth; clothes; attire: *India*.

karate [Jap], lit., empty hand; a Japanese system of unarmed combat, using hands and feet.

karateka [Jap], karate expert; karate devotee.

kari [Fr], curry. —**kari à l'indienne,** Indian curry: *cookery*.

karma [Skr], lit., work; the cumulative consequences of a person's acts in one earth life, considered as determining his or her lot in the next existence; the inexorable application of the law of cause and effect: *Buddhism*.

kartel [Cape Du], a kind of wooden hammock, used in ox wagons: *South Africa*.

Kartell [Ger; *pl.* Kartelle], orig., a written challenge, as to a duel; a written agreement between warring nations, esp. regarding the exchange of prisoners; a cartel; *econ.*, in Germany and Austria, a trade combine; trust.

katana [Jap], Japanese sword.

katar [Hind], a kind of short dagger: *India*.

κατ' ἔπος [Gr; kat' épos], word by word; accurately.

κατ' ἐξοχήν [Gr; kat' exokhén], preeminently: *par excellence*.

κατόπιν ἑορτῆς ἥκεις [Gr; katópin heortês hékeis], you are come after the feast (i.e., too late). Cf. POST FESTUM VENISTI.

kazak [Russ; *pl.* kazaku], cossack.

keddah [Hind]. See KHEDA.

keffiyeh [Ar]. Same as KAFFIYEH.

keine Pfiffe! [Ger], no nonsense!

kein Gedanke! [Ger], that is not to be thought of! no such thing! nonsense!

kein kluger Streiter hält seinen Feind gering [Ger], no prudent fighter thinks lightly of his foe: *Goethe*.

kein Kreuzer, kein Schweizer [Ger], no money, no Swiss: a reference to the Swiss mercenaries of former days.

kein Mensch muss müssen [Ger], lit., no man must must; no man is compelled to be compelled: *Lessing*.

kein Rauch ohne Feuer [Ger], no smoke without fire.

Kellner [Ger; *sing. & pl.; fem.* Kellnerin], waiter; servant at an inn.

kennst du das Land wo die Citronen blühn? [Ger], know'st thou the land where the lemon trees bloom?: *Goethe* (first line of Mignon's song in *Wilhelm Meister*).

képi [Fr], military cap, with visor.

χαῖρε [Gr; *pl.* χαίρετε; khaîre; khaírete], lit., rejoice; a salutation (1) *on meeting*, hail! welcome! (2) *on parting*, farewell! good-bye! (3) *on other occasions*, be of good cheer!

khalasi [Hind], sailor; also, general outdoor servant, who pitches tents, etc.; *mil.,* artilleryman: *India*.

khan [Ar & Pers], caravansary.

khan [Tatar], prince; lord; chief; also, a title: *Oriental*.

khana [Hind], food; dinner: *India*.

khanum [Turk], Oriental lady of rank; chief lady of a harem.

kharab [Hind], bad: opposite of *achcha*.

kharif [Hind & Ar], autumn; autumnal harvest, as of rice and cotton: *India*. Cf. RABI.

khatib [Ar], Muslim priest.

kheda *or* **keddah** [Hind], an enclosure for entrapping wild elephants.

χειρῶν νόμος [Gr; kheirôn nómos], lit., the law of hands; the law of might.

khidmutgar *or* **khitmutgar** [Anglo-Ind; Hind *khidmatgar*], male waiter or table servant, usually a Muslim.

χρήματ' ἀνήρ [Gr; khrḗmat' anḗr], money makes the man: *Pindar*.

χρήματα ψυχὴ βροτοῖσι [Gr; khrḗmata psykhḕ brotoîsi], a man's money is his life: *Hesiod*.

khubber [Anglo-Ind; Hind & Ar *khabar*], news; information; report.

khud [Anglo-Ind], steep hillside; deep valley.

khushi [Hind & Pers], pleasure; gladness; happiness; satisfaction; one's will and pleasure; as, hamari *kushi* hai, "it is my pleasure." The word *khushi*, in the form "kushi" or "cushy," was commonly used by British soldiers in India as an adjective. Thus, a *kushi* job is a pleasant or soft job. In this sense, "cushy" has passed into English.

khutbah [Ar], an address or sermon delivered, usually on a Friday, in the principal mosques: *Islam*.

kiang *or* **jiang** [Chin], river: common in Chinese geographical names.

kia ora! [Maori], be happy! be well! (a New Zealand toast).

kibbutz [Heb], a collective farm or settlement: *Israel*.

kibbutznik [Heb], a member of a *kibbutz: Israel*.

kibei [Jap], lit., returns to America; a son or daughter of Japanese immigrant parents, born in America but educated in Japan and then returned to live in America.

kibitka [Russ], a Tatar circular tent, usually of latticework and felt; also, a hooded vehicle on wheels or runners.

kibitz [Yiddish; *variant of* kibitzen], to look on and criticize; to meddle.

kiblah [Ar], the direction in which Muslims turn at prayer.

kiddush [Heb], lit., sanctification; a blessing or prayer recited over bread or wine, esp. on the eve of a Jewish Sabbath or festival.

kidhar? [Hind], whither? where?

kiku [Jap], chrysanthemum: *Japan.*

kikumon [Jap], Japanese imperial crest, in the form of an open chrysanthemum (*kiku*). Cf. KIRIMON.

kila *or* **killa** [Anglo-Ind; Hind *qil'a*], fort; fortress.

killadar [Anglo-Ind], governor or commandant of a fort.

kimchi [Kor], a spicy national dish: *Korea.*

kim-makiye [Jap], Japanese gold lacquer.

kimono [Jap], lit., clothes; a loose-fitting Japanese robe.

kindergarten [Ger], lit., children's garden; class or school for young children.

κινεῖν πᾶν χρῆμα [Gr; kineîn pân khrêma], to set everything in motion; leave no stone unturned: *Herodotus.*

kingyo [Jap], goldfish (*Carassius auratus*): *Japan.*

kirimon [Jap], Japanese imperial crest, representing three leaves of the paulownia tree (*kiri*) beneath three budding stems. Cf. KIKUMON.

kisen [Jap], steamship; steamboat: *Japan.*

kismet [Turk, *fr.* Ar *qismah*, portion], fate.

kis-waste? [Hind], on what account? why?

kitab [Hind & Ar], book; *Muslim law,* book of revealed religion.

kitna [Hind; *pl.* kitne], how much? how many?

kiwi [Maori], flightless bird: *New Zealand.*

kiva [Hopi], underground room in a pueblo.

Kladderadatsch [Ger], a mess; muddle.

Klagelied [Ger], song of lament; elegy; dirge.

Klang [Ger; *pl.* Klänge], clang; sound; *music & phonetics,* timbre; tone.

Klangfarbe [Ger], lit., clang tint; tone color; quality of sound.

Klatsch [Ger], smack; slap; crack, as of a whip; fig., gossip; chatter.

kleb [Russ], bread.

kleine Leiden [Ger], petty annoyances.

klein gewin brengt rijkdom in [Du], small gains bring riches in.

kloof [Du], gorge; deep glen: *South Africa.*

Klügler [Ger], pretender to wisdom; quibbler.

klutz [Yiddish], a clod; a bungler.

knesset [Heb], lit., gathering; Israeli parliament.

knout [Russ *knut*], a heavy whip.

Koh-i-noor *or* **Koh-i-nur** [Pers], lit., mountain of light; a famous Indian diamond.

kolkhoz [Russ], Soviet collective farm.

Kol Nidre [Aram], lit., all the vows; a prayer sung by Jews at the start of the service for the Day of Atonement.

κολοιὸς ποτὶ κολοιόν [Gr; koloiòs potì koloión], jackdaw with jackdaw; birds of a feather flock together.

komban-wa [Jap], good evening: a Japanese salutation.

konnichi-wa [Jap], good day: a Japanese salutation.

kop [Du], hill; mountain: *South Africa*.

Kopfschmerzen [Ger], headache.

kopje [Du], small hill or *kop*: *South Africa*.

kos [Hind], measure of distance, of about two miles: *India*.

kosher [Yiddish *fr.* Heb], lit., proper; prepared in accordance with Jewish dietary laws.

koto [Jap], long-necked zither with thirteen strings.

kowashi, mitashi [Jap], afraid, and yet itching to peep.

kowtow [Chin], lit., bump head; a ceremonial bow.

Kraft durch Freude [Ger], strength through joy; a youth project in Nazi Germany.

kräftig [Ger], strong; powerful; vigorous: *music*.

Krieg [Ger; *pl.* Kriege], war.

Kriegsminister [Ger], minister of war.

Kriegspiel *or* **Kriegsspiel** [Ger], German war game, in which blocks representing naval or military units are moved about on a map or table.

Kshatriya [Skr], the military caste, one of the four major divisions of the Hindu caste system: *India*.

κτῆμα ἐς ἀεί [Gr; ktêma es aeí], a possession for all time: *Thucydides*.

kto druhému jamu kope sám do nej padá [Slovak], who digs a grave for someone else falls into it himself.

kudos [Gr κῦδος], acclaim as result of achievement.

kukri [Hind], a curved Gurkha knife, broadening toward the point, used for everyday work and as a weapon: *India*.

Kultur [Ger], culture; civilization.

Kulturkampf [Ger], culture conflict (*or* battle for civilization); the struggle between the Roman Catholic Church and the German government concerning the ecclesiastical policy initiated by Bismarck in 1872. The conflict lasted for more than a decade, the government finally yielding to the vigorous opposition of the Clerical Party.

kumshaw [Pidgin]. Same as CUMSHAW.

kun [Chin & Jap], prince; lord; also, a polite form of address, placed after the name. Cf. SAMA and SAN.

kung fu [Chin], lit., boxing principles; Chinese method of unarmed combat developed by monks.

Kunst [Ger; *pl.* Künste], art.

Kursaal [Ger], lit., cure hall; a public hall for visitors at a famous watering place; pump room.

kursi [Hind], chair: *western India.* Cf. CHAUKI. —**kursi dena,** to offer a chair; give elevation to; show respect or regard for.

Kursivschrift [Ger], italics; italic type: *typog.*

kurz ist der Schmerz, und ewig ist die Freude [Ger], brief is the pain and eternal is the joy: *Schiller.*

kurzum [Ger], in short; to sum up.

kushti [Hind], Hindu wrestling, a method of self-defense somewhat resembling jiu jitsu.

kuskus *or* **kuskos** [Anglo-Ind; Hind *khaskhas*], an East Indian grass; also, its roots, used for making mats and screens; vetiver.

kutcha [Anglo-Ind], lit., raw; makeshift; temporary. Cf. PUCKA.

kvass [Russ], Russian beer.

kvell [Yiddish], to glow with pride.

kyaung [Burmese], Buddhist monastery: *Burma.*

Kyrie eleison [Gr Κύριε ἐλέησον], Lord, have mercy on us; words occurring in the rituals of the Eastern and Roman churches; also, a musical setting of this petition: *eccl.*

kyuji [Jap], waiter: *Japan.*

L

la almohada es buen consejo [Sp], the pillow is a good counselor.

la América del Norte [Sp], North America.

la América del Sur [Sp], South America.

la ausencia es madrasta del amor [Sp], absence is the stepmother of love.

la beauté sans vertu est une fleur sans parfum [Fr], beauty without virtue is a flower without perfume.

la belle dame sans merci [Fr], the beautiful lady without mercy.

labitur et labetur in omne volubilis aevum [L], (the stream) flows on and will forever flow: *Horace.*

la bonne blague! [Fr], what a joke!

laborare est orare [L], to work is to pray; work is worship.

labore et honore [L], by (*or* with) labor and honor.

labor ipse voluptas [L], work itself is a pleasure: *Manilius.*

labor omnia vincit [L], labor conquers all things: motto of *Oklahoma.*

laborum dulce lenimen [L], sweet solace of my toils: *Horace* (to his lyre).

labrador [Sp], laborer; farmer; countryman: *Sp. Am.*

la bride sur le cou [Fr], lit., bridle on neck; with free rein; unchecked; unrestrained.

labuntur et imputantur [L], (the moments) glide away and are set down to our account: *for a sundial.*

lac *or* **lakh** [Anglo-Ind], one hundred thousand, esp. of rupees. Cf. CRORE.

la carrière ouverte aux talents [Fr], the career (i.e., of arms) open to talent: *Napoleon.*

lâche [Fr], *adj.* loose, as a knot; slack; slovenly; cowardly; *n.* coward; dastard.

lâcheté [Fr], cowardice; also, laxity; slackness.

la codicia rompe el saco [Sp], cupidity breaks the sack; grasp all, lose all.

la commedia è finita [It], the comedy is ended: closing words of the opera *I Pagliacci.* Cf. TIREZ LE RIDEAU, LA FARCE EST JOUÉE.

la cosa marcha [Sp], lit., the thing goes (*or* marches); the affair is making progress.

lacrimae rerum [L], lit., the tears of things.

lacrimis oculos suffusa nitentis [L], her sparkling eyes bedewed with tears: *Virgil.*

la critique est aisée et l'art est difficile [Fr], criticism is easy and art is difficult: *Destouches.*

la cruz en los pechos y el diablo en los hechos [Sp], the cross on one's breast and the devil in one's deeds.

Ladino [Sp], lit., cunning; a language based on Old Spanish and written in a modified Hebrew alphabet, used by some Sephardic Jews. —**ladino** [Am Sp], mestizo; a person of mixed Spanish and Indian ancestry in the U.S., typically following Spanish customs and speaking Spanish; a vicious, unmanageable horse full of cunning.

La Divina Commedia [It], The Divine Comedy: title of Dante's immortal epic.

ladno [Russ], all right.

laesa maiestas [L], lese majesty; high treason.

laevus [L; *fem.* laeva], left; left-handed.

la fame non vuol leggi [It], hunger has (*or* knows) no laws.

la farce est jouée [Fr], the farce is over: *Rabelais* (last words). Cf. ACTA EST FABULA.

l'affaire s'achemine [Fr], the affair is progressing.

la fleur des pois [Fr], the height of fashion.

la fortune passe partout [Fr], fortune passes everywhere; the vicissitudes of fortune are felt everywhere.

la garde meurt et ne se rend pas [Fr], the guard dies and does not surrender: ascribed to *General Cambronne,* commander of the Old Guard at Waterloo. (Cambronne is commonly supposed to have used an expletive resembling the sound but not the meaning of *meurt* (dies) instead of the first three words of the quotation, but his real words were censored for posterity.)

lagniappe *or* **lagnappe** [Louisiana Fr], a trifling complimentary present given by a tradesman to a customer; gratuity: *Louisiana.* Cf. PILON.

lago [It, Pg, & Sp], lake.

λαγὼς καθεύδων [Gr; lagòs kathéudōn], a sleeping hare; a man with his weather eye open.

lagrimoso [It], tearfully; plaintively: *music.*

Lagting [Norw], upper house of the Norwegian legislature.

la haute politique [Fr], affairs of state.

laisser-aller [Fr], lit., let go; a letting go; unconstraint; unlimited freedom.

laisser-faire [Fr], lit., let act; a letting alone; noninterference, esp. by government in trade, industry, and individual action generally.

laissez-nous faire [Fr], let us alone.

lait [Fr], milk. —**au lait,** with milk. —**lait coupé,** milk and water.

laitance [Fr], milt; soft roe; milky fluid exuding from concrete newly laid under water.

laitue [Fr], lettuce.

lakh [Hind]. See LAC.

l'allegro [It], the cheerful (*or* merry) man.

lama [Tibetan *blama*], Buddhist monk of Tibet and Mongolia.

lamba [Hind; *fem.* lambi], long; tall. —**lamba chauki** *or (more correctly)* **lambi chauki,** long chair; an easy chair with extended arms that serve as a leg rest: called in western India *lamba* (or *lambi) kursi.*

lamé [Fr], fabric with metallic threads.

lamentando [It], lamenting; sorrowful: *music.*

lamentevole [It], plaintive; doleful: *music.*

l'amitié est l'amour sans ailes [Fr], "friendship is love without his wings": *Byron.*

lamentoso [It], doleful; sorrowful; mournful: *music.*

l'amour et la fumée ne peuvent se cacher [Fr], love and smoke cannot be hidden.

lamproie [Fr], lamprey.

lana caprina [L], goat's wool; a thing nonexistent (as goats have hair); trifle: *Horace* (adapted).

lanai [Hawa], veranda; porch.

la nation boutiquière [Fr], the nation of shopkeepers (i.e., England): epithet used by Napoleon Bonaparte in one of his speeches.

lance-flamme [Fr], flame thrower: *mil.*

landa [Sp], heath; moor. Cf. LANDE.

landau [Fr *fr.* Ger], four-wheeled carriage; baby carriage.

landdrost [Du], magistrate: *South Africa.*

lande [Fr], stretch of wasteland; moor; *pl.,* infertile lowlands near the sea, as in S.W. France.

Landsting [Dan], upper house, or senate, of the Danish legislature.

Landsturm [Ger], army reserve.

Landtag [Ger], legislature or diet of a German state; in Austria, a provincial assembly.

Landwehr [Ger], militia.

langage [Fr], language; speech; tongue. —**langage de carrefour,** lit., language of the crossroad; low, vulgar language. —**langage des halles,** language of the markets; billingsgate.

langouste [Fr], spiny lobster.

langsam [Ger], slow; slowly; not so fast! gently!

langue [Fr], tongue; language. —**langue d'oc,** lit., language of *oc* or "yes"; a Romance dialect spoken in the Middle Ages in southern France: so called because of the use of *oc* for the French affirmative. —**langue d'oïl,** lit., language of *oïl* or "yes"; a Romance dialect spoken in northern France: so called because of the use of *oïl* (later *oui*) for the French affirmative. —**langue maternelle,** mother tongue; native tongue or language. —**langue verte,** lit., green language; slang.

languente [It], languishing; faint: *music.*

languidamente [It], languidly; faintly: *music.*

la noche es capa de pecadores [Sp], night is the cloak of sinners.

la nuit tous les chats sont gris [Fr], at night, all cats are gray; in the dark, everyone looks alike.

la patience est amère, mais son fruit est doux [Fr], patience is bitter, but its fruit (or reward) is sweet: *Rousseau.*

la patrie de la pensée [Fr], the fatherland of thought (i.e., Germany): *Madame de Staël.*

lapereau [Fr; *pl.* lapereaux], young rabbit.

lapin [Fr], rabbit. —**lapin au kari** (*or* **cari**), curried rabbit: *cookery.*

lapis [L; *pl.* lapides], a stone. —**lapis philosophorum,** the philosophers' stone.

la pobreza no es vileza, mas inconveniencia [Sp], poverty is no shame, but an inconvenience.

la povertà è la madre di tutte le arti [It], poverty is the mother of all the arts; necessity is the mother of invention.

l'appétit vient en mangeant [Fr], appetite comes with eating.

la propriété c'est le vol [Fr], property is theft: *Proudhon.*

lapsus [L], a slip; blunder. —**lapsus calami,** a slip of the pen. —**lapsus linguae,** a slip of the tongue. —**lapsus memoriae,** memory lapse.

lar [L; *pl.* lares], tutelary deity; beneficent ancestral spirit. —**lares et penates,** household gods; the home. —**lar familiaris,** domestic or household deity, usually the spirit of the founder of the family.

l'arbre ne tombe pas du premier coup [Fr], the tree does not fall at the first blow.

la reine le veut [Fr], the queen wills it: formula of royal assent. In Norman French, the form was *la reyne le veult.* Cf. LE ROI LE VEUT.

largamente [It], broadly; in a broad style: *music.*

l'argent est un bon passe-partout [Fr], money is a good master key. See ARGENT.

larghetto [It], somewhat slow *or* slowly; between *adagio* and *largo: music.*

larghissimo [It], very slow: *music.*

largo [It], slow; solemn; also, slow, stately movement or piece: *music.*

larigo [Sp], on a Mexican saddle, a ring at each end of the cinch, through which the *látigos* pass; *Sp. Am. & southwestern U.S.* Cf. LÁTIGO.

la ringrazio [It], I thank you.

larka [Hind], boy: *India.*

larki [Hind], girl: *India.*

larmoyant [Fr; *fem.* larmoyante], tearful; weeping; lachrymose; fig., pathetic; sentimental; tragic.

lascar [Hind], East Indian sailor.

lascia parlare a me [It], leave speech to me: *Dante.*

lasciate ogni speranza voi ch'entrate [It], all hope abandon, ye who enter here: *Dante* (inscription over Hell, in the "Inferno").

lashkar [Hind & Pers], army; military camp; specif., a body of soldiers: *India.*

la speranza è il pan de' miseri [It], hope is the bread of the wretched.

lass das Vergang'ne vergangen sein [Ger], let bygones be bygones: *Goethe* (Faust's words to Margaret).

lateat scintillula forsan [L], perhaps a little spark (of life) may lurk unseen: motto of the *Royal Humane Society,* a society founded in London in 1774 for the rescue of drowning persons.

latet anguis in herba [L], a snake lies hidden in the grass.

λάθε βιώσας [Gr; láthe biósas], seek to live unnoticed: *Epicurus.*

lathi [Hind], club; heavy stick; quarterstaff: *India.*

látigo [Sp; *pl.* látigos], a strong strap fastened to the saddletree of a Mexican saddle, used for tightening the cinch: *Sp. Am. & southwestern U.S.* Cf. LARIGO.

latin de cuisine [Fr], spurious Latin. **—au bout de son latin,** at wit's end.

Latine [L], in Latin; as in Latin. **—Latine dictum,** spoken in Latin.

lato sensu [L], in a broad sense: opposite of *stricto sensu.*

la Trêve de Dieu [Fr], the Truce of God. Cf. TREUGA DEI.

lauda la moglie e tienti donzello [It], praise a wife and stay a bachelor; praise married life but remain single.

laudari a laudato viro [L], to be praised by a man (who is himself) praised: *Cicero* (quoted from Naevius).

laudator temporis acti [L], a praiser of times past; someone who prefers the good old days: *Horace.*

laudumque immensa cupido [L], and a boundless desire for praise (*or* passion for renown): *Virgil.*

laus Deo [L], praise be to God.

laus propria sordet [L], self-praise is base.

lá vão leis onde querem cruzados [Pg], laws go where dollars please.

lá vão os pés onde quer o coração [Pg], the feet go where the heart wills.

l'avenir [Fr], the future.

La Vergine Gloriosa [It], The Glorious Virgin.

la verità è figlia del tempo [It], truth is the daughter of time.

la vérité sort de la bouche des enfants [Fr], truth comes out of the mouth of little children. Cf. EX ORE PARVULORUM VERITAS.

laver la tête [Fr], lit., to wash the head; berate; reprimand.

la vertu est la seule noblesse [Fr], virtue is the only nobility.

la vida es sueño [Sp], life is a dream: *Calderón de la Barca.*

lazzarone [It; *pl.* lazzaroni], Neapolitan beggar or homeless idler.

l'chaim [Heb], to life; to your health.

le agradezco mucho [Sp], I am much obliged to you.

le beau monde [Fr], the fashionable world; society.

Lebensabend [Ger], evening of life.

leben und leben lassen [Ger], to live and let live.

leb(e) wohl *or* **leben sie wohl!** [Ger], farewell!

lebhaft [Ger], lively; animated: *music.*

le bois tortu fait le feu droit [Fr], crooked stick makes straight fire; the end justifies the means.

le bonheur semble fait pour être partagé [Fr], happiness seems made to be shared: *Racine.*

le bon motif [Fr], matrimony: *jocose.*

le bon temps viendra [Fr], the good time will come; there is a good time coming.

Le Bourgeois Gentilhomme [Fr], the commoner turned nobleman; the tradesman turned gentleman: title of comedy by *Molière.*

le chant du cygne [Fr], the swan song. See CHANT DU CYGNE.

l'échapper belle [Fr], to have a narrow escape.

leche [Sp], milk.

le coût en ôte le goût [Fr], the cost takes away the taste.

le crime fait la honte, et non pas l'échafaud [Fr], the crime makes the shame and not the scaffold; it's the crime that is the disgrace, not the scaffold: these words of *Corneille* were quoted in a letter written by Charlotte Corday, slayer of Marat, on the eve of her execution, July 17, 1793.

lector benevole [L], kind (*or* gentle) reader.

lectori benevolo [L], to the kind (*or* gentle) reader: *abbr.* L.B.

le dessous des cartes [Fr], the underside (i.e., the face) of the cards; (to be in on) the secret; behind the scenes.

Le Diable Boiteux [Fr], lit., the lame devil; the devil on two sticks (*or* on crutches): title character of play by *Le Sage.*

le droit du plus fort [Fr], the right of the strongest.

le fin mot [Fr], the main point; gist.

le fruit du travail est le plus doux plaisir [Fr], the fruit of toil is the sweetest pleasure: *Vauvenargues.*

legadero [Am Sp], stirrup strap on a Mexican saddle: *Mexico & southwestern U.S.*

legalis homo [L], a legal man; a man of full legal rights: *law.*

legatissimo [It], very smoothly: *music.*

legato [It], smoothly; flowingly; without breaks between the notes (*abbr.* leg.): *music.*

legatura [It], a tie or brace; slur: *music.*

legatus a latere [L], lit., a legate from the side (of the Pope); specially instructed papal legate.

legenda [L], things to be read.

le génie c'est la patience [Fr], genius is patience.

lege, quaeso [L], read, I pray you: formula inscribed by students at the head of their papers to invite reading by the instructor.

légèreté [Fr], lightness; nimbleness; slimness; fickleness; levity; frivolity.

leges mori serviunt [L], laws are subservient to custom.

leggiero [It], light; nimble; delicate: *music.*

legimus, ne legantur [L], we read that others may not read (said of reviewers and censors): *Lactantius.*

légionnaire [Fr], member of a legion; esp., member of the French Legion of Honor (*Légion d'honneur*).

λεγιὼν ὄνομά μοι [Gr; legiṑn ónomá moi], my name is Legion: *Mark* v. 9.

le grand Monarque [Fr], the Great Monarch (i.e., Louis XIV).

le grand oeuvre [Fr], the philosophers' stone.

legs [Fr; *pr.* lā], legacy; bequest.

legua [Sp], Spanish league, as a measure of distance, equivalent to 4.83 kilometers (2.63 miles); as a measure of area, equivalent to about 4,409 acres or 1,785 hectares: used in *Texas, the Philippines, Mexico,* etc.

Lehrer-seminar [Ger], training college for teachers.

Lehrgabe [Ger], talent for teaching.

Lehrjahre [Ger], years of apprenticeship. See WANDERJAHRE.

lei [Hawa], a floral garland.

leidenschaftlich [Ger], passionate; vehement; impassioned: *music.*

Leiermann [Ger], organ grinder.

Leitartikel [Ger], leading article; leader.

Leitmotif *or* **Leitmotiv** [Ger], leading theme or motif in a composition, esp. a theme identified with a certain character, idea, or situation, as in Wagnerian music dramas: *music.*

le jeu ne vaut pas la chandelle [Fr], the game is not worth the candle.

le jour viendra [Fr], the day will come.

le juste-milieu [Fr], the golden mean.

le meilleur vin a sa lie [Fr], even the best wine has its dregs.

le mieux est l'ennemi du bien [Fr], better is the enemy of good; leave well enough alone.

le moi est haïssable [Fr], the word "I" is hateful; egoism is odious: *Pascal.*

le monde [Fr], the world; society. **—le monde est le livre des femmes,** the world is women's (*or* woman's) book: *Rousseau.* **—le monde récompense plus souvent les apparences du mérite que le mérite même,** the world more often rewards the appearance of merit than merit itself: *La Rochefoucauld.* **—le monde savant,** the learned world.

le mot de l'énigme [Fr], the key to the mystery.

le mot juste [Fr], the exact word; the precise expression.

l'empire, c'est la paix [Fr], the empire is (*or* stands for) peace: *Prince Louis Napoleon* (afterwards *Napoleon III*), in a speech at Bordeaux, Oct. 9, 1852. The trend of events caused a German paper to give to the world the punning variant: *l'empire, c'est l'épée* (the empire is the sword). London *Punch,* viewing the military disasters and the load of taxation that must follow, concocted its own significant pun: *l'empire, c'est la pay.*

l'empire des lettres [Fr], the republic (lit., empire) of letters.

lentamente [It], slowly: *music.*

lentando [It], becoming slower; slackening; retarding: *music.*

lentille [Fr], lentil; also, freckle.

lento [It], slow; slowly. —**lento assai** *or* **lento molto,** very slow: *music.*

l'envoi [Fr], postscript to a literary composition; a short concluding stanza; envoy.

leone fortior fides [L], faith is stronger than a lion.

leonina societas [L], a leonine partnership; a partnership, legally invalid, in which one partner shares the losses but not the profits: *law.*

le pas [Fr], lit., the step; precedence; preeminence.

le petit caporal [Fr], the little corporal; Napoleon.

le point du jour [Fr], daybreak.

le premier pas [Fr], the first step.

le premier venu [Fr; *fem.* la première venue], the first comer; the man in the street; the first person one meets; anyone.

le revers de la médaille [Fr], the other side of the medal (coin).

le roi est mort, vive le roi! [Fr], the king is dead, long live the king!

le roi et l'état [Fr], the king and the state.

le roi le veut [Fr], the king wills it: formula of royal assent. In Norman French, the form was *le roy le veult.* Cf. LA REINE LE VEUT.

le roi s'avisera [Fr], the king will consider (*or* take under advisement): old formula of royal veto.

les absents ont toujours tort [Fr], the absent are always wrong (*or* in the wrong).

les affaires font les hommes [Fr], experience of affairs (*or* business) makes men.

les aristocrates à la lanterne! [Fr], to the lamppost with the aristocrats! string them up!

les bras croisés [Fr], with arms folded; doing nothing; idle; indifferent.

les convenances [Fr], the proprieties; good manners; etiquette.

les dessous des cartes [Fr], the undersides (i.e., the faces) of the cards; inside information.

les doux yeux [Fr], tender glances.

lèse-majesté [Fr], high treason.

les extrêmes se touchent [Fr], extremes meet: *Mercier.*

les jeux sont faits [Fr], the bets have been placed: *roulette.*

les larmes aux yeux [Fr], tears in one's (*or* the) eyes.

les murailles ont des oreilles [Fr], walls have ears.

les petites gens [Fr], humble folk.

le style est l'homme même [Fr], the style is the man himself: *Buffon.* A familiar variation of this aphorism is *le style, c'est l'homme,* the style is the man.

l'état, c'est moi [Fr], the state, it is I: a saying formerly attributed to *Louis XIV.*

l'étoile du nord [Fr], star of the north: motto of *Minnesota.*

le tout ensemble [Fr], the whole (taken) together; general effect.

letra de cambio [Sp], bill of exchange; bank draft.

lettre [Fr], letter; note; bill. **—lettre d'avis,** letter of advice: *abbr.* l.a.
—lettre de cachet, sealed official letter; a royal or arbitrary warrant
of arrest. **—lettre de change,** bill of exchange. **—lettre de créance,**
letter of credit; *pl.* credentials. **—lettre de crédit,** letter of credit:
abbr. l/cr.

levée en masse [Fr], a gathering (*or* rising) in a body; general rising.

leve fit quod bene fertur onus [L], lightly lies the load that is cheerfully
borne: *Ovid.*

lever de rideau [Fr], curtain raiser.

lever de séance [Fr], closing of a meeting.

le véritable Amphitryon est l'Amphitryon où l'on dîne [Fr], the real
Amphitryon is the Amphitryon where one dines (i.e., the provider
of the feast, whether known or not, is the real host): *Molière.*

le vrai n'est pas toujours vraisemblable [Fr], truth is not always probable; truth is stranger than fiction: *Boileau.*

levraut [Fr], young hare.

lex [L; *pl.* leges], law. **—lex loci,** the law of the place. **—lex mercatorum**
or **mercatoria,** mercantile law; law merchant. **—lex non scripta,**
unwritten law; the common law. **—lex scripta,** written law; statute
law. **—lex talionis,** the law of retaliation. **—lex terrae,** the law of the
land: *all law.*

l'homme n'est ni ange ni bête [Fr], man is neither an angel nor a
beast: *Pascal.*

l'homme propose, et Dieu dispose [Fr], man proposes, and God disposes.

liaison [Fr], connection; intimacy, esp. an illicit one; *mil.,* the communication established between units; a linking of operations.

liant [Fr; *fem.* liante], supple; flexible; complying; affable.

libeccio [It], the southwest wind.

liber [L; *pl.* libri], book: *abbr.* L. *or* lib.

liberamente [It], freely; liberally: *music.*

liberavi animam meam [L], I have freed (*or* relieved) my mind.

libertad y orden [Sp], liberty and order: motto of *Colombia.*

libertas [L], liberty. **—libertas et natale solum,** liberty and native land.
—libertas in legibus, liberty under the laws. **—libertas sub rege pio,**
liberty under an upright king.

liberté, égalité, fraternité [Fr], liberty, equality, fraternity (*or* brother-
hood): rallying cry of the French Revolution.

liberté toute entière [Fr], liberty wholly complete.

liberum arbitrium [L], free will; free choice.

libido [L; *pl.* libidines], desire; esp., secret desire; sex instinct: *psychol.*

libraire [Fr], bookseller.

librairie [Fr], bookstore; publishing house.

libret [Fr], booklet; memorandum book; bankbook; also, descriptive
catalogue; *theat.,* words of an opera; book of words.

libro cerrado no saca letrado [Sp], a closed book never makes a scholar.

licenciado [Sp], one holding a baccalaureate or licentiate; title of lawyer, *abbr.* lcdo.

licentia vatum [L], the license of the poets; poetic license.

licenza [It], license; freedom of style: *music.*

licet [L], it is permitted; it is legal.

Licht, Liebe, Leben [Ger], light, love, life: motto of *Herder.*

Liebchen [Ger], lit., little love; beloved; darling; sweetheart.

Liebe kann viel, Geld kann alles [Ger], love can do much, money can do everything; love is mighty, but money is almighty.

Liebesbote [Ger], harbinger of love.

Liebesliedchen [Ger], love ditty.

Liebeswonne [Ger], the bliss (*or* ecstasy) of love.

lieblich [Ger], lovely; charming; delightful; sweet.

Lieb und Leid [Ger], joy and sorrow.

Lied [Ger; *pl.* Lieder], a song; ballad; German lyric.

Liederkranz [Ger], wreath (*or* collection) of songs; German choral society; a type of cheese.

Lieder ohne Worte [Ger], songs without words.

Liedertafel [Ger; *pl.* Liedertafeln], lit., song table; men's singing club; glee club; choral society.

lièvre [Fr], hare. —**mémoire de lièvre,** bad memory.

lila tov [Heb], good night.

limae labor et mora [L], the toil and delay of the file; the tedious polishing and revision of a literary composition: *Horace.*

limande [Fr], the dab (fish).

limbus [L], lit., border; edge; hence, a region on the confines of hell; limbo. —**limbus fatuorum,** fools' paradise. —**limbus infantium,** infants' paradise; limbo for unbaptized children. —**limbus patrum,** the paradise of the fathers; a place for the souls of righteous men of pre-Christian times. —**limbus puerorum,** children's paradise.

l'inconnu [Fr], the unknown.

l'incroyable [Fr], the incredible.

linga sharira [Skr], astral counterpart of the physical body; ethereal double (*or* self): *theos.*

lingerie [Fr], linen articles, esp., women's underwear.

lingote [Sp], an ingot of metal.

linguae verbera [L], tongue lashings.

lingua franca [It], lit., Frankish language; a common language spoken in Mediterranean ports: Italian, mixed with French, Spanish, Greek, and Arabic; any language used as a common tongue among people of diverse speech.

lis litem generat [L], strife begets strife.

lis pendens [L], a pending suit: *law.*

List gegen List [Ger], cunning against cunning.

lit de justice [Fr], bed of justice; seat of justice; *Fr. hist.*, the king's throne at a formal session of parliament; also, the session itself.

litem lite resolvere [L], to settle strife by strife; explain one obscurity by another: *Horace* (adapted).

lite pendente [L], during the trial.

literati [L; *pl.*], men of letters; the learned class.

literatim [L], letter for letter; literally.

litterae humaniores [L], the humanities; polite letters; ancient classics: *abbr.* Lit. Hum.

litterae scriptae [L], written letters; manuscript.

littera scripta manet [L], the written letter remains.

littérateur [Fr], literary man; man of letters.

livraison [Fr], a part or number (of a book published in parts).

livre [Fr], book: *abbr.* liv.

llamar al pan, pan y al vino, vino [Sp], to call bread, bread and wine, wine; to call a spade a spade.

llanero [Am Sp], dweller on the *llanos,* or plains, of South America.

llano [Sp], vast plain or steppe in the northern part of South America.

llanura [Sp], a plain.

lluvia [Sp], rain.

Lobgesang [Ger], hymn of praise.

local or *(esp. in English, though erroneous as French)* **locale** [Fr], locality; scene of an event, operation, or of some characteristic feature.

locatio [L], a letting; leasing: *law.*

l'occasion fait le larron [Fr], opportunity makes the thief.

loco [L], in the place. —**loco citato,** in the place cited; in the passage already quoted: *abbr.* loc. cit. *or* l.c. —**loco laudato,** in the place cited with approval: *abbr.* loc. laud. —**loca supra citato,** in the place before cited: *abbr.* l.s.c.

loco [It], place; used to indicate a return to the normal pitch after an 8va transposition: *music.*

locos y niños dicen la verdad [Sp], children and fools speak the truth.

locum tenens [L; *pl.* locum tenentes], a substitute or deputy, esp. for a clergyman or physician.

locus [L; *pl.* loci], a place; written passage. —**locus citatus,** the passage quoted. —**locus classicus** [*pl.* loci classici], a classical passage; a standard or authoritative passage on a word or subject. —**locus communis** [*pl.* loci communes], lit., a commonplace; place of the dead; public place; fig., (usually *pl.*), a general argument. —**locus criminis** (*or* **delicti**), scene of the crime. —**locus in quo,** the place in which (*or* where); the place where a passage occurs. —**locus poenitentiae,** place (*or* opportunity) for repentance. —**locus sigilli,** the place of the seal: *abbr.* L.S. —**locus standi,** a place of standing; recognized standing or position; *law,* right to appear before a court; right to be heard.

lo dicho dicho [Sp], what I have said I stand by.

l'oeil du maître [Fr], the eye of the master.

loger le diable dans sa bourse [Fr], lit., to house the devil in one's purse; be penniless.

logion [Gr λόγιον; *pl.* logia], a traditional saying or maxim of a religious teacher; esp., a saying of Jesus unrecorded in the Gospels.

logos [Gr λόγος], word, speech, reason, narrative.

loma [Sp], a flat-topped hill or ridge of hills: *southwestern U.S.*

lomita [Sp], a small flat-topped hill; small *loma: southwestern U.S.*

longe [Fr], loin: *cookery.*

longe aberrat scopo [L], he wanders far from the goal; he is wide of the mark.

longe absit [L], far be it from me; God forbid.

longo intervallo [L], by (*or* at) a long interval.

longo sed proximus intervallo [L], the next, but after a long interval: *Virgil.*

longueur [Fr], length; prolixity; a lengthy or tedious passage or part.

loquitur [L], he (*or* she) speaks: *stage direction* (*abbr.* loq.).

l'ordre du jour [Fr], order of the day: *mil.*

lorette [Fr], a Parisian courtesan of a class living orig. near the Church of Notre Dame de Lorette.

lorgnette [Fr], eyeglasses held with a handle or attached to a chain.

lorgnon [Fr], eyeglass or eyeglasses; *pince-nez;* opera glasses.

los Estados Unidos [Sp], the United States.

loshka degtya ve bulke modje [Russ], one drop of tar spoils a barrel of honey.

los montes ven, y las paredes oyen [Sp], mountains see and walls hear.

lota [Hind], a small round vessel, usually of brass or copper: *India.*

Louis Quatorze [Fr], designating the styles of architecture, furniture, etc., that prevailed in the reign of Louis XIV of France.

Louis Quinze [Fr], designating the styles that prevailed in the reign of Louis XV of France.

Louis Seize [Fr], designating the styles that prevailed in the reign of Louis XVI of France.

Louis Treize [Fr], designating the styles that prevailed in the reign of Louis XIII of France.

loukoum [Turk *lukum*], fig paste, a Turkish confection.

loup-garou [Fr], werewolf; bugbear.

loustic [Fr], a wag; joker.

louvoyer [Fr], *naut.*, to tack; fig., to maneuver; dodge; sidestep.

loyal en tout [Fr], loyal in everything.

loyal je serai durant ma vie [Fr], I shall be loyal during my life (*or* as long as I live).

loyauté m'oblige [Fr], loyalty binds me.

loyauté n'a honte [Fr], loyalty has (*or* knows) no shame.

lua [Pg], moon.

luce lucet aliena [L], it shines with a borrowed light.

lucernam olet [L], it smells of the lamp.

lucidus ordo [L], clear (*or* perspicuous) arrangement: *Horace.*

lucri causa [L], for the sake of gain.

lucus a non lucendo [L], lit., a grove from not being light (a fanciful derivation of *lucus,* grove, from *lucere,* to shine); hence, any inconsequent or absurd derivation; explanation by contraries.

ludere cum sacris [L], to sport (*or* trifle) with sacred things.

ludi [Russ], people. See CHILOVEK.

lues [L], a plague; pestilence; contagious disease. **—lues venerea,** syphilis: *med.*

luge [Fr], small sled; single toboggan.

λύχνου ἀρθέντος, γυνὴ πᾶσα ἡ αὐτή [Gr; lúkhnou arthéntos, gynè pâsa hē autè], when the light is taken away, every woman is the same; in the dark all cats are gray.

l'ultima che si perde è la speranza [It], the last thing we lose is hope.

l'ultima sera [It], "the farthest gloom"; Death: *Dante* (tr. by Cary).

lumen naturale [L], light of nature; natural intelligence.

lumenque iuventae purpureum [L], lit., the purple light of youth; the radiant bloom of youth: *Virgil.*

luna [Sp & It], moon.

lune [Fr], moon.

l'union fait la force [Fr], union makes strength: motto of *Belgium.*

lupa [Tag], the earth; ground; land: *P.I.*

lupo affamato mangia pan muffato [It], a famished wolf eats moldy bread.

lupum auribus tenere [L], to hold a wolf by the ears; have a tiger by the tail.

lupus est homo homini [L], man is a wolf to his fellow man.

lupus in fabula [L], the wolf in the fable (i.e., talking of him, he appeared): *Terence.*

lupus pilum mutat, non mentem [L], the wolf changes his coat, not his disposition.

l'usage du monde [Fr], the way of the world.

lusingando *or* **lusingante** [It], alluring; soothing; caressing: *music.*

lustig [Ger], merry; gay; jovial.

Lustspiel [Ger], comedy.

lusus naturae [L], a freak of nature; a sport.

luttuosamente [It], mournfully; sadly: *music.*

luttuoso [It], mournful; doleful; sorrowful: *music.*

luxe [Fr], luxury; sumptuousness. **—de luxe,** sumptuous; elegant.

lux et veritas [L], light and truth: motto of *Yale University.*

lux in tenebris [L], light in darkness.

lux mundi [L], light of the world.

Luxuszug [Ger], first-class train: *abbr.* L.-Zug.

lux venit ab alto [L], light comes from above.

luz [Sp; *pl.* luces], light; also, *pl.* windows; learning; *engin.*, span, as of a bridge.

lycée [Fr], lyceum; high school.

M

mabap [Hind], lit., mother-father; parents; fig., benefactor; as, sahib *mabap* hai, "the sahib is my father and my mother" (i.e., my benefactor, standing as it were *in loco parentis*): *India*.

maboule [Fr], a fool: *Fr. mil. slang.*

macabre [Fr], grimly or grotesquely suggestive of death; gruesome; now naturalized in English, but in French used only in the phrase *danse macabre,* dance of death.

macédoine [Fr], a dish of mixed fruit or vegetables; fig., medley; hodgepodge.

ma chère [Fr; *fem.*], my dear. Cf. MON CHER.

machete [Sp], a heavy swordlike knife used in Spanish America.

machhli [Hind; *pr.* mŭch′lĭ], fish: *India.*

Macht ist Recht [Ger], might is right.

macte! [L], well done! bravo! good luck attend thee! **—macte animo!,** lit., be increased in courage; courage! **—macte virtute!,** lit., be increased in virtue; go on and prosper!

madame [Fr; *pl.* mesdames], lit., my lady; married woman; a title or form of address equivalent to *madam* or *Mrs.: abbr.* Mme., *pl.* Mmes.

Mädchen [Ger; *sing. & pl.*], maiden; maid; girl.

madeleine [Fr], a rich cake made of flour, sugar, eggs, brandy, and grated lemon peel: *cookery.*

mademoiselle [Fr; *pl.* mesdemoiselles], unmarried woman; a title or form of address equivalent to *Miss: abbr.* Mlle., *pl.* Mlles.

madère [Fr], Madeira wine; Madeira.

madrasa [Ar], Muslim school or college.

madre [It & Sp], mother.

maestosamente [It], majestically; with dignity: *music.*

maestoso [It], majestical; grandiose (*abbr.* maes.): *music.*

maestro [It; *pl.* maestri], lit., master; eminent musical composer, teacher, or conductor.

Mafia [It], secret terrorist and crime organization especially in Sicily and the U.S.

mafioso [It], member of the Mafia.

ma foi! [Fr], my faith! upon my word! indeed!

magasin [Fr], store; shop; warehouse. **—grand magasin,** department store.

maggiore fretta, minore atto [It], more haste, less speed.

magister [L], master. **—Magister Artium,** Master of Arts. **—magister ceremoniarum,** master of ceremonies. **—magister dixit,** the master has said so. **—magister ludi,** master of the games (in honor of the gods).

197

magistratus indicat virum [L], office shows the man.

magna civitas, magna solitudo [L], a great city (is) a great solitude.

magna cum laude [L], with great praise (*or* distinction): used esp. in a diploma to designate a grade of work higher than *cum laude* but lower than *summa cum laude.*

magnae spes altera Romae [L], another (*or* a second) hope of mighty Rome (orig. said of Ascanius, son of Aeneas; hence, used of any young man of promise): *Virgil.*

magna est veritas et praevalebit [L], truth is mighty and will prevail.

magna est vis consuetudinis [L], great is the force of habit: *Cicero.*

magna servitus est magna fortuna [L], a great fortune is a great slavery: *Seneca.*

magnas inter opes inops [L], poor amid great riches: *Horace.*

magni nominis umbra [L], the shadow of a great name: *Lucan.*

magno conatu magnas nugas [L], by great effort (to obtain) great trifles: *Terence.*

magnum bonum [L], a great good.

magnum in parvo [L], a great deal in a small space.

magnum opus [L; *pl.* magna opera], a great work; esp., a great literary undertaking; author's chief work; masterpiece.

magnum vectigal est parsimonia [L], economy is a great revenue: *Cicero.*

magnus ab integro saeculorum nascitur ordo [L], the mighty cycle of the ages begins its round anew: *Virgil.*

mahalo [Hawa], thank you.

maharaja [Hind & Skr], lit., great raja or king; Hindu ruling prince: *India.*

maharani [Hind], lit., great queen; wife of a maharaja; also, Hindu ruling princess of a native state: *India.*

maharishi [Skr]. See RISHI.

mahatma [Skr *mahātman*], lit., great-souled; in Buddhism and theosophy, an expert of the highest order: *India.*

mahayana [Skr], lit., great vehicle; school of Buddhism.

mahjong [Chin], lit., house sparrow; game played with small tiles: *China.*

Mahlzeit [Ger], meal. —**Mahlzeit!** (*in full,* **ich wünsche Ihnen eine gesegnete Mahlzeit,** may your meal be blessed), good digestion! I hope you have enjoyed your dinner: an expression used in some parts of Germany at the end of a meal.

maidan [Anglo-Ind], a plain; common; esplanade.

maigre [Fr], meager; lean; scanty; barren; specif., suitable for fast days; *cookery,* made without flesh meat or meat juices. —**jour maigre,** fish day; fast day. —**repas maigre,** a fish (*or* meatless) meal. —**soupe maigre,** a thin soup made without meat. —**sujet maigre,** barren subject.

main de justice [Fr], hand of justice.

mains froides, coeur chaud [Fr], cold hands, warm heart.

maintien [Fr], maintenance; preservation; also, behavior.

maintiens le droit [Fr], maintain the right.

maiores pennas nido [L], wings greater than the nest (i.e., soaring above the position in which one was born): *Horace.*

maire [Fr], mayor.

mairie [Fr], mayoralty; town hall.

maison [Fr], house; residence; establishment; firm. —**maison d'arrêt,** prison. —**maison de campagne,** country house (*or* seat). —**maison de chasse,** shooting lodge (*or* box). —**maison de force,** jail; house of correction. —**maison de rendez-vous,** house of assignation. —**maison de santé,** private hospital or asylum; sanatorium. —**maison de ville,** town house; city residence. —**maison meublée** (*or* **garnie**), furnished house.

maître [Fr], master. —**maître d'armes,** fencing master. —**maître de danse,** dancing master. —**maître des hautes oeuvres,** hangman: *jocose.* —**maître d'hotel,** head steward; hotel keeper. —**maître Jacques,** jack of all work; factotum.

maîtresse [Fr], mistress; sweetheart; also, teacher; landlady.

maîtrise [Fr], mastery; control. —**maîtrise de soi-même,** self-control.

maiusculae [L], large or capital letters, as in early Latin MSS.; majuscules; uncials: *paleog.* Cf. MINUSCULAE.

makanan [Malay], dinner.

μακάριόν ἐστιν μᾶλλον διδόναι ἢ λαμβάνειν [Gr; makárión estin mâllon didónai hē lambánein], it is more blessed to give than to receive: *Acts* xx. 35.

makimono [Jap], a scroll picture mounted on a roll, containing a series of pictures arranged horizontally. Cf. KAKEMONO.

mal [Fr], evil; injury; misfortune; disease; sickness. —**mal de dents,** toothache. —**mal de mer,** seasickness. —**mal de tête,** headache. —**mal du pays,** homesickness; nostalgia.

malade [Fr], *adj.* sick; ill; unwell; diseased; *n.* sick person; invalid. —**malade imaginaire,** imaginary invalid.

maladie [Fr], sickness; illness; disease. —**maladie noir,** hypochondria.

maladresse [Fr], awkwardness; tactless behavior; blunder.

mala fide [L], in bad faith; treacherously: opposite of *bona fide.*

mala fides [L], bad faith: opposite of *bona fides.*

malahini [Hawa], newcomer to Hawaii.

malaise [Fr], uneasiness; indisposition; vague, premonitory feeling of discomfort.

mala praxis [NL], malpractice.

mal à propos [Fr], ill-timed; unseasonable; out of place.

malchik [Russ; *pl.* malchikee], boy.

mal entendu [Fr], ill-conceived; ill-managed; misunderstood.

malentendu [Fr], misunderstanding; misconception; mistake.

male parta male dilabuntur [L], things ill-gotten are ill lost; ill-gotten, ill-spent; easy come, easy go: quoted from Naevius by *Cicero*.

malesuada fames [L], hunger that impels to crime: *Virgil*.

maleza [Sp], underbrush.

malgré nous [Fr], in spite of us.

malgré soi [Fr], in spite of oneself.

malheur ne vient jamais seul [Fr], misfortune never comes alone; misfortunes never come singly.

mali [Hind], gardener: *India*.

mali exempli [L], of bad example; of bad precedent.

malignum spernere vulgus [L], to scorn the noxious crowd: *Horace*.

malik [Hind], landowner; proprietor; cultivator: *India*.

malinconia [It], melancholy; sadness.

mali principii malus finis [L], the bad end of a bad beginning.

malis avibus [L], with unlucky birds; under bad auspices.

malo modo [L], in an evil manner.

malo mori quam foedari [L], I had rather die than be dishonored.

malpropre [Fr], dirty; untidy; slovenly.

malum [L; *pl.* mala], an evil. **—malum in se,** a thing evil in itself; a thing unlawful in itself, regardless of statute. **—malum prohibitum** [*pl.* mala prohibita], a prohibited evil or wrong; an act that is unlawful because forbidden by law (i.e., a legal crime though not necessarily a moral one): *both law*.

malus pudor [L], false modesty.

mamaloshen [Yiddish], mother tongue; Yiddish.

manada [Sp], drove of horses; herd of cattle; also, flock of sheep: *southern Texas & California*. Cf. REMUDA.

mañana [Sp], tomorrow. **—mañana será otro día,** lit., tomorrow will be another day; tomorrow may bring better luck.

mancando [It], failing; languishing; dying away (*abbr.* man. *or* manc.): *music*.

manchette [Fr], ornamental cuff; sleeve trimming; *typog.*, a side note.

mancia [It], tip; gratuity.

mandar não quer par [Pg], authority brooks no equal.

mandat [Fr], warrant; authority, mandate; power of attorney; also, money order.

mandorla [It; *pl.* mandorle], lit., almond; an almond-shaped, or pointed oval, design; esp., the *vesica piscis* (q.v.): *fine arts*.

ma neeshtana ha lila ha zay mee kol ha laylot? [Heb], lit., what is different this night from all other nights?; why is this night different from all other nights?

manège [Fr], school of horsemanship; horse training; horsemanship.

manet [L; *pl.* manent], he (*or* she) remains: *stage direction*. **—manet alta mente repostum,** it remains deep stored in the mind: *Virgil*. **—manet cicatrix,** the scar remains.

manger son blé en herbe [Fr], to eat one's corn in the blade; spend one's money before one has it.

mangia a tuo modo, vesti a modo d'altri [It], eat after your own fashion, dress like others.

mania a potu [L], mania from drinking; delirium tremens.

manibus pedibusque [L], with hands and feet; with might and main.

maniéré [Fr; *fem.* maniérée], affected; unnatural; mannered.

man kann Gold zu teuer kaufen [Ger], one can buy gold too dear.

mannequin [Fr], lay figure; mannequin; model.

mano [Sp], hand; *tech.*, a coat of paint or varnish. —**mano a mano,** hand in hand; familiarly. —**mano!,** to the right! (a direction in driving): *P.I.* Cf. SILLA.

manqué [Fr; *fem.* manquée], unsuccessful; resulting in failure, would-be.

man sagt [Ger], it is said; they say; *on dit.*

man spricht Deutsch [Ger], German spoken (here).

μάντις κακῶν [Gr; mántis kakôn], a prophet of evils.

mantón [Sp], large veil.

manu forti [L], with a strong hand; by main force.

manu propria [L], with one's own hand.

manus e nubibus [L], a hand from the clouds.

manus haec inimica tyrannis [L], this hand is an enemy to tyrants. See ENSE PETIT etc.

mao tai [Chin; *mao t'ai chiu: mao,* a family surname, *t'ai,* tower, *chiu,* liquor], a Chinese brandy, produced in Maotai, Guizhou (formerly Kweichow), China.

maquereau [Fr; *fem.* maquerelle], lit., mackerel; a pander; procurer: *slang.*

máquina [Sp], machine; engine; locomotive.

marabout [Fr], large bellying coffeepot or kettle.

maram [Mal], wood; timber: *India.*

mar bravo [Pg], heavy sea.

marbré [Fr], marbled; mottled.

marcato [It], marked; accentuated; distinct: *music.*

Märchen [Ger; *sing. & pl.*], folk tale; fairy story.

marchesa [It], marchioness.

marchese [It], marquis.

maréchal [Fr], field marshal: *mil.*

maréchale [Fr], field marshal's wife.

mare clausum [L], closed sea; a sea within the jurisdiction of a country.

mare liberum [L], an open sea; a sea open to all.

marginalia [L], marginal notes.

marhaba [Ar], health; to your health.

mariachi [Sp], a typical Mexican band or member thereof.

mariage [Fr], marriage. **—mariage de conscience,** lit., marriage of conscience; a marriage of persons who have been living unlawfully together as husband and wife; also, private marriage. **—mariage de convenance,** marriage of convenience; a marriage contracted from motives of interest. **—mariage de la main gauche,** left-handed marriage; morganatic marriage. **—mariage d'inclination,** love match.

marido [Sp], husband.

mariguana *or* **marihuana** [Mex], any of various Mexican plants having narcotic properties; also the narcotic itself, marijuana: *Mexico.* Cf. MESCAL.

marivaudage [Fr], writing in the style of Marivaux (18th-century dramatist and novelist); excessive refinement and preciosity; delicate sentimentalism and affectation.

marmite [Fr], pot; saucepan; *Fr. mil. slang,* bomb; shell (from a big gun).

marmiton [Fr], scullion; kitchen drudge.

marmouset [Fr], grotesque figure; fig., small boy; undersized man.

maro [Hind; imperative of *mārnā*], beat; strike; hit; kill. Spelled *marrow* in Kipling, and used by British soldiers for all forms of the verb; thus, "I'll *marrow* you this minute."

maroquin [Fr], Morocco leather; roan.

marque de fabrique [Fr], trademark.

marron [Fr], chestnut. **—marron d'Inde,** horse chestnut.

marrow [Anglo-Ind]. Same as MARO.

Mars gravior sub pace latet [L], a severer war lies hidden under peace.

martellato [It], lit., hammered; strongly marked: *music.*

marziale [It], martial; in warlike style: *music.*

marzipan [Ger], a type of cake made of pounded almonds, sugar, etc.: *cookery.*

masa [Sp], lit., dough; cornmeal: *southwestern U.S.*

mashallah [Ar], lit., what God has willed.

masjid [Ar], Islamic mosque.

massé [Fr], stroke with the cue held almost vertically: *billiards.*

massepain [Fr]. Same as MARZIPAN.

mässig [Ger], moderate; *music,* andante.

mastaba [Ar], ancient Egyptian tomb.

m'as-tu vu? [Fr], lit., have you seen me?; a person inordinately self-centered.

más vale saber que haber [Sp], it is better to know than to have; knowledge is better than wealth.

más vale ser necio que porfiado [Sp], better be ignorant than obstinate.

más vale tarde que nunca [Sp], better late than never.

más vale tener que desear [Sp], better to have than to desire.

matadero [Sp], slaughterhouse.

matador [Sp], the featured bullfighter; lit., killer (of the bull).

mata hari [Mal], a female spy; a fatal woman; lit., eye of the day (the sun).

maté [Sp], Argentinian tea.

matelassé [Fr], *adj.* quilted, or having a quilted pattern; as, *matelassé* silk. —**matelas,** a quilted dress fabric; pad; cushion.

matelot [Fr], sailor; seaman.

matelote [Fr], a kind of fish stew flavored with wine: *cookery.*

mater [L], mother. —**mater artium necessitas,** necessity is the mother of the arts; necessity is the mother of invention. —**Mater Dolorosa,** the sorrowing Mother; the Holy Mother sorrowing at the Cross.

materfamilias [L], mother of a family (*or* household).

materiam superabat opus [L], the workmanship was better than (*or* surpassed) the material: *Ovid.*

matériel [Fr], material; supplies and equipment; equipment and munitions of an army.

matois [Fr], *adj.* cunning; sly; *n.* cunning person; sly dog.

matre pulchra, filia pulchrior [L], a daughter more beautiful than her beautiful mother: *Horace.*

mattinata [It], a morning song; *aubade: music.*

maturato opus est [L], there is need for haste: *Livy.*

matz [Russ; *pl.* materi], mother.

matzo [Heb & Yiddish; *pl.* matzos], ritual unleavened bread: *Judaism.*

mauvais [Fr; *fem.* mauvaise], bad; ill; wicked; mischievous; adverse. —**mauvais goût,** bad taste. —**mauvaise honte,** false shame; diffidence; bashfulness. —**mauvaise plaisanterie,** ill-timed jest. —**mauvais livre,** dangerous or noxious book. —**mauvais quart d'heure,** bad quarter of an hour; a brief but unpleasant experience. —**mauvais sujet,** lit., bad subject; a worthless scamp; ne'er-do-well; black sheep. —**mauvaise tête,** hot-headed person. —**mauvais ton,** bad taste; bad style; ill breeding; vulgarity.

mavin *or* **maven** [Yiddish *fr.* Heb], an expert; a connoisseur.

maxima debetur puero reverentia [L], the greatest respect is due a child: *Juvenal.*

maximus in minimis [L], greatest in trifles; very great in trifling things.

maxixe [Pg], a Brazilian round dance, combining characteristics of the two-step and the tango.

maya [Skr], the visible world regarded as illusory, hiding the unseen reality; illusion; deceptive appearance: *Hinduism.*

mazagran [Fr], cold black coffee served in a glass.

mazel [Yiddish *fr.* Heb], luck. —**mazel tov!,** lit., good luck; congratulations!

mea culpa [L], my fault; by my fault.

mea virtute me involvo [L], I wrap myself up in my virtue: *Horace.*

mecate [Mex Sp], a rope made of hair or of maguey fiber.

médaille [Fr], medal. —**médaille d'honneur,** prize medal. —**médaille militaire,** military decoration.

medano [Sp], sand dune.

médecine expectante [Fr], medical treatment in which the cure is left largely to nature: *med.*

médecin, guéris-toi toi-même [Fr], physician, heal thyself: *Luke* iv. 23.

μηδὲν ἄγαν [Gr; mēdèn ágan], nothing too much; no excess. Cf. NE QUID NIMIS.

medice, cura te ipsum [L], physician, heal thyself: *Vulgate* (*Luke* iv. 23).

medicina [Sp], medicine.

mediocria firma [L], a middle course is the most secure; moderation is safer than extremes.

medio tutissimus ibis [L], in the middle course you will go most safely; a middle course will be safest: *Ovid.*

meditatio fugae [L], contemplation of flight: *law.*

medium tenuere beati [L], happy are they who have kept a middle course.

megillah [Yiddish *fr.* Heb], a long, complex story or explanation. —**Megillah** [Heb], lit., a scroll; each of five books of Jewish Scriptures, esp. the Book of Esther, read at the feast of Purim.

meglio un uovo oggi che una gallina domani [It], better an egg today than a chicken tomorrow.

mehr Licht! [Ger], more light: *Goethe* (last words).

mehtar *or* **mihtar** [Hind & Pers.; *fem.* mehtrani *or* mihtrani], orig., prince; now a euphemistic appellation for a sweeper or scavenger: *India.*

meine Ruh' ist hin, mein Herz ist schwer [Ger], my peace is gone, my heart is heavy: *Goethe* (Gretchen's song in *Faust*).

meines Bedünken [Ger], in my opinion; to my thinking.

mein Gott! [Ger], my God! for Heaven's sake!

mein Herr [Ger; *pl.* meine Herren], usual German form of address, equivalent to *Sir.*

me iudice [L], I being judge; in my opinion.

μὴ κρίνετε ἵνα μὴ κριθῆτε [Gr; mè krínete hína mè krithête], judge not, that ye be not judged: *Matthew* vii. 1.

mélange [Fr], mixture; medley; *pl.,* miscellaneous collection; miscellanea.

mêlé [Fr; *fem.* mêlée], mixed; miscellaneous.

mêlée [Fr], hand-to-hand fight; fray; skirmish; squabble; clash.

meliores priores [L], the better, the first; the better (men) first.

melioribus annis [L], in the better years; in happier times: *Virgil.*

me, me adsum qui feci [L], it is I, here before you, who did the deed: *Virgil.*

memento mori [L], remember you must die; an object (such as a skull) serving as a reminder of death.

μέμνησο ἀπιστεῖν [Gr; mémnēso apisteîn], remember to distrust.

mémoire [Fr], short autobiography; personal narrative; memory.

mémoire de lièvre [Fr], lit., a hare's memory; a bad or treacherous memory.

memorabilia [L], things worth remembering.

memor et fidelis [L], mindful and faithful.

memoria in aeterna [L], in everlasting remembrance.

memoria technica [L], artificial memory; a mnemonic system or contrivance; mnemonics.

memoriter [L], from memory; by heart.

memsahib [Anglo-Ind], a European married lady or mistress of a household in India.

ménage [Fr], household management; housekeeping; household. —**ménage à trois,** a trio frequently consisting of husband, wife, and wife's lover, or husband, wife, and husband's mistress.

mendacem memorem esse oportet [L], a liar should have a good memory: *Quintilian.*

mene, mene, tekel, upharsin [Aram], lit., numbered, weighed, divisions; "God hath numbered thy kingdom and finished it; thou art weighed in the balances, and art found wanting; thy kingdom is divided": the writing on the wall of Belshazzar's banquet hall (*Daniel* v. 25-28).

menina [Pg], young lady; miss.

meno *or* **men** [It], less. —**meno mosso,** less quick: *music.*

mens aequa in arduis [L], a mind undisturbed in adversities; equanimity in difficulties: *Horace* (adapted). Cf. AEQUAM SERVARE MENTEM.

mensa et toro [L], from bed and board: *law.*

mens agitat molem [L], mind moves (*or* animates) the mass; mind moves matter: *Virgil.*

Mensch werden ist eine Kunst [Ger], to become a man is an art.

mens conscia recti [L], a mind conscious of rectitude.

mens divinior [L], a mind of diviner cast; an inspired soul: *Horace.*

mens invicta manet [L], the mind remains unconquered.

mens legis [L], the spirit of the law.

mens rea [L], a guilty intent: *law.*

mens sana in corpore sano [L], a sound mind in a sound body: *Juvenal.*

mens sibi conscia recti [L], a mind conscious to itself of rectitude; a good conscience: *Virgil.*

Mensur [Ger], students' duel.

menteur à triple étage [Fr], a consummate liar.

menthe [Fr], mint.

mentis gratissimus error [L], a most delightful hallucination: *Horace.*

menu gibier [Fr], small game.

menus plaisirs [Fr], pocket money (i.e., money for small pleasures).

meo periculo [L], at my own risk.

meo voto [L], by my wish.

mépris [Fr], contempt; contumely.

méprisable [Fr], contemptible; despicable.

merci! [Fr], thanks! thank you!

meret qui laborat [L], he is deserving who is industrious.

merlan [Fr], whiting (fish).

merum sal [L], pure salt; genuine Attic wit.

mesa [Sp], a high plain or plateau, commonly bordering a river valley: *southwestern U.S.*

mésalliance [Fr], a misalliance; marriage with one of lower rank or social standing.

mescal [Am Sp *mezcal, fr.* Aztec *mezcalli*], a Mexican plant of the genus *Lophophora,* with medicinal and narcotic properties; also, an intoxicating drink distilled from various species of *Agave* or maguey: *Mexico & southwestern U.S.* Cf. MARIGUANA, SOTOL, and TEQUILA.

mesdemoiselles [Fr], *pl.* of MADEMOISELLE.

meshugah [Yiddish *fr.* Heb], crazy.

mesilla [Sp], a small *mesa* or plateau: *southwestern U.S.*

messa di voce [It], the gradual increase and decrease in loudness of a sustained note in singing (<>): *music.*

Messidor [Fr], in the Revolutionary calendar of the first French Republic, the tenth month of the year, from June 19 to July 18.

mestizo [Sp], a person of mixed ancestry, usually Indian and Spanish.

metate [Sp], primitive stone handmill, consisting of a concave stone or slab standing on legs of the same block, used for grinding corn, etc., with a kind of pestle: *Mexico & southwestern U.S.*

métayage [Fr], a system of share rent, by which the tenant gives usually half the produce to the owner, who supplies stock, tools, and seed.

métayer [Fr], one who farms on shares; a small farmer.

métier [Fr], calling; profession; line.

métif [Fr; *fem.* métive]. Same as MÉTIS.

métis [Fr; *fem.* métisse], one of mixed ancestry.

μέτρον ἄριστον [Gr; métron áriston], moderation is best: *Cleobulus.*

mettre à la question [Fr], to put to the rack; torture.

mettre au net [Fr], to make a fair copy.

mettre de l'eau dans son vin [Fr], lit., to put water in one's wine; lower one's pretensions.

mettre en question [Fr], to call in question; doubt.

meubles [Fr], movables; furniture; household goods.

meum et tuum [L], mine and thine: used to express rights of property.

mezzo [It; *fem.* mezza], middle; half; medium; moderate: *abbr.* m. —**mezzo voce,** with medium fullness of tone (*abbr.* M.V. *or* m.v.): *music.* —**mezzo forte,** moderately loud (*abbr.* mf.): *music.* —**mezzo piano,** moderately soft (*abbr.* mp.): *music.* —**mezzo termine,** a middle term or course; compromise.

mezzo-rilievo [It], half relief: *sculp.*

mi-carême [Fr], mid-Lent.

mi cuenta [Sp], my account: *abbr.* m/c.

midi [Fr], noon; noonday. **—Midi,** the south; southern France.

midinette [Fr], one of a class of young Parisian working women said to throng the streets at noon (*midi*).

mieux vaut tard que jamais [Fr], better late than never.

mignard [Fr; *fem.* mignarde], dainty; delicate; prettily engaging; also, affected; mincing.

mignardise [Fr], daintiness; delicacy; engaging ways, as of a child; delicate fondling; wheedling; also, affectation; mincing.

mihi cura futuri [L], my care is for the future.

mijaurée [Fr], an affected and finicky or conceited woman.

mijnheer [Du], usual Dutch form of address, equivalent to *Sir.*

mijoter [Fr], *cookery,* to simmer; *colloq.,* coddle; pamper.

mikado [Jap], the emperor of Japan.

mikva [Yiddish], ritual bath for women.

miles gloriosus [L], boastful soldier.

milieu [Fr], middle; medium; environment; sphere.

militat omnis amans [L], every lover serves as a soldier: *Ovid.*

militiae species amor est [L], love is a kind of military service: *Ovid.*

mille verisimili non fanno un vero [It], a thousand probabilities do not make one truth.

millier [Fr], metric ton.

minaccevolmente [It], in a threatening manner; menacingly: *music.*

minacciando [It], threateningly: *music.*

minauderie [Fr], lackadaisicalness; simpering; smirking; affectation; mincing manners.

minestrone [It], a thick soup, made with vegetables and pasta.

Minnenwerfer *or* **Minnen** [Ger], mine thrower; trench mortar: *mil.*

minusculae [L], small Roman letters in cursive script of the seventh to the ninth centuries; minuscules; hence, a small or lower-case letter: *paleog.* Cf. MAIUSCULAE.

minyan [Heb; *pl.* minyanim], in Judaism, the quorum of adult males necessary for holding public worship.

mi permetta [It], allow me; permit me.

mir [Russ], Russian village community; world; peace.

mirabile dictu [L], wonderful to relate: *Virgil.*

mirabile visu [L], wonderful to behold.

mirabilia [L], wonders; miracles.

miroir [Fr], mirror; looking glass.

miroton [Fr], stew of beef slices smothered in onions: *cookery.*

mirum in modum [L], in a wonderful manner; surprisingly: *Caesar.*

misce [L], mix: *pharm.*

miscebis sacra profanis [L], you will mingle sacred things with profane: *Horace.*

misce stultitiam consiliis brevem [L], mix a little folly with your wisdom: *Horace.* Cf. La Rochefoucauld's maxim, QUI VIT SANS FOLIE N'EST PAS SI SAGE QU'IL CROIT.

mise en scène [Fr], stage setting; surroundings of an event.

miserabile dictu [L], sad to relate.

miserabile vulgus [L], a wretched mob (*or* rabble).

misère [Fr], misery; poverty; want.

miserere mei [L], have mercy on me.

miseris succurrere disco [L], I am learning to help the distressed: *Virgil.*

Missa [L; *pl.* Missae], the Mass. **—Missa bassa,** Low Mass. **—Missa cantata,** Mass sung, but without deacon and subdeacon. **—Missa catechumenorum,** Mass of the catechumens. **—Missa fidelium,** Mass of the faithful. **—Missa solemnis,** High Mass: *all R.C.Ch.*

misterioso [It], mysterious: *music.*

mistral [Fr], dry, northerly cold wind: *southern France.*

misurato [It], measured; in strict time: *music.*

mit Ausdruck [Ger], with expression: *music.*

mit dem Wissen wächst der Zweifel [Ger], with knowledge grows doubt: *Goethe.*

mit der Dummheit kämpfen Götter selbst vergebens [Ger], with stupidity, the gods themselves contend in vain: *Schiller.*

mit Gewalt [Ger], by force.

mitis sapientia [L], ripe (*or* mellow) wisdom.

mitnichten [Ger], by no means.

mitrailleur [Fr], machine gunner: *mil.*

mitrailleuse [Fr], machine gun: *mil.*

Mittagsessen [Ger], dinner; midday meal.

mittimus [L], lit., we send; *law,* a warrant of commitment to prison; also, a writ to remove records from one court to another; *colloq.,* dismissal; discharge.

mitzvah [Yiddish, *fr.* Heb *misvah*], lit., commandment; precept; something that should be done; good deed.

miya [Jap], Shinto temple: *Japan.*

młode piwko szumi [Pol], youth is hard to pass.

mobile perpetuum [L], something in perpetual motion.

mode [Fr], style; fashion.

moderata durant [L], things used in moderation endure.

moderato [It], moderate; moderately fast (*abbr.* mod.): *music.*

modestie [Fr], modesty; *dressmaking,* a piece of lace, or other material, inserted in the low-cut neck of a dress.

modique [Fr], of little value.

modiste [Fr], dressmaker or milliner.

modo et forma [L], in manner and form.

modo praescripto [L], in the way directed; as directed.

modus [L; *pl.* modi], mode; manner; method. **—modus operandi,** manner of working (*or* operating). **—modus ponens,** inference from a hypothetical proposition in which the minor premise affirms the antecedent and the conclusion affirms the consequent; constructive hypothetical syllogism; e.g., if A is B, then C is D; but A is B, therefore C is D: *logic.* **—modus tollens,** destructive hypothetical syllogism, i.e., one in which the consequent is denied; e.g., if A is B, then C is D; but C is not D, therefore A is not B: *logic.* **—modus vivendi,** manner of living; a temporary working agreement or compromise between disputants, pending a settlement of the differences.

moeda corrente [Pg], current money; lawful money.

moelle de boeuf [Fr], beef marrow: *cookery.*

moeurs [Fr], manners; customs.

mofette [Fr], an exhalation of poisonous gas from a fissure in the earth; also, such a fissure; a skunk.

moglie [It], wife; spouse.

Moharram [Ar]. Same as MUHARRAM.

moisson [Fr], harvest.

môle [Fr], breakwater at entrance to port.

mole [Sp], spicy sauce of unsweetened chocolate: *Mexico.*

mole ruit sua [L], it falls down of its own bulk; it is crushed by its own weight: *Horace.*

molla *or* **mollah** [Turk]. Same as MULLAH.

mollemente [It], softly; gently: *music.*

mollia tempora [L], favorable times (*or* occasions). **—mollia tempora fandi,** favorable times for speaking: a misquotation of MOLLISSIMA FANDI TEMPORA.

mollissima fandi tempora [L], the most favorable times for speaking: *Virgil.*

molto [It], much; very. **—molto allegro,** very quick: *music.* **—molto fumo e poco arrosto,** much smoke and little meat; much cry and little wool.

mompe [Jap], baggy working trousers.

momzer [Yiddish], lit., a bastard; a detestable person.

mon [Jap], family badge: *Japan.* Cf. KIKUMON and KIRIMON.

mon ami [Fr; *fem.* mon amie], my friend.

mon cher [Fr; *masc.*], my dear. Cf. MA CHÈRE.

monde [Fr], the world of fashion; society; one's set or coterie.

mon Dieu! [Fr], lit., my God! good heavens! my goodness! gracious!

mono [Sp], monkey; cute: *colloq.*

monomachia [Gr μονομαχία], single combat; duel.

mon petit chou [Fr], lit., my little cabbage; my little darling.

monseigneur [Fr], form of address to princes and prelates; your Grace.

monsieur [Fr; *pl.* messieurs], lit., my lord; a title or form of address equivalent to *Sir* or *Mr.*: *abbr.* M., *pl.* MM. *or* Messrs.

montagnard [Fr; *fem.* montagnarde], mountaineer; highlander; *Fr. hist.*, a member of "the Mountain" (*le Montagne*), or extreme radical faction in the first French Revolution, so called because its delegates occupied the highest seats in the National Convention; member of mountain tribes friendly to the U.S. in Vietnam war.

montagnes russes [Fr], lit., Russian mountains; switchback railway; roller coaster.

montaña [Sp], mountain.

Montani semper liberi [L], Mountaineers are always free men: motto of *West Virginia.*

mont-de-piété [Fr; *pl.* monts-de-piété], lit., mount of piety; a public or municipal pawnshop.

monte de piedad [Sp], **monte di pietà** [It], public pawnbroking establishment. See MONT-DE-PIÉTÉ.

montrer patte blanche [Fr], lit., to show a white paw; prove one's identity.

monumentum aere perennius [L], a monument more lasting than brass: *Horace.*

moolvee [Anglo-Ind], Islamic doctor of law; also, teacher of Arabic.

moqueur [Fr; *fem.* moqueuse], *adj.* mocking; sneering; *n.* mocker; scoffer.

morbidezza [It], softness or delicacy; *fine arts,* lifelike delicacy in the representation of flesh tints; hence, extreme delicacy of treatment, in a literary or musical composition.

morceau [Fr; *pl.* morceaux], a piece; morsel; esp., a short musical or literary piece.

morcellement [Fr], division into parcels, as of land; parceling out; subdivision.

more [L], in the fashion (*or* style); after the manner (*or* way). —**more Anglico,** in the English fashion. —**more Hibernico,** in the Irish fashion. —**more maiorum,** after the manner of our ancestors. —**more meo,** in my own way. —**more Socratico,** after the manner of Socrates; dialectically. —**more solito,** in the usual (*or* customary) manner; as usual. —**more suo,** in his usual manner; in his own way.

more [Russ], sea.

morendo [It], dying away (*abbr.* mor.): *music.*

mores [L; *pl.* of *mos*], customs; habits; traditional rules of conduct; customary usages; unwritten laws.

Morgenessen [Ger], *in Switzerland,* breakfast.

morgen, morgen nur nicht heute, sagen alle faule Leute [Ger], tomorrow, tomorrow but never today, is what all lazy people say.

Morgenstunde hat Gold im Munde [Ger], lit., the morning hour has gold in its mouth; early to bed and early to rise makes a man healthy, wealthy, and wise. Cf. AURORA MUSIS AMICA EST.

morgue [Fr], haughtiness; arrogance; hauteur. —**morgue littéraire,** literary self-sufficiency.

morisco [Sp], *adj.* Moorish. —**Morisco,** *n.* Moor; a person of Moorish extraction in Spain.

morituri morituros salutant [L], those about to die salute those about to die.

morituri te salutamus [L], we who are about to die salute thee: the salutation of the gladiators to the Roman emperor.

mormorando [It], murmuring; whispering: *music.*

morne [Fr], *adj.* dull; doleful; dreary; melancholy.

morne [Fr], *n.* a rounded hill: *Fr. America.*

mors ianua vitae [L], death is the gate of life.

mors omnibus communis [L], death is common to all men.

mors ultima linea rerum est [L], death is the final goal of things; "for when Death comes, the power of fortune ends": *Horace* (tr. by Conington).

mortifié [Fr], made tender; well hung: said of meat.

mortis causa [L], by reason of (impending) death: *law.*

mort ou vif [Fr], dead or alive.

mortuo leoni et lepores insultant [L], even hares leap on (*or* insult) a dead lion.

morue [Fr], cod; codfish. Cf. CABILLAUD.

mos pro lege [L], custom for law; usage has the force of law.

mosso [It], moved; with motion; rapid; quicker. —**più mosso,** lit., more moved; with more movement or animation: *both music.*

mot [Fr], word; expression; witty or pithy saying. —**mot à mot** *(in translating)* or **mot pour mot** *(in repeating),* word for word; verbatim. —**mot d'écrit,** a short note; a line. —**mot de l'énigme,** the answer to the riddle; key to the mystery. —**mot de passe,** password. —**mot de ralliement,** countersign; password. —**mot d'ordre,** watchword; password. —**mot du guet,** watchword. —**mot d'usage,** word in common use. —**mot juste,** the precise (*or* exact) word. —**mot pour rire,** jest; joke; witty saying.

moti [Hind], pearl: *India.*

motif [Fr], in artistic composition, salient feature; central or dominant idea; theme or subject, esp., as elaborated in musical composition; motive; *dressmaking,* an appliqué design used in lace and other trimmings. —**le bon motif,** matrimony: *jocose.*

moto [It], movement; motion; energy. —**con moto,** with movement; with animation: *both music.*

motte [Fr], a clump or island of trees in a prairie: *U.S. (local).*

motu proprio [L], by one's own motion; of one's own impulse or accord.

mouchard [Fr], police spy; informer.

mouchoir [Fr], pocket handkerchief.

mouflon [Fr], wild sheep.

mouillé [Fr], lit., wet; softened in sound; palatalized.

moule [Fr], mussel.

moulin [Fr], mill; specif., a nearly vertical shaft in a glacier formed by water from the surface. —**moulin à paroles,** chatterbox. —**Moulin Rouge,** lit., red mill; famous Paris music hall.

moulinage [Fr], the act or process of twisting and doubling raw silk; silk throwing.

mousquetaire [Fr], musketeer.

mousse [Fr], cabin boy; ship boy: *naut.;* a light dessert made with whipped egg whites, whipped cream, etc.

mousseline [Fr], French muslin. —**mousseline-de-laine,** lit., muslin of wool; a light, untwilled, woolen dress material. —**mousseline-de-soie,** lit., muslin of silk, a thin silk fabric resembling chiffon.

mousseux [Fr], foaming; sparkling (as wine).

moutard [Fr], urchin; brat; youngster: *colloq.*

moutarde [Fr], mustard.

mouton [Fr], mutton; sheep.

moutonné [Fr; *fem.* moutonnée], fleecy; white with foam, as the sea.

Moyen-Age [Fr], Middle Ages.

mozzetta [It], short cape with a small hood, worn by dignitaries of the Roman Catholic Church; a mozetta.

muchacha [Sp], girl; lass.

muchacho [Sp], boy; lad.

mucho en el suelo, poco en el cielo [Sp], much on earth, little in heaven; rich here, poor hereafter.

mucho ruido, pocas nueces [Sp], much noise, few nuts.

muchos pocos hacen un mucho [Sp], many littles make a much: *Cervantes.*

mucke nicht! [Ger], not a word! not a sound!

muelle [Sp], quay; wharf; railroad platform.

muet comme un poisson [Fr], mute as a fish.

Muharram [Ar *muharran,* sacred, forbidden], first month of the Muhammadan calendar.

muita parra e pouca uva [Pg], great vineyard and few grapes.

muito falar, pouco saber [Pg], many words, little knowledge.

mujer [Sp], woman; wife.

mujer te doy pero no esclava [Sp], I give you a wife but not a slave.

mulatto [Sp *mulato*], a person of black and Caucasian ancestry.

muleta [Sp], short red cape used by matador in bullfight.

mullah [Ar *maulā*], one learned in Islamic laws and dogmas.

multa acervatim frequentans [L], crowding together a number of thoughts: *Cicero.*

multa docet fames [L], hunger teaches us many things.

multa fidem promissa levant [L], many promises lessen (*or* weaken) faith: *Horace.*

multa gemens [L], with many a groan; groaning oft: *Virgil.*

multa paucis [L], much in little; much (*or* many things) in few words.

multa petentibus desunt multa [L], to those who seek many things, many things are lacking; who covets much, wants much: *Horace.*

multa tulit fecitque [L], much has he suffered and done: *Horace.*

multi sunt vocati, pauci vero electi [L], many are called but few are chosen.

multum demissus homo [L], a very modest (*or* unassuming) man: *Horace.*

multum in parvo [L], much in little (*or* in small compass).

multum, non multa [L], much, not many: *Pliny.*

mumbo jumbo [Mandingo *mamagyombo*], fetish; sorcerer; gibberish: *colloq.*

munditiis capimur [L], we are captivated by neatness: *Ovid.*

mundus [L], world.

mundus vult decipi [L], the world wishes to be deceived.

municipio [Sp], town; civic administration.

munshi [Hind & Pers], a native secretary; teacher of languages, esp. of Urdu, Persian, and Arabic.

munus Apolline dignum [L], a gift worthy of Apollo: *Horace.*

mûr [Fr; *fem.* mûre], ripe; mature.

mûre [Fr], mulberry.

murshid [Ar], Islamic religious teacher; spiritual guide.

murus aëneus conscientia sana [L], a sound conscience is a wall of brass.

muscae volitantes [L], lit., flying flies; specks before the eyes; floaters.

Musik ist Poesie der Luft [Ger], music is the poetry of the air: *Jean Paul Richter.*

Musikverein [Ger], German musical society.

musjid [Ar]. Same as MASJID.

musnud [Anglo-Ind; Hind & Ar *masnad*], large cushion; throne. Cf. GADDI.

must [Anglo-Ind; Hind *mast*], *adj.* drunk; ruttish; sexually frenzied (said esp. of male elephants and camels); *n.* a state of periodical frenzy; also, an elephant or camel in this condition: *India.*

musti [Anglo-Ind; Hind *mastī*], drunkenness; intoxication; frenzy: sometimes used erroneously as an adjective in place of *must.*

mutanda [L], things to be altered.

mutare vel timere sperno [L], I scorn to change or fear.

mutatis mutandis [L], necessary changes being made; with appropriate alteration of details.

mutato nomine [L], the name being changed; under a changed name.

mutato nomine, de te fabula narratur [L], the name being changed, the story is told of you; with a mere change of name, the story applies to yourself: *Horace.*

mutig [Ger], courageous; stout-hearted. **—mutig!,** courage!

Mütterchen [Ger], old woman; granny.

mutum est pictura poëma [L], a picture is a silent poem (*or* a poem without words).

mutuus consensus [L], mutual consent.

muzh [Russ], husband; man.

muzhik [Russ; *fem.* muzhitshka], Russian peasant.

Mynheer [Du *mijnheer*], lit., my master; Dutch title or form of address equivalent to *Sir* or *Mr.*

N

nacelle [Fr], enclosure for protecting an engine.

Nachbeterei [Ger], blind adherence; unquestioning fidelity.

nach Canossa gehen wir nicht [Ger], we are not going to Canossa: *Bismarck* (referring to the humiliating submission of Emperor Henry IV to Pope Gregory VII at Canossa, Italy, in 1077).

nach Christo *or* **nach Christi Geburt** [Ger], after Christ; A.D.: *abbr.* n.Ch. Cf. VOR CHRISTO.

Nachdruck [Ger], emphasis: *music.*

nacheifern ist beneiden [Ger], to emulate is to envy: *Lessing.*

nachlässig [Ger], negligent; careless.

Nachmittag [Ger], afternoon: *abbr.* Nm.

nachmittags [Ger], in the afternoon; p.m.: *abbr.* Nm.

nach reiflicher Überlegung [Ger], after mature consideration.

Nachspiel [Ger], postlude.

Nacht [Ger], night.

Nachtmusik [Ger], serenade.

nach und nach [Ger], by degrees; little by little.

nacré [Fr], nacreous; pearly.

nage [Fr], swimming.

naïf [Fr; *fem.* naïve], artless; ingenuous; unaffected; natural.

naik [Hind], leader; chief; in a native regiment, a corporal: *India.*

naissance [Fr], birth; origin; dawn.

naissant [Fr], being born; beginning to be.

naïveté [Fr], native simplicity; ingenuousness; naturalness.

nämlich [Ger], namely; to wit.

nam tua res agitur, paries cum proximus ardet [L], when your neighbor's house is on fire, you are in danger yourself; "no time for sleeping with a fire next door": *Horace* (tr. by Conington).

nanook [Esk], polar bear.

não há de que [Pg], don't mention it: said in reply to "thanks."

não saber ler [Pg], not to know reading; not to know black from white.

não sei [Pg], I do not know.

napoleon [Fr], a pastry.

nat [Burmese], a spirit of the forest and the stream, believed in by the animists of India and Burma.

natale solum [L], native soil.

natio comoeda est [L], it is a nation of comic actors: *Juvenal* (of the decadent Greeks).

natura abhorret a vacuo [L], nature abhors a vacuum: *Descartes.*

natura il fece, e poi roppe la stampa [It], nature made him and then broke the mold: *Ariosto* (said of someone preeminent in a field of endeavor).

naturalia [NL], the sexual organs.

naturam expellas furca, tamen usque recurret [L], you may drive out Nature with a pitchfork, but she will always come back: *Horace.*

natura non facit saltum [L], nature makes no leap; there are no gaps in nature.

naturel [Fr; *fem.* naturelle], natural; innate.—**enfant naturel,** illegitimate child. —**au naturel,** lit., to the life; naturally; plain; plainly cooked.

natus ad gloriam [L], born to glory.

natus nemo [L], not a born soul; not a human being; nobody: *Plautus.*

naukar [Hind; *pl.* naukarlog], servant: *India.*

nautch [Anglo-Ind; Hind *nāch*], dance; esp., an entertainment provided by Hindu professional dancing girls.

navarin [Fr], lamb or mutton stew: *cookery.*

navet [Fr], turnip.

n'avoir pas le sou [Fr], not to have a sou; be penniless.

nawab [Hind & Ar], orig., viceregent or governor; title of a Muslim ruling prince; also, a courtesy title formerly conferred by the government on Muslims of high rank but without office: *India.*

nazim [Ar], administrator; military governor: *India.*

nazir [Hind & Ar], orig., an inspector; a native official of a civil court; also, the warden of a mosque: *India.*

ne admittas [L], do not admit.

nebech *or* **nebbish** [Yiddish], a hapless person; a weak, pathetic person.

Nebiim [Heb], in the Jewish Scripture, the books known as the "Prophets."

nec amor nec tussis celatur [L], neither love nor a cough can be hidden.

nec aspera terrent [L], not even hardships deter us.

nec caput nec pedes [L], neither head nor tail; in confusion.

nec cupias nec metuas [L], neither desire nor fear.

ne cede malis, sed contra audentior ito [L], yield not to misfortunes, but go more boldly to meet them: *Virgil.*

nécessaire [Fr], dressing case; workbox.

necessità il c'induce, e non diletto [It], necessity brings him here and not delight: *Dante.*

necessitas non habet legem [L], necessity has (*or* knows) no law.

nec habeo, nec careo, nec curo [L], I have not, I want not, I care not.

ne choisit pas qui emprunte [Fr], he who borrows chooses not (*or* has no choice).

nec male notus eques [L], a well-known knight; a knight of good repute.

nec mora nec requies [L], neither delay nor rest; without intermission: *Virgil.*

nec placida contentus quiete est [L], nor is he content with calm repose.

nec pluribus impar [L], not unequal to many; a match for the whole world: motto of *Louis XIV* of France.

nec prece nec pretio [L], neither by entreaty nor by bribe.

nec quaerere nec spernere honorem [L], neither to seek nor to despise honors.

nec scire fas est omnia [L], nor is it permitted to know all things: *Horace*.

nec tecum possum vivere, nec sine te [L], I can neither live with you nor without you: *Martial*.

nec temere nec timide [L], neither rashly nor timorously.

nec timeo nec sperno [L], I neither fear nor despise.

nec vixit male, qui natus moriensque fefellit [L], he has not lived ill who has been born and died unnoticed: *Horace*.

née [Fr], born: used in adding the maiden name of a married woman.

ne exeat (regno) [L], let him not go out (of the realm); a writ of restraint: *law*.

nefasti dies [L], in ancient Rome, days on which court judgment could not be pronounced nor general assemblies held; unlucky days.

ne fronti crede [L], trust not to appearances.

negatur [L], it is denied.

negligé [Fr], free and easy attire; state of undress; woman's dressing gown.

negligentemente [It], negligently; unconstrained: *music*.

nehmen Sie gefälligst Platz [Ger], pray be seated.

ne Iuppiter quidem omnibus placet [L], not Jupiter himself can please everyone.

νεκρὸς οὐ δάκνει [Gr; nekròs ou dáknei], a dead man does not bite; dead men tell no tales.

nella chiesa co' santi, ed in taverna co' ghiottoni [It], with saints in church and with gluttons in the tavern: *Dante*.

nello stile antico [It], in the ancient style.

nel mezzo del cammin di nostra vita [It], midway in the journey of our life: *Dante* (opening words of the "Inferno").

nemine contradicente [L], no one contradicting; unanimously: *abbr.* nem. con.

nemine dissentiente [L], no one dissenting; no one opposing: *abbr.* nem. diss.

nemo alius [L], no one else.

nemo bis punitur pro eodem delicto [L], no man is punished twice for the same offense.

nemo dat quod non habet [L], no one can give what he does not have.

nemo est heres viventis [L], no one is heir of a living man: *law*.

nemo me impune lacessit [L], no one assails me with impunity: motto of *Scotland* and of the *Order of the Thistle*.

nemo mortalium omnibus horis sapit [L], no mortal is wise at all times: *Pliny.*

nemo repente fuit turpissimus [L], no one ever was suddenly very base; no one ever became a villain all at once: *Juvenal.*

nemo solus satis sapit [L], no one is sufficiently wise by himself; two heads are better than one: *Plautus.*

nemo tenetur se ipsum accusare [L], no one is bound to accuse himself.

ne mozhet beet [Russ], it can't be true.

ne nimium [L], not too much; do nothing in excess.

ne obliviscaris [L], lest ye forget; do not forget.

ne plus ultra [L], not more beyond; the utmost point attained or attainable; acme; culmination.

ne puero gladium [L], (trust) not a sword to a boy; don't give a man's job to a boy.

neque semper arcum tendit Apollo [L], Apollo does not always keep his bow bent; high tension should be followed by relaxation: *Horace.*

ne quid detrimenti respublica capiat [L], (take care) that the republic (*or* state) receive no injury.

ne quid nimis [L], not anything too much; avoid excess.

ne quittez pas [Fr], hold the line (on the telephone).

nero-antico [It], black marble, found among Roman ruins.

nervi belli pecunia infinita [L], plenty of money is the sinews of war: *Cicero.*

nervus probandi [L], the sinew of proof; chief argument.

nervus rerum [L], the sinew of things.

nescio quid [L], I know not what.

nescit vox missa reverti [L], the word once spoken can never be recalled: *Horace.*

nessun maggior dolore che ricordarsi del tempo felice nella miseria [It], there is no greater grief than to remember times of happiness in the midst of wretchedness; "a sorrow's crown of sorrow is remembering happier things" (*Tennyson*): *Dante.*

n'est-ce pas? [Fr], isn't that so?

ne sutor supra crepidam iudicaret [L], let not the shoemaker criticize beyond his last; let the cobbler stick to his last: *Pliny* (the saying of the painter Apelles to a cobbler who criticized not only the shoes in a picture but the painting generally).

Ne Temere [L], lit., not rashly; a decree pronouncing as invalid all Roman Catholic marriages not celebrated before a priest and proper witnesses: *R.C.Ch.*

ne tentes, aut perfice [L], attempt not, or accomplish.

netsuke [Jap], a small piece of carved ivory or wood, used as a pouch toggle and the like: *Japan.*

netteté [Fr], cleanness; neatness; also clearness; distinctness.

neue Besen kehren gut [Ger], a new broom sweeps clean.

neue Menschen [Ger], lit., new men; upstarts; parvenus.

neuere Richtung [Ger], new, or modern, method; specif., the reform movement in the teaching of languages.

Neujahr [Ger], New Year.

névé [Fr], an expanse of partially compacted snow at the upper end of a glacier (a transitional stage between loose snow and glacier ice); field of granular snow.

n'è vero? [It], is it not true? isn't it so?

ne vile velis [L], incline to nothing base.

nez retroussé [Fr], upturned nose.

niais [Fr; *fem.* niaise], *adj.* silly; foolish; simple; *n.* simpleton.

niaiserie [Fr], foolishness; silliness; trifling; also, piece of foolishness; foolery; trifle; nonsense.

nichevo [Russ *nichebo*, nothing], it doesn't matter; don't mention it; nothing.

Nichts halb zu tun [Ger], to do nothing by halves.

nicht so redlich wäre redlicher [Ger], not so honest were more honest: *Lessing.*

nicht wahr? [Ger], isn't that so?

niente affatto [It], nothing at all.

ni firmes carta que no leas, ni bebas agua que no veas [Sp], never sign a paper you have not read, nor drink water you have not seen (*or* examined).

nigaud [Fr; *fem.* nigaude], booby; simpleton.

niger cycnus [L], black swan; prodigy. Cf. RARA AVIS IN TERRIS.

nihil [L], nothing. **—nihil ad rem,** nothing to the point; irrelevant. **—nihil amori iniuriam est,** there is no wrong that love will not forgive. **—nihil debet,** lit., he owes nothing; a plea denying a debt: *law.* **—nihil dicit,** lit., he says nothing; a common-law judgment when the defendant declines to plead or answer: *law.* **—nihil est ab omni parte beatum,** nothing is blessed in every respect (i.e., there is no perfect happiness): *Horace.* **—nihil ex nihilo,** nothing comes from nothing. **—nihil quod tetigit non ornavit,** he touched nothing he did not adorn. See NULLUM QUOD TETIGIT NON ORNAVIT (the correct form). **—nihil obstat,** there is no objection: *eccl.* **—nihil sub sole novum,** there is nothing new under the sun.

νίκη δ' ἐπαμείβεται ἄνδρας [Gr; níkē d' epameíbetai ándras], victory comes in turn to men (i.e., now to this man, now to that): *Homer.*

nil admirari [L], to be astonished at nothing: *Horace.*

nil agit exemplum, litem quod lite resolvit [L], an example is nothing to the purpose, which decides one controversy by creating another: *Horace.*

nil conscire sibi, nulla pallescere culpa [L], to be conscious of no wrongdoing, to turn pale at no crime (*or* with no guilt): *Horace.*

nil consuetudine maius [L], nothing is greater (*or* stronger) than custom: *Ovid.*

nil desperandum [L], nothing must be despaired of; never despair: *Horace.*

nil (*or* **nihil**) **dicit** [L], he says nothing; he makes no answer; the defendant has no defense: *law.*

nil fuit umquam sic impar sibi [L], nothing was ever so inconsistent with itself: *Horace.*

nil magnum nisi bonum [L], nothing is great unless good.

nil mortalibus arduum est [L], nothing is too difficult for mortals to accomplish: *Horace.*

nil nisi Cruce [L], naught save by the Cross.

nil sine Deo [L], nothing without God.

nil sine magno vita labore debit mortalibus [L], life has given nothing to man without great labor: *Horace.*

nil sine numine [L], nothing without divine will: motto of *Colorado.*

nil ultra [L], nothing beyond; the utmost limit.

ni l'un ni l'autre [Fr], neither the one nor the other.

nimium ne crede colori [L], trust not too much to a beautiful complexion (*or* to appearances): *Virgil.*

n'importe [Fr], it's no matter; it's of no consequence.

ninguno nace maestro [Sp], no one is born an expert.

niño [Sp; *fem.* niña], child.

nirvana [Skr], Buddhist state of grace and nondesire.

nisei [Jap], lit., second generation; a son or daughter of immigrant Japanese (*issei*) who is born and educated in America. Cf. KIBEI.

nisi [L], unless; if not; designating that a decree, order, rule, or the like, will become effective at a given time unless previously modified or rescinded: *law.* **—nisi Dominus frustra,** except the Lord (build the house, they labor) in vain: motto of *Edinburgh.* **—nisi prius,** lit., unless before; orig., a writ directing the sheriff to bring a jury to Westminster on a certain day, "unless before" that day, a justice of assizes should come to the county in question; hence, a *nisi prius* court is one held for the trial of civil cases before a judge and jury: *law.*

nisus [L], endeavor; effort; striving; conatus. **—nisus formativus,** creative effort; vital principle.

nitor in adversum [L], I press forward to the opposite side; I strive against opposition: *Ovid.*

Nivôse [Fr], in the Revolutionary calendar of the first French Republic, the fourth month of the year, from Dec. 21 to Jan. 19.

nizam [Hind, Turk, & Ar], lit., order; arrangement; *Turkey,* soldier (*or* soldiers) of the Turkish regular army; *India,* administrator; viceroy, esp. under the Moguls. **—Nizam,** title of the ruling prince of Hyderabad, formerly the largest native state in India.

nobilitas sola est atque unica virtus [L], virtue is the true and only nobility: *Juvenal.*

nobilitatis virtus non stemma character [L], virtue, not pedigree, is the distinguishing mark of true nobility.

noblesse [Fr], nobility; rank; the nobility. —**noblesse oblige,** rank imposes obligations.

nocet empta dolore voluptas [L], pleasures bought by pain are injurious: *Horace.*

Nochebuena [Sp], Christmas Eve.

nocte [L], at night: *abbr.* n.

Noël [Fr], Christmas; yuletide.

no es para tanto [Sp], it does not matter; it isn't important.

¿no es verdad? [Sp], isn't it true? isn't it so?

noeud [Fr], a bow; knot. —**noeud d'amour,** love knot; true lover's knot.

nogada [Am Sp], pecan candy: *southern Texas.*

no hay cerradura donde es oro la ganzúa [Sp], there is no lock where gold is the picklock; a golden key will open any door.

no hay pariente pobre [Sp], a poor relation has no existence: *Cervantes.*

no hay pero que valga [Sp], there are no buts that are worthwhile.

no hay que mentar la soga en casa del ahorcado [Sp], one must not talk about rope in the household of a person who has been hanged.

noir [Fr; *fem.* noire], black.

noisette [Fr], hazelnut.

noix [Fr; *pl.* noix], lit., walnut; a small lymphatic gland near the shoulder, as of a calf (*noix de veau*): *cookery.*

nolens volens [L], unwilling (or) willing; willy-nilly; perforce.

noli irritare leones [L], do not stir up the lions.

noli me tangere [L], touch me not: *Vulgate* (*John* xx. 17).

nolle prosequi [L], lit., to be unwilling to prosecute; an entry on the court record, denoting discontinuance or stay of proceedings, either wholly or in part (*abbr.* nol. pros.): *law.*

nolo contendere [L], lit., I do not wish to contest; in criminal cases, a plea by the defendant equivalent to that of "guilty" but without admitting guilt: *law.*

nolo espiscopari [L], I do not wish to be made a bishop: a phrase expressing refusal of a responsible office, esp. the royal offer of a bishopric.

nom [Fr], name. —**nom de demoiselle,** maiden name. —**nom de famille,** family name; surname. —**nom de guerre,** lit., war name; assumed name; pseudonym. —**nom de plume** [pseudo-French], pen name. —**nom de théâtre,** stage name. —**nom emprunté,** lit., borrowed name; assumed name.

nomen [L; *pl.* nomina], name. —**nomen atque omen,** a name and also an omen: *Plautus.* —**nomen genericum,** a generic name. —**nomen**

nudum [*pl.* nomina nuda], lit., naked name; a mere name without a proper description: *biol.* —**nomen specificum,** a specific name.

nomina stultorum parietibus haerent [L], the names of fools stick (*or* adhere) to the walls; fools' names and fools' faces are always found in public places.

nominis umbra [L], the shadow of a name.

non Angli sed angeli [L], not Angles but angels: *Pope Gregory the Great* (on seeing some British youths exposed for sale in the slave market at Rome).

non assumpsit [L], lit., he did not undertake; a general denial in an action of *assumpsit* (q.v.): *law.*

non avenu [Fr], (regarded as) not having taken place; *law,* null and void.

non capisco [It], I do not understand.

non compos (mentis) [L], not of sound mind.

non constat [L], it does not appear; the evidence is not before the court: *law.*

non cuivis homini contingit adire Corinthum [L], it is not given to every man to go to Corinth (a city noted for its luxury and lavishness): *Horace.*

non datur tertium [L], no third is given; there is no third choice.

non deficiente crumena [L], the purse not failing; while the money holds out: *Horace.*

non è così [It], it is not so.

non è guadagnare, beneficando uno, offender più [It], nothing is to be gained by offending many in order to do a kindness to one: *Machiavelli.*

non ens [L], the nonexistent; nonentity.

non esse [L], not to be; nonexistence.

non est [L], he (*or* it) is not.

non est inventus [L], he has not been found; a statement by the sheriff on return of a writ when the defendant is not to be found: *law.*

non est iocus esse malignum [L], there is no fun (*or* joking) where there is spite: *Horace.*

non est meus actus [L], it is not my act: *law.* Cf. *actus me invito,* etc., under ACTUS.

non est tanti [L], it is not worthwhile.

non est vivere, sed valere, vita [L], life is not mere living but the enjoyment of health.

nonetto [It], composition for nine; nonet: *music.*

non è vero? [It], isn't that true?

non fa caso [It], no matter; it's of no importance.

non generant aquilae columbas [L], eagles do not bear doves.

non ignara mali, miseris succurrere disco [L], not unacquainted with misfortune, I learn to aid the distressed: *Virgil.*

non importa [It], it doesn't matter.

non inferiora secutus [L], not having followed anything inferior: *Virgil*.

non intendo [It], I do not understand.

non libet [L], it does not please (me).

non liquet [L], it (i.e., the case) is not clear; not proven: *law*.

non mihi sed Deo et regi [L], not for myself but for God and the King.

non mi ricordo [It], I do not remember.

non multa, sed multum [L], not many things, but much.

non nobis, Domine [L], not unto us, O Lord: *Vulgate (Psalms* cxv. 1).

non nobis solum nati sumus [L], not for ourselves alone are we born: *Cicero*.

non nostrum inter vos tantas componere lites [L], it is not for me to settle such weighty controversies between you: *Virgil*.

nonobstant clameur de haro [Fr], notwithstanding the hue and cry.

non obstante [L], notwithstanding: *abbr.* non obst. —**non obstante veredicto,** notwithstanding the verdict; a judgment for the plaintiff, setting aside a verdict for the defendant: *law*.

non ogni giorno è festa [It], every day is not a holiday.

non olet [L], it does not have a bad smell (i.e., money, however come by).

non omne licitum honestum [L], not every lawful thing is honorable.

non omnia possumus omnes [L], we cannot all do all things: *Virgil*.

non omnis moriar [L], I shall not wholly die (i.e., my works will survive me): *Horace*.

non passibus aequis [L], not with equal steps: *Virgil*.

non placet [L], lit., it does not please: expressing a negative vote.

non possidentem multa vocaveris recte beatum [L], you cannot rightly call happy the man who possesses many things: *Horace*.

non possumus [L], lit., we cannot: a statement expressing inability to act or move in a matter.

non prosequitur [L], lit., he does not prosecute; a judgment where the plaintiff does not appear (*abbr.* non pros.): *law*.

non quis sed quid [L], not who but what.

non quo sed quomodo [L], not by whom but how.

non regioniam di lor, ma guarda e passa [It], "speak not of them, but look, and pass them by": *Dante* (tr. by Cary).

non revertar inultus [L], I shall not return unavenged.

non sans droict [OF], not without right: motto on *Shakespeare's* coat of arms.

non semper erit aestas [L], it will not always be summer; make hay while the sun shines.

non semper erunt Saturnalia [L], it will not always be Saturnalia (a Roman festival celebrated in December and lasting for several days); the carnival will not last forever.

non sequitur [L], it does not follow; illogical inference: *abbr.* non seq.

non sibi sed omnibus [L], not for himself (*or* oneself) but for all.

non sibi sed patriae [L], not for himself but for his country.

non sine numine [L], not without divine aid.

non si può far d'un pruno, un melarancio [It], you cannot make an orange tree out of a bramble bush.

non subito delenda [L], not to be suddenly (*or* hastily) destroyed.

non sum qualis eram [L], I am not what once I was: *Horace.*

non tali auxilio [L], not for such aid as this: *Virgil.*

nonum(que) prematur in annum [L], (and) let it be kept back (from publication) till the ninth year: *Horace.*

non v'è peggior ladro d'un cattivo libro [It], there is no robber worse than a bad book.

non vobis solum [L], not for you alone.

nosce te ipsum (*or* **teipsum**) [L], know thyself.

nosce tempus [L], know thy time.

noscitur a sociis [L], he is known by his companions.

nos duo turba sumus [L], we two are a crowd (*or* multitude): *Ovid.*

no se puede pedir peras al olmo [Sp], one cannot get pears from an elm tree.

nostro periculo [L], at our own risk.

nos vertus ne sont le plus souvent que des vices déguisés [Fr], our virtues are often only vices in disguise: *La Rochefoucauld.*

nota [It], a note. **—nota buona,** an accented note. **—nota cattiva,** an unaccented note. **—nota sensibile,** the leading note. **—nota sostenuta,** a sustained note: *all music.*

nota bene [L], note well; take notice: *abbr.* N.B.

notandum [L; *pl.* notanda], something to be noted; memorandum.

Not bricht Eisen [Ger], necessity breaks iron; necessity is the mother of invention.

note infamante [Fr], brand of infamy.

Not kennt kein Gebot [Ger], necessity knows no law.

Not lehrt Künste [Ger], necessity is the mistress of the arts.

Notre Dame [Fr], Our Lady; the Virgin Mary.

notturno [It], nocturne: *music.*

n'oubliez pas [Fr], do not forget.

nourri [Fr; *fem.* nourrie], nourished; full; copious.

nourrice [Fr], wet nurse; foster mother.

nous avons changé tout cela [Fr], we have changed all that: *Molière.*

nous avons tous assez de force pour supporter les maux d'autrui [Fr], we all have strength enough to bear the misfortunes of others: *La Rochefoucauld.*

nous dansons sur un volcan [Fr], we are dancing on a volcano.

nous maintiendrons [Fr], we will maintain; we will carry on.

nous verrons [Fr], we shall see. —**nous verrons ce que nous verrons,** we shall see what we shall see.

nouveau riche [Fr; *pl.* nouveaux riches], a man newly become rich; an upstart.

nouvelle [Fr; *pl.* nouvelles], news; tidings; also, a short story; novelette. —**quelles sont les nouvelles?,** what is the news?

nouvelle vague [Fr], lit., new wave; the film and literary phenomenon of the 1950's et seq.

novella [It; *pl.* novelle], a tale or narrative with an artistic plot and brevity of style, like the stories in Boccaccio's *Decameron.*

novena [L; *pl.* novenae], a nine days' devotion: *R.C.Ch.*

novia [Sp], fiancée; bride.

novio [Sp], fiancé; bridegroom.

novus homo [L; *pl.* novi homines], a new man; a man newly risen from obscurity; an upstart.

novus rex, nova lex [L], new king, new law.

noyade [Fr], wholesale execution by drowning, as in France during the Reign of Terror (1793-1794).

noyer [Fr], walnut tree.

nuance [Fr], shade; tint; subtle distinction or difference, as in meaning, color, etc.

nuda veritas [L], naked (*or* undisguised) truth: *Horace.*

nudis verbis [L], in plain words.

nudj [Yiddish], lit., to poke at; to pester, nag.

nudnik [Yiddish, *fr.* Russ *nudnyi*, tedious], an annoying person, a pest; a bore.

nudum pactum [L], a nude pact; an informal contract without consideration or without a cause and therefore invalid unless under seal: *law.*

nugae [L; *pl.*], trifles; unprofitable minutiae; compositions of a trivial and fugitive kind. —**nugae canorae,** melodious trifles (*or* nonsense): *Horace.*

nugis addere pondus [L], to add weight to trifles: *Horace.*

nugis armatus [L], armed with trifles.

nuisible [Fr], hurtful; injurious; noxious.

nul bien sans peine [Fr], no gain without pain.

nulla bona [L], no goods; no effects: *law.*

nulla dies sine linea [L], no day without a line; no day without something done.

nulla-nulla [Australian native], a hardwood club used by the Australian aborigines.

nulla nuova, buona nuova [It], no news is good news.

nulli desperandum, quamdiu spirat [L], no one is to be despaired of so long as he breathes; while there is life there is hope.

nulli secundus [L], second to none.

nullius addictus iurare in verba magistri [L], not pledged to swear to the words (*or* ipse-dixits) of any particular master: *Horace.*

nullius filius [L], nobody's son; an illegitimate son.

nullum quod tetigit non ornavit [L], there was nothing he touched that he did not adorn: from Dr. Johnson's epitaph on Goldsmith (*Qui nullum fere scribendi genus non tetigit, nullum quod tetigit non ornavit,* who left scarcely any kind of writing untouched, and nothing touched that he did not adorn).

numdah [Anglo-Ind; Hind *namdā*], lit., felt; a felt pad or coarse woolen covering, used under a saddle; saddle pad: *India.*

numini et patriae asto [L], I stand on the side of God and my country.

nunatak [Eskimo *nunaettak*], an insular outcrop of rock surrounded by a sheet of land ice.

nunca lo bueno fué mucho [Sp], the good was never plentiful: *Cervantes.*

nunca mucho cuesta poco [Sp], much never costs little.

nunc aut nunquam [L], now or never.

Nunc Dimittis [L], Simeon's canticle, *nunc dimittis servum tuum, Domine,* Lord, now lettest thou thy servant depart in peace: *Vulgate* (*Luke* ii. 29).—**nunc dimittis,** willingness, or permission, to depart; departure.

nunc est bibendum [L], now is the time for drinking.

nunc pro tunc [L], lit., now for then; designating a delayed action which takes effect as if done at the proper time: *law.*

nunquam dormio [L], I never sleep; I am ever watchful.

nunquam minus solus quam cum solus [L], never less alone than when alone: *Cicero.*

nunquam non paratus [L], never unprepared; always ready.

nuoc nam [Viet], sauce made from juice of fish.

nuptiae [L], nuptials; marriage.

nurimono [Jap], Japanese lacquerware.

nur zur Schau [Ger], only for show.

nusquam tuta fides [L], nowhere is fidelity sure; nowhere is there true honor: *Virgil.*

nyet [Russ], no.

O

obbligato [It], *adj.* lit., bound; indispensable; inseparably connected with the composition; *n.* an instrumental part of more or less importance, often used as an accompaniment to a vocal solo; as, a violin *obbligato: music.*

obi [Jap], lit., a belt; Japanese sash worn with a kimono by women and children.

obiit [L], he (*or* she) died: *abbr.* ob. —**obiit sine prole,** he (or she) died without issue: *abbr.* ob.s.p.

obiter [L], by the way; in passing; incidentally. —**obiter dictum** [*pl.* obiter dicta], an unofficial expression of opinion; a thing said by the way; incidental remark. —**obiter scriptum** [*pl.* obiter scripta], something written by the way; an incidental composition.

objet d'art [Fr; *pl.* objets d'art], an object of artistic value.

objets d'occasion [Fr], secondhand things.

oblast [Russ], province or district; in Soviet Russia, a regional soviet.

obra de común, obra de ningún [Sp], everybody's work is nobody's work; everybody's business is nobody's business.

obrigado [Pg], thank you; thanks.

obscuris vera involvens [L], shrouding truth in darkness (*or* in obscure terms): *Virgil.*

obscurum per obscurius [L], (explaining) an obscurity by something more obscure.

observandum [L; *pl.* observanda], a thing to be observed.

obsta principiis [L], resist the beginnings: preferably *principiis obsta.*

obstupui, steteruntque comae, et vox faucibus haesit [L], I was astounded, my hair stood on end, and my voice stuck in my throat: *Virgil.*

occasio furem facit [L], opportunity makes the thief.

occasionem cognosce [L], know your opportunity.

occupet extremum scabies [L], plague take the hindmost: *Horace.*

occurrent nubes [L], clouds will intervene.

octroi [Fr], grant; concession; toll; duty, esp. on commodities entering a town.

odalisque [Fr, *fr.* Turk ōdahliq, chambermaid], a female slave or concubine, esp. in the Sultan's seraglio during the old régime.

O dea certe! [L], O thou, who art a goddess surely!: *Virgil.*

Odelsting [Norw], lower house of the Norwegian legislature.

oderint dum metuant [L], let them hate, so long as they fear: *Cicero.*

O dignitosa coscienza e netta, come t'è picciol fallo amaro morso! [It], "O clear conscience, and upright! How doth a little failing wound thee sore": *Dante* (tr. by Cary).

odi profanum vulgus et arceo [L], I hate the unhallowed (or uninitiated) rabble and keep them far from me: *Horace*.

odium [L], hatred. **—odium aestheticum,** the bitterness of aesthetical controversy. **—odium medicum,** the hatred of (rival) physicians; the bitterness of medical controversy. **—odium musicum,** the hatred of (rival) musicians; the bitterness of musical controversy. **—odium theologicum,** the hatred of (rival) theologians; the bitterness of theological controversy.

odor lucri [L], lit., a whiff of money; expectation of gain.

odotsa [Basque, *fr. odei,* cloud, *otsa,* noise], thunder.

oeil [Fr; *pl.* yeux], eye.

oeil-de-boeuf [Fr; *pl.* oeils-de-boeuf], lit., ox eye; a small round window; bull's-eye.

oeil-de-perdrix [Fr; *pl.* oeils-de-perdrix], lit., partridge eye; a soft corn (on the foot).

oeillade [Fr], a glance; ogle; sheep's eye.

oeuf [Fr; *pl.* oeufs], egg. **—oeufs à l'indienne,** curried eggs. **—oeufs brouillés,** scrambled eggs. **—oeufs frais,** new-laid eggs. **—oeufs pochés,** poached eggs.

oeuvre [Fr], a work, esp. of art or literature; a substantial body of work comprising the lifework of one writer, composer, or artist.

O fama ingens, ingentior armis! [L], O great by report, greater in arms (*or* deeds).

officina [L], workshop; laboratory. **—officina gentium,** the workshop of the nations.

oficina [Sp], office; works; plant.

O fortunatos nimium, sua si bona norint! [L], O too happy they, if they but knew their blessings.

ofrecer mucho especie es de negar [Sp], to offer too much is a kind of denial.

ogni cane è leone a casa sua [It], every dog is a lion at home.

ogni debolo ha sempre il suo tiranno [It], every weakling always has his tyrant.

ogni medaglia ha il suo rovescio [It], every medal has its reverse side; there are two sides to every question.

ogni pazzo vuol dar consiglio [It], every fool is ready with advice.

ogni vero non è buono a dire [It], lit., every truth is not good to be told; it's better to keep quiet about certain things.

ohe! iam satis est [L], ho there! that is enough: *Horace*.

ohne Hast, ohne Rast [Ger], without haste, without rest: motto of *Goethe* (said originally of the sun).

ohne Überlegung [Ger], without consideration; inconsiderate.

ohne Wissen, ohne Sünde [Ger], without knowledge, without sin; where there is no knowledge there is no sin.

οἶκοι λέοντες ἐν μάχη δ' ἀλωπέκες [Gr; oíkoi léontes en mákhē d'alō-pékes], lions at home, foxes in a fight: *Aristophanes.*

O imitatores, servum pecus [L], O servile herd of imitators; "mean, miserable apes!": *Horace* (tr. by Conington).

οἶνος Ἀφροδίτης γάλα [Gr; oînos Aphrodítēs gála], wine is the milk of Aphrodite (goddess of love): *Aristophanes.*

ojo [Sp], lit., eye; a spring surrounded by rank grass or rushes, as in the arid wastes of Texas, New Mexico, and California; an oasis: *southwestern U.S.*

O laborum dulce lenimen [L], O sweet solace of labors: *Horace* (referring to Apollo's lyre).

olé [Sp], shout of encouragement and appreciation; bravo! hurrah!

olet lucernam [L], it smells of the lamp; it bears the mark of nightly toil. Cf. REDOLET LUCERNA.

oleum [L], oil. —**oleum addere camino,** to pour oil on the fire; add fuel to the flame; aggravate an evil: *Horace* (adapted).

omen faustum [L], an auspicious omen; a lucky sign.

O mihi praeteritos referat si Iuppiter annos [L], O that Jove would give me back the years that are past: *Virgil.*

om mani padme hum [Skr], a Buddhist invocation (beginning with the mystic syllable *om*), which may be freely translated, "O, the Jewel in the Lotus, Amen": used esp. by the Lamaists of Tibet.

omne bonum desuper [L], all good is from above.

omne ignotum pro magnifico [L], everything unknown is thought to be splendid (*or* magnificent): *Tacitus.*

omnem movere lapidem [L], to leave no stone unturned.

omne scibile [L], everything knowable.

omne solum forti patria est [L], every soil is a fatherland to a brave man: *Ovid.*

omne trinum (est) perfectum [L], every perfect thing is threefold.

omne tulit punctum qui miscuit utile dulci [L], he has gained (or carried) every point who has blended the useful with the agreeable: *Horace.*

omne vivum ex ovo [L], every living thing comes from an egg (*or* germ).

omnia ad Dei gloriam [L], all things for the glory of God.

omnia bona bonis [L], to the good all things are good.

omnia desuper [L], all things are from above.

omnia mea mecum porto [L], everything that is mine I carry with me.

omnia mors aequat [L], death levels all things: *Claudian.*

omnia munda mundis [L], to the pure all things are pure.

omnia mutantur, nos et mutamur in illis [L], all things change and we change with them.

omnia praeclara rara [L], all excellent things are rare: *Cicero.*

omnia suspendens naso [L], turning up his nose at everything.

omnia tuta timens [L], fearing all things, even those that are safe: *Virgil*.

omnia vanitas [L], all is vanity.

omnia vincit amor [L], love conquers all things: *Virgil*.

omnia vincit labor [L], labor overcomes all things.

omnibus hoc vitium est [L], all have this vice: *Horace*.

omnibus idem [L], the same to all men.

omnibus invideas, livide, nemo tibi [L], you may envy everybody, envious one, but nobody envies you.

omnis amans amens [L], every lover is demented.

omnium rerum principia parva sunt [L], the beginnings of all things are small: *Cicero*.

ὄναρ καὶ ὕπαρ [Gr; ónar kaì húpar], sleeping and waking; at all times.

on commence par être dupe, on finit par être fripon [Fr], one begins by being a dupe, one ends by being a rascal.

on connaît l'ami au besoin [Fr], a friend is known in need; a friend in need is a friend indeed.

onda [Sp], wave. —**onda corta,** shortwave length: *radio*. —**onda larga,** long-wave length: *radio*.

on dit [Fr], they say; it is said. —**on-dit,** a piece of hearsay; rumor.

on dit que Dieu est toujours pour les gros bataillons [Fr], they say God is always on the side of the big battalions: *Voltaire*.

o ni o wo tsukeru [Jap], to add tail to tail; to exaggerate and amplify.

on n'a rien pour rien [Fr], nothing is had for nothing.

on n'attrappe pas les mouches avec du vinaigre [Fr], one doesn't catch flies with vinegar.

on ne passe pas [Fr], no passing; no thoroughfare.

onorate l'altissimo poeta! [It], honor the bard sublime!: *Dante* (in the "Inferno," the greeting given to Virgil by his fellow poets).

ὄνου πόκαι [Gr; ónou pókai], ass's wool; something nonexistent.

on parle français [Fr], French is spoken (here).

on se l'arrache [Fr], he (she, it) is all the rage.

onus probandi [L], the burden of proof.

onus segni impone asello [L], lay the burden on the lazy ass.

on y va! [Fr], coming!

o occhi miei, occhi non già, ma fonti! [It], O eyes of mine, not eyes, but fountains now: *Petrarch*.

oo chiloveka virasta hyoot krilyah [Russ], a man feels ten feet tall.

oo lazhee karotkee nochee [Russ], a lie has short legs.

oont [Anglo-Ind; Hind *ūnt*], camel.

ope et consilio [L], with aid and counsel (applied to accessories to a crime): *law*.

o peior porco come a melhor glande [Pg], the worst pig eats the best acorn.

opéra bouffe [Fr], opera of farcical character.

opéra comique [Fr], lit., comic opera; light opera, usually with spoken dialogue.

operae pretium est [L], there is reward for the work; it is worth doing: *Terence.*

opera illius mea sunt [L], his works are mine.

opere citato [L], in the work quoted: *abbr.* op. cit. *or* o.c.

opere in medio [L], in the midst of the work.

operose nihil agunt [L], they are busy about nothing: *Seneca.*

opinionâtre [Fr], opinionated; stubborn.

opposuit natura [L], nature has opposed; it is contrary to nature.

opprobrium medicorum [L], the reproach (*or* disgrace) of the doctors; said of incurable diseases.

optima mors Parca quae venit apta die [L], the best death is that which comes on the day fixed by Fate: *Propertius.*

optimates [L], aristocracy of ancient Rome; hence, aristocracy or nobility in general.

optime [L], very good; most excellent.

optimi consiliarii mortui [L], the best counselors are the dead.

optimum obsonium labor [L], lit., work is the best means of getting a meal; work is the best relish (*or* sauce).

opum furiata cupido [L], frenzied lust for wealth: *Ovid.*

opus [L; *pl.* opera], a work; musical composition: *abbr.* op. —**opus artificem probat,** the work proves the craftsman; the workman is known by his work. —**opus operatum** [*pl.* opera operata], a task performed; a work wrought; *theol.,* inherent efficacy of the sacrament.

O quam cito transit gloria mundi! [L], oh, how quickly passes away the glory of the world!

oración breve sube al cielo [Sp], short prayers mount to heaven.

ora e sempre [It], now and always.

ora et labora [L], pray and work.

orando laborando [L], by prayer and by toil: motto of *Rugby School,* England.

ora pro nobis [L], pray for us.

orate fratres [L], lit., pray, brothers: *eccl.*

orate pro anima [L], pray for the soul (of).

oratio gravis [L], a telling speech; weighty address.

orationem concludere [L], to end a speech.

orator fit, poeta nascitur [L], the orator is made, the poet born.

orbis scientiarum [L], the circle of the sciences.

ordre dispersé [Fr], extended order; open order: *mil.*

ordre du jour [Fr], order of the day; agenda of a meeting.

ordre serré [Fr], close order: *mil.*

orégano [Sp], herb used in cooking.

orejones [Sp], dried fruit: *Sp. Am.*

ore rotundo [L], lit., with a round mouth; with well-turned speech: *Horace*.

ore tenus [L], merely from the mouth; by word of mouth; verbally: *law*.

orfèvrerie [Fr], goldsmith's work.

orge [Fr], barley.

origo mali [L], the origin of evil.

ornamenti [It], ornaments; embellishments; grace notes: *music*.

ornatamente [It], with embellishments; in a florid style: *music*.

orné [Fr; *fem.* ornée], adorned; ornamented.

ὀρνίθων γάλα [Gr; orníthōn gála], birds' milk; any marvelous good fortune.

oro è che oro vale [It], that is gold which is worth gold; all is not gold that glitters.

oro y plata [Sp], gold and silver: motto of *Montana*.

O rus, quando ego te aspiciam [L], O country (home of my childhood), when shall I behold thee! *Horace*. Cf. O UBI CAMPI!

os [L; *pl.* ora], a mouth; opening: *anat.*

os [L; *pl.* ossa], a bone: *anat. & zool.*

O Salutaris Hostia [L], O saving Victim; first words of hymn used at the beginning of the Benediction of the Blessed Sacrament: *R.C.Ch.*

O sancta simplicitas! [L], O, sacred simplicity!

os à ronger [Fr], a bone to pick.

osculum pacis [L], kiss of peace.

oseille [Fr], sorrel; sorrel leaves (used for certain sauces): *cookery*.

O senza brama sicura ricchezza! [It], oh, riches secure without hankering!: *Dante*.

O si sic omnia [L], oh, if all things were thus! oh, that he had always done or spoken thus!

osotre [Russ], sturgeon.

osteria [It; *pl.* osterie], inn; tavern.

ostinato [It], obstinate; unceasing: *music*.

óstrov [Russ], island.

otage [Fr], hostage; pledge; guarantee.

O tempora! O mores! [L], alas for the times! alas for the manners!: *Cicero*.

O terque quaterque beati [L], O thrice, yea four times happy they!: *Virgil*.

otia dant vitia [L], leisure begets vices.

otiosa sedulitas [L], leisurely assiduity; laborious trifling.

otio sepoltura dell'uomo vivo [It], idleness is the tomb of living man.

otium [L], leisure; ease. **—otium cum dignitate,** ease with dignity; dignified leisure: *Cicero*. **—otium sine dignitate,** leisure without dignity. **—otium sine litteris mors est,** leisure without literature (*or* books) is death.

ottava [It], octave: *music.*

ottava rima [It], stanza of eight lines with three rhymes.

O ubi campi! [L], oh, where are those plains (*or* fields): *Virgil* (recalling the tranquility of country life). Cf. O RUS, QUANDO EGO TE ASPICIAM.

oublier je ne puis [Fr], I can never forget.

oubliette [Fr, *fr. oublier,* to forget], a secret dungeon or cell, with an opening only at the top; also, a secret pit into which a victim could be thrown unawares.

οὐδεὶς γὰρ ὃν φοβεῖται φιλεῖ [Gr; oudeìs gàr hòn phobeîtai phileî], no one loves the man whom he fears: *Aristotle.*

οὐδὲν μάτην ἡ φύσις ποιεῖ [Gr; oudèn mátēn hē phúsis poieî], nature creates nothing in vain: *Aristotle.*

οὐδὲν πρᾶγμα [Gr; oudèn prâgma], it is no matter; it is of no consequence.

οὐδὲν πρὸς ἔπος [Gr; oudèn pròs épos], to no purpose; nothing to the purpose; not to the point.

οὐ δύνασθε θεῷ δουλεύειν καὶ μαμωνᾷ [Gr; ou dúnasthe theô douleúein kaì mamōnâ], ye cannot serve God and mammon: *Matthew* vi. 24.

ouï-dire [Fr], hearsay.

οὐκ ἐπ’ ἄρτῳ μόνῳ ζήσεται ὁ ἄνθρωπος [Gr; ouk ep’ ártō mónō zḗsetai ho ánthrōpos], man shall not live by bread alone: *Matthew* iv. 4.

οὐρανός [Gr; ouranós], the vault of heaven; the firmament; sky; also, heaven, the seat of the gods. —οὐρανὸς ἀστερόεις [ouranòs asteróeis], the starry firmament.

où sont les neiges d’antan [Fr], where are the snows of yesteryear?: *Villon.*

outrance [Fr], the extreme; excess; last extremity. —**à outrance,** to the death; to the bitter end.

outré [Fr; *fem.* outrée], extravagant; exaggerated; eccentric; bizarre; outraging propriety or decorum; indecorous.

outrecuidance [Fr], arrogance; presumption.

outre mer [Fr], beyond the sea.

ouvert [Fr; *fem.* ouverte], open.

ouverture [Fr], overture: *music.*

ouvrage de longue haleine [Fr], lit., a work of long breath; a work of time or of sustained effort; tedious task.

ouvrier [Fr; *fem.* ouvrière], workman; workingman; artisan.

oveja [Sp], a sheep.

oyev [Heb; *fem.* oyevet], enemy.

ózero [Russ], a lake.

P

pabulum Acheruntis [L], food for Acheron (said of one who deserves to die): *Plautus.*

pabulum animi [L], food of the mind; learning.

pace [L], by leave of; with all deference to. —**pace tanti viri,** by the leave of so great a man; if so great a man will pardon me: often used ironically. —**pace tua,** by your leave.

pacífico [Sp], a peaceable person; peace lover; specif., a Cuban or Filipino who did not take up arms against Spain.

pacta conventa [L], the conditions agreed upon; diplomatic pact.

pactum [L; *pl.* pacta], bargain; contract; agreement; pact. —**nudum pactum,** a nude pact; an informal contract without consideration. —**pactum illicitum,** an unlawful agreement. —**pactum vestitum,** an enforceable pact: *all law.*

padishah [Pers *pādshāh*], lit., protecting lord; great king; emperor: *Oriental.*

padre [Sp & Pg; *pl.* padres; also It; *pl.* padri], lit., father; Christian priest.

padrone [It; *pl.* padroni], master; Italian employment agent; godfather; head of a Mafia group.

paella [Sp], lit., pot; a Valencian dish made of rice, seafood, chicken, and vegetables.

pahar [Hind], mountain: *India.*

pahari [Hind], mountaineer; hillman: *India.*

pailles de parmesan [Fr], cheese straws: *cookery.*

pain [Fr], bread.

país [Sp], country; region; land.

paisano [Sp; *fem.* paisana], countryman; rustic; peasant.

paix [Fr], peace.

pájaro [Sp], bird.

pajero [Sp], dealer in straw; also, the pampas cat (*Felis pajeros*), a small wildcat inhabiting the pampas.

palabra [Sp], word; palaver. —**de palabra,** by word of mouth. —**palabra y piedra suelta no tiene vuelta,** word and stone once gone cannot be recalled.

palafitte [Fr], lake dwelling, built on piles. Cf. PFAHLBAUTEN.

palais [Fr], palace.

palang [Hind], bed; bedstead; esp., a European style of bedstead, as distinguished from *charpoy* (q.v.): *India.*

palazzo [It; *pl.* palazzi], palace.

palette [Fr], artist's holder for paints while painting.

palki [Hind], a long, closed litter in which the occupant may lie at full length; palanquin: *India.*

pallida mors [L], pale Death (part of the quotation *pallida mors aequo pulsat pede pauperum tabernas regumque turres,* pale Death, with impartial step, knocks at the cottages of the poor and the palaces of kings): *Horace.*

pallidus ira [L], pale with rage.

palmam qui meruit ferat [L], let him bear the palm who has deserved it: motto of *Lord Nelson.*

paloma [Sp], dove.

pan [Sp], bread.

panache [Fr], lit., plume; high spirits; verve; nobility of gesture.

panaché [Fr; *fem.* panachée], plumed; striped; variegated, as ice cream.

panais [Fr], parsnip.

Paname [Fr], Paris: *Fr. mil. slang.*

panee [Anglo-Ind; Hind. *pānī*], water; rain. —**panee lao,** bring water: *Kipling.*

panem et circenses [L], bread and the games of the circus; food and amusements (sole interests of the Roman plebeians): *Juvenal.*

paner [Fr], to crumb; dress with bread crumbs: *cookery.*

pani [Hind]. Same as PANEE.

panier [Fr], basket.

panier percé [Fr], lit., a pierced basket; spendthrift.

panneau [Fr], panel, as of a door; also, snare; trap.

pansupari [Hind], a chewing substance consisting of areca nut (*supari*) and other ingredients rolled up in a betel leaf (*pan*): fig., a small bribe: *India.*

πάντα δυνατὰ τῷ πιστεύοντι [Gr; pánta dunatà tô pisteúonti], all things are possible to him that believeth: *Mark* ix. 23.

πάντα καθαρὰ τοῖς καθαροῖς [Gr; pánta katharà toîs katharoîs], to the pure all things are pure: *Titus* i. 15.

pantalan [PI Sp], raised platform; wharf: *P.I.*

pantano [Sp], swamp; morass; marsh.

Pantoffel-regiment [Ger], petticoat government.

pantoufle [Fr], slipper.

Pantruche [Fr], Paris: *Fr. mil. slang.*

pañuelo [Sp], handkerchief; neckcloth; a starched square of cloth, folded triangularly, and worn around the neck.

panure [Fr], fine crumbs, as used for sprinkling over various baked dishes: *cookery.*

Panzer [Ger], lit., coat of mail; armor; a tank. —**Panzer division,** armored division: *mil.*

pão, pão: queijo, queijo [Pg], bread, bread; cheese, cheese; to call a spade a spade.

papeterie [Fr], box or case of stationery; also, stationer's shop.

papetier [Fr; *fem.* papetière], stationer.

papier-mâché [Fr], paper pulp material capable of being molded into various shapes.

papillon [Fr], butterfly.

papillote [Fr], a curl paper, so called because of its suggestion of a butterfly (*papillon*); *cookery,* an oiled or buttered paper wrapper, in which meat or fish is sometimes broiled or grilled. **—côtelette en papillote,** a cutlet cooked in a paper wrapper.

papirosa [Russ; *pl.* papirosi], cigarette.

papiya *or* **papiha** [Hind], the crested cuckoo. Called also *brain-fever bird* from its call, although Tagore says this nickname is "a sheer libel."

paquebot [Fr], ocean liner; steamer.

par accès [Fr], by fits and starts.

par accident [Fr], by chance.

par accord [Fr], by agreement; in harmony with.

parada [Sp], stop; stay.

parador [Sp], inn.

paralysis agitans [L], shaking palsy: *med.*

par amitié [Fr], by favor: *abbr.* p.a.

páramo [Sp], a high and usually treeless plateau in South America.

para todo hay remedio sino para la muerte [Sp], there is a remedy for everything except death: *Cervantes.*

par avance [Fr], in advance; by anticipation; beforehand.

par avion [Fr], by plane; airmail.

parbleu! [Fr], by Jove! egad! (a petty oath, a corruption of *par Dieu,* by God).

par boutades [Fr], by fits and starts.

parc [Fr], park.

parce, parce, precor [L], spare me, spare me, I pray.

parcere subiectis, et debellare superbos [L], to spare the vanquished and subdue the proud: *Virgil.*

par-ci par-là [Fr], here and there; now and then; at intervals.

par complaisance [Fr], by (*or* with) a readiness to oblige; out of politeness.

par contrecoup [Fr], as a consequence.

par dépit [Fr], out of spite.

pardonnez-moi [Fr], pardon me; I beg your pardon.

par écrit [Fr], in writing; in black and white.

par élans [Fr], by starts.

parem non fert [L], he endures no equal.

parendo vinces [L], you will conquer by obedience.

pareve [Yiddish *parev*], *of food or utensils,* suitable for use with both meat and dairy meals: *dietary laws.*

par excellence [Fr], preeminently; above all.

par exemple [Fr], for instance (*abbr.* p.ex.); indeed! upon my word! the idea!

par faveur [Fr], by favor.

parfleche [Can Fr], a raw hide, esp., of a buffalo, stripped of hair and dried; also, any article made of this.

par force [Fr], by force; by forcible means.

par hasard [Fr], by chance; accidentally.

pari [Maori], precipice: *New Zealand.*

pari mutuel [Fr; *pl.* paris mutuels], lit., mutual bet; a form of betting in which those who have backed the winner divide the money bet on the rest, less a small percentage.

pari passu [L], with (*or* at) equal pace; equally and simultaneously.

Paris vaut bien une messe [Fr], Paris is well worth a mass: attributed to *Henri IV* of France, on becoming a convert to Catholicism.

paritur pax bello [L], peace is produced by war.

parla bene, ma parla poco [It], speak well, but speak little.

parlando *or* **parlante** [It], in a speaking or declamatory manner: *music.*

par l'écoulement du temps [Fr], by the lapse of time.

par le droit du plus fort [Fr], by right of the strongest.

parlementaire [Fr], bearer of a flag of truce, authorized to negotiate terms of truce with the enemy.

parler à tort et à travers [Fr], to speak at random or thoughtlessly.

parler français comme une vache enragée [Fr], lit., to speak French like an enraged cow; murder the French language; also: **vache espagnole,** Spanish cow.

parlez du loup et vous verrez sa queue [Fr], speak of the wolf and you will see his tail; speak of the devil and he will appear.

par manière d'acquit [Fr], lit., by way of discharge; for form's sake; carelessly.

par moitiés [Fr], by halves.

par negotiis, neque supra [L], equal to his business and not above it: *Tacitus.*

par nobile fratrum [L], a noble pair of brothers; two just alike: *Horace.*

paroisse [Fr], parish; parish church.

parole d'honneur [Fr], word of honor: *esp. mil.*

paroles aigres [Fr], sharp words.

paroles en l'air [Fr], vain (*or* idle) words.

par oneri [L], equal to the burden.

par parenthèse [Fr], by way of parenthesis; by the way.

par pari refero [L], I return like for like; tit for tat.

par plaisir [Fr], for pleasure; for pastime.

par précaution [Fr], by way of precaution.

par principe [Fr], on principle.

par privilège [Fr], by way of privilege.

pars adversa [L], the opposing party.

par signe de mépris [Fr], as a token of contempt.

pars pro toto [L], part for the whole.

partage [Fr], share; portion; division; distribution.

partager le gâteau [Fr], lit., to share the cake; go halves.

part du lion [Fr], the lion's share.

partenaire [Fr], partner in a game or dancing.

partes aequales [L], equal parts: *abbr.* p.ae.

Parthis mendacior [L], more deceptive than the Parthians.

parti [Fr], party; side; part; specif., matrimonial candidate; match. —**esprit de parti,** party spirit. —**homme de parti,** party man. —**parti pris,** preconceived opinion; bias. —**un beau parti,** a good (matrimonial) match.

particeps criminis [L], an accomplice in a crime.

particulier [Fr], private individual.

partie [Fr], portion of a whole; part; also, party; body of persons; *games,* match; game. —**en partie,** in part; not entirely. —**partie carrée,** lit., square party; a pleasure party consisting of two couples. —**partie nulle,** drawn game.

partim [L], in part: *abbr.* p.

Partitur [Ger], a full score: *music.*

partout [Fr], everywhere.

parturiunt montes, nascetur ridiculus mus [L], the mountains are in labor; there will be brought forth—a ridiculous mouse: *Horace.*

parure [Fr], a set of decorative articles or ornaments for the person; a set of jewels.

parva componere magnis [L], to compare small things with great (adapted from the quotation *parvis componere magna solebam,* I am accustomed to comparing great things with small): *Virgil.*

parva leves capiunt animas [L], little minds are caught with trifles: *Ovid.*

parvenu [Fr; *fem.* parvenue], a person who has forced his way into a higher class; an upstart.

parvum parva decent [L], small things befit the small: *Horace.*

pas [Fr], a step; precedence. —**pas à pas on va loin,** step by step one goes far. —**pas de deux,** a dance for two. —**pas glissant,** lit., slippery step; ticklish affair. —**pas seul,** a dance for one person; solo dance.

pasce con gli occhi, e per l'orecchio beve [It], he feasts with his eyes and drinks through his ears.

pas de zèle! [Fr], don't be too zealous! See SURTOUT, MESSIEURS, PAS DE ZÈLE.

pasear [Sp], to take a walk; ride.

paseo [Sp], a walk; promenade; public walk: *Sp. Am. & southwestern U.S.*

pasha [Turk], Turkish title of honor.

paso a paso van lejos [Sp], step by step goes far.

paso doble [Sp], lit., double step; Spanish dance.

pas possible! [Fr], impossible! you don't say so!

passager [Fr], passenger.

passé [Fr; *fem.* passée], past; past one's prime; esp., past the period of a woman's greatest beauty; faded; withered; antiquated; behind the times.

passe-montagne [Fr; *pl.* passe-montagnes], a kind of combination scarf and helmet for protection against cold; balaclava.

passe-partout [Fr], master key; pass-key; *picture framing,* a cut-out mount used as a mat; also, a kind of light frame of glass and cardboard, with portrait or other picture between, the whole being held together with gummed strips.

passer une nuit blanche [Fr], to pass a sleepless night (lit., white night).

passetemps [Fr], pastime.

passez au large [Fr], pass at a distance; keep off; go round the other way.

pas si bête [Fr], not such a fool; not so green.

passim [L], everywhere; scatteredly: said of allusions, expressions, etc., found in all parts of a particular book or used by a given author.

passionato [It], passionate; impassioned: *music.*

passionnant [Fr; *fem.* passionnante], of absorbing interest; thrilling.

passons au déluge [Fr], let us pass on to the Deluge; let us get to the point: *Racine.*

passus [L; *pl.* passus], a portion or division of a poem or story; canto.

pasta [It], doughy substance from which spaghetti, ravioli, etc., are made; general name for all such dishes.

pas tant de rouscaille [Fr], not so much growling: *Fr. mil. slang.*

pastèque [Fr], watermelon.

pasticcio [It; *pl.* pasticci], lit., a pie; medley; hodgepodge; potpourri.

pastiche [Fr], medley; imitation (of an author or artist); *pasticcio.*

pastille [Fr], small round candy or medicine.

pastorale [It; *pl.* pastorali], piece of music of an idyllic or rustic character; a pastoral.

πάταξον μέν, ἄκουσον δέ [Gr; pátaxon mén, ákouson dé], strike, but hear me: reply of Themistocles to the Spartan commander.

pâte [Fr], paste; *ceramics,* the plastic mixture used in making pottery or porcelain. —**pâte dure,** hard paste used for porcelain. —**pâte feuilletée,** puff paste: *cookery.* —**pâte sur pâte,** lit., paste upon paste; white enamel applied in low relief to a previously prepared surface. —**pâte tendre,** soft paste in porcelain manufacture.

pâté [Fr], a pie; patty. —**pâté de foie gras,** goose liver loaf.

paterfamilias [L], father of a family; head of a household.

pater patriae [L], father of his country.

patetico [It], pathetic: *music.*

παθήματα μαθήματα [Gr; pathémata mathémata], sufferings are lessons: *Herodotus.*

pathétique [Fr], pathetic; full of pathos: *music.*

pathma [Beng], lotus flower.

pathya [Beng], poem.

patience passe science [Fr], patience surpasses knowledge.

patio [Sp], a court or courtyard; esp., an inner court open to the sky in a Spanish or Spanish American house.

pâtisserie [Fr], pastry; pastry business.

pâtissier [Fr; *fem.* pâtissière], pastry cook.

patres conscripti [L], conscript fathers; the Roman senators; the supreme authority: *abbr.* PP.C.

patria cara, carior libertas [L], country is dear, but liberty dearer.

patriae infelici fidelis [L], faithful to my unhappy country.

patria potestas [L], parental authority; the power of a Roman father over his family: *law.*

patrie [Fr], native land; fatherland.

patriis virtutibus [L], by ancestral virtues.

pattadi [Kan], district: *India.*

patte [Fr], paw (of an animal); foot (of a bird or of a glass); flap (of a pocket); leg (of an insect). —**patte de chien,** dog's paw. —**pattes de mouches,** fly tracks; scrawl. —**pattes de velours,** velvet paws, as of a cat with sheathed claws; fig., assumed gentleness; flattery; cajolery.

patte-d'oie [Fr; *pl.* pattes-d'oie], goosefoot; fig., crow's foot; also, intersection of several roads.

patte-pelu [Fr; *pl.* patte-pelus], lit., hairy paw; wolf in sheep's clothing; hypocrite.

pau [Hawa], over; finished.

paucis verbis [L], in (*or* with) few words; concisely.

paulo maiora canamus [L], let us sing of somewhat greater (*or* loftier) things: *Virgil.*

pauvre diable [Fr], poor devil; poor wretch.

pavé [Fr], pavement; also, a setting of jewels in which the stones are placed close together.

pax [L], peace; peace established by law. —**Pax Britannica,** British peace. —**Pax Dei** (*or* **Pax Ecclesiae**), Peace of God (*or* Peace of the Church); an attempt of the Church to lessen the evils of private warfare and to protect noncombatants, developing into what became known as the Truce of God. See TREUGA DEI. —**pax in bello,** peace in war. —**pax orbis terrarum,** the peace of the world; universal peace. —**pax paritur bello,** peace is produced by war. —**pax potior bello,** peace is more powerful than war. —**pax quaeritur bello,** peace is sought by war: motto of the *Cromwell* family. —**pax regis,** king's peace. —**Pax Romana,** Roman peace. —**pax vobiscum,** peace be with you.

payer la goutte [Fr], to stand a drink.

paysage [Fr], landscape; landscape painting.

pazdr'vlahyoo [Russ], congratulations!

pazhalsta [Russ], please; you're welcome.

paz y justicia [Sp], peace and justice: motto of *Paraguay.*

peccato [It], sin; pity. **—che peccato!,** what a pity!

peccavi [L; *pl.* peccavimus], I have sinned (*or* been to blame); hence, *n.* a confession of guilt.

pêche [Fr], peach.

pectus est quod disertos facit [L], it is the heart that makes men eloquent: *Quintilian.*

pedir peras al olmo [Sp], to look for pears on the elm; expect impossibilities: *Cervantes.*

peignoir [Fr], woman's loose dressing gown.

pela boca morre o peixe [Pg], the fish dies by its mouth; a closed mouth makes a wise head.

pelean los ladrones y descúbrense los hurtos [Sp], thieves quarrel, and thefts are discovered.

Pelio imponere Ossam [L], to pile Ossa on Pelion; pile difficulty on difficulty.

Pelion imposuisse Olympo [L], to have piled Pelion on Olympus: *Horace.* See preceding entry.

pelota [Sp], lit., ball; a Spanish game played in a court.

pelure [Fr], lit., peel; rind; a hard thin paper, as sometimes used for postage stamps.

peña [Sp], rock; cliff.

pena de azote [Sp], public flogging.

penchant [Fr], strong inclination; liking (for).

pendeloque [Fr], pendant; earring.

pendente lite [L], pending the suit.

pendule [Fr], pendulum clock.

penetralia mentis [L], the secret recesses of the mind.

pensa molto, parla poco, e scrivi meno [It], think much, speak little, and write less.

pensée [Fr], a thought; notion; maxim. **—pensée creuses,** idle fancies; airy notions.

pensez à moi [Fr], think of me.

pensieroso [It], pensive; musing: *music.*

pension [Fr], boarding house, esp. on the Continent; board and lodging; boarding school; *mil.,* officers' mess. **—en pension,** as a boarder.

pensionnat [Fr], boarding school.

peón [Sp], day laborer; farm worker: *archaic.*

pequeño [Sp; *fem.* pequeña], little; small.

per [L], through; by means of; by; for; for each.

per accidens [L], by accident; by chance; *logic,* not following from the nature of the thing but from some external circumstance.

per ambages [L], by circuitous ways; indirectly; circumlocution.

per angusta ad augusta [L], through difficulties to honor.

per annum [L], by the year; annually.

per aspera ad astra [L]. See AD ASTRA PER ASPERA.

per capita [L], lit., by heads; for each person.

percé [Fr; *fem.* percée], pierced; in holes; out at elbows. **—il est bas percé,** he has holes in his stockings; he is low in funds.

per centum [L], by the hundred; per cent.

per contante [It], for cash.

per contra [L], on the contrary; on the other side (as of an account).

per curiam [LL], by the court (as a whole): *law.*

perdendo *or* **perdendosi** [It], dying away; growing fainter and slackening speed (*abbr.* per., perd., *or* perden.): *music.*

per diem [L], (so much) by the day; daily.

perdoar é vencer [Pg], to forgive is to conquer.

perdre son latin [Fr], lit., to lose his Latin; be unable to make anything (of it); rack one's brains in vain.

perdrix [Fr], partridge.

perdu [Fr; *fem.* perdue], *adj.* lit., lost; lost to view; concealed; invisible; in ambush; *mil.*, in a dangerously advanced position; exposed; forlorn; *n.* one who is concealed or in ambush; *mil.*, one of a forlorn hope. **—enfants perdus,** lit., lost children; a forlorn hope: *mil.*

père [Fr], father: often used after French surname to distinguish father from son. Cf. FILS. **—père aux écus,** moneyed man. **—père de famille,** father of a family; paterfamilias.

pereant qui ante nos nostra dixerunt [L], deuce take those who said our smart sayings before us: *Donatus.*

per essentiam [L], essentially.

per eundem [L], by the same (judge).

pereunt et imputantur [L], they (the hours or years) pass away and are counted against us: *for a sundial.*

per fas et nefas [L], through right and wrong.

perfervidum ingenium [L], ardent temper (*or* disposition).

per gradus [L], step by step.

pericoloso [It], dangerous.

periculum fortitudine evasi [L], by courage I have escaped danger.

periculum in mora [L], danger in delay.

per incuriam [L], through carelessness.

per interim [L], in the meantime.

per iocum [L], in jest.

periódico [Sp], newspaper; periodical.

periuria ridet amantum Iuppiter [L], Jove laughs at lovers' perjuries: *Tibullus.*

per mare per terram [L], by (*or* through) sea and land.

per me [It], for my part; as for me.

per mensem [L], (so much) by the month; monthly.

per mese [It], by the month; monthly.

per mille [L], by the thousand.

per mio avviso [It], in my opinion.

permis de séjour [Fr], permission to reside.

permitte divis caetera [L], leave the rest to the gods: *Horace.*

per pares [L], by one's peers: *law.*

per procurationem [L], by proxy; by the action of: *abbr.* p.p. *or* per pro.

perro [Sp; *fem.* perra], dog. **—perro del hortelano,** the gardener's dog; dog in the manger.

perro que ladra no muerde [Sp], the barking dog doesn't bite.

perruque [Fr], wig; periwig; fig., prejudiced old man.

per saltum [L], by a leap; at a single bound.

per se [L], by (*or* in) itself; intrinsically.

perseverando [L], by persevering.

persiflage [Fr], ironic mockery.

persifleur [Fr], a banterer; ironic mocker.

persil [Fr], parsley.

persona [L], person. **—persona ficta,** a fictitious person. **—persona grata,** an acceptable person; a welcome guest. **—persona gratissima,** a most acceptable person. **—persona muta,** a silent actor. **—persona non grata,** an unacceptable (*or* objectionable) person; specif., a diplomatic representative who is unwelcome to the foreign government to which the representative is assigned.

per stirpes [L], by stocks (*or* families): *law.*

per totam curiam [LL], by the entire court; unanimously.

per tot discrimina rerum [L], through so many vicissitudes of fortune (lit., crises of events): *Virgil.* See PER VARIOS CASUS.

per troppo dibatter la verità si perde [It], by too much debating truth is lost (*or* obscured).

per varios casus, per tot discrimina rerum [L], through many mishaps, through sundry perilous experiences (*or* vicissitudes of fortune): *Virgil.*

per viam [L], by way of. **—per viam dolorosam,** by the sorrowful path.

per vias rectas [L], by straight roads; by direct ways.

pervoiya mahyah [Russ], May Day.

pesante [It], heavily; gravely; impressively: *music.*

peso [Sp], weight; load; dollar. **—peso duro,** lit., hard dollar; Spanish dollar. **—peso muerto,** dead load: *engin.* **—peso neto,** net weight: *abbr.* p.° nto.

pessimi exempli [L], of a very bad example.

petit [Fr; *masc.*], little; small; minor; inferior; unimportant; mean; *law,* petty. **—en petit,** in miniature; on a small scale. **—petit blanc** [*pl.* petits blancs], lit., small white; in French foreign possessions, a middle-class European. **—petit à petit l'oiseau fait son nid,** little by little the bird makes her nest. **—petit bourgeois,** small tradesman; professional. **—petit caporal,** little corporal; Napoleon. **—petit chaudron, grands oreilles,** little pitchers (have) big ears. **—petit maître,** lit., little master;

fop; dandy; coxcomb; ladies' man. **—petit mal,** a mild form of epilepsy. **—petit point,** small stitch used in needlepoint. **—petit souper,** little supper; informal supper for a few close friends. **—petit verre,** a small glass, esp. of liqueur.

petit-bleu [Fr], lit., small blue; telegram form, as used for sending messages by pneumatic tubes in Paris.

petite [Fr; *fem.*], little; small; trim. **—petite amie,** small friend; girl friend; mistress. **—petite maîtresse** [*pl.* petites maîtresses], lady of studied elegance; female dandy. **—petite pièce,** a short play; afterpiece.

petitio principii [L], begging of the question.

petit-lait [Fr], whey.

petits-chevaux [Fr], lit., little horses; a gambling game.

petits pois [Fr], little peas; green peas.

petits soins [Fr], small attentions.

petto [It; *pl.* petti], the breast; bosom; chest. **—in petto,** within one's own breast; in secret. **—voce di petto,** chest voice: *music.*

peu à peu [Fr], little by little; by degrees.

peu de bien, peu de soin [Fr], little wealth, little care; few wares, few cares.

peu de chose [Fr], a trifle.

peu de gens savent être vieux [Fr], few people know how to be old: *La Rochefoucauld.*

peut-être [Fr], perhaps.

pezzo [It; *pl.* pezzi], piece; excerpt; musical selection.

Pfahlbauten [Ger; *pl.*], lake dwellings. Cf. PALAFITTE.

φάρμακον νηπενθές [Gr; phármakon nēpenthés], a drug that brings forgetfulness after grief; the nepenthe of the gods.

φιλοσοφία ὄρεξις τῆς θείας σοφίας [Gr; philosophía órexis tês theías sophías], philosophy is a yearning after heavenly wisdom: *Plato.*

phúl [Hind], a flower: *India.*

φύσει σοφὸς μὲν οὐδείς [Gr; phúsei sofòs mèn oudeís], none are wise by nature (*or* natural instinct): *Aristotle.*

piacere [It], please. **—a piacere,** at pleasure; ad lib.: *music.*

piacevole [It], pleasing; in a pleasing manner: *music.*

pia fraus [L], a pious fraud: *Ovid.*

piangendo [It], weepingly; plaintively: *music.*

pianissimo [It], very soft; very softly (*abbr.* pp.): *music.*

piano [It], soft; softly (*abbr.* p.): *music.*

piazza [It], place; open square; market place; *U.S.,* veranda.

picador [Sp], participant in bullfight who spears the bull from horseback.

Pickelhaube [Ger], spiked helmet.

picot [Fr], one of the small projecting loops forming an edging on lace and the like.

pièce [Fr], piece; portion; fragment; document; apartment; roast (of meat); cannon; *colloq.,* person. **—pièce à pièce,** bit by bit. **—pièce de**

circonstance, a composition written for a special event. **—pièce de résistance,** the principal dish of a meal: also used figuratively. **—pièce de théâtre,** a play. **—pièce d'occasion,** a piece for a special occasion. **—pièce justificative,** voucher; document used as supporting evidence: *law.* **—pièces de batterie,** heavy ordnance: *mil.*

pied [Fr], foot. **—pied poudreux,** lit., dusty foot; a tramp.

pied-à-terre [Fr; *pl.* pieds-à-terre], a resting place; temporary lodging.

pied noir [Fr], French person born in Algeria; French exile from Algeria.

piedra [Sp], stone; gravel; mass of stones; *med.,* a disease of the hair, characterized by stony nodules.

piège [Fr], snare; trap.

Pietà [It], a representation of the Virgin Mary holding the dead body of Christ: *fine arts.*

pietra dura [It], lit., hard stone; the stones used in Italian mosaics: *fine arts.*

pietra mossa non fa muschio [It], a rolling stone gathers no moss.

piffero [It; *pl.* pifferi], a fife; also, an organ stop with a similar tone: *music.*

pilau *or* **pilaw** [Pers], an Oriental dish of rice mixed with fowl, meat, or fish, and highly seasoned: *cookery.*

pilon [Sp *pilón*], lit., sugar loaf; small gratuity given by a tradesman to a customer, esp. on payment of an account: *southwestern U.S.* Cf. LAGNIAPPE.

pimiento [Sp], the Spanish sweet pepper.

piña [Sp], pineapple; pine cone; also, short for **piña cloth,** a fabric made from the fibrous leaves of the pineapple plant.

pince-nez [Fr; *sing. & pl.*], eyeglasses with a spring to grip the nose.

πῖνε καὶ εὐφραίνου [Gr; pîne kaì eufraínou], drink and be merry: *Palladas.*

pinole [Sp], parched maize, ground and mixed with sugar and spices, and much used as food: *Mexico & southern U.S.*

pinxit [L], lit., he (*or* she) painted it: appended to artist's name on a picture (*abbr.* pinx.).

piolet [Fr], ice axe, as used by Alpine climbers.

pique [Fr], resentment; vexation.

piquer des deux [Fr], to spur with both heels; put spurs to one's horse; *colloq.,* to go very fast; strive hard.

pirogi [Russ], potato-filled pastries.

pirozhki [Russ], meat-filled pastries.

pis aller [Fr], lit., to go worst; last resource; makeshift.

piscem natare docere [L], to teach a fish how to swim.

pisco [Sp *fr.* Quechua], high-quality anisette from the Andes.

pisé [Fr], masonry; a method of building by ramming clay between molds.

pishu [Can Fr *pichou*], the Canadian lynx.

piso [Sp], pavement; floor; story; *mining,* lower face of a stratum.
—**piso bajo,** ground floor: *abbr.* p.b.

piste [Fr], trace; track; footprint; scent.

piton [Fr], screw ring; eyebolt; *mountaineering,* a bar or stanchion used
for fixing ropes on precipitous slopes; also, a steep peak.

più [It], more. —**più allegro,** quicker. —**più lento,** slower. —**più mosso,**
more animated; quicker: *all music.*

più tosto mendicanti che ignoranti [It], better be beggars than be
ignorant; better starve the body than the mind.

pizzicato [It], plucked by the fingers instead of being played with the
bow; also, a passage so played: *music.*

place [Fr], place; room; square; rank or stand for cabs and taxis.
—**place!,** make way! make room! clear the way! —**place aux dames,**
make way (*or* room) for the ladies. —**place forte,** fortified town;
stronghold. —**place publique,** public (*or* market) square; marketplace.

placebo [L], lit., I shall please; *R.C.Ch.,* first antiphon in the vespers
for the dead; *med.,* an innocuous prescription given merely to please
a patient.

placidaque ibi demum morte quievit [L], and there at length he reposed
in tranquil death: *Virgil.*

placitum [LL; *pl.* placita], decree; decision: *law.*

plafond [Fr], ceiling. —**une araignée dans le plafond,** lit., a spider in
the ceiling; a bee in one's bonnet.

plage [Fr], beach; shore.

plaidoyer [Fr], plea of counsel for the defense; *pl.,* pleadings: *Fr. law.*

plainte [Fr], complaint.

plaisanterie [Fr], pleasantry; jesting; jest; joke.

plaque [Fr], plated metal; electroplate.

plat [Fr], a dish of food.

plata [Sp], silver.

playa [Sp], shore; strand; beach; in New Mexico, Arizona, and Texas,
a level tract of silt and mud caused by the drying up of a flooded
area.

plaza [Sp], public square; also, fortified place.

plein [Fr], full.

plein air [Fr], the open air.

pleno iure [L], with full right (*or* authority).

plie [Fr], plaice.

plissé [Fr; *fem.* plissée], *adj.* plaited; gathered; *n.* plaiting; kilting;
gathering.

plus aloës quam mellis habet [L], he has more of gall (lit., of aloes)
than of honey; the bitter outweighs the sweet: *Juvenal.*

plus ça change, plus c'est la même chose [Fr], the more it changes,
the more it is the same thing.

plus on est de fous, plus on rit [Fr], the more merrymakers, the more fun; the more the merrier.

plus royaliste que le roi [Fr], more royalist than the king.

plus sage que les sages [Fr], wiser than the wise.

plus salis quam sumptus [L], more of good taste than expense; more tasteful than costly: *Nepos.*

plus tôt [Fr], sooner; earlier.

plutôt [Fr], rather; in preference.

Pluviôse [Fr], in the Revolutionary calendar of the first French Republic, the fifth month of the year, from Jan. 20 to Feb. 18.

poca favilla gran fiamma seconda [It], a small spark produces a large flame: *Dante.*

poca roba, poco pensiero [It], little wealth, little care.

pocas palabras [Sp], few words.

poco [It], little (in quantity); a little; somewhat. —**poco a poco,** little by little; by degrees. —**poco allegro,** somewhat quick. —**poco forte,** somewhat loud. —**poco più lento,** somewhat slower: *all music.*

poco tiempo [Sp], pretty soon; one moment!

poêle *or* **poile** [Fr], stove.

poesis est vinum daemonum [L], poetry is devil's wine.

poeta nascitur, non fit [L], a poet is born, not made.

pogrom [Yiddish *fr.* Russ], lit., devastation; organized massacre.

poi [Hawa], a dish made from the root of the taro or kalo plant, which is cooked, pounded, and left to ferment before eating.

poilu [Fr], lit., hairy, unshaven; French soldier in W. W. I.

ποιμανεῖ αὐτοὺς ἐν ῥάβδῳ σιδηρᾷ [Gr; poimaneî autoùs en rhábdō sidērâ], he shall rule them with a rod of iron: *Revelations* ii. 27.

point d'appui [Fr], point of support; prop; fulcrum; *mil.,* any point upon which troops are formed; base.

point de réunion [Fr], place of meeting; *rendezvous.*

point du jour [Fr], daybreak.

point et virgule [Fr], semicolon.

poireau [Fr], lit., a leek; wart; stupid fellow: *Fr. mil. slang.*

poissarde [Fr], a market woman of the lowest class; fishwife: notorious for their part in the French Revolutionary riots.

poisson [Fr], fish. —**poisson d'avril,** lit., fish of April; mackerel; April-fool joke.

poitrine [Fr], chest; breast; bosom. —**poitrine d'agneau,** breast of lamb.

poivrade [Fr], pepper sauce.

poivre [Fr], pepper.

polder [Du], a tract of low-lying land reclaimed by dikes.

póle [Russ], field; ground.

polenta [It], a thick porridge made of cornmeal or, occasionally, of semolina, with grated cheese and other condiments, the whole being cut into slices, which are sometimes lightly fried in oil or butter.

polisson [Fr; *fem.* polissonne], *adj.* low; coarse; libidinous; *n.* vagabond urchin; reprobate; blackguard; low fellow.

politesse [Fr], politeness; civility; kindness.

politico [It & Sp], politician.

politique [Fr], politician; specif., opportunist.

πολλὰ μεταξὺ πέλει κύλικος καὶ χείλιος ἄκρου [Gr; pollà metaxù pélei kýlikos kaì kheílios ákrou], there's many a slip 'twixt cup and lip: *Aristotle*.

pollice verso [L], with thumb turned (downward); the signal by which spectators condemned a vanquished gladiator to death.

pollo [Sp], chicken. —**arroz con pollo,** chicken with rice.

πολλοὶ γάρ εἰσιν κλητοὶ ὀλίγοι δὲ ἐκλεκτοί [Gr; polloì gár eisin klētoì olígoi de eklektoí], for many are called, but few are chosen: *Matthew* xxii. 14.

pompadour [Fr], hair style named after Madame de Pompadour.

pompiere [It; *pl.* pompieri], fireman.

pomposo [It], pompous; grandiose (*abbr.* pomp.): *music*.

pondere non numero [L], by weight not by number.

pons [L; *pl.* pontes], a bridge; *anat.,* a part connecting two parts. —**pons asinorum,** asses' bridge (fifth proposition of the first book of Euclid); hence, anything difficult for beginners. —**pons Varolii,** in the higher vertebrates, a band of transverse nerve fibres on the ventral surface of the brain: *anat. & zool.*

ponticello [It], bridge of string instrument: *music*.

pontificalia [L; *pl.*], vestments and insignia of a bishop; pontificals.

pont-levis [Fr], drawbridge.

poonghie *or* **pongyi** [Burmese *hpōng-gyi,* great glory], Buddhist monk: *Burma*. Cf. TALAPOIN.

populus me sibilat, at mihi plaudo [L], the people hiss me, but I applaud myself: *Horace*.

populus vult decipi, ergo decipiatur [L], the populace wants to be deceived, therefore let it be deceived.

porc [Fr], hog; pork.

por ciento [Sp], per cent: *abbr.* p%.

por favor [Sp], please.

por ferrocarril [Sp], by rail.

porro unum est necessarium [L], still there is one thing necessary.

portamento [It], a slur or glide from one note to another: *music*.

portato [It], carried; sustained: *music*.

porte-cochère [Fr], carriage entrance; courtyard gateway; erroneously, carriage porch.

portefeuille [Fr], portfolio.

portemonnaie [Fr], small flat purse or pocketbook.

portière [Fr], curtain hung over door or doorway.

pôrto [Pg], port. —**pôrto de mar,** seaport.

po-ruski [Russ], in Russian.

posada [Sp], an inn; hotel.

posément [Fr], sedately; calmly; steadily.

poser pour le torse [Fr], to show off one's figure.

poseur [Fr; *fem.* poseuse], an affected person.

ποσὶ καὶ χερσίν [Gr; posì kaì khersín], with feet and hands; with might and main.

posse comitatus [L], the power of the county; a body of men who may be summoned by the sheriff to assist in preserving the public peace; popularly, a posse.

posse videor [L], I seem to be able; I think I can.

possunt quia posse videntur [L], they can because they seem to be able to: *Virgil.*

post bellum auxilium [L], aid after the war (i.e., assistance offered too late).

post cibum [L], after meals: *abbr.* (*in prescriptions*) p.c.

post cineres gloria sera venit [L], after one is reduced to ashes, fame comes too late: *Martial.*

post diem [L], after the (appointed or proper) day: *law.*

poste de secours [Fr], lit., post (*or* station) of aid; emergency station; advanced dressing station: *mil.*

post equitem sedet atra cura [L], black care sits behind the horseman (i.e., even the rich man cannot escape his cares): *Horace.*

poste restante [Fr], lit., remaining post; to be held in the post office until called for: used in addressing letters.

post factum nullum consilium [L], after the deed, no advice is useful.

post festum venisti [L], you have come after the feast.

post hoc ergo propter hoc [L], after this, therefore because of this: an illogical reasoning.

postiche [Fr], *adj.* superadded (as ornament inappropriately added to a completed work); misplaced; artificial; counterfeit; sham; also, provisional; acting; *n.* an imitation.

post litem motam [L], after litigation began: *law.*

post meridiem [L], after midday: *abbr.* p.m.

post mortem [L], after death: *abbr.* P.M.

post nubila, Phoebus [L], after the clouds, the sun.

post obitum [L], after death.

post proelia praemia [L], after battles come rewards.

post tenebras lux [L], after darkness, light.

post terminum [L], after the conclusion.

post tot naufragia portum [L], after so many shipwrecks, the harbor (*or* port).

postulata [L; *pl.*], fundamental assumptions; postulates.

potage [Fr], soup. —**potage à la queue de boeuf,** ox-tail soup. —**potage au gras,** meat soup. —**potage de printanier,** clear soup with spring vegetables: *all cookery.*

pot-au-feu [Fr], a thick soup or stew of meat and vegetables.

potiche [Fr], vase or jar of Oriental porcelain.

potin [Fr], an alloy of copper, zinc, lead, and tin; pot metal; *colloq.,* petty gossip.

potiron [Fr], pumpkin.

pot pourri [Fr], lit., rotten pot; combination of incongruous elements; a stew: *cookery.*

pouding [Fr], pudding.

poularde [Fr], fat pullet; capon.

poulet [Fr], young chicken. —**poulet rôti,** roast chicken.

pour acquit [Fr], received; settled; paid: written at the foot of a receipted bill, etc.

pour ainsi dire [Fr], so to speak.

pour bien désirer [Fr], to desire good.

pourboire [Fr], gratuity; tip.

pour couper court [Fr], to cut the matter short; be brief.

pour dire adieu [Fr], to say good-bye: *abbr.* p.d.a.

pour encourager les autres [Fr], to encourage the others.

pour faire rire [Fr], to raise a laugh.

pour faire ses adieux [Fr], to take one's leave; say goodbye: *abbr.* p.f.s.a.

pour faire visite [Fr], to pay a visit; make a call: *abbr.* p.f.v.

pour jamais [Fr], forever.

pour le mérite [Fr], for merit.

pourparler [Fr], an informal preliminary discussion; parley; conference.

pour passer le temps [Fr], to pass the time away.

pour prendre congé [Fr], to take leave: *abbr.* p.p.c.

pourquoi? [Fr], why? for what reason?

pour rire [Fr], in jest; for fun.

pour toujours [Fr], forever.

pour tout dire [Fr], in a word.

pour tout potage [Fr], lit., for every soup; in all; all told.

pour y parvenir [Fr], to attain the objective.

poussé [Fr], the upstroke of a bow: *music.*

pousse-café [Fr], a liqueur taken after coffee; esp., a varicolored drink of several liqueurs appearing in layers.

pousse-l'amour [Fr], aphrodisiac.

pousser à bout [Fr], lit., to push to extremity; provoke beyond endurance.

poussière [Fr], dust.

poussin [Fr], chick; young chicken.

pow wow [Algon *pow waw*], conference; a tribal meeting.

pozo [Sp], a spring or natural well: *southwestern U.S.*

praam [Du], a flat-bottomed boat or lighter used in the Netherlands and on the Baltic.

Prachtausgabe [Ger], deluxe edition: *abbr.* Pr.-A.

Prado [Sp], lit., meadow; fashionable boulevard in Madrid; also, a similar boulevard or promenade elsewhere; as, the *Prado* in Havana; also, Spanish national museum of art in Madrid.

praecognitum [L; *pl.* praecognita], something foreknown, esp. a branch of knowledge necessary to the understanding of something else.

praedium [L], land; landed property: *law.*

praefervidum ingenium Scotorum [L], the ardently serious temperament of the Scots.

praemonitus, praemunitus [L], forewarned, forearmed.

praesto et persto [L], I stand in front and I stand firm.

praeteriti anni [L], bygone years.

Prairial [Fr], in the Revolutionary calendar of the first French Republic, the ninth month of the year, from May 20 to June 18.

Pralltrilier [Ger], a kind of shake or trill; an inverted mordent: *music.*

pranzo [It], dinner.

pravda [Russ], truth. —**Pravda,** name of a newspaper published in the U.S.S.R.

precibus infimis [L], with abject prayers: *Livy.*

précieuse [Fr; *fem.*], *adj.* precious; overnice; affectedly refined; *n.* conceited woman; euphuist. —**précieuse ridicule,** ridiculous *précieuse:* from the title of Molière's play *Les Précieuses Ridicules,* satirizing the affected precision of the literary women of his day.

precipitando [It], hurriedly: *music.*

précis [Fr; *sing. & pl.*], summary; abstract.

preciso [It], with precision: *music.*

preghiera [It], prayer; supplication.

prego [It], please; you are welcome.

première [Fr], leading woman (as in a play); also, first performance; first night.

première danseuse [Fr; *fem.*], first or leading female dancer in a ballet.

prendetevi cura [It], take care of yourself.

prend-moi tel que je suis [Fr], take me as I am.

prendre la balle au bond [Fr], to take the ball at the rebound; take time by the forelock; grasp opportunity.

prendre la lune avec les dents [Fr], lit., to seize the moon with the teeth; aim at impossibilities.

prendre le mors aux dents [Fr], to take the bit in the teeth; fly into a passion; apply oneself unrestrainedly; buckle down.

prenez garde! [Fr], take care! beware!

presa [It], lit., a taking; seizure; in a canon, a mark (:*S̈*: , +, or ✳) indicating the point at which the successive voice parts are to take up the theme: *music.*

pré-salé [Fr; *pl.* prés-salés], salt-marsh-fed mutton.

presidio [Sp], garrison town; army post; also, Spanish penal settlement: *Sp. Am. & southwestern U.S.*

prestance [Fr], commanding appearance; bearing; carriage; presence.

prestissimo [It], very quick; very quickly: *music.*

presto [It], quickly; more rapid than *allegro: music.* —**presto e bene, non si conviene,** quickly and well do not agree; haste makes waste.

presto maturo, presto marcio [L], soon ripe, soon rotten.

prêt d'accomplir [Fr], ready to accomplish.

pretium [L], worth; value; price; reward. —**pretium affectionis,** lit., the price of feeling (*or* affection); the sentimental value as distinct from the intrinsic or market value: *law.* —**pretium laborum non vile,** no mean reward for the labors: motto of *Order of the Golden Fleece.* —**pretium periculi,** premium for insurance. —**pretium puellae,** lit., the price of a maiden; among early Teutonic and other races, the marriage price demanded by a woman's guardian: *law.*

prêt pour mon pays [Fr], ready for my country.

preux chevalier [Fr], a gallant knight.

prévenance [Fr], ingratiating manner; thoughtful attention; readiness to oblige.

prévôt [Fr], provost.

prie-dieu [Fr; *sing. & pl.*], prayer desk; kneeling desk.

prima [It; *fem.*], *adj.* first; chief; principal. —**prima buffa,** principal female comic singer or actress. —**prima donna** [*now naturalized;* It *pl.* prime donne], principal female singer in an opera. —**prima volta,** first time: *music.*

prima facie [L], at first view; (based) on the first impression.

prima inter pares [L], first among her equals.

primeur [Fr], first of the season (said of fruit, flowers, etc.); hence, early news; fig., freshness; bloom; first love.

primo [L], in the first place; first.

primo [It; *masc.*], *adj.* first; chief; principal; *n.* the first or principal part, as in a duet: *music.* —**primo basso,** chief bass singer. —**primo tenore,** chief tenor singer. —**primo uomo** *or* **prim'-omo,** principal actor or male singer.

primo intuiti [L], at the first glance.

primum cognitum [L], the first thing known.

primum mobile [L], lit., the first moving thing; in the Ptolemaic system, the outermost sphere, carrying with it the contained spheres in its daily revolution; hence, the prime source of motion; mainspring.

primum non nocere [L], first of all, do no harm; *medical aphorism,* take care that the remedy is not worse than the disease.

primus inter pares [L], first among his equals.

principe [It, Sp, & Pg], prince.

principia, non homines [L], principles, not men.

principibus placuisse viris non ultima laus est [L], to have won the approbation of eminent men is not the lowest praise: *Horace.*

principiis obsta [L], resist the beginnings; check the evil at the outset: *Ovid.*

printanier [Fr; *fem.* printanière], with early spring vegetables: *cookery.*

prior tempore, prior iure [L], first in time, first by right; first come, first served.

pris au dépourvu [Fr], taken unawares; caught napping.

prise [Fr], lit., a taking; capture; prize; bite; dose; pinch (as of snuff); *pl.,* close quarters. —**en prise,** in danger of capture; exposed. —**hors de prise,** out of reach; out of danger. —**prise de bec,** dispute; quarrel; words.

pris sur le fait [Fr], caught in the act.

pristinae virtutis memores [L], mindful of the valor of former days.

Privatdozent [Ger; *pl.* Privatdozenten], in German universities, a teacher or lecturer licensed by the university, but not on the regular staff.

prix [Fr], price; prize. —**prix fixe,** fixed price. —**prix honnête,** reasonable price.

proa [Malay *prāū*], outrigger sailing canoe.

pro aris et focis [L], for our altars and our hearths; for civil and religious liberty.

probatum est [L], it has been proved (*or* tried).

probitas laudatar et alget [L], honesty is promised and freezes (*or* is left to starve): *Juvenal.*

probitas verus honor [L], honesty is true honor.

pro bono publico [L], for the public good (*or* weal).

probum non poenitet [L], the upright man does not repent.

procès [Fr], lawsuit.

procès-verbal [Fr; *pl.* procès-verbaux], official report; record of proceedings; minutes; *Fr. law,* a written authenticated statement of fact in support of a charge.

pro confesso [L], as if confessed: *law.*

procul, O procul este, profani! [L], begone! begone! ye profane (*or* uninitiated)!: *Virgil.*

procureur [Fr], attorney. —**procureur general,** public prosecutor.

pro Deo et Ecclesia [L], for God and the Church.

prodesse quam conspici [L], to be of service rather than to be gazed at.

pro Ecclesia et Pontifice [LL], for Church and Pope.

pro et contra [L], for and against.

profanum vulgus [L], the profane herd; unhallowed multitude.

pro forma [L], for the sake of form; as a matter of form.

pro hac vice [L], for this occasion only.

projet [Fr], project; plan; scheme; design; first sketch; draft as of a proposed treaty. —**projet de loi,** legislative bill.

proletaree fsyoch stran, soyadinyatsyes! [Russ], workers of the world, unite!: translation of last words of *The Communist Manifesto*; in German: *Proletarier aller Länder, vereinigt euch!*

pro libertate patriae [L], for the liberty of my country.

pro memoria [L], for a memorial.

pro mundi beneficio [L], for the benefit of the world: motto of *Panama*.

prôneur [Fr; *fem.* prôneuse], enthusiast; long-winded preacher.

pronto [Sp], soon; quickly; promptly; [It], hello! (*on the telephone*).

pro nunc [L], for now.

pronunciamiento [Sp], proclamation; public declaration; esp., a manifesto issued by revolutionists.

pro patria [L], for one's country. —**pro patria et rege,** for country and king.

propositi tenax [L], firm of purpose.

propria quae maribus [NL], things appropriate to males (*or* husbands): part of a rule on gender in old Latin grammars; fig., the rudiments of Latin.

proprie communia dicere [L], to utter stock ideas as one's own; utter commonplaces as if original.

propriétaire [Fr], owner; proprietor (*or* proprietress).

propriété littéraire [Fr], literary property; copyright.

proprio iure [L], of his own right: *law.*

proprio motu [L], by one's own motion or initiative; spontaneously.

proprio vigore [L], of one's own strength; by its own force; independently.

propter hoc [L], on this account.

pro pudor [L], for shame!

pro rata [L], according to rate (*or* proportion); proportional or proportionally.

pro rege et patria [L], for king and country.

pro rege, lege, et grege [L], for king, for law, and for the people; for ruler, rule, and ruled.

pro re nata [L], for an occasion as it arises; for a special emergency; when required: *abbr.* (*in prescriptions*) p.r.n.

pro salute animae [L], for the welfare of the soul.

prosciutto [It; *pl.* prosciutti], dry-cured spiced ham, usually sliced thin for serving.

proscrit [Fr], outcast; outlaw.

proshchái *or* **proshcháite** [Russ], goodbye; farewell; adieu.

prosit [L & Ger], lit., may it do you good; your health! —**prosit Neujahr!** [Ger], a happy New Year to you! —**prosit tibi!** [L], may it be well with thee!

Prost Mahlzeit! [Ger], lit., may your meal be blessed; applesauce!: *colloq.*

pro tanto [L], for so much; to that extent; so far.

protégé [Fr; *fem.* protégée], one under the protection or patronage of another.

pro tempore [L], for the time being; temporarily: *abbr.* pro tem.

provenance [Fr], source; origin; provenance.

pro virili parte [L], lit., for a man's part; to the utmost of one's ability; as well as one is able.

provocant [Fr; *fem.* provocante], provoking; exciting; instigating.

proxime accessit [L; *pl.* accesserunt], he (*or* she) came very near (winning a prize, etc.): *abbr.* prox. acc.

proximo [L], in the next month after the present one: *abbr.* prox.

próximo pasado [Sp], last month: *abbr.* pp.^do.

proximus ardet Ucalegon [L], Ucalegon's house, next door, is on fire: *Virgil.* (Ucalegon, in the *Iliad*, was a counselor of Priam.)

prudens futuri [L], thoughtful of the future.

prudens quaestio dimidium scientiae [L], the half of knowledge consists in being able to put the right question: *Bacon.*

prud'homme [Fr], lit., a wise and prudent man; specif., a member of a French board of arbitration for the settlement of labor disputes.

prueba [Sp], proof: *typog.*

pruina [L], hoarfrost.

pruneau [Fr; *pl.* pruneaux], prune; French dried plum.

ψεκάδες ὄμβρον γεννῶνται [Gr; psekádes ómbron gennôntai], many drops make the rain (*or* a shower).

publice [L], publicly.

pucka, pukka, *or* **pakka** [Anglo-Ind], lit., ripe; cooked; thorough; hence, permanent; durable; well-built; substantial; solid; genuine: opposite of *kutcha.*

pueblo [Sp], lit., town; people; an Indian or Spanish village; esp., an Indian village consisting of communal houses built of stone or adobe, often several stories high, as in New Mexico and Arizona; *P.I.,* a territory or district corresponding to a county or township.

puente [Sp], bridge; by extension, raft; *nav.,* deck.

puerto [Sp], port; harbor.

pug [Anglo-Ind; Hind *pag,* foot], footprint; spoor.

puggree [Anglo-Ind; Hind *pagrī*], turban.

pugi [Anglo-Ind; Hind *pagī*], tracker.

pugnis et calcibus [L], with fists and heels; with all one's might.

puîné [Fr; *fem.* puînée], younger: opposed to *aîné.*

puja [Hind & Skr], worship; esp., Hindu idol worship; any religious rite: *India.*

pujari [Hind], worshiper; specif., a priest in charge of a Hindu temple: *India.*

pulka [Finnish *pulkka*], traveling sleigh used by Laplanders.

pulmo [L; *pl.* pulmones], lung.

pulque [Mex Sp], a Mexican intoxicating beverage made from the sap of the maguey.

pulvis et umbra sumus [L], we are but dust and shadow: *Horace.*

pulwar [Hind], a light, keelless riverboat: *India.*

puna [Quechua], a cold, desert plateau in the Andes of Peru and Bolivia.

punctatim [L], point for point.

punctum [L; *pl.* puncta], a point; dot; speck; puncture; minute area distinguished from the surrounding surface: used in various scientific phrases. —**punctum caecum,** the blind spot of the eye: *anat.* —**punctum saliens,** salient point. —**punctum vegetationis,** the growing point: *bot.*

Punica fides [L], Punic faith; treachery.

puntilla [Sp], narrow lace edging; lacelike decoration.

pupule [Hawa], crazy.

purée [Fr], thick soup of vegetables, fish, etc., boiled to a pulp and put through a sieve. —**purée de pois,** pea soup. —**purée d'oignons,** onion soup: *all cookery.*

pur et simple [Fr], pure and simple; unqualified; unconditional; absolute.

πῦρ μαχαίρα μὴ σκαλεύειν [Gr; pûr makhaíra mè skaleúein], don't poke the fire with a sword: *Pythagoras.*

purohit [Hind], Hindu family priest: *India.*

pur sang [Fr], pure blood; aristocratic birth or descent; thoroughbred.

Putsch [Ger; *pl.* Putsche], a riot; insurrection; armed uprising.

putti [It], lit., children; little boys; representations of nude Cupidlike children in Italian art and sculpture.

puttoo [Hind *pattu*], a coarse fabric made from the hair of the Kashmir goat.

puy [Fr], a conical hill of volcanic origin, found esp. in Auvergne, France.

pyorrhea alveolaris [L], Riggs' disease; inflammation and suppuration of the gums.

Q

qua [L], insofar as; in the capacity of.

quae amissa salva [L], things lost are safe.

quae fuerunt vitia mores sunt [L], what once were vices are now customs (*or* common manners).

quae nocent docent [L], things that injure instruct.

quaere [L], *v.* inquire; question; *n.* a question; query: *abbr.* qu.

quaeritur [L], it is sought; the question arises.

quaestio vexata [L; *pl.* quaestiones vexatae], vexed question, one debated at length.

quae sursum volo videre [L], I desire to see the things that are above.

quae vide [L], which (things) see: *abbr.* qq.v.

Quai d'Orsay [Fr], French Foreign Office: from the street in which it is located.

qualche volta è virtu tacere il vero [It], it is sometimes a virtue to conceal the truth.

qualis ab incepto [L], such as from the beginning: *Horace* (adapted).

qualis artifex pereo [L], what an artist dies in me: *Nero* (shortly before his death).

qualis rex, talis grex [L], like king, like people.

qualis vita, finis ita [L], as is the life, so is the end.

quamdiu se bene gesserit [L], so long as he conducts himself well; during good behavior.

quam parva sapientia mundus regitur! [L], with how little wisdom the world is governed!

quamprimum [L], as soon as possible; forthwith.

quam proxime [L], as nearly as possible.

quam te Deus esse iussit [L], what God commanded you to be.

quand même [Fr], even though; notwithstanding; all the same.

quando la nave è perda, tutti son piloti [It], when the ship is lost, all become pilots.

quandoque bonus dormitat Homerus [L], sometimes even good Homer nods: *Horace.*

quanti est sapere! [L], what a grand thing it is to be wise!: *Terence.*

quantum [L; *pl.* quanta], *n.* a concrete quantity; specified amount.

quantum [L], *adv.* as much as; how much. **—quantum libet,** as much as you please: *abbr. (in prescriptions)* q.l. *or* q.lib. **—quantum meruit,** as much as he (*or* she) deserved. **—quantum mutatus ab illo!,** how changed from what he once was!: *Virgil* (adapted). **—quantum placet,** as much as you please: *abbr. (in prescriptions)* q.pl. *or* q.p. **—quantum sufficit,** as much as suffices; a sufficient quantity: *abbr. (in prescriptions)* q.s. *or* quant. suff. **—quantum valeat,** as much as it may be worth.

—quantum valebat, as much as it was worth. **—quantum vis,** as much as you will: *abbr.* q.v.

quare impedit [L], lit., why does he hinder?: *law,* a writ issued against the objector in a case of disputed right of presentation to a benefice.

quarte [Fr], a certain position in fencing; carte.

quartier [Fr], a quarter. **—quartier général,** headquarters: *mil.*

quasi dicat [L], as if one should say: *abbr.* q.d.

quasi dictum [L], as if said: *abbr.* q.d.

quasi dixisset [L], as if he had said.

Quatsch [Ger], twaddle; bosh.

quattrocento [It], Italian art and literature of the 15th century.

que besa su mano (*or* **sus manos**) [Sp], lit., who kisses your hand (*or* your hands); yours respectfully (*abbr.* q.b.s.m. *or* Q.B.S.M.).

que besa sus pies [Sp], lit., who kisses your feet; yours respectfully (*abbr.* q.b.s.p. *or* Q.B.S.P.): complimentary close of a Spanish letter to a lady.

que diable allait-il faire dans cette galère? [Fr], what the devil was he going to do in that galley?: *Molière;* whatever was he going to do there?

que Dieu vous bénisse [Fr], God bless you.

que Dios guarde [Sp], may God keep him: *abbr.* Q.D.G.

que en Gloria esté [Sp], may he be in Glory: *abbr.* Q.E.G.E.

que en paz descanse [Sp], may he (*or* she) rest in peace: *abbr.* q.e.p.d.

que faire? [Fr], what is to be done?

que ha? [Pg], what is the matter?

¿que hay? [Sp], what's up? what's the matter?

¿que hay de nuevo? [Sp], what's new?

¿qué hora es? [Sp], what time is it?

que horas são? [Pg], what time is it?

quelle affaire! [Fr], what a to-do!

quelle bêtise! [Fr], what an absurdity!

quelles sont les nouvelles? [Fr], what is the news?

quelli studi ch'immortal fanno le mortal virtudi [It], those studies that make mortal virtues immortal: *Ariosto* (said of history).

quelque chose [Fr], something; a trifle.

quelqu'un [Fr; *fem.* quelqu'une], somebody; someone.

quel temps fait-il? [Fr], what is the weather like?

quel temps il fait! [Fr], what weather this is!

quel toupet! [Fr], what effrontery! what cheek! See TOUPET.

quem canta, seus males espanta [Pg], he who sings drives away his misfortunes.

quem di diligunt adolescens moritur [L], whom the gods love dies young: *Plautus.*

que m'importe? [Fr], what is that to me?

quem Iuppiter vult perdere, prius dementat [L], whom Jupiter wishes to destroy, he first makes mad.

que n'ai-je le temps! [Fr], oh, that I had the time!

quenelle [Fr], forcemeat ball: *cookery.*

¿qué pasa? [Sp], what's going on?

¿qué quiere? [Sp], what do you want?

querela [L; *pl.* querelae], bill of complaint; also, a court action: *law.*

querelle d'Allemand [Fr], lit., German quarrel; groundless quarrel.

querido [Sp; *fem.* querida], *adj.* beloved; dear; *n.* darling; lover; *fem.* also (esp. in Sp. Am. and P.I.), a mistress; a loose woman. —**querido mío** *or* **querida mía,** my dear; my darling; my love.

que sais-je? [Fr], what do I know?: motto of *Montaigne.*

que son raros los deseados [Sp], few men are missed: *Gracian y Morales.*

qu'est-ce que c'est? [Fr], what is this? what is that?

¿qué tal? [Sp], how goes it?: *colloq.*

que temps fait-il? [Fr], what sort of weather is it?

queue [Fr], tail; train of a gown; line of persons.

¡qué vergüenza! [Sp], how outrageous! how scandalous!

que voulez-vous? [Fr], what do you want?

que vous faut-il? [Fr], what do you need?

qui a bu boira [Fr], he who has drunk will drink again.

qui aime bien châtie bien [Fr], who loves well chastises well.

quia timet [L], because he fears (designating various bills and writs in equity): *law.*

qui capit ille facit [L], he who takes it to himself has done it; if the shoe fits, wear it.

quicquid delirant reges, plectuntur Achivi [L], whatever folly their kings commit, it is the Greeks themselves who suffer.

quicunque vult servari [L], whosoever will be saved: beginning of the Athanasian Creed (commonly called the *quicunque vult*).

quidam [L], an unknown person; somebody.

qui desiderat pacem, praeparet bellum [L], who wishes for peace, let him make ready for war.

quid faciendum? [L], what is to be done?

quid hoc sibi vult? [L], what does this mean?

quid leges sine moribus vanae proficiunt? [L], what can idle laws avail in the absence of morals?: *Horace.*

quid novi? [L], what is the news?

qui docet discit [L], he who teaches learns.

qui dort, dîne [Fr], he who sleeps, dines; sleeping is as good as eating.

quid pro quo [L], something in return; equivalent; compensation; consideration.

quid rides? Mutato nomine, de te fabula narratur [L], why do you laugh? Change the name, and the story is told of you: *Horace.*

quid sit futurum cras, fuge quaerere [L], avoid asking what tomorrow will bring forth: *Horace.*

quid times [L], what do you fear? what are you afraid of?

quid verum atque decens [L], what is true and becoming: *Horace.*

quien calla otorga [Sp], silence gives consent.

quien canta sus males espanta [Sp], he who sings chases away his troubles.

¿quién es? [Sp], who is it?

quien más sabe más calle [Sp], who knows most says least.

quien mucho abarca poco aprieta [Sp], who grasps much holds little; grasp all, lose all.

quien no sabe, no vale [Sp], who knows nothing is worth nothing.

¿quién sabe? [Sp], who knows?

quien te cubre te descubre [Sp], whoever covers you discovers you.

quieta non movere [L], not to move quiet things; don't stir things at rest; let sleeping dogs lie.

qui facit per alium facit per se [L], he who does a thing through another does it himself; a man is legally responsible for his agent.

qui invidet minor est [L], he who envies is the inferior.

qui laborat orat [L], he who labors prays.

qui le sait? [Fr], who knows? Cf. CHI LO SA?

qui m'aime aime mon chien [Fr], who loves me loves my dog.

qu'importe? [Fr], what does it matter?

qui n'a santé n'a rien [Fr], he who has not health has nothing.

qui nimium probat nihil probat [L], he who proves too much proves nothing.

qui non proficit deficit [L], he who does not advance loses ground (*or* fails).

qui perd, pèche [Fr], he who loses, sins (*or* offends); the loser is always deemed to be wrong.

quiproquo [Fr], a mistake; blunder.

quis custodiet ipsos custodes? [L], who shall guard the guards themselves?: *Juvenal.*

qui se ressemblent s'assemblent [Fr], those who resemble each other, assemble together; birds of a feather flock together.

qui s'excuse s'accuse [Fr], who excuses himself accuses himself.

quis fallere possit amantem? [L], who can deceive a lover?: *Virgil.*

quisque sibi proximus [L], everyone is nearest to himself.

quis separabit? [L], who shall separate (Great Britain from Ireland)?: motto of the *Order of St. Patrick.*

qui stat, caveat ne cadat [L], let him that standeth take heed lest he fall: *Vulgate* (*I Corinthians* x. 12).

qui tacet consentit [L], he who is silent consents.

qui tam [L], lit., who as well (first words of clause); action to recover, brought by an informer in conjunction with the government: *law.*

qui timide rogat docet negare [L], he who asks timidly courts denial: *Seneca.*

qui transtulit sustinet [L], he who transplanted sustains: motto of *Connecticut.*

qui trop embrasse mal étreint [Fr], who grasps too much clasps ill; grasp all, lose all.

qui trop se hâte reste en chemin [Fr], who hurries too much rests on the way; slow and sure wins the race.

qui uti scit ei bona [L], that man should have wealth who knows how to use it: *Terence.*

qui va la? [Fr], who goes there?

qui vit sans folie n'est pas si sage qu'il croit [Fr], who lives without folly is not as wise as he thinks: *La Rochefoucauld.*

qui vive? [Fr], who goes there? —**être sur le qui vive,** to be on the alert.

qui vivra verra [Fr], who lives will see.

quoad [L], as to; as regards; so far as. —**quoad hoc,** as to this; as regards this particular matter; in this respect; as far as this goes. —**quoad minus,** as to the lesser matter. —**quoad ultra,** as regards the past.

quo animo? [L], with what intention?

quocunque modo [L], in whatsoever manner; in whatever way.

quocunque nomine [L], under whatever name.

quod absurdum est [L], which thing is absurd.

quod avertat Deus! [L], which may God avert! God forbid!

quod bene notandum [L], which is to be well marked (*or* especially noted).

quod erat demonstrandum [L], which was to be demonstrated: *abbr.* Q.E.D.

quod erat faciendum [L], which was to be done: *abbr.* Q.E.F.

quod est [L], which is: *abbr.* q.e.

quod hoc sibi vult? [L], what does this mean?

quodlibet [L], lit., what you please; a debatable point; a subtlety.

quod non opus est, asse carum est [L], what is not necessary is dear at a penny.

quod sciam [L], as far as I know: *Cicero.*

quod scripsi scripsi [L], what I have written I have written.

quod vide [L], which see: *abbr.* q.v.

quo fas et gloria ducunt [L], where duty and glory lead.

quo Fata vocant [L], whither the Fates call (*or* summon).

quo iure? [L], by what right?

quomodo? [L], in what manner? by what means? how?

quondam [L], former; formerly.

quo pax et gloria ducunt [L], where peace and glory lead.

quorum pars magna fui [L], of which things I was an important part: *Virgil.*

quot homines tot sententiae [L], so many men, so many minds (*or* opinions): *Terence.*

quot servi tot hostes [L], so many servants, so many enemies.

quousque tandem? [L], how long, pray? to what lengths?: *Cicero.*

quo vadis? [L], whither goest thou?

R

rabat [Fr], a clerical linen collar; also, a neckband with flaps, as worn by ecclesiastics in France; *hunting,* beating for game.

rabi [Hind], spring (season); spring crop or harvest, as of wheat, barley, hemp, indigo, and vegetables: *India.*

râble [Fr], the back and loins (the barons) of certain quadrupeds, esp. of a hare or rabbit; baron. **—râble de lièvre rôti,** roast baron of hare: *both cookery.*

rabota [Russ], work.

rabotnik [Russ; *pl.* rabotniki], worker.

raccomandare il lardo alla gatta [It], to trust the bacon to the cat.

raccontalo al portiere [It], tell it to the doorman; tell it to the Marines.

raccroc [Fr], pure chance; lucky hit; fluke, as at billiards.

raconte cela à ta soeur [Fr], tell that to your sister. Cf. RACCONTALO.

raconteur [Fr; *fem.* raconteuse], a teller of anecdotes; storyteller; narrator.

raddolcendo [It], becoming softer (*abbr.* raddol.): *music.*

radoteur [Fr; *fem.* radoteuse], driveler; dotard.

rafale [Fr], squall; *mil.,* violent fusillade; barrage.

raffiné [Fr; *fem.* raffinée], refined; delicate; subtle; consummate; finished.

rafraîchissements [Fr], refreshments; cooling beverages, fruits, ices, etc.

raide [Fr], stiff; stern; rigid; inflexible.

raifort [Fr], horseradish.

railleur [Fr; *fem.* railleuse], banterer; josher (*slang*).

raison [Fr], reason; proof; ground; argument; consideration; justice; right; *law,* claim; *com.,* firm; company; also, firm's name or style. **—bonne raison,** good grounds. **—raison d'état,** reason of state. **—raison d'être,** reason for existence. **—raison sociale** *or* **raison de commerce,** official name or style of a firm. **—sans raison,** groundless; groundlessly. **—vous avez raison,** you are right.

raisonné [Fr; *fem.* raisonnée], lit., reasoned; rational; methodical; analytical; classified; systematically arranged. **—catalogue raisonné,** a catalogue arranged according to subjects, with explanatory details and notes.

raj [Hind], rule; dominion.

rajah *or* **raja** [Hind], orig., king; Hindu ruling prince; native chief; also, a title of rank: *India & Malaysia.*

rajeunissant [Fr; *fem.* rajeunissante], giving a youthful look to; rejuvenescent.

rajeunissement [Fr], a growing or making young again; rejuvenation.

râle [Fr], an abnormal, rattling sound accompanying that of respiration. **—râle de la mort,** death rattle: *med.*

rallentando [It], slackening; gradually slower (*abbr.* ral., rall., *or* rallo.): *music.*

Ramadan [Ar], ninth month of the Muslim year; also, the great religious fast held each day during this period, from dawn to sunset.

rambla [Sp], ravine; avenue (Barcelona).

ramo [Sp & It], branch (in all senses).

ramollissement [Fr], a softening, esp. of the brain; *colloq.*, quasi-imbecility.

rana [Hind], Hindu ruling prince; rajah: *India.*

ranchería [Sp], dwelling place of a *ranchero;* herdsman's hut or a collection of such huts; also, an Indian settlement: *Sp. Am. & southwestern U.S.*

ranchero [Sp], herdsman; ranchman: *Sp. Am. & southwestern U.S.*

rancho [Sp], a rude hut or group of huts for stockmen and laborers; also, a ranch; stock farm (as distinguished from *hacienda*): *Sp. Am. &* (in the second sense) *southwestern U.S.*

rançon [Fr], ransom.

rani *or* **ranee** [Hind], Hindu queen; wife of a *rana: India.*

rann [Norw], house.

ranz des vaches [Swiss dial.], pastoral song played on the alpenhorn by Swiss herdsmen.

rapin [Fr], a painter's pupil; art student; *colloq.*, dauber.

rappel [Fr], drum call to arms or quarters: *mil.*

rapport [Fr], harmonious relationship; agreement; harmony; correspondence; affinity; sympathetic contact. **—en rapport,** in accord; in sympathy.

rapprochement [Fr], the act of bringing (*or* coming) together; reconciliation, reestablishment of friendly relations, esp. between countries.

rara avis [L; *pl.* rarae aves], a rare bird; prodigy. **—rara avis in terris nigroque simillima cycno,** a rare bird upon the earth and very like a black swan; a strange prodigy; unusual person or thing: *Juvenal.*

rari nantes [L], a few (shipwrecked sailors at sea) swimming here and there: *Virgil.*

Raskolnik [Russ; *pl.* Raskolniki], dissenter; nonconformist; esp., a seceder from the Greek Church.

rassemblement [Fr], lit., an assembling; fall in! rally!: *mil.*

Rast macht Rost [Ger], rest makes (*or* breeds) rust.

rata [LL], rate; individual share.

Rathaus [Ger], town hall.

ratione domicilii [L], by reason of domicile: *law.*

ratione soli [L], by reason of the soil: *law.*

Ratskeller [Ger], orig., in Germany, a town-hall cellar commonly used as a beer room and restaurant; hence, **rathskeller** [*naturalized in U.S.*], a bar or restaurant on the German model.

Raum für alle hat die Erde [Ger], the earth has room for all: *Schiller.*

ravigote [Fr], a thick sauce of stock containing herbs, lemon juice, and white wine: *cookery*.

ravissant [Fr; *fem.* ravissante], ravishing; charming.

ravissement [Fr], ravishment; rapture; transport.

razzia [Fr], a plundering excursion, as practiced by African Muslims; foray; raid; fig., a clean sweep.

re [L], in the matter of; concerning: used for *in re*.

Realpolitik [Ger], practical politics.

Realschule [Ger; *pl.* Realschulen], a nonclassical secondary school.

rebozo [Sp], a kind of shawl or mantilla worn by women in Mexico and Spanish America generally, covering the head and shoulders and sometimes part of the face.

réchauffé [Fr], a warmed-over dish; rehash (*lit. & fig.*).

recherché [Fr; *fem.* recherchée], sought out with care; choice; exquisite; highly finished; rare; out of the ordinary.

recitando [It], in the style of recitation; declamatory: *music*.

recitativo [It], recitative, as in the narrative parts of oratorios and operas. **—recitativo accompagnato,** accompanied recitative. **—recitativo parlando,** recitative more nearly resembling speech. **—recitativo secco,** recitative accompanied only by occasional chords. **—recitativo stromentato,** recitative with orchestral accompaniment.

réclame [Fr], the securing of notoriety; advertising; advertisement; newspaper puff.

recoupé [Fr], lit., recut; characterizing a rose diamond or other gem with 36 facets (*rose recoupé*).

recru [Fr; *fem.* recrue], worn out with fatigue; spent.

recte et suaviter [L], justly and mildly.

recto [L], right-hand page. Cf. VERSO.

rectus [NL; *pl.* recti], any of various straight muscles: *abbr.* of *rectus musculus,* straight muscle.

rectus in curia [L], upright in the court; with clean hands; blameless.

reçu [Fr], received; also, receipt.

recueil [Fr], literary collection *or* compilation; selection; miscellany. **—recueil choisi,** choice collection.

reculade [Fr], falling back; retreat.

reculer pour mieux sauter [Fr], lit., to go back in order to leap better; await a better opportunity.

rédacteur [Fr], editor (of a newspaper).

rédaction [Fr], editing; also, editorial department.

redan [Fr], fortification ending in a protruding angle.

Reden ist Silber, Schweigen ist Geld [Ger], speech is silver, silence is gold.

redingote [Fr], long jacket, reaching almost to knees.

redintegratio amoris [L], the renewal of love.

redire ad nuces [L], to return to the nuts; resume childish interests.

redivivus [L], restored to life; resuscitated; renewed.

redolet lucerna (*or* **lucernam**) [L], it smells of the lamp: said of any labored literary work. Cf. OLET LUCERNAM.

reductio ad absurdum [L], reduction to absurdity; proof of the falsity of a conclusion or principle by reducing it to its logical absurdity.

reductio ad impossibile [L], reduction to impossibility; an impossible conclusion.

réduit [Fr], an interior stronghold or retreat within a fortification.

refait [Fr], drawn game.

reflet [Fr], reflection; luster; *ceramics,* brilliancy of surface; special glaze. —**reflet métallique,** metallic luster. —**reflet nacré,** iridescent luster, like that of mother-of-pearl.

regarder de haut en bas [Fr], lit., to look at from top to bottom (*or* from head to foot); regard scornfully.

regard farouche [Fr], fierce look.

regards distraits [Fr], vacant looks.

Regenmantel [Ger], raincoat.

régie [Fr], administration of taxes and public works; excise office; in France and some other European states, the department having sole control of tobacco, salt, and other government monopolies.

Regierung [Ger], government; administration; executive power.

Regina Caeli [L], Queen of Heaven; The Virgin Mary.

regium donum [L], a royal gift (*or* grant).

règlement [Fr], a regulation; rule.

regnant populi [L], the people rule: motto of *Arkansas.*

Reich [Ger; *pl.* Reiche], empire; realm; esp., the former German Empire and, from 1918 until after World War II, the German Republic (*Deutsches Reich*).

Reichsbank [Ger], formerly the central banking institution of Germany.

Reichsmark [Ger], monetary unit of Germany from 1925 to 1948.

Reichsrat [Ger], formerly, the upper house of the German parliament; state council.

Reichstag [Ger], imperial parliament; prior to 1918, the lower house of the German legislature; under the Republic, the national diet, or House of Representatives.

Reichswehr [Ger], the German armed forces, 1919 to 1933.

Reifeprüfung [Ger], examination for leaving-certificates; in German first-class secondary boys' schools, a leaving examination entitling the successful candidate to enter any German university without taking any further test or matriculation.

reine-claude [Fr; *pl.* reines-claude], greengage plum.

re infecta [L], the business being unfinished.

relâche [Fr], intermission; relaxation; discontinuance; *theat.,* no performance; closed.

relata refero [L], I tell the tale as it was told to me.

relaxe [Fr], stoppage of proceedings: *law.*

relevé [Fr; *fem.* relevée], raised; exalted; noble; *cookery,* highly seasoned.

religieuse [Fr], a nun.

religieux [Fr], monk; friar; brother.

religio laici [L], a layman's religion.

religio loci [L], the awesome sanctity of the place: *Virgil.*

religiosamente [It], religiously; devotionally: *music.*

religioso [It], religious; devout: *music.*

reliquiae [L], the remains.

rem acu tetigisti [L], you have touched the thing with a needle; you have hit the nail on the head.

remar contra a maré [Pg], to row against the tide.

remerciement *or* **remercîment** [Fr], thanks; words of thanks.

remettez la baïonnette [Fr], unfix bayonets!: *mil.*

remettez-vous [Fr], compose yourself.

remisso animo [L], with mind relaxed; listlessly.

remis velisque [L], with oars and sails; with might and main.

remonta [Sp], a fresh horse; supply of saddle horses: *southwestern U.S.*

remontado [Sp], lit., that has fled to the mountains; specif., an indigenous person who has fled from civilization; also, one of the tribesmen of the northern Philippines: *P.I.*

rémoulade [Fr], a sauce or dressing resembling mayonnaise: *cookery.*

remplissage [Fr], filling; fig., padding; trash.

remuant [Fr; *fem.* remuante], restless, fidgety; unquiet.

remuda [Sp], the saddle horses collectively, as on a ranch; relay of remounts.

rencontre [Fr], an encounter; a hostile meeting; also a casual meeting; rencounter.

render pane per focaccia [It], to return bread for bun; give tit for tat.

rendez-moi mon reste [Fr], give me my change.

rendez-vous [Fr], appointment; tryst.

rendu [Fr; *fem.* rendue], lit., rendered; exhausted; done up; spent (as a horse).

renommé [Fr; *fem.* renommée], renowned; celebrated.

renovate animos [L], renew your courage.

renovato nomine [L], by a revived name.

rente [Fr], yearly income; revenue; pension. **—rentes sur l'État,** interest on Government stocks; also, the stocks themselves; funds.

rentier [Fr; *fem.* rentière], one who has an income from investments; stockholder; annuitant; independent gentleman.

renversé [Can Fr], lit., overturned; specif., a tract of forest covered with trees felled by storms.

renvoi [Fr], dismissal; discharge; *law,* adjournment; also, sending before another judge; *typog.,* reference mark.

repartimiento [Sp], distribution; partition; also, an allotment or assessment; in early Spanish America, a grant of land with the people on it, made by the conquerors to their adherents, with right of peonage.

repas maigre [Fr], a meatless meal. See MAIGRE.

repertorium [L; *pl.* repertoria], a catalogue.

repetatur [L], let it be repeated: *abbr.* repet.

Repetent [Ger; *pl.* Repetenten], a tutor; coach: *Ger. univ. cant.*

replicato [It], repeated; doubled: *music.*

répondez, s'il vous plaît [Fr], answer, please: *abbr.* R.S.V.P. Cf. UM ANTWORT WIRD GEBETEN.

répondre en Normand [Fr], to reply like a Norman; give an evasive answer.

repos! [Fr], at ease! stand easy!: *mil.*

repoussage [Fr], the art or process of hammering out metal on the reverse side, as in *repoussé* work.

repoussé [Fr], formed in relief: said of ornamental metal work hammered on the reverse side.

représaille [Fr], reprisal; retaliation.

reprise [Fr], repetition; continuation.

République Française [Fr], the French Republic: *abbr.* R.F.

requiescat in pace [L; *pl.* requiescant], may he (*or* she) rest in peace: *abbr.* R.I.P.

requiescit in pace [L], he (*or* she) rests in peace.

rerum primordia [L], the first beginnings (*or* elements) of things.

res [L; *pl.* res], a thing; matter; affair; point; a cause or action. —**res adiudicata** *or* **res iudicata,** a thing or matter already settled; a decided case: *law.* —**res alienae,** things belonging to others. —**res angusta domi,** straitened circumstances at home: *Juvenal.* —**res corporales,** corporeal (*or* tangible) things: *law.* —**res est ingeniosa dare,** giving requires good sense: *Ovid.* —**res est sacra miser,** a person in distress is a sacred object. —**res est solliciti plena timoris amor,** love is full of anxious fears: *Ovid.* —**res gestae,** things done; deeds; transactions; exploits; *law,* the material facts; attendant circumstances. —**res in cardine est,** lit., the matter is on the hinge; the affair is hanging in the balance. —**res incorporales,** things incorporeal (*or* intangible): *law.* —**res ipsa loquitur,** the thing speaks for itself. —**res iudicata,** a decided case: *law.* See RES ADIUDICATA. —**res iudicata pro veritate accipitur,** a case decided is considered as just: *law.* —**res mobiles,** movable things: *law.* —**res nihili** (*or* **nullius**), a thing of naught; nonentity. —**res rustica,** a country matter.

resa [Sw], journey; travel; voyage.

réseau [Fr; *pl.* réseaux], network; netlike pattern; *lace making,* fine-meshed ground or foundation; *astron.,* network of small squares used to facilitate measurements in stellar photography; *optics,* diffraction grating.

respice finem [L], look to (*or* consider) the end.

respondeat superior [L], let the superior answer; let the principal answer for the acts of his agent: *law.*

respublica [L], commonwealth; state; republic.

restaurateur [Fr], restaurant owner.

résumé [Fr], summary; abstract.

resurgam [L], I shall rise again.

rete [L; *pl.* retia], lit., net; vascular network; plexus: *anat.*

retenue [Fr], reserve; discretion; self-control.

retroussé [Fr], turned up: said esp. of the nose.

revanche [Fr], revenge; retaliation; also, return match; second game.
—**en revanche,** by way of retaliation; in requital; in return.

réveillon [Fr], midnight repast or revel, esp. on Christmas eve.

revenons à nos moutons [Fr], let us return to our sheep; let us return to our subject.

re vera *or* **revera** [L], in truth; in fact.

rêveur [Fr; *fem.* rêveuse], dreamer; daydreamer.

rêveusement [Fr], dreamingly; pensively.

revocate animos [L], recover your courage: *Virgil.*

revolutsya [Russ; *pl.* revolutsiee], revolution.

revolutsyaner [Russ; *pl.* revolutsyaneree], revolutionary.

revue [Fr], review; inspection; survey.

rex bibendi [L], king of the revels.

rex non potest peccare [L], the king can do no wrong.

rex nunquam moritur [L], the king never dies.

rex regnat sed non gubernat [L], the king reigns but does not govern.

rey nuevo, ley nueva [Sp], new king, new law.

rez-de-chaussée [Fr], ground floor.

ῥοδοδάκτυλος ἠώς [Gr; rhododáktulos ēós], rosy-fingered morn (*or* dawn): *Homer.*

rhythmus [Gr ῥυθμός, rhuthmós], measured motion; rhythm.

riant [Fr; *fem.* riante], laughing; cheerful; pleasing.

ribák ribaká vidyet izdaleká [Russ], a fisherman sees another fisherman from afar; birds of a feather.

ribyonik [Russ], child.

ric-à-ric [Fr], in driblets.

richt euch! [Ger], dress (ranks)!: *mil.*

rideau [Fr; *pl.* rideaux], curtain; screen; *mil.*, a height commanding a fortified position; also, a protective ridge around a camp.

ride bene chi ride l'ultimo [It], he laughs well (*or* best) who laughs last.

ridentem dicere verum quid vetat? [L], what hinders one from speaking the truth, even while laughing?: *Horace.*

ridere in stomacho [L], to laugh inwardly; laugh up one's sleeve.

ride si sapis [L], laugh, if you are wise: *Martial.*

ridiculus mus [L], a ridiculous mouse. See PARTURIUNT MONTES.

ridotto [It; *pl.* ridotti], orig., a fashionable club or pleasure resort, devoted to dancing, dining, and (often) dissipation; a public entertainment with music and dancing, often in masquerade, very popular in England in the 18th century; *music,* an adaptation of a piece from the full score.

rien de plus éloquent que l'argent comptant [Fr], nothing is more eloquent than ready money; money talks.

rien n'est beau que le vrai [Fr], nothing is beautiful but the truth.

rifacimento [It; *pl.* rifacimenti], a remaking; refurbishing; esp., a remodeled form of a literary or musical composition.

rigolo [Fr], amusing; jolly: *colloq.*

rigor mortis [L], lit., rigor of death; the temporary stiffening of the body after death.

Rigsdag [Dan], the Danish legislature.

rilievo [It], projection from a background; relief: *sculp.*

rinforzando [It], lit., reinforcing; strengthening; imparting additional stress (*abbr.* rf., rfz., *or* rinf.): *music.*

rio [It; *pl.* rii], rivulet; brook; specif., one of the smaller canals, or water streets, in Venice.

rio [Pg], river. —**rio abaixo,** downriver. —**rio arriba,** upriver.

río [Sp], river. —**río abajo,** downriver. —**río arriba,** upriver.

ripaille [Fr], feasting; carousal; debauch; riotous living. Cf. BOMBANCE. —**faire ripaille,** to feast; junket; revel; carouse.

ripieno [It], lit., filling up; supplementary; additional (i.e., executed by several performers to increase the mass effect): *music.*

ripopée [Fr], slops; bad wine; hodgepodge; medley.

riposatamente [It], restfully; calmly: *music.*

rira bien qui rira le dernier [Fr], he laughs best who laughs last.

rire entre cuir et chair [Fr], lit., to laugh between skin and flesh; laugh up one's sleeve.

rire jaune [Fr], lit., to laugh yellow; laugh on the wrong side of one's mouth; force a laugh.

risaldar [Hind], commander of an Indian cavalry regiment.

ris de veau [Fr], calf's sweetbread; sweetbread.

rishi [Skr], Hindu sage or seer; inspired poet, esp., one of the seven ancient sages to whom the Vedic hymns were originally revealed; *pop.,* a Hindu ascetic. —**maharishi,** a Hindu teacher of mystical knowledge.

Risorgimento [It], lit., resurrection; the Revival of Learning in Italy in the 14th and 15th centuries; *politics,* the awakening of Italian nationalism, culminating in complete unification and independence in 1870.

risotto [It], an Italian mixed dish consisting of rice, broth, onions, cheese, meat, etc.: *cookery.*

risqué [Fr; *fem.* risquée], risky; improper; indelicate.

rissolé [Fr; *fem.* rissolée], browned, as by frying: *cookery.*

risum teneatis, amici? [L], could you help laughing, my friends?: *Horace.*

risus [L], a laugh; laughter.

risvegliato [It], awakened; lively; with renewed animation: *music.*

ritardando [It], retarding; becoming gradually slower (*abbr.* rit. *or* ritard.): *music.*

ritenuto [It], held back; gradually slackening speed (*abbr.* rit. *or* ritten.): *music.*

ritornello [It], a brief instrumental prelude or refrain; ritornelle: *music.*

ritratto [It; *pl.* ritratti], portrait; representation.

Ritter [Ger; *sing. & pl.*], knight. **—Ritter der traurigen Gestalt,** knight of the woeful countenance (i.e., Don Quixote).

rituale [L], manual for priests; ritual: *R.C.Ch.*

rivière [Fr], river; stream; *jewelry,* many-stringed necklace of precious stones, esp. diamonds.

rixatur de lana saepe caprina [L], he often quarrels about goat's wool; he quarrels about anything or nothing: *Horace.*

riz [Fr], rice.

robe de chambre [Fr], dressing gown.

robe de cour [Fr], court dress.

robe de nuit [Fr], nightdress.

rocaille [Fr], artificial rockwork, as for gardens.

roche moutonnée [Fr; *pl.* roches moutonnées], a knob or knoll of rock rounded like the back of a sheep, as the result of glacial action.

rodeo [Sp], cattle roundup with tests of range skills.

rôdeur [Fr], prowler.

rodina [Russ], native land.

rognon [Fr], kidney.

rôle d'équipage [Fr], list of the crew; muster roll; roster.

rolpens [Du], tripe and minced beef mixed together and usually eaten fried.

roman à clef [Fr], lit., novel with a key; novel in which real personages are depicted as fictional.

romanza [It], a romance; a short musical composition, usually suggestive of a love song; ballad: *music.*

rompez le pas! [Fr], break step!: *mil.*

rompez les rangs! [Fr], lit., break ranks; dismiss!: *mil.*

ropa [Sp], clothing; wearing apparel.

rosalia [It], the successive repetition of a phrase or motif, each time being transposed a step or half step higher or, occasionally, lower: *music.*

rosbif [Fr], roast beef.

rose du Barry [Fr], a rose tint used on Sèvres porcelain.

rossignol [Fr], nightingale; *Canada,* the song sparrow. **—rossignol d'Arcadie,** jackass.

roti [Hind], bread: *India.*

rôti [Fr], a roast; roast meat.

rotura [Sp], rupture; *geol.,* fault; break.

roture [Fr], plebeian rank; state of being a *roturier; Fr. Can. law,* tenure of feudal land by a commoner, subject to an annual charge or rent.

roturier [Fr; *fem.* roturière], *n.* one not of noble birth; plebeian; commoner; *Fr. Can. law,* one holding real property by *roture; adj.* plebeian; of mean birth.

roublard [Fr; *fem.* roublarde], *adj.* cunning; knowing; *n.* a cunning or knowing person; one who knows how to get out of a scrape.

roué [Fr], debauchee; profligate; rake.

rouelle de veau [Fr], fillet of veal.

rouge et noir [Fr], lit., red and black; a gambling game played on a table having red and black diamond-shaped compartments, on which the stakes are laid. Called also *trente et quarante.*

roulade [Fr], trill; florid vocal passage, sung to one syllable: *music;* also, a slice of meat rolled about a filling and cooked: *cookery.*

rouleau [Fr; *pl.* rouleaux], a roll; coil; cylindrical roll of coins wrapped in paper.

roux [Fr], brown butter sauce or thickening: *cookery.*

rovine [It], ruins.

ruade [Fr], kick, as of a horse; sudden unexpected attack.

ruat caelum [L], though the heavens fall; let the heavens fall!

rubato [It], lit., robbed; designating the lengthening of one note at the expense of another, in a free metrical rendering. **—tempo rubato,** a departure from strict metrical time in the above manner: *both music.*

Rückblick [Ger], backward glance; retrospect.

Rucksack [Ger], knapsack, as carried by hikers and mountain climbers.

rudera [L], rubbish, as from demolished buildings; debris.

rudis indigestaque moles [L], a rude and undigested (*or* formless) mass: *Ovid.*

rue [Fr], street.

ruego de rey, mando es [Sp], a king's request is a command.

Ruhe, Ruhe! [Ger], order, order!

ruiné [Fr; *fem.* ruinée], ruined; worn out; spoiled.

rumal [Hind & Pers], handkerchief or head covering; also, an East Indian fabric of silk or cotton.

rumba [Sp; also spelled *rhumba*], a Cuban dance.

rusé [Fr; *fem.* rusée], wily; designing; artful; sly.

ruse contre ruse [Fr], wile against wile.

ruse de guerre [Fr], stratagem of war.

rus in urbe [L], the country in a city: *Martial.*

ruvidamente [It], roughly; ruggedly: *music.*

ryo [Jap], inn.

ryot [Anglo-Ind; Hind *ra'iyat*], native cultivator; peasant.

S

sabra [Heb], native-born Israeli; a desert pear ("prickly on the outside, soft on the inside").

sabot [Fr], wooden shoe; clog; also, a top (plaything).

sabotage [Fr], orig., the making of *sabots;* specif., malicious waste, or damage perpetrated by discontented workmen, esp. while ostensibly carrying on their accustomed work.

saboteur [Fr; *fem.* saboteuse], orig., a clumsy worker or bungler; one who practices *sabotage.*

sabreur [Fr], swashbuckler; swordsman; dashing cavalry officer.

sacamuelas [Sp], dentist; *colloq.*, lit., tooth puller. **—miente más que un sacamuelas,** he lies more than a tooth puller.

sacate [Sp]. Same as ZACATE.

sacco pieno rizza l'orecchio [It], a full sack pricks up its ear.

sacré [Fr; *fem.* sacrée], sacred; also sometimes "damned," when preceding a noun.

sacré bleu [Fr], an oath: confound it!

Sacrum Romanum Imperium [L], the Holy Roman Empire: *abbr.* S.P.I.

saepe stilum vertas [L], often turn the stylus (and make erasures with the blunt end on the waxen tablets); correct freely, if you wish to write anything meritorious: *Horace.*

saeva indignatio [L], fierce wrath: *Virgil.*

saevis tranquillus in undis [L], calm amid the raging waters.

safar [Hind], a journey; travel: *India.*

safari [Ar *safarīy*], lit., of a trip; hunting expedition, usually for big game.

sage [Fr], wise; prudent; virtuous; *of children,* well behaved. **—femme sage,** virtuous woman.

sage-femme [Fr; *pl.* sages-femmes], midwife.

sage mir mit wem du gehst und ich werde dir sagen wer du bist [Ger], tell me with whom you go, and I'll tell you who you are.

sagesse [Fr], wisdom; discretion; *of children,* good behavior; *of animals,* gentleness.

sagouin [Fr; *fem.* sagouine], squirrel monkey; fig., untidy person; sloven.

sahib *or* **saheb** [Hind & Ar], orig. (in Arabic), friend; (in Hindustani), lord; ruler; master; gentleman; a title of respect equivalent to *Sir* or *Mr.,* formerly used by indigenous inhabitants in addressing or referring to an Englishman or other European, and placed after the surname or office; as, Morton *Sahib,* Colonel *Sahib;* also used after titles of rank; as, Rajah *Sahib.* See also BURRA SAHIB and CHOTA SAHIB.

sahibah [Hind & Ar], a lady; mistress; madam: *India.*

sahih salamat [Hind], safe and sound.

saignant [Fr; *fem.* saignante], lit., bleeding; underdone; rare: *both cookery.*

sain et sauf [Fr], safe and sound.

sais [Hind & Ar]. Same as SYCE.

sake [Jap], Japanese rice wine.

saki [Per], cupbearer.

sakura [Jap], cherry tree; cherry blossom.

sal [L], salt. **—sal amarum,** lit., bitter salt; Epsom salt. **—sal Atticum,** Attic salt; keen and delicate wit. **—sal catharticus** [NL], Epsom salt. **—sal culinarius,** common salt. **—sal gemmae,** rock salt. **—sal sapit omnia,** salt seasons everything.

sala [Sp], hall; saloon; the large room or reception hall in the front part of a house.

salaam *or* **salam** [Ar], lit., peace; ceremonious salutation; obeisance; compliment or compliments. **—salaam aleikum,** peace be unto (*or* with) you: *Muslim salutation.*

salamat [Tag], a word said by way of thanks or welcome: *P.I.*

salame [It; *pl.* salami], salt meat; salt pork; sausage.

salamet ilah [Turk], go in peace.

salaud [Fr], an insulting epithet: bastard; slut.

sale [Fr], *adj.* dirty; soiled; foul; coarse; *of colors,* dull; *n.* a dirty or coarse person.

salé [Fr; *fem.* salée], salted; salt; corned; *of speech,* biting; pungent; also, coarse; indelicate. **—un propos salé,** a coarse remark.

salero [Sp], saltcellar; winning ways: *colloq.*

salida [Sp], exit.

salière [Fr], saltcellar.

salle [Fr], hall; room. **—salle à manger,** dining room. **—salle d'armes,** school of arms; fencing school. **—salle d'attente,** waiting room. **—salle de danse,** dance hall; dancing school. **—salle d'étude,** study; schoolroom. **—salle des pas perdus,** lit., hall of the lost footsteps; outer hall of a court of law.

salmis [Fr], ragout of previously cooked game: *cookery.*

salon [Fr], reception room; drawing room; a gathering of distinguished guests at the home of a lady of fashion; also, art exhibition; specif., **le Salon,** the annual exhibition in Paris of the works of living artists.

saloperie [Fr], sluttishness; filth; ribaldry; also, a thing (as wine) of execrable quality.

sal sapit omnia [L], salt seasons everything.

sal si puedes [Sp], lit., get out if you can; a trap; a dangerous part of town.

saltarello [It; *pl.* saltarelli], a lively Italian dance, with a hop at the beginning of each measure.

saltimbanco [It], mountebank; quack.

saltimbanque [Fr], mountebank; clown; also, quack; charlatan.

saltimbocca [It], lit., (it) leaps into the mouth; a dish of rolled slices of veal, prosciutto, and herbs.

salud [Sp], health; to your health!

saludos [Sp], greetings.

salus per Christum Redemptorem [L], salvation through Christ the Redeemer.

salus populi suprema lex esto [L], let the welfare of the people be the highest (*or* supreme) law: motto of *Missouri.*

salut! [Fr], greetings!

salute [It], health; to your health!

salva conscientia [L], without compromising one's conscience.

salva dignitate [L], without compromising one's dignity.

salva fide [L], with safety to one's honor; without breaking one's word.

salvam fac reginam, O Domine [L], God save the queen.

salva res est [L], the matter is safe: *Terence.*

salve! [L; *pl.* salvete!], hail! welcome! God save you!

salvo iure [L], saving the right; without prejudice.

salvo ordine [L], with due regard to one's rank (*or* order).

salvo pudore [L], without offense to modesty.

salvo sensu [L], without violation of sense.

salvum fac regem, O Domine [L], God save the king.

sama [Jap], a Japanese title or form of address, placed after the name of an exalted personage; as, Shaka *Sama* (i.e., Sakyamuni, the Buddha), Tenshi *Sama* (lit., Son of Heaven, the Mikado). For ordinary persons *sama* becomes *san* (q.v.).

samadh [Hind], lit., profound meditation; self-immolation; also, a tomb or shrine on the grave of a religious mendicant, saint, spiritual teacher, or yogi.

samadhi [Hind], in *yoga,* a state of deep trance, a sign of the complete identification of soul with reality.

samisen [Jap], a guitarlike instrument with three strings: *Japan.*

samizdat [Russ; *abbr.* of *samoizdatel'stvo,* self-publishing house], self-publishing, i.e. illegal or clandestine publishing in the U.S.S.R.

samo [Jap; also *sumo*], national style of wrestling, as practiced by Japanese professionals: distinguished from *jiu jitsu,* a method of self-defense. —**samo-tori,** wrestler.

samovar [Russ], metal urn to boil water for tea.

sampan [Chin], lit., three planks; Oriental skiff, propelled by sculls or, sometimes, a sail.

samurai [Jap; *sing. & pl.*], a member of the military caste in feudal Japan; also, this caste collectively. Cf. SHIZOKU.

san [Jap], a Japanese title or form of address equivalent to *Mr.,* placed after the name; as, Togo *San.* It is also used to represent *Mrs.* and *Miss,* when no confusion is likely to arise. Thus, "Mrs. Togo" would be *Togo San* (or more fully, *Togo San no okusama,* lit., Mr. Togo's lady);

"Miss Togo" would be *Togo San* (or more fully, *Togo San no ojosan,* lit., Mr. Togo's young lady), while, if her personal name alone were used, the form would be *O— San;* as, *O Kiku San* (lit., the honorable Miss Chrysanthemum).

sancte et sapienter [L], with holiness and wisdom.

sanctum sanctorum [L], holy of holies; *colloq.,* a private room or retreat; den.

sanft [Ger], soft; gentle: *music.*

sang-de-boeuf [Fr], lit., ox's blood; a dark-red color found on old Chinese porcelain; ox blood.

sang-froid [Fr], lit., cold blood; coolness; composure; calmness; nonchalance.

sanglier [Fr], boar; wild boar.

sangre [Sp], blood. **—sangre azul,** blue blood. **—sangre fría,** cold blood.

sangría [Sp], wine punch with fruit and soda water.

sannyasi [Hind & Skr], lit., abandoner; one who has abandoned all worldly desires; Hindu religious mendicant and ascetic: *Hinduism.* Cf. FAKIR.

sans [Fr], without. **—sans âme,** spiritless. **—sans appel,** without appeal. **—sans cérémonie,** without ceremony; informally. **—sans changer,** without changing. **—sans détour,** straightforward; sincere; sincerely. **—sans Dieu rien,** without God, nothing. **—sans doute,** without doubt; doubtless. **—sans façon,** without ceremony; offhand; informally; outspokenly. **—sans faute,** without fail. **—sans gêne,** unconstrained; unceremonious; free-and-easy. **—sans le sou,** without a *sou;* penniless. **—sans mélange,** unmixed; fig., unalloyed; pure. **—sans pareil,** without equal; matchless. **—sans peine,** without difficulty; readily; easily. **—sans peur et sans reproche,** without fear and without reproach; chivalrous. **—sans phrase,** without circumlocution; in a word. **—sans raison,** without reason; groundless; groundlessly. **—sans souci,** without care; happy-go-luckyism; unconcern. **—sans tache,** without spot (*or* blemish); stainless.

sans-culotte [Fr; *pl.* sans-culottes], lit., without breeches; a term of reproach given by the aristocrats to the extreme republicans (wearers of pantaloons instead of knee breeches) in the first French Revolution; hence, a violent revolutionist.

sansei [Jap], lit., third generation; a grandchild of Japanese immigrants to America. Cf. NISEI.

sans-gêne [Fr], absence of constraint; coolness; offhandedness; familiarity; also, an unceremonious and coolly familiar person.

santé [Fr], health. **—corps de santé,** medical staff. **—maison de santé,** private asylum; sanatorium.

Santiago y a ellos! [Sp], Santiago (St. James) and at them!: Spanish battle cry, especially of the *conquistadores.*

Santo [Sp; *fem.* santa], saint; also a saint's image.

Saorstát [Irish], Free State. —**Saorstát Eireann,** Irish Free State.

sapere aude [L], dare to be wise: *Horace.*

sapiens dominabitur astris [L], the wise man will be master of (*or* will rule) the stars.

sapperment [Ger], a German oath: corr. of *Sakrament,* sacrament; the devil! the dickens!

sarai [Hind & Pers]. Same as SERAI.

sardana [Sp], Spanish dance from Catalonia.

sarishtadar [Hind & Pers], lit., record-keeper; registrar; secretary.

sarkar [Hind], the government, esp. the Indian government; supreme authority; as a title, equivalent to "master," "lord."

Sartor Resartus [L], the tailor retailored; the patcher repatched: title of a book by *Carlyle.*

sashimi [Jap], lit., pierce flesh; a prepared dish of thinly sliced raw fish served with grated radish, soy sauce, etc.

sastrería [Sp], tailor shop.

sat-bhai [Hind], lit., seven brothers; a species of thrush, commonly seen in groups of seven.

sat cito, si sat bene [L], soon enough, if but well enough: a saying of *Cato's.*

sate [Mal], marinated meat cooked on skewers.

sati [Hind & Skr]. Same as SUTTEE.

satis eloquentiae, sapientiae parum [L], enough eloquence but too little wisdom.

satis quod sufficit [L], what suffices is enough; enough is as good as a feast.

satis superque [L], enough and too much (*or* more than enough); enough and to spare.

satis verborum [L], enough of words; enough said.

sat pulchra, si sat bona [L], beautiful enough, if (she is) good enough; handsome is as handsome does.

Saturnia regna [L], the reign of Saturn; the golden age: *Virgil.*

sauce [Fr], sauce; relish; food dressing. —**sauce à la menthe,** mint sauce. —**sauce au beurre,** butter sauce. —**sauce aux câpres,** caper sauce. —**sauce béarnaise,** warm mayonnaise and mustard sauce. —**sauce blanche,** white sauce. —**sauce financière,** madeira wine sauce with truffles. —**sauce hollandaise,** warm butter, egg yolk, and lemon sauce. —**sauce meunière,** browned butter, parsley, and lemon sauce. —**sauce piquante,** a sharp, pungent sauce. —**sauce relevée,** rich, highly seasoned sauce. —**sauce verte,** green sauce: *all cookery.*

saucisse *or* **saucisson** [Fr], lit., sausage; a long canvas tube filled with powder, for use as an emergency fuse: *mil.*

Sauerbraten [Ger], pot roast of marinated beef.

sauf erreur ou omission [Fr], errors or omissions excepted: *abbr.* s.e.o.o.

sault [OF], orig., a leap; rapid on a river: *Fr. Can.*

saumon [Fr], salmon.

sauna [Fin], steam bath.

sauté [Fr; *fem.* sautée; *pl.* sautés *or* sautées], quickly fried with a small quantity of fat: *cookery.*

sauvage [Fr], savage; wild; untamed; fig., uncultivated; unsociable; delighting in solitude.

sauve qui peut [Fr], save (himself) who can. —**sauve-qui-peut,** precipitate flight; complete rout.

savant [Fr; *fem.* savante], *adj.* learned; erudite; skillful. —**une main savante,** a skillful hand.

savant [Fr; *fem.* savante], *n.* man of learning; scholar; esp., eminent scientist. —**les savants,** the literati; the learned.

savate [Fr], a French method of boxing, in which the feet are used as well as the fists.

savio contra tempo è pazzo [It], a sage out of season is a fool.

savoir-faire [Fr], lit., a knowing how to do; readiness in doing the right thing; tact; address.

savoir gré [Fr], to be grateful; appreciate.

savoir-vivre [Fr], lit., a knowing how to live; good manners; being at one's ease in society; good breeding.

sayonara! [Jap], lit., if that be so (we shall meet again); goodbye!

saz [Turk], a string instrument.

sbirro [It; *pl.* sbirri], policeman.

sbrigatevi [It], make haste.

scampi [It], large shrimps; prawns.

scandalum magnatum [L; *pl.* scandala magnata], lit., scandal of magnates; defamation of exalted personages: *abbr.* scan. mag.

scena [It], a scene in an opera; also, a dramatic recitative interspersed with melodic passages: *music.*

Schadenfreude [Ger], malicious joy (at another's misfortune).

Schalkheit [Ger], roguishness; guile; wile.

schapska [Pol *czapka*], flat-topped cavalry helmet: *mil.*

schatchen [Yiddish]. Same as SHADCHEN.

Schein vergeht, Wahrheit besteht [Ger], appearance passes away, truth abides.

Schelm [Ger; *pl.* Schelme *or* Schelmen], rogue; rascal; knave.

Schelmerei [Ger], roguery; rascality.

schepen [Du], Dutch alderman or magistrate.

scherzando [It], in a playful manner: *music.*

Scherz bei Seite [Ger], joking apart; seriously.

scherzo [It; *pl.* scherzi], lit., pleasantry; sport; jest; a sprightly passage or movement, usually following a slow one in a sonata or symphony: *music.*

Schiedam [Du town], Holland gin.

Schiff [Ger; *pl.* Schiffe], lit., ship; galley: *typog.*

schip [Du; *pl.* schepen], ship.

schipperke [Du], lit., little boatman (because used as watchdog on boats); a small, tailless, short-haired lapdog, originating in Holland.

schizzo [It; *pl.* schizzi], a sketch.

schlafen Sie wohl! [Ger], good night! sleep well!

Schläger [Ger], German student's dueling sword.

Schlagobers [Ger], whipped cream.

Schlagwort [Ger], lit., striking word; catchword; slogan.

schlemiel [Yiddish], bungler; fool; born loser; person for whom nothing turns out right.

schlep [Yiddish]. Same as SHLEP.

schleppend [Ger], dragging; drawling: *music.*

Schlimmbesserung [Ger], lit., bad improvement; correction for the worse; spoiling of a text.

schlock [Yiddish]. Same as SHLOCK.

Schloss [Ger; *pl.* Schlösser], castle; seat; manor.

Schluss [Ger], conclusion. —**Schluss folgt,** concluded in our next.

schmaltz *or* **shmaltz** [Yiddish], lit., cooking fat; excessive sentimentality.

Schmalz [Ger], melted fat; sentimental mush.

Schmerz [Ger; *pl.* Schmerzen], pain; grief.

Schnapps [Ger], lit., a dram of liquor; any of various distilled liquors.

schnell [Ger], quick; rapid: *music.*

Schnellzug [Ger; *pl.* Schnellzüge], forced march; also, express train.

Schönheit vergeht, Tugend besteht [Ger], beauty fades, virtue (*or* chastity) stays.

Schrecklichkeit [Ger], frightfulness; terrorism.

schuit *or* **schuyt** [Du], a Dutch vessel, usually sloop-rigged, used on the canals and along the coast.

Schutzstaffel [Ger], blackshirts; elite police and later military units of Nazi Germany; *abbr.* S.S.

Schwarm [Ger; *pl.* Schwärme], a swarm; cluster; *colloq.:* object of admiration or adoration; hero; idol; pet.

Schwärmerei [Ger], enthusiasm; ecstasy; wild devotion; fanaticism.

schwärmerisch [Ger], enthusiastic; visionary; fanatical.

schweigen Sie [Ger], be quiet; hold your tongue.

Schweinehund [Ger], an insulting epithet: swine.

scienter [L], knowingly; willfully: *law.*

scientia [L], knowledge; science. —**scientia popinae,** the art of cookery. —**scientia scientiarum,** the science of sciences.

scintillante [It], sparkling: *music.*

scio cui credidi [L], I know in whom I have believed.

sciolto [It], in a free and independent manner: *music.*

scire facias [L], lit., cause it to be known (i.e., show cause); a writ to enforce, annul, or vacate a judgment, patent, or other matter of record (*abbr.* sci. fa.): *law.*

scordato [It], put out of tune: *music.*

scordatura [It], the intentional tuning of a stringed instrument in an irregular manner: *music.*

scorrendo [It], gliding: *music.*

scribendi recte sapere est et principium et fons [L], the foundation and source of writing well is to be wise; "sound judgment is the ground of writing well": *Horace* (tr. by the Earl of Roscommon).

scribere iussit amor [L], love bade me write: *Ovid.*

scribere scientes [L], skilled in writing.

scribimus indocti doctique [L], learned and unlearned, we all write: *Horace.*

scripsi [L], I have written.

scripsit [L], he (*or* she) wrote (it).

scrutin [Fr], ballot; voting. —**scrutin d'arrondissement,** a method of voting by which the elector votes for one or more representatives for his own district only. —**scrutin de liste,** voting for a group of departmental representatives collectively.

sculpsit [L], he (*or* she) carved or engraved (this work): *abbr.* sc. *or* sculp. (usually following the artist's name).

scusi! *or* **scusate!** *or* **scusatemi!** [It], pardon! I beg pardon! pardon me! excuse me!

scuto bonae voluntatis tuae coronasti nos [L], with the shield of thy good will thou hast encompassed us: one of the mottoes of *Maryland.*

sdegno [It], disdain; indignation.

sdegnoso [It], disdainful; scornful: *music.*

séance [Fr], a spiritualist meeting.

se battre contre des moulins [Fr], to fight against windmills.

seconda volta [It], second time: *music.*

secrétaire [Fr], an escritoire; secretary (in all senses).

secundum [L], according to: *abbr.* sec. —**secundum artem,** according to art (*or* rule); scientifically; also, artificially: *abbr.* sec. art. —**secundum formam statuti,** according to the form of the statute. —**secundum genera,** according to classes. —**secundum legem,** according to law: *abbr.* sec. leg. —**secundum naturam,** according to nature; naturally; not artificially: *abbr.* sec. nat. —**secundum ordinem,** in order; orderly; in an orderly manner. —**secundum quid,** lit., according to something; in some one respect only; with limitations. —**secundum regulam,** according to rule: *abbr.* sec. reg. —**secundum usum,** according to usage. —**secundum veritatem,** according to truth; universally valid.

securus iudicat orbis terrarum [L], the whole world judges in safety (i.e., its judgment is unswayed by fear): *St. Augustine.*

se defendendo [L], in defending himself (*or* herself).

sed haec hactenus [L], but so much for this.

se Dio ti lasci, lettor, prender frutto di tua lezione [It], may God vouchsafe thee, reader, to gather fruit from this thy reading: *Dante.*

seditio civium hostium est occasio [L], the disaffection of the citizens is the opportunity of the enemy.

séduisant [Fr; *fem.* séduisante], seductive; bewitching.

segno [It], lit., a sign; the sign 𝄋 or 𝄌 indicating the beginning or end of a repetition: *music.*

s'égosiller [Fr], to make oneself hoarse with talking; bawl loud and long; strain one's voice.

segue [It], follows; play the following like the preceding: *music.*

seguidilla [Sp], a lively Spanish tune and dance, in triple time.

seguro servidor [Sp; *pl.* seguros servidores], (your) faithful servant; yours truly: *abbr.* s. s. *or* S. S., *pl.* ss.ss. *or* SS.SS.

se habla español [Sp], Spanish spoken (here).

Sehnsucht [Ger], passionate desire; longing; yearning.

sehr verbunden [Ger], much obliged.

seigneur [Fr], feudal lord. —**en grand seigneur,** in lordly style.

séjour [Fr], stay; sojourn; residence.

sel [Fr], salt; also, wit.

selamat [Mal], peace.

selamat datang [Mal], greetings (to the one arriving).

selamat djalan [Mal], goodbye (to the one leaving).

selamat tinggal [Mal], goodbye (to the one staying).

selbst getan ist wohl getan [Ger], self-done is well done; if you wish a thing well done, do it yourself.

selbst ist der Mann [Ger], self is the man; self do, self have.

selig [Ger], blessed; happy; hence, deceased; late: *abbr.* sel.

selle [Fr], saddle. —**selle de mouton,** saddle of mutton.

sellette [Fr], culprit's stool (*or* seat); fig., stool of repentance.

selon [Fr], according to. —**c'est selon,** that depends. —**selon les règles,** according to rule; according to the regulations. —**selon moi,** in my opinion.

semel abbas, semper abbas [L], once an abbot, always an abbot.

semel et simul [L], once and together.

semel insanivimus omnes [L], we have all been mad once (*or* at some time).

semel pro semper [L], once for all.

semper [L], always. —**semper ad eventum festinat,** he always hastens to the dénouement (*or* crisis): *Horace.* —**semper avarus eget,** the miser is ever in want. —**semper eadem** [*fem.*], always the same: motto of *Queen Elizabeth.* —**semper et ubique,** always and everywhere. —**semper felix,** always happy (*or* fortunate). —**semper fidelis** [*pl.* fideles], always faithful. —**semper idem** [*masc. & neut.*], always the same. —**semper paratus,** always ready. —**semper timidum scelus,** crime is always fearful. —**semper vivit in armis,** he ever lives in arms.

semplice [It], simply; without embellishments: *music.*

sempre [It], always; continually; in the same manner throughout (*abbr.* semp.): *music.*

senatus consultum [L], a decree of the senate.

Senatus Populusque Romanus [L], the Senate and People of Rome: *abbr.* S.P.Q.R.

senda [Sp], footpath; path; trail.

senex bis puer [L], an old man is twice a boy.

senhor, senhora, senhorita [Pg], Portuguese titles of courtesy equivalent to the Spanish SEÑOR, SEÑORA, SEÑORITA.

seniores priores [L], elders first.

se non è vero, è ben trovato [It], if it is not true, it is well imagined (*or* cleverly invented).

señor [Sp; *pl.* señores], a Spanish title or form of address equivalent to *Sir* or *Mr.*, used with the family name (*abbr.* Sr. or Sor., *pl.* Srs. or Sres.): also, gentleman. —**Señor Don** [*fem.* Señora Doña], a Spanish title given to a gentleman, and prefixed to his full name: *abbr.* Sr. D., *fem.* Sra. D.ª. Cf. DON.

señora [Sp; *pl.* señoras], a Spanish title or form of address equivalent to *Madam* or *Mrs.* (*abbr.* S.ª *or* Sra.); also, lady; wife.

señorita [Sp; *pl.* señoritas], a Spanish title or form of address equivalent to *Miss* (*abbr.* Srta. *or* Sta.); also, young lady.

señorito [Sp], young gentleman; master (courtesy title).

se novim godom [Russ], happy new year!

sens dessus dessous [Fr], upside down; topsy-turvy.

sensé [Fr; *fem.* sensée], sensible; reasonable.

sensible [Fr], sensitive; impressible.

sensu bono [L], in a good sense.

sensu malo [L], in a bad sense.

sentir con los pocos, y hablar con los más [Sp], think with the few, speak with the many: *Gracián y Morales.*

senza [It], without: *abbr.* sen. —**senza organo,** without organ. —**senza replica,** without repetition. —**senza sordini,** without mutes; with the loud pedal. —**senza stromenti,** without instruments. —**senza tempo,** without strict time: *all music.*

separatio a mensa et toro [L], separation from bed and board; legal separation: *law.*

separatio a vinculo matrimonii [L], separation from the bond of marriage; divorce: *law.*

sepoy [Anglo-Ind; Hind & Pers *sepāhī*], an indigenous soldier; esp., an infantryman; indigenous policeman.

seppia [It], squid. Cf. CALAMARO.

seppuku [Jap]. Same as HARA-KIRI.

septetto [It], a composition for seven instruments or voices; septet: *music.*

septimana [L], a week.

sepultus [L], buried: *abbr.* S.

se queres aprender a orar, entra no mar [Pg], if you wish to learn how to pray, put to sea.

sequitur [L], lit., it follows; a logical inference: *abbr.* seq.

sequiturque patrem non passibus aequis [L], he follows his father, but not with equal steps: *Virgil* (said of Ascanius, little son of Aeneas).

sequor non inferior [L], I follow, but am not inferior.

sérac [Swiss Fr], a type of white cheese; a pinnacle of ice, formed by the crossing of crevasses in a glacier; hence, sérac ice, a field of wedged masses of icy pinnacles in broken confusion.

serai [Hind & Pers], resthouse for travelers; caravansary.

serape [Sp], Mexican blanket, with opening for the head, worn as an outer garment in place of an overcoat: *Sp. Am.*

serdab [Ar], lit., ice cellar; a secret chamber in an ancient Egyptian tomb, usually containing a statue of the deceased.

serein [Fr], a very fine rain, falling from a clear sky after sunset; evening mist.

seriatim [NL], serially; point by point; in regular order.

serón [Sp], pannier; hamper.

sero sapiunt Phryges [L], the Phrygians became wise too late.

sero sed serio [L], late, but seriously.

sero venientibus ossa [L], (only) the bones for those who come late; first come, first served.

serra [Pg], sierra; mountain range; saw.

serus in caelum redeas [L], late may you return to heaven; may you live long.

servabo fidem [L], I will keep faith.

serva iugum [L], preserve the yoke.

servare modum [L], to keep within bounds.

servata fides cineri [L], faithful to the memory of my ancestors.

servus [L; *pl.* servi], slave; serf; servant. —**Servus Servorum Dei,** Servant of the Servants of God: title of the Pope.

sesquipedalia verba [L], words a foot and a half long; very long words.

sestetto [It], a composition for six instruments or voices; sextet or sestet: *music.*

sestra [Russ], sister.

se tu segui tua stella, non puoi fallire al glorioso porto [It], if thou follow thy star, thou canst not miss the glorious haven: *Dante.*

seul à seul [Fr], alone; by oneself; in private.

se vi piace [It], if you like; as you please.

sforzando *or* **sforzato** [It], lit., forcing or forced; with emphasis; with additional accent (*abbr.* sf., sfz., *or* sforz.): *music.*

sfumato [It], lit., smoked; with indistinct outlines: said of a painting.

sgraffito [It; *pl.* sgraffiti], decoration of frescoes or pottery by scratching through an outer layer of stucco or plaster to show a different-colored ground; graffito decoration: *fine arts.*

shabash! [Hind], bravo! well done!

shadchen [Yiddish], marriage broker; matchmaker.

shahin *or* **shaheen** [Hind & Ar], Indian falcon.

shaitan [Hind & Ar], Satan; the Devil; an evil spirit; *colloq.,* a devilish person or animal.

shaktha [Beng], worshiper of Kali: *India.*

shalom [Heb], peace; hello; goodbye.

shaman [Russ], medicine man or priest in Siberian or North American Indian tribes.

shamianah *or* **shamiyanah** [Hind & Pers], awning; canopy; large tent, with open sides: *India.*

shammes [Yiddish], a caretaker of a synagogue.

sharab [Hind & Ar], wine; spirit: generic word.

shashlyk [Russ], kebob; shashlik.

shegetz [Yiddish; *pl.* shkotzim], non-Jewish boy. Cf. SHIKSA.

sheik [Ar *shaikh*], lit., old or venerable man; tribal leader.

sher [Hind & Pers; *fem.* sherni], tiger.

shereef *or* **sherif** [Ar], Muslim prince, chieftain, or high dignitary.

shibboleth [Heb], lit., a stream; a custom or use of language distinctive of a particular group; slogan.

shikar [Hind], hunting, esp. of big game; chase; also, game; booty.

shikari [Hind], indigenous hunter, esp. of big game; sportsman: *India.*

shikata ga nai [Jap], what's the use: expression of resignation; you can't fight city hall.

shikker [Yiddish], *n.* a drunk; *adj.* drunk.

shiksa [Yiddish], non-Jewish girl. Cf. SHEGETZ.

shintiyan [Ar *shintīān*], a type of loose trousers worn by Muslim women.

shizoku [Jap], the military or landed-gentry class of modern Japan, corresponding to the *Samurai;* the upper middle class, between the *kuwazoku* or nobles and the *heimin* or common people; also, a member of this class. Cf. SAMURAI.

shkola [Russ], school.

shlep [Yiddish], to carry or pull with effort; drag, move slowly; drag one's heels. **—shlepper** *or* **schlepper,** a person of no importance.

shlock [Yiddish], shoddy or defective merchandise.

shlump [Yiddish], a crude, careless, or unclean person; a slob.

shmaltz [Yiddish]. Same as SCHMALTZ.

shmendrik [Yiddish], a timid, ineffectual person; a fool.

shmooz [Yiddish], a long, friendly chat; also, a verb for intimately chatting.

shoji [Jap], slides of wood and paper, or of glass, enclosing a room in a Japanese house; movable partitions.

shtik [Yiddish], a part; piece; a performer's special piece of business; an attention-getting device; a devious trick.

sic [L], thus: put in brackets after a doubtful word or expression in a quoted passage to indicate that the original is being faithfully followed.

sic donec [L], thus until.

sic eunt fata hominum [L], thus go the destinies of men.

sic in originali [L], thus in the original.

sic iter ad astra [L], such is the way to the stars (i.e., to immortal fame): *Virgil.*

sic iubeo [L], so I order.

sic me servavit Apollo [L], thus Apollo preserved me: *Horace.*

si componere magnis parva mihi fas est [L], if I may be allowed to compare small things with great: *Ovid.*

sic passim [L], so everywhere; so here and there throughout.

sic semper tyrannis [L], ever thus to tyrants: motto of *Virginia.*

sic totidem verbis [L], thus in as many words.

sic transit gloria mundi [L], so passes away the glory of the world.

sicut ante [L], as before.

sicut meus est mos [L], as is my habit: *Horace.*

sicut patribus, sit Deus nobis [L], may God be with us as with our fathers: motto of *Boston, Mass.*

sic volo sic iubeo [L], thus I will, thus I command: *Juvenal.*

sic vos non vobis [L], thus do ye, but not for yourselves; you do the work but another takes the credit: *Virgil,* who wrote four incomplete lines beginning thus, as a challenge to Bathyllus to complete them, his rival having claimed authorship of an anonymous couplet written (by Virgil) on the palace door in honor of Augustus. Bathyllus failed to finish the lines. Virgil then supplied the remainder and established his title to the original couplet.

si Deus nobiscum, quis contua nos? [L], if God be with us, who shall be against us?

si Dieu n'existait pas, il faudrait l'inventer [Fr], if God did not exist, it would be necessary to invent him: *Voltaire.*

si Dieu veult [OF], if God so wills it.

si diis placet [L], if it pleases the gods.

siècle [Fr], century; age —**siècle d'or,** golden age (esp., the reign of Louis XIV). —**siècles des ténèbres,** the Dark Ages.

sierra [Sp], lit., saw; mountain range.

si fait! [Fr], yes, indeed!

si fortuna iuvat [L], if fortune favors.

signor [It], man of rank; gentleman; Italian title of address equivalent to *Mr.:* used before a man's name.

signora [It; *pl.* signore], an Italian title or form of address equivalent to *Madam* or *Mrs.;* also, a lady.

signor dell' altissimo canto [It], lord (*or* monarch) of the loftiest poetry: *Dante* (of Homer).

signore [It; *pl.* signori], an Italian title or form of address equivalent to *Sir* or *Mr.;* also, a gentleman.

signorina [It; *pl.* signorine], an Italian title or form of address equivalent to *Miss;* also, a young lady.

signorino [It; *pl.* signorini], young gentleman; master (courtesy title).

si je puis [Fr], if I can.

si jeunesse savait, si vieillesse pouvait [Fr], if youth but knew, if age but could.

sile et philosophus esto [L], be silent and be a philosopher; hold your tongue and you will pass for a philosopher.

silentium altum [L], deep silence.

silent leges inter arma [L], laws are silent in time of war: *Cicero.*

silla [Sp], chair; saddle; *geol.,* a rounded elevation.

s'il vous plaît [Fr], if you please: *abbr.* s.v.p.

simagrée [Fr], grimace; pretense; *pl.,* affected or lackadaisical manners; affectation.

simba [Swa], lion.

similia similibus curantar [L], like cures like.

similiter [L], in like manner.

si monumentum requiris, circumspice [L], if you seek his monument, look around: epitaph of *Sir Christopher Wren* in St. Paul's, London, of which he was the architect.

simpatico [It], sympathetic; congenial.

simpkin [Anglo-Ind], champagne: corr. of the English word.

simplex munditiis [L], plain in (thy) neatness; elegant in simplicity: *Horace.*

simpliciter [L], absolutely; without reserve.

sin [Russ; *pl.* sinovya], son.

sindhu [Beng], the sea: *India.*

sine [L], without. **—sine anno,** without the date: *abbr.* s.a. **—sine cortice natare,** to swim without corks; need no assistance. **—sine cruce, sine luce,** without the Cross, without light. **—sine cura,** without obligation or care (i.e., without the responsibilities of office, but with the benefits). **—sine die,** without a day being appointed (i.e., indefinitely adjourned): *abbr.* s.d. **—sine dubio,** without doubt. **—sine ictu,** without a blow. **—sine invidia,** without envy. **—sine ioco,** without jesting; seriously. **—sine ira et studio,** without anger and without partiality. **—sine loco, anno, vel nomine,** without place, year, or name: *abbr.* s.l.a.n. **—sine loco et anno,** without place and year: said of books without imprint and date of publication. **—sine legitima prole,** without lawful issue; *abbr.* s.l.p. **—sine mascula prole,** without male issue: *law.* **—sine mora,** without delay. **—sine nervis,** without strength (*or* force); weak. **—sine nomine,** without name; *abbr.* s.n. **—sine odio,** without hatred.

—sine omni periculo, without any danger. **—sine praeiudicio,** without prejudice. **—sine proba causa,** without approved cause. **--sine prole,** without issue (*or* offspring): *abbr.* s.p. **—sine qua non,** lit., without which not; an indispensable condition; a necessity.

sinfonia [It; *pl.* sinfonie], symphony: *music.*

singe [Fr], monkey; *Fr. mil. slang,* canned beef; canned meat.

singerie [Fr], apishness; grimaces; apish tricks; mimicry; affected ways.

singillatim *or* **singulatim** [L], one by one; singly.

Singspiel [Ger], operetta with spoken dialogue; a dramatic representation with incidental music.

sinistra manu [L], with the left hand.

sino [It], to; as far as. **—sino al segno,** to the sign: *both music.*

si parla italiano [It], Italian spoken (here).

si parva licet componere magnis [L], if it be allowable to compare small things with great: *Virgil.*

si peccavi, insciens feci [L], if I have sinned, I have done so unwittingly: *Terence.*

si piace [It], at pleasure.

si quaeris peninsulam amoenam, circumspice [L], if thou seekest a beautiful peninsula, look around: motto of *Michigan.*

si quieres el huevo, sufre la gallina [Sp], if you want the egg, bear with the hen.

si quis [L], if anyone.

sirocco [It], hot, humid wind: *Southern Italy & Mediterranean.*

si sic omnes! [L], if all (did) thus!

si sit prudentia [L], if there be prudence.

siste, viator! [L], stop, traveler!

sit pro ratione voluntas [L], let will stand for reason: *Juvenal.*

sit tibi terra levis [L], may the earth lie lightly upon thee.

sit ut est, aut non sit [L], let it be as it is, or let it not be.

sit venia verbis [L], pardon my words.

si vis amari ama [L], if you wish to be loved, love: *Seneca.*

si vis pacem, para bellum [L], if you desire peace, prepare for war.

sjambok [Afrik], heavy leather whip: *South Africa.*

skazhee mnye kto tvoi droog, ee ya skazhoo kto tee [Russ], tell me who your friend is, and I'll tell you who you are.

σκιᾶς ὄναρ [Gr; skiâs ónar], the dream of a shadow: said of anything fleeting or unreal. **—σκιᾶς ὄναρ ἄνθρωποι** [skiâs ónar ánthropoi], men are the dream of a shadow: *Pindar.*

slāinte [Gael], to your health.

slalom [Norw], lit., sloping path; zigzag skiing.

slava bogoo [Russ], thank God!

smaniantate [It], furious; passionate: *music.*

smert' za vorotami ne zhdet [Russ], death keeps no calendar.

smorzando *or* **smorzanto** [It], dying away (*abbr.* smorz.): *music.*

soavemente [It], sweetly; gently; tenderly: *music*.

sobriquet [Fr], nickname; assumed name.

Sociedad Anónima [Sp], impersonal partnership; joint stock company; corporation: *abbr*. S.A.

Sociedad en Comandita [Sp], limited partnership: *abbr*. S. en C.

société [Fr], society; company. —**société anonyme,** joint stock company. —**société de commerce,** trading company. —**société en commandite,** limited liability company, consisting of acting and silent partners. See COMMANDITE.

socius criminis [L], partner in crime.

so du mir, so ich dir [Ger], as thou me, so I thee; measure for measure.

sogenannt [Ger], so-called; would-be: *abbr*. sog.

soggetto [It; *pl*. soggetti], subject; theme: *music*.

sogleich [Ger], immediately; coming! (said in reply to a call).

so Gott will [Ger], please God.

soi-disant [Fr], self-styled; pretended; would-be.

soigné [Fr; *fem*. soignée], carefully done; highly finished; elegantly simple (as a dress); well-groomed.

Sokol [Bohem], lit., falcon; Czechoslovak gymnastic society; also, one of its members.

sola iuvat virtus [L], virtue alone assists one.

solano [Sp], a hot, easterly wind.

sola nobilitas virtus [L], virtue alone is true nobility.

sola salus servire Deo [L], our only safety is in serving God.

sola topi [Anglo-Ind], sun helmet, made from the pith (*sola*) of an East Indian plant: sometimes incorrectly written *solar topi*.

sola virtus invicta [L], virtue alone is invincible.

soldado [It & Sp], soldier.

soldato, acqua, e fuoco, presto si fan luoco [It], soldier, water, and fire soon make room for themselves.

solem quis dicere falsum audeat? [L], who would dare to call the sun a liar?: *Virgil*.

solfatara [It], lit., sulfur mine; a volcanic region in which vapors and sulfurous gases escape through various vents.

solfeggio [It; *pl*. solfeggi], sol-fa singing exercise; solmization: *music*.

soli Deo gloria [L], to God alone be glory.

solitudinem faciunt, pacem appellant [L], they make a solitude and call it peace; they crush the rebellion by putting the populace to the sword: *Tacitus*.

sol lucet omnibus [L], the sun shines on all; everyone is entitled to enjoy certain natural advantages.

Soll und Haben [Ger], debit and credit.

solus [L; *fem*. sola], alone: used in stage directions.

solventur risu tabulae [L], the bills (of indictment) are dismissed with laughter; the case breaks down and you are laughed out of court: *Horace.*

solvitur ambulando [L], it is solved by walking; the problem is settled by action (i.e., the theoretical by the practical).

son [Sp], a Latin American dance.

sonatina [It], short sonata: *music.*

songe-creux [Fr], dreamer; visionary.

sono maggiori gli spaventi che i mali [It], fears are greater than the evils feared.

son saint frusquin [Fr], lit., one's blessed toggery; one's all: *colloq.*

Sopherim [Heb], Jewish scribes or teachers of the law.

sopra [It], above. **—come sopra,** as above.

sordamente [It], in a muffled manner; softly: *music.*

sordino [It; *pl.* sordini], a mute (as for a violin).

sordo [It], muted; muffled: *music.*

sortes Virgilianae [L], divination by the random selection of passages from Virgil.

sospirando *or* **sospirante** [It], sighing; longing: *music.*

sospiroso [It], sighing; doleful: *music.*

sostenuto [It], sustained; in a sustained manner (*abbr.* sos. *or* sost.): *music.*

sot à triple étage [Fr], lit., fool to the third story; a consummate fool.

sotnia [Russ *sotnya*], lit., a hundred; a squadron of a Cossack cavalry regiment.

sotol [Mex], a Mexican yuccalike plant of the genus *Dasylirion,* from which an intoxicating drink is distilled; also, the drink itself: *Mexico & southwestern U.S.* Cf. MESCAL and TEQUILA.

sottise [Fr], silliness; foolishness; something stupid or foolish.

sotto la bianca cenere, sta la brace ardente [It], under the white ash, the glowing embers lie.

sotto voce [It], in an undertone.

soubrette [Fr], waiting-maid, esp. an intriguing, coquettish, and meddlesome maid in a comedy: *theat.*

soufflée [Fr], lit., puffed; made light and fluffy, usually by including well-whipped whites of eggs; as omelette *soufflée;* also, a delicate dish made in this manner: *cookery.*

souffleur [Fr], lit., blower (*or* whisperer); prompter: *theat.*

soupçon [Fr], a suspicion; minute quantity; a mere trace or dash; a taste.

soupe [Fr], soup; broth. **—soupe de l'Inde,** mulligatawny soup. **—soupe grasse,** meat soup. **—soupe maigre,** a thin vegetable soup.

souper [Fr], supper.

soupir [Fr], a sigh; breath; *music,* crotchet rest.

sous tous les rapports [Fr], in all respects.

soutache [Fr], a kind of narrow braid.

soutane [Fr], a cassock.

sowar [Anglo-Ind *sawar*], cavalryman; trooper; orderly.

soyez ferme [Fr], be firm; be staunch.

spahi [Fr], formerly, an indigenous cavalryman of the French army in Algeria.

spakonoi nochee [Russ], good night.

Sparen bringt Haben [Ger], saving brings having; a penny saved is a penny earned.

spargere voces in vulgum ambiguas [L], to spread equivocal rumor among the multitude: *Virgil.*

spasiba [Russ], thank you.

speciali gratia [L], by special favor.

spectemur agendo [L], let us be judged by our actions.

spem pretio non emo [L], I do not give money for mere hopes: *Terence.*

sperat infestis, metuit secundis [L], he hopes in adversity, and fears in prosperity: *Horace.*

speravi [L], I have hoped.

spero meliora [L], I hope for better things: *Cicero.*

spes [L], hope. —**spes bona,** good hope: motto of former *Cape Colony.* —**spes gregis,** the hope of the flock: *Virgil.* —**spes mea Christus,** Christ is my hope. —**spes mea in Deo,** my hope is in God. —**spes sibi quisque,** let each be a hope unto himself; each must rely upon himself alone: *Virgil.* —**spes tutissima coelis,** the safest hope is in heaven.

spianato [It], lit., leveled; even; smooth: *music.*

spiccato [It], distinctly detached; half-staccato (a direction for bowing): *music.*

spirito [It], spirit; fire: *music.*

spiritoso [It], spiritedly; with spirit: *music.*

spirituel [Fr; *fem.* spirituelle], lit., spiritual; ethereal; intellectual; witty; *fem.,* designating a woman of grace, charm, and delicacy of mind.

spiritus [L], spirit; a breathing; aspirate. —**spiritus asper,** rough breathing: *Gr. gram.* —**spiritus lenis,** smooth breathing: *Gr. gram.*

splendide mendax [L], nobly mendacious; untruthful for a good object: *Horace.*

spolia opima [L], the richest spoils; the arms stripped from a defeated commander, in single combat; hence, supreme achievement.

sponte sua [L], of one's own accord; unsolicited.

sportula [L; *pl.* sportulae], lit., small basket; the basket in which ancient Romans placed provisions, or an equivalent in money, donated to their clients and dependents; hence, gratuity; largess; present.

spretae iniuria formae [L], the insult to her slighted beauty: *Virgil.*

sputnik [Russ], lit., co-traveler; satellite.

Stabat Mater [L], lit., the Mother was standing; Latin hymn, or its musical setting, inspired by the sufferings of the Holy Mother at the Crucifixion.

staccato [It], detached; disconnected (opposite of *legato*): *music*.

Stadt [Ger; *pl*. Städte], town; city.

Staffage [Ger], figures in a landscape; subordinate additions in a work of art; decorative accessories.

staffetta [It], courier; express messenger.

stakhanovite [*fr*. Russ], a worker who exceeds production norms: *fr*. Alexei G. Stakhanov, a Russian miner.

stanitza *or* **stanitsa** [Russ], herd; flock; Cossack village.

stans pede in uno [L], standing on one foot (i.e., standing in an oratorical position with the weight on one foot): *Horace*.

stare super antiquas vias [L], to stand on the old paths.

starets [Russ; *pl*. startsy], a holy man; spiritual adviser.

state zitto [It], be quiet; hold your tongue.

stat fortuna domus virtute [L], the fortune of the house stands by its virtue.

statim [L], immediately; at once.

stat magni nominis umbra [L], he stands, the shadow of a great name.

stat promissa fides [L], the promised faith remains.

stat pro ratione voluntas [L], will stands for reason.

status quo *or* **status in quo** [L], the state in which (anything is); existing conditions; unchanged position.

status quo ante bellum [L], the state (condition) existing before the war.

sta, viator, heroem calcas [L], stop, traveler, you tread on a hero's dust.

stemmata quid faciunt [L], what do pedigrees avail? what is the use of long pedigrees?: *Juvenal*.

steppe [Russ *step'*], great grassy plain.

στέργει γὰρ οὐδεὶς ἄγγελον κακῶν ἐπῶν [Gr; stérgei gàr oudeìs ággelon kakôn epôn], no one loves the bearer of bad news: *Sophocles*.

stesso [It], the same: *music*.

stet [L], let it stand: *editor's mark*.

stet fortuna domus! [L], may the fortune of the house endure!

stet pro ratione voluntas [L], let my will stand as a reason.

stets ist die Sprache kecker als die Tat [Ger], speech is even bolder than deed.

Steuer [Ger; *pl*. Steuern], tax; rate; impost; duty.

stiacciato [It], very low relief, as on coins: *sculp*.

stille Woche [Ger], Passion Week.

stinguendo [It], dying away: *music*.

stoep [Du], covered porch or veranda; stoop: *South Africa*.

stoomboot [Du; *pl*. stoombooten], steamer; steamboat.

Storting [Norw], Norwegian legislature.

strada [It], street.

straná [Russ], land; country; region.

Strasse [Ger], street.

stratum super stratum [L], layer upon layer.

strenua inertia [L], energetic idleness; masterly inactivity: *Horace* (adapted).

strepitoso [It], noisy; loud; impetuous: *music*.

stretto [It; *pl.* stretti], strait; in a fugue, the part where the subject and answer overlap; in an opera or oratorio, a quickening of the tempo at the end of a movement: *music*.

stricto sensu [L], in a strict sense: opposite of *lato sensu*.

strictum ius [L], strict law; the strict letter of the law.

stringendo [It], in accelerated time: *music*.

stromenti [It], instruments. —**stromenti da arco,** bow instruments; strings. —**stromenti da fiato,** wind instruments. —**stromenti da percossa,** percussion instruments. —**stromenti da tasto,** keyboard instruments. —**stromenti di corda,** string instruments: *all music*.

Stube [Ger; *pl.* Stuben], room; sitting room. —**Stubenleben,** sedentary life. —**Bierstube,** beerhall. —**Weinstube,** wine room in a tavern; wine shop.

Stück [Ger; *pl.* Stücke], a piece.

Stückchen [Ger], a little piece; scrap; *music,* air.

studiis et rebus honestis [L], by honorable pursuits and studies.

studium immane loquendi [L], an insatiable need for talking: *Ovid* (adapted).

stupa [Skr], Buddhist monument or shrine; a tope.

Sturm und Drang [Ger], storm and stress; a period of revolt and unrest, esp. in German literature, during the latter part of the 18th century.

sua cuique sunt vitia [L], every man has his own vices.

sua cuique utilitas [L], to everything its own use: *Tacitus*.

sua cuique voluptas [L], every man has his own pleasures.

sua munera mittit cum hamo [L], he sends his gifts with a hook attached; a sprat to catch a mackerel.

suave mari magno [L], how pleasant (when) on the great sea... (beginning of the verse *Suave mari magno turbantibus aequora ventis, E terra magnum alterius spectare laborem!,* How pleasant when, on the vast deep, the winds have lashed the waters into billows, to witness—from the land—the perils of another!): *Lucretius*.

suaviter et fortiter [L], gently and firmly.

suaviter in modo, fortiter in re [L], gentle in manner, resolute in deed.

subahdar [Hind & Pers], orig., governor of a province; viceroy; in an Indian regiment, a native officer corresponding to a captain: *India*.

subaudi [L], supply (implied word or words) by means of subaudition; read between the lines; understand: *abbr.* sub.

sub colore iuris [L], under color of law.

sub cruce candida [L], under the pure white Cross.

sub cruce salus [L], salvation under the Cross.

sub dio (*or* **divo**) [L], under the open sky; in the open air. Cf. SUB IOVE.

sub ferula [L], under the rod.

sub hoc signo vinces [L], under this sign thou shalt conquer. See IN HOC SIGNO VINCES.

sub initio [L], at the beginning.

sub Iove [L], lit., under Jupiter; in the open air. Cf. SUB DIO. —**sub Iove frigido,** under cold Jupiter; under the cold sky.

subitamente [It], suddenly; at once: *music.*

subito [It], quickly; immediately; in haste: *music.*

sub iudice [L], before the judge (*or* court); under judicial consideration.

sublata causa, tollitur effectus [L], when the cause is removed the effect is removed.

sub lege libertas [L], liberty under the law.

sublimi feriam sidera vertice [L], with head uplifted I shall strike the stars: *Horace.*

sub modo [L], in a qualified sense.

sub poena [L], under penalty.

sub rosa [L], under the rose; confidentially.

sub sigillo [L], under seal (of confession); in the strictest confidence.

sub silentio [L], in silence; privately.

sub specie [L], under the appearance of. —**sub specie aeternitatis,** under the aspect of eternity: *Spinoza.*

sub spe rati [L], in the hope of a decision.

sub tegmine fagi [L], beneath the canopy of the spreading beech: *Virgil.*

sub voce *or* **sub verbo** [L], under the word (in reference to dictionaries, etc.): *abbr.* s.v.

succès d'estime [Fr], lit., success of esteem; success with more honor than profit, as of a play.

sucre [Fr], sugar. —**sucre en morceaux,** sugar cubes.

su cuenta [Sp], your account: *abbr.* s/c.

sudadero [Sp], lit., a sweating-place; a crack or fissure in a well or water tank, through which water is escaping: *southwestern U.S.*

sudarka *or* **sudarushka** [Russ], sweetheart; mistress.

suerte [Sp], lit., chance or lot; formerly a portion of land (about 27 acres) for which settlers drew lots; now, any small lot: *southwestern U.S.* —**suerte está echada,** the die is cast.

sufficit [L; *pl.* sufficiunt], it is enough.

suggestio falsi [L], suggestion of a falsehood; indirect lie; misrepresentation. Cf. SUPPRESSIO VERI SUGGESTIO FALSI.

sui generis [L], of its (his, her, or their) own kind; in a class by itself; unique.

sui iuris [L], in one's own right; of full legal capacity: *law.*

suisse [Fr; *fem.* suissesse], native of Switzerland; Swiss; also, head porter, as of a mansion.

suis stat viribus [L], he stands by his own strength.

suivante [Fr], waiting woman or maid; lady's maid.

suivez [Fr], follow; a direction to the accompanist to follow the soloist: *music.* —**suivez raison,** follow reason.

suivre son penchant [Fr], to follow one's bent.

sujet [Fr], subject; individual; reason; topic. —**mauvais sujet,** worthless fellow; scamp; black sheep. —**sujet maigre,** barren subject.

σύκινη μάχαιρα [Gr; súkinē mákhaira], a sword of fig wood; fig., a weak and ineffective argument.

sukiyaki [Jap], dish of sliced meat, soybean curd, and vegetables, all cooked together in a broth of soy sauce, sake, and sugar.

summa cum laude [L], with the highest praise (*or* distinction): used esp. in a diploma to designate work of the highest merit.

summa petit livor [L], it is the highest (*or* noblest) things that envy assails: *Ovid.*

summa summarum [L], the sum of sums; the sum of all things.

summo studio [L], with the greatest zeal: *Cicero.*

summum bonum [L], the supreme good.

summum genus [L; *pl.* summa genera], the highest genus: *logic.*

summum ius [L], the highest law (i.e., strict law as distinguished from equity): *law.* —**summum ius, summa iniuria,** the highest law, the highest injustice; the rigor (*or* strict enforcement) of the law may be the height of injustice: *Cicero* (adapted).

sumo [Jap]. Same as SAMO.

sumptibus publicis [L], at public expense.

συναγάγετε τὰ περισσεύσαντε κλάσματα [Gr; sunagágete tà perisseúsante klásmata], gather up the fragments that remain: *John* vi. 12.

sunt bona, sunt quaedam mediocria, sunt mala plura [L], some things are good, some middling, but more are bad: *Martial.*

sunt lacrimae rerum, et mentem mortalia tangunt [L], here are tears for human things (*or* sufferings) and mortal woes touch the heart; "the sense of tears in mortal things": *Virgil* (tr. Matthew Arnold).

sunyasî [Anglo-Ind]. Same as SANNYASI.

suo iure [L], in one's own right.

suo loco [L], in its proper place.

suo Marte [L], by one's own prowess (*or* exertions).

suo periculo [L], at his (*or* one's) own peril.

supari [Hind], areca nut; betel nut. Cf. PANSUPARI.

supercherie [Fr], deception; hoax; fraud; as, literary *supercherie.*

superstitione tollenda religio non tollitur [L], religion is not got rid of by eliminating superstition: *Cicero.*

suppressio veri [L], a suppression of the truth; concealment of facts. —**suppressio veri suggestio falsi,** suppression of the truth is suggestion of falsehood.

supra [L], above; beyond; before; formerly: *abbr.* sup. —**supra vires,** beyond one's powers.

sura *or* **surah** [Ar], a chapter of the Koran, of which there are 114: *Islam.* Cf. FATIHAH.

sûrement va qui n'a rien [Fr], he goes surely (*or* safely) who has nothing to lose.

sur espérance [Fr], in hope.

surgit amari aliquid [L], something bitter rises; no joy without alloy: *Lucretius.*

sur-le-champ [Fr], lit., on the field; immediately.

sur le tapis [Fr], on the carpet; under discussion or consideration.

sursum corda [L], lift up your hearts.

surtout [Fr], above all; especially; chiefly. —**surtout, messieurs, pas de zèle,** above all, gentlemen, no zeal: *Talleyrand* (advice to his subordinates).

su seguro servidor [Sp], your faithful servant; yours truly: *abbr.* s.s.s. *or* S.S.S.

sushi [Jap], a dish of thinly sliced raw fish and cooked rice served with soy sauce and vegetables.

suspendens omnia naso [L], turning up the nose at everything; sneering at everything: *Horace.*

suspensio per collum [L], lit., suspension by the neck; execution by hanging: *abbr.* sus. per col.

suspiria de profundis [L], sighs from the depths (of the soul).

Süsschen [Ger], sweetmeat; also, sweetheart; darling.

sussurrando *or* **sussurrante** [It], murmuring; whispering: *music.*

sutor, ne supra crepidam [L], cobbler, stick to your last. See NE SUTOR SUPRA CREPIDAM.

suttee [Anglo-Ind; Hind *satī*, faithful wife], the Hindu custom of a widow's sacrifice of herself on the funeral pyre of her husband; also, a woman who does this.

suum cuique [L], to each his own.

suus cuique mos [L], everyone has his own custom (*or* particular habit).

svegliato [It], sprightly; in a sprightly manner; briskly: *music.*

svelte [Fr], slender; slim; supple; lissome: said of the female figure.

Swadeshi [Hind], lit., (of) own country; designating a nationalist movement for the promotion and exclusive use of native manufactures and the boycott of foreign, esp. British, goods: *India.*

Swami [Skr], lit., master; a religious teacher; mystic.

Swaraj [Skr], self-government; home rule: *India.*

syce [Anglo-Ind; Hind *sāis*], a groom.

szálloda [Hung], hotel.

T

tabac *or* **tabac à fumer** [Fr], tobacco; smoking tobacco.

tabatière [Fr], snuff box.

tabi [Jap], a thick-soled sock with a division for the big toe, for convenience in wearing a Japanese sandal. —**tabi issoku,** a pair of socks.

tabla [Hind], a small hand-drum.

table [Fr], table. —**table à manger,** dining table. —**table d'hôte** [*pl.* tables d'hôte], lit., host's table; a common table for guests at a hotel; a meal at a fixed hour and price: distinguished from *à la carte.*

tableau vivant [Fr; *pl.* tableaux vivants], living picture.

tablier [Fr], apron or pinafore; also, an apronlike part of a woman's dress.

taboo [Tongan & Polynesian; also spelled *tabu* and *tapu*], a prohibition of an act or use of an article.

tabula rasa [L; *pl.* tabulae rasae], an erased (*or* blank) tablet; clean slate; fig., the mind at birth.

tace! [L], be silent!

tacent; satis laudant [L], their silence is praise enough: *Terence.*

tacet [L], lit., it is silent; a direction indicating silence of a part through a particular movement: *music.*

tache [Fr], spot; stain; blotch; freckle. —**tache de naissance,** birthmark; mole.

tâche [Fr], task; job. —**à la tâche,** by the job.

tâcheron [Fr], piece worker; workman employed by the job.

tacitum vivit sub pectore vulnus [L], the wound unuttered lives deep within the breast: *Virgil.*

tack för maten [Sw], thanks for the food (said after eating).

taedium vitae [L], weariness of life.

Tageblatt [Ger; *pl.* -blätter], daily paper.

tai chi chuan [Chin], Chinese unarmed combat.

taihoa [Maori], by and by; presently: *New Zealand.*

taille écrasé [Fr], a squat figure.

tailleur [Fr; *fem.* tailleuse], tailor; cutter; *in card games,* dealer.

tais-toi *or* **taisez-vous** [Fr], hold your tongue! be silent! be quiet!

tajo [Sp], lit., a cut or incision; trench for the collection of water in a dry season: *southwestern U.S.*

taka-makiye [Jap], Japanese raised lacquer.

tak for mad [Dan], thanks for the food (said after eating).

takk for maten [Norw], thanks for the food (said after eating).

Tal [Ger; *pl.* Täler], valley; vale; glen.

talis qualis [L], such as it is.

talmouse [Fr], *cookery*, a kind of cheesecake; *colloq.*, a slap; whack.

tal padrone, tal servitore [It], like master, like man.

tal para cual [Sp], tit for tat.

Talweg [Ger], lit., valley way; road through (*or* along) a valley.

tamale *or* **tamal** [Mex Sp; *pl.* tamales], a Mexican dish of corn and chopped meat seasoned with red peppers.

tamasha [Hind], entertainment; spectacle; show; fête: *India.*

tam charosho g'dje nas nyet [Russ], lit., there is good where we are not; someplace else is always better.

tam Marte quam Minerva [L], as much by Mars as by Minerva; as much by war as by wisdom.

tandem fit surculus arbor [L], a shoot at length becomes a tree.

tangere ulcus [L], to touch the sore (*or* sore spot): *Terence.*

Tannenbaum [Ger], pine tree; Christmas tree.

tantae molis erat [L], so vast a work it was; so great was the difficulty of the enterprise: *Virgil.*

tantaene animis caelestibus irae? [L], can wrath so great dwell in heavenly minds?: *Virgil.*

tantas componere lites [L], to settle such great disputes.

tante [Fr], aunt; also, pawnbroker.

tant mieux [Fr], so much the better.

tanto [It], so much; as much: *music.* —**allegro non tanto,** lively, but not too quick: *music.* —**tanto buono che val niente,** so good that it's good for nothing. —**tanto a quanto,** ever so little.

tant pis [Fr], so much the worse.

tant s'en faut [Fr], lit., so much is wanting; far from it.

tant soit peu [Fr], ever so little.

Tantum Ergo [L], lit., so great, therefore; a Eucharistic hymn: *R.C.Ch.*

tantum quantum [L], just as much as (is required).

tantus amor scribendi [L], such a passion for writing: *Horace.*

tao [Chin], the way; the road; the philosophy of Taoism.

tapadera *or* **tapadero** [Sp], lit., lid or cover; a leather guard or hood covering each of the stirrups of a Mexican saddle.

tapage [Fr], uproar; noise; racket; also, flashy display.

tapageur [Fr], noisy fellow.

tápalo [Mex Sp], a scarf or shawl made of a coarse material.

tapotement [Fr], tapping rapidly with the tips of the fingers in massage.

tarantella [It], a Neapolitan dance.

tardamente [It], slowly; lingeringly: *music.*

tardando [It], lingering; gradually slackening the pace: *music.*

tartane [Fr], one-masted coasting vessel, with lateen sail, used in the Mediterranean; tartan.

tartine [Fr], slice of bread, spread with butter or jam; fig., long, tedious speech or article.

tartufe [Fr], hypocrite.

τὰ σῦκα σῦκα, τὴν σκάφην σκάφην λέγειν [Gr; tà sûka sûka, tèn skáphēn skáphēn légein], lit., to call figs figs and a tub a tub; call a spade a spade.

Taubenpost [Ger], pigeon post; conveyance of letters by carrier pigeon.

Tausch ist kein Raub [Ger], exchange is no robbery.

Täuschung [Ger], deception; fraud; illusion; disappointment.

taz a taz [Sp], tit for tat.

tazza [It; *pl.* tazze], a large, saucer-shaped cup or vase, esp. one mounted on a pedestal.

teatro [Sp], theater.

tedesco [It; *pl.* tedeschi], *adj. & n.* German: used esp. of art. **—tedesco furor,** German fury; the wild impetuosity of the Germans: *Petrarch.*

Te Deum Laudamus [L], We praise thee, O God; an ancient hymn, of unknown authorship.

teeshi yedesh, dolshe budish [Russ], lit., the slower you go, the farther you go; more haste, less speed.

te hominem esse memento [L], remember thou art a man.

te huis [Du], at home.

Te Igitur [L], lit., thee therefore; first part of the eucharistic canon in the Latin liturgy: *eccl.*

te iudice [L], you being the judge; in your judgment.

tekel, upharsin [Aram], thou art weighed in the balances and art found wanting; thy kingdom is divided: *Daniel* v. 25. See MENE, MENE, TEKEL, UPHARSIN.

telega [Russ *telyega*], a Russian four-wheeled springless wagon.

tel est notre bon plaisir [Fr], such is our good pleasure.

tel maître, tel valet [Fr], like master, like man.

tel père, tel fils [Fr], like father, like son.

tel qui rit vendredi dimanche pleurera [Fr], he who laughs on Friday will weep on Sunday; laugh today and cry tomorrow (i.e., laughter is akin to tears): *Racine.*

telum imbelle sine ictu [L], a feeble spear (thrown) without effect; hence, a weak and ineffectual argument: *Virgil.*

tema [Sp], theme; subject.

témoin [Fr], witness.

tempi passati [It], times past, bygone days.

tempo [It], time. **—tempo commodo** (*or* **comodo**), in moderate time. **—tempo di ballo,** in dance time. **—tempo di marcia,** in march time. **—tempo di menuetto,** in minuet time. **—tempo giusto,** in correct time. **—tempo primo,** first time; in the time of the original movement. **—tempo rubato,** lit., stolen time; the lengthening of some notes at the expense of others: *all music.*

tempora mutantur nos et mutamur in illis [L], the times are changed, and we are changed with them.

tempori parendum [L], one must yield to (*or* move with) the times.

tempura *or* **tenpura** [Jap], lit., fried food; shrimps fried in oil.

tempus [L], time. —**tempus anima rei,** time is the soul of the business; time is the essence of the contract. —**tempus edax rerum,** time, the devourer of all things: *Ovid.* —**tempus fugit,** time flies: *Virgil.* —**tempus in ultimum,** to the last extremity. —**tempus ludendi,** the time for play. —**tempus omnia revelat,** time reveals (*or* uncovers) all things. —**tempus rerum imperator,** time is sovereign over all things.

tena koe? [Maori], how do you do?: *New Zealand.*

tenax et fidelis [L], steadfast and faithful.

tenax propositi [L], tenacious (*or* firm) of purpose.

teneramente [It], tenderly: *music.*

tener es temer [Sp], to have is to fear: *Ramón de Campoamor.*

tenerezza [It], tenderness: *music.*

tener l'anima co' denti [It], to hold the soul with the teeth; be at the last gasp.

tenez! [Fr], hold! take it! look! look here! listen! one moment! (a word expressing astonishment or calling attention). —**tenez bon!,** hold! hold out! hold fast! stick to it!

tenez cela pour fait [Fr], consider it done.

tenore [It; *pl.* tenori], tenor. —**tenore buffo,** a tenor who sings comic parts. —**tenore leggiero,** a light tenor. —**tenore robusto,** a powerful tenor: *all music.*

tentanda via est [L], the way must be tried: *Virgil.*

tenuto [It], held; sustained (*abbr.* ten.): *music.*

tepee [Dakota *tipi*], a round tent made of skins.

tequila [Sp], a Mexican alcoholic drink distilled from the maguey or other *mescal*-yielding plant.

ter [L], thrice; three times.

tera [Jap], Buddhist temple: *Japan,* usually prefixed by "o" when said.

teres atque rotundus [L], smooth-polished and rounded (i.e., perfect and round as a ball); a man polished and complete: *Horace.*

terminus ad quem [L], the end (*or* limit) to which; finishing point; point of destination.

terminus ante quem [L], lit., point (in time) before which; established time or date before which an event must have occurred.

terminus a quo [L], the end (*or* limit) from which; starting point.

terminus post quem [L], lit., point (in time) after which; established time or date after which an event must have occurred.

ter quaterque beatus [L], thrice and four times blessed: *Virgil.*

terra [L], the earth; earth; soil. —**terra es, terram ibis,** dust thou art, unto dust shalt thou return: *Vulgate (Genesis* iii. 19). —**terra firma,** solid earth; dry land; a firm footing. —**terra incognita** [*pl.* terrae incognitae], an unknown land; a region or subject of which nothing is known.

terrae filius [L; *pl.* terrae filii], son of the soil; man of lowly birth.

terrine de foie gras [Fr], goose liver cooked in earthenware.

Tersanctus [L], lit., thrice holy; holy, holy, holy; the Trisagion.

tertium quid [L], a third something; something intermediate, as between mind and matter.

terza rima [It; *pl.* terze rime], lit., a third or triple rhyme; arrangement of interlocked triplets, as in Dante's *Divina Commedia*.

terzetto [It], a trio, esp. a vocal one: *music*.

tessitura [It], lit., texture; weaving; the compass embraced by the majority of tones, esp. in a vocal composition: *music*.

teste [L], by the evidence (of); witness: *law*.

tête [Fr], head. —**tête baissée,** lit., head lowered; headlong; precipitately. —**tête carrée,** lit., square head; a German: *Fr. slang*. —**tête de veau,** calf's head. —**tête exaltée,** overexcited; overelated. —**tête montée,** excited.

tête-à-tête [Fr], *n.* lit., head to head; a private conversation or interview; also, a settee for two; *adj.* private; confidential; *adv.* privately; confidentially. —**en tête-à-tête,** face to face; in private.

tête-de-pont [Fr; *pl.* têtes-de-pont], bridgehead: *mil.*

tetigisti acu [L], you have touched it with a needle; you have hit the nail on the head: *Plautus*.

Teufel [Ger], devil.

textus receptus [L], the received text: *abbr.* text. rec.

thag [Hind; *pr.* t'hŭg], a garroter; highwayman; thug.

thakur [Hind], orig., a deity or idol; man of rank or authority; Rajput chief.

thakurdwara [Hind], Hindu temple: *India*.

θάλαττα! θάλαττα! [Gr; thálatta! thálatta!], the sea! the sea!: *Xenophon*.

θάρσει, ἔγειρε, φωνεῖ σε [Gr; thársei, égeire, phōneî se], be of good cheer, rise, he calleth thee: *Mark* x. 49.

thé dansant [Fr], lit., tea dancing; a tea at which there is dancing.

θεῶν ἐν γούνασι κεῖται [Gr; theôn en goúnasi keîtai], it lies on the knees of the gods: *Homer*.

θεὸς ἐκ μηχανῆς [Gr; theòs ek mēkhanês], a god from the machine: *Lucian*. See DEUS EX MACHINA.

Thermidor *or* **Fervidor** [Fr], in the Revolutionary calendar of the first French Republic, the eleventh month of the year, from July 19 to Aug. 17.

thon [Fr], tuna.

tibi seris, tibi metis [L], you sow for yourself, you reap for yourself; as you sow, so shall you reap: *Cicero*.

tidama [Wolof], goodbye: *West Africa*.

tienda [Sp], tent; awning; hence, booth; shop.

tiene el miedo muchos ojos [Sp], fear has many eyes.

tiens! [Fr], same as TENEZ! also, hello! indeed! to be sure! —**tiens! tiens!,** really! you don't say so! —**un tiens vaut deux tu l'auras,** one here-it-is is worth two you-will-have-its.

tiens à la vérité [Fr], stick to (*or* maintain) the truth.

tiens à ta foy [OF], hold to (*or* keep) thy faith.

Tiergarten [Ger], game preserve; zoological garden.

tierras [Sp], lands; particles of earth or rock containing ore: *mining.*

tiers état [Fr], the third estate; the common people or *bourgeoisie,* as distinguished from the nobility and clergy in France before the Revolution.

tige [Fr], trunk; shank; shaft, as of a column; *bot.,* stalk; stem.

τίκτει τὸ κόρος ὕβριν [Gr; tíktei tò kóros húbrin], satiety begets (*or* breeds) insolence: *Theognis.*

tilak [Hind], Hindu caste mark: *India.*

timbale [Fr], kettledrum; *cookery,* a mold shaped like a kettledrum; hence, a seasoned dish prepared in such a mold.

timbre [Fr], quality of tone; tone color: *music.*

timbre-poste [Fr; *pl.* timbres-poste], postage stamp: *abbr.* t.p.

time Deum, cole regem [L], fear God, honor the king.

timeo Danaos et dona ferentes [L], I fear the Greeks even (when they are) bringing gifts: *Virgil.*

timet pudorem [L], he fears shame.

timor addidit alas [L], fear gave him wings: *Virgil.*

timor mortis morte peior [L], the fear of death is worse than death.

timoroso [It], timorous; with hesitation: *music.*

timpani [It], kettledrums. —**timpani coperti,** muffled drums.

tinaja [Sp], large earthen water jar; specif., a water hole or cavity where water collects during the rainy season: *southwestern U.S.*

tintouin [Fr], tingling of the ears; uneasiness; anxiety; trouble.

tirage au sort [Fr], drawing lots.

tirailleur [Fr], sharpshooter; skirmisher: *mil.*

tirasse [Fr], pedal coupler on an organ: *music.*

tiré à quatre épingles [Fr], lit., drawn to four pins; neat as a pin; well-groomed.

tirer d'affaire [Fr], to help out of trouble; extricate.

tirer le diable par la queue [Fr], lit., to pull the devil by the tail; lead a struggling existence.

tirez le rideau, la farce est jouée [Fr], ring down the curtain, the farce is over: *Rabelais* (said to have been his last words). Cf. LA COMMEDIA È FINITA.

tisane [Fr], infusion; decoction, esp. a medicinal one. —**tisane de champagne,** light champagne.

τίς οὖν ἄρξει τοῦ ἄρχοντος [Gr; tís oûn árxei toû árkhontos], who will rule the ruler?: *Plutarch.*

tjenare [Sw; *fem.* tjenarinna], servant.

toccata [It], a brilliant piece or prelude for the organ or harpsichord: *music*.

toches *or* **tokus** [Yiddish], the buttocks.

toda [Heb], thank you.

todai, moto kurashi [Jap], just below the candlestick is the darkest place of all; one has to go abroad to get news of home.

τὸ δ᾽ εὖ νικάτω [Gr; tò d᾽ eû nikáto], may the right prevail: *Aeschylus*.

todkrank [Ger], sick to death; fatally ill.

todo cae en el dedo malo [Sp], everything falls on the sore finger.

todo el mundo es uno [Sp], all the world is one: *Cervantes*.

todos contra el caído [Sp], everyone is against the fallen.

toga candida [L], the white toga or robe worn by Roman candidates for office, such applicants being known as *candidati* (*fr. candidatus*, white robed).

toga praetexta [L], a white robe bordered with purple, worn by Roman magistrates and freeborn children.

togata [L], in ancient Rome, a freed woman; also, prostitute: so called because they wore the toga, instead of the *stola* worn by Roman matrons.

toga virilis [L], the manly toga; the dress of manhood (assumed by Roman boys at the age of fourteen, in place of the *toga praetexta*).

τὸ ὅλον [Gr; tò hólon], the whole; the universe: *Plato*.

tohunga [Maori], soothsayer; priest: *New Zealand*.

toison d'or [Fr], the Golden Fleece: a Spanish and Austrian order of knighthood.

τὸ καλὸν καὶ τὸ αἰσχρόν [Gr; tò kalòn kaì tò aiskhrón], the beautiful and the base; virtue and vice. Cf. HONESTUM ET TURPE.

tokohia? [Maori], how many?: *New Zealand*.

tokus [Yiddish]. Same as TOCHES.

toldo [Sp], a skin tent or rude shelter used by South American Indians.

tomare! [Jap], halt!

tombé des nues [Fr], fallen from the clouds; fig., greatly surprised.

tomber de la poêle dans le feu [Fr], to fall from the frying pan into the fire.

ton [Fr], tone; style; fashion; vogue.

Tonart [Ger], key; mode: *music*.

Tonbild [Ger], tone picture; representation by sound; musical tableau; also, phonetic figuration of a sound.

Tondichter [Ger], lit., tone poet; composer: *music*.

tonga [Anglo-Ind; Hind *tāngā*], a light two-wheeled four-seated vehicle drawn by ponies: *India*.

τὸν θεὸν φοβεῖσθε, τὸν βασιλέα τιμᾶτε [Gr; tòn theòn phobeîsthe, ton basiléa timâte], fear God, honor the king: *I Peter* ii. 17.

tope [Anglo-Ind; Hind *tōp*], Buddhist monument or shrine. Cf. STUPA.

tope là [Fr, *fr. toper*, to cover an adversary's stake; agree], agreed! done!

topi [Hind], hat; helmet; sun helmet. Written also *topee*.

τὸ πρέπον [Gr; tò prépon], that which is seemly; propriety; decorum.

toreo [Sp], bullfighting.

torero [Sp], bullfighter on foot.

torii [Jap], Japanese gate, commonly built before the entrance to a Shinto shrine.

toro [Sp; *pl.* toros], bull. **—corrida de toros,** bullfight.

torsk [Dan], fresh cod.

torta [Sp & It], tart; pie.

Torte [Ger], a rich cake.

tortilla [Sp], a Mexican cornmeal cake, unleavened, and baked on a heated stone or iron; in Spain, an omelette.

tortue [Fr], turtle. **—tortue claire,** clear turtle soup.

tosto [It], quick; rapid: *music.*

Totenmarsch [Ger], funeral march.

Totentanz [Ger], dance of death.

τῷ θεῷ δόξα [Gr; tô theô dóxa], glory to God.

tot homines quot sententiae [L], so many men, so many minds. The form used by Terence, *quot homines tot sententiae,* is preferred.

totidem verbis [L], in so many words; in these very words.

toties quoties [L], as often as; on each occasion; repeatedly.

totis viribus [L], with all one's might.

toto caelo [L], lit., by the whole heaven; by an immense distance; diametrically opposed.

totum [L], the whole. **—totum in eo est,** all depends on this.

totus in toto, et totus in qualibet parte [L], complete as a whole, and complete in every part: said of the human heart.

totus teres atque rotundus [L], entire, smooth, and round; complete in itself: *Horace* (adapted).

toujours en vedette [Fr], ever on guard: motto of *Frederick the Great.*

toujours gai [Fr], always gay.

toujours perdrix [Fr], always partridge; partridge at every meal; too much of a good thing.

toujours prêt [Fr], always ready.

toujours propice [Fr], always favorable.

toupet [Fr], tuft of hair; fig., effrontery; presumption; cheek. **—quel toupet!,** what effrontery! what cheek!

tour [Fr], a turn; tour; trick; feat. **—tour à tour,** alternately. **—tour d'adresse,** legerdemain. **—tour de coquin,** knavish trick. **—tour de force,** feat of strength (*or* skill). **—tour de main,** sleight of hand. **—tour du bâton,** perquisites; pickings.

tourelle [Fr], turret.

tournedos [Fr], a choice cut of beef fillet.

tourner casaque [Fr], to turn one's coat; change sides.

tournure [Fr], contour of a figure; characteristic shape or outline; figure; appearance; cast; fig., turn of mind; distinguishing style.

tourte [Fr], tart; pie.

tous frais faits [Fr], all expenses paid.

τοὺς πτωχοὺς γὰρ πάντοτε ἔχετε μεθ' ἑαυτῶν [Gr; toùs ptōkhoùs gàr pántote ékhete meth' heautôn], for the poor always ye have with you: *John* xii. 8.

tous songes sont mensonges [Fr], all dreams are lies (*or* illusions).

tout à coup [Fr], suddenly.

tout à fait [Fr], entirely; wholly; quite.

tout à l'heure [Fr], presently; in a moment; also, just now; only a moment ago.

tout au contraire [Fr], quite to the contrary.

tout à vous [Fr], wholly yours; yours truly.

tout beau [Fr], gently; not so fast.

tout bien ou rien [Fr], lit., everything well or nothing; all or nothing.

tout comprendre c'est tout pardonner [Fr], to understand all is to pardon all: *Madame de Staël.*

tout court [Fr], quite short; abruptly; *of name, etc.,* without addition; simply; only that and nothing more.

tout de même [Fr], all the same; in the same manner; even so; nevertheless.

tout d'en haut [Fr], everything (is) from above.

tout de suite [Fr], immediately.

tout d'un coup [Fr], all of a sudden; all at once.

tout d'une pièce [Fr], all of a piece.

tout ensemble [Fr], the whole taken together; general effect.

tout est frit [Fr], it's all over.

tout est perdu hors l'honneur [Fr], all is lost save honor.

tout est pris [Fr], all is taken.

tout fait [Fr], ready made; fig., cut and dried.

tout lasse, tout casse, tout passe [Fr], everything wearies (*or* bores), everything breaks, everything passes away.

tout le monde [Fr], all the world; everybody. **—tout le monde est sage après coup,** everybody is wise after the event.

tout lui rit [Fr], everything smiles on him.

tout mon possible [Fr], everything in my power.

tout nu [Fr], stark naked.

tout ou rien [Fr], all or nothing.

tout vient à point à qui sait attendre [Fr], everything comes in time to him who knows how to wait.

tout vient de Dieu [Fr], everything comes from God.

tovarishch [Russ; *fem.* tovarishcha], comrade.

tov shem tov mee shemen tov [Heb], lit., better a good name than good oil; a good name is worth more than riches.

trabajo [Sp], work; labor; *engin.*, stress.

tracasserie [Fr], annoyance; bickering; quarrel; worry; also, chicanery; trickery.

traducteur [Fr], translator.

traduction [Fr], translation.

traduttori traditori [It], translators are traitors.

tragédienne [Fr], an actress who plays tragic roles; tragic actress.

Träger der Litteratur [Ger], lit., the bearers of literature; the representative writers of a literary period.

trahit sua quemque voluptas [L], his own delight draws each man; each man acts on his own taste: *Virgil.*

traînard [Fr], straggler; loiterer.

train de luxe [Fr], train of exceptional comfort; special train.

trait d'union [Fr], hyphen: *typog.*

traiter de haut en bas [Fr], to treat with scorn.

tranchant [Fr; *fem.* tranchante], cutting; trenchant; decisive.

tranchée [Fr], trench; drain; cut; excavation; *pl.,* throes; pains, as of labor.

tranquillamente [It], tranquilly: *music.*

transeat in exemplum [L], let it pass into a precedent (*or* example).

transi [Fr; *fem.* transie], chilled; benumbed. **—transi de froid,** numb with cold. **—un amoureux transi,** a bashful lover.

trattoria [It; *pl.* trattorie], restaurant.

Träume sind Schäume [Ger], dreams are froth; dreams are empty.

travaux forcés [Fr], forced labors; penal servitude.

traviesa [Sp], lit., the distance across; crosstie; railroad sleeping car.

trayf *or* **treyf** [Yiddish], contrary to Jewish dietary laws; not kosher.

trecento [It], lit., three hundred (*used for* thirteen hundred); the fourteenth century in Italian art and literature.

tre corde [It], lit., three strings; in piano music, release of the soft pedal: *music.* Cf. UNA CORDA.

tremando *or* **tremolando** [It], tremulously; in a *tremolo* manner: *music.*

tremolo [It], a trembling or quavering; tremulous effect: *music.*

trente et quarante [Fr], lit., thirty and forty. Same as ROUGE ET NOIR.

tres irmãos, tres fortalezas [Pg], three brothers, three fortresses.

tressaillir de joie [Fr], to leap for joy.

Treuga Dei (*or* **Treva Dei**) [L], Truce of God; from the 10th to 13th centuries, the suspension of hostilities and of every act of private warfare during certain days and holy seasons, under penalty of excommunication and other means of enforcement. See PAX DEI.

trêve [Fr], truce. **—trêve à ces niaiseries,** no more of these fooleries. **—trêve de compliments,** a truce to compliments. **—Trêve de Dieu,** Truce of God. See TREUGA DEI. **—trêve de plaisanteries,** a truce to joking.

treyf [Yiddish]. Same as TRAYF.

triage [Fr], sorting; sifting; selection.

tria iuncta in uno [L], three joined in one: motto of the *Order of the Bath,* Great Britain.

tricot [Fr], knitted vest; sweater.

triennium [L; *pl.* triennia], period of three years.

Trinkgeld [Ger], lit., drink money; gratuity; tip.

Trinklied [Ger], drinking song.

tripe de roche [Fr], a kind of moss growing on rocks in northern latitudes; rock tripe.

tripotage [Fr], medley; jumble; mess; also, intrigue.

triste [Fr], sad; melancholy; dull.

tristesse [Fr], sadness; melancholy; dullness.

tristezza [It], sadness; melancholy; pensiveness: *music.*

tristis eris si solus eris [L], you will be sad if you remain alone: *Ovid.*

trium literarum homo [L], a thief. See HOMO TRIUM LITERARUM.

triumpho morte tam vita [L], I triumph in death, as in life.

trivial [Fr; *fem.* triviale], lit., trivial; vulgar; slangy.

trivoie [Fr], junction of three roads.

Troia fuit [L], Troy was. Same as FUIT ILIUM.

troika [Russ, *fr. troe,* three], a special wagon drawn by three horses harnessed side by side; a triumvirate.

trôleur [Fr; *fem.* trôleuse], tramp; vagrant; *fem.,* prostitute.

tromba [It; *pl.* trombe], trumpet.

trop de cuisiniers gâtent la sauce [Fr], too many cooks spoil the sauce.

trop de hâte gâte tout [Fr], too much haste spoils everything; more haste, less speed.

troppo [It], too much: *music.*

Tros Tyriusque mihi nullo discrimine agetur [L], Trojan and Tyrian shall be treated by me with no difference (*or* discrimination): *Virgil.*

trottoir [Fr], sidewalk.

trouble-fête [Fr; *masc. & fem.*], a killjoy.

trouée [Fr], opening; gap; breach.

trousse [Fr], lit., truss; bundle; specif., a case or container, as for surgical instruments, razors, etc.

trousseau [Fr; *pl.* trousseaux], bride's special wardrobe.

trouvaille [Fr], lucky find; godsend; windfall.

truditur dies die [L], one day is pushed onward by another: *Horace.*

truffe [Fr], truffle.

truite [Fr], trout. **—truite au bleu,** brook trout. **—truite de lac,** lake trout. **—truite saumonée,** salmon trout.

truité [Fr; *fem.* truitée], spotted; speckled; specif., having a crackled glaze (as certain porcelain).

tsimmis [Yiddish], a compote; a confusing, troublesome, prolonged, or embarrassing situation or condition.

tsunami [Jap], lit., harbor wave; tidal wave.

T.S.V.P. [Fr], please turn (the page); *abbr.* form of *tournez s'il vous plaît.*

tuan [Malay], lord; master; sir: a title of respect in the Malay Archipelago and Indonesia.

tu, Domine, gloria mea [L], thou, O Lord, art my glory.

tuebor [L], I will defend.

tué raide [Fr], lit., killed stiff; killed outright.

tulipe noir [Fr], black tulip; a rarity.

tulwar [Anglo-Ind; Hind *talwār*], curved saber, as used by the Sikhs.

tundra [Lapp *tundar*, hill], treeless area in arctic and subarctic regions.

tu ne cede malis, sed contra audentior ito [L], yield not to misfortunes, but march more boldly to meet them: *Virgil.*

tu nihil invita dices faciesve Minerva [L], naught wilt thou say or do when Minerva is unwilling: *Horace.* Cf. INVITA MINERVA.

tu quoque [L], thou also; you too; you're another.

Turnfest [Ger], gymnastic exhibition.

Turnhalle [Ger], gymnasium.

Turnverein [Ger], gymnastic or athletic club or association.

tutamen [L; *pl.* tutamina], protection; protective pact.

tutoiement [Fr], the use of *tu* in place of *vous*, in familiar address.

tutor et ultor [L], protector and avenger.

tutta [It; *fem.*], all; whole. —**tutta forza,** with full force: *music.*

tutti [It; *pl.*], all (i.e., all the performers together): *music.*

tutti i gusti son gusti [It], all tastes are tastes; no accounting for tastes.

tutto di novello par bello [It], everything new seems beautiful.

tuum [L], yours; your property. —**tuum est,** it is yours. —**tuum est?,** is it yours?

tyaktena bhunjithah [Skr], thou shalt gain by giving away: from the *Upanishad.*

τυφλὸς δὲ τυφλὸν ἐὰν ὁδηγῇ ἀμφότεροι εἰς βόθυνον πεσοῦνται [Gr; typhlòs, dè typhlòn eàn hodēgê, amphóteroi eis bóthunon pesoûntai], and if the blind lead the blind, both shall fall into the ditch: *Matthew* xv. 14.

Tyrolienne [Fr], a Tyrolese peasant dance or song.

U

ua mau ke ea o ka aina i ka pono [Hawa], the life of the land is established in righteousness: motto of *Hawaii*.

über allen Gipfeln ist Ruh [Ger], over all the heights is rest: *Goethe*.

Übergang [Ger], a crossing; passage; *music*, transition; modulation from one key to another.

Überleitung [Ger], a transitional passage in a composition: *music*.

übermässig [Ger], excessive; superfluous; *music,* augmented.

Übermensch [Ger; *pl.* Übermenschen], superhuman being; superman.

uberrima fides [L], superabounding faith; implicit trust (*or* reliance).

Überschlagen [Ger], the crossing of the hands on the keyboard: *music*.

ubi amici, ibi opes [L], where there are friends, there is wealth.

ubi bene, ibi patria [L], where it is well with me, there is my country.

ubi homines sunt, modi sunt [L], where there are men, there are manners.

ubi ius incertum, ibi ius nullum [L], where the law is uncertain, there is no law; uncertainty destroys law.

ubi lapsus? quid feci? [L], where have I fallen (*or* where have I made a slip)? what have I done?

ubi libertas, ibi patria [L], where there is liberty, there is my country.

ubi mel, ibi apes [L], where honey is, there are the bees.

ubique [L], everywhere. **—ubique patriam reminisci,** everywhere to remember our country.

ubi sunt [L], short for *ubi sunt qui ante nos fuerunt?* (where are those who lived before us?).

ubi supra [L], lit., where above; in the place (in book, etc.) above-mentioned.

Übung [Ger; *pl.* Übungen], practice; exercise; study (as in music). **—Übung macht den Meister,** practice makes the master; practice makes perfect.

Uhr [Ger; *pl.* Uhren], clock; time of day; hour; o'clock: *abbr.* U. **—wieviel Uhr ist's?,** what time is it?

uhuru [Swa], freedom.

uitlander [Du], outlander; foreigner; esp., any European other than a Boer: *South Africa*.

ukehé [Nav], thank you.

Ulk [Ger; *pl.* Ulke], fun; frolic; trick; hoax.

ultima ratio [L], final argument; force. **—ultima ratio regum,** last argument of kings; resort to arms; war.

ultima Thule [L], farthest Thule; utmost limit: *Virgil*. Also any unknown land or region.

ultimo [L], in the month preceding the present one: *abbr.* ult.

ultimum vale [L], a last farewell.

ultimus heres (*or* **haeres**) [L], the last (*or* final) heir: *law.*

ultimus regum [L], the last of the kings.

ultimus Romanorum [L], the last of the Romans.

ultra [L], beyond; farther; more than. —**ultra licitum,** beyond what is permitted. —**ultra posse nemo obligatur,** no one is bound to do more than he can. —**ultra valorem,** beyond the value: *law.* —**ultra vires,** beyond one's power; transcending authority conferred by law: *law.*

uma no mimi ni nembutsu [Jap], pouring prayers into a horse's ears (i.e., taking useless trouble).

um Antwort wird gebeten [Ger], an answer is requested: *abbr.* u.A.w.g. —**um gefällige Antwort wird gebeten,** the favor of an answer is requested: *abbr.* u.gefl.A.w.g.

umbra [L; *pl.* umbrae], shade; shadow.

Umfang [Ger], circumference; range; *music,* compass.

umiak *or* **oomiak** [Esk], a large Eskimo boat made of skins over a wooden framework, and usually paddled by women.

umore [It], humor; playfulness: *music.*

um so besser [Ger], so much the better.

Umstimmung [Ger], a change of mind; a change of tuning or key: *music.*

una corda [It], lit., one string; in piano music, with the soft pedal (*abbr.* u.c.): *music.*

una et eadem persona [L], one and the same person.

un amoureux transi [Fr], a bashful lover.

un argent fou [Fr], no end of money.

una scopa nuova spazza bene [It], a new broom sweeps clean.

una voce [L], with one voice; unanimously.

una volta [It], once: *music.* —**una volta furfante, e sempre furfante,** once a rogue, always a rogue.

un bienfait n'est jamais perdu [Fr], a kindness is never lost.

un cabello hace sombra [Sp], a single hair casts a shadow.

un cheval qui n'a ni bouche ni éperon [Fr], a horse that obeys neither rein (lit., mouth) nor spur.

un clavo a otro saca [Sp], one nail drives out another.

un coup de hasard [Fr], a stroke of luck.

un coup de soleil [Fr], sunstroke.

und [Ger], and: *abbr.* u. —**und andere,** and others: *abbr.* u.a. —**und andere mehr** *or* **und anderes mehr,** and others; and other things besides: *abbr.* u.a.m. —**und damit Punktum!,** lit., and therewith a period (*or* end); enough; let's have no more of it; and there's an end of it! —**und so weiter,** and so forth; et cetera: *abbr.* u.s.w. *or* usw.

Undank ist der Welt Lohn [Ger], ingratitude is the world's payment.

une affaire flambée [Fr], a ruined affair; lost enterprise.

une araignée dans le plafond [Fr], lit., a spider in the ceiling; a bee in one's bonnet.

une bonne bête [Fr], a good-natured fool.

une femme grosse [Fr], a pregnant woman.

une fois n'est pas coutume [Fr], once is not a habit; one swallow does not make a summer.

une grosse femme [Fr], a stout (*or* fat) woman.

une main savante [Fr], a skillful hand.

un freddo amico è mal sicuro amante [It], a cold friend makes an uncertain lover.

Ungeduld [Ger], impatience; also, an impatient person.

Unglück [Ger], misfortune; ill luck.

unguibus et rostro [L], with claws and beak; tooth and nail.

unguis in ulcere [L], a claw in the wound (i.e., to keep it open); a knife in the wound.

un homme averti en vaut deux [Fr], a man who is warned is equal to two (unwarned); forewarned, forearmed.

un homme de bonne foi [Fr], an honest man.

un homme qui parle deux langues vaut deux hommes [Fr], a man who speaks two languages is worth two men.

uni aequus virtuti, atque eius amicis [L], friendly to virtue alone and to the friends of virtue: *Horace.*

unica virtus necessaria [L], virtue is the only thing necessary.

Unitas Fratrum [L], lit., unity of brethren; official name of Moravian Church.

unius dementia dementes efficit multos [L], the madness of one drives many mad.

Universität [Ger; *pl.* Universitäten], university.

un je servirai [Fr], one I will serve.

Unkraut vergeht nicht [Ger], lit., weeds do not perish; ill weeds thrive.

un mal chiama l'altro [It], **un mal llama a otro** [Sp], one evil summons another; misfortunes never come singly.

uno animo [L], with one mind; unanimously.

un' occhio alla padella, uno alla gatta [It], one eye on the frying pan, one on the cat.

uno ictu [L], at one blow.

uno saltu [L], in one leap; at a single bound.

uno tiene la fama, y otro carda la lana [Sp], one gets the credit, and another cards the wool; one does the work, someone else gets the credit.

un poète manqué [Fr], a would-be poet.

un propos salé [Fr], a coarse remark.

unrecht Gut gedeiht nicht [Ger], ill-gotten gain never thrives.

unrein [Ger], dirty; out of tune: *music.*

un roy, une foy, une loi [OF], one king, one faith, one law.

unruhig [Ger], restless; agitated.

un sot à triple étage [Fr], lit., a fool to the third story; a consummate blockhead.

un style serré [Fr], a terse style.

unt [Hind], camel. See OONT.

untar o carro [Pg], to oil the cart.

unter den Linden [Ger], lit., under the linden trees; formerly a fashionable street in Berlin.

unter der Hand [Ger], lit., under the hand; secretly.

Unterseeboot [Ger], lit., undersea boat; a submarine; specif., U-boat (i.e., [formerly] a German or Austrian submarine).

unter vier Augen [Ger], lit., under four eyes; tête-à-tête; between ourselves.

un tour de fripon [Fr], a knavish trick.

un uomo litterato ne val due [It], a man of learning is worth two without.

unverhofft kommt oft [Ger], the unforeseen often happens.

uomo amante, uomo zelante [It], a loving man, a jealous man.

uomo da molto [It], man of weight.

uomo solitario o e bestia o angelo [It], a solitary man is either a brute or an angel.

urbem latericiam invenit, marmoream reliquit [L], he found the city (Rome) brick and left it marble: *Suetonius* (of Caesar Augustus).

urbi et orbi [L], to the city (Rome) and to the world: words formerly accompanying a special Papal benediction.

urceus [L], earthenware jug; pitcher; urn.

Ursprache [Ger], a primitive language; esp., primitive Aryan.

usine [Fr], factory; works.

usque ad aras [L], to the very altars; to the last extremity. Cf. AMICUS USQUE AD ARAS.

usque ad nauseam [L], even to nausea; even so far as to disgust.

usted [Sp; *pl.* ustedes], you: *abbr.* Vd., Ud., *or* V., *pl.* Vds., Uds., *or* VV.

usus est tyrannus [L], custom is a tyrant.

usus loquendi [L], usage in speaking.

ut ameris, amabilis esto [L], that you may be loved, be lovable; to gain love, show love to others: *Ovid.*

ut apes geometriam [L], as bees (practice) geometry.

utcumque placuerit Deo [L], as it shall please God.

ut dictum [L], as directed: *abbr.* ut dict.

ut homo est, ita morem geras [L], as a man is, so must you humor him; suit the manner to the man: *Terence.*

utile dulci [L], the useful with the agreeable: *Horace.*

utinam noster esset [L], would that he were ours.

ut infra [L], as (shown or stated) below: *abbr.* u.i.

uti possidetis [L], lit., as you possess; with the possessions you at present hold: *law.*

ut mos est [L], as the custom is: *Juvenal.*

ut pictura poesis [L], poetry is like a painting: *Horace.*

ut pignus amicitiae [L], as a pledge (*or* token) of friendship.

ut prosim [L], that I may be of use (*or* service); that I may do good.

ut quocunque paratus [L], prepared on every side.

utrum horum mavis accipe [L], take whichever you prefer.

ut supra [L], as (shown or stated) above: *abbr.* u.s.

uyezd [Russ], district or county; in Soviet Russia, a county soviet.

úzhin [Russ], supper.

V

vaca [Sp], cow.

vache [Fr], cow. —**vache à lait,** a milking cow.

vacher [Fr], cowherd; cattle tender; *vaquero.*

vacherie [Fr], lit., cowhouse; dirty trick; an island in the swamps of the lower Mississippi region: *Louisiana.*

vacuo *or* **in vacuo** [L], in a vacuum.

vacuus cantat coram latrone viator [L], the traveler who has an empty purse sings in the face of the robber.

vada [Russ]. Same as VODA.

vade in pace [L], go in peace.

vadium mortuum [L], a mortgage: *law.*

vado [Sp], a ford.

vae soli [L], woe to the solitary man: *Vulgate* (*Ecclesiastes* iv. 10).

vae victis [L], woe to the vanquished: *Plautus.*

vagitus [L], the first cry of a newborn child: *med.*

vagón [Sp], wagon; railroad car (*or* carriage). —**vagón cama,** railway sleeping car.

vaguada [Sp], waterway.

vaille que vaille [Fr], whatever it may be worth; at all events; for better or worse.

vairagi [Skr], lit., one devoid of passion; *bairagi* (q.v.).

vakil *or* **vakeel** [Hind], an ambassador; deputy; agent; in India, esp., an indigenous attorney or pleader.

vale [L; *pl.* valete], farewell.

valeat quantum valere potest [L], let it pass for what it is worth.

vale la pena [Sp], it is worthwhile.

valet ancora virtus [L], virtue avails as an anchor; virtue is a strong anchor.

valet de chambre [Fr], a valet; personal servant.

valet de pied [Fr], footman; flunky.

valete ac plaudite [L], farewell and applaud: said by Roman actors at the end of a piece.

¡válgame Dios! [Sp], God bless me; great Heavens!

valgus [L; *pl.* valgi], a bowlegged person.

valle d'abisso dolorosa [It], valley of the woeful abyss: *Dante.*

valuta [It], value; worth; esp., currency value in international exchange.

vanitas vanitatum, omnia vanitas [L], vanity of vanities, all is vanity: *Vulgate* (*Ecclesiastes* i. 2).

vaquero [Sp], herdsman; cowboy.

vara [Sp], lit., staff or rod; a linear measure varying from 33 to 34 inches; in Cuba and P.I., as in Spain, equal to 33.38 inches: *Sp. Am.*

vareuse [Fr], a pea jacket for men; jumper.

vargueno [Sp], decorative boxlike cabinet or writing desk.

varia lectio [L; *pl.* variae lectiones], variant reading.

variazioni [It], variations: *music.*

variorum notae [L], notes of various commentators.

varium et mutabile semper femina [L], woman is ever a fickle and changeable thing: *Virgil.*

varón de Dios [Sp], virtuous, saintly man.

vas [L; *pl.* vasa], vessel; duct: *anat.* **—vas deferens** [*pl.* vasa deferentia], a spermatic duct: *anat. & zool.*

vaso malo nunca cae de mano [Sp], a worthless vase never slips from the hand.

vaso vuoto suona meglio [It], an empty vase (*or* vessel) makes the most noise.

va-t'en! [Fr], go away! be off!

Vaterland [Ger], fatherland; specif., Germany.

vaya con Dios [Sp], go with God; farewell.

váyase [Sp], go away!

vaurien [Fr], a good-for-nothing; worthless fellow; scamp. Cf. GAR-NEMENT.

veau [Fr], calf; veal; also, lazy fellow; *bookbinding,* calf; calfskin.

vectigalia nervi sunt rei publicae [L], revenues are the sinews of the state: *Cicero* (adapted).

vedi Napoli, e poi mori [It], see Naples and then die.

vega [Sp], open tract of country; fertile plain.

Vehmgericht [Ger; *pl.* Vehmgerichte], a medieval secret tribunal, esp. of Westphalia.

veille [Fr], lit., watching; sleeplessness; vigil; also, the day before; eve.

veilleuse [Fr], night light.

velis et remis [L], with sails and oars; by every means possible.

veloce [It], with great rapidity: *music.*

velouté [Fr], lit., velvety; *cookery,* soft and smooth to the palate; as, sauce *velouté.*

vel prece vel pretio [L], either with prayer or with price; for either love or money.

velut aegri somnia [L], like a sick man's dreams: *Horace.*

veluti in speculum [L], even as in a mirror.

vena [L; *pl.* venae], a vein. **—vena cava** [*pl.* venae cavae], one of the large veins that discharge into the right cardiac auricle: *anat.*

venaison [Fr], venison.

venalis populus venalis curia patrum [L], the people and the senators are equally venal; every man has his price.

Vendémiaire [Fr], in the Revolutionary calendar of the first French Republic, the first month of the year, Sept. 22 to Oct. 21.

vender gato por lebre [Pg], to sell cat for hare.

vendidit hic auro patriam [L], this man sold his country for gold.

venenum in auro bibitur [L], poison is drunk from a golden cup: *Seneca;* no one bothers to poison poor people.

venez au fait [Fr], get to the point.

venez ici [Fr], come here.

venga aquí [Sp], come here.

venga lo que viniere [Sp], come what may.

venga qui [It], come here.

venia necessitati datur [L], indulgence is granted to necessity; necessity knows no law.

venienti occurrite morbo [L], meet the approaching disease; prevention is better than cure.

venire (facias) [L], lit., (make) to come; a writ or judge's order, instructing the sheriff to summon a jury: *law.*

Venite [L], lit., come ye; a musical setting of the 95th Psalm (94th in the Douay version), beginning, in Latin, *Venite, exultemus Domino,* "O come, let us sing unto the Lord."

venit summa dies et ineluctabile tempus [L], the last day (of Troy) has come and the inevitable hour (*or* doom): *Virgil.*

veni, vidi, vici [L], I came, I saw, I conquered: *Julius Caesar* (message to the senate, announcing his defeat of Pharnaces, king of Pontus, 47 B.C.).

venta [Sp], roadside inn; a sale.

ventana [Sp], window; window shutter.

vente [Fr], sale. **—en vente,** on sale; now ready (said of a book). **—vente au rabais,** sale at reduced prices.

ventis secundis [L], with favorable winds.

Ventôse [Fr], in the Revolutionary calendar of the first French Republic, the sixth month of the year, from Feb. 19 to March 20.

ventre à terre [Fr], lit., belly to ground; at full speed.

vera causa [L], a true cause.

vera incessu patuit dea [L], by her gait the true goddess was revealed: *Virgil.*

verbatim et literatim [L], word for word and letter for letter.

verbera, sed audi [L], strike, but hear me; lash but listen.

Verbi Dei Minister [L], Preacher of the Word of God: *abbr.* V.D.M.

verbis ad verbera [L], from words to blows.

verboten [Ger], forbidden; prohibited; illicit.

verbum (sat) sapienti [L], a word to the wise (is enough): *abbr.* verb. sap. *or* verb. sat.

verchovnoi sovyet S.S.S.R. [Russ], Supreme Soviet of the U.S.S.R.; the legislature of the Soviet Union.

verdad [Sp], truth; reality. **—¿no es verdad?** *or* **¿verdad?,** isn't it true? isn't it so? **—verdad es verde,** truth is green.

verdeckte Märsche [Ger], stolen marches.

Verein [Ger], association; company; society; club: *abbr.* Ver.

Vereinigte Staaten [Ger], United States: *abbr.* Ver. St.

verger [Fr], orchard; fruit garden.

vergonha [Pg], shame!

veritas [L], truth. —**veritas entis** [LL], lit., truth of being; metaphysical truth. —**veritas nunquam perit,** truth never dies. —**veritas odium parit,** truth begets hatred: *Ausonius.* —**veritas omnia vincit,** truth conquers all things. —**veritas praevalebit,** truth will prevail. —**veritas signi,** truth of a symbol. —**veritas temporis filia,** truth is the daughter of time. —**veritas victrix,** truth the conqueror. —**veritas vincit,** truth conquers.

veritatem dies aperit [L], time reveals the truth.

veritatis simplex oratio est [L], the language of truth is simple: *Seneca.*

vérité sans peur [Fr], truth without fear.

Verlag [Ger], publishing house.

Verlagsbuchhändler [Ger], publisher.

vermoulu [Fr; *fem.* vermoulue], worm-eaten; crumbling into dust.

vernaccia [It], an Italian white wine, made esp. in Sardinia.

Vernunft [Ger], reason; understanding; sense.

verre [Fr], glass; tumbler.

verrückt [Ger], crazy.

versal [Sp; *pl.* versales], capital letter: *typog.*

versalilla [Sp], small capital: *typog.*

Versammlung [Ger], assembly; meeting.

vers libre [Fr], free verse.

Verstand [Ger], understanding; intelligence; sense; discernment.

verstimmt [Ger], in bad temper; out of tune: *music.*

verso [L], left-hand page; opposed to RECTO.

verte [L], turn; turn the page.

verweile doch! du bist so schön! [Ger], ah, still delay—thou art so fair!: *Goethe.*

vesania [L], insanity: *med.*

vesica piscis [L], lit., fish bladder; an oval aureole often surrounding the figure of Christ and the saints in early Christian art.

Vesperbrot [Ger], afternoon tea; light afternoon meal.

vestigia [L; *pl.* of *vestigium*], footsteps; tracks; traces; vestiges. —**vestigia morientis libertatis,** the footprints of expiring liberty. —**vestigia nulla retrorsum,** no footsteps backward: *Horace* (adapted). —**vestigia terrent,** the footprints frighten me (part of the quotation containing Reynard's reply to the sick lion's invitation, *quia me vestigia terrent, omnia te adversum spectantia, nulla retrorsum,* "I'm frightened at those footsteps: every track leads to your home, but ne'er a one leads back"): *Horace* (tr. by Conington).

veteris vestigia flammae [L], remnants of an ancient flame: *Virgil* describing Dido's rekindled passion for Aeneas.

vettura [It; *pl.* vetture], Italian four-wheeled carriage; automobile.

vetturino [It; *pl.* vetturini], driver; proprietor or driver of an automobile (*vettura*).

veuf [Fr], widower.

veuve [Fr], widow: *abbr.* v^e.

vexata quaestio [L], a disputed (*or* vexed) question.

v'gloobeene dooshee [Russ], in one's heart of hearts.

via [L; *pl.* viae], way. —**via amicabili,** in a friendly way. —**via crucis, via lucis,** the way of the Cross is the way of light. —**Via Lactea,** the Milky Way. —**via media,** a middle way (*or* course). —**via militaris,** a military road. —**via trita est tutissima,** the beaten path is the safest. —**via trita, via tuta,** the beaten path, the safe path.

viaje [Sp], journey; voyage; travel; trip.

viajero [Sp], traveler; wayfarer.

vibrato [It], vigorous; also, pulsation of tone, as in violin playing or in emotional singing: *music.*

vi capisco [It], I understand you.

vice versa [L], the order being changed; conversely: *abbr.* V.V.

vicisti, Galilaee [L], thou hast conquered, O Galilean: *Julian the Apostate* (on his deathbed).

victi vicimus [L], conquered, we conquer.

victoria concordia crescit [L], victory is increased by concord.

victoriae gloria merces [L], glory is the reward of victory.

victrix fortunae sapientia [L], wisdom is the victor over fortune: *Juvenal.*

vidana [Sing], village chief.

vida sin amigos muerte sin testigos [Sp], friendless in life, friendless (lit., without witnesses) in death.

vide [L], see: a direction. —**vide ante,** see before. —**vide et crede,** see and believe. —**vide infra,** see below: *abbr.* v.i. —**vide post,** see after this. —**vide supra,** see above: *abbr.* v.s. —**vide ut supra,** see as above; see the above statement.

vide [Fr], open (of strings): *music.*

videlicet [L], lit., one may see; namely; in other words; to wit: *abbr.* viz.

video meliora proboque deteriora sequor [L], I see and approve of the better things; I follow the worse: *Ovid.*

videtur [L], it appears; it seems.

vidit et erubuit lympha pudica Deum [L], the modest water saw its God and blushed: referring to Christ's first miracle.

vieille [Fr], old woman.

vieja [Cuban Sp, *fr.* Sp *vieja mujer,* old woman], any of various parrot fishes.

viejo [Sp; *fem.* vieja], *adj.* old; *n.* old man.

viele Kinder, viel Segen [Ger], many children, many blessings.

vielle [Fr], medieval viol; also, hurdy-gurdy: *music.*

vierhändig [Ger], four-handed; *music,* for four hands.

vierkleur [Du], the four-colored flag of the former South African Republic.

vierstimmig [Ger], composed for four voices or parts; in four parts: *music.*

vi et armis [L], by strength and by arms; by main force.

vieux [Fr; *fem.* vieille], old; aged. —**du vieux temps,** quite old-fashioned. —**vieux comme le monde,** old as the hills (lit., the world). —**vieux garçon,** old bachelor.

vif [Fr; *fem.* vive], alive; animated; sprightly.

vigilantibus [L], to the watchful.

vigilate et orate [L], watch and pray.

vigneron [Fr], wine grower.

vigoroso [It], with vigor: *music.*

vigueur de dessus [Fr], strength from on high.

vilius argentum est auro, virtutibus aurum [L], silver is of less value than gold, gold (less) than virtue.

villeggiatura [It], country holidays.

vin [Fr], wine. —**vin d'honneur,** lit., wine of honor; wine drunk in honor of a distinguished guest. —**vin du pays,** wine of the area (lit., of the country). —**vin ordinaire,** cheap table wine; red ink (*slang*). —**vin pur,** wine without water added.

viña [Sp], vineyard.

vinaigre [Fr], vinegar. —**vinaigre de toilette,** aromatic vinegar.

vincam aut moriar [L], I will conquer or die.

vincere aut mori [L], to conquer or die.

vincet amor patriae laudumque immensa cupido [L], love of country will prevail and the boundless passion for glory (of renown): *Virgil.*

vincit amor patriae [L], love of country conquers (i.e., outweighs all other considerations).

vincit omnia veritas [L], truth conquers all things.

vincit qui patitur [L], he conquers who endures.

vincit qui se vincit [L], he conquers who conquers himself.

vincit veritas [L], truth conquers.

vinculum matrimonii [L], the bond of marriage.

vindex iniuriae [L], an avenger of wrong.

vingt et un *or* **vingt-un** [Fr], lit., twenty-one; the game of blackjack.

vinho velho, e amigo velho [Pg], old wine and old friend.

vino tortus et ira [L], racked by wine and anger: *Horace.*

viola da gamba [It], lit., viol for the leg; an early form of cello: *music.*

viola d'amore [It], lit., viol of love; a bass viol of the 17th and 18th centuries, with a soft and sympathetic tone: *music.*

violino [It; *pl.* violini], violin: *abbr.* v.

violone [It], the double bass; contrabass: *music.*

vir bonus dicendi peritus [L], a good man skilled in the art of speaking.

vires acquirit eundo [L], it gains strength by going; it acquires strength as it advances: *Virgil* (of fame).

virescit vulnere virtus [L], virtue flourishes from a wound.

viret in aeternum [L], it flourishes forever.

vir et uxor [L], husband and wife.

Virgilium vidi tantum [L], Virgil I have only seen: *Ovid.*

virginibus puerisque [L], for maidens and boys: *Horace.*

Virgo [L], the Virgin. —**Virgo Sapientissima,** Virgin Most Wise. —**Virgo Sponsa Dei,** Virgin Bride of the Lord.

virgola [It; *pl.* virgole], comma.

virgule [Fr], comma. —**point et virgule,** semicolon.

viribus unitis [L], with united strength.

viritim [L], man by man.

vir sapit qui pauca loquitur [L], that man is wise who talks little.

virtus [L], manly excellence; virtue; valor. —**virtus ariete fortior,** virtue is stronger than a battering ram. —**virtus est militis decus,** valor is the soldier's glory (*or* honor). —**virtus in actione consistit,** virtue consists in action. —**virtus in arduis,** virtue (*or* valor) in difficulties. —**virtus incendit vires,** virtue kindles one's strength. —**virtus laudatur et alget,** virtue is praised and is left to freeze (*or* starve). —**virtus millia scuta,** virtue is a thousand shields. —**virtus nobilitat,** virtue ennobles. —**virtus non stemma,** virtue, not pedigree. —**virtus post nummos,** virtue after money. —**virtus probata florescit,** virtue flourishes in trial. —**virtus requiei nescia sordidae,** lit., virtue, knowing nothing of base leisure; virtue doesn't know the meaning of relaxation. —**virtus incendit vires,** virtue kindles one's strength. —**virtus semper viridis,** virtue is always green; virtue never fades. —**virtus sola nobilitat,** virtue alone can ennoble. —**virtus vincit invidium,** virtue overcomes envy.

virtute et armis [L], by valor and arms: motto of *Mississippi.*

virtute et fide [L], by virtue and faith.

virtute et labore [L], by virtue and toil.

virtute et opere [L], by virtue and industry.

virtute fideque [L], by virtue and faith.

virtute, non astutia [L], by virtue, not by craft.

virtute, non verbis [L], by virtue, not by words; by character, not by speech.

virtute, non viris [L], by virtue, not by men.

virtute officii [L], by virtue of office.

virtute quies [L], in virtue there is tranquility.

virtute securus [L], secure through virtue.

virtuti nihil obstat et armis [L], nothing can withstand valor and arms.

virtuti non armis fido [L], I trust to virtue and not to arms.

virtutis amore [L], from love of virtue.

virtutis avorum praemium [L], the reward of the valor of my ancestors.

virtutis fortuna comes [L], fortune is the companion of valor: motto of the *Duke of Wellington.*

virum volitare per ora [L], lit., to fly through the mouths of men; spread like wildfire: *Ennius.*

vis [L; *pl.* vires], force; power; strength. **—vis a fronte,** a propelling force from before. **—vis a tergo,** a propelling force from behind. **—vis comica,** comic power (*or* talent): *Suetonius.* **—vis conservatrix,** the preservative power. **—vis consilii expers mole ruit sua,** force without discretion (*or* judgment) falls by its own weight: *Horace.* **—vis inertiae,** the power of inertia; passive resistance to force applied. **—vis maior,** superior force; inevitable accident: *law.* **—vis medicatrix,** healing power. **—vis medicatrix naturae,** the healing power of nature. **—vis mortua,** dead force; force that does no work: *mech.* **—vis poetica,** poetic force (*or* genius). **—vis unita fortior,** power is strengthened by union; union is strength. **—vis vitae,** vital force. **—vis viva,** living force; kinetic energy: *mech.*

visage fardé [Fr], a painted face; fig., a dissembling countenance.

vis-à-vis [Fr], *adv.* lit., face to face; opposite; facing; *n.* one facing another, as in dancing or at table; also, a passenger vehicle with seats facing each other.

vita brevis, ars longa [L], life is short and art is long.

vitae via virtus [L], virtue is the way of life.

vitam impendere vero [L], to risk one's life for the truth: *Juvenal.*

vita sine litteris mors est [L], life without literature (*or* books) is death.

vite [Fr], lively; quick; quickly: *music.*

vitiis nemo sine nascitur [L], no one is born without faults.

viuda [Sp], widow: *abbr* V.^da.

viuva rica com um olho chora, e com outro repica [Pg], a rich widow weeps with one eye and signals with the other.

viva! [It & Sp], long live; hurrah: a cry or salute. **—viva il rè!,** long live the king!

vivace [It], in a lively manner; with spirit: *music.*

vivamus, mea Lesbia, atque amemus [L], let us live, my Lesbia, and let us love one another: *Catullus.*

vivandier [Fr; *fem.* vivandière], in Continental armies, a provisioner; a sutler.

vivant rex et regina! [L], long live the king and queen!

viva quien vence [Sp], long live the winner; hurrah for the winning side.

vivat regina! [L], long live the queen!

vivat respublica! [L], long live the republic!

vivat rex! [L], long live the king!

viva voce [L], by the living voice; oral or orally; *colloq.,* oral examination.

vive *or* **vivat!** [Fr], hurrah! huzza!

vive la bagatelle! [Fr], long live trifles (or frivolity)! —**vive la République!,** long live the Republic! —**vive l'empereur!,** long live the emperor! —**vive le roi!,** long live the king!

vive memor leti [L], live mindful of death: *Persius.*

vivendi causa [L], cause of living; source of life.

vivere est cogitare [L], to live is to think: *Cicero.*

vivere sat vincere [L], to conquer is to live enough.

vive ut vivas [L], live so that you may (truly) live.

vive, vale! [L], long life to you, farewell!: *Horace.*

vivida vis animi [L], the living force of the mind.

vivit post funera virtus [L], virtue lives after (or survives) the grave: *Tiberius Caesar.*

vivo [It], with life; in a lively manner: *music.*

vivre au jour le jour [Fr], to live from day to day; enjoy the present; live from hand to mouth.

vivre ce n'est pas respirer, c'est agir [Fr], living is not breathing but doing: *Rousseau.*

vivre et laisser vivre [Fr], to live and let live.

vivres de réserve [Fr], emergency rations: *mil.*

vix ea nostra voco [L], I can scarcely call these things our own.

vixere fortes ante Agamemnona [L], there lived great men before Agamemnon: *Horace.*

vixit... annos [L], has lived (so many) years: *abbr.* v.a.

vlei [Afrik], land where water collects in rainy seasons; swampy tract; marsh: *South Africa.*

voce [It], voice. —**voce bianca,** lit., white voice; voice of a woman or child. —**voce di petto,** chest voice. —**voce di testa,** head voice. —**voce granita,** firm, powerful voice. —**voce mista,** mixed voice. —**voce pastosa,** soft, rich, and flexible voice. —**voce spiccata,** voice with clear enunciation. —**voce velata,** veiled voice; a voice slightly obscured.

voda *or* **vada** [Russ], water.

vodka [Russ], lit., little water; a strong alcoholic beverage.

vogue la galère! [Fr], lit., row the galley! come what may! here goes!

voilà [Fr], behold! there! look! there it goes (or comes)! there it is! here you are! —**voilà tout,** that is all. —**voilà une autre chose,** that's another thing; that's quite a different matter. —**vous voilà bien!,** you are now in deep trouble.

voile [Fr], *n.m.* veil; *n.f.* sail.

voina [Russ], war.

voir dire [OF], lit., to say the truth; an oath given by witnesses that they will tell the truth in regard to questions concerning their competency: *law.*

voir le dessous des cartes [Fr], to see the underside (i.e., the face) of the cards; be in on the secret.

voiture [Fr], carriage; vehicle.

voiturier [Fr], carrier; wagoner; driver.

voix [Fr], voice; tone; vote; suffrage. **—aux voix!,** put it to the vote! divide! **—voix céleste.** Same as VOX ANGELICA. **—voix criarde,** shrill voice. **—voix larmoyante,** tearful voice.

Vokal [Ger; *pl.* Vokale], vowel.

volador [Sp], a Californian flying fish.

volaille [Fr], poultry; fowl.

volant [Fr; *fem.* volante], *adj.* flying; floating; *n.* flounce (of a dress); sail (of a windmill).

volante [It], flying; with light rapidity: *music.*

volata [It], lit., a flight; a series of rapid notes embellishing a melody: *music.*

volat hora per orbem [L], time flies through the world.

vol-au-vent [Fr], lit., flight in the wind; a shell of puff paste filled with a ragout: *cookery.*

volée [Fr], flight; volley; discharge; shower; peal (of bells).

volens et potens (*or* **valens**) [L], willing and able.

volente Deo [L], God willing.

volenti non fit iniuria [L], no injustice (*or* injury) is done to a consenting party: *law.*

voleur [Fr], thief. **—au voleur!,** stop thief!

Volk der Dichter und Denker [Ger], nation of poets and thinkers (the Germans).

Volkskammer [Ger], chief legislature of the German Democratic Republic.

Volkslied [Ger; *pl.* Volkslieder], folk song; popular ballad.

vollstimmig [Ger], for full orchestra or chorus; polyphonic: *music.*

voló golondrino [Sp], the swallow has flown; the opportunity has fled.

volo non valeo [L], I am willing but unable.

volonté [Fr], will. **—à volonté,** as one wishes. **—dernières volontés,** last will and testament.

volontieri [It], willingly; gladly.

volost [Russ], a district including several villages; rural district; in Soviet Russia, a rural soviet.

volta [It; *pl.* volte], turn; turning; time. **—due volte,** twice. **—prima volta,** first time. **—seconda volta,** second time. **—una volta,** once: *all music.*

volte-face [Fr], reversal (*or* change) of policy; a facing about: *lit. & fig.*

volteggiando [It], crossing the hands in playing the piano: *music.*

volti [It], turn over. **—volti subito,** turn (the page) quickly (*abbr.* v.s.): *music.*

voltigeur [Fr], lit., a vaulter; rifleman; light infantryman: *Fr. hist.*

voluntas habetur pro facto [L], the will is taken for the deed.

voluptates corporis [L], the pleasures of the body; sensual pleasures.

volventibus annis [L], lit., with revolving years; as the years rolled on.

vom Hundert [Ger], per cent: *abbr.* v.H.

von der Liebe kann man nicht leben [Ger], one cannot live on love alone; the flames of love won't boil the pot.

von einem Ochsen kann man nur Rindfleisch verlangen [Ger], from an ox you can get only beef.

von oben [Ger], from the top: *abbr.* v.o.

von unten [Ger], from the bottom: *abbr.* v.u.

voortrekker [Du], pioneer: *South Africa.*

vorbei sind diese Träume [Ger], past are these dreams; these dreams are gone beyond recall: *Schiller.*

vor Christo *or* **vor Christi Geburt** [Ger], before Christ; B.C.: *abbr.* v.Ch. Cf. NACH CHRISTO.

vorigen Monats [Ger], last month: *abbr.* v.M.

vormittags [Ger], in the forenoon: *abbr.* vorm.

Vorrede [Ger], preface; prefatory discourse.

Vorspiel [Ger], prelude; overture: *music.*

Vorstellung [Ger; *pl.* Vorstellungen], presentation; representation; performance; esp., a mental image; conception; idea.

vorwärts! [Ger], forward!: *mil.*

Vorwort [Ger], preface; preamble; foreword.

vota vita mea [L], my life is devoted.

vouloir prendre la lune avec les dents [Fr], to want to seize the moon with the teeth; aim at impossibilities.

vous avez raison (*or* **tort**) [Fr], you are right (*or* wrong).

vous l'avez voulu, vous l'avez voulu, George Dandin [Fr], you wanted it, you wanted it, George Dandin (i.e., it is your own fault): in Molière's *George Dandin*, the lament of a man who has married above his station.

vous y perdrez vos pas [Fr], you will lose your labor (lit., your step).

vox [L; *pl.* voces], voice. **—vox angelica,** an organ stop producing a sound of stringlike quality: *music.* **—vox audita perit, litera scripta manet,** the voice that is heard perishes, the letter that is written abides; the spoken word perishes but the written word remains. **—vox barbara,** an incorrectly formed word; hybrid. **—vox clamantis in deserto,** the voice of one crying in the wilderness: *Vulgate* (*John* i. 23). **—vox clandestina,** whisper. **—vox et praeterea nihil,** a voice and nothing more; sound without sense. **—vox faucibus haesit,** the voice stuck in the throat; he was dumb with amazement: *Virgil.* **—vox humana,** an organ stop somewhat resembling the human voice: *music.* **—vox populi** [*pl.* voces populi], the voice of the people. **—vox populi, vox Dei,** the voice of the people is the voice of God. **—vox stellarum,** the voice of the stars; music of the spheres.

voyageur [Fr], a traveler; voyager; specif., an employee of a fur company engaged in transporting men and goods from outlying posts; a boatman or trapper: *Canada.*

voyelle [Fr], vowel.

voyez! [Fr], see! look!: *abbr.* v.

voyons! [Fr], let us see! come! now! now then!

vraisemblable [Fr], *adj.* likely; probable; plausible; *n.* likelihood; probability; appearance of truth.

vraisemblance [Fr], verisimilitude; probability.

vrouw [Du], woman; housewife; madam.

vuelo [Sp], flight, as of an airplane.

vuelta [Sp], a turn; return; *mech.,* revolution. —**a vuelta de correo,** by return mail. —**andar a vueltas,** to struggle; to endeavor. —**a vuelta de ojo,** quickly; in a jiffy. —**dar una vuelta,** to take a walk or ride. —**de la vuelta,** brought forward. —**no tiene vuelta de hoja,** there are no two ways about it.

vulgo [L], commonly.

vulgus amicitias utilitate probat [L], the common herd values friendships for their usefulness: *Ovid.*

vultus est index animi [L], the face is the index of the soul (*or* mind).

W

Wacht [Ger; *pl.* Wachten], *naut.,* watch; *mil.,* guard.

Wächterlied [Ger], watchman's song; aubade.

Waffenstillstand [Ger], truce; armistice.

wagon-lit [Fr; *pl.* wagons-lits], railway sleeping car.

wahine [Hawa], woman.

Wahrheit [Ger], truth. —**Wahrheit gegen Freund und Feind,** truth in spite of friend and foe: *Schiller.* —**Wahrheit und Dichtung,** truth and poetry: popular but erroneous transposition of Goethe's subtitle (*Dichtung und Wahrheit*) to his autobiography.

wahrscheinlich [Ger], probable; likely.

walla *or* **wallah** [Anglo-Ind; Hind *wala*], a word affixed to a noun or verb to denote the agent, doer, or occupational connection, corresponding to the English suffix *-man;* as, punkah-*walla,* the man who works a punkah; *colloq.,* fellow; person.

Wanderjahre [Ger; *pl.*], years of travel; years in which a journeyman traveled to gain more experience, following his *Lehrjahre,* his years of apprenticeship.

Wanderlust [Ger], passion for traveling; desire to see the world.

wan sui *or* **wan sei** [Chin], lit., 10,000 years; long live...

warum? [Ger], why? wherefore? —**warum nicht?,** why not? —**warum nicht gar!,** you don't say so! by no means!

was du liebst, das lebst du [Ger], what thou lovest, that thou livest: *Fichte.*

was gibt es? [Ger], what is the matter?

was gibt es neues? [Ger], what's new?

was ich nicht loben kann, davon sprech ich nicht [Ger], what I cannot praise, of that I do not speak: *Goethe.*

was ist das Leben ohne Liebesglanz [Ger], what is life without the light of love: *Schiller.*

Wasser [Ger], water.

was uns alle bändigt, das Gemeine [Ger], that which enthralls us all— the commonplace: *Goethe.*

Weihnachten [Ger], Christmas.

Weinstube [Ger; *pl.* Weinstuben], wine room in a tavern; wine shop.

Wein, Weib, und Gesang [Ger], wine, woman, and song.

Weltanschauung [Ger] lit., world view; conception of life or of the world in all its aspects; philosophy of life.

Weltgeschichte [Ger], world history; universal history.

Weltkrieg [Ger], world war.

weltmüde [Ger], world weary; disgusted with life.

Weltpolitik [Ger], international policy; foreign policy seeking economic and territorial expansion on a worldwide scale.

Weltschmerz [Ger], world sadness; vague discontent with the way life is proceeding; romantic discontent; pessimistic melancholy.

Weltweisheit [Ger], world wisdom; philosophy of life.

wenig [Ger], little. **—ein wenig schneller,** somewhat faster: *music.*

wenn man den Esel nennt, kommt er gerennt [Ger], when you speak of the donkey, he comes running.

wer am Wege baut, hat viele Meister [Ger], he who builds by the roadside has many foremen.

wer im Glashaus sitzt, soll nicht mit Steinen werfen [Ger], he who sits in a glass house should not throw stones.

Werk [Ger; *pl.* Werke], work; production.

wer rastet rostet [Ger], who rests rusts; if you rest, you rust.

wer zuletzt lacht, lacht am besten [Ger], who laughs last laughs best.

Widmung [Ger], dedication.

wie befinden Sie sich? [Ger], lit., how do you find yourself? how do you do? how are you?

wie geht's? [Ger], how goes it? how do you do?

Wiegenlied [Ger; *pl.* Wiegenlieder], cradle song; lullaby.

wie gewöhnlich [Ger], as usual; in the customary manner.

wie gewonnen, so zerronnen [Ger], as won, so spent; easy come, easy go.

wie Gott in Frankreich leben [Ger], lit., live like God in France; be very happy; be in a good situation.

wie heissen Sie? [Ger], what is your name?

Wirtshaus [Ger], inn; tavern.

Witwe [Ger; *pl.* Witwen], widow; dowager.

Witwer [Ger; *sing. & pl.*], widower.

wohin? [Ger], whither?

wohl! [Ger], lit., well; aye, aye, sir!

Wohlgefühl [Ger], a pleasant feeling.

wohlgetan überlebt den Tod [Ger], well-done outlives death.

wo ich nicht irre [Ger], if I am not mistaken.

wollte Gott! [Ger], would to God!

wollt ihr immer leben? [Ger], would you live forever?: *Frederick the Great* (to his guards on their hesitating to expose themselves to almost certain death).

Wörterbuch [Ger; *pl.* Wörterbücher], wordbook; dictionary.

wozu das? [Ger], what is that for? why that?

wozu dient das? [Ger], what is the use of that?

Wurst [Ger; *pl.* Würste], sausage. **—Wurst wider Wurst,** tit for tat.

Y

yad rochetset yad [Heb], lit., you help me, and I'll help you; one hand washes the other.

yafa shteeka lechachamin, kal vachomer lateepsheem [Heb], silence is beautiful in wise people and even more so in fools; silence is golden for the wise, essential for fools.

yah vahs loobloo [Russ], I love you.

yamen *or* **yamun** [Chin], formerly official residence of a mandarin; departmental headquarters: *China*.

yarmulke [Yiddish], skullcap worn by male Orthodox Jews.

yashmak [Turk *yāshmāq*], double veil worn by Muslim women in public.

yelick [Turk *yelek*], bodice.

yenta [Yiddish], a gossipy woman; a vulgar, coarse, carping woman.

yeux [Fr; *pl.* of *oeil*], eyes.

yoga [Skr], lit., union; ascetic Hindu philosophy aimed at achieving union with the supreme soul of the universe; also, exercises to promote physical and spiritual well-being.

yogi [Hind], a devotee of *yoga;* Hindu ascetic.

yojan [Hind], Hindu measure of distance, usually about five miles.

yuga [Skr], one of the four ages or cycles of the world: *Hinduism*.

yurt [Turkic, home], circular movable tent used in northern & central Asia.

Z

zacate [Sp], grass grown for forage; fodder.

zaftig [Yiddish], pleasantly plump.

zaftrek [Russ], breakfast.

Zahltag kommt alle Tag [Ger], payday comes every day.

zaibatsu [Jap], lit., wealth family; great industrial cliques.

zambomba [Sp], kind of crude rustic drum.

zamindar *or* **zemindar** [Hind], landholder; land tax collector: *India.*

zamindari [Hind], office and estates of a *zamindar;* real estate: *India.*

zampogna [It], bagpipe.

zanja [Sp], ditch; trench; esp., irrigation ditch or canal.

zanjero [Sp], man in charge of *zanjas.*

zapatera [Sp], shoemaker's wife; also, a defective olive, esp. one spoiled in curing.

zapatería [Sp], shoemaker's shop; shoe store.

zapatero [Sp], shoemaker. **—zapatero, a tus zapatos,** shoemaker, keep to your shoes; cobbler, stick to your last.

zapatilla [Sp], light shoe or pump; slipper.

zapato [Sp], shoe.

¡zape! [Sp], scat!

zapote [Mex Sp]. Cf. CHAPOTE.

zarf [Ar], lit., sheath or case; a metallic stand for a *finjan,* or Oriental coffee cup.

zart [Ger], *music,* tender; soft; delicate; also, fond; affectionate; *of colors,* pale; subdued.

zartem Ohre, halbes Wort [Ger], to a quick ear, half a word (is enough).

Zartgefühl [Ger], delicacy of feeling; tact.

zärtlich [Ger], tender; delicate; loving; fond.

zayat [Burmese], lit., a stopping-place to eat in; inn; public shelter or resthouse: *Burma.*

zdrávstvui! *or* **zdrávstvuite!** [Russ], a salutation for all occasions, equivalent to "good morning," "good day," etc.

Zeichen [Ger; *sing. & pl.*], mark; sign.

Zeitgeist [Ger], the spirit of the age; cultural climate; moral and intellectual trend of any particular period.

Zeitung [Ger; *pl.* Zeitungen], newspaper; gazette; journal.

zelosamente [It], ardently; with energy: *music.*

zeloso [It], with energy: *music.*

Zen [Jap], lit., religious meditation; mystical Japanese Buddhist sect.

zenana [Hind], the apartments reserved for women in a household: *India.*

zhená [Russ], wife; spouse; woman.

zhenshena [Russ; *pl.* ludi, people], woman.

ziemlich [Ger], considerable; rather; as, *ziemlich schnell,* rather fast: *music.*

zierlich [Ger], decorative; elegant; graceful; dainty; neat.

zillah [Hind], administrative division; collectorate; judicial district: *India.*

zingano *or* **zingaro** [It; *pl.* zingani *or* zingari], gypsy.

ζωή καὶ ψυχή [Gr; zóē kaì psukhḗ], my life and soul: term of affection.

ζωή μοῦ [Gr; zóē moû], my life; my dearest.

ζωή μοῦ, σὰς ἀγαπῶ [Gr; zóē moû, sàs agapô], my life, I love you!

> Hear my vow before I go,
> ζώη μοῦ, σὰς ἀγαπῶ.
> —BYRON, "Maid of Athens."

zögernd [Ger], hesitating; slackening in time: *music.*

Zoll [Ger; *pl.* Zolle], an inch: *abbr.* Z.

Zoll [Ger; *pl.* Zölle], toll; duty; custom; custom house.

Zollverein [Ger], customs union.

ζῶμεν ἀλογίστως προσδοκῶντες μὴ θανεῖν [Gr; zômen alogístōs, pros-dokôntes mè thaneîn], thoughtlessly we live, thinking death will never come: *Menander.*

zonam perdidit [L], he has lost his girdle (in which money was kept); he is ruined: *Horace.*

zonam solvere [L], to untie the girdle (a mark of maidenhood, laid aside at a Roman marriage ceremony); marry a maiden.

zornig [Ger], angry; hasty; passionate.

zufolo [It], a small flute or flageolet; esp., one used to teach birds to sing.

Zugzwang [Ger], lit., move compulsion; forced to move; a situation in which a player cannot make an effective move; also, the move made: *chess.*

zum Beispiel [Ger], for example: *abbr.* z.B.

zum ersten [Ger], in the first place. **—zum ersten! zum zweiten! zum dritten und letzen!,** going! going! gone!

zu Paaren [Ger], in couples.

Zuschrift [Ger; *pl.* Zuschriften], letter; dedication, as of a book.

zut [Fr], exclamation conveying annoyance, refusal, scorn, etc.

zu viel Demut ist Hochmut [Ger], too much humility is pride.

zwar weiss ich viel, doch möcht' ich alles wissen [Ger], true, I know much, but I should like to know everything: *Goethe.*

Zweigesang [Ger; *pl.* Zweigesänge], duet.

zwei Seelen und ein Gedanke, zwei Herzen und ein Schlag [Ger], two souls and one thought; two hearts and one beat; "two souls with but a single thought, two hearts that beat as one": *Friedrich Halm* (pseudonym of Baron von Münch-Bellinghausen, author of *Der Sohn der*

Wildnis or, as it was called on the American stage, *Ingomar the Barbarian,* from which this quotation is taken).

zweitens [Ger], secondly.

zwischen Amboss und Hammer [Ger], between anvil and hammer.

zwischen Freud' und Leid ist die Brücke nicht weit [Ger], between joy and sorrow the bridge is narrow.

Zwischenmusik [Ger], incidental music; a waiting move: *chess.*

Zwischenspiel [Ger], interlude; intermezzo.

Zwischenstück [Ger], a piece inserted; insertion; *theat.,* interlude.

zwischen uns sei Wahrheit [Ger], let truth be between us: *Goethe.*

Index

abandon, with: **con abbandono**
abbey: **abbaye**
abbot
  once an ~ always an ~: **semel abbas**
able
  as well as one is ~: **pro virili**
  can because they seem ~: **possunt**
aboard, all: **en voiture**
abomination, crush the: **écrasez
    l'infâme**
about: **circa; circiter; circum**
above: **en haut; sopra; supra**
  all things are from ~: **omnia
    desuper**
  as ~: **come sopra; sopra; ut supra**
aboveboard: **carte**
abridgment: **abrégé**
abroad
  go ~ to get news of home: **todai**
abruptly: **tout court**
absence: **abest; absence**
  ~ is love's stepmother: **la ausencia**
  ~ of air: **air**
  cat's ~: **absent**
  conspicuous by ~: **briller**
absent
  being ~: **absente**
  the ~ are always wrong: **gli assenti;
    les absents**
absentminded: **distrait**
absinthe: **génépi**
absolutely: **simpliciter**
absorbing: **passionnant**
abstract, in: **in abstracto**
absurd: **ab absurdo**
  ~ derivation: **lucus**
  which is ~: **quod absurdum**
absurdity: **ad absurdum; bêtise**
abundance
  ~ made me poor: **inopem**
  ~ of words: **copia verborum**
  out of the ~: εκ γαρ (ek gàr); **ex
    abundantia**
abuse is no argument against use: **abu-
    sus; ex abusu**
academy: **accademia**
accident: **casus; d'occasion; hasard;
    par hasard; per accidens**

acclaim as a result of achievement:
    kudos
accompaniment: **accompagnamento;
    Begleitung**
  without ~: **a capella**
accompanist: **accompagnatore**
accomplice: **particeps**
accomplishment: **agrément; arts
    d'agrément**
accord
  in ~: **en rapport; rapport**
  of its own ~: **ex proprio motu**
  one's own ~: **ex mero motu**
according to: **apud; secundum; selon**
account
  current ~: **cuenta**
  my ~: **mi cuenta**
  on ~: **à compte**
  on this ~: **propter**
  your ~: **su cuenta**
accurately: **ad amussim**
Acheron never lets go: **et l'avare**
acid, nitric: **aqua**
acknowledgment of a claim: **cognovit**
acme: **ne plus**
acquaintance: **conocido**
acrid: **âcre**
across: **à travers**
act
  do what's been done: **actum agere**
  in the ~: **in actu**
  it's not my ~: **non est meus**
  thoughtless ~: **étourderie**
  unlawful ~: **malum**
action
  ~ against my will: **actus**
  ~ delayed: **nunc pro**
  judged by our ~s: **spectemur**
  unostentatious ~: **faire sans**
activity
  much ~ small result: **molto**
actor
  comic ~: **buffo**
  principal ~: **primo**
  silent ~: **persona**
actress
  comic ~: **comédienne**
  tragic ~: **tragédienne**

actual: **actus; de facto; in esse**
added: **additum**
addition: **allonge; Beilage**
address, familiar: **tutoiement**
adherence, blind: **Nachbeterei**
adjournment: **aggiornamento**
  adjourned indefinitely: **sine**
administration: **régie**
administrator: **intendente; nazim;**
    nizam
admiral: **amiral**
admiration is not the same for all
        men: **denique non**
admit
  do not ~: **ne admittas**
  I ~: **concedo**
admittance, no: **défense d'entrer**
advancing
  who does not advance loses ground:
    qui non
advantage: **ex usu**
adversity, repel: **adversa**
advertisement: **annonce; Anzeige;**
    réclame
affable: **liant**
affair: **affaire**
  ~ of state: **la haute**
  casual love ~: **amoretto**
  love ~: **affaire**
  new ~s new counsels: **à nouvelles**
  ruined ~: **affaire; une affaire**
  the ~ is progressing: **la cosa;**
    l'affaire
  ticklish ~: **pas**
affectation: **maniéré; minauderie**
  ~ of a person: **poseur**
  ~ of behavior: **singerie**
  ~ of devotion: **béguinage**
  ~ of simplicity: **faire l'ingénu**
affectionate: **afectuoso**
  most ~: **afectísimo**
affiliated: **affilié**
affinity: **rapport**
affliction affects us less: **damna**
affront: **camouflet**
Africa, always something new out of:
    ex Africa
after: **dopo**
  ~ all: **am Ende**
  ~ this, therefore because of this:
    post hoc
afternoon: **après-midi; Nachmittag;**
    post meridiem
  good ~: **boa tarde; buenas tardes;**

    dobre din
  in the ~: **nachmittags**
again: **ancora; encore; etiam atque;**
    iterum
against: **adversus**
Agamemnon, great men lived before:
    vixere
age: **aetatis**
  ~ considers, youth essays: **das Alter**
  foolishness and wisdom in ~: **en**
    vieillissant
  golden ~: **Saturnia; siècle**
  now the Golden A~ returns: **iam**
    redit
  on the threshold of old ~: **επι**
    γηραος (epì gḗraos)
agenda: **ordre du**
agent: **commissionnaire**
agitation: **agitato**
agreeable: **agréable; délicat; gustoso**
agreed: **d'accord; es bleibt; tope là**
agreement: **accordo; Ausgleich; con-**
    cordat; entente
  unlawful ~: **pactum**
aid
  ~ and counsel: **ope et**
  not for such ~ as this: **non tali**
aide, military: **aide-de-camp**
aim: **en joue**
  ~ at impossibilities: **prendre la lune;**
    vouloir
air
  ~ of distinction: **air**
  ~s, put on: **faire l'homme**
  in the open ~: **en plein; im Freien;**
    sub dio; sub Iove
  mountain ~: **afflatus**
  open ~: **aire; al fresco; im Freiern;**
    plein air
airmail: **correo; par avion**
airplane: **avion**
alarm: **alerte**
alas: **ahimè; eheu; hélas; heu pietas;**
    O tempora
alehouse: **Bier; brasserie**
alert: **en alerte; qui vive**
  on the ~: **alerte**
alienation, mental: **égarement**
alive: **vif**
all: **tutta; tutti**
  above ~: **surtout**
  ~ at once: **tout d'un**
  ~ depends on this: **totum**
  ~ is taken: **tout est pris**

~ of that kind: **id genus omne; tout d'une**

~ or nothing: **tout bien; tout ou**

~ right: **bahut; ladno**

~ together: **en masse; pour tout potage**

grasp ~ lose ~: **la codicia; quien mucho; qui trop embrasse**

if ~ did thus: **si sic omnes**

in ~: **chou**

understand ~ pardon ~: **tout comprendre**

Allah, in the name of: **bismillah**

alley: **allée**

blind ~: **cul-de-sac; impasse**

alliance: **entente**

triple ~: **Dreibund**

allowance, make: **al amigo**

almond: **almendra; amande**

~ shape: **mandorla**

almoner: **aumonier**

almost: **à peu près; seul; solus**

alone

better ~: **antes só**

let us ~: **laissez-nous**

never less ~ than when ~: **nunquam minus**

alternately: **tour**

always: **semper; sempre**

ambassador: **vakil**

ambiguity of expression: **double entente**

ambiguous: **équivoque**

ambush: **embuscade; guet-apens**

ambusher: **embusqué**

amends: **amende**

American: **gringo**

amicably: **à l'amiable**

amount, specified: **quantum**

amusing: **rigolo**

ancestors, in the manner of our: **hoc erat in more**

anchovy: **anchois**

and

~ also: **ac etiam**

~ elsewhere: **et alibi**

~ everything of that kind: **et hoc; et id**

~ others: **et alii; und**

~ so forth: καὶ τα (kaì tà); **und**

~ so of the like: **et sic de similibus**

~ so of the rest: **et sic de ceteris**

~ the following: **et sequens**

~ the like: **et similia**

anew: **de integro; de nouveau; de novo**

angels, not Angles but: **non Angli**

anger: **zornig**

~ and tears: **inde irae**

~ is a brief madness: **ira furor**

~ so great in heavenly minds: **tantaene**

in ~: **en courroux**

without ~: **sine**

animal

two-legged ~ without feathers: **animal bipes**

animated: **caloroso**

animatedly: **animato; bewegt; moto**

animation

with ~: **con moto**

with more ~: **mosso**

annals: **annales**

annotations: **Anmerkungen**

annoyance, deliberate: **avoir le diable**

annoyances: **kleine**

annoying: **embêtement**

how ~: **das ist Pech**

annually: **per annum**

another

~ exactly the same: **alter idem**

~ point of view: **alio**

~ way must be tried: **alia tendenda**

answer, give evasive: **répondre**

antonym: **antonyme**

anxiety: **tintouin**

anyone: **le premier venu**

if ~: **si quis**

apart: **à part; in disparte**

apartment: **appartement; garçonnière; garni**

apartments, women's: **zenana**

aphrodisiac: **pousse-l'amour**

Apollo preserved me: **sic me**

apologize: **faire l'amende**

appeal

~ for understanding: **argumentum**

without ~: **sans**

appearance: **air; tournure**

~ deceives: **decipit**

deceptive ~: **decipimur**

distinguished ~: **air**

first ~: **début; débutant**

no trusting ~s: **fronti nulla; ne fronti; nimium**

under the ~ of: **sub specie**

world rewards ~: **le monde**

appendix: **Anhang**

vermiform ~: **appendix vermiformis**
appetite: **à bon appétit**
  ~ comes from eating: **l'appétit**
  no sauce like ~: **il n'est sauce**
appetizer: **apéritif; canapé; hors-**
    d'oeuvre
applauder, hired: **claque; claqueur**
applause, making of: **claquer**
application of oneself: **prendre le mors**
appointment: **rendez-vous**
appreciation, to feel: **savoir gré**
apprenticeship, years of: **Lehrjahre**
approval
  to have won ~ of eminent men:
    principibus
apricot: **abricot**
  peach ~: **abricot-pêche**
apronlike: **en tablier**
Arcadia
  both from ~: **Arcades ambo**
  even I am in ~: **et ego**
  I too was born in ~: **auch ich war**
arch, triumphal: **arc de triomphe**
archduke: **Erzherzog**
architecture: **Baukunst**
  ~, frozen music: **die Baukunst**
  German school of ~: **Bauhaus**
ardent: **ardente; perfervidum**
ardently: **ardentemente; praefervidum**
ardor: **élan; empressement; estro**
area, enclosed: **enclave**
argument
  ~ proving ignorance, absurdity, etc.:
    argumentum
  chief ~: **nervus probandi**
  ineffectual ~: συκινη (súkinē);
    telum
  who proves too much proves noth-
    ing: **qui nimium**
aria, short: **arietta; cavatina**
aristocracy: **optimates**
aristocrat: **Junker**
  to the lamppost with the ~s: **les**
    aristocrates
armchair: **fauteuil**
armored division: **Panzer**
arms
  ~ and the man: **arma virumque**
  let ~ yield: **cedant**
  open ~: **à bras**
  put down your ~: **Gewehre**
  receive ~: **arma accipere**
  side ~: **armes blanches**
  stack ~: **formez**

to ~: **aux armes**
under ~: **in armis**
army: **lashkar**
  ~ cook: **cuistot**
  ~ post: **presidio**
  ~ reserve: **Landsturm**
  call to ~ service: **arrière-ban**
  German ~: **Reichswehr**
around, all: **attorno**
arrangement, clear: **lucidus**
arrest, under: **arrêt; aux arrêts**
arrogance: **hauteur; hubris;**
    outrecuidance
  aristocratic ~: **Junkerei**
  ~ in prosperity: εντυχων
    (**eutukhôn**)
arrow: **flèche**
arroyo: **coulée**
art: **Kunst**
  ~ even to maligning: **est ars**
  ~ is long: **ars est longa**
  ~ of cookery: **scientia**
  fine ~s: **beaux arts**
  he will adorn the ~s: **artes**
  new ~: **Art Nouveau**
  true ~ conceals: **ars est celare**
  with ~ the mistress: **arte magistra**
artichoke: **artichaut**
article, lead: **Leitartikel**
artist
  an ~ must live: **die Kunst**
  what an ~ dies in me: **qualis artifex**
as
  ~ if one should say: **quasi dicat**
  ~ if said: **quasi dictum; quasi**
    dixisset
  ~ much as it may be worth:
    quantum
  ~ much as you please: **quantum**
  ~ you please: **se vi**
  ~ you possess: **uti possidetis**
  ~ you sow: **tibi**
  ~ you were: **autant**
  ~ you will: **a vostro beneplacito**
ascetic: **sannyasi**
ask and it shall be given you: αιτειτε
    (**aiteîte**)
asparagus: **asperge**
ass
  ~ at the lyre: **asinus ad**
  ~ beautiful to an ~: **asinus asino**
  ~ remains an ass: **ein Esel**
  stubborn ~: **à dur âne**
  wool of an ~: ονον (**ónou**)

assembly, sound general: **battre**
assertion, mere: **gratis dictum**
assiduity, leisurely: **otiosa**
assignee, rights of: **assignatus**
assistance, need no: **sine**
assistant: **aide; ayudante**
associates: **entourage**
association, loan: **credit foncier**
assumptions: **postulata**
assurance, with: **à plomb**
astonishment
~ at nothing: **nil admirari**
I was astounded: **obstupui**
Athanasius against the world:
Athanasius
atrocious: **affreux**
attack: **attacca**
attainment
~ of an object: **pour y**
~ of what he attempts: **consequitur**
attempt
~ not made: **ne tentes**
first ~: **coup**
attention: **Achtung; atento; garde à**
~ to one's own affairs: **age quod; il faut cultiver**
~ to serious matters: **amoto**
small ~s: **petits soins**
to pay ~: **assister**
attorney: **procureur**
attractive: **alléchant**
at which: **ad quem**
audacity: **de l'audace**
August: **août**
aunt: **tante**
aureole, oval: **vesica**
author: **autore**
authoritatively: **ex cathedra**
authority: **droit**
~ brooks no equal: **mandar**
~ to inquire: **inquirendo**
on good ~: **de bonne part**
parental ~: **patria potestas**
supreme ~: **patres**
unlimited ~: **carte**
with full ~: **pleno iure**
automobile: **vettura**
~ body: **carrosserie**
autumn: **kharif**
avenger
~ of wrong: **vindex**
may some ~ arise: **exoriare**

avenue: **alameda; avenida**
average, annual: **communibus**
avocado: **avocat**
avoidance
~ of asking what tomorrow brings: **quid sit**
~ of excess: **ne quid nimis**
~ of perils of leisure: **fuyez**
award: **accolade**
awkwardness: **maladresse**
axe is laid unto the root of the trees: η αξινη (hē axínē)

babbler: **babillard**
baby: **bébé**
baccalaureate: **baccalauréat**
bachelor: **célibataire; garçon; en garçon**
old ~: **vieux**
back
~ again: **de retour; de vuelta**
~ and loins: **râble**
~ of a page: **folio**
~ to ~: **dos à**
backwards: **à rebours; à reculons**
backwoods: **boondocks**
bad: **kharab; mauvais**
~ to worse: **de mal**
spare the ~, injure the good: **bonis nocet**
badge: **chaprás**
bagpipe: **zampogna**
bail: **cautionnement**
bakery: **boulangerie**
balance, hanging in the: **res**
ball
country ~: **bal**
fancy-dress ~: **bal**
masked ~: **bal**
ballad: **frottola**
ballet ensemble: **corps**
balloon, trial: **ballon**
ballot: **scrutin**
band
guerrilla ~: **comitadji**
Mexican ~: **mariachi**
bandit: **bandido**
banished: **aqua**
bank: **crédit mobilier**
~ draft: **letra**
~ note: **billet**

banquet: **bara**
banterer: **persifleur; railleur**
bard, honor the: **onorate**
bare-headed: **en cheveux**
bargain: **bandobast; bon marché;**
    pactum
barge: **chaland**
barium sulfate: **blanc fixe**
barley: **orge**
baron: **Freiherr**
  ~ of hare: **râble**
barracks: **cuartel**
barrage: **rafale**
barroom: **Bier; cantina; estaminet;**
    Stube
basket: **corbeille; panier**
bass: **bar** (fish); **basso** (singer)
  double ~: **contrabasso; violone**
bassoon, double: **contrafagotto**
bastard: **filius; momzer**
bath: **ghusl; hammam; mikvah**
  steam ~: **sauna**
battle, pitched: **bataille**
Bavarian: **bavarois**
bay: **abra; anconada; bahía; baia**
bayonet, fix: **baïonnette; das**
    Seitengewehr
bayonets, unfix: **Bajonett; remettez la**
beach: **plage; playa**
bean: **fève; frijol; haba; haricot**
bear: **baloo**
  kill ~ before selling it: **il ne fait pas**
    vendre
  polar ~: **nanook**
bearded: **barbu**
beard well lathered: **barba bagnata**
bearer of flag of truce: **parlementaire**
bearing: **allure**
beating: **frottée**
beat, musical: **battuta**
beautiful
  the ~ and the base: **τo καλov (tò**
    kalòn)
  to be ~ it's necessary to suffer: **il**
    faut souffrir
beauty
  artificial ~: **beauté d'emprunt**
  ~ and marriage: **chi nasca**
  ~ and pride: **es soberbia**
  ~ fades, virtue stays: **Schönheit**
  ~ is a flower, fame a breath: **forma**
    flos
  ~ without virtue: **la beauté**
  death of ~: **auch das Schöne; forma**

    bonum
trail of ~: **bik'é**
bed: **charpoy; palang**
  ~ and board: **a mensa; mensa et**
bedroom: **chambre**
bedtime: **hora decubitus**
beech, beneath the spreading: **sub**
    tegmine
beef: **carne**
  ~ fillet: **tournedos**
  ~ slices: **miroton**
  ~ steak: **bifteck**
  jerked ~: **charqui**
  ribs of ~: **côtes**
  roast ~: **rosbif**
bee in one's bonnet: **plafond; une**
    araignée
beer: **Bier; bière; Frühschoppen**
  ~ hall: **Stube**
bees practice geometry: **ut apes**
beet: **betterave**
  ~ soup: **borshch**
before: **en avant; par avance**
  as ~: **sicut ante**
  ~ death: **ante mortem**
beggar: **lazzarone**
  better to be a ~: **è meglio un buon**
beginning: **ab initio; ab origine; ab**
    ovo; capo; initio; sub initio
  ~ and end: **Αλφα (álpha)**
  ~s of all things: **omnium**
  ~ to end: **ab ovo usque; da capo**
  every ~ is cheerful: **aller Anfang ist**
    heiter
  every ~ is difficult: **aller Anfang ist**
    schwer
  from the ~: **a principio; da capo**
  good ~: **à bonne commencement**
  in the ~: **in principio**
  lacks ~: **caret**
  resist the ~s: **obsta**
  well begun, half done: **αρχη ημισν**
    (arkhḕ hémisu); barba bagnata;
    buen principio; dimidium
behavior
  good ~: **quamdiu**
  overweening or arrogant ~: **hubris**
  tactless ~: **gaffe**
behind: **en queue**
being
  be what you seem to be: **esto quod**
  let it be as it is: **sit ut**
  Supreme B~: **ens**
  to be: **esse**

what God commanded you to be:
quam te
who has not, is not: **chi non ha**
belief: **credite**
~ because of absurdity: **credo quia absurdum**
~ because of impossibility: **credo quia impossibile**
~ makes all possible: παντα δυνατα **(pánta dunatà)**
let Apella believe it: **credat**
power of ~: **crede quod**
bell: **cloche; Glocke**
~ ringer: **carillonneur**
small ~: **clochette**
beloved: **Liebchen; querido**
below: **infra**
as ~: **ut infra**
belt: **banda; ceinture**
beneficiary of a trust: **cestui**
benefit of the world: **pro mundi**
bent not broken: **flecti**
be rather than seem: **esse quam**
besides: **au reste; d'ailleurs**
best: **au mieux**
all the ~: **fservyo charoshevo**
~ is good enough: **das Beste**
oldest is ~: **azeite**
bet
~s have been placed: **les jeux**
I ~ it's so: **je gage**
betrothed: **fiancé**
better: **bien mieux**
~ ask than lose your way: **è meglio domandar**
~ is the enemy of good: **le mieux**
~ once than never: **è meglio una**
~ or worse: **vaille**
the first is ~: **meliores**
betters, give way to: **da locum**
betting: **pari mutuel**
~ marks the fool: **gageure**
between: **inter**
beware: **prenez**
~ he's vicious: **faenum**
let him ~: **caveat**
bewilderment: **désorienté; égaré; éperdu**
bias: **parti**
bidding: **enchère**
bigness: **gros**
bill: **conto**
~ of exchange: **lettre**
legislative ~: **projet**

quash the ~: **cassetur**
true ~: **billa vera**
billiards: **massé**
billingsgate: **langage**
bills, post no: **défense d'afficher**
bird: **kiwi; pájaro**
~ makes her nest little by little: **petit**
~ thinks: **à chaque oiseau**
gallows ~: **gibier**
birds
~ of a feather: **gens; κολοιος (ko-loiòs); qui se ressemblent; ribàk**
~ of prey: **dos aves**
birth: **geboren; née; naissance**
~ certificate: **extrait**
birthright: **droit**
bishop: **évêque**
bit
~ by bit: **pièce**
bitter ~: **outrance**
biter is bitten: **captantes**
bitter: **amargoso**
something ~ rises: **surgit**
bitterness: **amari; amertume; odium**
~ outweighs sweetness: **plus aloës**
bittersweet: **aigre-doux; dolce-piccante**
bizarre: **outré**
black: **dhu; kala; noir**
~ and white: **par écrit**
blackguard: **drôle**
blackmail: **chantage**
blackmailer and twister of laws: **extortor**
blackshirts: **Shutzstaffel**
blameless: **integer; rectus in**
blank: **in bianco**
blanket: **kammal; serape**
bless: **bentsh**
~ you: **benedicite**
it is more ~ed to give: μακαριον **(makárión)**
thrice ~ed: **ter quaterque**
blessing: **kiddush**
blind
the ~ lead the blind: τυφλος **(typhlòs)**
Venetian ~: **jalousie**
blinds, lower the: **bassez les stores**
blockhead: **Dummkopf**
blond: **blondin**
blood: **sangre**
~ and iron: **Blut**
~ from a stone: **ab asino; dalla**
blue ~: **sangre**

cold ~: **à froid; sangre**
bloodthirsty: **acharné**
blow: **coup**
  ~ of a stick: **à coups de bâton**
  bold ~: **coup**
  one ~: **de un golpe; de un tirón;**
    uno ictu
  without a ~: **sine**
blue: **bleuâtre**
  dark ~: **gros**
  deep ~: **bleu foncé**
blunder: **lapsus**
  make a ~: **faire un impair**
  more than ~, a crime: **c'est plus**
  social ~: **gaucherie**
bluntly: **de but en**
blushed so the affair is safe: **erubuit**
boar: **sanglier**
  ~ head: **hure**
board
  ~ of directors: **conseil**
  sounding ~: **abat-voix**
boarder: **en pension; pension**
boasting: **gasconnade**
boat: **bateau; caïque; embarcación;**
    gál; praam; pulwar; schuit;
    umiak
bodice: **yelick**
body: **corps; corpus; cuerpo**
  astral counterpart of the ~: **linga**
  better ~ starved than the mind: **più**
    tosto
  form of ~ after death: **kama rupa**
bodyguard: **garde**
boiler: **chaudière**
boldly: **audaciter; deciso**
boldness: **audax**
bombshell: **bombe**
bonbon: **cosaque**
bond, marriage: **vinculum**
bondage, sweet: **ηδυ (hēdu)**
bone: **os**
  to pick a ~: **os à ronger**
book: **Buch; Heft; kitab; liber; livre**
  ~ binder: **Buchbinder**
  ~ binding: **Buchbinderkunst**
  ~ censorship: **Index Expurgatorius**
  ~ cover: **Banddeckel**
  ~ plate: **ex libris**
  ~ prize: **detur**
  ~ seller: **bouquiniste; Buchhändler;**
    libraire
  ~ store: **Buchhandlung; librairie**
  closed ~: **libro**

dangerous ~: **mauvais**
destiny of a ~: **habent sua**
never judge a ~ by its cover: **al**
    teestakel
no robber worse than a bad ~: **non**
  v'è
Old Testament ~: **megillah**
where the ~ opens: **ad aperturam**
  libri
booklet: **libret**
bookworm: **helluo**
border: **limbus**
boredom: **ennui**
  bored: **ennuyé**
  boring: **ennuyeux**
borrower has no choice: **ne choisit**
borrowing makes sorrowing: **Borgen**
boss: **baas**
bottle: **fiaschetta**
  scent ~: **flacon**
bottom, from the: **von unten**
bouillon, wine: **court-bouillon**
boulevard: **Boule-Miche; Prado**
bound: **uno saltu**
bounds, keep within: **servare**
bow: **noeud**
  ceremonial ~: **kowtow**
  two strings to one's ~: **duplici**
  violin ~: **arco; Bogen**
  with the ~: **coll' arco**
  with the stick of the ~: **collegno**
box: **caisse; caja; cassette**
  money ~: **cagnotte**
boxing: **savate**
boy: **chokra; garçon; larka; malchik;**
    muchacho
  cabin ~: **mousse**
  little ~: **chico**
  to maidens and ~s: **virginibus**
  trust not a sword to a ~: **ne puero**
brace: **braguero**
bracket: **cul-de-lampe**
braggart: **faux; hâbleur**
bragging: **hâblerie**
braid: **soutache**
brain: **cervelle**
  long hair, little ~: **cabello**
brains, calf's: **cervelle**
  rack one's ~: **perdre**
brake: **freno**
branch: **ramo**
brandy: **aqua; eau; mao tai**
  apple ~: **calvados**

brat: **moutard**
brave and faithful: **fortis et**
bravely and uprightly: **fortiter et**
bravery: **fortitudini**
  ~ and arms: **virtute et armis**
brazenness: **chutzpah**
brazier: **brasero; hibachi**
bread: **brioche; challa; chapati;**
    croissant; kleb; pain; pan;
    roti
  ~ and circus games: **panem**
  broken ~: **brisé**
  loaf of ~: **baguette**
  slice of~: **tartine**
  unleavened ~: **matzo**
break
  ~ in ranks: **rompez les rangs**
  ~ in step: **rompez le pas**
breakfast: **almuerzo; aruchat; bara;**
    chhota; colazione; déjeuner; de-
    juma; Frokost; Frühstuck; Mor-
    genessen; zaftrek
breakwater: **môle**
breast
  in the ~: **in pectore**
  within one's ~: **in petto**
breath: **fiato**
breeches: **bragas; chausses; culotte;**
    jodhpurs
breeze: **aura**
brevity
  briefly: **en peu**
  to be brief: **pour couper**
  to the understanding, a few words
    suffice: **intelligenti**
bride: **novia**
bridegroom: **novio**
bridesmaid: **dame d'honneur**
bride's wardrobe: **trousseau**
bridge: **pons; ponticello** (of string in-
    strument)**; puente**
bridgehead: **tête-de-pont**
brigade: **brigada**
brigand: **haiduk**
brightness: **chiarezza**
  more brightly from out of darkness:
    clarior e
brilliant: **brillante**
brilliantly: **di bravura**
bring with you: **duces**
briskly: **svegliato**
bristling: **brosse**
broadly: **largamente**
broiled: **grillé**

broom
  new ~ sweeps clean: **neue Besen;**
    una scopa
broth: **bouillon**
brother: **brat; Bruder; frangin; frate;**
    frater; hermano
brothers: **Gebrüder**
  three ~, three fortresses: **tres**
brought forward: **vuelta**
browned: **rissolé**
brush: **brosse**
brushlike: **en brosse**
brusqueness: **brusquerie**
Brussels sprouts: **chou**
bud: **bourgeon**
Buddhism, Japanese sect of: **Zen**
Buddhist
  ~ invocation: **om mani**
  ~ monastery: **kyaung**
  ~ priest: **bosan**
buddy: **copain**
buffalo
  ~ fish: **besugo**
  water ~: **carabao**
bugaboo: **croque-mitaine**
bugle: **Flügelhorn**
building
  block of ~s: **corps**
  detached ~: **corps**
  he pulls down, he builds up: **diruit**
bulb, light: **bombilla**
bull: **toro**
  fleeing ~: **huyendo**
bullfighting: **toreo**
  bullfight: **corrida; toro**
  bullfighter: **matador; picador; torero**
  matador's attendants: **cuadrilla**
bull's-eye: **oeil-de-boeuf**
bundle: **Fascio; trousse**
bungler: **klutz; schlemiel**
burden
  ~ of proof: **onus probandi**
  equal to the ~: **par oneri**
  heavy ~: **à chacun**
  lay the ~ on the lazy ass: **onus segni**
buried: **sepultus**
burlesque: **burletta**
bush, beat about the: **battre**
bushel: **fanega**
business: **beigebunden**
  ~ is ~: **affaire**
  ~ manager: **gérant**
  ~ people: **gens**
  equal to his ~: **par negotiis**

everybody's ~, nobody's ~: **obra**
pastry ~: **pâtisserie**
unfinished ~: **re infecta**
butcher, pork: **charcutier**
buts are not worthwhile: **no hay pero**
butter: **beurre; ghee**
  browned ~: **au beurre roux; sauce**
butterfly: **papillon**
buttocks: **derrière; toches**
buttonhole: **boutonnière**
buttress, flying: **arc-boutant**
buyer: **emptor**
  ~ beware: **emptor**
by
  ~ and ~: **al-ki; taihoa**
  ~ the way: **à propos; en passant;**
    par parenthèse
  ~ way of: **per viam**
bygones be bygones: **lass**
bystander: **assistant**

cab: **fiacre**
cabaret: **bal musette**
cabbage: **chou**
  ~ twice over is death: δις κραμβη
    (dìs krámbē)
  with ~: **aux choux**
cabin: **cabane; cabine; camarote; choza**
cackle: **caquet**
cactus: **bisagre; bisnaga**
cadence: **cadenza**
  deceptive ~: **inganno**
Caesar
  ~ or nothing: **aut Caesar**
  render unto ~: αποδοτε (apódote)
cake: **baba au rhum; chupatty;**
    dariole; gâteau; madeleine;
    marzipan; massepain; Torte
calamities, series of: Ιλιας (Iliàs); **Ilias**
    malorum
calendar of events: **fasti**
calf, golden: **adorer**
call: **dit**
  I can scarcely ~ these mine: **vix**
calm: **saevis**
  stay ~: **aequam servare**
camel: **oont**
cameo: **camaïeu**
Canada: **bois**
  upper ~: **Haut-Canada**
canal: **acequia**
  ~ overseer: **zanjero**
  irrigation ~: **zanja**
candle: **cierge**

burn the ~: **brûler la**
candy: **nogada; pastille**
  ~ dish: **bonbonnière**
cannibal: **caribe**
canon: **chanoine**
canopy: **baldacchino**
Canossa, we're not going to: **nach**
    Canossa
canteen keeper: **cantinier**
canter: **aubin**
canyon: **cañada; cañoncito**
cap: **beret; berretta; képi**
cape: **cabo; mozzetta; muleta**
  red ~: **bonnet rouge**
  woman's ~: **faldetta**
capital, small: **versalilla**
capon: **chapon; poularde**
caprice: **capriccio**
captains
  two ~ sink the ship: **due capitani**
captivation
  ~ by kitchen aroma: **captus**
  ~ by neatness: **munditiis**
capture: **prise**
car: **cabriolet; carrozza; coche**
  sleeping ~: **traviesa; vagón; wagon-**
    lit
caravan stopping-place: **caravanserai;**
    khan
card: **carte**
  ~ game: **baccarat; bésigue; brelan;**
    juego de; vingt
  shuffle ~s: **battre**
  visiting ~: **carte**
cardinal: **chapeau**
care: **con cura**
  black ~: **atra**
  ~ brings gray hairs: **aura facit**
  ~ of: **en casa de**
  take ~: **gardez bien; gare; guarda-**
    tevi; prendetevi
  take ~ that republic not be injured:
    ne quid detrimenti
career: **carrière; la carrière**
carelessness: **déboutonné; nachlässig**
  through ~: **per incuriam**
caretaker: **shammes**
carnival won't last forever: **non semper**
    erunt
carouse: **ripaille**
carriage: **berline; calèche; calesa; car-**
    rosse; dormeuse; gark; gharry;
    landau

carry on and keep yourselves for better times: **durate et**
cart: **charrette**
~ before the horse: **currus**
oil the ~: **untar**
ox ~: **bail**
two-wheeled ~: **carreta**
cartel: **Kartell**
Carthage must be destroyed: **delenda
est**
carved it: **sculpsit**
case
~ decided: **res**
~ of conscience: **casus**
~ within stipulations: **casus**
celebrated ~: **cause**
in an analogous ~: **in pari**
in any ~: **jedenfalls**
omitted ~: **casus**
small ~: **étui**
undecided ~: **adhuc sub iudice**
cash: **argent; per contante**
~ works wonders: **argent**
cask is easily rolled when empty:
dolium
cassock: **soutane**
cast: **dramatis**
caste: **ját**
~ mark: **tilak**
military ~: **Kshatriya**
castle: **alcázar; château; Schloss**
~ in the air: **bâtir; far almanacchi**
cat: **billi; chat; gato**
one eye on frying pan, one on ~:
un' occhio
scalded ~ is afraid of cold water:
gato escaldado
sell ~ for hare: **vender**
sleeping ~ doesn't catch mouse:
chat; gato que
trust bacon to ~: **raccomandare**
catalogue: **catalogue; Index Librorum;
raisonné; repertorium**
catalpa: **bois**
catchword: **Schlagwort**
cathedral: **Dom**
cattle: **ganado**
caught
~ in the act: **pris sur**
~ napping: **pris au**
cauliflower: **choufleur**
cause: **causa**
~ ceases, effect ceases: **cessante**
~ removed, effect removed: **sublata**

~ to effect: **a priori**
final ~: **causa**
hidden ~: **causa**
I have good ~: **j'ay**
immediate ~: **causa**
remote ~: **causa**
secondary ~: **causa**
show ~: **scire**
true ~: **causa; vera causa**
without approved ~: **sine**
caution, excessive: **ex abundante**
cavalcade: **cabalgada**
cavalry: **caballería**
~ commander: **risaldar**
~man: **sowar; spahi**
~ squadron: **sotnia**
dashing man of the ~: **beau sabreur**
ceiling: **plafond**
celery: **celeri**
cellar, town-hall: **Ratskeller**
cemetery: **campo; Friedhof**
censor: **censor**
center
~ of the road: **ad filum viae**
~ of the stream: **ad filum aquae**
century: **siècle**
close of 19th ~: **fin**
ceremony: **bar mitzvah; bas mitzvah;
cérémonie**
certainly: **jawohl**
certificate: **bene exeat; certificado**
cessation of fire: **cessez**
chair: **calesin; jampan; kursi; lamba;
sedan; silla**
challenge: **appel**
chamber: **câmara; cámara; serdab**
Star C~: **Camera**
champagne: **simpkin; tisane**
chance, by: **par accident**
change
all things and people ~: **omnia
mutantur**
~s being made: **mutatis**
give me my ~: **rendez-moi**
I scorn to ~: **mutare**
more it ~s, more it's the same: **plus
ça**
we've ~d all that: **nous avons
changé**

channel, sluggish: **bayou**
chant: **accentus**
chanting: **cantillatio**
chaparral: **ceja**
chapel: **capilla; chapelle; Kapelle**
chapter, closed: **chose jugée**
characteristic: **ben trovato; cachet**
character not speech: **virtute, non verbis**
charcoal: **charbon; fusain**
  ~ burner: **carbonaro; charbonnier**
chariot, Italian medieval: **carroccio**
charm, personal ~: **charisma**
charming: **lieblich; ravissant**
charmingly: **à ravir**
chase: **caccia**
  who ~s another does not sit still: **die een ander**
chat: **causerie; shmooz**
chatterbox: **moulin**
chatter, idle: **bavardage; paroles en**
cheap: **à bon marché**
cheaply: **à bon compte; à peu de frais**
check: **échec**
cheek, what: **quel toupet; toupet**
cheer: **banzai**
  be of good ~: θαρσει (thársei)
  ~ up: **frisch auf**
cheerfully: **freudig**
cheese: **camembert; Liederkranz**
  ~ straws: **pailles**
cheesecake: **talmouse**
cherry: **cereza**
  ~ blossom: **sakura**
chess, forced move in: **Zugzwang**
chest: **petto; poitrine**
chestnut: **castaña; marron**
  ~ horse: **alezan**
  horse ~: **marron**
chewing-substance: **pansupari**
chicken: **arroz; cacciatore; pollo**
  chick: **poussin**
  roast ~: **poulet**
  young ~: **poulet**
chief: **aga; capo; caudillo; naik; prima; thakur; vidana**
child: **bachcha; bambino; enfant; niño; ribyonik**
  ~ of fortune: **fortunae filius**
  non-Jewish ~: **shegetz; shiksa**
  out of the mouth of a ~: **ex ore**
  spoiled ~: **enfant**
  terrible ~: **enfant**

childbirth, before: **antepartum**
childhood: **ab incunabilis; enfance**
children: **diti; putti**
  class for ~: **kindergarten**
  many ~ many blessings: **viele**
chilled: **transi**
chimes: **Glockenspiel**
chimney: **chimenea**
  ~ stack: **corps**
  fireless ~: **chimenea**
Chinese
  ~ idol: **joss**
  ~ style: **à la chinoise**
chivalrous: **sans**
chivalry, code of: **Bushido**
choice: **crème; recherché**
  no third ~: **non datur**
choir, cathedral: **Domchor**
chop, loin: **côtelette**
chosen, many called but few: **multi sunt; πολλοι γαρ (polloì gár)**
Christ
  after ~: **dopo; nach Christo**
  before ~: **ante Christum; avanti; vor Christo**
  body of ~: **corpus**
  ~ have mercy: **Christe**
  ~, my hope: **spes**
  cross of ~: **Christi**
  for ~ and Church: **Christo**
  in ~'s name: **in Christi**
Christmas: **Noël; Weihnachten**
  ~ Eve: **Nochebuena**
  ~ tree: **Tannenbaum**
  Merry ~: **fröhliche; Joyeux**
chrysanthemum: **kiku**
Church
  bosom of the ~: **bercail**
  for ~ and Pope: **pro Ecclesia**
churchman: **homme**
cider: **kvass**
cigarette: **cigarillo; papirosa**
cipher, mere: **c'est un zéro**
circle
  ~ course: **chukker**
  ~ of the sciences: **orbis**
  vicious ~: **circulus**
circumference: **Umfang**
circumlocution: **circuitus**
circumstance
  according to ~: **cela est selon**
  I try to make ~s yield to me: **et mihi**
  straitened ~s: **res**

citizen: **citoyen; cittadino; grazhdanyin**
  fellow ~: **concitoyen**
  substantial ~: **bon bourgeois**
city: **ciudad; górod**
  great ~, great solitude: **magna
    civitas**
civilian: **gens togata**
civilization: **civilitas; Kultur**
clamor of the forum: **forensis**
clasp: **barrette**
class
  lower ~es: **gens**
  middle ~: **bourgeois; bourgeoisie;
    petit**
  military ~: **shizoku**
  upper middle ~: **bourgeoisie; haute
    bourgeoisie**
classmate: **condiscipulus**
clay takes any form: **argilla**
cleaned: **décrotté**
clearing, grassy: **brûlée**
clemency belongs to the brave: **inest
  clementia**
clergy: **ad clerum; gens**
clerk: **commis; dependente;
  escribiente**
cleverness of thought: **bien trouvé**
clinker-built: **à clin**
clique: **camarilla**
  great industrial ~s: **zaibatsu**
cloak, dust: **cache-poussière**
clock: **pendule**
closet: **camarín**
closure: **clôture**
cloth
  golden ~: **drap**
  good ~ sells itself: **el buen**
clothes: **frusques; kapra; ropa**
  Sunday ~: **endimanché**
clouds
  ~ will intervene: **occurrent**
  in the ~: **in nubibus**
  remove the ~ from your brow:
    deme supercilio
club: **nulla-nulla**
  athletic ~: **Turnverein**
  literary ~: **Gelehrten-verein**
clump of trees: **motte**
coachman: **cocher; cochero**
coals
  ~ to Newcastle: γλαυκας (glaûkas);
    in silvam
  hauled over the ~: **être sur**

coarse: **polisson**
coarseness: **grossièreté; salé; un
  propos**
coast
  ~ guard: **guardacoste; garde-côte**
  ~ is clear: **die Luft**
coat: **houppelande; justaucorps**
coaxing: **câlin**
cobbler
  ~, stick to your last: **ne sutor; sutor;
    zapatero**
cock of the walk: **der Hahn**
cod: **cabillaud; morue; torsk**
coda, short: **codetta**
coffee: **café**
  black ~: **café**
  ~ cup: **finjan**
  ~ party: **Kaffeeklatsch**
  ~ plantation: **cafetal**
  iced ~: **mazagran**
cofferdam: **batardeau**
cognates: **cognati**
coin: **décime; dinero; écu; escudo**
  other side of the ~: **le revers**
cold: **gros**
  numb with ~: **transi**
coldly: **freddamente**
collaborator: **collaborateur**
collapse: **débâcle; écroulement**
collar: **rabat**
colleague: **confrère**
  society of ~s: **collegium**
collection, choice: **recueil**
college, teacher training: **Lehrer-
  seminar**
colon: **Doppelpunkt; due**
color
  lower the ~s: **baisser le drapeau**
  neutral in ~: **écru**
  tone ~: **timbre**
combat, unarmed: **karate; kung fu; tai
  chi**
combination
  ~ of political groups: **bloc**
  ~ scarf and helmet: **passe-montagne**
  incongruous ~: **pot pourri**
come
  ~ here: **haere; idhar; venez ici;
    venga aquí**
  ~ what may: **venga lo; vogue**
  ~ ye: **Venite**
comedy: **Lustspiel**
  ~ is ended: **la commedia**
  sentimental ~: **comédie**

comfort: **gemach**
comical: **drôle**
coming: **on y va**
comity: **comitas**
comma: **virgola; virgule**
command: **hukm**
commander, knight: **comendador**
committee: **comité**
commoner: **bourgeois; Le Bourgeois;
     roturier**
commonly: **vulgo**
commonplace: **banalité**
   ~s as if original: **proprie**
   what enthralls us all, the ~: **was uns**
commotion, what a: **quelle affaire**
communion, Easter: **devoir**
compact, social: **contrat**
companion: **compañero**
   drinking ~: **Bier**
   he is known by his ~s: **noscitur**
   lady's ~: **dame de**
   pleasant ~: **comes**
   travel ~: **compagnon**
companionship, sweet: **dulce
     sodalicium**
company: **compagnie; compañía; Ge-
     sellschaft; société; Verein**
   in ~: **en suite**
   joint-stock ~: **Aktiengesellschaft;
     société**
   limited liability ~: **commandité;
     société**
   trading ~: **société**
comparison
   ~ of small things with great: **si com-
     ponere; si parva**
   to make a ~: **confer; parva
     componere**
competing, not: **hors concours**
competition: **concours; concurrence**
complaint: **audita; plainte; querela**
complete: **totus; totus in**
complexion, fair: **beau teint**
compliments, with author's: **avec les;
     hommage**
composer: **compositeur; Tondichter**
composition: **étude; nonetto; opus;
     pastorale; pezzo; pièce**
composure: **aequanimiter**
compote: **tsimmis**
comprehension: **Auffassung**
compromise: **mezzo**
   uncompromising: **intransigeant**
comrade: **camarade; Kamerad;**

   tovarishch
   good ~: **bon camerade**
comradeship: **camaraderie**
concealment: **camouflage; suppressio**
conceded, from what has been: **ex
     concesso**
concerning: **in re; re**
   ~ all things and more: **de omnibus**
   ~ everything knowable and more:
     de omni re
concert, morning: **aubade**
concerto
   ~ with two or more soloists:
     concertante
   small ~: **concertino**
concession: **octroi**
concessionaire: **concesionario;
     concessionnaire**
concise
   ~ly: **paucis**
   trying to be ~, become obscure:
     brevis
conclusion: **Schluss**
   after the ~: **après coup; après la
     pluie; post terminum**
   impossible ~: **reductio ad
     impossibile**
concrete: **bêton**
concubine: **odalisque**
condemnation of what they do not un-
     derstand: **damnant**
condition
   ~s before the war: **status quo ante**
   existing ~s: **status quo**
   indispensable ~: **causa; conditio;
     sine**
conductor: **chef d'orchestre; Kapell-
     meister; maestro**
confederacy: **Bund**
conference: **pourparler; pow wow**
confession: **pro confesso**
   I confess: **confiteor**
confidence
   ~ begets confidence: **fides facit**
   in ~: **entre nous**
   in strictest ~: **sub sigillo**
confidentiality: **sub rosa**
configuration: **Gestalt**
confinement: **accouchement**
conflict of opinions: **Kampf der**
confound it: **cospetto**
confusion: **dérangement; désarroi; nec
     caput**

congenial: **simpatico**
congratulations: **mazel; pazdr'vlahyoo**
connoisseur: **cognoscente; connaisseur; gourmet**
conquer
   ~ed: **victi**
   ~s who conquers himself: **vincit qui
      se**
   ~s who endures: **vincit qui patitur**
   I came, I saw, I ~ed: **veni, vidi**
   I remain un~ed: **invictus**
   I will ~ or die: **vincam**
   to ~ is to live enough: **vivere sat**
conqueror: **conquistador**
conquest
   ~ by degrees: **gradatim**
   ~ by obedience: **parendo**
   ~ of self: **bis vincit**
   ~ or death: **aut vincere; vincere**
conscience
   before the tribunal of ~: **in foro**
   ~ good as thousand witnesses:
      conscientia
   good ~: **mens sibi**
   nothing stronger than ~: **nil
      consuetudine**
   O clear ~: **O dignitosa**
   sound ~: **murus**
   without compromising ~: **salva
      conscientia**
consciousness of wrongdoing: **nil
   conscire**
consent: **agrément**
   common ~: **communi consensu**
   ~ makes law: **consensus facit**
   mutual ~: **mutuus**
   universal ~: **consensus omnium**
consequence: **contrecoup; karma; par
   contrecoup**
   it is of no ~: ονδεν πραγμα (**oudèn
      prâgma)**
conservative: **conservateur**
conservatory: **conservatoire**
considerable: **ziemlich**
consideration
   after ~: **nach reiflicher**
   under ~: **sur le tapis**
   under judicial ~: **sub iudice**
consider it done: **tenez cela**
consistency: **esprit**
conspiracy
   who covers you discovers you: **quien
      te**

constabulary: **gendarmerie**
constancy: **basis**
constellation: **Canis Maior; Canis
   Minor**
consumer from birth: **fruges**
contemplation of flight: **in meditatione; meditatio**
contempt: **mépris**
   token of ~: **par signe**
contentment surpasses riches:
   contentement
contents of a vat: **cuvée**
contract: **contrat**
   conditional ~: **contrat**
   informal ~: **nudum; pactum**
   private ~: **de gré; gré**
   reciprocal ~: **contrat**
contractor: **entrepreneur**
contradiction: **contradictio; démenti**
contrary
   on the ~: **au contraire; e contrario;
      im Gegenteil; per contra**
   quite to the ~: **tout au**
controversy not for me to settle: **non
   nostrum**
convenience: **a vostro commodo; ex
   commodo**
conversation: **conversazione; tête-à-tête**
conversely: **vice**
convict: **forçat**
conviviality: **goguette**
cook: **bawarchi**
   bad ~: **gâte-sauce**
   head ~: **chef**
   pastry ~: **pâtissier**
   too many ~s: **trop de cuisiniers**
cooking
   plain ~: **bourgeois; cuisine; naturel**
   well cooked: **bien cuit**
coolness: **sans-gêne**
   ~ of evening: **au frais**
copper: **cobre**
copy: **exemplaire; exemplum; extrait**
   certified ~: **extrait**
   make a ~: **mettre au**
copyright: **propriété littéraire**
cordon, sanitary: **cordon sanitaire**
cord, ornamental: **fourragère**
Corinth, not every man goes to: **non
   cuivis**
cornmeal: **masa**
   ~ cake: **tortilla**

corn on the foot: **oeil-de-perdrix**
corporal: **caporal**
corporation: **Sociedad Anónima**
corps, diplomatic: **corps**
Corpus Christi, feast of: **fête**
corral: **atajo**
correction
  ~ for good writing: **saepe**
  ~ for the worse: **Schlimmbesserung**
  ~ of manners by laughing: **castigat**
corruption of best is worst: **corruptio**
cossack: **cosaque; kazak**
cost: **au prix; coûte**
  ~ takes away taste: **le coût**
  ~ what may: **à tout prix**
  very ~ly: **à prix**
costume: **costumé**
cottage: **chalet; chaumière**
cotton: **algodón**
couch: **chaise**
council: **conseil**
  ~ member: **camarista**
counsel overnight: **besser Rat**
count: **comte; conde; Graf**
countenance
  dissembling ~: **visage**
  open ~ means thoughts withheld: **il volto**
countersign: **mot**
countess: **comtesse; condesa; Gräfin**
counting house: **comptoir**
country: **país; straná**
  ~ and king: **pro patria**
  ~ has customs: **chaque pays; en cada**
  ~ in a city: **rus in**
  ~ is dear, liberty dearer: **patria cara**
  ~, when shall I behold thee: **O rus**
  for one's ~: **pro patria**
  in the ~: **à la campagne**
  not for himself but for his ~: **non sibi sed patriae**
  our home, our ~: **hic domus**
  sold ~ for gold: **vendidit**
  sweet and fitting to die for one's ~: **dulce et decorum**
  where well with me, there my ~: **ubi bene**
countryman: **paisano**
county: **uyezd**
couples, in: **zu Paaren**
courage: **coraggio; macte; mutig**
  ~ and discretion: **animus et prudentia**
  ~ and faith: **animo et fide**
  ~ and prudence: **fortitudine**
  ~ as means to escape danger: **periculum fortitudine**
  ~ not craft: **animo non**
  ~ without fear: **courage**
  recover your~: **revocate**
  renew your ~: **renovate**
  to the brave and faithful, nothing is difficult: **forti et**
courageous: **mutig**
courier: **estafette**
course
  in a middle ~: **in medio**
  middle ~: **via**
  middle ~ safest: **medio**
course, of: **bien entendu**
court: **adalat; per curiam**
  approach the ~: **accedas**
  before the ~: **in facie**
  C~ of Common Pleas: **Bancus Communium**
  ~ wishes to consider: **curia**
  in full ~: **in banco**
  in open ~: **in curia**
  out of ~: **ex curia**
courtesan: **bona roba; cocotte; cortesias; femme; fille; lorette**
courtier: **homme**
courtyard: **cortile; patio**
cove: **barachois; ensenada**
cover, under: **à couvert**
covering: **cachepot**
covetousness: **alieni**
  who covets much wants much: **multa petentibus**
cow: **inkomo; vaca; vache**
cowardice: **lâcheté**
cowboy: **charro; gaucho; vaquero**
cowherd: **vacher**
cowl: **cagoule; capuce**
  ~ does not make the monk: **cucullus**
crab: **crabe**
crack: **sudadero**
crackled: **craquelé**
cradle: **berceau**
crawfish: **écrevisse**
crazy: **amok; meshugah; pupule; verrückt**
cream: **crème**
  ice ~: **crème**
  whipped ~: **crème; Schlagobers**

credit
  one does work, the other gets ~:
    uno tiene
creditors, flee one's: **faire un trou**
cremation, willing: **suttee**
crest: **kikumon; kirimon**
crevasse: **Bergschrund**
crime: **crimen**
  ~ always fearful: **semper**
  ~ equalizes: **facinus**
  ~ is the mistake: **le crime**
  ~ of falsification: **falsi**
criminal identification system:
    bertillonage
criticism: **critique**
  ~ is easy, art difficult: **la critique**
  critics wrangle, question undecided:
    grammatici
  excessive ~: **flak**
crook: **gonif**
cross: **croix; crux**
  bravely bear the ~: **fortiter geret**
  ~ is my anchor: **crux**
  ~ is the touchstone of faith: **fidei**
    coticula
  ~ on breast and devil in deeds: **la**
    cruz
  hope in the ~: **in hoc signo spes**
  I hope in the ~: **in cruce**
  naught save by the ~: **nil nisi**
  Southern ~: **crux**
  tau ~: **crux**
  T-shaped ~: **crux**
  under the pure ~: **sub cruce**
    candida
  way of the ~: **via**
  without the ~: **sine**
  X-shaped ~: **crux**
crossing of hands on keyboard: **Über-**
  schlagen; volteggiando
crossroad: **carrefour**
crow: **corbeau**
  ~ like the egg: **cual**
  flight of the ~: **à vol**
  till ~s turn white: **εως (héos)**
crowd
  in a ~: **en foule**
  scorn the noxious ~: **malignum**
crown of light: **corona**
crumbs: **panure**
  dress with ~: **paner**

  with buttered ~: **au gratin**
crushed: **accablé; mole ruit**
crushing: **écrasement**
crust of buttered crumbs: **gratin**
cry
  ~ before hurt: **ante tubam**
  ~ of battle: **beauséant**
  first ~: **vagitus**
cuckold: **cocu; cornuto**
cuckoo: **papiya**
cucumber: **concombre**
cuff: **manchette**
cultism: **culteranismo**
culture
  ~ climate: **Zeitgeist**
  ~ conflict: **Kulturkampf**
cunning: **Ladino; matois; roublard**
  ~ against ~: **List**
cup: **tazza**
cupbearer: **saki**
cup holder: **zarf**
cupid, infant: **amorino**
curlers, in: **en papillotes**
currant: **groseille**
curry: **kari**
curtain: **portière; rideau**
  ~ raiser: **lever de rideau**
cushion: **gaddi**
custard: **flan**
custody
  ~ of the law: **custodia**
  in ~: **in custodia**
custom: **ad usum; ut mos**
  according to ~: **ex more**
  ~ decides the issue: **consuetudo pro**
  ~ is a tyrant: **usus est**
  once vices and now ~s: **quae fuerunt**
  power of ~: **gravissimum**
customary: **de règle**
customer
  know one's ~s: **connaître**
  regular ~: **habitué**
customs: **moeurs**
  ~ house: **alfandega; dogana; douane**
  ~ official: **douanier**
  ~ union: **Zollverein**
cut: **coupure**
  ~ting off: **abscissio infiniti**
  loin ~: **carré**
cutlet: **côtelette; papillote**
cycle
  ~ of the ages: **magnus ab**
  ~ of the world: **yuga**

dagger: **katar**
daily: **per diem**
daintiness: **mignardise**
dainty: **mignard**
dale: **hondonado**
dam: **barrage**
damage: **dégât**
  malicious ~: **sabotage**
  what ~: **ad quod damnum**
damn, I don't give a: **je m'en fous**
dance: **allemand; baile; bal; cachucha;**
    cancan; carmagnole; cotillon;
    danse; farandole; flamenco; ja-
    rabe tapatio; kantikoy; maxixe;
    nautch; pas; paso doble; rumba;
    saltarello; sardana; seguidilla;
    son; tarantella; Tyrolienne
  belly ~: **danse**
  ~ attendance: **faire antichambre;**
    faire le pied
  ~ on a volcano: **nous dansons**
  ~ step: **chassé; coupé; entrechat**
  ~ style: **da ballo**
  pantomimic ~: **ballet**
  rope ~: **danse**
  solo ~: **pas**
  tea ~: **thé dansant**
dancer: **danseur; ghawazi**
  ballet ~: **ballerina; coryphée; dan-**
    seuse; figurant
  leading ~: **première danseuse**
dancing: **dansant**
danger: **periculum in; prise**
  common ~: **commune periculum**
  ~ when neighbor's house is on fire:
    nam tua
  without ~: **sine**
dangerous: **dangereux; pericoloso**
daring: **hardiesse**
Dark Ages: **siècle**
darkness: **in tenebris**
  shrouding truth in ~: **obscuris**
darling: **chou**
dart: **banderilla**
  ~ thruster: **banderillero**
  steel ~: **fléchette**
dash: **brûler le**
date: **a dato**
daughter: **anac; doch; figlia; fille;**
    hija
  ~ married, ~ lost: **hija**
  ~ more beautiful than her beautiful
    mother: **matre**
daughter-in-law: **belle-fille**

dawn
  friend of the Muses: **aurora musis**
  rosy-fingered ~: ροδοδακτνλος ηως
    (rhododàktulos)
day: **dies; jour**
  after the appointed ~: **post diem**
  appointed ~: **dies**
  before the ~: **ante diem**
  ~ of wrath: **dies**
  ~ to ~: **au jour le; de die; jour**
  ~ will come: **le jour**
  every ~ is a little life: **jeder Tag**
  every ~ is not a holiday: **non ogni**
  fast ~: **jour; maigre**
  few ~s: **ad paucos**
  from that ~: **a die**
  good ~: **guten tag; konnichi-wa**
  good ~, good work: **bon jour, bonne**
  in my younger ~s: **consule**
  I've lost a ~: **diem perdidi**
  last ~: **venit summa**
  lucky and unlucky ~s: **fasti et**
  lucky ~: **dies**
  no ~ without doing something:
    nulla dies
  one ~ pushed onward by another:
    truditur
  past ~s: **die schönen Tage**
  unlucky ~: **dies; nefasti**
daybreak: **all' alba; le point; point du**
  before ~: **ante lucem**
daylight: **au jour; jour**
  in broad ~: **en plein**
dead: **abiit ad; ad patres; décédé**
  ~ are the best counselors: **optimi**
  ~ men tell no tales: νεκρος
    (nekròs)
  ~ or alive: **mort ou**
  of the ~, nothing but good: **de**
    mortuis
  those about to die salute those about
    to die: **morituri morituros**
  we who are about to die salute you:
    morituri te
  when I am ~, let earth be mingled
    with fire: εμον **(emoù)**
  whom the gods love dies young: ον
    οι θεοι **(hòn hoi theoì); quem di**
deadlocked: **accroché**
deal
  great ~ in small space: **magnum in**
dealer: **Händler**
  old-clothes ~: **fripier**
  secondhand ~: **brocanteur**

straw ~: **pajero**
dean: **doyen**
dear
  extravagantly ~: **hors de prix**
  my ~: **ma chère; mon cher; mon**
    petit; querido; ζωη μον (zóē
    moû)
death: **debitum; Furst; Heimgang; in**
  extremis
  after ~: **post mortem; post obitum**
  best ~: **optima mors**
  by reason of ~: **mortis**
  dance of ~: **Totentanz**
  ~ blow: **coup**
  ~ certificate: **extrait**
  ~ is common to all men: **mors**
    omnibus
  ~ is farthest goal: **mors ultima**
  ~ is the gate of life: **mors ianua**
  ~ keeps no calendar: **smert'**
  ~ knocks: **aequo pulsat**
  ~ levels all things: **omnia mors**
  ~ of a bad thing: **cosa mala**
  ~ or victory: **aut mors**
  ~ preferable to dishonor: **malo mori**
  ~ rattle: **râle**
  ~ reflects one's life: **como se vive**
  honorable ~ better than a base life:
    honesta mors
  I triumph in ~: **triumpho**
  live mindful of ~: **vive memor**
  marked for ~: **Acheruntis**
  memory of ~: **dulces moriens**
  natural ~: **belle mort; bene decessit**
  pale D~: **pallida**
  reposed in tranquil ~: **placidaque**
  same man will be loved after ~:
    extinctus
  the doctor after ~: **après la mort**
  to be forgotten is the ~ of ~: **el**
    olvido
  well done outlives ~: **wohlgetan**
debatable point: **quodlibet**
debauchee: **roué**
debit and credit: **Soll und**
debris: **rudera**
debt: **aes alienum; debitum**
  arrest for ~: **contrainte**
deceit: **dolus**
  ~ of husband: **coiffer**
  permissible ~: **dolus**
  unlawful ~: **dolus**
deception
  more deceptive than the Parthians:

    Parthis
decisive: **tranchant**
declamatory: **aria parlante; parlando;**
  recitando
decorated: **décoré**
decoration
  ~ by scratching: **sgraffiti**
  window ~: **chambranle**
decree: **arrêt; decretum; Ne Temere;**
  placitum; senatus
dedication: **Widmung; Zuschrift**
deed
  ~ once done: **capo**
  ~s manly, words womanly: **fatti**
  ~s match words: **dictis**
  ~s not words: **facta**
  great ~s: **hauts faits**
  I did the ~: **me me**
  no advice helps after the ~: **post**
    factum
defamation of exalted personages:
  scandalum
defects, only great men have great: **il**
  n'appartient
defend
  in ~ing himself: **se defendendo**
  I will ~: **tuebor**
defendant not found: **non est inventus**
defense
  ~ of the conduct of one's life:
    apologia
  no ~: **nil dicit**
  strong ~: **aes triplex**
deference: **pace**
  ~ is not abandonment:
    aufgeschoben
deficiency much to be regretted: **hiatus**
definitely: **in terminus**
degraded, socially: **déclassé**
degree
  Bachelor of Arts: **Artium**
    Baccalaureus
  Bachelor of Letters: **Bachelier ès**
    lettres
  Bachelor of Science: **Bachelier ès**
    sciences
  Master of Arts: **Artium Magister;**
    magister
  same ~: **ad eundem**
deity of a place: **genius**
dejected: **abattu**
delay
  delight in ~: **verweile**
  in ~: **in mora**

without ~: **sine**
delegate: **député**
deletions: **delenda**
deliberation: **consilio non**
delicacy: **beccafico; délicatesse; morbidezza**
delicate: **zärtlich**
delicately: **delicato**
delight
  ~ of battle: **gaudium**
  ~ of mankind: **deliciae**
delighted: **enchanté**
delirium tremens: **dementia; mania**
delivery
  after ~: **après livraison**
  general ~: **correo; en lista**
deluge, after us the: **après nous**
delusion: **Irrwahn**
den: **sanctum**
denial
  ~ to recover damages: **non assumpsit**
  it is denied: **negatur**
  offering too much is akin to ~: **ofrecer**
denims: **dungaree**
denouement, hastening to: **semper**
dentist: **sacamuelas**
depart
  ~ed: **abiit; excessit**
  they ~: **exeunt**
  willingness to ~: **Nunc Dimittis**
department: **département**
departure: **Abschied; rubato**
  ~ platform: **gare**
deposit: **in deposito**
  sandy ~: **batture**
depression: **affaissement**
depths, out of the: **de profundis**
deranged: **aliéné; berserk**
descendants will pluck your fruit: **carpent**
descent to hell is easy: **facilis descensus**
desert: **desierto**
deserved
  ~ as much as: **quantum**
  having well ~: **bene meritus**
deservedly: **à bonnes**
deserving, well: **bene merenti**
design: **ex proposito**
  he ~ed it: **invenit**
  illuminated ~: **enluminure**

designer, dress: **couturier**
desire: **appetitus; el deseo; laudumque**
  anything ~d: **desideratum**
  ~ nor fear: **nec cupias**
  limit your ~: **certo voto**
  live with unconcealed ~: **aperto**
  one of my ~s: **hoc erat in votis**
desk
  prayer ~: **prie-dieu**
  writing ~: **vargueno**
despair: **au désespoir**
  never ~: **nil desperandum**
desperation: **éperdument**
despicable: **méprisable**
destination: **terminus ad**
destroyed, not to be hastily: **non subito**
detached: **spiccato; staccato**
determined, I am: **infixum**
deuce take those: **pereant**
deviation: **détour**
devil: **diable; diantre; diavolo; shaitan; Teufel**
  be~ed: **à la diable**
  ~ and the deep: **entre la**
  ~ behind the Cross: **detrás**
  ~ in him: **il a le diable**
  ~ on crutches: **Le Diable**
  D~'s advocate: **advocatus; avvocato**
  ~ to pay: **der Teufel**
  poor ~: **pauvre**
  speak of the ~: **falando; parlez du**
  young saint and old ~: **giovane santo**
devotion, nine days': **novena**
devout: **andächtig; religioso**
diagram: **épure**
dialectically: **more**
dialect, Romance: **langue**
diamond
  ~ cut ~: **ruse contre**
  rough ~: **brut; diamant**
diary: **journal**
dice, throw of the: **coup**
dictionary: **Handwörterbuch; Wörterbuch**
died: **feu; gestorben; obiit**
die is cast: **alea; iacta; suerte**
different as day and night: **jour**
difficult: **difficile**
difficulty
  crucial ~: **deo dignus**
  ~ needing intervention of a god: **dignus**
  for beginners, ~: **pons**

pile ~ on ~: **Pelio; Pelion**
dignity
   beneath one's ~: **infra**
   without compromising ~: **salva dignitate**
diligently: **con diligenza**
diminishing, gradually: **diminuendo; ritenuto; tardando**
dinner: **aruchat; bara; comida; dîner; jantar; khana; makanan; Mittagsessen; pranzo**
dinnerless: **dîner**
direction: **modo praescripto; ut dictum**
   from ~: **dirige nos**
directly: **per vias**
director: **direttore**
dirge: **Klagelied**
dirty: **malpropre; sale**
disabled: **hors de combat**
disaffection of citizens: **seditio**
discernment, keen: **flair**
disciple: **Jünger**
disciplined: **aguerri**
discontent, romantic: **Weltschmerz**
discontinuance of legal proceedings: **nolle**
discourse to clergy: **concio**
disdainful: **sdegnoso**
disease: **ciguatera; lues; piedra; pyorrhea**
   contagious ~: **lues**
   deficiency ~: **beriberi**
disembowelment: **hara-kiri**
disgrace of the doctors: **opprobrium**
disguise: **fardé**
disgust: **dégoût**
dish
   extra ~es: **assiette**
   principal ~: **pièce**
   side ~: **entremets**
disk: **bobèche**
dismissal: **renvoi**
dismount: **absitzen**
disorder: **à l'abandon**
display: **échaufaudage; étalage**
dispute: **démêlé**
   settle ~s: **componere; tantas**
dissenter: **Raskolnik**
distance, from a: **ex longinquo**
distinction
   make overly subtle ~s: **fendre**
   subtle ~: **nuance**
   with ~: **cum laude**

distressed, I'm learning to help the: **miseris**
district: **arrondissement; barrio; Gau; oblast; pattadi; volost; zillah**
disuse: **desuetudo**
ditch: **cuneta**
ditty, love: **Liebesliedchen**
divide and rule: **divide**
divination by passages from Virgil: **sortes**
Divine Comedy: **Divina Commedia; La Divina**
divinity, present is: **die Gegenwart**
divisions numbered and weighed: **mene mene**
divorce: **separatio a vinculo**
do
   ~ everything possible: **faire le possible**
   ~ nothing: **far niente**
   I ~ that you may ~: **facio ut facias**
   I ~ that you may give: **facio ut des**
Doctor
   ~ of Both Laws: **Iuris Utriusque; doctor**
   ~ of law: **moolvee**
dog: **Bouvier; Hund; perro; schipperke**
   barking ~: **perro que**
   beware of the ~: **cave canem; chien**
   ~ in the manger: **canis in; perro**
   every ~ is a lion at home: **ogni cane**
   sleeping ~: **chat; il ne faut pas é-veiller; quieta**
   vicious ~: **à méchant**
doing
   ~ as others do: **hurler avec**
   what the devil was he ~ there: **que diable**
doleful: **lamentoso; sospiroso**
done
   ~ to a turn: **cuit**
   well ~!: **brava; bravo; euge**
   well ~ is twice ~: **cosa ben**
donkey, speak of the: **wenn**
don't
   ~ hang up: **ne quittez**
   ~ mention it: **il n'y a pas de quoi; não hà**
   ~ speak of them: **non regioniam**
   ~ you wish you get it: **ja prosit**
door: **darwaza**
   closed ~s: **à huis**
doorkeeper: **concierge; huissier**

office of the ~: **conciergerie**
double: **doppio**
doubt: **mettre en**
  in ~: **entre dos; in ambiguo; in dubio**
  room for ~: **ambigendi**
doubtless: **sans**
doubtlessly: **sine**
dove: **paloma**
downfall: **déchéance**
downriver: **rio; río**
down with: **abajo; à bas**
dozen: **douzaine**
draft
  let a ~ be made: **fiat haustus**
  rough ~: **brouillon**
drag: **shlep**
dragging: **schleppend**
drama: **drame**
draw
  ~s back to leap better: **il se recule**
  he drew it: **delineavit**
drawbridge: **pont-levis**
drawing: **dibujo**
dream
  ~ all are lies: **tous songes**
  ~ beyond recall: **vorbei**
  ~ of a shadow: σκιας (skiâs)
  empty ~s: **Träume**
  like a sick man's ~s: **velut**
  sick man's ~s: **aegri**
dreamer: **rêveur; songe-creux**
dress
  ceremonial ~: **grande toilette**
  court ~: **robe de cour**
  full ~: **grande tenue**
  in full ~: **en grande tenue; en grande toilette**
dressmaker: **couturière; modiste**
driblets: **ric-à-ric**
drink
  ~ and be merry: πινε (pîne)
  ~ or depart: **aut bibat;** η πιθι (è pîthi)
  now's the time for ~ing: **nunc est**
  over a ~: **inter**
  stand a ~: **goutte; payer**
dripping hollows stone: **gutta**
driveler: **radoteur**
driver: **gharry-wallah; vetturino; voiturier**
drop by drop: **goutte**
drove
  ~ of horses: **caballada**

in ~s: **gregatim**
drown someone and you will be drowned: **al d'ataift**
drug that brings forgetfulness: φαρμακον (phármakon)
drum: **bongo; tabla; zambomba**
  ~ call: **rappel**
  muffled ~s: **timpani**
drunk: **barracho; shikker**
  half ~: **entre deux**
drunkard: **briago**
drunkenness: **être gris; musti**
dubbing: **dégras**
duchess: **duchesse**
duck: **canard; canne-de-roche**
duckling: **caneton**
duct, spermatic: **vas**
duel: **affaire; die Mensur; monomachia**
  students' ~: **Mensur**
duet: **duo; Zweigesang**
duke: **duc; Herzog**
dumb with amazement: **vox**
dune: **medano**
dungeon: **cachot; oubliette**
dupe will end a rascal: **on commence**
durable: **aere perennius**
during: **durante**
dust: **poussière**
  ~ thou art: **terra**
  we're but ~ and shadow: **pulvis**
Dutch: **hollandais**
duty: **devoir; être de jour**
  do my ~: **faire mon**
  ~ and glory: **quo fas**
  ~ come what may: **fais ce que**
dweller, plains: **llanero**
dwelling: **demeure**
  lake ~: **palafitte; Pfahlbauten**
dying away: **diluendo; morendo; perdendo; smorzando; stinguendo**

each
  ~ man led by own taste: **trahit**
  ~ uses its natural weapon: **dente lupus**
  to ~ his own: **cuique; suum**
eager: **empressé**
eagle
  ~ doesn't bear doves: **Adler; non generant**
  ~ doesn't catch flies: **aquila**
  ~ in the clouds: αετος (aetòs)

ear
  ~s pricked up: **arrectis**
  grate on one's ~s: **écorcher**
  turn a deaf ~: **faire la sourde**
early to bed and early to rise:
    Morgenstunde
earnest: **ernst**
earth: **terra**
  ~ has room for all: **Raum**
  ~ smiles: **angulus**
  may the ~ lie lightly on you: **sit tibi**
  move the ~: δος (**dós**)
earthenware, glazed: **faïence**
ease: **repos**
  ~ and rest to the weary: **detur**
easily: **de plano; sans**
east, pressure toward the: **Drang**
eastward: **au levant**
easy: **facile**
  ~ come, ~ go: **male parta; wie**
    gewonnen
  it's ~ to be generous with another's:
    facile largiri
eat
  ~ after your own fashion: **mangia**
  excessive love of ~ing: **gourmandise**
  tell me what you ~, I'll tell you what
    you are: **dis-moi**
  they who ~ the fruit of the soil: οι
    αρουρης (**hoì aroúrēs**)
eccentricity: **bizarrerie**
economy is a great revenue: **magnum**
    vectigal
editing: **rédaction**
edition: **Auflage**
  deluxe ~: **Prachtausgabe**
  first ~: **editio princeps**
  revised ~: **Ausgabe**
  sumptuous ~: **édition de luxe**
editor: **Herausgeber; rédacteur**
editorial: **article**
editorship: **gérance**
eel: **anguille; carapo**
  conger ~: **anguille**
  ~ by the tail: **anguillam cauda**
effect: **causa**
  ~ of high explosives: **brisance**
  ~ to cause: **a posteriori**
  general ~: **ensemble; le tout; tout**
    ensemble
  no ~: **nulla bona**
effort
  creative ~: **nisus**
  great ~: **magno conatu**

  one's all: **son saint**
  one's own exertions: **suo Marte**
  vain ~s: **battre**
egg: **huevo; oeuf**
  boiled ~: **oeuf**
  curried ~: **oeuf**
  ~ for an ox: **donner un**
  if you want the ~: **si quieris**
  new-laid ~s: **oeuf**
  poached ~s: **oeuf**
  scrambled ~s: **oeuf**
eggplant: **aubergine**
egoism is odious: **le moi**
either ... or: **aut ... aut**
elation: **exalté**
elbowroom: **avoir les coudées**
elder: **aîné**
  ~s first: **seniores**
elegance in simplicity: **simplex**
elegant: **luxe**
elegantly: **elegantemente**
elements, first: **rerum**
elephant
  ~ enclosure: **kheda**
  ~ goad: **ankus**
  ~ troubled about a fly: ο ελεφας
    (**ho eléphas**)
elite, intellectual: **die geistige;**
    intelligentsia
elixir of life: **elixir**
eloquence, enough: **satis eloquentiae**
elsewhere, from: **aliunde**
Elysian Fields: **Champs**
emaciation: **décharnement**
embarrassment of riches: **embarras**
embellishment: **abbellimento; fregia-**
    tura; ornamenti
  vocal ~: **coloratura**
  with ~: **ornatamente**
embers, under the ash lie: **soto la**
embroider: **broder**
embroidery, openwork: **broderie**
emergency, in an: **en cas; événement**
eminent: **distingué**
eminently: **éminemment**
emperor: **mikado; padishah**
  long live the ~: **vive la**
emphasis: **Nackdruck**
  with ~: **ben marcato**
emphatically: **enfaticamente; sforzando**
empire: **Reich**
  ~ and liberty: **imperium et**
  ~ stands for peace: **l'empire c'est**
  Holy Roman E~: **Sacrum**

employee: **empleado**
emulation: **à l'envi**
　to emulate is to envy: **nacheifern**
enamel
　~ work: **champlevé; cloisonné**
　white ~: **pâte**
enamored: **épris**
enclosure, engine: **nacelle**
encore: **bis**
encourage others: **pour encourager**
end: **ad finem; fin; fine**
　all's well that ~s well: **Ende gut; exi-**
　　tus acta
　beginning of the ~: **c'est le com-**
　　mencement; commencement
　consider the ~: **avise; finem; respice**
　~ crowns the work: **finis**
　~ justifies the means: **le bois**
　~ of bad beginning: **mali principii**
　~ of discussion: **cadit**
　in the ~: **en fin de**
　to the ~: **al fine**
endlessly: **ad infinitum**
endorsement: **visé**
endowment: **dotación**
enemy: **hostis humani; oyev**
　fewer enemies the better: **de los**
　permissible to learn from an ~: **fas**
　　est
energetic: **energico**
energetically: **energicamente;**
　　zelosamente
energy
　kinetic ~: **vis**
　with ~: **zeloso**
engraved it: **insculpsit**
enlightenment: **Aufklärung**
enough: **assai; bas; basta; sufficit**
　~ already: **iam satis**
　~ and to spare: **satis superque**
　~ for contentment: **assez à qui**
　~ is as good as a feast: **satis quod**
　~ is ~: **assai basta**
　~ said: **satis verborum**
enraged: **enragé**
entertainment: **divertissement;**
　　tamasha
enthusiasm: **Schwärmerei**
enthusiast: **prôneur**
enthusiastic: **schwärmerisch**
enthusiastically: **avec entrain**
entirely: **in toto; tout à fait**
entrance: **entrada; entrata**
　carriage ~: **porte-cochère**

entreaty nor bribe: **nec prece**
environment: **milieu**
envy
　~ assails the noblest things: **summa**
　　petit
　~ is blind: **caeca**
　~ is the foe of honor: **hostis honori**
　who envies is the inferior: **qui**
　　invidet
　without ~: **sine**
　you may ~ everybody: **omnibus**
　　invideas
epigram: **épigramme**
epilepsy: **petit**
Epiphany eve: **Befana**
equal
　endures no ~: **parem**
　without ~: **hors de pair**
equality: **égalité**
　~ and simultaneity: **pari passu**
　~ of terms: **d'égal**
equally: **egualmente**
equanimity in difficulties: **mens aequa**
equilibrium: **in equilibrio**
equity follows the law: **aequitas**
　　sequitur
erased: **biffé**
error: **écart; égarement**
　~ excepted: **erreur; Irrtümer; sauf**
　~ to be corrected: **corrigendum**
　printer's ~: **Druckfehler**
　to err is human: **errare; hominis;**
　　humanum
escape: **échappée**
　~ from the mind: **ex animo**
　narrow ~: **l'échapper**
essence: **esencia**
essentially: **per essentiam**
established, well: **ben ficcato**
estate
　country ~: **hacienda**
　third ~: **tiers**
estrangement: **éloignement**
eternal, be thou: **esta perpetua**
eternity: **Ewigheit**
etiquette: **les convenances**
Eton—may it flourish: **floreat**
Eurasian: **chee-chee**
evening, good: **bonsoir; buenas**
　　noches; erev; guten Abend;
　　komban-wa
　~ of life: **Lebensabend**
event: **casus; événement**
　~s: **à tout hasard; en tout cas**

I speak of well-known ~s: **haud ignota**

passing ~: **actualité**

even though: **quand même**

everlasting, let it be: **esto perpetuum**

everybody: **ad unum; tout le**

~ is wise after the event: **tout le**

everyone

~ has his hobby: **chacun a sa**

~ has his own custom: **suus**

~ is against the fallen: **todos**

~ is nearest to himself: **quisque sibi**

~ is the product of his own deeds: **cada uno es hijo**

~ pulls for his own side: **chacun tire**

~ to his own taste: **chacun à son**

everything

~ from above: **tout d'en**

~ has its time: **cada coisa; tout vient à**

~ hits a sore finger: **todo cae**

~ in my power: **tout mon**

~ knowable: **omne scibile**

~ mine I carry with me: **omnia mea**

~ new seems beautiful: **di novello; tutto di**

~ passes: **deficit; tout lasse**

~ smiles on him: **tout lui rit**

~ unknown is taken as magnificent: **omne ignotum**

everywhere: **partout; passim; ubique**

evidence

~ not before the court: **non constat**

in ~: **en évidence**

evil: **malum**

endure this ~: **hoc sustinete**

~ and a half: **à malin**

~ at the outset: **principiis**

of two ~s, choose the lesser: **de duobus**

one ~ always follows another: **δεχεται (dékhetai)**

origin of ~: **origo mali**

prophet of ~: **μαντις (mántis)**

source of ~: **fons malorum**

sufficient unto the day is the ~: **αρκετον (arketón)**

thing ~ in itself: **malum**

exactly: **giustamente**

exaggeration and amplification: **o ni o**

examination, school: **Reifeprüfung**

example: **exemple**

~ decides controversy, creates another: **nil agit**

~s are odious: **exempla sunt**

for ~: **exempli; zum Beispiel**

of very bad ~: **pessimi**

excellence: **arete**

always to excel: **αιεν (aién)**

~ is hard to get: **difficilia quae**

manly ~: **virtus**

rarity of ~: **omnia praeclara**

excellency: **excellence**

Excellent, Most: **Excelentísimo**

exception

~ being made: **exceptis**

~ proves the rule: **einmal; exceptio probat**

exceptional: **hors de ligne**

exchange

~ is no robbery: **cambio; Tausch**

stock ~: **bourse**

excited: **tête**

over~: **tête**

exclamation: **caramba; zut**

exclamation point: **Ausrufungszeichen**

execution

~ by hanging: **suspensio**

wholesale ~: **noyade**

exercise, singing: **solfeggio**

exhalation of poisonous gas: **mofette**

exhausted: **épuisé; ich bin ganz; rendu**

existence: **ens**

lead a struggling ~: **tirer le diable**

struggle for ~: **Kampf ums**

exit: **salida**

expenditures and receipts: **data et**

expense: **frais**

cover one's ~s: **faire ses frais**

great ~s: **à grands frais**

household ~s: **bouche; dépense**

incidental ~s: **faux; frais**

incur ~s: **faire des frais**

paid ~: **tous frais**

public ~: **sumptibus**

experience

~ deserves credence: **experto**

~ makes men: **les affaires**

~ teaches: **experientia**

unpleasant ~: **mauvais**

experiment on a worthless body: **fiat experimentum**

expert: **mahatma; mavin**

camouflage ~: **camoufleur**

karate ~: **karateka**

no one's born an ~: **ninguno**

explanation: **éclaircissement; exposé**

long ~: **megillah**
exposed: **en prise**
expression: **Ausdruck; espressione**
  stereotyped ~: **cliché**
expressive: **espressivo**
expressively: **con espressione; mit Ausdruck**
expressly: **expressio verbis**
expurgated: **in usum Delphini**
extent, to that: **pro tanto**
extermination: **ad internecionem**
extreme: **ad extremum**
  ~s meet: **les extrêmes**
extremity
  ~ of apse: **chevet**
  to the last ~: **tempus; usque ad aras**
eye: **oeil**
  ~ for an ~: **Auge um; ayeen**
  ~ of the master: **l'oeil**
  twinkling of an ~: **clin; en un clin**
eyebolt: **piton**
eyeglasses: **lorgnette; lorgnon; pince-nez**
eyes: **yeux**
  ~ front: **fixe**
  ~ of mine: **che non**
  ~ of mine, fountains now: **o occhi**
  ~ right: **Augen rechts**
  four ~ better than two: **cuatro**

fabric
  metallic ~: **lamé**
  woolen ~: **mousseline; puttoo**
face
  ~ graven on her heart: **haerent**
  ~ is the index of the soul: **vultus**
  ~ to ~: **barba a; bouche; en tête-à-tête; front à; tête-à-tête**
  on its ~: **ex facie**
  put a good ~ on it: **faire bonne**
fact: **eo ipso; ipso facto**
  accomplished ~: **fait accompli**
  ~s of a crime: **corpus**
  I deal with ~s: **hypotheses**
  known ~: **donnée**
factory: **fábrica; usine**
failure: **coup; culbute**
  failing: **mancando**
  ~ of issue: **defectus**
  ~ to meet an appointment: **faire faux**

fail, without: **à coup sûr; faute; sans**
fair: **feria**
fairly: **de bonne guerre**
faith
  article of ~: **de fide**
  bad ~: **mala fides**
  defender of the ~: **fidei defensor**
  ~ and love: **fide et amore**
  ~ before understanding: **fides ante**
  ~ confers a crown when approved: **fides probata**
  ~ does not fear: **fides non**
  ~ for duty: **foy pour**
  ~ hath saved thee: **η πιστις (he pístis)**
  ~ in everything: **foi en**
  ~ in life: **glaube**
  ~ is all: **foy est**
  ~ is stronger than a lion: **leone**
  ~ is the sister of justice: **iustitiae soror**
  ~ must be kept: **fides servanda**
  ~ not arms: **fide, non armis**
  ~ remains: **stat promissa**
  ~ will bring increase: **haec generi**
  give to ~: **da fidei**
  good ~: **bona fides; bonne foi; de bonne foi**
  in bad ~: **mala fide**
  in good ~: **bona fide**
  I promise in good ~: **bona fide**
  I will keep ~: **servabo**
  keep the ~: **gardez la; tiens à ta**
  strong through ~: **ex fide**
faithful: **ad finem**
  always ~: **semper**
  ~ and courageous: **fidus et**
  ~ but unlucky: **fiel**
  ~ in both: **in utroque**
  ~ to my ancestors: **servata**
  ~ to my unhappy country: **patriae**
  mindful and ~: **memor et**
  reward is sure to the ~: **fideli**
faithfully: **fideliter**
falcon: **shahin**
fall
  ~ far short: **il s'en faut**
  ~ in: **en ligne; rassemblement**
  ~ into a trap: **donner dans**
  ~ prey to Scylla: **incidis**
fallacy of the consequent: **fallacia**
falling, beware of: **cave ne**
false: **faux; jhuta**
  ~ in one, ~ in all: **falsus**

fame
  ~ after death: **post cineres**
  ~ spread by deeds: **famam**
  may his ~ live: **fama semper**
familiarly: **mano**
family: **per stirpes**
  ~ badge: **mon**
  ~ council: **conseil**
  ~ name: **apellido; nom**
famous: **célèbre; digito**
fanatic: **fanatico**
fancies, idle: **pensée**
fan, sports: **aficionado; fanático**
far
  as ~ as: **sino**
  as ~ as I know: **quod sciam**
  as ~ as possible: **in toto**
  as ~ as this goes: **quoad**
  ~ from it: **tant s'en**
farce
  the ~ is over: **la farce; tirez le
    rideau**
  tragic ~: **flebile ludibrium**
fare, good: **grande chère**
farewell: **leb(e) wohl; vale; vaya**
  ~ and applaud: **valete**
  ~ for now: **hasta luego**
  last ~: **ultimum**
farfetched: **à perte**
farm: **ferme; heredad; kibbutz;
  kolkhoz**
farmer: **fermier; hacendero; kibbutznik; labrador; peón**
farther: **ultra**
fascism: **Fascismo**
fascist: **Fascista**
fashion: **mode**
  after the ~: **ad instar**
  ~ed it: **excudit**
  height of ~: **la fleur**
  high ~: **haut ton**
  in the English ~: **more**
  in the ~ of: **more**
  in the Irish ~: **more**
  out of ~: **démodé**
  set the ~: **den Ton**
fashionable: **à la mode; chi chi**
faster: **accelerando**
fastidious: **dégoûté**
fasting: **dharna**
fat: **gras**
fate: **kismet**
Fates
  ~ find a way: **Fata viam**

~ lead the willing: **Fata volentem**
~ oppose: **Fata obstant**
whither the ~ call: **quo Fata**
father: **bába; père**
  ~ of a family: **paterfamilias; père**
  ~ of his country: **pater patriae**
  I rejoin your ~: **je vais**
  like ~ like son: **el hijo; hijo; κακον
    (kakoû); tel père**
  miserly ~, spendthrift son: **a padre**
fatherland: **Vaterland**
fattening: **gavage**
fault: **faute**
  ~ most fortunate: **felix culpa**
  it's your own ~: **vous l'avez**
  my ~: **mea culpa**
  no one is born without ~: **vitiis**
  to find ~: **fronder**
faultfinder: **frondeur**
favor: **beneficium; de gratia; ex gratia;
  par amitié; par faveur**
  acceptance of ~: **beneficium**
  special ~: **speciali**
  through mere ~: **ex mera gratia**
favorable, always: **toujours propice**
favorite: **protégé**
fear: **quia**
  ~ betrays: **degeneres**
  ~ concealed by daring: **audendo**
  ~ curbs the tongue: **εμποδιζει
    (empodízei)**
  ~ gave him wings: **timor addidit**
  ~ greater than the evils ~ed: **sono**
  ~ Greeks bringing gifts: **timeo**
  ~ has many eyes: **tiene**
  ~ nor desire: **nec timeo**
  ~ of all things: **omnia tuta**
  ~ of burned child: **durch Schaden;
    empta; expertus; gebranntes**
  ~ of death, worse than death: **timor
    mortis**
  ~ plus curiosity: **kowashi**
  more ~ than shame: **con màs**
  to have is to ~: **tener es**
  what do you ~: **quid times**
  why ~ before the trumpet sounds:
    cur ante
fearlessly, faithfully, fruitfully: **fortiter,
  fideliter**
feast
  ~ with eyes: **pasce**
  recline at ~s: **epulis**
  you are come after the ~: **κατοπιν
    (katópin); post festum**

feasting: **bombance; ripaille**
feat of skill: **tour**
features, not the same in all: **facies**
feeble: **fiacco**
feeling: **Empfindung; Gefühl**
 pleasant ~: **Wohlgefühl**
fees, professional: **honoraires**
feet go where heart wills: **lá vão os**
felicity of expression: **curiosa**
fellow
 good ~: **bon enfant**
 good-natured ~: **bonhomme**
 jolly ~: **ein lustiger**
 noisy ~: **tapageur**
 sharp-witted ~: **épice; fine épice**
feminine, eternal: **das Ewig-Weibliche;
 Ewig-Weibliche**
fence gracefully: **avoir les armes**
fencing: **escrime**
 ~ foil: **fleuret**
 ~ master: **maître**
 ~ position: **quarte**
fennel: **fenouil**
fern: **capillaire**
ferociously: **fieramente**
fertilizer: **guano**
festival: **fête; jour**
 outdoor ~: **fête**
few
 ~ know how to be old: **peu de gens**
 ~ men are missed: **que son**
 select ~: **élite**
fibers, transverse nerve: **pons**
fictions please if they resemble truth:
 ficta
fidelity
 ~ and confidence: **fide et fiducia**
 ~ and fortitude: **fide et fortitudine**
 ~ and justice: **fides et**
 ~ is of God: **fidélité**
field: **campo; póle**
 ~ of granular snow: **névé**
field marshal: **maréchal**
 wife of ~: **maréchale**
fields, where are those: **O ubi**
fierce: **acerbus**
fife: **piffero**
fighter
 partisan ~: **guerrilla**
 prudent ~ takes foe seriously: **kein
 kluger**
fig paste: **loukoum**
figure: **Staffage**
 show off one's ~: **poser**

squat ~: **taille**
figured: **chiffré**
fillet: **filet**
 veal ~: **rouelle**
filling: **remplissage**
filth: **saloperie**
finally: **en somme**
fingers, plucked by the: **pizzicato**
finicky: **chercher**
finished: **pau**
 it is ~: **consummatum**
fire: **faire feu; feu; fuego; fuoco**
 between ~s: **entre deux**
 ~ extinguisher: **extincteur**
 ~ not extinguished by ~: **il fuoco**
 ~ poked with a sword: πυρ
 μαχαιρα (**pûr makhaíra**)
 ~ screen: **garde-feu**
 ~ tests gold: **ignis aurum**
 light a ~: **faire du feu**
 never set the world on ~: **il n'a pas**
 poetic ~: **estro**
 scathing ~: **feu**
 spread like wild ~: **virum**
 under ~: **en fuego; fuego**
 with ~: **con fuoco**
firearms: **armes à feu**
fireman: **pompiere**
fireworks: **feu**
firmness: **constantia; fermeté**
 be firm: **soyez**
 firm of purpose: **propositi; tenax
 propositi**
first: **come prima; primo**
 easily ~: **facile princeps**
 ~ among her equals: **prima inter**
 ~ among his equals: **primus**
 ~ born: **erstgeboren**
 ~ come, first served: **prior; sero
 venientibus**
 ~ consider, then venture: **erst wägen**
 ~ do no harm: **primum non**
 ~ in order: **imprimis**
 ~ of the season: **primeur**
 ~ performance: **première**
 ~ thing known: **primum cognitum**
 ~ time: **prima; tempo; volta**
 from the ~: **a primo**
fish: **machhli; poisson**
 flounder: **carrelet**
 flying ~: **volador**
 parrot ~: **vieja**
 plaice: **plie**
 shad: **alose**

sturgeon: **baliki; beluga; esturgeon; osotre**
teach a ~ to swim: **delphium natare; piscem**
whitebait: **blanchailles**
whiting: **merlan**
fissure: **falla**
fitness: **convenance**
fits and starts: **à bâtons; boutade; par accès; par boutades**
fitted: **encastré**
fit to paint: **à peindre**
flag: **drapeau**
　South African ~: **vierkleur**
flame
　feed the ~: **alere**
　~ thrower: **Flammenwerfer; lance-flamme**
flap of wings: **coup**
flash
　~ in the pan: **faux**
　~ of wit: **concetto**
flask: **flacon**
flatter: **faire pattes**
flatterer: **flatteur**
flattery: **eau; patte**
fleece: **moutonné**
flight: **volée; vuelo**
　precipitate ~: **sauve**
　she flies: **alis**
flogging, public: **pena de**
floor
　first ~: **au premier**
　fourth ~: **au troisième**
　ground ~: **piso; rez-de-chaussée**
　main ~: **bel étage**
　second ~: **au second**
floridly: **fioreggiante**
flourish
　~ed: **floruit**
　~es: **fioritura; viret in**
　he ~es upon ancestral honors: **avito**
　may it ~: **floreat**
flow: **flux**
　~ing: **délié**
　~ on forever: **labitur**
flower: **fleur; phúl**
　~ arrangement: **ikebana**
　~ stand: **jardinière**
　lily: **fleur**
　lotus: **pathma**

flowerets of thought: **flosculi**
flowers: **flores**
flowery: **fiorito**
fluency of speech: **facilité de**
fluent: **geläufig**
fluently: **currente**
flunky: **valet de pied**
flute: **chalumeau; zufolo**
　like a ~: **en flûte**
fly
　~ does not enter a closed mouth: **en boca**
　~ has a belly: **i mucha**
　~ has anger: **habet et musca**
flying: **volant**
fodder: **zacate**
fogy, old: **culotte**
folk, humble: **gens; les petites**
follow: **suivez**
　~ fate's decree: **data fata**
　~ one's bent: **suivre**
　~s his father: **sequiturque**
　~ thy star: **se tu segui**
　it ~s: **segue**
following but not inferior: **sequor**
folly, king's: **quicquid**
food: **chow**
　dish of ~: **couscous; enchilada; fondue; macédoine; paella; plat; risotto; saltimbocca; sashimi; sukiyaki; sushi; tamale**
　~ for the gallows: **pabulum Acheruntis**
　~ for the gods: βρωμα (brôma); **deorum**
　Hawaiian ~: **poi**
　infant's ~: **bouillie**
　more mouths than ~: **hay más**
fool: **bête; maboule; shmendrik**
　every ~ is pleased: **à chaque fou**
　every ~ offers advice: **ogni pazzo**
　~ found in public places: **nomina**
　~ goes in crowds of ~s: **à la presse**
　~ in the house: **basta d'un pazzo**
　~ must be taught by experience: **eventus; experientia**
　~ never has gray hair: **glupi**
　~ of the first water: **c'est un sot**
　~s run to opposite extremes: **dum vitant**
　~ who holds his tongue: **fou qui**
　good-natured ~: **bonne bête; une bonne**
　learned ~s: **i pazzi**

not such a ~: **bête; pas si bête**
to be a ~: **être un sot**
fooleries, no more of these: **trêve**
foolishness: **sottise**
foot: **pied**
   ~ warmer: **chauffe-pieds;**
      chaufferette
   on ~: **à pied**
   standing on one ~: **stans**
footprint: **pug**
   ~ frightens me: **vestigia**
   ~ of expiring liberty: **vestigia**
footsteps: **vestigia**
for and against: **pro et**
forbearance: ανεχον (anékhou)
forbidden: **verboten**
force: **ad baculum; de haute; forza;**
     fuerza; mit Gewalt; ultima ratio
   death ~: **vis**
   electromotive ~: **fuerza**
   ~ of arms: **à main armée**
   ~ of the term: **ex vi**
   ~ without discretion: **vis**
   in ~: **en vigueur**
   propelling ~: **vis**
   superior ~: **force; vis**
   vital ~: **élan vital; vis**
   with full ~: **tutta**
forced: **forzando**
forcefully: **con forza**
forcemeat: **andouillette; boudin; bou-**
     lette; farce; godiveau; quenelle
forcibly: **par force**
ford: **vado**
forehead, door of the mind: **frons**
foreigner: **eenostrahnyets; extranjero;**
     haole; uitlander
foreman: **capataz**
forenoon, in the: **vormittags**
forever: **à jamais; in aeternum; in in-**
     finitum; in perpetuum; pour ja-
     mais; pour toujours
   ~ and ever: **in saecula**
forewarned, forearmed: **praemonitus;**
     un homme averti
forfeit: **dédit**
forget
   don't ~: **n'oubliez**
   I'll never ~: **je n'oublierai**
   lest ye ~: **ne obliviscaris**
forgiveness
   ~ is conquest: **perdoar**
   ~ of others: **ignoscito**

fork: **fourchette**
form
   as a matter of ~: **pro forma**
   for the sake of ~: **par manière**
former: **ci-devant**
fortification: **redan**
fortress: **alcazaba; kila**
fortunate
   with the ~, all things ~: **in beato**
fortunately: **heureusement**
fortune
   follow ~: **fortuna sequatur**
   ~ favors fools: **fortuna favet fatuis**
   ~ favors the bold: **audentes**
   ~ favors the brave: **fortes; fortuna**
     favet fortibus
   ~ follows the better man: **fortuna**
     meliores
   ~ gives too much to many: **fortuna**
     multis
   ~ is great slavery: **gran casa; grande**
     fortune; magna servitus
   ~ is mine in fair fight: **fortuna mea**
   ~ is the companion of valor: **virtutis**
     fortuna
   ~ makes a fool of him: **fortuna**
     nimium
   ~ of the house: **stat fortuna**
   ~ passes everywhere: **la fortune**
   ~ to whom ~ yields: **cui Fortuna**
   I commit the rest to ~: **fortunae**
     cetera
   if ~ favors: **si fortuna**
   may the ~ of the house endure: **stet**
     fortuna
   unflinching before the blows of ~:
     ben tetragono
   while ~ lasted: **dum fortuna**
forum, clamor of the: **forensis**
forward: **age; en avant; vorwärts**
foundation of justice: **fundamentum**
founding, from the: **ab urbe**
foundling: **enfant**
fountain: **fuente; jet d'eau**
   drink from pure ~s: **integros**
four-handed: **vierhändig**
foursome: **partie**
fours, on all: **à quatre pattes**
fox, sly as a: **chytry**
fraction: **Bruch**
fragments, gather up: συναγαγετε
   (sunagágete)

framework: **cadre**
France, southern: **midi**
frankly: **bonnement; candide**
fraud: **supercherie; Täuschung**
 ~ to conceal ~: **fraus est**
 pious ~: **pia fraus**
freak: **coup; jeu; lusus**
freedom: **Freiheit ist; licenza**
 ~ is on the mountains: **auf den**
 ~ rushed upon the sword: **in ferrum**
 unlimited ~: **laisser-aller**
freeloader: **darmoyed**
freely: **à plaisir; liberamente**
 ~ and independently: **sciolto**
freethinker: **esprit**
French
 ~ Directory: **Directoire**
 ~ Foreign Office: **Quai**
 ~ land measure: **arpent**
 ~ person born in Algeria: **pied noir**
 ~ political party: **Fronde**
 ~ Republic: **République**
 ~ Revolutionary months: **Brumaire; Floréal; Frimaire; Fructidor; Germinal; Messidor; Nivôse; Pluviôse; Prairial; Thermidor; Vendémiaire; Ventôse**
 ~ spoken: **ici on; on parle**
 in ~: **Gallice**
frenzy, poetic: **furor poeticus**
frequenter of boulevards: **boulevardier**
fresco, finishing coat in: **intonaco**
fresh: **frisch**
freshet: **crecida**
freshly: **frescamente**
freshness: **fraîcheur**
 ~ of youth: **beauté du**
frets and fumes: **il jette**
fricassee with white sauce: **blanquette**
fried: **frit; sauté**
friend: **ami; amigo; chaver; compadre; droog**
 bosom ~: **alter ego; ami**
 false ~: **ami**
 ~ as far as the altars: **amicus usque**
 ~ at court: **ami**
 ~ in need: **al bisogno; on connaît**
 ~ is a second self: **amicitia semper; o φιλος (ho phílos)**
 ~ of the court: **amicus curiae**
 ~ of the human race: **amicus humani**
 ~ of the people: **ami**

 ~ proved by adversity: **amici**
 like a ~: **en ami**
 my ~: **mon ami**
 trusted ~: **fidus Achates**
friendless in life and death: **vida**
friendly to virtue and friends of virtue: **uni**
friends
 many acquaintances, few ~: **conocido**
 many ~ when prosperous: **donec**
 one mind among ~: **anima**
 tell me your ~, I'll tell you who you are: **dime con; Sage mir; skazhee**
 where ~, there wealth: **ubi amici**
friendship: **amitié**
 ~ always of benefit: **amicitia semper**
 ~ is love without wings: **l'amitié**
 ~ without deceit: **amicitia sine**
 token of ~: **ut pignus**
 while the pot boils, ~ lives: **fervet olla**
fright: **frousse**
frightened: **avoir du guignon**
frightfulness: **Schrecklichkeit**
frill: **balayeuse**
fritter: **beignet**
frivolity, long live: **vive la**
frizzed: **crêpé**
front: **façade**
frost: **gelée**
frozen: **frappé**
fruit
 dried ~: **orejones**
 forbidden ~: **i frutti**
 ~ cooked with sugar: **compote**
 ~ of toil: **le fruit**
 judge a tree by its ~: **fructu**
frying: **friture**
fugue: **fuga**
 short ~: **fughetta**
full: **plein**
fully: **en plein; in pleno**
fun
 for ~: **aus Scherz; pour rire**
 in ~: **en badinant**
functions: **funzioni**
fundamentally: **au fond**
funds, low in: **il est bas; percé**
furnished: **garni**
furniture: **meubles**
 ~ leg: **cabriole**
future: **in futuro; l'avenir**

for the ~: **in futuro**
thoughtful of the ~: **prudens futuri**

gaiety: **gaieté**
gaily: **festivamente; gaiement**
gain
  expectation of ~: **odor lucri**
  for ~: **lucri**
  ill-gotten ~: **unrecht**
gale: **coup**
Galilean, thou hast conquered: **vicisti**
gallantly: **galantemente**
gambol: **gambade**
game: **jeu; juego; mahjong; pelota;**
      petits-chevaux
  drawn ~: **partie; refait**
  gambling ~: **trente**
  ~ not worth the candle: **le jeu**
game (animals or birds): **gibier**
  feathered ~: **gibier**
  ~cock: **coq**
  small ~: **gibier; menu**
gamekeeper: **garde-chasse**
gamin: **gavroche**
gangster, Parisian: **apache**
gap: **trouée**
garden: **jardin**
  botanical ~: **jardin**
gardener: **mali**
garland: **lei**
garlic, with: **à la provençale**
garnet: **grenat**
gasoline: **essence**
gasp, last: **à l'extrémité; outrance; te-**
    ner l'anima
gate: **torii**
  ~ of the mind: **ianuae**
gathered: **plissé**
gathering, fashionable: **belle assemblée**
gay: **giocoso**
geniality: **bonhomie**
genius
  ~ is patience: **le génie**
  poetic ~: **vis**
Gentile: **goy**
gentle: **sanft**
  ~ in manner: **suaviter in**
gentleman: **babu; Don; gentilhomme;**
    gospodar; gospodin; Herr;
    homme
  shopkeeper turned ~: **bourgeois**
  young ~: **señorito; signorino**
gentlemanly: **genre**
gently: **tout beau**

~ and firmly: **suaviter et**
genuine: **pucka**
genus, highest: **summum genus**
German: **boche; tedesco**
  ~ Empire: **Deutsches Reich**
  ~ manner: **al tedesco**
  ~ National Bank: **Reichsbank**
  ~ spoken: **man spricht**
  wild impetuosity of ~s: **tedesco**
Germany: **la patrie**
  ~ above all: **Deutschland**
gesture, magnanimous: **beau geste**
getting on well: **il conduit**
gibberish: **baragouin; galimatias**
gibe: **coup**
giblets: **abatis**
gift: **cadeau**
  gave as a ~: **dono dedit**
  ~ I bear: **haec tibi**
  ~ of gab: **avoir la langue**
  ~ of God: **dante**
  ~ with hook attached: **sua munera**
  ~ worthy of Apollo: **munus**
gin: **Schiedam**
giraffe: **kameel**
girdle of Venus: **cingulum**
girl: **chokri; devochka; larki;**
    Mädchen; muchacha
  adolescent ~: **Backfisch**
  artless ~: **ingénue**
  coquettish ~: **soubrette**
  dancing ~: **almah; bai; bayadère;**
    geisha
  good-natured ~: **ein gutes**
  working ~: **grisette**
gist: **le fin**
give
  ~ and it shall be ~n unto you: **date**
    et
  ~r makes gifts precious: **auctor**
    pretiosa
  ~ that you may do: **do ut facias**
  ~ that you may ~: **do ut des**
  he will ~ who gave: **dabit qui**
  I gave you a wife, not a slave: **mujer**
  let it be ~n to the fairest: **detur**
  let it be ~n to the more worthy:
    detur
  who ~s quickly ~s twice: **bis dat;**
    chi dà
giving
  ~ requires good sense: **res**
  thou shalt gain by ~: **tyaktena**

glad, I am: **das freut**
glance: **aperçu**
  first ~: **prima facie; prima vista; primo intuiti**
  loving ~s: **faire les yeux**
  tender ~s: **les doux**
glass: **verre**
  ~ and luck: **Glück und**
  in ~: **in vitro**
  liqueur ~: **petit**
glide: **portamento**
gliding: **glissando; scorrendo**
glistening: **chatoyant**
gloom, farthest: **l'ultima sera**
glory
  born to ~: **natus ad**
  G~ be on high: **Gloria**
  ~ is the reward of victory: **victoriae**
  ~ is the shadow of virtue: **gloria**
  ~ of the world passes away: **sic transit**
  ~ of the world passes quickly: **O quam**
  ~ to God: **τω θεω (tô theô)**
  ~ to God alone: **soli Deo**
  ~ to God in the highest: **δοξα (dóxa)**
  ~ too late: **cineri**
  may he be in G~: **que en Gloria**
  no path of flowers leads to ~: **aucun chemin**
glutton: **croqueur; Epicuri; fresser; gourmand**
go: **haere; jao**
  ~ away: **allez-vous-en; haere; imshi; va-t'en; váyase**
  ~ back again: **haere**
  ~ing, ~ing, gone: **zum ersten**
  ~ quickly: **jaldi**
  ~ slowly: **ahista**
  ~ the mass is over: **ite**
  it ~es without saying: **cela va; das versteht**
  let's ~: **allons; andiamo**
  who ~es softly ~es safely: **chi va piano**
  who ~es there: **qui va**
  who has nothing to lose ~es safely: **sûrement**
goat: **bakra**
goblin: **esprit**
go-cart: **carretón**
God: **Adonai; Allah; deva; kami**
  all things for the glory of ~:
    omnia ad
  everything comes from ~: **tout vient de**
  fear ~: **crains; time; τον θεον (tòn theòn)**
  for ~ and King: **non mihi**
  gift of ~: **ex dono**
  give unto ~: **Deo date**
  ~ and Church: **pro Deo**
  ~ and fatherland and friends: **Deo, patriae**
  ~ and federation: **Dios y**
  ~ and king: **a Deo et rege**
  ~ and my right: **Dieu et**
  ~ and union and liberty: **Dios unión**
  ~ as my leader: **Deo duce**
  ~ be merciful: **Deus misereatur**
  ~ Best, Greatest: **Deo, Optimo**
  ~ be with us as with our fathers: **sicut patribus**
  ~ be with you: **Deus vobiscum; Dhia bith**
  ~ bless me: **válgame**
  ~ bless you: **Dio vi; que Dieu**
  ~ defend me: **defiéndame**
  ~ defends the right: **Dieu défend**
  ~ deliver me from a man of one book: **Dios me**
  ~ enriches: **ditat**
  ~ forbid: **astagh-fer; Deus avertat; Dieu m'en; Gott bewahre; longe absit; quod avertat**
  ~ grant: **Deus det; Dieu le**
  ~ has conferred these comforts: **deus nobis haec**
  ~ has smiled: **annuit**
  ~ helping: **Deo adiuvante; iuvante**
  ~ helps the poorly dressed: **Dios ayuda**
  ~ is great: **Allah akbar**
  ~ is the chief good: **Deus est summum**
  ~ keep him: **que Dios**
  ~ keep you: **Dieu vous**
  ~ listens to short prayers: **breve orazione**
  ~ made us and we are struck with wonder: **hízonos**
  ~ not chance: **Deo, non**
  ~ on the side of big battalions: **on dit que Dieu**
  ~ opposes the haughty: **górdym**
  ~ out of a machine: **deus ex machina; θεος εκ (theòs ek)**

~ pays: **Bóg**

~ preserve you from a reconciled friend: **guarde-vos**

~ rules all things: **Deus est regit**

~ save the king: **salvum**

~ save the queen: **salvam**

~ sent forth His breath: **afflavit Deus**

~ so wills: **si Dieu veult**

~ steers the ship: **Deus gubernat**

~ takes care of flowers: **flores**

~ tempers: **à brebis**

~ vouchsafe thee to profit from reading: **se Dio**

~ warning: **Deo monente**

~ who wounds gives medicine: **Dios que**

~, why hast thou forsaken me: **Eli, Eli**

~ will end these troubles: **dabit Deus**

~ willing: **Deo volente; inshallah; volente**

~ will provide: **Deus providebit**

~ wills it: **Deus vult; Gott will**

~ within us: **est deus**

~ with us: **Dieu avec; Gott mit**

~ with us and who against us: **Deus nobiscum; si Deus**

~ would be invented: **si Dieu n'existait**

greater glory of ~: **ad maiorem**

in ~ everything: **en Dieu est tout**

in ~ have I trusted: **in Deo**

in ~ my trust: **en Dieu est ma**

I seek ~: **je ne cherche**

mighty fortress is our ~: **Ein' feste**

mindful of ~: **Dei memor**

my ~: **mein Gott; mon Dieu**

my hope is in ~: **spes**

our only safety is in serving ~: **sola salus**

pleased ~: **utcumque**

please ~: **so Gott**

praise be to ~: **laus Deo**

Preacher of the Word of ~: **Verbi**

rejoice in ~: **Iubilate**

Servant of the Servants of ~: **servus**

submit to ~: **cede**

thank ~: **à Dios gracias; Deo gratias; Gott sei; grâce à; gracias a; slava bogoo**

to the Unknown ~: αγνωστω (agnóstō)

Truce of ~: **la Trêve; Treuga; trêve**

We praise thee O ~: **Te Deum**

what ~ has willed: **mashallah**

where ~ is, nothing is lacking: **dove Dio**

will of ~: **à la volonté; fiat Dei**

with ~'s favor: **Deo favente; Deo iuvante**

without ~ nothing: **sans**

worship ~ serve king: **Deum cole**

would to ~: **wollte**

ye cannot serve ~: ον δυνασθε (ou dúnasthe)

goddess: **devi**

~ revealed by her gait: **incessu; vera incessu**

O thou who art a ~: **O dea**

gods: **dii**

~ help the stronger: **deos**

~ of vengeance act in silence: **die Rachegötter**

~ see virtuous deeds: **di pia**

household ~: **di penates; lar**

if it pleases the ~: **si diis**

it lies on the knees of the ~: θεων εν (theôn en)

leave the rest to the ~: **permitte**

to the ~ otherwise: **dis aliter**

under direction of the ~: **dis ducibus**

godsend: **c'est une**

gold: **aurum**

all that glitters is not ~: **es ist nicht; oro è che**

craving for ~: **auri sacra**

~ and silver: **oro y**

~ too dear: **man kann**

where ~ speaks, every tongue is silent: **dove l'oro**

Golden Fleece: **toison**

goldfish: **kingyo**

good: **achcha; bon; charosho**

according to what is right and ~: **ex aequo**

common ~: **commune bonum**

do ~ to all: **faze**

for the public ~: **pro bono**

~ and fine: **bonne et**

~ for nothing: **garnement; vaurien**

~ was never plentiful: **nunca lo**

great ~: **magnum bonum**

it is ~ for us to be here: καλον (kalón)

preferred to be rather than seem ~:

esse quam
public ~: **bonum publicum**
so ~ that ~ for nothing: **tanto**
supreme ~: **summum bonum**
to desire ~: **pour bien**
to the ~ all things are good: **omnia bona**
very ~: **ding hao; optime**
where no ~ is: **daar niets**
goodbye: **addio; adeus; adieu; adiós; aloha; arrivederci; até a; auf Wiedersehen; au revoir; bene vale; do svidaniya; proshchài; sayonara; selamat djalan; selamat tinggal; tidama**
to say ~: **pour dire; pour faire ses**
without saying ~: **insalutato**
goodness
~ is from above: **omne bonum**
~ repays good deed: **bien con**
goods: **de bonis asportatis; géneros**
among the ~: **in bonis**
~ not administered: **de bonis non**
movable ~: **bona; res**
perishable ~: **bona**
unclaimed ~: **bona**
gooseberry: **groseille**
gooseflesh: **cutis**
gorge: **kloof**
gossip: **bavard; caquet; chronique; Klatsch**
gossiping: **caquetrie**
government: **Regierung; sarkar**
petticoat ~: **Pantoffel-regiment**
self-~: **Swaraj**
violent change in ~: **coup**
governor: **beg; beglerbeg; killadar**
~'s wife: **gouvernante**
gown, dressing: **peignoir; robe de chambre**
grace: **grazia**
~ of God: **Dei gratia; gratia Dei**
~ of pleasing: **gratia placendi**
state of ~: **nirvana**
your G~: **monseigneur**
graceful: **disinvolto; gentile; grazioso; zierlich**
gracefully: **con grazia; graziosamente**
gradually: **allmählich; di grado; gradatim**
grandchild: **sansei**
grandfather: **grand-père**
grandiose: **maestoso; pomposo**
grandmother: **baba; babushka;**

grand-mère
grant, royal: **regium**
grass: **atocha; kuskus**
gratitude, token of: **hommage**
gratuity: **buonamano; cumshaw; gratificación; lagniappe; mancia; pilon; pourboire; sportula; Trinkgeld**
gravedigger: **fossoyeur**
grave for another: **kto druhému**
gravel: **casquijo**
gravely: **pesante**
gravy: **jus**
natural ~: **au jus**
great: **bara; grande; grosso**
~ and good: **haut et**
~ by report, ~er in deeds: **O fama**
~est to least: **a maximis**
so ~ therefore: **Tantum Ergo**
Greek to me: **das kommt; eso es chino**
greengage: **reine-Claude**
greenhorn: **blanc-bec**
greetings: **saludos; salut**
greeting, warm: **beso las manos; beso los pies**
Gregorian
~ chant: **cantus planus**
~ melody: **cantus firmus**
grenade, hand: **granada**
grief: **chagrin; duolo**
great ~s are silent: **i gran**
~s find utterance: **curae**
no greater ~: **nessun**
renew unspeakable ~: **infandum renovare**
unspeakable ~: **infandum regina**
groaning: **multa gemens**
grocer: **épicier**
groom: **syce**
groomed, well: **soigné**
grooved: **cannelé**
grotesque: **marmouset**
ground, barren: **borrasca; maigre; sujet**
groundless: **raison; sans**
grounds, good: **bonne raison; raison**
group with common interests: **cénacle**
grouse: **coq**
grove: **bocage; bosque**
grow
~s as it goes: **crescit eundo**
~ slowly and die quickly: **corpora**

growling, stop: **pas tant**
gruesome: **macabre**
guarantee: **del credere**
guard: **garde**
  ever on ~: **toujours en**
  ~ dies but does not surrender: **la
    garde**
  mounted ~: **garde**
  rural ~: **garde**
  who shall ~ the ~s: **quis custodiet**
guardian: **custos**
guests, have: **Fremd**
guide: **cicerone**
  spiritual ~: **guru**
guilt
  accused person pleads ~y: **habemus**
  actions do not make ~: **actus**
  who keeps silent admits ~: **chi tace
    confessa**
guitar: **samisen**
gully: **arroyo; couloir; donga**
gum: **goma**
gun: **banduk; bouche; chassepot;
  flingot**
  ~ bearer: **askari**
  machine ~: **mitrailleuse**
  machine ~ner: **mitrailleur**
gymnasium: **Turnhalle**
gymnastics
  ~ exhibition: **Turnfest**
  ~ society: **Sokol**
gypsy: **gitano; zingano**
  non~: **gorgio**

habit
  as is ~: **sicut meus**
  great force of ~: **magna est vis**
  ~ is second nature: **consuetudo
    quasi**
hail: **ave; hare; jambo**
  ~ and farewell: **ave**
  ~ Caesar: **ave**
  ~ god of Triumph: **io Triumphe**
  ~ Krishna: **hare**
  ~ Mary: **ave**
hair
  ~ style: **chevelure; coiffure;
    pompadour**
  hangs by a ~: **de pilo**
  tuft of ~: **toupet**
half: **à demi; à moitié; demi; Hälfte;
  par moitiés**
hall: **sala; salle**
  outer ~ of a law court: **salle**

town ~: **ayuntamiento; hôtel de
  ville; mairie; Rathaus**
hallucination, delightful: **mentis**
halo: **Heiligenschein**
halt: **tomare**
halter, head portion of: **jaquima**
halves, go: **partager**
ham: **jambon; jamón; prosciutto**
hammer and anvil: **entre l'enclume;
  inter; zwischen Amboss**
hammock: **kartel**
hamper: **serón**
hand: **ad manum; camay; mano**
  cold ~s and warm heart: **froides;
    mains**
  for four ~s: **à quatre mains**
  ~, an enemy to tyrants: **manus haec**
  ~ from the clouds: **manus e**
  ~s up: **Hände**
  ~ to ~: **corps**
  I commend my spirit into Thy ~s:
    in manus
  one ~ washes the other: **eine Hand;
    yad rochetset**
  on the other ~: **e contra**
  right ~: **derecha; destra; droite**
  shake ~s: **dextras**
  skillful ~: **une main**
  strong ~: **manu forti**
  with both ~s: **à deux**
  with left ~: **colla sinistra; sinistra**
  with one's own ~: **manu propria**
  with right ~: **colla destra**
handball, Basque: **jai alai**
handbook: **Handbuch**
handkerchief: **pañuelo; rumal**
handmill: **metate**
handrail: **barandilla; garde-fou**
handsome is as handsome does: **sat
  pulchra**
hangman: **maître**
hangover: **calavera**
Hannibal
  ~ at the gates: **Hannibal**
  weigh the dust of ~: **expende**
haphazard: **geratewohl**
happily: **feliciter**
happiness: **bonheur; le bonheur**
  domestic ~: **Hausglück**
  earthly ~: **das irdische**
  ~ from a middle course: **medium**
  ~ not from possessions: **non
    possidentem**
  no perfect ~: **nihil**

happy: **selig**
  always ~: **semper; toujours gai**
  ~ is he who understands causes: **felix qui**
  H~ New Year: **prosit; se novim godom**
  O ~ they: **O fortunatos**
  O thrice yea four times ~: **O terque**
  very ~: **wie Gott**
harbinger: **avant-coureur**
harbor: **puerto**
  ~ master: **garde-port**
hardness: **dur**
  hard to boil, hard to eat: **duro de**
hardships
  ~ don't deter us: **nec aspera**
  through ~: **ad astra**
hare: **lièvre**
  ~s insult a dead lion: **mortuo**
  young ~: **levraut**
harm: **damnum**
  no ~ intended: **absit omen**
  whom will it ~: **cui malo**
harmony: **concentus**
  in ~: **par accord**
harshly: **duramente**
harvest: **cosecha; moisson**
  ~ truly is bountiful: **ο μεν θερισμος (ho mèn therismòs)**
hash: **hachis**
haste
  ~ makes waste: **presto**
  make ~: **festina; jaldi; sbrigatevi**
  more ~ and less speed: **blinder; eile mit; maggiore; teeshi; trop de hâte**
  need for ~: **maturato**
  without ~: **ohne Hast**
hat: **chapeau-bras; jipijapa**
hate
  let them ~ so long as they fear: **oderint**
  pet ~: **bête**
hatred
  ~ of rival physicians, theologians: **odium**
  without ~: **sine**
hats off: **Hut ab**
haughtiness: **morgue**
haughty: **imperioso**
haunt, Muses' lonely: **avia**
have
  ~ and distribute: **habere et**
  I ~ not, want not, care not:

  nec habeo
hazelnut: **noisette**
head: **caput; tête**
  big ~: **gros**
  calf's ~: **tête**
  fat ~ and lean brains: **capo**
  ~ covering: **haik**
  ~ in the clouds: **caput**
  ~ of a boar, salmon, etc.: **hure**
  ~ over heels: **Hals**
  ~ to heel: **a capite; de pied**
  ~ uplifted, strike the stars: **sublimi**
  so many ~s: **autant de têtes**
  square ~: **tête**
  two ~s are better than one: **εις (hês); nemo solus**
headache: **Kopfschmerzen; mal**
headdress, Arab: **kaffiyeh**
headman: **dato**
headquarters: **comandancia; yamen**
headstrong: **entêté**
health: **marhaba; salud; salute; santé**
  be well: **kia ora**
  to your ~: **slâinte**
  who has not ~ has nothing: **qui n'a**
  your ~: **alla salute; alla vostra; a su salud; a vostra salute; à votre santé; a vuestra; Gesundheit; kan pei; prosit**
heap: **in cumulo**
  many grains make a ~: **ex granis**
  out of a ~: **ex acervo**
hearsay: **de auditu; de oídos; dictum de dicto; ouï-dire**
heart
  bottom of the ~: **ab imo; imo**
  broken ~: **désolé**
  content ~: **à coeur joie**
  ~ makes men eloquent: **pectus**
  ~-shaped: **en coeur**
  in one's ~: **v'gloobeenye dooshee**
  lift up your ~: **sursum**
  one ~ and one way: **cor unum**
  opening of one's ~: **épanchement**
  two ~s that beat as one: **zwei Seelen**
heartbreak: **crève-coeur**
hear the other side: **audi alteram; audiatur**
heartiness: **entrain**
heartrending: **déchirant**
heat: **calore**
heath: **landa**
heating: **chauffage**
heaven: **Himmel**

~ at last: **denique caelum**
~ can't bend: **flectere**
~ is rest: **in caelo quies**
~ is salvation: **in caelo salus**
~ send better times: **di meliora**
~s fall: **ruat**
~ the seat of the gods: ουρανος **(ouranós)**
short prayers mount to ~: **oración**
strength from ~: **caelitus; vigueur**
heavenly secrets: **arcana caelestia**
heir: **heres**
final ~: **ultimus heres**
hell: **enfer; jahannan**
~ has its rights: **die Hölle**
hello: **aloha; ciao; selamat datang; zdrávstvui**
helmet: **casque; Pickelhaube; schapska; sola topi; topi**
help: **aiuto; à moi; à mon secours; au secours**
~ from on high: **auxilium ab**
~ offered too late: **post bellum**
~ out of trouble: **tirer d'affaire**
~ yourself: **aide-toi**
he not with me is against me: ο μη ων **(ho mè òn)**
herb: **orégano**
herbarium: **hortus**
herd: **manada; stanitza**
here: **aquí**
~ and everywhere: **hic et ubique**
~ and now: **hic et nunc**
~ and there: **ça et; hin und her; par-ci**
~ begins: **incipit**
~ ends: **explicit**
~ I am and ~ I stay: **j'y suis**
~ is buried: **ci-gît; hic iacet; hic sepultus**
~ I stand: **hier stehe**
~ is that bore again: **ecce**
~ is the proof: **ecce**
~ lies the difficulty: **hic iacet**
~, there, and everywhere: **ab hoc**
~ the speech ended: **hic finis fandi**
~ today and gone tomorrow: **heute rot**
heresy, suspected of: **il sent le fagot**
hero: **bahadur; Schwarm**
no man is a ~ to his valet: **es gibt; il n'y a pas de héros**

heroic: **eroico**
herring: **hareng**
hesitating: **zögernd**
higher: **excelsior**
highest, in the: **in excelsis**
Highness: **Altesse; Alteza**
highway: **calzado; carretera**
hill: **alto; cerro; colina; coteau; falda; kop; loma; morne; puy**
small ~: **kopje; lomita**
him, just like: **cela est digne**
himself, said it: **ipse**
Hindu
~ ascetic: **yogi**
~ ascetic philosophy: **yoga**
~ spring festival: **Holi**
hint: **demi-mot**
historian is a prophet looking backward: **der Historiker**
history: **Geschichte**
world ~: **Weltgeschichte**
world's ~: **die Weltgeshichte**
hit: **maro**
he is ~: **hoc habet**
lucky ~: **coup; raccroc**
hoarfrost: **pruina**
hoarse: **fioco**
hoarseness: **fiochezza**
hoax: **canard**
hoaxer: **blagueur**
hobby: **dada**
hodgepodge: **pot pourri; ripopée**
hog: **cerda**
holding
hold fast: **tenez**
~ directly from the Crown: **in capite**
to be held in the post office: **poste restante**
to hold and not be held: **habere non**
hole, water: **alberca**
holiday: **congé; Feiertag; festa; fiesta; jour**
country ~s: **villeggiatura**
~ mood: **en fête**
holiness
~ and wisdom: **sancte**
thrice holy: **Tersanctus**
home: **à la maison; chez; Heimat; in casa; te huis**
~ and a pleasing wife: **domus et**
~ of a ranchero: **ranchería**
~ of one's own: **avoir un chez; chez**
no place like ~: **eigner**
not ~: **darwaza**

sweet H~: **dulce Domum**
Homer nods: **aliquando; dormitat;**
    quandoque
homesickness: **mal**
honesty
  ~ is the best policy: **ehrlich**
  ~ is true honor: **probitas verus**
  ~ praised and left to starve: **probitas**
    laudatur
  not so honest, more honest: **nicht so**
honey
  one drop of tar spoils a barrel of ~:
    loshka
  where there's ~, there are the bees:
    ubi mel
honor: **izzat**
  add to ancestral ~: **decori**
  ~ alters manners: **honores**
  ~ and defense: **decus**
  ~ and fatherland: **honneur**
  ~ carries responsibility: **honos habet**
  ~ follows unsolicited: **invitum**
  ~ is from the Nile: **honor est**
  ~ is my guide: **el honor**
  ~ is the reward of virtue: **honor**
    virtutis
  ~ not lost: **tout est perdu**
  ~ nourishes the arts: **honos alit**
  military ~: **a cuspide; médaille**
  neither seek nor despise ~: **nec**
    quaerere
  nowhere is there true ~: **nusquam**
  on one's ~: **ex bona**
  through difficulties to ~: **per**
    angusta
  to whom ~ is due: **à chaque saint;**
    al hombre
  upon my ~: **bei meiner**
  word of ~: **ein Mann; parole**
  your ~: **huzur**
honorable, not everything lawful is:
    non omne
honorary: **honoris**
hook or crook: **à bis; de bric**
hope: **Hoffnung; spes**
  abandonment of ~: **lasciate**
  forlorn ~: **enfant; perdu**
  good ~: **spes**
  ~ and fear: **inter**
  ~ and God: **espérance et Dieu**
  ~ for better things: **spero**
  ~ in adversity and fear in prosper-
    ity: **sperat**
  ~ in God: **espérance en Dieu**

~ in heaven: **spes**
~ is not broken: **at spes**
~ is the bread of the wretched: **la**
    speranza
~ is the last thing we lose: **l'ultima**
    che
~ of a decision: **sub spe**
~ of Rome: **magnae spes**
~ of the flock: **spes**
I don't pay for ~: **spem**
I have ~d: **speravi**
in ~: **sur espérance**
while I breathe I ~: **dum spiro**
while there's life there's ~: **dum vita**
    est; hasta la; nulli desperandum
horn: **corno**
  blow one's own ~: **faire claquer**
  English ~: **cor anglais; corno**
hornets, stir up: **irritabis**
horrible
  ~ to relate: **horribile dictu**
  ~ to see: **horribile visu**
hors d'oeuvre: **antipasto**
horse: **bronco; caballo; cheval**
  fresh ~: **remonta**
  good ~: **à bon cheval**
  neither rein nor spur a ~ that
    obeys: **un cheval**
horseback: **a caballo**
  on ~: **à cheval**
horsehair: **cerda**
horseman: **caballero; jinete**
horsemanship: **haute école; manège**
  military ~: **école**
horseplay: **jeu**
horseradish: **raifort**
horses, saddle: **remuda**
hospital: **bet choleem; hôpital**
  chief ~: **hôtel-Dieu**
  Paris veterans' ~: **Hôtel des**
    Invalides
host: **hôte**
  the real ~: **le véritable**
hostage: **otage**
hostility, during: **flagrante bello**
hot: **garm**
hotel: **gostínnista; Hof; szálloda**
hour: **Uhr**
  ~ flies: **fugit hora; hora fugit**
  ~ for prayer: **horae canonicae**
  I mark none but shining ~s: **horas**
  leisure ~s: **heures perdues; horae**
    subsicivae
  passing ~s are counted against us:

pereunt
use each ~: **Gebraucht**
house: **casa; dacha; dom; igloo; maison; rancheria; rann**
  boarding ~: **pension**
  coach ~: **cochera**
  furnished ~: **maison**
  ~ and home: **Haus und**
  ~ next door on fire: **iam proximus; proximus**
  H~ of Lords: **Domus Procerum; Herrenhaus**
  ~ of prostitution: **bordello; maison**
  ice ~: **glacière**
  little ~: **caseta; casetta; casita**
  town ~: **maison**
  within the walls of a ~: **intra parietes**
household: **ménage**
housekeeper: **balabustah; femme**
housewife: **Hausfrau**
how: **quomodo**
  ~ are you: **come state; come va; comment allez-vous; comment ça; cómo está; cómo le; cómo vai; kak delah; qué tal; tena; wie geht's**
  ~ changed from what he was: **quantum**
  ~ many: **combien; tokohia**
  ~ much: **kitna; quantum**
hubbub: **brouhaha**
hue and cry: **haro**
human being: **homo**
Human Comedy: **comédie**
humanities: **litterae humaniores**
humming: **fredonnement**
humor: **umore**
hundred: **per centum**
hunger
  ~ impelling to crime: **malesuada**
  ~ is the best sauce: **il n'est chère**
  ~ knows no laws: **la fame**
  ~ teaches many things: **multa docet**
hunter: **byadha; cacciatore**
hunting: **safari; shikar**
hurdy-gurdy: **vielle**
hurrah: **enviva; hoch; macte; olé; shabash; vive**
hurriedly: **in fretta; precipitando**
husband: **esposo; marido; muzh**
  dear ~: **caro sposo**
  ~ and wife: **vir et**
  ~ and wife and lover: **ménage**

hut: **hogan**
Hydra, you are wounding a: **νδραν (hýdran)**
hymn of praise: **Lobgesang**
hyphen: **Bindestrich; Divis; trait**
hypochondria: **maladie**
hypocrisy: **cafardise**
hypocrite: **patte-pelu; tartufe**
hypocritically: **à la Tartuffe**
hypothesis: **ex hypothesi**

I am
  ~ not what once I was: **non sum**
  ~ sorry: **es tut**
ice: **barf; glace**
  ~ axe: **piolet**
  ~ bomb: **bombe**
  ~ cream: **crème**
idea, fixed: **idée**
ideal of perfection: **beau idéal**
identity, prove one's: **montrer**
idle: **désoeuvré; les bras**
idleness: **désoeuvrement; fainéantise; geschäftiger; operose**
  energetic ~: **strenua**
  ~ is the tomb of living man: **otio sepoltura**
  pleasant ~: **dolce**
idler: **badaud; flâneur**
if
  ~ I can: **si je puis**
  ~ you please: **s'il vous plaît**
ignoramus has no doubts: **chi niente**
ignorance
  gross ~: **ignorance**
  ~ is better than obstinacy: **más vale ser**
  ~ of point in dispute: **ignoratio elenchi**
  ~ of the facts: **ad ignorantium**
  ~ of the law excuses no one: **ignorantia facti; ignorantia legis**
  not know black from white: **não ha**
  where ~ is bliss: **ignoti**
  who knows nothing is worth nothing: **quien no**
ill
  fatally ~: **todkrank**
  great ~ness, great remedies: **aux grands**
  he's ~: **aegrotat**
ill-bred: **de mauvais genre**
ill-timed: **mal à propos**
illusion: **maya**

~ brief, repentance long: **der Wahn**
optical ~: **deceptio**
imaginative: **fantaisiste**
imbecile: **bécasse; impos**
imitation: **pastiche**
imitators, O servile herd of: **imitatores; O imitatores**
immediately: **sogleich; statim; sur-le-champ; tout de suite**
immigrant
    Japanese ~: **issei**
    second-generation ~: **kibei; nisei**
    third-generation ~: **sansei**
immortality: **à l'immortalité**
impatience: **Ungeduld**
impatiently: **umpazientemente**
imperceptibly: **insensibilmente**
impetuosity: **impeto**
    with ~: **con impeto**
impetuous: **impetuoso**
implication: **implicite**
important, begin with the: **ab Iove**
impossibilities, expect: **pedir**
impossibility: **c'est la mer**
impossible: **pas possible**
impressive: **frappant**
impromptu: **ex tempore**
improvement, room for: **cela laisse**
improvisation: **improvvisatore**
impulse, of one's own: **motu**
impunity, no one assails me with: **nemo me**
incarnate: **Incarnatus**
inch: **Zoll**
incidentally: **obiter**
inclination: **gré; penchant**
incline to nothing base: **ne vile**
income: **rente**
inconsiderate: **ohne Überlegung**
inconvenience: **ab inconvenienti**
increase and multiply: **crescite**
increase, gradual: **messa**
incredible: **c'est vraiment; incroyable; l'incroyable**
incriminate: **accusare**
indeed: **ma foi; tiens**
indelicate: **grivois**
independently: **proprio vigore**
index
    subject ~: **index rerum**
    word ~: **index verborum**
Indian: **indio**
indictment: **acte d'accusation**
indignation: **sdegno**

~ produces verse: **facit indignatio**
indirectly: **per ambages**
indiscretion: **faux**
indispensable: **obbligato**
individual, private: **particulier**
indolent on holiday: **ignavis**
indoors: **à l'intérieur**
indulgence: **a buen bocado**
    with your ~: **cum bona**
industrious and deserving: **meret**
industry
    to ~, nothing impossible: **industriae**
infamy, brand of: **note**
infantryman, light: **franc-tireur**
inference
    illogical ~: **non sequitur**
    logical ~: **sequitur**
inferior, not having followed anything: **non inferiora**
infidel: **infiel**
infinity, to: **ad infinitum; in infinitum**
informally: **en famille; sans**
information
    inside ~: **les dessous**
    supplementary ~: **apparatus criticus**
informed: **au courant**
informer: **mouchard**
infuriated: **forcené**
infusion: **tisane**
ingenuous: **naïf**
ingot: **lingote**
ingratitude is the world's payment: **Undank**
inhabitant: **habitant**
inheritance, damaging: **damnosa**
iniquity, sink of: **colluvies**
injurious: **nuisible**
injustice
    no ~ to a consenting party: **volenti**
inlet, sea: **fjord**
inn: **albergo; auberge; fonda; Gasthaus; Gasthof; guingette; osteria; parador; posada; ryo; Wirtshaus; zayat**
innkeeper: **aubergiste**
inopportune: **cela tombe mal**
Inquisition, sentence of the: **auto-da-fé; auto-de-fe**
insanity: **dementia; vesania**
inscription: **dédicace**
insertion: **Zwischenstück**
insofar: **qua**
insolence, satiety breeds: **τικτει (tíktei)**
inspiration: **afflatus; Begeisterung;**

mens divinior
instance, for: **exemple; par exemple**
instigating: **provocant**
instigator: **agent**
instrument, musical: **baja; bandurria;**
    fiato; inflatilla; koto; stromenti
instrument, surgical: **écraseur**
insult: **incartade; spretae**
    swallow ~s: **avaler; couleuvre**
insurance premium: **pretium**
insurrection: **Putsch**
intellect, powerful: **ein starker**
intellectual: **homme**
intelligence: **Verstand**
    natural ~: **lumen**
intent, guilty: **mens rea**
intention
    hell paved with ~s: **di buona**
    ~ and fact: **animo et facto**
    ~ of stealing: **animus furandi**
    ~ of taking: **animus capiendi**
    with that ~: **eo animo**
    with what ~: **quo animo**
intentional: **absichtlich**
intentionally: **à dessein**
interest
    ~ of one side: **ex parte**
    ~ on Government securities:
        rente
    resume childish ~s: **redire**
interlude: **entracte; Zwischenspiel**
intermission: **relâche**
    without ~: **nec mora**
interpreter: **dubash**
intersection: **patte-d'oie**
interval
    frequent ~s: **haud longis**
    long ~: **longo intervallo**
intervention, providential: **coup; deus**
        ex
intimacy: **liaison**
intrigue: **brigue**
    amorous ~s: **bonne fortune**
intrinsically: **per se**
introduction: **Einleitung**
invaluable: **impayable**
inventory: **inventario**
investigation: **enquête**
invoice: **factura**
Ireland
    ~ forever: **Erin go**
    long live ~: **Eirëann**
iridescent: **gorge-de-pigeon; reflet**
Irish Free State: **Saorstát**

iron
    branding ~: **gancho**
    ~ and blood: **Eisen und**
    ~ sharpened by ~: **ferrum**
ironwood: **bois**
irrelevant: **à propos; nihil**
irresolutely: **à tâtons**
irritating: **agaçant**
irritation: **agacement**
island: **île; óstrov**
islet, rocky: **farallon**
isolated: **détaché**
Israeli, native-born: **sabra**
issue, without: **sine**
it
    ~ is all over: **actum est; adieu la voi-**
        ture; ce n'est fait; damit; es ist
        rein; frit; fuimus; tout est frit
    ~ is all the same: **c'est égal**
    ~ is as well to try: **bene est**
    ~ is easy to add to things: **facile est**
    ~ is not so: **non è così**
    ~ is permitted: **licet**
    ~ is settled: **il n'y pas à dire**
    ~ is so: **ita est**
    ~ is too much: **è troppo**
    ~ seems: **videtur**
    ~ will go on: **ça ira**
Italian: **italien**
    14th century ~ art and literature:
        trecento
    15th century ~ art and literature:
        quattrocento
    16th century ~ art and literature:
        cinquecento
    ~ manner: **italice**
    ~ spoken: **si parla**
italics: **Kursivschrift**
Italy unredeemed: **Italia**
itch for writing: **cacoëthes**
itself, in: **in se**

jackass: **rossignol**
jacket: **chaqueta; redingote**
    pea ~: **vareuse**
jail: **calabozo; cárcel; maison**
January: **janvier**
jar, water: **tinaja**
javelins, we too have hurled: **et nos**
        quoque
jealousy, professional: **jalousie**
jelly, currant: **gelée**
jest: **scherzo**
    ill-timed ~: **mauvais**

in ~: **per iocum**
Jesus Savior of Men: **Iesus**
jewel: **bijou; joya; parure**
   ~ in a dunghill: **haki-dame**
jewelry setting: **pavé**
Jewish
   ~ dietary laws: **kosher**
   quorum for ~ worship: **minyan**
jingoist: **chauvinist**
job: **colocación; tâche**
John the Baptist Day: **Johannistag**
joining, skillful: **callida**
joke: **mot; plaisanterie**
   April-fool ~: **poisson**
   practical ~s are ~s of boors: **giuco**
   practical joking: **brimade**
   what a ~: **blague; la bonne; quelle
     bêtise**
joker: **diseur; farceur; loustic**
jolting: **cahotage**
journal, trade: **Handelsblatt**
journey: **resa; safar; viaje**
   day's ~: **jornada**
   pleasant ~: **bon voyage; buon viag-
     gio; Glück auf den**
   prosperous ~: **glückliche**
Jove: **parbleu**
jovial: **gioviale**
joy
   ~ and sorrow: **Lieb und; zwischen
     Freud'**
   ~ eternal after brief pain: **kurz**
   ~ of living: **joie**
   ~ shared ~ doubled: **geteilte**
   leap for ~: **tressaillir**
   let us then be ~ful: **gaudeamus**
   malicious ~: **Schadenfreude**
joyous: **gaudioso**
joyousness: **allégresse**
judge: **cadi; hakim; juez; juge**
   before a ~: **coram**
   ~ condemned when the guilty is ac-
     quitted: **iudex**
   ~ not: μη κρινετε (**mè krínete**)
   ~ of elegance: **arbiter elegantiae**
   merciful ~ and cruel people: **juiz**
   out of thine own mouth will I ~
     thee: εκ του (**ek toû**)
judgment
   in your ~: **te iudice**
   ~ for plaintiff: **non obstante**
   ~ of God: **iudicium Dei**
   ~ unswayed by fear: **securus**
   ~ where plaintiff absents himself:

     non prosequitur
   of mature ~: **emunctae**
juggling: **escamotage**
July: **juillet**
junction: **trivoie**
June: **juin**
junior: **cadet; chhota**
Jupiter
   ~ can't please everyone: **ne Iuppiter**
   ~ the Thunderer: **Iuppiter**
jurisdiction
   establishing ~: **iurisdictionis**
   ~ of an alcalde: **alcaldía**
   supreme ~: **ius**
jury, unless before a: **nisi**
just
   ~ and loyal: **droit**
   ~ will flourish: **indignante**
justice
   ~ but not for my family: **justicia
     mas**
   ~ of case decided: **res**
   ~ to all: **iustitia omnibus**
   let ~ be done: **fiat iustitia**
   tenacious of ~: **iustitiae tenax**
justly: **à bon droit; droit; recte**

kale, sea: **chou**
Kali, worshipper of: **shaktha**
keep off: **passez**
kettle: **chaudron; marabout**
kettledrum: **timbale; timpani**
key: **clavis**
   golden ~: **dádivas; no hay
     cerradura**
   ~ to the mystery: **le mot de; mot**
   master ~: **passe-partout**
kick: **ruade**
kidney: **rognon**
killed outright: **tué raide**
killjoy: **trouble-fête**
kind
   in ~: **in genere**
   of the same ~: **eiusdem farinae;
     eiusdem generis**
kindly: **gemütlich**
kindness: **Gemütlichkeit**
   in all ~: **bona gratia**
   ~ is never lost: **un bienfait**
   ~ produces ~: **gratia gratiam**
king: **badshah**
   better a good ~: **antes bom Rei**
   I and my ~: **ego et**
   in the K~'s Bench: **in banco regis**

in the ~'s name: **de par**
~ and country: **pro rege**
~ and state: **le roi et**
~ can do no wrong: **rex non**
~ is dead, long live the ~: **le roi est**
~ is like his people: **qualis rex**
~ never dies: **rex nunquam**
~ of the revels: **rex bibendi**
~ reigns, does not govern: **rex regnat**
K~'s Bench: **Bancus Regis**
~ will consider: **le roi s'avisera**
~ wills it: **le roi le**
long live the ~: **hoch lebe; viva; vivat rex; vive la**
long live the ~ and queen: **vivant**
new ~ new law: **novus rex; rey**
one ~, one faith, one law: **un roy**
serve the ~ willingly: **de bon vouloir**
speak of the ~ of Rome: **hablando**
today ~ tomorrow nothing: **aujour-d'hui roi**
kingdom of the blind: **au royaume**
kiss
~ of peace: **osculum**
~ of the mouth touches not the heart: **bacio**
kitchen: **bawarchi; cuisine**
~ utensils: **batterie**
knapsack: **alforja; Rucksack**
knave
arrant ~: **fripon**
~ always suspects ~ry: **el malo**
kneeling: **à genoux**
knife: **belduque; chhuri; cuchillo; dah; kukri; machete; unguis**
knight
fearless and stainless ~: **chevalier sans**
gallant ~: **preux**
~ of good repute: **nec male**
~ of the woeful countenance: **chevalier; Ritter**
knoll: **roche**
know: **connaître**
I don't ~: **não sei**
I ~ him inside and out: **intus**
I ~ in whom I've believed: **scio cui**
I ~ not what: **nescio**
nor permitted to ~ all: **nec scire**
well ~est thou this: **ben lo sai**
what do I ~: **que sais-je**
who ~s: **chi lo; quién sabe; qui le**
who ~s most says least: **quien más**

knowingly: **scienter**
knowledge: **scientia**
half of ~: **prudens quaestio**
~ brings doubt: **mit dem**
~ is better than wealth: **más vale saber**
~ of much: **zwar**
meager ~: **curta**
with full ~: **en connaissance**
without ~: **ohne Wissen**
Koran, chapter of: **fatihah; sura**
kosher, not: **treyf**

labor
~ and honor: **labore**
~ conquers all things: **labor omnia; omnia vincit labor**
~ in vain: **nisi**
~s past are pleasant: **iucundi**
O sweet solace of ~: **O laborum**
pains for one's ~: **avoir l'aller**
unpaid ~: **corvée**
vain ~: **frustra**
you will lose your ~: **vous y**
laborer: **bracero**
~ is worthy of his hire: αξιος (áxios)
lace: **picot; puntilla**
lacquer
gold ~: **kim-makiye**
raised ~: **taka-makiye**
lacquerware: **nurimono**
ladder: **échelle**
ladderlike: **en échelle**
ladies only: **dames seules**
lady: **domina; Dona; Doña; Donna**
charming ~: **charmante**
harem ~: **khanum**
~ in waiting: **dame du**
~ of studied elegance: **petite**
~ without mercy: **la belle**
young ~: **menina**
lake: **jheel; lago; ózero**
lamb: **abbacchio; agneau**
breast of ~: **poitrine**
L~ of God: **Agnus Dei**
spring ~: **agneau**
lame: **boiteux**
lamprey: **lamproie**
lampshade: **abat-jour**
lamp, smells of the: **lucernam; olem; redolet**
land: **ancón; lupa; praedium; straná; tierras**

cultivated ~: **arado**
dry ~: **terra**
~ of the unbelievers: **in partibus**
~ tract: **ejido**
low~: **polder**
native ~: **natale; patrie; rodina**
unknown ~: **terra; ultima Thule**
landlord: **Hausherr; malik; zamindar**
landmark: **baken**
landscape: **paysage**
landslide: **éboulement**
lane: **callejón**
language: **Ladino**
common ~: **lingua franca**
~ of truth is simple: **veritatis**
murder the French ~: **parler français**
primitive ~: **Ursprache**
languishing: **languidamente**
lantern at noon: **il porte**
lanyard: **aiguillette**
lapse: **lapsus; par l'écoulement**
lariat: **botón; cabestro**
lark: **alouette**
last: **à la fin; enfin**
for the ~: **au dernier**
~ of the kings: **ultimus regum**
~ of the Romans: **ultimus Romanorum**
~ resort: **dernier ressort; en dernier; en désespoir; pis**
late
better ~ than never: **más vale tarde; mieux**
seriously ~: **sero sed**
lately: **di fresco**
Latin
in ~: **Latine**
rudiments of ~: **propria**
spoken in ~: **Latine**
spurious ~: **latin**
with ~, a horse, and money: **con latín**
lattice: **cancelli; enrejado**
laugh
~ed out of court: **solventur**
~ if you're wise: **ride si**
~ on wrong side of the mouth: **rire jaune**
~s best who ~s last: **il rit; ride bene; rira bien; wer zuletzt**
~ today and cry tomorrow: **tel qui**
~ up one's sleeve: **ridere; rire entre**
to raise a ~: **pour faire rire**

laughing: **riant**
laughter: **éclat; risus**
helpless ~: **risum**
Homeric ~: **ασβεστος (ásbestos)**
ill-timed ~: **γελως (gélos)**
~ not always sign of ease: **ce n'est pas**
laundress: **blanchisseuse**
laureate, poet: **Hofdichter**
law: **de iure; dharma; fuero; ipso iure; ius; lex**
against the form of ~: **contra formam**
against the nations' ~: **contra ius**
arising from ~: **ex lege**
body of ~: **corpus; halachah**
canon ~: **corpus; ius**
civil ~: **corpus; ius**
common ~: **ius; lex**
divine ~: **ius**
extreme ~: **ius**
highest ~: **summum ius**
international ~: **droit; ius**
~ arises out of fact: **ex facto**
~ by what right: **quo iure**
~ does not concern itself with trifles: **de minimis**
~ is hard but the ~: **dura lex**
~ is mighty but necessity mightier: **Gesetz**
~ is subservient to custom: **leges**
~ of might: **χειρων (kheirôn)**
~ of nature: **ius**
~ of retaliation: **lex**
~ of the land: **iudicium parium**
~s are silent in time of war: **silent leges**
~s go where dollars please: **lá vão leis**
learned in ~: **iuris peritus; mullah**
mercantile ~: **lex**
practice of the court is ~: **cursus**
Roman ~: **corpus**
spirit of the ~: **mens legis**
statute ~: **lex**
such is the ~: **ita lex**
uncertainty destroys ~: **ubi ius**
under both ~s: **in utroque iure**
under color of ~: **sub colore**
under protection of ~: **in gremio**
usage has the force of ~: **mos**
what can idle ~s do without morality: **quid leges**
with this ~: **hac lege**

lawsuit: **procès**
lawyer: **abogado; avocat; gens;**
    homme; licenciado
  good ~ is bad neighbor: **bon avocat**
layer on layer: **stratum**
lazy: **fainéant**
lead
  I ~: **dirigo**
  juvenile ~: **jeune**
leader: **condottiere; der Führer; duce;**
    dux gregis; Führer; Il Duce; in-
    duna; jefe
  ~ of the deed was a woman: **dux**
    femina
  tribal ~: **sheik**
leadership: **Führerschaft**
  collective ~: **junta**
leaf: **feuillet**
leap: **per saltum**
  ~s and bounds: **di salto**
learn
  I still ~: **ancora**
  ~ or depart: **aut disce**
learned: **femme; le monde; savant**
learning: **pabulum animi**
  all ~ from one: **ab uno disce; ex**
    uno
leasing: **locatio**
leather: **chamois; maroquin**
  molded ~: **cuir-bouilli**
leave: **congé**
  all ~: **exeunt**
  go on ~: **aller en permission**
  he ~s: **exit**
  ~ well enough alone: **actum ne**
    agas; il meglio
  on ~: **congé; en congé**
  to take ~: **pour prendre**
lecture: **conférence**
leek: **poireau**
left: **à gauche; izquierda; laevus**
legacy: **legs**
legate, papal: **legatus**
legerdemain: **tour**
leggings: **chivarras; gamache; jambière**
legionnaire: **légionnaire**
legislature: **Bundesrat; Folketing; knes-**
    set; Lagting; Landsting; Land-
    tag; Odelsting; Reichsrat;
    Reichstag; Rigsdag; Storting;
    Volkskammer
legs, horse's hind: **gigot**
leisure
  dignified ~: **otium**

  ~ begets vices: **otia**
  ~ without books is death: **otium**
  ~ without dignity: **otium**
  sweet to unbend on occasion: **desi-**
    pere; dulce est
leisurely: **à loisir**
length: **longueur**
  to what ~s: **quousque**
Lent: **carême**
  mid-~: **mi-carême**
lentil: **lentille**
less: **meno**
  from the ~: **a minori**
lessee: **huurder**
lesson, object: **Anschauungsunterricht**
letter: **billet; chit; lettre**
  capital ~s: **maiusculae; versal**
  initial ~: **Anfangsbuchstabe**
  ~ for ~: **literatim**
  ~ of the alphabet: **Buchstabe**
  ~ of the law: **strictum**
  lower-case ~: **minusculae**
  turned ~s: **caractères; Fliegenkopf**
  written ~ remains: **littera scripta**
lettuce: **laitue**
level
  ground ~: **à fleur de terre; chaus-**
    sée; fleur
  water ~: **à fleur d'eau; fleur**
liar
  consummate ~: **menteur**
  ~s should have a good memory:
    mendacem
liberty: **libertad; libertas; sub lege**
  civil and religious ~: **pro aris**
  complete ~: **liberté toute**
  ~, equality, fraternity: **liberté, égalité**
  ~ of my country: **pro libertate**
  where ~, there my home: **ubi**
    libertas
librarian: **bibliothécaire; Bibliothekar**
library: **Bibliothek; bibliothèque**
license, poetic: **licentia**
lie
  ~ down: **hinlegen**
  ~ has short legs: **oo lazhee**
  ~ of a flattering tongue: **blandae**
  ~s more than a dentist: **sacamuelas**
  ~ to discover truth: **dizer**
life
  for ~: **ad vitam**
  ~ and soul: ζωη και (z$\acute{o}$ē kaì)
  ~ comes from an egg: **omne vivum**
  ~ has given man nothing without la-

bor: **nil sine magno**
~ I love you: ζωη μον σας (zōē moû sàs)
~ is a dream: **la vida**
~ is a kind of death when evil: **genus est**
~ is devoted: **vota**
~ is earnest: **ernst**
~ is enjoyment of health: **non est vivere**
~ is love: **das Leben**
~ is short and art is long: **o βιος (ho bíos); vita brevis**
~ of the land is established in righteousness: **ua**
~ of the party: **boute-en-train**
~ without books is death: **vita sine**
~ with you or without you: **nec tecum**
long ~ to you, farewell: **vive, vale**
look to the end of a long ~: **ορα τελος (hóra télos)**
luxurious ~: **dolce vita**
midway through ~: **nel mezzo**
sedentary ~: **Stube**
source of ~: **vivendi**
spark of ~ may lurk unseen: **lateat**
springtime of ~: **des Lebens**
to ~: **l'chaim**
lifelike: **ad vivum**
life-size: **grandeur**
light: **leggiero; luz**
a burning ~: εκεινος (ekeînos)
accidental ~: **échappée**
false ~: **faux**
let there be ~: **fiat lux**
~ after darkness: **post tenebras**
~ and fluffy: **soufflée**
~ and love and life: **Licht**
~ and shade: **chiaroscuro**
~ and truth: **lux et**
~ from above: **a deo lux; lux venit**
~ in darkness: **lux in**
~ of the world: νμεις εστε το φως (humeîs este tò phôs); **lux mundi**
~ received from hence: **hinc lucem**
more ~: **mehr**
night ~: **veilleuse**
northern ~s: **aurora borealis**
shines with borrowed ~: **luce**
southern ~s: **aurora australis**
lightly: **agevole**
~ lies the load cheerfully

borne: **leve**
lightness: **légèreté**
like: **ad modum**
~ cures ~: **similia**
likely: **vraisemblable; wahrscheinlich**
likeness of all: **ad instar**
limbo for unbaptized children: **limbus**
limbs of the dismembered poet: **disiecti membra poetae**
limitations, with: **secundum**
limited: **borné**
lindens, under the: **unter den**
line
I have a long ancestral ~: **avi**
I wrote these ~s: **hos ego**
lined: **doublé**
linen soiled should be washed in private: **il faut laver**
lining: **doublure**
lion: **simba**
don't stir up ~s: **noli irritare**
~ at home and fox in a fight: οικοι λεοντες (oíkoi léontes)
~ is known by his claw: **ex ungue**
liqueur: **aguardiente; calvados; chicha; crème; pisco; pousse-café**
liquid: **fluidus**
liquor: **guarapo; mescal; pulque; Schiedam; schnapps; sotol; tequila; vodka**
listener
good ~: **a buen entendedor**
who listens will yield: **castello; che dà**
listlessly: **remisso animo**
lists: **champ clos**
literally: **à la lettre; au pied**
literary phenomenon of 1950s: **nouvelle vague**
literary writings: **belles-lettres**
literati: **savant**
litigation
before ~: **ante litem**
~ begun: **post litem**
litter: **cacolet; dooli; kajawah; palki**
little: **pequeño; petit; petite; poco; wenig**
add ~ to: **adde parvum**
ever so ~: **tanto; tant soit**
in ~: **in piccolo**
~ by ~: **a poco a poco; nach und; peu à peu; poco**
very ~: **fort peu**

live
  he has ~d (so many) years: **vixit**
  I have ~d and loved: **ich habe**
  I ~ in hope: **je vis**
  I ~ in the word: **en parole**
  let us ~, my Lesbia: **vivamus**
  ~ and let ~: **leben und; vivre et**
  ~d in obscurity, ~d in security: **bene qui**
  ~ from day to day: **in diem; vivre au**
  ~ resolutely: **im Ganzen**
  ~ so you truly ~: **vive ut; vivre ce**
  ~ sumptuously: **faire ripaille**
  long may he ~: **hoch soll; wansei**
  may you ~ long: **serus in**
  not ~d ill: **nec vixit**
  seek to ~ unnoticed: λαθε (**láthe**)
  thoughtlessly we ~: ζωμεν (**zômen**)
  to ~ is to think: **vivere est**
  while we ~, let's ~: **dum vivimus**
  would you ~ forever: **wollt ihr**
lively: **allegro; desto; lebhaft; risvegliato; tanto**
liver: **foie; pâté; terrine**
living
  among the ~: **inter**
  ~ in arms: **semper**
load, dead: **peso**
loader: **cargador**
loaf about: **battre**
loafing: **flânerie**
lobster: **homard; langouste**
locality: **local**
lode: **filon**
lodge, shooting: **maison**
lodging: **chawl; hospice; hôtel garni; pied-à-terre**
lofty: **erhaben**
logic: **ars artium**
loin: **longe**
loincloth: **dhoti**
loneliness: **Einsamkeit**
longing: **Sehnsucht**
long-legged: **bien fendu; fendu**
look: **dekko; voilà; voyez**
  downcast ~: **air**
  embarrassed ~: **air**
  fierce ~: **farouche; regard farouche**
  forbidding ~: **air**
  ~ here: **tenez**
  ~ out: **cuidado**
  sorrowful ~: **air**
looks
  good ~: **beaux yeux; bonne mine**

  vacant ~: **regards distraits**
loose: **lâche**
loquacity: **flux**
lord: **daimio; khan; kun; seigneur**
  before our ~: **coram**
  great Spanish ~: **grande**
  L~ be with you: **Dominus vobiscum**
  L~ direct us: **Domine**
  L~ have mercy on us: **Kyrie**
  L~ is my light: **Dominus illuminatio**
  ~ of the loftiest poetry: **signor dell'**
  L~'s Supper: **Cena**
  L~ thou art my glory: **tu, Domine**
  L~ will provide: **Dominus providebit**
  not unto us O L~: **non nobis Domine**
  whom the L~ loveth he chasteneth: ον γαρ (**hòn gàr**)
lordly: **en grand seigneur; seigneur**
loss
  at a ~: **à perte**
  ~ without injury: **damnum**
  unknown ~: **amissum**
  who loses, sins: **qui perd**
lost: **adiratum; perdu**
lot: **suerte**
  drawing ~s: **tirage**
loud: **à haute**
  as ~ as possible: **forte**
  ~ and then soft: **forte**
  moderately ~: **mezzo**
  very ~: **forte; fortissimo**
  with decreasing ~ness: **calando; decrescendo**
  with increasing ~ness: **crescendo**
louver: **abat-sons; abat-vent**
love: **ahava; amore**
  accursed ~: **amor sceleratus**
  all's fair in ~ and war: **jeder Vorteil**
  boy's ~: **amor de niño**
  ecstasy of ~: **Liebeswonne**
  happy days of ~: **die schöne Zeit**
  harbinger of ~: **Liebesbote**
  I ~ as I find: **amo ut**
  I ~ forever: **j'aime**
  I ~ you: **yah vahs loobloo**
  ~ and prudence: **amar y saber**
  ~ and smoke cannot be hidden: **l'amour**
  ~ at first sight: **coup**
  ~ bade me write: **scribere iussit**
  ~ begets ~: **amor gignit**
  ~ conquers all things: **omnia**

vincit amor
~ feeds on ~: **amor solo**
~ has no choice: **amor no tiene**
~ is a form of military service:
    militiae
~ is a teacher: **amor magnus**
~ is blind: **amore; credula res**
~ is full of anxious fears: **res**
~ is mighty but money almighty:
    Liebe
~ is powerful: **amour fait**
~ knot: **noeud**
~ letter: **billet-doux**
~ lyric: **ghazal**
~ match: **mariage**
~ me and ~ my dog: **qui m'aime**
~ nor a cough can be hidden: **nec**
    amor
~ of country leads: **ducit**
~ of country outweighs all: **vincit**
    amor
~ of country will prevail: **vincet**
~ of money: **amor nummi**
~ of money grows: **crescit amor**
~ of one's fatherland: **dulcis amor**
~ of one's neighbor: **amor proximi**
~ of possessing: **amor habendi**
~ or money: **vel prece**
~ passionately: **aimer**
~ rules: **amor regge**
~s me, ~s me not: **il m'aime**
~s well who never forgets: **bien ama**
~ thy neighbor: αγαπα (**agápa**)
~ will forgive any wrong: **nihil**
madly in ~: **éperdu**
make ~ to: **conter**
one cannot live on ~ alone: **von der**
renewal of ~: **amantium;**
    redintegratio
serious ~ affair: **grande passion**
to gain ~ show ~: **ut ameris**
well ~d: **bien-aimé**
what's life without ~: **was ist das**
what thou ~st, that thou livest: **was**
    du
who ~s much says little: **chi ama**
    assai
who ~s trusts: **chi ama, crede**
who ~s well chastises well: **qui aime**
with ~: **amore; con amore**
lover: **amant; amoroso; cavaliere; cher**
    ami; cicisbeo; innamorato
act the ~: **faire l'amant**
bashful ~: **transi; un amoureux**

every ~ is a soldier: **militat**
every ~ is demented: **omnis**
~ of good living: **bon vivant**
~s are lunatics: **amantes**
who can deceive a ~: **quis fallere**
low-cut: **décolletage; décolleté**
loyal
~ as long as I live: **loyal je**
~ in everything: **loyal en**
~ to God and king: **Deo et**
loyalty
love ~: **aymez**
~ binds me: **loyauté m'oblige**
~ has no shame: **loyauté n'a**
luck: **mazel**
bad ~: **coup**
good ~: **bene vale; bonne chance;**
    buena suerte; Glück auf
lacked ~: **faltóle**
stroke of ~: **hasard; un coup de**
    hasard
lullaby: **bayushki; berceuse;**
    Wiegenlied
lunch: **almôço; aruchat; déjeuner**
lung: **pulmo**
luster: **reflet**
luxury: **luxe**
lynch him: **à la lanterne**
lynx: **pishu**

machine: **máquina**
decapitation ~: **guillotine**
mad
~ness of one drives many ~: **unius**
~ or composing verses: **aut insanit**
we've all been ~: **semel insanivimus**
whom Jupiter wants to destroy, he
    first makes ~: **quem Iuppiter**
madam: **sahibah; señora; signora**
made, ready: **tout fait**
madman
~ thinks everybody else mad:
    insanus
never defy a ~: **il ne faut jamais**
Mafia member: **mafioso**
magic: **jadu**
magistracy, Spanish: **corregimiento**
magistrate: **corregidor; gens; land-**
    drost; schepen
magnolia, East Indian: **champak**
maid: **bonne; criada; fille; suivante**
lady's ~: **femme**
remain an old ~: **coiffer**

maiden, marry a: **zonam solvere**
mail
  pigeon ~: **Taubenpost**
  return ~: **a vuelta; vuelta**
mailbox: **Briefkasten**
mainspring: **primum mobile**
maintain, I will: **je maintiendrai**
maize: **pinole**
majestically: **maestosamente**
make
  he made it: **fecit**
  ~ way: **place**
malaria: **kala**
malice: **diablerie**
malinger: **faire le malade**
malpractice: **mala praxis**
man: **chilovek; hombre; homme;
    homo**
  angry ~: **ab irato**
  behold the ~: **ecce;** ιδον **(idoù)**
  best ~: **garçon**
  brave ~: **fortis cadere**
  cheerful ~: **l'allegro**
  civil ~: **homme; honnête**
  every ~ for himself: **a poco pan;
    chacun pour**
  every ~ has his pleasures: **sua cui-
    que voluptas**
  every ~ has his price: **venalis**
  every ~ has his vices: **sua cuique
    sunt**
  every ~ is architect of his own for-
    tune: **chacun est; faber; jeder ist**
  every ~ is subject to the law: **cada
    uno tiene**
  fit ~: **idoneus**
  handsome ~ is not wholly destitute:
    bel hombre no
  honest ~: **homme; honnête; un
    homme de**
  honest ~ need fear nothing: **cassis**
  I am a ~: **homo**
  I'm a plain ~: **Davus**
  I'm looking for a ~: **hominem**
  intelligent ~: **hombre**
  ladies' ~: **petit**
  lazy ~: **abends**
  lazy young ~: **giovane ozioso**
  literary ~: **homme**
  loving ~ is a jealous ~: **uomo
    amante**
  ~ about town: **bon viveur;
    gommeux**
  ~ by ~: **viritim**

  ~ feels ten feet tall: **oo chiloveka**
  ~ is a wolf to fellow men: **lupus est**
  ~ is but a breath and a shadow:
    ανθρωπος **(anthropós)**
  ~ is either brute or god: η θηριον
    (ē thēríon)
  ~ is known by his drink, pocket, and
    anger: **adam**
  ~ is lent not given to life: **homo**
  ~ is neither angel nor beast:
    l'homme n'est
  ~ is not punished twice for same of-
    fense: **nemo bis**
  ~ is to ~ either god or wolf: **homo**
  ~ is what he eats: **der Mensch**
  ~ made of money: **écu**
  ~ newly risen from obscurity: **novus
    homo**
  ~ of full legal rights: **legalis**
  ~ of great learning: **homo**
  ~ of honor: **galant homme; galantu-
    omo; homme**
  ~ of learning is worth two without:
    un uomo
  ~ of letters: **littérateur; literati**
  ~ of low origin: **filius; terrae**
  ~ of no account: **ein unbedeutender**
  ~ of no party: **homo**
  ~ of one book: **hombre; homo**
  ~ of property: **hacendado**
  ~ of the world: **homme**
  ~ of two languages is worth two
    men: **un homme qui**
  ~ of virtue and loyalty: **homo**
  ~ of wealth can't escape cares: **post
    equitem**
  ~ of weight: **uomo da**
  ~ preaches best who lives best: **bien
    predica**
  ~ proposes and God disposes:
    l'homme propose
  ~ shall not live by bread alone: ονκ
    επ' **(ouk ep')**
  ~ skilled in speech: **vir bonus**
  ~ with weather eye open: λαγως
    (lagòs)
  modest ~: **multum demissus**
  moneyed ~: **père**
  no ~ is compelled: **kein Mensch**
  party ~: **homme; parti**
  penniless ~ has nothing to lose:
    cantabit
  polished ~: **ad unguem**
  poor ~ is happy with little: **homem**

poor ~ is not liable for costs: **in
    forma**
power will prove a ~: αρχη ανδρα
    (arkhĕ ándra)
remember thou art a ~: **te hominem**
resourceful ~: **homme**
saintly ~: **varón**
skilled ~ trusted in his art: **cuilibet**
solitary ~: **uomo solitario**
straw ~: **homme**
suit manner to the ~: **ut homo**
to become a ~ is an art: **Mensch**
upright ~ doesn't repent: **probum**
upright ~ firm of purpose: **iustum**
wise and prudent ~: **prud'homme**
wise ~ talks little: **vir**
worthy ~: **honnête**
wounded ~: **blessé**
young ~: **Jüngling**
mandate: **mandat**
mane: **crinière**
manger: **crèche**
mania: **cacoëthes**
manner
    after the ~: **à la**
    aristocratic ~: **bel air**
    contrary to ~s: **contra bonos**
    delightful ~s: **dolce**
    evil ~: **malo modo**
    good ~s: **bienséance; savoir-vivre**
    ingratiating ~: **prévenance**
    in like ~: **similiter**
    in lively ~: **vivace; vivo**
    in playful ~: **scherzando**
    ~ and form: **modo et**
    ~ of living: **modus**
    ~ of our ancestors: **more**
    ~ of speaking: **façon**
    ~ of working: **modus**
    melodious ~: **arioso**
    singing ~: **cantando**
manuscript: **Handschrift; litterae
    scriptae**
map: **carte**
marble
    black ~: **nero-antico**
    yellow ~: **giallo**
march
    forced ~: **Schnellzug**
    funeral ~: **Totenmarsch**
    stolen ~es: **verdeckte**
marchioness: **marchesa**
mark: **Zeichen**
    shoots wide of the ~: **longe aberrat**

marked: **marcato**
marked, strongly: **martellato**
market: **chauk**
marquis: **marchese**
marriage: **mariage; nuptiae**
    early ~ long love: **frühe**
    ~ bond: **a vinculo**
    ~ broker: **schatchen; shadchen**
    ~ certificate: **extrait**
    ~ is an evil that most men welcome:
        γαμος **(gámos)**
    ~ is the road to repentance: γαμειν
        (gameîn)
    ~ of conscience: **mariage**
    ~ of convenience: **convenance;
        mariage**
    ~ with one of lesser standing:
        mésalliance
    morganatic ~: **mariage**
    what God hath joined together: **o
        ovv o (ho oûn ho)**
marrow: **amourette; moelle**
marry and be tamed: **casarás**
Mars, Field of: **Campus; champ de**
marsh: **vlei**
martial: **marziale**
marvelous: ορνιθων **(orníthōn)**
marvelously: **à merveille**
Mary holding Christ: **Pietà**
masonry: **pisé**
Mass: **Missa**
    High ~: **grand-messe; Hochamt;
        Missa**
    Low ~: **Missa**
    sung ~: **Missa**
mass
    ~es: **hoi polloi (οι πολλοι)**
    rude and formless ~: **rudis**
massacre: **pogrom**
master: **balabos; bwana; dueño; magis-
    ter; maître; padrone; sahib; tuan**
    dancing ~: **maître**
    great ~: **bara**
    like ~ like man: **tal padrone; tel
        maître**
    ~ has said so: **magister**
    ~ of ceremonies: **magister**
    ~ of himself: **compos sui**
    ~ of the games: **magister**
    not pledged to any ~: **nullius
        addictus**
    school~: **caji**
masterpiece: **capo; chef-d'oeuvre;
    magnum opus**

mastery: **maître**
  ~ passes for egoism: **die Meisterschaft**
match: **cerilla**
  good ~: **parti**
  ~ for the whole world: **nec pluribus**
matchless: **sans**
material: **barège; plaque**
matrimony: **le bon motif; motif**
matter: **res**
  ejected ~: **eiectamenta**
  it doesn't ~: **nichevo; n'importe; no es para; non importa**
  lesser ~: **quoad**
  ~s little to me: **cela m'importe**
  no ~: **non fa**
  printed ~: **impresos**
  quite another ~: **c'est tout**
  rural ~: **res**
  the ~ is safe: **salva res**
  what does it ~: **qu'importe**
  what is the ~: **que ha; que hay; was gibt**
  worthless ~: **corpus**
  you're making a bad ~ worse: **νδραν (hýdran)**
matters: **e re nata**
  serious ~ tomorrow: **εις ανριον (eis aúrion)**
mature: **mûr**
maxim of a religious teacher: **logion**
May Day: **pervoiya**
mayor: **alcalde; maire**
me
  leave that to ~: **c'est mon; lascia**
  take ~ as I am: **prend-moi**
meager: **maigre**
meal: **Mahlzeit**
  after ~s: **post cibum**
  before ~s: **ante cibum**
  enjoy your ~: **Mahlzeit**
  fish ~: **maigre**
  fixed price ~: **table**
  may your ~ be blessed: **Prost**
  meatless ~: **repas**
mean
  golden ~: **aurea mediocritas; juste-milieu; le juste-milieu**
  what does this ~: **quid hoc; quod hoc**
means: **fuerza**
  by every ~: **à toute force; velis**
  by no ~: **mitnichten**
  live by desperate ~: **e flamma**

meantime: **ad interim; en attendant; per interim**
measure
  beyond ~: **à toute outrance; extra modum**
  linear ~: **vara**
  ~ for ~: **so du**
  ~ in all things: **est modus**
  ~ of distance: **kos; legua; yojan**
  ~ of time: **ghurry**
measured: **misurato**
meat: **carne**
  broiled ~: **châteaubriant; churrasco**
  marinated ~ dish: **sate**
  ~ in spicy sauce: **chile**
  roasted ~: **kabab**
  stewed ~: **bouilli**
meatball: **boulette**
medal: **médaille**
meddle: **kibitz**
medicine: **medicina**
meditation, profound: **samadh**
medley: **farrago; fatras**
meeting: **rencontre; Versammlung**
  closing of ~: **lever de séance**
  happy ~: **coetus**
  spiritualist ~: **séance**
  till we meet again: **do svidaniya**
melancholy: **il penseroso; malinconia; morne**
melody: **cabaletta; cantilena**
  with the ~: **col canto**
member
  ~ of Arab anti-Israel organization: **fedaya**
  ~ of Japanese military caste: **samurai**
memorandum: **bordereau; notandum**
memorial, for a: **pro memoria**
memory: **mémoire; memoriter**
  bad ~: **lièvre; mémoire de**
  blessed ~: **beatae**
  from ~: **ex capite**
  in ~ of: **in memoriam**
  ~ aid: **aide-mémoire**
  ~ is a test of pleasure: **die Probe**
men
  like able ~: **en habiles**
  ~ at arms: **gens**
  ~ of lesser merit: **di minores**
  ~ of wit: **beaux esprits**
  ~ who pretend to knowledge: **barbae tenus**
  military ~: **gens**

old ~ twice children: **bis pueri;
senex**
outstanding ~: **di maiores**
so many ~: **autant d'hommes**
so many ~ so many opinions: **quot
homines; tot homines**
what insignificant creatures ~ are:
homunculi
where there are ~ there are manners: **ubi homines**
Wise M~: **Dreikönige**
younger ~ for labors: **iuniores**
menacingly: **minaccevolmente**
mendicant: **bairagi; bhikku; fakir**
mention of one and exclusion of the
other: **expressio unius**
menu: **carte**
from the ~: **à la carte**
merchandise, shoddy: **shlock**
merchant: **comerciante**
mercy: **à la grâce**
~ on me: **ελεησον (eléēsón);
miserere**
merit: **à bon chien**
for ~: **pour le**
meritorious: **bonae**
merry: **lustig**
mess: **Kladderadatsch; tripotage**
message: **dépêche**
messenger: **chaprási; staffetta**
metal
hammering out ~: **repoussage**
pot ~: **potin**
method: **modus**
new ~: **neuere**
metropolis: **Haupstadt**
mezzanine: **entresol**
middle: **in medias res; mezzo**
in the ~: **au beau; in medio; opere
in medio**
~aged: **entre deux**
M~ Ages: **Moyen-Age**
midst of things: **in mediis rebus**
middleman: **homme**
midwife: **sage-femme**
might
~ and main: **remis**
~ makes right: **der Stärkste; Macht**
with all one's ~: **pugnis; totis**
with ~ and main: **à corps perdu;
manibus; ποσι και (posì kaì)**
militia: **garde; Landwehr**
milk: **lait; leche**
spilled ~: **hin ist**

with ~: **au lait**
Milky Way: **via**
mill: **moulin**
ore ~: **arrastre**
red ~: **moulin**
sugar ~: **central**
million: **conto**
ten ~: **crore**
milt: **laitance**
mind
balanced ~: **animus non**
brilliant ~: **bel esprit**
calm ~: **aequo animo**
change of ~: **Umstimmung**
disordered ~: **esprit**
I have freed my ~: **liberavi**
in the ~: **in intellectu**
it remains stored in the ~: **manet**
little ~s are caught with trifles:
parva leves
living force of the ~: **vivida**
~ conscious of integrity: **conscia;
mens conscia**
~ moves matter: **mens agitat**
~ remains unconquered: **mens
invicta**
narrow ~: **esprit**
not of sound ~: **non compos**
secret recesses of the ~: **penetralia**
sound and vigorous ~: **integra**
sound ~ in sound body: **mens sana**
sound of ~: **compos mentis**
mine: **fougade**
sulfur ~: **solfatara**
mine and thine: **meum**
Minerva being unwilling: **invita**
miniature, in: **en petit; petit**
minister
~ of state: **diwan**
~ of war: **Kriegsminister**
mint: **menthe**
minutes: **procès-verbal**
miracles: **mirabilia**
mirror: **miroir**
as in a ~: **veluti**
miscellany: **collectanea**
mischance: **contretemps**
misdemeanor: **délit**
miser is ever in want: **semper**
misery: **misère**
~ is the heritage of Adam: **esa es**
misfortune: **Unglück**
blessed ~: **benedetto**
~ doesn't come singly: **ein Unglück;**

malheur; un mal
~ is better forgotten: **il vaut**
~ tries men: **explorant**
not unacquainted with ~: **non ignara**
we can bear ~s of others: **nous avons tous**
yield not to ~: **ne cede; tu ne**
mishaps, through many: **per varios**
mislead: **jeter de la**
misplaced: **déplacé; postiche**
misrepresentation: **suggestio**
miss: **san; señorita; signorina**
mistake: **malentendu; quiproquo**
mistaken, if I'm not: **wo ich**
mister: **mein Herr; mijnheer; mon-sieur; Mynheer; san; señor; si-gnor; signore**
mistress: **belle amie; maîtresse**
misunderstanding: **brouillerie**
misunderstood: **mal entendu**
mix: **misce**
mixed: **mêlé**
mixture: **mélange**
let a ~ be made: **fiat mistura**
mnemonics: **memoria technica**
mob: **attroupement**
mockery, ironic: **persiflage**
mode: **Tonart**
model: **mannequin**
moderate: **mässig; moderato**
moderation
~ is best: αριστον (áriston); μετρον (métron)
~ is safer than extremes: **mediocria**
modesty: **ad verecundiam; modestie**
false ~: **malus**
~ has died: αιδως ολωλεν (aidòs ólōlen)
mold, fluted: **cannelon**
molding: **cavetto; cyma recta; cyma reversa**
moment: **eo instante**
~s glide away: **labuntur**
spare ~s: **à ses moments**
Monarch, Great: **le grand Monarque**
money: **argent; barato; moeda**
borrowed ~: **argent**
German ~: **Reichsmark**
man's ~ is his life: χρηματα (khrémata)
~ doesn't smell: **non olet**
~ gives rank and beauty: **et genus**
~ is a master key: **l'argent**

~ is master or slave: **imperat**
~ is money's brother: **il danaro**
~ is necessary: **il faut de l'argent**
~ is the sinews of war: **nervi**
~ makes the man: χρημματ' (khrémat')
~ not advice: **dineros y**
~ order: **giro**
~ or your life: **Geld oder**
~ rules the world: **Geld regiert**
~ talks: **rien de plus**
no end of ~: **un argent**
pin ~: **argent**
pocket ~: **menus**
rolling in ~: **être cousu**
spend ~ before one has it: **manger**
while ~ holds out: **non deficiente**
monk: **fraile; lama; poonghie; religieux**
monkey: **bandar; mono; singe**
month
in this ~: **hoc mense**
last ~: **próximo; vorigen**
~ preceding this one: **ultimo**
next ~ after this: **proximo**
of this ~: **huius mensis**
this ~: **corriente**
monthly: **per mensem; per mese**
monument
he erected this ~: **hoc monumentum**
if you seek his ~: **si monumentum**
I have raised a ~: **exegi**
~ more lasting than brass: **monumentum**
mood, merry: **être en goguettes; goguette**
moon: **lua; luna; lune**
howl at the ~: **hurler à**
Moor: **morisco**
Moorish: **morisco**
Moravian Church: **Unitas**
more: **più**
let's have no ~: **und**
~ than ever: **de plus**
~ the merrier: **je mehr; plus on**
~ to it than meets the eye: **il y a anguille**
morels, with: **aux morilles**
morning, good: **boker; bom dia; bon-jour; buenos días; Dhia duit; dobre utra; guten Morgen; zdrávstvui**
Moro who takes Muslim oath: **juramentado**

morsel: **bouchée**
mortals, nothing too difficult for: **nil
    mortalibus**
mortar: **Minnenwerfer**
mortgage: **vadium**
mortification: **couleuvre**
mosque: **masjid**
moss: **tripe**
most: **al più**
mother: **madre; mater; materfamilias;
    matz**
  foster ~: **nourrice**
  fostering ~: **alma mater**
  ~ dear: **Mütterchen**
  ~-in-law: **belle-mère**
  ~ was standing: **Stabat**
  sorrowing ~: **mater**
motion, perpetual: **mobile**
mottled: **marbré**
mountain: **Berg; boondocks; Gebirg;
    montaña; pahar**
  ~ of light: **Koh-i-noor**
  ~ out of molehill: **elephantem**
  ~ pass: **ghat**
  ~ range: **serra; sierra**
  ~s in labor bring forth a mouse:
    parturiunt
  ~s see and walls hear: **los montes**
mountaineer: **montagnard; pahari**
  ~s always free men: **Montani**
mournful: **luttuoso**
mournfully: **con dolore; flebilmente**
mourning: **annus**
mouse, ridiculous: **ridiculus**
mouth: **boca; bouche; os**
  closed ~: **pela**
  make the ~ water: **faire venir**
  ~ of honey and heart of gall: **bôca
    de mel**
movement: **intermezzo; moto**
  nationalist ~: **Swadeshi**
much
  as ~ as required: **tantum quantum**
  many littles make a ~: **muchos**
  ~ and not many: **multum non**
  ~ has he suffered and done: **multa
    tulit**
  ~ in little: **multa paucis; multum in**
  ~ never costs little: **nunca mucho**
  ~ noise and few nuts: **mucho ruido**
  ~ obliged: **bien obligé; sehr**
  too ~: **troppo**
  too ~ of a good thing: **toujours
    perdrix**

too ~ to choose from: **embarras**
mud: **fango**
muffled: **sordo**
Muhammadan
  ~ calendar: **Muharram**
  ~ prayer: **kiblah**
  ~ robe: **jubbah**
Muhammad, flight of: **hegira**
mulberry: **mûre**
mule, lead: **cencerro**
multitude
  baseborn ~: **ignobile**
  profane ~: **profanum**
  we two are a ~: **nos duo**
munitions: **apparatus belli; matériel**
murmuring: **mormorando**
muscle: **rectus**
mush: **polenta**
  sentimental ~: **Schmalz**
mushroom: **champignon; chanterelle**
music
  brilliant piece of ~: **toccata**
  incidental ~: **Zwischenmusik**
  ~ is poetry of the air: **Musik**
  ~ of the spheres: **vox**
  natural sign in ~: **bécarre**
  virtuoso ~: **bravura**
musketeer: **mousquetaire**
Muslim
  ~ calendar month: **Ramadan**
  ~ festival: **bairam**
  ~ judge: **cadi**
  ~ title: **hafiz**
muslin: **mousseline**
mussel: **coquille; moule**
mustard: **moutarde**
mute: **muet; sordino**
  ~d: **gedämpft**
  with the ~: **con sordino**
mutton: **pré-salé**
  ~ legs: **gigot**
mysterious: **misterioso**
mystic: **Swami**

nag: **nudj**
nail: **clou**
  hit ~ on head: **rem acu; tetigisti**
  one ~ drives out another: **un clavo**
naked: **cuerpo; en cueros; en cuerpo;
    in puris; tout nu**
name: **eo nomine; nom; nomen**
  generic ~: **nom**
  good ~ is better than riches: **bonne
    renommée; tov shem**

illustrious ~: **clarum et**
in the ~ of: **in nomine**
maiden ~: **nom**
~ being changed: **mutato nomine**
~ is John: **Ioannes**
~ is Legion: λεγιων (**legiòn**)
official ~: **raison**
pen ~: **nom**
revived ~: **renovato**
shadow of a ~: **magni nominis; nominis; stat magni**
specific ~: **nomen**
stage ~: **nom**
under whatever ~: **quocunque nomine**
what is your ~: **cómo se llama; wie heissen**
without place, year, or ~: **sine**
namely: **nämlich; videlicet**
nape of the neck: **chignon**
Napoleon: **le petit; petit**
narcotic: **bhang; marihuana**
narrative with brevity of style: **novella**
nation
~ of comic actors: **natio**
~ of poets and thinkers: **Volk**
~ of shopkeepers: **la nation**
natural: **naturel**
naturally: **au naturel; secundum**
naturalness: **naïveté**
nature
contrary to ~: **opposuit**
drive out ~ with a pitchfork: **naturam**
~ abhors a vacuum: **natura abhorret**
~ creates nothing in vain: ονδεν ματην (**oudèn máten**)
~ knows her purpose: **die Natur**
~ made him and then broke the mold: **natura il**
~ makes no leaps: **natura non**
wild ~: **ferae**
nausea: **ad nauseam**
even to ~: **usque ad nauseam**
near, came: **accessit; proxime**
nearly as may be: **cy près; quam proxime**
neatness: **netteté**
necessarily: **ex necessitate**
necessary, one thing: **porro**
necessity
~ brings him here: **necessità**
~ is a powerful weapon: **ingens telum**

~ is mistress of the arts: **Not lehrt**
~ is the mother of invention: **la povertà; mater; Not bricht**
~ knows no law: **necessitas; Not kennt; venia**
neck: **col**
necktie: **cravate**
need, direst: **die höchste**
needle: **aiguille**
needlepoint stitch: **petit**
neglect, excusable: **culpa**
negligence: **culpa**
gross ~: **crassa; culpa**
nerve, have a: **avoir du toupet**
nest, feather one's: **faire ses choux**
network: **réseau**
~ of triangles: **canevàs**
vascular ~: **rete**
never: **ad kalendas; jamais de**
~ behind: **jamais arrière**
~ mind: **das schadet; das tut nichts**
nevertheless: **eppur; tout de même**
newcomer to Hawaii: **malahini**
news: **izvestiya; khubber**
no ~ is good: **nulla nuova**
newspaper: **periódico**
section of a ~: **feuilleton**
new, what's: **que hay de; was gibt es neues**
New Year: **Neujahr**
New Year's Day: **capo; jour**
next but after a long interval: **longo sed**
nickname: **sobriquet**
night: **Nacht; nocte**
good ~: **boa noite; bon soir; gute Nacht; lila; schlafen; spakonoi nochee**
Holy N~: **heilig**
~ different from other ~s: **ma neeshtana**
~ is the cloak of sinners: **la noche**
~ makes all cats gray: **la nuit**
pass a sleepless ~: **passer**
Twelfth N~: **Dreikönigsabend**
nightcap: **bonnet de**
nightclub: **discothèque**
nightdress: **robe de nuit**
nightingale: **rossignol**
nimble: **affilié**
no: **nyet**
~ more: **il n'y en a plus**
~ thank you: καλως (**kalôs**)
nobility: **hidalguía; noblesse**

French ~: **ancienne noblesse**
~ lies in worth: **Adel sitzt**
noble
  ~ is as ~ does: **edel ist**
  ~ of birth and ~ of soul: **adelig**
nobleman: **boyar; hidalgo**
  great ~: **grand seigneur**
nobody: **natus nemo**
nocturne: **notturno**
noise: **bruit**
noisy: **strepitoso**
nonchalance: **insouciance; sang-froid**
nonentity: **non ens; res**
nonexistence: **non esse**
nonsense: **baliverne; baste; coq-à-l'âne;**
    kein Gedanke; niaiserie
  amorous ~: **fleurette**
  melodious ~: **nugae**
  no ~: **keine Pfiffe**
nook, shady: **kala**
noon: **midi**
  before ~: **ante meridiem**
no one
  ~ can give what he does not have:
    nemo dat
  ~ dissenting: **nemine dissentiente**
  ~ else: **nemo alius**
  ~ ever became a villain suddenly:
    nemo repente
  ~ is heir of a living man: **nemo est**
  ~ loves a man he fears: **ονδεις**
    (oudeìs)
  ~ loves the bearer of bad news:
    στεργει (stérgei)
  ~ must accuse himself: **nemo**
    tenetur
  ~ must do more than he can: **ultra**
North America: **la América del Norte**
nose, upturned: **nez**
nostalgia: **Heimweh**
not
  he is ~: **non est**
  ~ by whom but how: **non quo**
note: **lettre; nota**
  accented ~: **nota**
  grace ~: **acciaccatura; appoggiatura**
  leading ~: **nota**
  short ~: **mot**
  sustained ~: **Aushaltung; nota**
  unaccented ~: **nota**
notebook: **cahier**
notes
  commentators' ~: **variorum**
  in the ~: **in notis**

marginal ~: **marginalia**
rapid musical ~: **volata**
with ~: **cum notis**
nothing: **niente; nihil**
  ~ beyond: **nil ultra**
  ~ by halves: **Nichts halb**
  ~ can shake the upright man:
    impavidum
  ~ can withstand valor and arms: **vir-**
    tuti nihil
  ~ done and no mistakes: **chi non fa**
  ~ for ~: **on n'a rien**
  ~ from ~: **aus nichts; de nihilo; ex**
    nihilo; nihil
  ~ gained offending many: **non è**
    guadagnare
  ~ great unless good: **nil magnum**
  ~ he touched he did not adorn:
    nullum
  ~ in excess: **ne nimium**
  ~ is beautiful but truth: **rien n'est**
    beau
  ~ learned and ~ forgotten: **ils n'ont**
    rien
  ~ new under the sun: **nihil**
  ~ relating to man is alien: **humani**
  ~ so inconsistent: **nil fuit**
  ~ too much: **μηδεν (mēdèn)**
  ~ ventured and ~ gained: **chi non**
    s'arrischia
notice: **avis; aviso**
  ~ to the reader: **avis au**
  take ~: **nota bene**
notwithstanding: **non obstante**
  ~ the hue and cry: **nonobstant**
  ~ these things: **his non**
nourished: **nourri**
novelette: **nouvelle; novella**
novel in which real persons figure un-
    der disguise: **roman**
now: **in praesenti**
  for ~: **pro nunc**
  ~ and always: **et nunc; ora e sempre**
  ~ or never: **nunc aut**
  ~ then: **voyons**
nudge: **coup**
null and void: **non avenu**
nun: **religieuse**
nurse: **amah; ayah**
nut: **supari**
nutshell: **in nuce**

oath: **gros; iusiurandum; juramento;**

sacré bleu; voir dire
Moro who takes Muslim ~:
   juramentado
oats, sow wild: **fredaine**
object
  ~ of artistic value: **objet**
  ~ unsuited: **delphinum silvis**
objection, no: **nihil**
obligatory: **de rigueur**
obliged, I am much: **estimo; le**
   agradezco
obscurity
  explain one ~ by another: **litem;**
   obscurum
obstetrician: **accoucheur**
occasion, for this: **pro hac**
ocean: **ingens**
octave: **all' ottava; in alto; ottava**
odds and ends: **chop suey**
offense: **delictum**
  without ~ to modesty: **salvo pudore**
  youthful ~: **Jugendsünde**
offhand: **brevi**
office: **cabinet; daftar**
  I refuse the ~: **nolo episcopari**
  ~ shows the man: **magistratus**
  ~ without pay: **Amt ohne**
  resigned from ~: **functus**
officer: **jemadar; subahdar**
  commanding ~: **comandante**
  police ~: **faujdar; ispravnik; sbirro**
official: **nazir**
  embassy ~: **attaché; chargé**
  public ~: **fonctionnaire**
offspring, without: **sine**
ogle: **oeillade**
oil: **aceite; oleum**
  ~ on the fire: **oleum**
old: **viejo; vieux**
  we grow ~: **alt wird**
older, younger learns from: **a bove**
old-fashioned: **altmodisch; du vieux;**
   vieux
olive: **aceituna**
Olympus, Pelion on: **imponere**
omen
  good ~: **bonum omen; de bon**
   augure
  ~ of better times: **auspicium**
ominous: **de mauvais augure**
once: **una volta; volta**
  ~ and together: **semel et**
  ~ for all: **semel pro**
  ~ more: **ancora**

one
  number ~: **dai ichi**
  ~ and the same: **una et**
  ~ by ~: **singillatim**
  ~ nor the other: **ni l'un**
  ~ out of many: **e pluribus**
  ~ to all: **ab uno ad**
  ~ who flees from civilization:
   remontado
  ~ who mines with others' means:
   aviado
  the ~: **cestui**
onions, with: **aux oignons**
open: **à jour; ouvert; vide**
opening: **débouché**
openly: **ex professo**
openness: **glasnost'**
opera: **drame**
  farcical ~: **opéra bouffe**
  light ~: **opéra comique**
operetta: **Singspiel**
opinion
  in my ~: **à mon avis; meines; me**
   iudice; per mio; selon
  unofficial expression of ~: **obiter**
opportune: **cela tombe bien**
opportunity
  better ~: **reculer**
  know your ~: καιρον **(kairòn);**
   occasionem
  missed ~: **voló golondrina**
  one here-it-is is worth two you-will-
   have-its: **tiens**
  ~ makes the thief: **l'occasion;**
   occasio
opposed, diametrically: **toto**
opposite: **vis-à-vis**
  ~ cured by ~: **contraria**
opposition
  in ~: **ex adverso**
  I strive against ~: **nitor**
opulence: **abondance**
oral: **viva voce**
orange tree is not made out of a
   bramble: **non si può**
oration, funeral: **éloge**
orator
  an ~ is made, a poet born: **orator fit**
  good ~ convinces himself: **é buon**
orchard: **huerta; verger**
orchestra, for full: **vollstimmig**
order: **im Auftrage; Ruhe**
  close ~: **ordre serré**
  extended ~: **ordre dispersé**

in ~: **en règle**
inverse ~: **hysteron; inverso**
money ~: **giro**
~ of the day: **l'ordre**
out of ~: **dérangé**
orderliness: **esprit**
orderly: **secundum**
ordnance: **pièce**
portable ~: **jingal**
organ
  ~ grinder: **Leiermann**
  ~ pedal coupler: **tirasse**
  ~ stops: **vox**
organism, in the: **in vivo**
organization, Italian secret: **carbonaro; Mafia**
origin, humble: **fossoribus orti**
ornamented: **orné**
ornament, floral: **fleuron**
others, with many: **cum multis**
ourselves, between: **entre quatre; inter; unter vier**
ours, would he were: **utinam**
outcome gives deeds their name: **der Ausgang**
outcrop: **affleurement; afloramiento; crestón; floración**
outlaw: **caput; dacoit; proscrit**
  ~ band: **comitiva**
  ~ed: **hors la**
outline: **ébauche; galbe**
outpouring: **épanchement**
outrageous, how: **qué vergüenza**
outrigger: **proa**
outside: **à l'extérieur; dehors; extra muros**
outward: **ad extra**
oven bottom: **cul-de-four**
overalls, leather: **chaparajos**
over and above: **de sobra**
overcoat: **capote**
overseer: **caporal**
oversight: **bévue**
overthrow, complete: **bouleversement**
overture: **ouverture; Vorspiel**
overturned: **renversé**
owner: **propriétaire**
ox: **bail**
  get beef from an ~: **von einem**
  old ~ plows straight: **boi velho; buey**
oxblood: **sang-de-boeuf**
oyster: **huître**
  ~ patty: **bouchée**

pace, walking: **gehend**
pack up: **faire sa malle; faire ses paquettes**
pact
  diplomatic ~: **pacta**
  enforceable ~: **pactum**
pad, saddle: **numdah**
page
  left-hand ~: **verso**
  please turn ~: **T.S.V.P.**
  right-hand ~: **recto**
pain: **Schmerz**
  a fault gives ~: **come t'è**
  no gain without ~: **nul**
painter, I too am a: **anch' io**
paint-holder: **palette**
painting
  he painted it: **pinxit**
  method of ~: **gouache; guazzo**
palace: **palais; palazzo**
  golden ~ disturbs one's rest: **aurea rumpunt**
palatable: **cela se laisse**
palm, let him bear the: **palmam**
palsy: **paralysis**
pampering: **gâterie**
pamphlets: **fliegende**
pancake: **blin; blintze; crêpe**
panel, ornamental: **gaku**
pan into the fire: **de fumo; tomber**
pants: **caleçon**
paper
  curl ~: **papillote**
  daily ~: **Tageblatt**
  never sign a ~ unread, nor drink water unexamined: **ni firmes**
  ~ pulp: **hari-nuki; papier-mâché**
paradise
  children's ~: **limbus**
  ~ of fathers: **limbus**
  ~ of fools: **limbus**
paragraph: **Abschnitt**
  new ~: **alinéa**
parasite: **Graeculus**
pardon me: **pardonnez-moi; prosteet-sye; scusi; sit venia**
parents: **mabap**
Paris: **Paname; Pantruche**
  ~ is worth a mass: **Paris**

parish: **paroisse**
park: **parc**
parsley: **persil**
parsnip: **panais**
part: **shtik**
  aggregate of ~s: **complexus**
  an important ~: **quorum**
  divine the whole from a ~: **ex pede**
  equal ~s: **partes**
  in four ~s: **vierstimmig**
  in ~: **partie; partim**
  on this ~: **in hac**
  ~ for the whole: **pars pro**
  ~ of a book published in ~s:
    livraison
  ~ of the regalia: **inter**
  scattered ~s: **disiecta membra**
  showy ~: **beau rôle**
partition: **cloison; repartimiento; shoji**
partly: **en partie**
partner: **partenaire; socius**
  silent ~: **commanditaire**
partnership
  invalid ~: **leonina**
  limited ~: **Sociedad en**
partridge: **perdrix**
party
  opposing ~: **pars adversa**
  small ~: **comité; petit**
passage: **foramen; Übergang**
  classical ~: **locus**
  ~ already quoted: **loco**
  quoted ~: **locus**
passenger: **passager**
passing
  no ~: **on ne passe**
  they shall not pass: **ils ne passeront**
passion: **affetto; emportement; Feuer**
  ~ for glory is the torch of the mind:
    fax
  ~ for traveling: **Wanderlust**
  ~ for writing: **tantus**
  ~ swells: **fervens**
  P~ Week: **stille**
  tender ~: **belle passion**
  with much ~: **con molto**
  with ~: **appassionato; con calore**
passionate: **feuerig; focoso; impotens;**
    irato; leidenschaftlich; passio-
    nato; smaniatamente
passionately: **adiramente; calore;**
    furioso

password: **mot; shibboleth**
past, as regards the: **quoad**
paste: **pasta; pâte**
pastime: **passetemps**
pastries, meat-filled: **pirozhki**
pastry: **napoléon; pirogi**
  potato-filled ~: **pirogi**
pasture: **agostadero**
patent: **brevet**
patented: **breveté**
path: **senda**
  ~ of an unnoticed life: **fallentis**
  safe ~: **via**
  stand on the old ~s: **stare**
pathetic: **affettivo; doloroso; patetico;**
    pathétique
patience
  ~ is bitter but its reward sweet: **la**
    patience
  ~ surpasses knowledge: **patience**
patiently: **con pazienza**
patriotism: **amor patriae**
patty: **croustade; pâté**
pauperism, glittering: **glänzendes**
pause: **fermata**
pavement: **firme; piso**
paw: **patte**
pawnshop: **mont-de-piété; monte**
payday comes every day: **Zahltag**
pay, half: **demi-solde**
paymaster: **bukhshi**
payment, annual: **cens**
  ~ made: **acquit; pour acquit**
pea: **dal**
  green ~: **petits poix**
  ~s and rice: **dalbhat**
  ~s in a pod: **comme deux**
  with green ~s: **aux petit pois**
peace: **candida; mir; paix; Pax; paz;**
    salaam; selamat; shalom
  against the ~: **contra pacem**
  breach of ~: **Friedensbruch**
  British ~: **Pax**
  go in ~: **salamet; vade**
  in ~: **in pace**
  king's ~: **Pax**
  may he rest in ~: **requiescat; que en**
    paz
  ~ is gone and heart is heavy: **meine**
  ~ lover: **pacífico**
  ~ maintained by arms: **arma pacis;**
    arma tuentur
  ~ produced by war: **paritur; Pax**
  Roman ~: **Pax**

universal ~: **Pax**
where ~ and glory lead: **quo pax**
who wants ~ prepares for war: **qui desiderat**
without making ~: **infecta**
peach: **pêche**
pear: **beurré**
  no ~s from an elm: **no se**
pearl: **moti**
pearly: **nacré**
peasant: **Bauer; Bonhomme; conta-dino; fellah; muzhik; ryot**
  ~ uprising: **Jacquerie**
peck: **almud**
pedal, with the loud: **senza**
peddler: **camelot**
pedigrees
  what do ~ avail: **stemmata**
peel: **pelure**
peers: **per pares**
  before one's ~: **coram**
peevish: **acariâtre**
penalty: **amende**
  under ~: **sub poena**
pendant: **pendeloque**
pending: **in fieri; lis pendens**
peninsula, beautiful: **si quaeris**
penniless: **loger; sans**
  be ~: **loger; n'avoir**
penny
  ~ saved and ~ earned: **Sparen**
  ~ to Belisarius: **date obulum**
pensive: **pensieroso**
pensively: **rêveusement**
people: **demos**
  common ~ and friendship: **vulgus**
  monkey ~: **bandarlog**
  ~ hiss me but I applaud myself: **po-pulus me**
  ~ of rank: **gens**
  ~ rule: **regnant**
  ~ want bread and the circus: **duas**
  ~ want to be deceived: **populus vult**
  ~ who live in glass houses: **wer im**
  sometimes the common ~ see aright: **interdum**
  to the ~: **ad populum**
pepper: **poivre**
  sweet ~: **pimiento**

per cent: **por ciento; vom**
perfection is threefold: **omne trinum**
performance: **Vorstellung**
performer: **artiste**
perhaps: **peut-être**
peril, one's own: **suo periculo**
perjuries, Jove laughs at lovers': **periuria**
perjury: **crimen**
permission
  allow me ~: **mi permetta**
  beyond ~: **ultra**
  ~ of so great a man: **pace**
  ~ to reside: **permis**
  what pleases us is permissible: **erlaubt**
  with your ~: **avec votre; con per-messo; pace**
perquisites: **bâton; tour**
perseverance: **perseverando**
  he runs far who never turns: **corre**
persimmon: **chapote**
person: **chal; persona; walla**
  acceptable ~: **persona**
  against the ~: **in personam**
  among other ~s: **inter**
  bowlegged ~: **valgus**
  condemned ~: **condamné**
  delivered in ~: **en propria**
  each ~: **per capita**
  fictitious ~: **persona**
  hapless ~: **nebech**
  hot-headed ~: **mauvais**
  important ~: **gros**
  in one's own ~: **in propria persona**
  in ~: **in persona**
  most acceptable ~: **persona**
  newly successful ~: **arriviste**
  ~al action dies with the ~: **actio**
  ~ in distress is sacred: **res**
  ~ of mixed ancestry: **chicano; cré-ole; criollo; Ladino; mestizo; métif; métis; mulatto**
  ~ who benefits: **cestui**
  self-centered ~: **m'as-tu**
  unacceptable ~: **persona**
  unemployed ~: **chômeur**
  wise ~: **chachem**
personal: **ad hominem**
pest: **nudnik**
pheasant: **faisan**
philosopher: **abnormis**
philosophy: **ancilla; Weltanschauung; Weltweisheit**

~ is a yearning after heavenly wisdom: φιλοσοφια (philosophía)

physician: **hakeem**
~ heal thyself: ιατρε (iatré); **médecin guéris-toi; medice**

piano: **cembalo**
for the ~: **a cembalo**

picker, rag: **chiffonnier**

pickles: **achar**

picture: **Abbildung; kakemono**
living ~: **tableau**
~ is a silent poem: **mutum**
~ scroll: **makimono**
pretty as a ~: **fait à peindre**
tone ~: **Tonbild**

pie: **torta; tourte**

piece: **morceau; pièce; Stück**

pier: **jetée**

pierced: **percé**

pig: **cochon**
every ~ has its Martinmas: **cada porco**
~ in a poke: **chat; ego spem**
worst ~ eats best acorn: **o peior**

pike: **brochet**

pilgrimage: **hadj**

pill, gild the: **dorer**

pillow is a good counselor: **la almohada**

pinch, in a: **au besoin**

pineapple: **piña**

pinion: **aileron**

pinnacle, ice: **sérac**

pin, neat as a: **tiré**

pint, two-thirds of a: **chupa**

pioneer: **voortrekker**

pipe, smoking: **chibouk**

pitcher: **aiguière**
little ~s have big ears: **petit**

pitch, French standard: **diapason**

pity
thousand pities: **es ist ewig**
to ~: **ad misericordiam**
what a ~: **peccato**

place: **eo loci; loco; locus**
hiding ~: **cachette**
in another ~: **in alio**
in its original ~: **in situ**
in ~ of: **in loco**
in the first ~: **ante omnia; erstens; zum ersten**
in the ~: **loco**
in the same ~: **ibidem**
in this ~: **hoc loco**

meeting ~: **point de**
~ cited: **in loco; ubi supra**
~ of a parent: **in loco**
proper ~: **suo loco**
public ~: **locus**
sweet resting ~: **amitié**
this ~: **ad hunc**

plague take the hindmost: **occupet**

plain: **boschveld; llano; llanura; maidan; mesa; steppe; vega**

plainly: **nudis**

plaintive: **flebile; lamentevole**

plaintively: **piangendo**

plan: **dessin**

plant
Andean ~: **frailejon**
dock ~: **canaigre**
forage ~: **alfilaria**
soap ~: **amole**

plaster: **emplastrum**

plate: **assiette**

plateau: **altiplano; páramo; puna**
small ~: **mesilla**

platform: **estrade; pantalan**
arrival ~: **gare**
sleeping ~: **kang**
speaker's ~: **bema**

Plato is my friend: **amicus Plato**

play: **pièce**
~ fair: **de bonne lutte**
~ is ended: **acta est**
~ out of tune: **détonner**
short ~: **petite**

player, wind instrument: **Bläser**

playful: **folâtre; giochevole; giocondo**

plea
declines ~: **nihil**
~ denying a debt: **nihil**
~ equivalent to "guilty": **nolo contendere**
~ for the defense: **plaidoyer**

pleasant on the great sea: **suave**

please: **bitte; dozho; pazhalsta; piacere; por favor; prego**
hard to ~: **exigeant**
I shall ~: **placebo**
it doesn't ~ me: **non libet**
~ forward: **a reexpedir; faire suivre**

pleasing: **aimable; piacevole**

pleasingly: **affabile**

pleasure: **a beneplacito; ad libitum; al piacere; a piacere; khushi; piacere; si piace**
for ~: **par plaisir**

giving ~: **delectando**
~ bought by pain: **nocet**
~ in remembering: **haec olim**
~ in weeping: **est quaedam**
~ of seeing you again: **au plaisir**
~ short, repentance long: **court plaisir**
~ to dine without paying: **gran placer**
~ to remember: **forsan**
sensual ~: **voluptates**
with ~: **avec plaisir; con piacere**
pledge
in ~: **in vadio**
love ~: **gage**
plotter: **intrigant**
plot, unraveling of a: **dénouement**
pluck and gather: **carpere**
plumed: **panaché**
plumpness: **embonpoint**
pleasantly plump: **zaftig**
pocket, out of his own: **de bonis propriis**
poem: **Gedicht; haiku; pathya**
poet: **Dichter**
~ is born, not made: **poeta**
would-be ~: **un poète**
poetry: **ars poetica**
~ and truth: **Dichtung**
~ is devil's wine: **poesis**
~ is like a painting: **ut pictura**
point: **punctum**
get to the ~: **aller au fait; venez au**
growing ~: **punctum**
let's get to the ~: **passons**
make one's ~: **faire une trouée**
~ by ~: **punctatim; seriatim**
salient ~: **punctum**
same ~: **ad idem**
starting ~: **terminus a quo**
to the ~: **ad rem**
to the highest ~: **ad summum**
poison: **aqua**
~ from a golden cup: **bibere; venenum**
police, secret: **Gestapo**
policy
change of ~: **démarche**
reversal of ~: **volte-face**
polished
~ and complete: **teres**
~ without facets: **en cabochon**
polishing and revision: **limae**
politeness: **politesse**

out of ~: **par complaisance**
~ costs nothing: **berretta**
politician: **politico; politique**
politics
international ~: **Weltpolitik**
practical ~: **Realpolitik**
pomegranate: **granada**
pomp: **faste**
pompous: **fastoso**
pond: **barachois; charco; estanque**
poodle, French: **caniche**
poor
~ amid great riches: **magnas inter**
you always have the ~ with you: **τους πτωχους (toùs ptōkhoùs)**
poppy: **chicalote**
popular: **couru**
porch: **lanai**
pork: **porc**
porridge: **atole**
port: **pôrto**
~ after shipwrecks: **post tot**
porter: **hamal**
portfolio: **portefeuille**
portion: **partie; passus**
portrait: **imagines; ritratto**
Portuguese
~ noble: **fidalgo**
~ titles of courtesy: **senhor**
posse: **posse comitatus**
possession
~ for all time: **κτημα (ktēma)**
~ is better than desire: **más vale tener**
~ is nine points of the law: **beati**
post
military ~: **corps**
~ office: **correo; dak; Hauptpost; hôtel des postes**
posted: **affichée**
poster: **affiche**
postlude: **Nachspiel**
postman: **Briefträger; facteur**
postscript: **l'envoi**
pot: **chatti; marmite**
potentially: **in posse; in potentia**
potpourri: **mélange; pasticcio; pot pourri**
pottery: **fictilia**
made of ~: **fictilis**
potter has grudge against potter: **και κεραμευς (kaì keramèus)**

poultry: **volaille**
pouting: **bouderie; faire la moue**
poverty
  one that cannot endure ~: **indocilis**
  ~ has no shame: **a pobreza**
  ~ is not a shame: **la pobreza**
power
  according to my ~: **à ma puissance**
  beyond one's ~: **supra; ultra**
  comic ~: **vis**
  healing ~: **vis**
  nature's healing ~: **médecine; vis**
  preservative ~: **vis**
  within the ~: **intra vires**
practice makes perfect: **exercitatio;**
     Übung
praise
  ~d by a man ~d: **laudari**
  ~ married life and stay single:
     lauda
  ~r of times past: **laudator**
  self-~ is base: **laus propria**
  with great ~: **magna cum**
  with highest ~: **summa cum**
prance: **caracoler**
prank: **fredaine**
pray
  ~ and work: **ora et**
  ~ brothers: **orate fratres**
  ~ed well, strived well: **bene orasse**
  ~ for us: **ora pro**
  to learn to ~, put to sea: **se queres**
  watch and ~: **vigilate**
  who labors ~s: **qui laborat**
prayer: **preghiera**
  abject ~s: **precibus**
  ~ and toil: **orando**
precaution, by way of: **par précaution**
precedence: **pas**
  have ~: **avoir le pas**
precedent
  bad ~: **mali exempli**
  let it become ~: **transeat**
preciosity: **marivaudage**
precious: **précieuse**
precipice: **pari**
precipitately: **tête**
precisely: **preciso**
preeminence: **le pas**
preeminently: **κατ' εξοχην (kat' exo-**
    khēn); par excellence
preface: **avant-propos; Vorrede;**
    Vorwort
pregnant: **enceinte**

prejudice
  excite ~: **in invidiam**
  to ~: **ad invidiam**
  without ~: **salvo iure**
prelude: **intrada; ritornello**
preparation
  without ~: **à livre; ex abrupto**
prepared: **ad utrumque; animis; in om-**
    nia; in utrumque; ut quocunque
  ~ plainly: **à la maître**
presence: **prestance**
  in the ~ of : **coram**
present: **actuel; adsum; ex dono**
  enjoy the ~: **carpe**
  for the ~: **de praesenti**
presently: **tout à l'heure**
presents, wedding: **corbeille**
preservation: **maintien**
preserves: **confiture**
  with ~: **aux confitures**
pretense: **simagrée**
pretensions
  lower one's ~: **mettre de**
  make ~: **die Saiten**
pretty: **chouette; hübsch; joli**
prevention better than cure: **venienti**
price
  fixed ~: **prix**
  marriage ~: **pretium**
  reasonable ~: **honnête; prix**
pride
  glow with ~: **kvell**
  too much humility is ~: **zu viel**
priest: **abbé; bosan; curé; imam; kan-**
    nushi; khatib; padre; pujari; pu-
    rohit; shaman; tohunga
prima donna: **diva**
prime, past one's: **passé**
prince: **der Fürst; maharaja; nawab;**
    nizam; principe; rajah; rana;
    shereef
  crown ~: **dauphin**
princely: **en prince**
princess: **maharani**
principle
  on ~: **par principe**
  general ~s: **generalia**
  ~s not men: **principia**
print: **estampe**
printed and published by: **Druck**
printer: **Buchdrucker**
printing: **ars artium; Buchdruck;**
    Druck

prison: **conciergerie; maison**
prisoner: **détenu**
privacy
  in private: **in camera**
  who builds by the roadside has many
    foremen: **wer am**
privately: **sub silentio**
privilege
  by way of ~: **par privilège**
  with ~: **cum privilegio**
prize: **médaille; prix**
  once lost, then ~d: **bien perdu**
pro-American: **americanista**
problem settled by action: **solvitur**
procession: **cortège**
proclamation: **pronunciamiento**
procurer: **maquereau**
procuress: **conciliatrix; entremetteuse**
prodigy: **niger; rara**
produce, home: **dapes**
profane begone: **procul**
profession: **de son; métier**
proficient: **au fait**
progress, in: **en train**
prohibition: **taboo**
project: **projet**
promises
  too many ~ weaken faith: **multa
    fidem**
prompter: **souffleur**
pronghorn: **berrendo**
proof: **argumentum; épreuve; prueba**
  printer's ~: **bozza**
proofreader: **correcteur**
proper: **comme il**
property: **bona**
  I take my ~ where I find it: **je
    prends**
  ~ is theft: **la propriété**
Prophets: **Nebiim**
proportional: **pro rata**
propriety: **décence**
prosecutor: **procureur**
prospect, in: **in prospectu**
prosperity has many friends: **εντυχια
  (eutukhía); felicitas**
prostitute: **cocotte; fille; joro; togata;
  troleur**
protection: **amparo; tutamen**
protector and avenger: **tutor**
proud: **fier**
  overthrow the ~: **debellare**

proved: **probatum**
proverb: **dicton**
providence, favoring: **benigno**
provisioner: **vivandier**
provoke: **pousser**
  ~ beyond endurance: **il m'a poussé**
provost: **prévôt**
prowler: **rôdeur**
proxy: **per procurationem**
prudence, if there be: **si sit prudentia**
prune: **pruneau**
pseudonym: **nom**
publicly: **coram; in oculis; publice**
publisher: **éditeur; Verlagsbuchhändler**
publishing
  ~ house: **Verlag**
  underground ~: **samizdat**
pudding: **pouding**
  black ~: **boudin**
puffed out: **bouffant**
pumpkin: **courge; potiron**
pun: **calembour; jeu**
punch: **coup**
punishment presses hard: **culpam**
pupil: **chela; in statu pupillari**
  day ~: **externe**
pure: **pur; sans**
  to the ~, all things are ~: **omnia
    munda; παντα καθαρα (pánta
    katharà)**
purpose
  for this ~: **ad hoc**
  to no ~: **ουδεν προς (oudèn pròs)**
purse: **ad crumenam; portemonnaie**
pursue: **chasser**
push forward: **boutez**
puzzle of critics, doctors: **crux**
Pyrenees, no longer any: **il n'y a plus**

quack: **saltimbanco; saltimbanque**
quail: **caille**
quantity
  small ~: **goutte**
  sufficient ~: **quantum**
quarrel: **prise**
  groundless ~: **querelle**
  lover's ~s: **amantium**
  ~ about anything or nothing:
    rixatur
quavering: **tremolo**
queen: **begum; rani**
  long live the ~: **vivat regina**
  ~ wills it: **la reine**
question: **quaere**

begging the ~: **petitio**
beside the ~: εξω τον (éxō toû)
disputed ~: **vexata**
~ arises: **quaeritur**
~ mark: **Fragezeichen**
two sides to every ~: **ogni medaglia**
vexed ~: **quaestio**
quibbling: **chicane**
quick: **hurtig; schnell; tosto; vite**
  less ~: **meno**
  ~er: **mosso; più**
  ~ly: **presto; pronto; subito; vuelta**
  rather ~er: **andantino**
  very ~: **allegro; molto**
  very ~ly: **prestissimo**
quickening: **affrettando**
quicksilver: **azogue**
quiet: **calmato; schweigen; state**
quietly: **commodo**
quilt, eiderdown: **duvet**
quilted: **matelassé**
quotation marks: **Anführungszeichen; Gänsefüsschen; guillemet**

rabbit: **lapin**
  curried ~: **lapin**
  young ~: **lapereau**
rabble: **faex**
  I hate the ~: **odi profanum**
  please the ~: **ad captandum**
  wretched ~: **miserabile vulgus**
race
  ~ of poets: **genus irritabile**
  separation of ~s: **apartheid**
  slow and sure wins the ~: **qui trop se**
rage: **acharnement**
  all the ~: **on se**
  pale with ~: **pallidus**
  ~ for speaking: **furor loquendi**
  ~ for writing: **furor scribendi**
  ~ supplies arms: **furor arma**
ragout: **brandade; civet; salmis**
raid: **razzia**
rail: **ferrocarril; por ferrocarril**
raillery: **badinage; blague**
railroad: **chemin de fer; Eisenbahn; ferrocarril; ferrovia**
  ~ car: **vagón**
  ~ platform: **muelle**
  ~ station: **Bahnhof; estação; gare**

rain: **lluvia; serein**
rainbow: **arc-en-ciel**
raincoat: **imperméable; Regenmantel**
raised: **relevé**
ranch: **rancho**
  cattle ~: **estancia**
ranchman: **estanciero; ranchero**
random: **alla ventura; à tort et; aufs Geratewohl**
rank
  dress ~s: **richt euch**
  plebeian ~: **roture**
  ~ imposes obligation: **noblesse**
ransom: **rançon**
rapid: **sault**
rapidity, with great: **veloce**
rapidly: **con prestezza**
rapture: **ravissement**
rare: **saignant**
rarity: **cygne; tulipe**
rascal: **coquin**
rash: **écervelé**
  neither ~ly nor timorously: **nec temere**
rather: **plutôt**
rational: **raisonné**
ration, emergency: **vivres**
ravine: **barranco; rambla**
raw: **brut**
rawhide: **parfleche**
reach
  out of ~: **hors de prise; prise**
  within ~: **à la portée; a tiro**
read
  ~ I pray you: **lege**
  we ~ that others may not: **legimus**
reader
  gentle ~: **lector**
  to the gentle ~: **lectori**
readiness, in: **in procinctu; in promptu**
reading
  erroneous ~: **falsa lectio**
  variant ~: **varia**
ready: **à la main; bereit; fertig; prêt pour**
  always ~: **nunquam non; semper; toujours prêt**
  I am ~: **je suis**
  ~ to accomplish: **prêt d'accomplir**

real estate: **finca; zamindari**
realization, from possibility to: **a posse**
really: **tiens**
rear: **arrière; en arrière**
rearguard: **arrière-garde**
rearing: **encabritada**
reason: **à bon raison; raison; Vernunft**
  creature of ~: **ens**
  for whatever ~: **ex quocunque**
  ~ for existence: **raison**
  ~ for silence: **βονς (boûs)**
  ~ of domicile: **ratione domicilii**
  ~ of state: **raison**
  ~ of the soil: **ratione soli**
  stronger ~: **a fortiori**
reasonable: **à propos; sensé**
rebellion crushed by killing everyone:
  solitudinem
receipt: **accepta; acquit**
received: **reçu**
reception: **durbar**
  good ~: **bon accueil**
recipient: **bénéficiaire**
recitative: **recitativo**
reckonings old lead to disputes new: **à**
  vieux
recommendation for good face: **auxi-**
  lium non
reconciliation: **rapprochement**
record, official: **dossier**
recut: **recoupé**
red and black: **rouge**
redemption: **anno**
red-handed: **en flagrant; flagrante de-**
  licto; in flagrante
reduction to absurdity: **reductio ad**
  absurdum
reef: **cayo**
reference: **ad referendum**
refined: **raffiné**
refrain thou must: **entbehren**
refreshments: **rafraîchissements**
refugee: **émigré; gîte**
regard
  ~s: **égards**
  ~ scornfully: **regarder**
  with due ~: **salvo ordine**
regime, old: **ancien régime**
register: **daftar**
  official ~: **cadastre**
  ~ above F: **in altissimo**

registered: **contrôlé**
registrar: **greffier**
regulations, according to: **selon**
regulator, pitch: **capotasto**
rehash: **réchauffé**
reinforcing: **rinforzando**
rejoice: **χαιρε (khaîre)**
rejuvenating: **rajeunissant**
relation who is poor does not exist: **no**
  hay pariente
relaxation of tension: **détente**
relief: **rilievo**
  formed in ~: **repoussé**
  half ~: **mezzo-rilievo**
  high ~: **alto-rilievo; haut-relief**
  hollow ~: **cavo-rilievo; intaglio**
  low ~: **bas-relief; basso-rilievo**
  very low ~: **stiacciato**
religion
  layman's ~: **religio laici**
  ~ not eliminated: **superstitione**
religiously: **religiosamente**
relish: **sauce**
reluctantly: **à contre coeur**
remainder wanting: **desunt caetera**
remains: **reliquiae**
  he ~: **manet**
remaking: **rifacimento**
remedy: **aegrescit**
  ~ for everything except death: **para**
    todo
  ~ worse than the disease: **graviora**
    quaedam
remember
  I don't ~: **non mi**
  ~ to distrust: **μεμνησο (mémnēso)**
  ~ you must die: **memento**
remembrance, everlasting: **in perpe-**
  tuam; memoria in
reminiscence: **Erinnerung**
remnants of an ancient flame: **veteris**
renewed: **redivivus**
renowned: **renommé**
repeated: **replicato**
  ~ and continues to please: **decies**
repeatedly: **toties**
repentance
  opportunity for ~: **locus**
  ~ costs dear: **caro cuesta**
  stool of ~: **sellette**
repercussion: **contrecoup**
repetition: **reprise**
  let it be repeated: **repetatur**
  ~ of a motif: **rosalia**

stale ~s: **crambe**
reply requested: **répondez; um**
    Antwort
report
  evil and good ~: δια δνσφημιας
    (**dià dusphēmías**)
  official ~: **compte rendu**
  ~ flies: **fama volat**
repose, nor content with calm: **nec**
    placida
reprimand: **laver**
reprisal: **représaille**
republic
  long live the ~: **vivat respublica;**
    vive la
  ~ of letters: **l'empire des**
reputation
  acquire a good ~: **acquista buona**
  reputable rather than showy: **ho-**
    nesta quam
  ~ is a cloak: **buena fama**
request of king is a command: **ruego**
required, when: **pro re nata**
resentment: **pique**
reservation, mental: **arrière-pensée**
reservoir: **aljibar**
resident, Hawaiian: **kamaina**
residue: **caput**
  sugar cane ~: **bagasse**
resolute in action, gentle in manner:
    fortiter in re
resort: **ridotto**
resources, from one's: **ex propriis**
respect: **hommage**
  in all ~: **sous tous**
  in ~: **intuitu**
  ~ due a child: **maxima**
  show ~: **kursi**
  whose hands I kiss: **cuyos**
responsibilities, without: **sine**
rest
  good night's ~: **bonsoir**
  over all the heights is ~: **über**
  ~ can rust: **wer rastet**
  restfully: **riposatamente**
  ~ house: **serai**
  ~ in peace: **en paz; requiescat;**
    requiescit
  restless: **remuant; unruhig**
  ~ makes rust: **Rast**
restaurant: **café; trattoria**
  ~ owner: **restaurateur**

restraint in jests: **adhibenda**
result: **Facit**
retaliation, in: **en revanche**
retire: **aller planter**
retirement title: **emeritus**
retreat: **reculade; réduit**
retrospect: **ex post; Rückblick**
return
  happy ~: **felice**
  I shall not ~ unavenged: **non**
    revertar
  let us ~ to our subject: **revenons**
revelation: **exposé**
revel, midnight: **réveillon**
revenge: **revanche**
revenues are sinews of the state:
    vectigalia
review: **revue**
revise: **incudi**
revival: **Risorgimento**
revolution: **revolutsya**
revolutionary: **revolutsyaner; sans-**
    culotte
reward
  ~ after battle: **post proelia**
  ~ for labors: **pretium**
  ~ of the valor of my ancestors: **vir-**
    tutis avorum
Rhine, watch on the: **die Wacht**
rhymes: **bout-rimés**
rhyme, triple: **terza**
rhythm: **rhythmus**
ribbon, blue: **cordon bleu**
rice: **arroz; pilau; riz**
  fried ~: **chow fan**
rich
  newly ~: **nouveau**
  oh ~es secure: **O senza**
  ~ here, poor hereafter: **mucho en**
  ~ in lands, ~ in money: **dives**
    aegris
  small gains bring ~es: **klein gewin**
ridge: **arête; cuesta**
riffraff: **canaille**
rifle: **jezail**
right: **iure**
  divine ~: **iure**
  dress ~: **à droit, alignement**
  husband's ~: **iure; ius**
  just ~: **au bon**
  maintain the ~: **maintiens le**
  may ~ prevail: το δ' εν (**tò d' eû**)
  not without ~: **non sans**
  of his own ~: **proprio iure**

one's own ~: **sui iuris; suo iure**
private ~s: **droit**
property ~: **ius**
real ~: **ius**
~!: **mano**
~ against a thing: **in rem**
~ and forward: **droit**
~ and not a gift: **iure**
~ forfeited by disuse: **ex desuetudine**
~ of pledge: **ius**
~ of possession: **ius**
~ of relationship: **iure; ius**
~ of resumption of status: **ius**
~ of the crown: **iure**
~ of the first night: **droit; ius primae**
~ of the soil: **ius**
~ of the strongest: **le droit; par le droit**
~ to be heard: **locus**
~ well: **bel et**
royal ~: **ius**
through ~ and wrong: **per fas**
to the ~: **à droite**
you're ~: **raison; vous avez**
ring, cinch: **larigo**
riot: **émeute**
ripped: **décousu**
rising
general ~: **levée**
I shall rise again: **resurgam**
risk: **hasard**
one's own ~: **meo periculo**
our only ~: **nostro**
risky: **risqué**
ritual: **rituale**
rival I embrace in order to choke: **j'embrasse**
river: **kiang; rio; río; rivière**
~ crossed, saint forgotten: **el río**
road: **camino; daan; doróga**
military ~: **via**
~ to ruin: **der Weg**
royal ~: **camino**
valley ~: **Talweg**
roast: **rôti**
pot ~: **Sauerbraten**
robbed: **rubato**
robber: **bandolero**
robbery, highway: **bandolerismo**
robe
episcopal ~s: **in pontificalibus**
Japanese ~: **kimono**

white ~: **toga candida; toga praetexta**
rock: **Fahlband; nunatak; peña**
rod
~ of iron: **ποιμανει (poimaneî)**
under the ~: **sub ferula**
rogue: **Schelm**
once a ~ then always a ~: **una volta**
roguish: **espiègle**
roguishness: **Schalkheit; Schelmerei**
roll: **croissant; rouleau**
roller coaster: **montagnes russes**
Roman
beware of a ~: **hunc tu**
I am a ~: **civis**
romance: **romanza**
Rome
found ~ brick, left it marble: **urbem**
Senate and people of ~: **Senatus**
smoke, wealth, din of ~: **fumum**
roof, flat: **azotea**
room: **chambre; kiva; Stube**
dining ~: **salle**
drawing ~: **salon**
dressing ~: **boudoir**
guest ~: **chambre**
school~: **salle**
suite of ~s: **enfilade**
visitor's ~: **Kursaal**
waiting ~: **salle**
wine ~: **Stube**
rooster: **coq**
~ on his own dunghill: **hardi**
rope: **mecate**
~ in the home of someone hanged: **no hay que**
rose, I flourish in the: **en la**
roster: **rôle**
roughly: **ruvidamente**
roundup, cattle: **rodeo**
row, violent: **chahut**
royalist
more ~ than the king: **plus royaliste**
rubbish: **débris**
rub, there's the: **c'est là le diable; hoc opus, hic labor**
ruin: **culbuter; délabrement**
he is ~ed: **zonam perdidit**
~ed: **ruiné**
~s: **rovine**
~s have perished: **etiam perire**
rule: **règlement**
rule (dominion): **raj**
ruler: **archon; dey; emir**

for ~, rule, and ruled: **pro rege lege**
who will rule the ~: τις ουν (**tís oûn**)
rumor: **on dit**
  nothing swifter than ~: **fama nihil**
  ~ is an evil than which nothing is swifter: **fama malum**
  spread ~: **spargere**
runner
  good ~ is never captured: **jamais bon**
rupture: **rotura**
Russian, in: **po-ruski**
rustic: **à la villageoise; campagnard; hirtlich**
rustle: **frou-frou**

saber: **tulwar**
sack pricks up its ears: **sacco**
sacred: **sacré**
  mingle ~ with profane: **miscebis**
  trifle with ~ things: **ludere**
sad: **dolente; triste**
  ~ to relate: **miserabile dictu**
  you'll be ~ if alone: **tristis**
saddle: **aparejo; selle**
  sit in two ~s: **duabus**
saddletree: **fuste**
sadly: **luttuosamente**
sadness: **tristesse; tristezza**
safe
  ~ and sound: **sahih; sain**
  ~ by taking heed: **cavendo**
  ~ty in this: **in hoc salus**
sage: **kanwa; rishi**
  ~ out of season is a fool: **savio**
said
  it is ~: **dicitur; on dit**
  no sooner ~ than done: **aussitôt; gesagt**
  ~ and done: **dicho; dictum ac**
  ~ only once: **hapax**
  well ~: καλως (**kalôs**)
sailor: **gens; khalasi; lascar; matelot**
saint: **Santo**
  ~ in church, glutton in tavern: **nella**
sake
  for ~ of pleasing: **ad captandum**
  for ~ of the joke: **ioci**
sale: **venta; vente**
  on ~: **vente**

salesman, traveling: **commis-voyageur**
salivation: **flux**
salmon: **saumon**
salt: **sal; sel**
  common ~: **sal**
  Epsom ~: **sal**
  pure ~: **merum**
  rock ~: **sal**
  ~cellar: **salero; salière**
  ~ed: **salé**
  ~ of the earth: υμεις εστε το αλας (**humeîs este tò hálas**)
  ~ seasons everything: **sal sapit**
  with a grain of ~: **cum grano**
saltpeter: **caliche**
salute: **coup; feu**
salvation: **a cruce**
  ~ in God alone: **in solo**
  ~ through Christ: **salus per**
  ~ under the cross: **sub cruce salus**
same: **idem; istesso; per eundem; stesso**
  ~ to all men: **omnibus idem**
  ~ way by different steps: **gradu**
sample: **échantillon**
sanatorium: **Heilanstalt; maison; santé**
sanctity of the place: **religio loci**
sandal: **geta**
sand, building on: **in arena**
sandwich, grilled: **croque-monsieur**
Santiago and at them: **Santiago**
sash: **obi**
Satan, get thee behind me: **apage; heb' dich**; νπαγε (**húpage**)
satellite: **sputnik**
sauce: **béchamel; mole; nuoc; ravigote; rémoulade**
  brown ~: **roux**
  butter ~: **au beurre fondu; sauce**
  caper ~: **sauce**
  cream ~: **béchamel**
  green ~: **sauce**
  mayonnaise and mustard ~: **sauce**
  mint ~: **sauce**
  pepper ~: **poivrade**
  white ~: **sauce**
  wine ~: **sauce**
saucepan: **bain-marie; cazoba**
sauerkraut: **choucroute**
sausage: **Bratwurst; choucroute; salame; saucisse; Wurst**

sausagelike: **boudiné**
savage: **sauvage**
save all and risk all: **Alles zu retten**
saved, whosoever will be: **quicunque**
saving one life, as good as saving the
    world: **ha matseel**
Savior: **der Heiland; Heiland**
say
  beware what you ~: **cave quid**
  it goes without ~ing: **il va**
  ~ goodbye: **adieu**
  ~ no more: **brisons-là**
  ~ what one feels: **fari quae**
  they ~: **man sagt**
scandal: **esclandre; fama clamosa**
scapegoat: **bouc**
scarf: **écharpe; foulard; tápalo**
scar remains: **cicatrix; manet**
scat: **zape**
scattered
  ~ here and there: **apparent**
  thinly ~: **clair semé**
scene: **scena; locus**
  behind the ~s: **le dessous**
  make a ~: **faire un esclandre**
  the ~ is a failure: **hic funis**
scholar: **savant**
scholarship: **beca**
school: **bet sefer; dojo; école; Internat;**
    madrasa; shkola
  agricultural ~: **ferme**
  boarding ~: **pensionnat**
  commercial ~: **Handelshochschule**
  day ~: **externat**
  fencing ~: **escrime; salle**
  found a ~: **faire école**
  high ~: **Gymnasium; lycée;**
    Realschule
  law ~: **école**
  military ~: **école**
  ~ of dance: **salle**
science of sciences: **scientia**
scientifically: **secundum**
scissors: **ciseaux**
scoffer: **moqueur**
scope: **Bereich; Partitur**
scornfully: **con sdegno**
scorn, treat with: **traiter**
scorpion: **alacrán**
scoundrel: **drôle**
scout: **coureur; explorador**
scrap: **Stückchen**
scrawl: **griffonnage; patte**
screen: **écran**

sun ~: **chick**
scullion: **marmiton**
sea: **more; sindhu**
  beyond the ~: **outre mer**
  closed ~: **mare clausum**
  heavy ~: **mar bravo**
  open ~: **mare liberum**
  ~ and land: **per mare**
  ~ slug: **bêche-de-mer**
  the ~: θαλαττα **(thálatta)**
  those who cross the ~: **caelum**
seal
  harp ~: **brasseur**
  place for the ~: **locus**
seaport: **pôrto**
search for a great Perhaps: **je m'en**
    vais chercher
seasickness: **mal**
season, out of: **hors de saison**
seat: **banquette**
  ~ of justice: **lit de**
  upholstered ~: **banquette**
seated: **nehmen**
secondly: **zweitens**
second to none: **nulli secundus**
secret: **dessous**
  in ~: **ianuis**
  know the ~: **connaître; voir le**
  state ~: **arcana imperii**
secretary: **munshi; sarishtadar;**
    secrétaire
secretly: **à la sourdine; cachette; en**
    cachette; petto; unter der
security, with: **avec nantissement**
sedately: **posément**
seductive: **séduisant**
see: **vide**
  I want to ~ things that are above:
    quae sursum
  ~ above: **vide**
  ~ and believe: **vide**
  ~ below: **vide**
  ~ing better things: **video**
  ~ Naples, then die: **vedi**
  ~n before: **déjà vu**
  we'll ~ what we'll ~: **nous verrons**
seizure: **presa**
selection: **excerpta; recueil**
self
  as for me: **per me**
  compose your~: **remettez-vous**
  in spite of one~: **malgré soi**
  I pardon my~: **egomet**
  literary ~-sufficiency: **morgue**

not for one~ but for all: **non sibi
sed omnibus**
not for ourselves alone are we born:
non nobis solum
other ~: **alter ego**
reliance on ~: **cada uno es artífice;
spes**
save him~ who can: **sauve**
second ~: **alter ipse**
~-control: **maîtrise; retenue**
~ do and ~ have: **selbst ist**
~ done and well done: **selbst getan**
~-evident: **cela saute**
who does a thing through another
does it him~: **qui facit**
who excuses him~ accuses him~:
qui s'excuse
semicolon: **point et**
sense
broad ~: **lato**
common ~: **ad iudicium**
in a bad ~: **sensu malo**
in a good ~: **sensu bono**
in a qualified ~: **sub modo**
in this ~: **hoc sensu**
strict ~: **stricto**
without violation of ~: **salvo sensu**
sensitive: **sensible**
separate: **divisi**
who shall ~: **quis separabit**
separation, legal: **separatio a mensa**
septet: **septetto**
serenade: **Nachtmusik**
serene: **heiter**
serf: **adscriptus**
seriously: **au grand; au sérieux; Scherz
bei; sine**
sermon: **khutbah**
servant: **farash; gens; naukar; tjenare;
valet de chambre**
~ depart: **Nunc Dimittis**
so many ~s: **quot servi**
service
in ~: **en condition**
I serve: **ich dien**
one I will serve: **un je**
~ vs. being gazed at: **prodesse**
that I may be of ~: **ut prosim**
servitude, penal: **travaux**
settee: **causeuse**
setting, stage: **mise en**
settle it: **accordez**
sex
fair ~: **das schöne**

~ instinct: **libido**
~ organs: **naturalia**
sexually frenzied: **must**
sextet: **sestetto**
shack: **chantier**
shadow: **umbra**
single hair casts a ~: **un cabello**
shame: **haro; vergonha**
false ~: αιδως ονκ (aidòs ouk);
mauvais
fear ~: **craignez; timet**
for ~: **fi donc; pro pudor**
~ in distrust of friends: **il est plus
honteux**
~ to him who thinks evil of it: **honi
soit**
shapeliness: **belle tournure**
share: **partage**
individual ~: **rata**
lion's ~: **part du**
~cropper: **métayer**
~cropping: **métayage**
~holder: **actionnaire**
sharpshooter: **bersagliere; tirailleur**
shawl: **rebozo**
sheep: **mouton; oveja**
black ~: **mauvais; sujet**
wild ~: **mouflon**
sheet: **feuille**
shell: **concha; coquille**
puff-paste ~: **vol-au-vent**
shellac: **goma**
shellfish: **coquillage**
shelter: **abri**
sheltered: **à l'abri**
shield
either with or upon this ~: η ταν (è
tàn)
~ is the safety of leaders: **forte
scutum**
~ of thy good will hath encompassed us: **scuto**
ship: **Schiff; schip; tartane**
great ~: **grande nao**
~ of many pilots: **barco**
when the ~ is lost all become pilots:
quando la
shirt: **camisa**
shoal: **barra**
shoe: **chaussures; espadrille;
zapato**
if the ~ fits: **qui capit**
~ polish: **cirage**
~ store: **zapatería**

well shod: **bien chaussé**
wooden ~: **sabot**
shoemaker: **zapatero**
　~'s son: **à fils de**
　~'s wife: **zapatera**
shoots, pine: **bourgeon**
shop: **boutique; dukan**
　~girl: **midinette**
　~keeper: **banya**
　tailor ~: **sastrería**
　wine ~: **Weinstube**
shortcut: **atajo**
　~ is the roundabout way:
　　compendia
short, in: **ad summam; bref; kurzum**
shortwave: **onda**
shot, big: **cane grosse**
shoulder: **épaule**
　cold ~: **chasse-cousins**
show
　fine ~ and small return: **belle
　　montre**
　only for ~: **nur zur**
　~ horse: **concours**
　~ off: **frou-frou**
shower, many drops make a: **ψεκαδες
　　(psekádes)**
shrill: **criard**
shrimp: **camarón; crevette; scampi;
　　tempura**
shrine: **châsse; stupa; tope**
shrub
　caper ~: **câpre**
　chamiso ~: **chamisal**
shudder to relate it: **horresco**
shut in: **claquemuré**
sick: **malade**
sickness: **mal; maladie**
side: **parti**
　change ~s: **casaque; tourner**
　on either ~: **ex utraque**
　~step: **louvoyer**
　~walk: **acera; trottoir**
　split one's ~s: **crever**
sigh: **soupir**
　~ from the depths: **suspiria**
　~ing: **sospirando**
sight: **à vue**
　out of ~, out of mind: **absens; aus
　　den Augen; cuan**
sign: **segno**
　from the ~: **dal segno**
　in this ~ thou shalt conquer: **in hoc
　　signo vinces**

lucky ~: **omen faustum**
to the ~: **sino**
under bad ~s: **malis avibus**
under favorable ~s: **bonis avibus**
under this ~ thou shalt conquer:
　　sub hoc
signal for surrender: **chamade**
signature: **firma**
silence: **chup; chut; favete; tace; tacet;
　　tais toi**
　deep ~: **silentium altum**
　~ gives consent: **chi tace accon-
　　sente; quien calla; qui tacet**
　~ is golden for the wise: **yafa**
　~ is praise enough: **tacent**
　~ speaks louder than words: **cum
　　tacent**
silliness: **badauderie**
silly: **niais**
silver: **plata**
silverware: **gin-zaiku**
simmer: **mijoter**
simple: **einfach**
simpleton: **benêt; bêta; fantoccino;
　　gobe-mouches; nigaud**
simplicity
　O sacred ~: **O sancta**
　with ~: **con semplicità**
simply: **semplice**
sin: **peccato**
　I have ~ned: **peccavi**
　unwitting ~: **si peccavi**
sincere: **innig**
sincerely: **ex animo**
sincerity gives wings: **candor**
sinew of things: **nervus rerum**
sing
　~ing: **Gesang**
　~ of loftier things: **paulo**
　~ unto the Lord: **cantate**
　sung by the cantorial side: **cantoris**
　sung by the decanal side: **decani**
　traditional Italian ~ing: **bel canto**
　who ~s chases away troubles: **quem
　　canta; quien canta**
singed: **flambé**
singer: **cantante; chanteuse**
　ballad ~: **Bänkelsänger**
　chief male ~: **primo**
　female ~: **cantatrice**
　male ~: **cantatore**
　principal female ~: **prima**

sirloin: **aloyau**
sister: **frangine; hermana; sestra**
sisterhood in the Netherlands: **béguine**
sister-in-law: **belle-soeur**
skepticism, I detest: **incredulus**
sketch: **croquis; esquisse; schizzo**
~book: **cahier; croquis**
skewer: **brochette**
~ed: **en brochette**
skiff: **sampan**
skiing, zigzag: **slalom**
skill: **Fertigkeit**
skim: **effleurer**
skinflint: **il tondrait**
skirmish: **échauffourée; escarmouche;
   mêlée**
skullcap: **berrettina; calotte; yarmulke**
sky, under the cold: **sub Iove**
slackening: **allentando; rallentando**
slander: **coup**
slang: **langue**
slashed: **fendu**
slate, clean: **tabula**
slaughter: **battue**
slaughterhouse: **matadero**
slave: **servus**
   ~ recently set free: **hesterni**
slayer of infidels: **ghazi**
sled: **luge; pulka**
sleep
   ~ing and waking: **οναρ (ónar)**
   ~ing is as good as eating: **qui dort**
   ~ on it: **in nocte**
   ~ out: **decoucher**
   sup well and ~ well: **chi ben
   twilight ~: **Dämmerschlaf**
sleight of hand: **tour**
slender: **svelte**
slice of fish: **darne**
slip
   ~ of the pen or tongue: **lapsus**
   ~ twixt cup and lip: **πολλα μεταξυ
      (pollà metaxù)**
slipper: **chinela; pantoufle; zapatilla**
slippery: **glissant**
slob: **sagouin; shlump**
slow: **adagio; ahista; langsam**
   rather ~: **adagietto**
   ~er: **più**
   ~ing: **lentando**
   ~ly: **larghetto; lentamente; lento;
      tardamente**
   very ~: **grave; larghissimo; lento**

sluice: **abito**
slur: **coulé; legatura**
slut: **salaud**
sly one: **c'est un fin**
small things befit the small: **parvum**
smelt: **éperlan**
smiles (of the waves): **ανηριθμον
      (anérithmon)**
smoke: **humo**
   in ~: **in fumo**
   no ~ without fire: **kein Rauch**
   no smoking: **défense de fumer**
   ~d: **sfumato**
   where there's ~, there's fire: **flamma**
smooth: **glacé; spianato**
smoothly: **equabilmente; legato**
   very ~: **legatissimo**
smuggler: **contrabandista**
snack: **dim sum; goûter**
snail: **escargot**
snake
   ~ in one's bosom: **colubrem**
   ~ in the grass: **anguis; latet**
   worse than a ~: **cane peius**
snarls at everybody: **il aboie**
sneering at everything: **suspendens**
snipe: **bécassine**
snows of yesteryear: **où sont**
snuffbox: **tabatière**
so
   everywhere ~: **sic passim**
   ~ far as: **quoad**
   ~ I order: **sic iubeo**
   ~ much: **tanto**
   ~ much for this: **sed haec**
   ~ much the better: **tant mieux; um
      so**
   ~ much the worse: **tant pis**
so-called: **sogenannt**
society: **le monde; monde**
   choral ~: **Liederkranz; Liedertafel**
   fashionable ~: **beau monde; bon
      ton; die schöne Welt; élégant;
      gens; le beau**
   high ~: **grand monde; haut monde**
   music ~: **Musikverein**
   well-bred ~: **bonne compagnie**
sock: **tabi**
sofa: **canapé**
soft
   increasing ~ness: **raddolcendo**
   moderately ~: **mezzo**
   ~ly: **dolcemento; doucement; molle-
      mente; piano; sordamente**

very ~ly: **pianissimo**
softening: **ramollissement**
soil
  all ~ fatherland to the brave: **omne solum**
  attached to the ~: **glebae**
sojourn: **séjour**
solace of my toils: **laborum**
soldier: **bashi-bazook; chasseur; gora; poilu; sepoy; soldado**
  boastful ~: **miles**
  ~ and water and fire make room for themselves: **soldato**
  ~ employed as policeman: **gendarme**
solemn: **largo**
sombrero ornament: **chapa**
somebody: **quelqu'un; quidam**
  ~ a nobody: **aliquis**
someplace else is always better: **tam charosho**
something: **aliquid; quelque**
  indescribable ~: **je ne sais quoi**
  ~ foreknown: **praecognitum**
  ~ in return: **quid pro**
  ~ is better than nothing: **besser ein; besser vas; meglio**
  ~ is rotten in Denmark: **Etwas ist; hay un**
  ~ written by the way: **obiter**
  third ~: **tertium**
somewhat: **etwas**
  ~ faster: **wenig**
  ~ hoarse: **fiochetto**
  ~ loud, quick, slower: **poco**
son: **anac; figlio; filho; filius; fils; hijo; sin**
  illegitimate ~: **filius; naturel; nullius filius**
  ~ of heroes: **heroum**
  thou, too, my ~: **και συ (kaì sú)**
sonata, short: **sonatina**
song: **aria; aubade; canzone; carmagnole; carmen; chanson; chansonnette; chant; Lied; mattinata**
  drinking ~: **chanson; Trinklied**
  folk ~: **Volkslied**
  pastoral ~: **ranz**
  ~s without words: **Lieder ohne**
  spring ~: **Frühlingslied**
  swan ~: **chant; le chant**
  watchman's ~: **Wächterlied**
son-in-law: **beau-fils**
soon
  pretty ~: **poco tiempo**

~ as possible: **aufs eheste; quamprimum**
~ enough: **assez tôt**
~ enough if but well enough: **sat cito**
~ ripe ~ rotten: **cito; presto maturo**
sooner: **plus tôt**
soothing: **lusingando**
sorcerer: **mumbo**
sorrel: **oseille**
sorrowful: **lamentando**
sorrowfully: **affanato**
sorrow, path of: **per viam**
sort: **genre**
  all this ~: **hoc genus**
sorting: **triage**
so-so: **comme ci; couci-couci**
soul: **anima; atman**
  base ~: **âme de boue**
  divine ~: **anima**
  feeds his ~: **animum**
  great ~s suffer in silence: **grosse Seelen**
  human ~: **anima**
  lost ~: **âme damnée**
  pray for the ~: **orate pro anima**
  the ~ shudders: **animus meminisse**
  welfare of the ~: **pro salute**
sound: **Klang**
  rattling ~: **râle**
  softened in ~: **mouillé**
  ~ing alike: **idem**
  ~ quality: **Klangfarbe**
  ~ without sense: **vox**
soup: **Bauernsuppe; borshch; bouillabaisse; consommé; garbure; gras; julienne; maigre; minestrone; potage; purée; soupe**
  clear ~: **julienne; potage**
  meat ~: **gras; potage; soupe**
  mulligatawny ~: **soupe**
  onion ~: **purée**
  ox-tail ~: **potage**
  pea ~: **purée**
  turtle ~: **tortue**
  vegetable ~: **soupe**
source: **provenance**
  ~ and origin: **fons et**
South America: **la América del Sur**
sovereignty
  before the sovereign: **coram**
  ~ within a ~: **imperium in**
Soviet, Supreme: **verchovnoi**

spade
  call a ~ a ~: **appeler les choses; appeler un chat; das Ding; llamar; pâo pâo; τα σνκα (tà sûka)**
Spaniard: **español**
spare me: **parce**
spark
  small ~ large flame: **poca favilla**
  ~ling: **scintillante**
sparrow in hand: **ein Sperling**
speaking
  he speaks: **loquitur**
  I have spoken: **dixi**
  so to speak: **pour ainsi**
  Spanish spoken: **se habla**
  ~ without thinking: **hablar**
  ~ words of good omen: **dicamus**
  speaks for itself: **res**
  speak thoughtlessly: **parler à**
  speak well but speak little: **parla**
  usage in ~: **usus loquendi**
  who speaks too much: **chi parla**
spear: **assegai**
species: **Geschlect**
  lowest ~: **infima**
speckled: **truité**
specks before the eyes: **muscae**
speculation: **à forfait**
  successful ~: **coup**
speech: **langage**
  end ~: **orationem**
  incoherent ~: **arena sine**
  ~ is bolder than deed: **stets**
  ~ is silver, silence gold: **Reden**
  telling ~: **oratio gravis**
  well-turned ~: **ore rotundo**
speed: **jaldi**
  a little faster: **ein wenig**
  as fast as one's legs can carry one: **à toutes jambes**
  faster: **accelerando**
  full ~: **à fond; a toda; fuerza; ventre**
spendthrift: **bourreau; panier percé**
spice: **épice**
spikes: **chevaux-de-frise**
spinach: **épinard**
spinster: **femme**
spirit: **djinn; esprit; Geist; spirito; spiritus**
  ancestral ~: **lar**
  and with thy ~: **et cum**
  animating ~: **esprit**
  high ~s: **fort en**

particle of divine ~: **divinae**
party ~: **esprit; parti**
~ed and not dull: **excitari**
~less: **sans**
~ of the forest: **nat**
~ of the universe: **anima**
~ that always denies: **ich bin der**
with ~: **con spirito; spiritoso**
spiritual: **geistig; spirituel**
spit: **broche**
  cooked on a ~: **à la broche**
spite: **dépit; par dépit**
  in ~ of us: **malgré nous**
  no fun where ~: **non est iocus**
splendor: **éclat**
spoiled: **gâté**
spoils, richest: **spolia**
spontaneously: **de proprio; proprio motu**
sportsman: **shikari**
spot: **tache**
  blind ~: **punctum**
  touch a sore ~: **tangere**
spree, go on a: **faire la noce**
spring (season): **ojo; rabi**
spring (water): **fontein**
spy: **mata hari**
spying: **espionnage**
squad: **escouade**
squadron: **escadrille**
squandered: **gaspillé**
square: **place**
  open ~: **piazza**
  public ~: **agora; piazza; plaza**
squash: **calabazilla; courge**
squid: **calamaro; seppia**
squire, country: **gentilhomme**
squirrel: **ardilla**
staff: **état-major**
  medical ~: **corps; santé**
stagecoach: **diligence**
stage, on the: **en scène**
stainless: **sans**
staircase: **escalier**
stale: **fade**
stamp, postage: **Briefmarke; timbre-poste**
stand
  I ~ firm: **praesto**
  I ~ on the side of God: **numini**
  let it ~: **stet**
  ornamental ~: **étagère**
  ~ up: **auf**
  who ~eth take heed lest he fall:

qui stat

stanza
  last ~: **envoi**
  ~ of eight lines and three rhymes:
    ottava rima
star: **estrella; étoile**
  ~ of the north: **étoile; l'étoile**
  ~s my camp, God my light: **astra
    castra**
  to the ~s: **ad astra**
  under the ~s: **à la belle**
starfish: **étoile**
starts: **élan; par élans**
state: **estado; respublica**
  I am the ~: **l'état**
  most corrupt ~ has most laws:
    corruptissima
  same ~ as before: **in statu quo**
statement: **communiqué**
  I withdraw this ~: **hoc indictum**
statesman: **homme**
station
  emergency ~: **poste de**
  police ~: **chauki**
  ~ master: **chef de gare; gare**
stationer: **papetier**
stationery, box of: **papeterie**
steadfast
  ~ and faithful: **tenax et**
  we'll carry on: **nous maintiendrons**
steak: **entrecôte**
steal
  ~ the pig, give away the feet: **hurtar
    el**
  ~ to give to God: **hurtar para**
stealthily: **à la dérobée; à l'échappée**
steamship: **Dampfboot; kisen; paque-
    bot; stoomboot**
step
  dangerous ~: **glissant**
  first ~: **le premier pas**
  first ~ costs: **c'est le premier; ce
    n'est que; il n'y a que**
  not with equal ~s: **non passibus**
  ~ by ~: **per gradus**
  ~ by ~ goes far: **pas; paso a**
  ~ to Parnassus: **gradus ad**
  unequal ~s: **haud passibus**
stern: **raide**
stew: **daube; étuvée; miroton; pot-au-
    feu**
  fish ~: **matelote**
  lamb ~: **navarin**
  rabbit ~: **gibelotte; Hasenpfeffer**

steward, head: **maître**
stick: **bâton**
  heavy ~: **lathi**
stiff: **empesé; guindé**
stiffening of body after death: **rigor
    mortis**
stirrup
  ~ guard: **tapadera**
  ~ strap: **legadero**
stitched: **broché**
stockholder: **rentier**
stock market, bull: **haussier**
stomach when empty seldom scorns
    food: **ieiunus**
stone: **lapis; piedra**
  leave no ~ unturned: κινειν (ki-
    neîn); **omne movere**
  mosaic ~: **pietra dura**
  philosophers' ~: **lapis; le grand
    oeuvre**
  precious ~: **cabochon**
  rolling ~ gathers no moss: **pietra
    mossa**
  split a ~: **à pierre**
stop: **arrêtez; fermatevi; gemach;
    halte-là; parada**
  ~ thief: **au voleur**
  ~ traveler: **siste; sta, viator**
stoppage: **relaxe**
store: **estanco; magasin**
  department ~: **magasin**
  grocery ~: **bodega**
  pork ~: **charcuterie**
  ~house: **étape**
  tobacco ~: **estanco**
storm and stress: **Sturm**
story: **étage**
  an old ~: **connu**
  improper ~: **grivois**
  ~teller: **raconteur**
  tell stories: **conter**
  the ~ applies to you: **de te fabula;
    mutato nomine de; quid rides**
stove: **poêle**
straggler: **traînard**
straightforward: **détour; sans**
straight on: **gerade**
strait: **stretto**
stranger: **Fremd; Fremmed; hospes**
strap, saddle: **látigo**
strawberry: **fraise**
straw, not worth a: **cio non**
stream
  troubled ~ is fisherman's gain: **fiume**

street: **calle; rue; strada; Strasse**
strength: **vis**
  acquires ~ as it advances: **vires**
  stands by his own ~: **suis stat**
  ~ and arms: **vi et**
  ~ through joy: **Kraft**
  unequal military ~: **impari**
  with united ~: **viribus**
  you may break, not bend me:
      frangas
stretcher: **brancard**
  ~ bearer: **brancardier**
stride
  giant ~: **à pas**
  great ~s: **à grands pas**
strife begets strife: **lis litem**
strike
  ~ but hear me: παταξον (pátaxon);
      verbera
  ~ while the iron is hot: **battre**
string: **corda**
  one ~: **una corda**
  three ~s: **tre corde**
  treble ~: **chanterelle**
strive hard: **piquer**
striving: **certamina; nisus**
stroke: **coup**
  master ~: **coup**
strong: **kräftig**
  ~ vinegar from sweet wine: **forte**
stronghold: **place**
struggle: **vuelta**
stubborn: **opinionâtre**
stubbornness: **entêtement**
student: **élève**
  ~ of art: **rapin**
  university ~ group: **Burschenschaft**
studies
  change ~: **abeunt**
  honorable ~: **studiis**
  ~ make mortal virtues immortal:
      quelli
studio: **atelier**
study: **étude**
stuff, same old: **cantilenam**
stupid: **bête**
stupidity: **balourdise**
  with ~ the gods contend: **mit der**
style: **façon; ton**
  American ~: **à l'américaine**
  ancient ~: **nello**
  church ~: **da cappella**
  Dutch ~: **à la hollandaise**
  English ~: **à l'anglaise**

flowing melodic ~: **cantabile**
free ~: **capriccioso**
French ~: **à la française**
grand ~: **grandioso**
Greek ~: **à la grecque**
hunting ~: **alla caccia**
in grand ~: **en grand**
Irish ~: **à l'irlandaise**
Italian ~: **à l'italienne**
Louis XIII ~: **Louis Treize**
Louis XIV ~: **Louis Quatorze**
Louis XV ~: **Louis Quinze**
Louis XVI ~: **Louis Seize**
military ~: **à la militaire**
Parisian ~: **à la parisienne**
Russian ~: **à la russe**
self-~d: **soi-disant**
Spanish ~: **à l'espagnole**
Spanish singing ~: **cante**
Swedish ~: **à la suédoise**
terse ~: **un style**
the ~ is the man: **le style**
Viennese ~: **à la viennoise**
stylish: **chic**
subdivision: **morcellement**
  territorial ~: **guberniya**
subject: **soggetto; sujet; tema**
sublime to the ridiculous: **du sublime**
submarine: **Unterseeboot**
subscription: **abonnement**
substantially: **en effet**
substitute: **badli; locum**
suburb: **afueras; banlieue; faubourg**
succeed: **faire son**
success
  ~ comes to him: **alcança**
  ~ of esteem: **succès**
such
  ~ as from the beginning: **qualis ab**
  ~ as it is: **talis**
  ~ is our pleasure: **tel est**
  ~ is the way to fame: **sic iter**
suddenly: **subitamente; tout à coup**
sufferings are lessons: παθηματα
      (pathémata)
sugar: **azúcar; sucre**
sugarberry: **bois**
suicide: **felo-de-se**
suit: **ad sectam**
  for the ~: **ad litem**
  in his own ~: **in propria causa**
  pending ~: **pendente lite**
  ~ to recover damages: **assumpsit**
suitable for use with meat and dairy:

pareve
sum
~ of all things: **summa summarum**
~ up: **en résumé**
summarily: **acervatim**
summary: **précis; résumé**
summer: **été**
in the height of ~: **en plein**
it won't always be ~: **non semper erit**
one swallow does not make a ~: **une fois**
sumptuous: **de luxe**
sun
in the ~: **au soleil**
~ after clouds: **post nubila**
~ seen for the last time: **je m'en vais voir**
~ shines on everybody: **et sceleratis; sol lucet**
who dares call the ~ a liar: **solem**
with undazzled eye to the ~: **illaeso**
sunstroke: **coup; un coup de soleil**
superfluous: **übermassig**
superior must answer: **respondeat**
superman: **Übermensch**
superstition: **Aberglaube**
supper: **Abendessen; ceia; cena; petit; souper; úzhin**
supplement: **Beiblatt**
supplementary: **ripieno**
support: **appui**
point of ~: **point d'appui**
supported: **appoggiato**
sure, I'm not: **je ne sais trop**
surface
on a level ~: **in plano**
prepared ~: **gesso**
surfeited: **blasé**
surprise
greatly ~d: **tombé**
surprisingly: **mirum**
surrender: **baisser le pavillon; ergebet**
~ of goods: **cessio**
surroundings: **alentours**
survival
I survived: **j'ai vécu**
tossed by waves but does not sink: **fluctuat**
survivors: **hibakusha**
suspicion: **soupçon**
sustained: **continuato; portato; sostenuto; tenuto**

swamp: **ciénaga; pantano**
swashbuckler: **sabreur**
swear to the words of the master: **iurare**
sweater: **chandail; tricot**
sweep before one's own door: **jeder fege**
sweeper: **mehtar**
sweet: **dolce**
what is useful is ~: **dulce quod**
sweetbread: **ris de**
sweetheart: **bon ami; sudarka; Süsschen**
sweetly: **amabile; soavemente**
sweetmeat, crisp: **croque-en-bouche**
sweetness: **douceur**
with ~: **con dolcezza**
swimming: **nage**
swindle: **escroquerie**
swindler: **chevalier d'industrie; fripon**
swindling: **estafa**
swine: **Schweinehund**
swish: **frou-frou**
Swiss: **suisse**
no money, no ~: **kein Kreuzer**
sword: **espada; estoque; katana; Schläger**
by the ~ seeks repose: **ense petit**
~ and plow: **ense et**
swordsman: **homme**
syllogism: **modus**
symphony: **sinfonia**
symptom: **indicium**
synthetic: **Ersatz**
syphilis: **lues**
syrup: **jarabe**

table: **table**
tacitly: **ex tacito**
tact: **savoir-faire; Zartgefühl**
tactless: **gauche**
tail: **queue**
tailor: **tailleur**
~ retailored: **Sartor**
tainted: **hasardé**
taint, slight: **haut goût**
take
~ whichever you prefer: **utrum**
~ who can: **capiat**
tale: **conte; fabliau**
folk ~: **Märchen**
old wives' ~: **aniles; conte**
talent
~ develops: **es bildet**

~ for teaching: **Lehrgabe**
talk: **bát**
  great flow of ~: **copia fandi**
talker: **causeur; diseur**
  idle ~: **diseur**
talking, insatiable need for: **studium**
tall: **lamba**
tan: **beige**
tandem: **flèche**
tank: **depósito; Panzer** (weapon)
tapping: **tapotement**
tarragon: **à l'estragon**
tart, crisp: **croquante**
task: **opus; ouvrage; tâche**
taste: **ad gustum; friandise; goût**
  bad ~: **mauvais**
  good ~: **bon goût**
  more ~ful than costly: **plus salis**
  no accounting for ~: **tutti i**
  no disputing ~: **al ta'am; de gustibus**
  refined ~: **goût**
  ~fully: **con gusto; gustosamente**
taunt: **coup**
tavern: **bodega**
  ~ owner: **cabaretier**
tax: **Steuer**
tea: **cha; maté**
  afternoon ~: **Vesperbrot**
teach
  learn through ~ing: **discere**
  ~ that you may learn: **doce ut**
  who ~es learns: **qui docet**
  you ~ old men: **ante barbam**
teacher: **Privatdozent; Sopherim**
  religious ~: **murshid**
tearful: **larmoyant**
tearfully: **lagrimoso**
tearless: **δακρυ (dákru')**
tears: **fondre**
  hence these ~: **hinc illae**
  sparkling eyes bedewed with ~: **lacrimis**
  ~ for suffering: **sunt lacrimae**
  ~ in one's eyes: **les larmes**
  ~ of things: **lacrimae**
telegram: **petit-bleu**
tell
  ~ before they ~: **antes de**
  ~ it to your grandmother: **cuénta-selo; das kannst; raccontalo; raconte**
  ~ me: **fac ut**
  ~ me in good faith: **dic bona**

telling
  ~ as it was told to me: **relata**
  ~ a thing incredible: **io dirò**
temperature, room: **chambré**
temper, control: **compesce**
temple: **devalaya; miya; tera; thakurdwara**
tempo
  slower ~: **ritardando**
  with the ~: **colla parte**
temporarily: **pro tempore**
tenant
  ~ farmer: **fermier**
  ~ farming: **fermage**
tender: **zart**
  made ~: **mortifié**
  ~ly: **affettuoso; teneramente**
  ~ness: **carità; tenerezza**
tenor: **tenore**
  comic ~: **tenore**
  light ~: **tenore**
tension
  ~ followed by relaxation: **neque**
  ~ of strings: **incordamento**
tent: **kibitka; shamianah; tepee; tienda; toldo; yurt**
  ~ walls: **kanat**
terms
  I accept the ~: **hac mercede**
  in plain ~: **en bon**
terror everywhere: **horror**
terseness is needed: **est brevitate**
test, crucial: **experimentum**
testing: **essayage**
test tube: **éprouvette**
text
  German ~: **Fraktur**
  received ~: **textus**
thank
  give ~s: **grateas agere**
  many ~s: **grand merci**
  ~ you: **arigato; blagodar'woo vas; danke; gracias; grazie; ich danke; laringrazio; mahalo; merci; obrigado; remerciement; salamat; spasiba; tack; tak; takk; toda; ukehé**
thankful: **blagodarnee**
that
  ~ depends: **c'est selon; selon**
  ~ is: **das ist; id est**
  ~ is to say: **c'est-à-dire; das heisst**
  ~'s all: **cetera desunt; voilà**
  ~'s another thing: **voilà**

~'s easy enough: **das ist keine**
~'s enough: **ohe**
~'s impossible: **eta vazmozhna**
~'s just it: **c'est bien ça**
~'s splendid: **das ist eine**
~'s too bad: **das ist aber**
~'s war: **c'est la guerre**
~ which I beheld: **ciò ch'io**
~ which is seemly: **το πρεπον (tò prépon)**
~ will do: **das tut's**
~ will never do: **das geht**
theater: **comédie; teatro**
 ~ box: **baignoire**
theatrical company: **corps**
Thee therefore: **Te Igitur**
theme: **motif**
 leading ~: **Leitmotif**
themselves, among: **inter**
there and back: **hin und zurück**
therefore: **ergo**
thicket: **chaparral**
thief: **chor; homo; trium; voleur**
 set a ~ to catch a ~: **à corsaire; à fripon**
 thieves quarrel and thefts discovered: **pelean**
thigh: **cuisse**
thing
 a ~ belonging to others: **res**
 a ~ in itself: **Ding an**
 better ~s: **ad meliora**
 intangible ~s: **res**
 in the nature of ~s: **in rerum**
 latest ~: **dernier cri**
 like and dislike the same ~s: **idem velle**
 many ~s wanting: **desunt multa**
 noteworthy ~s: **bona**
 not many ~s but much: **non multa**
 one ~ needs another: **alterum alterius**
 one ~ with another: **du fort**
 other ~s besides: **und**
 other ~s equal: **ceteris**
 secondhand ~s: **objets**
 seek higher ~s: **altiora peto**
 some good ~s and some middling and more bad: **sunt bona**
 take ~s as they come: **à la guerre**
 tangible ~: **res**
 the ~ defined: **definitum**
 ~s come to those who wait: **die Zeit**
 ~s lost are safe: **quae amissa**

~s that injure instruct: **quae nocent**
~s to be altered: **mutanda**
~s to be read: **legenda**
~s used in moderation endure: **moderata**
~s worth remembering: **memorabilia**
~ that pleases is half sold: **chose qui**
~ to be observed: **observandum**
think
 I ~ I can: **posse videor**
 I ~ therefore I am: **cogito**
 ~ much, speak little, write less: **pensa**
 ~ of me: **pensez**
 ~ with few and speak with many: **sentir**
this
 do ~: **hoc age**
 look for ~: **hoc quaere**
 without ~: **absque**
thong: **babiche**
thoroughbred: **pur sang**
thoroughfare: **corso**
 no ~: **hier geht**
thoroughly: **à fond**
thought: **pensée**
 crowding ~s: **multa acervatim**
thousand: **per mille**
 hundred ~: **lac**
thread: **filum**
threat, empty: **fulmen**
threateningly: **minacciando**
three
 ~ in one: **tria**
 ~ year period: **triennium**
threshold, on the: **in limine**
throat, pronounced in the: **grasseyé**
throne: **guddee; musnud**
throng, venal: **grex**
throwing
 silk ~: **moulinage**
 throw handle after hatchet: **echar el; jeter le manche**
thrush: **sat-bhai**
thrust home: **coup**
thug: **goon; thag**
thumbs down: **pollice**
thunder: **Donner; odotsa**
thunderation: **Donner**
thunderbolt: **brutum; coup**
 ~ snatched from heaven: **eripuit**
thus
 if all things were ~: **O si sic**
 ~ do they all: **così fan**

~ go men's destinies: **sic eunt**
~ in as many words: **sic totidem**
~ in the original: **sic in**
~ I will and ~ I command: **sic volo**
~ until: **sic donec**
thyself, know: γνωθι (**gnôthi**); **nosce te**
tidbit: **bonne bouche; bouche**
tide, row against the: **remar**
tiger: **bagh; sher**
~ by the tail: **lupum**
time: **hoc tempore; tempo; tempus**
accelerated ~: **stringendo**
a good ~ coming: **le bon temps**
all in good ~: **cela viendra**
always the right ~: **è sempre**
appointed ~: **à point**
bide ~: **boiteux**
correct ~: **tempo**
dance ~: **tempo**
favorable ~s: **mollia**
from ~ to ~: **de temps**
give things ~: **dà tempo**
happier ~: **melioribus**
in a short ~: **en poco**
in exact ~: **giusto**
in ~: **à point; a tempo**
know thy ~: **nosce tempus**
loss of ~: **dispendia**
march ~: **tempo**
minuet ~: **tempo**
moderate ~: **tempo**
moderately brisk ~: **allegretto**
moderately slow ~: **andante**
nick of ~: **cela arrive**
not too quick ~: **allegro**
oh that I had ~: **que n'ai-je**
one must move with the ~s: **tempori**
other ~s: **autres temps**
past ~s: **tempi**
present ~: **actualmente**
quick ~: **alla breve**
right ~: **dextro; iusto**
second ~: **seconda; volta**
stolen ~: **tempo**
strict ~: **a battuta**
take ~ by the forelock: **prendre la balle**
the good ~ comes but once: **il tempo**
three ~s: **ter**
~ after which an event must have occurred: **terminus post**
~ before which an event must have occurred: **terminus ante**

~ devourer of all things: **tempus**
~ flies: **fugit irreparabile; tempus; volat hora**
~ for play: **tempus**
~ having elapsed: **elapso**
~ is flying while I speak: **dum loquor**
~ is gold: **el tiempo es**
~ is of the essence: **tempus**
~ is sovereign over all: **tempus**
~ never hangs heavy: **ein Gelehrter**
~ of war: **inter**
~ reveals all things: **tempus**
~ reveals the truth: **veritatem**
~ runs and everything runs after it: **el tiempo corre**
~s are changed: **tempora**
~s most favorable for speaking: **mollissima**
~ speeds away: **dum loquimur**
to pass ~: **pour passer**
until another ~: **hasta otra**
what ~ is it: **qué hora; que horas; Uhr**
timid: **timoroso**
who asks ~ly courts denial: **qui timide**
tin: **estaño**
tinderbox: **briquet**
tint, rose: **couleur; rose du**
tipsy: **im Rausche**
tit for tat: **à bon chat; par pari; render; tal para; taz; Wurst**
title
Japanese ~: **sama**
Turkish ~ of honor: **pasha**
under this ~: **hoc titulo**
toast: **croûte**
cube of ~: **croûton**
toastmaster: **arbiter bibendi**
to a T: **ad unguem;** εις ουυχα (**eis ónykha**)
tobacco: **tabac**
today
~ not tomorrow: **hodie, non cras**
~'s: **du jour**
two weeks from ~: **d'aujourd'hui en quinze**
toga, man's: **toga virilis**
together: **ensemble**
toggle: **netsuke**
toilet
public ~: **chalet**
~s: **cabine**

toll: **Zoll**
tomb: **mastaba**
tomorrow: **apopo; mañana**
 another day ~: **mañana**
 till ~: **hasta mañana**
 to be taken ~: **cras mane**
 ~ but never today: **morgen**
 ~ we'll believe: **cras credemus**
tone
 medium fullness of ~: **mezzo**
 prolong a ~: **filar**
 subdued ~: **a mezzo**
 ~s in rapid succession: **arpeggio**
tongue: **langue**
 an ox on the ~: **bos**
 evil ~s: **a malas**
 hold your ~: **chup**
 hold your ~ and pass for a philosopher: **sile et**
 mother ~: **langue; mamaloshen**
 ~ lashings: **linguae**
ton, metric: **millier**
toolbox: **nécessaire**
tooth
 ~ache: **mal**
 ~ and nail: **unguibus**
 ~pick: **cure-dent**
 with disdainful ~: **dente superbo**
top: **cumbre**
 from the ~: **von oben**
 ~ to bottom: **de fond; de haut en**
topsy-turvy: **bouleversé; darunter; sens**
tormenter, self-: **Heauton**
torrent: **fiumara**
torture: **mettre à**
touch
 ~ed nothing he did not adorn: **nihil**
 ~ me not: **noli me**
town: **municipio; Stadt**
 skip ~: **filer**
towpath: **camino**
towrope: **cordelle**
traces: **vestigia**
track: **piste**
tracker: **pugi**
trade
 coasting ~: **cabotage**
 free ~: **Freihandel**
 jack of all ~s: **homme; maître**
trademark: **marque**
tradesman: **petit**
 every ~ praises his own wares: **jeder**
  Krämer
 prosperous ~: **bourgeois**

train: **Luxuszug**
 early ~: **Frühzug**
 special ~: **train**
 through ~: **Durchgangszug**
tramp: **pied; trôleur**
trance: **samadhi**
tranquility in virtue: **virtute quies**
tranquilly: **tranquillamente**
transactions: **res**
transition: **Überleitung**
translation: **traduction**
translator: **traducteur**
 ~s are traitors: **traduttori**
transplant
 who ~ed sustains: **qui transtulit**
transport: **dak**
trap: **panneau; piège; sal si**
 caught in one's own ~: **arte perire**
trapper: **coureur**
traveler: **viajero; voyageur**
 ~s lie: **à beau mentir**
 ~ with empty purse: **vacuus**
 weary ~: **fessus**
treachery: **fides Punica; Punica**
treason, high: **crimen; laesa; lèse-**
  majesté
treasure
 where your ~, there your heart:
  οπον γαρ (**hópou gár**)
treatise: **Abhandlung**
tree
 a shoot becomes a ~: **tandem**
 a ~ does not fall at one blow:
  l'arbre
 do you know where lemon ~s
  bloom: **kennst**
 dwarf ~: **bonsai**
 fern ~: **amau**
 knockaway ~: **anaqua**
 like fruit ~s: **de tal**
 linden ~: **bois**
 mahogany ~: **caoba**
 olive ~: **aceituno**
 poplar ~: **alamo**
 South American ~: **chicha**
 spruce ~: **abeto; épinette**
 striped maple ~: **bois**
 sycamore ~: **bois**
 ~less area in arctic regions: **tundra**
 walnut ~: **noyer**
tremulously: **tremando**
trench: **boyau; tajo; tranchée**
trial
 during the ~: **lite pendente**

~ by ordeal: **Dei iudicium**
tribunal: **Vehmgericht**
trick: **inganno; Ulk**
  dirty ~: **vacherie**
  knavish ~: **tour; un tour**
  play ~s: **faire des siennes; faire le
    diable**
  stage ~: **coup; jeu**
  under fair words lies a ~: **debaixo**
tricolor: **drapeau**
trifle: **lana; peu de chose**
  add weight to ~s: **nugis addere**
  armed with ~s: **nugis armatus**
  greatest in ~s: **maximus**
  laborious ~s: **difficiles nugae**
  melodious ~s: **nugae**
  ~s are not to be despised: **inest sua**
  ~s lead to evils: **hae nugae**
trill: **gorgheggio; Pralltriller; roulade**
trinket: **bibelot; bijouterie; breloque**
trio: **terzetto**
tripe and beef: **rolpens**
triumph sung before victory: **ante
    victoriam**
trivial: **trivial**
trouble: **embarras**
  taking useless ~: **uma**
  you're in ~: **voilà**
troublesome: **fâcheux**
trousers: **mompe; shintiyan**
trout: **truite**
Troy
  Trojan and Tyrian treated alike: **Tros**
  ~'s day is over: **fuit Ilium; Troia**
  where once was ~: **et campos**
truant, play: **faire l'école**
truce: **trêve; Waffenstillstand**
truck: **autocamión; camion**
trudge about: **battre**
true
  if not ~ then well imagined: **se non
    è**
  isn't it ~: **n'est-ce; n'è vero; nicht
    wahr; no es verdad; non è vero;
    verdad**
  it can't be ~: **ne mozhet**
  it's too ~: **è pur**
  ~ and becoming: **quid verum**
  ~ because impossible: **certum est**
  ~ till death: **fidelis**

truffle: **truffe**
truly: **en vérité**
trumpet: **tromba**
trunk: **tige**
trust
  implicit ~: **uberrima**
  in ~: **in commendam**
  I ~: **confido; cruce; je me fie; vir-
    tuti non**
  ~ but take care whom: **fide sed**
  ~ geese with the lettuce: **dare in**
  ~ in the Lord: **in te**
trustee: **curateur**
truth: **pravda; verdad; veritas;
    Wahrheit**
  abiding nature of ~: **Schein**
  in following the ~: **en suivant**
  in ~: **re vera**
  let ~ be between us: **zwischen uns**
  metaphysical ~: **veritas**
  naked ~: **nuda veritas**
  not always good to tell the ~: **ogni
    vero**
  promptness and ~: **celeritas**
  risk one's life for ~: **vitam**
  sometimes a virtue to conceal ~:
    qualche
  stick to the ~: **tiens à la**
  thousand probabilities do not make
    one ~: **mille**
  ~ and poetry: **Wahrheit**
  ~ begets hatred: **veritas**
  ~ conquers: **veritas; vincit omnia;
    vincit veritas**
  ~ from children and fools: **locos**
  ~ in spite of friend and foe:
    Wahrheit
  ~ in wine: **εν οινω (en oíno); in
    vino**
  ~ is green: **verdad**
  ~ is lost in too much debating: **per
    troppo**
  ~ is mighty: **magna est veritas**
  ~ is stranger than fiction: **le vrai**
  ~ is the daughter of time: **la verità;
    veritas**
  ~ never dies: **veritas**
  ~ of a symbol: **veritas**
  ~ out of the mouths of children: **la
    vérité**
  ~ shall make you free: **η αληθια
    (hē aléthia)**
  ~ will prevail: **veritas**
  ~ without fear: **vérité**

what prevents speaking the ~:
  ridentem
where the ~ is, there is God: **donde
  está**
tuba: **corno**
tumult: **cohue**
tuna: **thon**
tune
  intentional irregular tuning:
    scordatura
  out of ~: **unrein; verstimmt**
  put out of ~: **scordato**
turban: **puggree**
turkey
  stewed ~ hen: **dinde**
  tom ~: **coq; dindon**
  ~ hen: **dinde**
turn: **gruppetto; tour; verte; volta;
  vuelta**
  at every ~: **à tout propos**
  cooked to a ~: **à point**
  good ~: **à beau jeu**
  my ~ today and yours tomorrow:
    heute mir; hodie mihi
  my ~ tomorrow: **cras mihi**
  ~ over: **volti**
  ~ed: **bloqué**
  ~ed up: **retroussé**
  ~ing up his nose at everything: **om-
    nia suspendens**
  your ~: **à vous**
  your ~ to deal: **c'est à vous à
    donner**
  your ~ to speak: **c'est à vous à
    parler**
turnip: **navet**
turret: **tourelle**
turtle, mock: **fausse**
tutor: **Docent; Repetent**
twaddle: **babillage; barbouillage;
  Quatsch**
twice: **bis; due; volta**
  ~ as fast: **doppio**
  ~ as much: **alterum tantum**
twig, bent: **adeo in teneris**
twilight: **demi-jour; entre chien; inter**
twin: **jumelle**
twine: **ficelle**
two: **due**
  for ~: **à deux**
  ~ just alike: **par nobile**
type, printing: **Brotschrift**
tyrant
  ever thus to ~s: **sic semper**

every weakling has his ~: **ogni
  debolo**
~s make rebels: **i tiranni**

ultraradicalism: **intransigeance**
umbrella: **en-tout-cas**
unaccommodating: **désobligeant**
unanimously: **nemine contradicente;
  per totam; una voce; uno animo**
unawares: **au dépourvu**
unceasing: **ostinato**
unchanging: **sans**
unconcern: **sans**
unconstrained: **dégagé; negligentemente; sans**
undated: **sine**
underbrush: **maleza**
understand: **subaudi**
  I don't ~: **non capisco; non intendo**
  I ~ you: **vi capisco**
undertone: **sotto**
underwear, women's: **lingerie**
undeveloped: **in ovo**
undressed: **déshabillé; en déshabillé**
uneasiness: **malaise**
unemployment: **chômage**
unexpectedly: **à l'improviste**
unforeseen: **imprevisto; unverhofft**
uniformly: **aequabiliter**
union: **Anschluss**
  ~ is strength: **iuncta; l'union; vis**
unique: **sui generis**
united: **coniunctis**
  U~ States: **estado; los Estados;
    Vereinigte**
unit, reserve: **corps**
unity in essential things: **in necessarius**
universe: **το ολον (tò hólon)**
university: **Universität**
unknown: **ignotus; inconnu; l'inconnu**
  ~ explained by the still more ~:
    ignotum
unmarried, while: **dum sola**
unnamed: **sine**
unpleasantness: **désagrément**
unprejudiced: **sine**
unprepared: **illotis**
unproven: **non liquet**
unpublished: **inédit; inedita**
  ~ until the ninth year: **nonum(que)**

unreservedly: **à coeur ouvert**
unrestrained: **la bride**
unsaid, be it: **indictum**
unsolicited: **sponte**
unsuccessful: **manqué**
untruthful for good purpose:
    splendide
unusual: **bizarre; insolite; rara**
unwelcome: **de trop**
unwillingly: **ab invito**
upon: **dessus**
upriver: **rio; río**
uproar: **diable; tapage**
upstart: **homme; neue Menschen;**
    parvenu
upstroke: **poussé**
up-to-date: **aggiornamento; être à jour**
upturned: **cabré**
urn: **samovar; urceus**
usage
  bad ~: **ex malis**
  ordinary ~: **ius**
use
  in ~: **in usu**
  to everything its own ~: **sua cuique**
    utilitas
  ~ is second nature: **qui a bu**
  what is the ~: **à quoi bon; shikata;**
    wozu dient
useful with the agreeable: **omne tulit;**
    utile
usual: **à l'ordinaire; al solito; more;**
    wie gewöhnlich
utmost, to the: **à outrance**

vacuum, in a: **in vacuo; vacuo**
vain, in: **en pure**
valid, universally: **secundum**
valley: **khud; Tal**
  ~ of the abyss: **valle**
valor
  mindful of ~: **pristinae**
  ~ in difficulties: **virtus**
  ~ is soldier's glory: **virtus**
valuable: **de prix**
value: **ad valorem; valuta**
  beyond the ~: **ultra**
  of little ~: **modique**
  sentimental ~: **pretium**
vane, weather: **girouette**
vanguard: **avant-garde**
vanity: **amour propre**
  all is ~: **omnia vanitas**
  ~ of vanities: **vanitas**

vanquished
  spare the ~, subdue the proud:
    parcere
variation: **variazioni**
vase, porcelain: **potiche**
vaulter: **voltigeur**
veal: **veau**
vegetable: **groente**
  ~s, meat, and noodles: **chow mein**
  with spring ~s: **printanier**
vehement: **heftig**
vehemently: **focosamente**
vehicle: **tonga; voiture**
  covered ~: **carromata**
  horse-drawn ~: **char-à-bancs**
veil: **mantón; voile; yashmak**
vein: **vena**
vellum, in: **en vélin**
velvety: **velouté**
venison: **chevreuil; venaison**
  jugged ~: **civet**
veranda: **stoep**
verbatim: **mot**
verse, free: **vers libre**
verve: **panache**
very: **di molto**
vessel: **lota; vas**
  empty ~: **vaso vuoto**
  fishing ~: **chasse-marée**
  porous ~: **alcarraza**
vestments: **pontificalia**
vibratory: **vibrato**
vice
  all have this ~: **omnibus hoc**
  ~ thrives: **alitur**
vicissitudes, through so many: **per tot**
    discrimina
Victim, O saving: **O Salutaris**
victory
  Pyrrhic ~: **Καδμεια (kadmeía)**
  ~ comes in turn to men: **νικη (níkē)**
  ~ is increased by concord: **victoria**
view
  bird's-eye ~: **à vue**
  general ~: **coup**
vigil: **veille**
vigorously: **vigoroso**
villa: **dacha**
village: **aldea; basti; derévnya; Dorf;**
    Dorp; mir; pueblo; stanitza
villager: **aldeano**
vinegar: **vinaigre**
  not catch flies with ~: **on n'attrappe**
vineyard: **viña**

great ~ and few grapes: **muita**
viol: **viola da gamba**
  bass ~: **viola d'amore**
violin: **violino**
Virgil, I have only seen: **Virgilium**
Virgin
  Blessed ~: **Beata; heilig**
  Glorious ~: **La Vergine**
  ~, Bride of the Lord: **Virgo**
  ~ Mary: **Notre Dame; Regina**
  ~ Most Wise: **Virgo**
virtue
  after money, ~: **virtus**
  ancestral ~: **patriis**
  from love of ~: **virtutis amore**
  I wrap myself in ~: **mea virtute**
  ornament and reward of ~: **et decus**
  secure through ~: **virtute securus**
  ~ alone can ennoble: **virtus**
  ~ alone helps: **sola iuvat**
  ~ alone is invincible: **sola virtus**
  ~ alone is nobility: **sola nobilitas**
  ~, always green: **virtus**
  ~ and faith: **virtute et fide; virtute**
    fideque
  ~ and industry: **virtute et labore;**
    virtute et opere
  ~, a thousand shields: **virtus**
  ~ consists in action: **virtus**
  ~ doesn't know the meaning of re-
    laxation: **virtus**
  ~ ennobles: **virtus**
  ~ flourishes from a wound: **virescit**
  ~ flourishes in trial: **virtus**
  ~ grows under oppression: **crescit**
    sub
  ~ increased: **macte**
  ~ is a strong anchor: **valet ancora**
  ~ is praised and left to starve: **virtus**
  ~ is stronger than a battering ram:
    virtus
  ~ is the mark of nobility: **nobilitatis**
    virtus
  ~ is the only nobility: **la vertu**
  ~ is the only thing necessary: **unica**
  ~ is the true nobility: **nobilitas sola**
  ~ is the way of life: **vitae**
  ~ is worth more than silver or gold:
    vilius
  ~ kindles strength: **virtus**
  ~, not craft: **virtute, non astutia**
  ~, not men: **virtute, non viris**
  ~ of authority: **ex auctoritate**
  ~ of office: **ex officio; virtute officii**

  ~ overcomes envy: **virtus**
  ~ rejoices in trial: **gaudet**
  ~s often vices in disguise: **nos vertus**
  ~ survives the grave: **vivit**
visibly: **à vue**
visit, to pay a: **pour faire visite**
vivacity: **brio**
  with ~: **con brio**
voice: **voce; voix; vox**
  chest ~: **petto; voce**
  head ~: **voce**
  mixed ~: **voce**
  powerful ~: **tenore; voce**
  rich ~: **voce**
  slightly obscured ~: **voce**
  strain one's ~: **s'égosiller**
  two ~s: **a due**
  ~ crying in the wilderness: **vox**
  ~ of the people: **vox**
  ~s of women and children: **voce**
  ~ with clear enunciation: **voce**
  with the ~: **colla voce**
volume: **Band**
  folio ~: **in-folio**
  small ~: **Bändchen**
voluntarily: **aus freien; de plein**
vote
  negative ~: **non placet**
  put it to a ~: **aux voix; voix**
voucher: **pièce**
vow, according to one's: **ex voto**
vowel: **Vokal; voyelle**
vulgarity: **langage; mauvais**

waggishness: **espièglerie**
wagon: **araba; telega**
  ammunition ~: **fourgon**
  three-horse ~: **troika**
waistband: **cummerbund**
waiter: **camarero; cameriere; Kellner;**
    khidmutgar; kyuji
walk
  public ~: **paseo**
  take a ~: **pasear; vuelta**
walls
  ~ have ears: **les murailles**
  within the ~: **intra muros**
walnut: **noix**
wanting, thou art found: **tekel**
want of something better: **faute**
wantonly: **de gaieté**
war: **Blitzkrieg; guerre; jihad; Krieg;**
    ultima ratio; voina
  act of ~: **casus**

at ~: **en guerre**
before the ~: **ante bellum**
deadly ~: **bellum lethale**
holy ~: **jihad**
lightning ~: **Blitzkrieg**
magnificent but not ~: **c'est magnifique**
not permitted to blunder twice in ~: **bis peccare**
outbreak of ~: **in limine**
paper ~fare: **guerre**
stratagem of ~: **ruse de**
~ commenced is hell unchained: **guerra cominciata**
~ fosters ~: **der Krieg**
~ game: **Kriegspiel**
~ hidden under peace: **Mars**
~ horse: **cheval**
~ is sweet: **dulce bellum**
~ of all against all: **bellum omnium**
~ of extermination: **bellum internecinum**
~s abominated by mothers: **bellaque**
~s horrid ~s: **bella**
~ tax: **décime**
~ to the death: **guerra a la; guerre**
~ vs. wisdom: **tam Marte**
world ~: **Weltkrieg**
wardrobe: **armoire**
warehouse: **almacén; entrepôt**
warning: **avertissement; in terrorem**
warrant of commitment to prison: **mittimus**
warrior: **berserker; guerrero; impi**
wasteland: **lande**
watch: **Wacht**
I'm ever ~ful: **nunquam dormio**
on ~: **aux aguets**
to the ~ful: **vigilantibus**
~man: **garde**
~tower: **atalaya**
~word: **mot**
water: **acqua; agua; aqua; eau; panee; voda; Wasser**
boiling ~: **aqua**
deep ~: **charco**
distant ~: **acqua**
distilled ~: **aqua**
holy ~: **agua; asperges; eau**
ice ~: **barf**
in deep ~: **en plein**
pure rain~: **aqua**
running ~: **agua; eau**
shallow body of ~: **charca**

spring ~: **aqua; eau**
stagnant ~: **eau**
still ~: **acqua; agua; aqua; del agua; eau**
sweetened ~: **eau**
troubled ~: **agua**
~ carrier: **aguador; bhisti**
~ in a sieve: **cribro**
~ is best: **αριστον (áriston)**
~ saw its God and blushed: **vidit**
~way: **vaguada**
~ well: **cenote**
wonderful ~: **aqua**
you're writing in ~: **in aqua**
watercress: **berro; cresson**
with ~: **aux cressons**
watermelon: **pastèque**
wave: **onda**
long ~: **onda**
tidal ~: **tsunami**
way: **tao; via**
a ~ must be tried: **tentanda**
best ~: **aufs beste**
clear the ~: **gare**
feel one's ~: **aller à tâtons**
find or make a ~: **aut inveniam**
in a friendly ~: **via**
in his own ~: **more**
in whatever ~: **quocunque modo**
no two ~s: **vuelta**
on the ~: **chemin faisant; en route; in transitu**
~ of the world: **l'usage**
we
~ cannot: **non possumus**
~ can't all do all: **non omnia**
~ have been: **fuimus**
weak: **sine**
wealth
little ~ and little care: **peu de bien; poca roba**
lust for ~: **opum**
riches make the man: **divitiae**
who knows how to use ~ should have ~: **qui uti**
weariness: **taedium**
weather
bad ~: **candelia; gros**
what's the ~: **quel temps fait-il; que temps**
what ~ this is: **quel temps il fait**

weaving: **tessitura**
wedge drives wedge: **cuneus**
weeds do not perish: **Unkraut**
week: **septimana**
~ from today: **d'aujourd'hui en huit**
weight: **arroba; peso**
net ~: **peso**
~ not number: **pondere**
welcome: **accueil; ben venuto; bienvenue; faire accueil; salve**
~ home: **ben tornato**
~ misfortune if you come alone:
bien vengas
welfare of the people is the supreme
law: **salus populi**
well: **bien; pozo; wohl**
get ~: **gute Besserung**
may it go ~ with thee: **prosit**
pretty ~: **assez bien**
really ~: **allons**
very ~: **à la bonne; benissimo; bien;
bravissimo**
~ and good: **baste**
well-being: **bene esse**
well-bred: **de bon genre**
werewolf: **loup-garou**
wharf: **embarcadero**
what
he knows ~'s ~: **er hat**
not who but ~: **non quis**
~ do you want: **qué quiere; que
voulez-vous; que vous**
~ever is done for good men: **bonis
quod**
~ God hath joined together: **o ονν o
(ho oûn ho)**
~ I can't praise I don't discuss: **was
ich**
~ I've said I stand by: **lo dicho**
~ I've written, I've written: **quid
scripsi**
~'s going on: **qué pasa**
~'s not necessary is dear at a penny:
quod non
~'s put off is not lost: **ce qui est**
~'s that for: **wozu das**
~'s that to me: **que m'importe**
~'s the news: **nouvelle; quelles; quid
novi**
~'s this: **qu'est-ce que**
~'s to be done: **que faire; quid
faciendum**
~ will be will be: **che sarà**
where: **kidhar**

~ are those who lived before us: **ubi
sunt**
~ have I fallen, what have I done:
ubi lapsus
whetstone for the wits: **cos**
whey: **petit-lait**
which
from ~: **a quo**
of ~: **cuius**
~ is: **quod est**
~ is to be noted: **quod bene**
~ see: **quae vide; quod vide**
~ was to be demonstrated: **quod
erat demonstrandum**
~ was to be done: **quod erat
faciendum**
whim: **boutade; ghiribizzo**
whimsical: **ghiribizzoso**
whip: **azote; chabuk; chicote; knout;
sjambok**
whippoorwill: **bois**
whisper: **vox**
~ing: **sussurrando**
whither: **wohin**
~ thou goest: **quo vadis**
whitish: **blanchâtre**
who
~ as well: **qui tam**
~ benefits by it: **cui bono**
~ is it: **quién es**
whole: **totum**
for the ~: **in solidum**
on the ~: **à tout prendre; au bout
du compte**
wholesale: **en bloc**
why: **kis-waste; pourquoi; warum**
~ not: **warum**
widow: **veuve; viuda; Witwe**
merry ~: **die lustige**
rich ~ weeps with one eye, signals
with other: **viuva**
widower: **veuf; Witwer**
wife: **esposa; Frau; moglie; zhená**
dear ~: **cara sposa**
~ of the doge: **dogaressa**
wig: **perruque**
wild: **cerrero; farouche**
will: **a capriccio; ad arbitrium; à discrétion; à volonté; volonté**
free ~: **liberum**
let ~ stand as a reason: **hoc volo; sit
pro; stet pro**
no ill ~: **absit invidia**
nothing without divine ~: **nil sine**

Deo; nil sine numine
pray for a strong ~: **fortem**
Thy ~ be done: **fiat voluntas**
where there's a ~: **a chi vuole; celui
    qui**
~ and testament: **volonté**
~ of the people: **iure**
~ stands for reason: **stat pro**
~ taken for deed: **voluntas**
with a ~: **entrain**
willing
~ and able: **volens**
~ but unable: **volo non**
~ or unwilling: **bon gré; gré; nolens**
willingly: **con mucho; de bon gré; de
    bonne grâce; de bonne volonté;
    gré; volontieri**
will-o'-the-wisp: **ignis fatuus; Irrlicht**
wily: **rusé**
wind: **Föhn; mistral; sirocco; solano**
device for cutting off ~: **abat-vent**
favorable ~s: **ventis**
ill ~: **é cattivo**
northerly ~: **bise; mistral**
southwest ~: **libeccio**
windfall: **aubaine; bonne fortune;
    trouvaille**
winding: **en caracole**
windmills, tilt against: **se battre**
window: **ventana**
wine: **madère; sharab; vernaccia; vin**
cheap ~: **vin**
even the best ~ has dregs: **le
    meilleur**
good ~: **à bon vin; a buon vino;
    buon vino; bonum vinum**
old ~ and old friend: **vinho**
racked by anger and ~: **vino**
red ~: **barbera; eau**
rice ~: **sake**
~ and woman and song: **Wein, Weib**
~ grower: **vigneron**
~ is the milk of love: **οινος (oînos)**
~ list: **carte**
~ punch: **sangría**
~ without water: **vin**
with ~: **à la bordelaise**
wings larger than the nest: **maiores**
winner, long live the: **viva quien**
winter, in the depth of: **en plein**
wisdom: **sagesse**
dare to show ~: **aude; sapere**
mix folly with ~: **misce stultitiam**
ripe ~: **mitis**

~ and courage: **consilio et animis**
~ and prudence: **consilio et
    prudentia**
~ is easier for others: **il est plus
    aisé**
~ is justified by her works: **και
    εδικαιωθη (kaì edikaióthē)**
~ is the foundation of writing well:
    scribendi
~ is victor over fortune: **victrix**
with how little ~: **quam parva**
wise: **sage**
how grand to be ~: **quanti**
no mortal is always ~: **nemo
    mortalium**
none are ~ by instinct: **φνσει
    (phúsei)**
Phrygians became ~ too late: **sero
    sapiunt**
who lives without folly is not so ~:
    qui vit
~ man will rule the stars: **sapiens**
~r than the ~: **plus sage**
wiseacre: **Klügler**
wish: **meo voto**
as one ~es: **volonté**
having got one's ~: **compos voti**
wit
at ~s' end: **au bout de son; aux
    abois; latin**
keen and delicate ~: **sal**
~s' end: **latin de**
~ without discretion: **ingenio**
witchcraft: **Hexerei**
withered: **flétri**
within: **ab intra**
without: **ab extra; sans; senza; sine**
witness: **assister; in testimonium; té-
    moin; teste**
witticism: **bon mot; jeu**
woe
~ to the solitary man: **vae soli**
~ to the vanquished: **vae victis**
wolf
~ by the ears: **auribus**
~ changes his coat: **lupus pilum**
~ in the fable: **lupus in**
~ on one side: **hac urgent**
~ when famished eats moldy bread:
    lupo
wolverine: **carcajou**
woman: **bibi; femme; mujer; vrouw;
    wahine; zhenshena**
cleaning ~: **femme**

fat ~: **une grosse**
fickle and changeable ~: **Donna;**
    varium
finicky ~: **mijaurée**
gossipy ~: **yenta**
in the dark every ~ is the same:
    λυχνον (**lúkhnou**)
literary ~: **bas bleu; Blaustrumpf**
look for the ~: **cherchez**
market ~: **dames de; poissarde**
married ~: **dueña; femme; madame;**
    memsahib
old ~: **vieille**
pregnant ~: **gros; une femme**
stout ~: **gros**
unappreciated ~: **femme**
unmarried ~: **femme; Fräulein;**
    mademoiselle
virtuous ~: **femme; honnête; sage**
~ beautiful above with a fish's tail:
    desinit
~ chaser: **coureur**
~ is made of glass: **es de vidrio**
~ of dubious character: **demi-**
    mondaine
womb, in the: **in utero; in ventre**
wonderful
    ~ to behold: **mirabile visu**
    ~ to relate: **mirabile dictu**
wood: **bois; cahoy; maram**
wool
    go for ~ and return shorn: **fuése; ir**
    por
    ~ is better than the sheep: **è meglio**
    donar
word: **ad hanc vocem; logos; mot;**
    palabra
common ~: **mot**
exact ~: **le mot juste; mot**
fair ~s cost nothing: **bien hablar**
few ~s: **pocas**
half a ~: **zartem**
in a ~: **pour tout dire; sans**
incorrectly formed ~: **vox**
in so many ~s: **totidem**
many ~s little knowledge: **muito**
mum's the ~: **bouche**
not a ~: **mucke**
no ~s when Minerva's unwilling: **tu**
    nihil
offend in ~s: **intra verba**
sharp ~s: **paroles aigres**
so many ~s: **in totidem**
speak vain ~s: ανεμωλια (**anemólia**)

spoken ~ perishes but writing re-
    mains: **vox**
the very ~s: **ipsissima**
under the ~: **sub voce**
very long ~s: **sesquipedalia**
winged ~s: επεα (**épea**); **geflügelte**
without breaking one's ~: **salva fide**
~ and stone: **palabra**
~ beyond recall: **irrevocabile**
~ for ~: **ad verbum**; κατ' επος (**kat'**
    épos)
~ for ~ and letter for letter:
    verbatim
~ of mouth: **de palabre; ore tenus;**
    palabra
~ once spoken: **et semel; nescit**
~s do not feed cats: **belle parole**
~s that burn: **ardentia verba**
~s to blows: **a verbis; verbis**
~ to the wise: **dictum sapienti;**
    verbum
work: **kam; rabota; trabajo; Werk**
goldsmith's ~: **orfèvrerie**
in the ~ quoted: **opere citato**
overwhelmed with ~: **écrasé de**
rock ~: **rocaille**
this ~, this pursuit: **hoc opus, hoc**
~ is carried on briskly: **fervet opus**
~ is pleasure: **labor ipse**
~ is the best sauce: **optimum**
~ is worship: **laborare**
~ is worth doing: **operae pretium**
~ of art or literature: **oeuvre**
~ prospers: **adiuvante Deo**
~ so vast: **tantae**
~ stoppage: **hartal**
~ together: **gung ho**
you do the ~: **sic vos**
worker: **rabotnik**
outstanding ~: **stakhanovite**
piece ~: **tâcheron**
~s of the world, unite: **proletaree**
workman: **ouvrier**
~ is known by his work: **opus**
~ship better than the material:
    materiam
works
his ~ are mine: **opera illius**
my ~ will survive me: **non omnis**
workshop: **officina**
world: **mundus**
against the ~: **contra mundum**
knowing nothing of the ~: **i no uchi**
the ~ is his who has patience: **il**

mondo
the ~ is one: **todo el**
the ~ is woman's book: **le monde**
to Rome and the ~: **urbi**
~ full of fools: **ce monde**
~ of ours: **o κοσμος (ho kósmos)**
~ of women of doubtful reputation:
   demi-monde
~ weary: **weltmüde**
~ wishes to be deceived: **mundus
   vult**
worm-eaten: **vermoulu**
worn out: **recru**
worry: **tracasserie**
worse and worse: **de pis; immer**
worship: **bhakti; puja**
worst: **au pis**
~ is yet to come: **graviora manent**
worth: **pretium**
let it pass for what it's ~: **valeat**
~ all of them: **instar**
~ that wins more favor: **gratior**
worthless: **dare pondus**
~ness of any object: **de lana**
~ vase never breaks: **vaso malo**
worthwhile: **vale la**
not ~: **non est tanti**
wound
incurable ~: **immedicabile**
nursing a ~: **aeternum servans**
~ unuttered lives deep within:
   tacitum
wounded: **amoché**
wraith: **Doppelgänger**
wrangling: **criaillement**
wrath
fierce ~: **saeva**
~ of brothers is ~ of devils: **ira de**
~ of kings is always heavy: **gravis
   ira**
wrestler: **samo; sumo**
wrestling: **jiu jitsu; judo; kushti;
   samo; sumo**
wretched to be detected: **deprendi**
writ
~ against an objector: **quare**
~ of arrest: **capias; lettre**
~ of restraint: **ne exeat**
~ to call up court records: **certiorari**
~ to execute a judgment: **fieri facias**
~ to inquire into sanity: **de lunatico;
   inquirendo**
~ to summon a jury: **venire**
writer: **écrivain; gens; homme**

representative ~: **Träger**
Spanish ~s of the cultist school:
   cultos
writing
he wrote it: **scripsit**
I have written: **scripsi**
skilled in ~: **scribere scientes**
wall ~s: **graffiti**
we all write: **scribimus**
~ is the best memory: **escritura**
~ surface: **codex**
wrong, actionable: **ex delicto**
wrongly or rightly: **à tort ou à**

yam: **camote**
yarn, spins a good: **il brode**
year: **annus**
bygone ~s: **praeteriti**
for many ~s: **ad multos annos**
great ~: **annus**
he lived (so many) ~s: **annos**
in the ~: **anno; im Jahre**
in this ~: **hoc anno**
of this ~: **huius anni**
O that Jove would give back ~s: **O
   mihi**
tender ~s: **a teneris**
travel ~s: **Wanderjahre**
wonderful ~: **annus**
~ after the building of Rome: **anno**
~ of our Lord: **anno**
~ of the Hegira: **anno**
~ of the reign: **anno**
~ of the world: **anno**
~s rolling on: **volventibus**
yellow: **jaune**
pale ~: **feuille-morte**
yes: **da**
~ indeed: **si fait**
yoke, preserve the: **serva**
you: **usted**
not for ~ alone: **non vobis**
~ are right: **avete ragione**
~ are what ~ are: **du bist**
~ are wrong: **avete torto**
~ don't say: **warum**
~ too: **tu quoque**
~ too, Brutus: **et tu, Brute**
younger: **puîné**
youngster: **gosse**
yours: **tuum**
is it ~: **tuum**
it's ~: **tuum**
respectfully ~: **que besa**

~ truly: **atento; seguro; su seguro;**
   tout à vous
youth: **Bursch; giovanezza;**
   Junge
   bloom of ~: **lumenque**
   fashionable ~: **jeunesse**
   if ~ but knew: **si jeunesse**
   purple light of ~: **di giovinezza**

~ hard to pass: **młode**

zeal
   above all, no ~: **surtout**
   don't be too ~ous: **pas de**
   with greatest ~: **summo**
zoo: **Tiergarten**